HODGES'

HARBRACE

HANDBOOK

Writing

HODGES'

HARBRACE
HANDBOOK

FIFTEENTH EDITION

Cheryl Glenn
The Pennsylvania State University

Robert Keith Miller
University of St. Thomas

Suzanne Strobeck Webb
Texas Woman's University

and
Loretta Gray
Central Washington University

John C. Hodges
Late, The University of Tennessee, Knoxville

THOMSON
HEINLE

Australia Canada Mexico Singapore Spain United Kingdom United States

THOMSON

HEINLE

The Hodges' Harbrace Handbook, Fifteenth Edition
*Cheryl Glenn, Robert Keith Miller, Suzanne Strobeck Webb, Loretta Gray,
John C. Hodges*

Publisher: *Michael Rosenberg*
Acquisitions Editor: *Dickson Musslewhite*
Development Editor: *Michell Phifer*
Production Editor: *Lianne Ames*
Director of Marketing: *Lisa Kimball*
Marketing Manager: *Katrina Byrd*

Manufacturing Manager: *Marcia Locke*
Compositor: *Carlisle Communications, Ltd.*
Project Manager: *Lifland et al., Bookmakers*
Copyeditor: *Jane Hoover*
Cover/Text Designer: *Linda Beaupre*
Printer: *RR Donnelley & Sons Company*

Printed in the United States of America.
1 2 3 4 5 6 7 8 9 10   07 06 05 04 03

For more information contact Heinle, 25 Thomson Place, Boston, Massachusetts 02210 USA, or you can visit our Internet site at http://www.heinle.com

For permission to use material from this text or product contact us:

Tel	1-800-730-2214
Fax	1-800-730-2215
Web	www.thomsonrights.com

0-8384-0345-X (InfoTrac® College Edition)

Library of Congress Cataloging-in-Publication Data

Hodges' Harbrace handbook / Cheryl Glenn ... [et al.].—15th ed.
      p. cm.
   Includes bibliographical references and index.
   ISBN 0-8384-0345-X
   1. English language—Grammar—Handbooks, manuals, etc. 2. English language—Rhetoric—Handbooks, manuals, etc. I. Title: Harbrace handbook. II. Hodges, John Cunyus, 1892-1967. III. Glenn, Cheryl.

PE1112.H6 2003
808'.042—dc21   2003049918

Contents

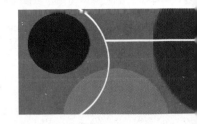

M Mechanics

Chapter 11 Abbreviations, Acronyms, and Numbers 195 **ab/ac/n**

P Punctuation

Chapter 12 The Comma 208 **,**

D Spelling and Diction

S Effective Sentences

 **Writing**

Preface

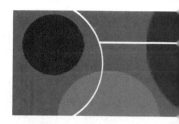

What are the origins of English handbooks?

The first English handbook of grammar rules and conventions was Edwin A. Abbott's 1874 *How to Write Clearly.* Abbott's aim was to help his classics students at the City of London School produce more fluent English translations of their Greek and Latin lessons, and his handbook was the first college-level text to equate clear writing with the mastery of specific rules, fifty-six of them, to be precise. In the United States, *How to Write Clearly* became wildly popular—not in classics, but in English composition courses, because it provided easy-to-use error-based rules for writers.

With the 1862 Morrill Act, the federal government provided funding for the establishment of Mechanical and Agricultural Colleges (which later became the major state universities), and the university population in the United States exploded. Higher education was no longer reserved for the sons and daughters of the upper classes. College writing classes suddenly expanded from thirty to one hundred students—a flood of students who needed to learn how to write correctly—and teachers desperately sought ways to handle the paper load of weekly themes. *How to Write Clearly,* along with a number of other popular rule-governed and exercise-based handbooks, tried to meet this need. The handbook had established itself as the *sine qua non* of writing instruction.

How did the *Harbrace Handbook* get started?

The book you have in your hands is not the first handbook, but, since 1941, it has served as the paradigm for all the successful handbooks that followed. In the 1930s, John C. Hodges obtained federal funding to support his study of the frequency of errors in college students' essays. Hodges, an English professor at the University of Tennessee, collected some twenty thousand student papers that had been marked by sixteen different professors of rhetoric from all over the United States. Then, working with a cadre of graduate students, he counted and analyzed the errors in those papers, creating a taxonomy that he used to organize the 1941 *Harbrace Handbook of English* into thirty-five sections.

A masterpiece of organized minimalism, easily accessible to teachers and students alike, the *Harbrace Handbook of English* captured the attention of both groups, as it responded to their needs in a material way. In the preface to that first edition, Hodges wrote:

> The *Harbrace Handbook of English* is a guide to the correction of student themes and also a text for use in class. It presents well-known subject matter in an easily usable form, and thus lightens the instructor's task of grading papers. The book contains only thirty-five major sections. To determine the sections actually needed (and consequently the numbers to appear in the correction chart), twenty thousand freshman themes were tabulated according to the corrections by sixteen instructors.

What makes *Hodges' Harbrace Handbook* so good?

Firmly established as the granddaddy of all handbooks, the *Harbrace Handbook of English* evolved into *Hodges' Harbrace Handbook,* Fifteenth Edition, which continues the Hodges tradition of up-to-date reliability and practicality. Like all of its predecessors, this edition of *Hodges' Harbrace Handbook* responds to the material needs of teachers and students. Still providing teachers with a simplified method for marking student papers, this handbook also gives both teachers and students the ease of reference and attention to detail that have made the Harbrace handbooks the standard of reliability. Maintaining its longstanding commitment to helping students make the best decisions in terms of grammar, style, punctuation, and mechanics, this "grammar first" handbook guides them as they develop their abilities as writers. In fact, *Hodges' Harbrace Handbook* provides priorities for any writing course, on any topic of composing or editing.

What's new about this edition?

This edition differs from the previous ones in a readily apparent way: a cleaner, clearer design. The new design enhances the handbook's overall accessibility and signals substantive changes in content.

- **Consideration of the Rhetorical Situation** Perhaps the most significant substantive change is this edition's attention to the rhetorical situation—to the writer, the audience, the message, the context, and the exigence (the specific reason for writing). Decisions about the most effective information to include, the best arrangement of that information, and the most appropriate grammatical choices all grow out of an understanding of the rhetorical situation.

- **Thoroughly Revised Grammar, Mechanics, and Punctuation Chapters** Given the emphasis on the rhetorical situation, all of these chapters have been reconceived; all of the exercises are new, and most of them have been rewritten as continuous discourse on lively and informative topics. Nearly all of the examples have been replaced with ones germane to students of all ages and the problems they encounter in their writing and editing.

    Chapter 1, "Sentence Sense," introduces grammar terms and topics that help students understand the rhetorical choices they make when they write sentences. This chapter thus prepares students to craft effective sentences as well as to revise common errors.

Chapter 7, "Verbs," provides essential information not only on the forms of verbs but also on their use. Students learn that even their choice of tense or voice affects the meaning their writing expresses.

■ **Revamped Writing Chapters** Attention to the rhetorical situation has invigorated all of the writing chapters, whether totally revamped or completely new, for the contemporary rhetorical situation includes writing with technology and writing across the disciplines. The following chapters have been thoroughly revised in light of contemporary composition pedagogy, while maintaining those aspects of traditional rhetorical theory that are still widely respected.

Chapter 8, "E-documents," formerly titled "Document Design," has been refocused to emphasize writing for the Web. Making liberal use of visuals, this chapter helps students understand that principles of good design are rhetorical and can be applied to produce effective, attractive Web pages, easy-to-read email messages, and final copy for paper documents.

Chapter 32, "Planning and Drafting Essays," guides students through the process of discovering appropriate topics, writing clear thesis statements, arranging their ideas, and developing initial drafts. At every step, students are encouraged to make decisions based on their audience and their purpose for writing.

Chapter 33, "Revising and Editing Essays," helps students understand the importance of revising their written work—of seeing it again—in terms of the overall rhetorical situation. Besides emphasizing editing and proofreading, this chapter encourages students to share their work with peers (whether fellow students or colleagues) and teaches them how to respond productively to the writing of others.

Chapter 36, "Writing Arguments," covers the basics found in any good argument chapter. But, in this edition, the chapter also addresses different kinds of arguments: deliberative (*What is the best course of action?*) and judicial (*What happened?*), as well as invitational (*I want to explain my point of view so that you understand—and then I'd like to understand your point of view*).

Chapter 38, "Evaluating Sources Online and in Print," provides guidelines for assessing the credibility of a text by determining the credentials of its author(s) and publisher (or sponsoring organization). Because students regularly use the Web for research, an entire section is devoted to the process of evaluating the timeliness, content, and credibility of Web sites. Finally, this chapter explains the difference between writing that is biased and writing that is imbued with committed values.

- **New Writing-across-the-Curriculum Chapter** Because rhetorical situations exist across the disciplines and in the workplace—not just in first-year writing classes—this edition has a new chapter that serves to complement chapter 42, "Writing to Interpret Literature" and chapter 43, " Writing in Business," which have been separated for this edition.

  Chapter 41, "Writing Academic Discourse," looks at how disciplinary cultures differ with respect to what they consider evidence to be, how they use evidence, their language and writing style, and their documents and formats. This chapter also introduces students to the concepts of qualitative and quantitative evidence and thick and thin description.

  Chapter 43, "Writing in Business," has been revised to help students with the transition from academic writing to workplace writing by showing a model business proposal along with a sample letter of application and résumé linked to that proposal.

- **Expanded Style Guides for Researched Writing** Of course, we maintain our thorough coverage of the style guidelines from the Modern Language Association (MLA) and the American Psychological Association (APA). MLA coverage includes

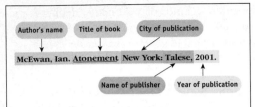

Author's name Title of book City of publication

McEwan, Ian. Atonement. New York: Talese, 2001.

Name of publisher Year of publication

updates from the very latest edition (2003) of the *MLA Handbook for Writers of Research Papers.* In addition, however, we now include *The Chicago Manual of Style* (CMS). (In fact, *Hodges' Harbrace Handbook* itself is edited according to *The Chicago Manual of Style,* which is the style guide used by most publishers.) Furthermore, all explanations of citations have an easy-to-use directory and color-edged pages to help students find exactly the type of citation they are looking for in the style guide they are using. And each type of citation (book, article, or computer source) is represented visually so that students may better understand its major components and how they are arranged.

■ **New Student Papers (and an emphasis on student writing)** Given our commitment to the rhetorical situation, we feature student papers for all of the writing chapters. In chapters 32 and 33, you'll find a new student essay on balancing school and work, "Working toward a Degree." The ideas for the essay originate in brainstorming, develop through drafts that include a peer-reviewed version, and come to fruition as a strong example of student writing. We've also included new student papers for each of the style guides—MLA, APA, and CMS (the latter available online). And three of the student papers illuminate different angles on the coffee

need to remember is that our schoolwork must always be your our first priority. *I think you should keep your pronouns consistent. Since you started with the second-person voice, why not stick with it?* Keeping this in mind, as with most things in life, your own individual sacrifices in this balancing act will determine your success. One of the sacrifices that you might have to make is the need to limit or carefully schedule the time that you spend with your friends. Since you are trying to show how work at school is both manageable and beneficial for a college student, maybe you shouldn't begin your evidence with such a negative example. Keep a consistent tone. Not all sacrifices need to be so difficult though. A small sacrifice you can make is to bring your schoolbooks along with you to work and utilize your work breaks to get a heads-up head start on your nightly schoolwork. In addition, since part of your time is already committed to your employers. You you will need to get a good handle on your school schedule and plan ahead to determine the time you need to work on various assignments. *This section seems kind of vague. I think it would be better if you gave some of your own personal experiences with planning in order to show specific examples of this point.* This sacrifice however will have positive repercussions as it will encourage you to form early study and time management habits. *This is a good point, but I wonder if it might fit better on page three where you begin to discuss the positive repercussions of part-time work on the college experience.*

While it is important to make such sacrifices in balancing a part-time job with success in school, you need not put all of the pressure on yourself. In fact, a key factor in minimizing such pressure is to choose a job where you work for an understanding employer. *I don't like the way this is worded, it implies that you are putting pressure on the employer. Maybe rephrase "there are ways to limit the pressure that you might feel."* This is not always an easy task and is certainly easier said than done. You can, however, take advantage of the resources available to you such as older students, advisors, and internship coordinators in finding a student-friendly employer. You should look for an employer that understands the need to put schoolwork first and who values scholarship in employees. A good place to look for such an employer is in university-run businesses where supervisors are advised to view employees as students first and foremost. Planning ahead around exam or paper weeks, you should also look for a job that offers flexibility and variability in scheduling culture, a topic we feel is relevant to students' lives: "Starbucks in Vienna: Coffee Cultures at a Crossroads" appears as the MLA paper; "Roxy's Coffee Shop," as the business plan; and "Just Coffee: A Proposal in the Classical Arrangement," as a sample argument.

- **"Beyond the Rule" Boxes** To help all students—whether English is their native, second, or third language—we've in-

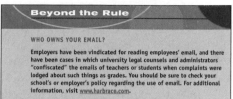

Beyond the Rule

WHO OWNS YOUR EMAIL?

Employers have been vindicated for reading employees' email, and there have been cases in which university legal counsels and administrators "confiscated" the emails of teachers or students when complaints were lodged about such things as grades. You should be sure to check your school's or employer's policy regarding the use of email. For additional information, visit www.harbrace.com.

cluded "Beyond the Rule" boxes, which will enrich students' understanding of the rules and conventions that substantiate the effectiveness of their rhetorical choices. The boxes link directly to our new Web site, www.harbrace.com, and provide additional information on quirks of grammar, punctuation, and mechanics, rules, and conventions. These boxes also suggest alternative rhetorical choices for writing.

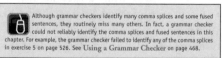

Although grammar checkers identify many comma splices and some fused sentences, they routinely miss many others. In fact, a grammar checker could not reliably identify the comma splices and fused sentences in this chapter. For example, the grammar checker failed to identify any of the comma splices in exercise 5 on page 526. See Using a Grammar Checker on page 468.

- **Computer Boxes** To support students' facility in all kinds of electronic

writing, we've included numerous computer boxes that provide useful information about working with electronic media. The use of technology in writing is integrated throughout the handbook.

- **Globe Boxes** The number of English-as-a-global-language boxes has doubled since the last edition. These

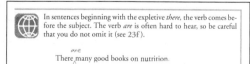

In sentences beginning with the expletive *there*, the verb comes before the subject. The verb *are* is often hard to hear, so be careful that you do not omit it (see 23f).

             are
There many good books on nutrition.

boxes identify common areas of confusion caused by native language differences, but they also address concerns that may arise for all students as they draft, revise, and edit their work.

Supplements

Instructor Supplements

Instructor's Flex-Files
Flex-Files are designed to give you maximum flexibility in planning and customizing your course. Providing an abundance of instructor materials, the Flex-Files consist of two main sections. "Part One: Questions for Teachers" raises a variety of pedagogical questions (and gives possible solutions) for you to consider in teaching your course with this handbook. "Part Two: Sample Syllabi and Activities" offers a sample syllabus with possible assignments for a semester-long course and a sample syllabus with possible assignments for a quarter-long course. Additionally, this section contains sample in-class collaborative learning activities, technology-oriented activities, and critical thinking and writing activities. The Flex-Files also include the following supplementary materials: (1) an ESL insert aimed at helping mainstream instructors teach writing effectively to their ESL students, (2) an insert on disability issues as they relate to teaching first-year composition, (3) the Answer Key for the exercises in the handbook, and (4) the Answer Key for the College Workbook.

Diagnostic Test Package
Built into Thomson Learning's BCA (Thomson Learning's grade book), the Diagnostic Test Package includes online testing correlated to this handbook. This package contains sample TASP and CLAST tests for instructors to deliver in a lab, at home, or in the class; practice versions of the TASP and CLAST tests for students; and general diagnostic tests designed to help instructors and programs place students in the appropriate writing course.

Instructor's Correction Chart

To make marking your students' papers easier, you can prop up on your desk the oversized, laminated chart listing all of the sections of the handbook and showing the editing symbols correlated to them.

Student Supplements

Hodges' Harbrace Handbook CD-ROM

A fully interactive version of the handbook, this CD-ROM includes over 200 animated examples of the most important choices and conventions for writers. Interactive versions of all the handbook's exercises are tied into a course management system and, where appropriate, automatically graded. In addition, the CD-ROM contains several other useful resources.

Electronic "Beyond the Rule" Resources Designed to guide students as they make rhetorical choices in the context of ever-evolving rules for Standardized English, the "Beyond the Rule" boxes address usage conventions that are in flux and provide additional information on points of writing and grammar. The electronic materials direct students to additional online resources as well as to electronic exercises designed to help them identify the best language choice among several options, according to their rhetorical situation.

Model Student Paper Library Animated and interactive as they move through the writing process, three student papers demonstrate proper use of MLA, APA, and CMS citation and documentation styles, respectively. The model student paper library also provides interactive examples of the research process and online research activities. In addition, this library contains student papers demonstrating each of the rhetorical methods as well as models of arguments based on Aristotelian, Rogerian, and Toulmin approaches.

Hodges' Harbrace Handbook Web Site

The free companion Web site provides links, sample syllabi, quizzing and testing, sample paper library, and other student and instructor resources.

Heinle InSite

Heinle InSite is an online writing resource for students, instructors, and program administrators. Within one integrated program, students can submit papers, review and respond to peers' papers, and work on writing and grammar problems by linking directly to online handbook content. As a component of InSite's paper-portfolio service, an "originality" checker enables students to check their own drafts for properly quoted and paraphrased material prior to final submission. Additionally, students can conduct online research with access to InfoTrac® College Edition, a database of more than 3,800 scholarly and popular sources with more than 10 million articles. Instructors using InSite can assign, view, and grade student papers and peer reviews and track all grades with a built-in course management system. Program administrators can view and track student progress from an individual- to a system-wide level.

InfoTrac® College Edition

Indispensable to writers of research papers, Info-Trac® College Edition offers students around-the-clock access to a database of more than 3,800 scholarly and popular sources with more than 10 million articles, providing information on almost any topic.

The Resourceful Reader, Sixth Edition

Offering a balance of classroom favorites and seldom- or never-before-reprinted pieces, *The Resourceful Reader* is a rhetorically arranged reader that has been completely reshaped in the sixth edition to be in line with current rhetorical theory. The pedagogical apparatus accompanying each reading addresses global issues of meaning, purpose, audience, and rhetorical strategy as well as local issues of language, style, grammar, punctuation, and mechanics. An instructor's manual accompanies the reader.

Writer's Resources CD-ROM, Version 2.0

This CD-ROM has more than 4,500 interactive exercises and activ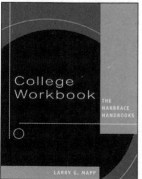ities, including many with animation and audio clips. A new section covers all stages of the writing process from prewriting to the final draft. Four student peers provide commentary on the writing process as they proceed through each stage. In addition, through the word-processing application being used by the student, the CD-ROM can launch over a hundred customized writing templates that guide the user through writing exercises in sentence, paragraph, and essay creation. More than an electronic exercise program, Writer's Resources helps students develop the skills necessary for choosing effective words, writing structurally balanced sentences, and developing detailed paragraphs as well as for writing a summary, an analysis, and an argumentative essay.

College Workbook

Twenty-seven units in five parts correspond to chapters of the handbook and cover grammar, punctuation, usage, style, and writing. This printed workbook combines exercises with

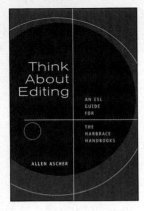

clear examples and explanations that supplement the information and exercises found in the handbook.

Think About Editing: An ESL Guide

A self-editing manual for ESL writers, *Think About Editing* is designed to help intermediate to advanced students edit their writing to correct grammar, structure, and usage. The manual is prefaced with a correlation guide that links its units to corresponding sections in *Hodges' Harbrace Handbook*.

Dictionaries

The following dictionaries are available for a nominal price when bundled with the handbook: *The Merriam-Webster Dictionary; Merriam-Webster's Collegiate Dictionary,* Eleventh Edition;

and *Heinle's Newbury House Dictionary of American English with Integrated Thesaurus.* The latter was created especially for ESL students.

Acknowledgments

Who wrote this handbook?

John C. Hodges carried forward his vision of a useful handbook for many editions of the *Harbrace Handbook*—and his influence continues with every edition. With the fifth edition, he was assisted by Mary E. Whitten (North Texas State University—now University of North Texas), who guided the book from the sixth through the tenth editions. Suzanne S. Webb (Texas Woman's University) joined the handbook on the tenth edition to enhance its rhetorical elements and add a section on logical thinking. In the eleventh edition, Winifred Bryan Horner (Texas Christian University) and Robert K. Miller (University of St. Thomas) joined the team, so that Win could add her rhetorical expertise and Bob could rework the research paper chapter.

The twelfth, thirteenth, and fourteenth editions profited from the three-person team of Sue, Win, and Bob, with remarkable results. Three new chapters, "Writing Arguments," "Reading and Thinking Critically," and "Writing under Pressure" were included in the handbook. By the fourteenth edition, the *Harbrace Handbook* appeared in three different versions to meet the growing diversity of handbook users: *Hodges' Harbrace Handbook* continued to emphasize grammar first, while *The Writer's Harbrace Handbook* and *The Writer's Harbrace Handbook,* Brief Edition, as their titles suggest, gave primary emphasis to writing, thereby rounding out the family of Harbrace handbooks.

With Win's retirement, rhetoric and composition specialist Cheryl Glenn (The Pennsylvania State University) and linguist Loretta Gray (Central Washington University) joined Sue and Bob to produce what we all hope is the best edition so far.

Who helped?

The fifteenth edition of this handbook and the other two versions took shape during a two-day meeting in Boston with members of the Heinle editorial staff. For their collective ideas, enthusiasm, support, and wise counsel, we remain grateful. In particular, we thank Michael Rosenberg, Publisher, whose pride in the Harbrace family of handbooks never wavered as he supported a new author team and its new ideas through many months of work. We're all grateful to Dickson Musslewhite, Acquisitions Editor, who worked tirelessly to put together our highly successful team—and then tapped his seemingly endless good humor to put up with each of us! On a number of occasions, he plied a tired author team with more ideas and, therefore, more work, but he always tempered his direction with the goodwill and good sense that characterize the best of rhetors. Stephen Marsi, Editorial Assistant, kept track of all our travels and expenses—and, most important, our reimbursements—for which we are grateful. The indispensable Katrina Byrd, Marketing Manager, advised us on ways to clarify the handbook's classic and new features; Lianne Ames, Production Editor, helped to bring this huge project to completion. Jane Hoover carried out the copyediting, typemarking, and proofreading with style and care. And Linda Beaupre gave the book its clear and aesthetically pleasing interior design and a cover that travels effortlessly into the twenty-first century. Without the help and support of these amazingly imaginative people, we simply could not have produced this edition of the *Hodges' Harbrace Handbook*.

But it is Michell Phifer, Senior Development Editor Extraordinaire, to whom we each owe a special thanks. A scrupulously careful editor—and our constant intellectual companion—Michell successfully managed to herd the likes of us four academics. On a daily or often a twice- or thrice-daily basis, she prodded our thinking about each chapter and about the project as a whole, massaged our sometimes convoluted writing and thinking into accessible prose, nudged us to improve what we thought were good (but clearly not good enough) exercises, and challenged us to locate more effective examples of professional and student writing. Michell was always on our team and guided our collaboration until the very last minute, until the presses rolled.

The successful completion of our work would not have been possible without the research assistance of Keith Gibson and the clerical help of Danielle Luzzo, both at The Pennsylvania State University. In addition, this project benefited from the support and encouragement of those overseeing our university schedules and workloads: Patsy Callaghan, Chair of the Department of English, and Liahna Armstrong, Dean of Arts and Humanities, both at Central Washington University; and Hugh Burns, Chair of English, Speech, and Foreign Languages at Texas Woman's University. Lou Thompson, Dene Grigar, and Rae Murphy of Texas Woman's University offered support and suggestions.

We would also like to thank the students whose indefatigable efforts went into the model student papers new to this edition: Melissa Schraeder and Nicole Hester, The Pennsylvania State University; Laura Klocke, Andy Pieper, and Nikki Krzmarzick, University of St. Thomas; and Roxanne Kirkwood, Texas Woman's University. Aaron Munk, Seattle University, created the student Web site. For writing and revising—and revising some more—we remain indebted to you. After all, good student writing, the kind that you have produced, is what this book is all about.

And we cannot forget our valued and amazingly imaginative colleague, Robert Yagelski at The State University of New York at Albany, who served as our technology consultant for this entire project. A consummate professional, Bob helped us envision chapter 5, "E-writing," and provided more good information than we could possibly use for each of the computer boxes.

Heartfelt appreciation is also due another consummate professional, Patrick Bizzaro, East Carolina University, who helped us realize the writing-across-the-curriculum chapters and kept us on track with them. We are the beneficiaries of his generosity, his good-humored and tireless reading and rereading, and his vast understanding of the subject.

We want to thank those colleagues who reviewed *Hodges' Harbrace Handbook* throughout the course of its development. Their astute comments, frank responses, and thoughtful suggestions helped shape what is the final version—until the next edition. We thank them for taking the time out of their already busy schedules to help us.

Specialty Reviewers

For writing across the curriculum, Patrick Bizzaro, *East Carolina University,* and Christopher Thaiss, *George Mason University;* for technology and composition, Samantha Blackmon, *Purdue University,* and Rebecca Rickley, *Texas Tech University;* for library research, Marianne Hageman, *University of St. Thomas;* for grammar, Martha Kolln, *The Pennsylvania State University;* for argumentation, Marie Secor, *The Pennsylvania State University;* for ESL, Tony Silva, *Purdue University;* and for research, Helen Schwartz, *Indiana University–Purdue University Indianapolis*

Handbook Reviewers

Stephen Calatrello, *Calhoun Community College;* Janice Cooke, *University of New Orleans;* Cecile deRocher, *Georgia State University;* Donna Gessell, *North Georgia College and State University;* Judith Hanley, *Wilbur Wright College;* David Mulry, *Odessa College;* James Richardson, *Morehouse College;* David Rieder,

University of Texas at Arlington; Paula Ross, *Gadsden State Community College;* and Michael Sirmons, *Austin Community College*

Focus Group Participants

Victoria Anderson and Joseph Janangelo, *Loyola University;* Vinson Burdette, *Tri-County Technical College;* Maria Clayton, *Middle Tennessee State University;* Michelle Eble and Lynée Gaillet, *Georgia State University;* Gabi Gautreaux and Kim McDonald, *University of New Orleans;* Karen Grossaint, *Regis University;* Elizabeth Howells, *Armstrong Atlantic State University;* John Hyman, *American University;* Trish Jenkins, *University of Alaska-Anchorage;* Raymonda Johnson, *Harold Washington College;* Peggy Jolly, *University of Alabama at Birmingham;* Sandee McGlaun and Linda Williams, *North Georgia College and State University;* and Patricia Webb, *Arizona State University*

Manuscript Reviewers

Sue Beebe and Michael Hennessy, *Southwest Texas State University;* Suzanne Bordelon, *San Diego State University;* Lauren Coulter, *University of Tennessee at Chattanooga;* James Crawford, *Walters State Community College;* Peter England, *Blinn College;* Cynthia Haynes, *University of Texas at Dallas;* Patricia Lonchar, *University of the Incarnate Word;* Rebecca Marez, *Del Mar College;* Cindy Moore, *St. Cloud State University;* Fiona Paton, *The State University of New York at New Paltz;* Chere Peguesse, *Valdosta State University;* Deborah Coxwell Teague, *Florida State University;* Freddy Thomas, *Virginia State University;* Donna Winchell, *Clemson University*

Finally, we are grateful to our friends and families. Although our faces toward the screen meant our backs toward you, you were never far from our thoughts. After all, without you, our work would be neither possible nor worthwhile.

To all of you reading this preface and using or considering using this handbook for the first time, know that we're grateful to you, too. In fact, if you have advice for how we might improve the next edition, write us c/o Heinle, English Editorial Department, 25 Thomson Place, Boston, MA 02210.

Cheryl Glenn
Robert Miller
Suzanne Webb
Loretta Gray

JUNE 2003

Grammar

Using a Grammar Checker

Most word-processing programs have features that help writers identify many grammar errors as well as various problems
with usage and style. But these grammar checkers have significant limitations. They usually will identify

- fused sentences, sometimes called run-on sentences (chapter 3),
- missing apostrophes in contractions (chapter 15),
- some misused prepositions (chapter 20), and
- wordy or overly long sentences (chapter 21).

However, grammar checkers frequently miss

- sentence fragments (chapter 2),
- problems with modifiers (chapter 4),
- problems with pronoun-antecedent agreement (chapter 6),
- errors in subject-verb agreement (chapter 6), and
- misused or missing commas (chapter 12).

Since these problems weaken your credibility as a writer, you should
never rely solely on a grammar checker to find them. Grammar checkers
cannot distinguish between true errors and choices you make deliberately
to suit your rhetorical situation (see chapter 32). Used carefully, a grammar checker can be a helpful tool, but keep the following advice in mind.

- Adjust the settings on your grammar checker to look only for
  errors you make frequently. (However, even if used in this way,
  a grammar checker may miss some errors.)
- Always evaluate any sentences flagged by a grammar checker to
  determine whether there is in fact a problem.
- Carefully review the revisions proposed by a grammar checker
  before accepting them. Sometimes, the proposed revisions
  create entirely new errors.
- Use a grammar checker only in addition to your own reading.
  When in doubt, consult the appropriate chapters in this
  handbook.

Sentence Sense

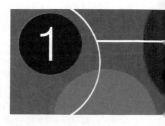

Sentences serve a number of purposes. Writers state facts or report information with **declarative sentences.** They give instructions with **imperative sentences.** Questions, or **interrogative sentences,** introduce topics and elicit information. **Exclamatory sentences** express emotion.

Declarative The runners from Kenya won the race.

Imperative Compare their times with the record.

Interrogative Who were those runners whose victory surprised the world?

Exclamatory What a tough race that was!

For guidelines on how to punctuate sentences, see chapter 17. To write effective sentences, though, you will also benefit from knowing their essential elements.

Beyond the Rule

SENTENCE TYPES

Each type of sentence can be used for a variety of purposes. For example, imperative sentences are used not only to give directions, but also to make suggestions (Try using a different screwdriver), **to issue invitations** (Come in), **to extend wishes** (Have a good time), **and to warn others** (Stop). **For further discussion of sentence types, visit www.harbrace.com.**

This chapter will help you

- identify the parts of speech (**1a**),
- recognize the subject and predicate (**1b**),
- identify verbs (**1c**),
- identify subjects and complements (**1d**),
- recognize basic sentence patterns (**1e**),
- recognize phrases (**1f**),
- recognize clauses (**1g**), and
- use different sentence forms (**1h**).

For explanations of any unfamiliar terms, consult the **Glossary of Terms**.

1a | **Knowing the parts of speech can help you discuss writing.**

When you look up a word in the dictionary, you will often find it followed by one or more of these labels: *adj., adv., conj., interj., n., prep., pron.,* and *verb.* These are the abbreviations for the traditional eight parts of speech: *adjective, adverb, conjunction, interjection, noun, preposition, pronoun,* and *verb.* The definition of a word depends on which of these labels it follows. When labeled as a noun, the word *turn* has several meanings, one of which is "curve" (*We were surprised by the turn in the road*). When *turn* is labeled as a verb, one of its possible meanings is "to change color" (*The leaves have turned*).

By learning the eight parts of speech, not only will you be able to use a dictionary effectively, you will also be able to understand feedback your readers provide as well as strengthen the responses you give to fellow writers. Someone reading your work, for example, may suggest that you use more action verbs. And you may note, as you read another's work, that it would be improved by balancing abstract nouns with concrete nouns.

Beyond the Rule

COUNTING PARTS OF SPEECH

The eight parts of speech were established in the eighteenth century. However, it took over two thousand years to reach that many categories. At first, there were only two parts of speech: nouns and verbs. The number slowly grew—and is still growing. You may have even used a grammar book that includes more than eight parts of speech. New categories such as *determiners* and *expletives* are widely recognized. To learn more about how parts of speech are identified and counted, visit www.harbrace.com.

(1) Verbs usually express action or being.

Thousands of verbs are **action verbs.** Just think of everything you do in one day: wake, eat, drink, wash, walk, drive, study, work, laugh, smile, talk, and so on. In contrast, only a few verbs express being or experiencing. Called **linking verbs,** these include *be, seem, become* and the sensory verbs *look, taste, smell, feel,* and *sound.* Both action verbs and linking verbs are frequently accompanied by **auxiliary verbs**—verbs that add subtle meaning to a main verb, such as information about time, ability, or certainty (**have** studied, **will** study, **can** study, **must be** studying). For more information on verbs, see **1c** and chapter 7.

The base form of most action verbs fits into this frame sentence:

    We should _____ (it). [With some verbs, *it* is not used.]

The base form of most linking verbs fits into this frame sentence:

    It should _____ good (terrible, blue, fine).

(2) Nouns usually name people, places, things, and ideas.

Proper nouns are specific names and are capitalized: *Bill Gates, Redmond, Microsoft Corporation.* **Common nouns,** also called *generic nouns,* refer to any member of a class or category: *person, city, company.* Common nouns that have singular and plural forms are called **count nouns:** *book, books.* **Noncount nouns** have only one form: *furniture, bacon.* **Collective nouns** such as *team, committee,* and *faculty* are either singular or plural, depending on the context (see **6a**). To learn how your choice of nouns can enhance your writing, see **20a**.

Most nouns fit into this frame sentence:

(The) _____ is important (unimportant, interesting, uninteresting).

(3) A pronoun takes the place of a previously mentioned noun or noun phrase.

A pronoun may substitute for a noun that occurs earlier in a sentence. This noun is called an **antecedent.**

Dan said **he** will have the report done by Friday.

A pronoun may also substitute for an antecedent noun phrase.

They bought the old, decrepit house because they thought **it** had charm.

The antecedent for a pronoun may also be found in a preceding sentence.

The students worked in the field for an entire semester. At the end of the school year, **they** reported their findings at the Undergraduate Research Conference.

The pronouns in the preceding examples are called **personal pronouns.** However, there are other types of pronouns as well: **indefinite, possessive, relative, interrogative, intensive,** and **reflexive.** For a detailed description of pronouns, see chapter **5.** For information on pronoun-antecedent agreement, see **6b.** Pronoun reference is discussed in chapter **28.**

(4) An adjective modifies a noun or a pronoun.

Adjectives most commonly modify nouns: *spicy* food, *cold* day, *special* price. Sometimes they modify pronouns: *blue* ones, anyone *thin.* Although adjectives usually precede the nouns they modify, they occasionally follow them: *enough* time, time *enough.* Adjectives that directly precede or follow nouns or pronouns are called **attributive adjectives. Predicate adjectives** are adjectives that follow linking verbs (such as *be, seem,* and *become*):

The <u>moon</u> is **full** tonight.

<u>He</u> seems **shy.**

Nouns sometimes function as adjectives.

The **marble** is from Italy. [*Marble* is a noun functioning as a noun.]

An incredible **marble** statue was hidden in the basement. [*Marble* is a noun functioning as an adjective.]

Adjectives usually answer one of these questions: *Which one? What kind of . . . ? How many? What color or size or shape (and so on)?* For a detailed description of adjectives, see **4a.**

Traditionally forming a subclass of adjectives, **articles** mark words as nouns. There are three articles: *a, an,* and *the.* This small group is now considered by many grammarians to be a subclass of **determiners** (see the Glossary of Terms).

Most adjectives fit into one of these frame sentences:

He told us about a/an _____ dog (person, idea).

The dog (person, idea) is very _____.

(5) Adverbs modify verbs, adjectives, and other adverbs.

Adverbs most frequently modify verbs. They provide information about time, manner, place, and frequency, thus answering one of these questions: *When? How? Where? How often?*

The conference <u>starts</u> **tomorrow.** [time]

I **rapidly** <u>calculated</u> the cost. [manner]

We <u>will meet</u> **here.** [place]

They **frequently** <u>work</u> late on Thursdays. [frequency]

Adverbs that modify verbs can often move from one position in a sentence to another. Compare the positions of *yesterday* and *carefully* in the following sentences.

Yesterday the team <u>traveled</u> to St. Louis.

The team <u>traveled</u> to St. Louis **yesterday.**

He **carefully** <u>removed</u> the radio collar.

He <u>removed</u> the radio collar **carefully.**

Most adverbs that modify verbs fit into this frame sentence:

They _____ moved (danced, walked) across the room.

Adverbs also modify adjectives and other adverbs by intensifying or otherwise qualifying the meanings of those words.

I was **somewhat** <u>surprised</u>. [modifying an adjective]

He was **unusually** <u>generous</u> [modifying an adjective]

The changes occurred **quite** <u>rapidly</u>. [modifying an adverb]

The team played **surprisingly** <u>well</u>. [modifying an adverb]

For more information on adverbs, see **4b**.

(6) Prepositions set up relationships between words.

A **preposition** is a word that combines with a pronoun, noun, or noun phrase to create a **prepositional phrase**. A prepositional phrase functions as an adjective or an adverb.

The tourists went on a tour **of** <u>the old city</u>. [adjectival]

With <u>much difficulty</u>, we completed the project. [adverbial]

The editor wrote comments **in** <u>the margin</u>. [adverbial]

Common one-word prepositions are *on, in, at, to, for, over,* and *under.* Common **phrasal prepositions** (prepositions consisting of more than one word) are *except for, because of, instead of,* and *according to.* For a list of prepositions and more information on prepositional phrases, see **1f(4)**.

(7) Conjunctions are connectors.

Conjunctions connect words or groups of words. There are two types of conjunctions: coordinating conjunctions and subordinating conjunctions. **Coordinating conjunctions** join words or groups of words of equal status; that is, they link a noun to a noun, an adjective to an adjective, a phrase to a phrase, and so on.

The game was <u>dangerous</u> **yet** <u>appealing</u>. [connecting adjectives]

They foraged for food <u>at dawn</u> **and** <u>at dusk</u>. [connecting prepositional phrases]

There are seven coordinating conjunctions. Use the made-up word *fanboys* to help you remember them.

F	A	N	B	O	Y	S
for	and	nor	but	or	yet	so

Correlative conjunctions (or **correlatives**), a subset of coordinating conjunctions, consist of two parts. The most common correlative conjunctions are *both . . . and, either . . . or, neither . . . nor,* and *not only . . . but also.*

The defeat left me feeling **both** <u>sad</u> **and** <u>angry</u>. [connecting adjectives]

Either <u>Pedro</u> **or** <u>Jeanie</u> will introduce the guest speaker. [connecting nouns]

Subordinating conjunctions join dependent clauses to main clauses. (See **1g** for a discussion of main clauses.)

The river rises **when** the snow melts.

Common subordinating conjunctions are *because, although, when,* and *if.* For a longer list of subordinating conjunctions and more information on dependent clauses, see **1g**. To learn how to use coordination and subordination to improve sentences, see chapter **24**.

(8) Interjections are expressions of surprise or strong feeling.

Interjections are most commonly used either before a sentence or at the beginning of a sentence or main clause to indicate surprise, dread, or some other strong emotion. Interjections are generally followed by a comma or an exclamation point.

Wow! Your design is astounding.

Oh no, you can't be telling the truth.

Exercise 1

Identify the part of speech of each word in the sentences below. Make sure you consider how the word is used in the sentence.

1. After we had finished lunch, we piled into a minivan and explored the valley.
2. A narrow river runs through it.
3. The tour guide drove very slowly because the road was old and rutted.
4. We stopped at a roadside stand for fresh figs, and, oh, were they good!
5. While we were there, we bought flowers for the guide.

1b | A sentence contains a subject and a predicate.

A sentence consists of two parts: a **subject** and a **predicate.**

SUBJECT + PREDICATE

The subject is generally someone or something that either performs an action or is described.

The <u>**quarterback**</u> + passed the ball to his wide receiver. [subject performs an action]

<u>**He**</u> + is talented. [subject is described]

The predicate expresses the action initiated by the subject or makes a comment about the subject.

> The goalie + **has blocked** the shot. [predicate expresses the action]
>
> She + **is quick.** [predicate makes a comment about the subject]

The central components of the subject and the predicate are often called the **simple subject** (the main noun or pronoun) and the **simple predicate** (the main verb and any accompanying verbs). They are underlined in the examples above.

Compound subjects and compound predicates include a connecting word such as *and, or,* or *but.*

> **The Republicans and the Democrats** are debating the issues. [compound subject]
>
> The candidate **stated his views on abortion but did not discuss stem-cell research.** [compound predicate]

Generally, sentences have the pattern subject + predicate. However, writers often vary this structure to provide emphasis or cohesion.

> He + elbowed his way into the lobby and paused. [subject + predicate]
>
> From a far corner of the lobby came + shrieks of laughter. [predicate + subject]

In the second sentence, the predicate contains information related to the first sentence and is thus placed at the beginning of the sentence. Placing the subject at the end of the sentence allows it to be emphasized. To learn how writers commonly vary sentence structure, see chapters **29** and **30**.

Exercise 2

Identify the subject and the predicate in each sentence, noting any compound subjects or compound predicates.

1. A naturalist gave us a short lecture on the Cascade Mountains.
2. He showed slides of mountain lakes and heather meadows.
3. Douglas fir predominates in the Cascade forests.
4. Mountaineers and artists have long considered the North Cascades the most dramatic mountains of the range.
5. Timberlines are low because of the short growing season.
6. Mt. Rainier is the highest volcano in the range.
7. The waxing and waning of the glaciers have eroded the mountain walls.
8. Hikers to this area should pack warm clothing.
9. My friend lent me his map of the Pacific Crest Trail.
10. The trail begins in southern California and ends in British Columbia.

Exercise 3

Bring to class a paragraph of at least five sentences. In each sentence, label the subject and the predicate. Place an asterisk by any sentence that does not follow the subject + predicate pattern.

1c | The central part of the predicate is the verb.

A verb indicates action or signals a state of being (see **1a(1)** and chapter 7). A verb may be a single word, or it may be accompanied by one or more auxiliary verbs, also called *helping verbs*. The most common auxiliaries are *be (am, is, are, was, were, been), have (has, had),* and *do (does, did, done).* Others, including *can, may,* and *might,* are called **modal auxiliaries.** These auxiliary verbs convey various meanings, such as ability or possibility.

> They **have been working** as volunteers. [verb with two auxiliaries]
>
> They **might work** as volunteers. [verb with modal auxiliary expressing possibility]

Other words, usually adverbs, may intervene between the auxiliary and the main verb.

> They have **always** worked as volunteers.
>
> Have you **ever** volunteered?

Because verbs are essential parts of a sentence, be precise when choosing them. Exactness is a characteristic of good writing. (See chapter **20**.)

Exercise 4

Review the sentences in exercise 2, identifying all main verbs and auxiliary verbs.

1d | Subjects and complements take different positions in a sentence.

In most sentences, the subject refers to someone or something performing an action and usually appears before the verb.

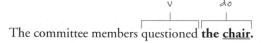

The chair of the committee presented his plans for the new year.

Complements are parts of a sentence required by the verb to make the sentence complete. For example, the sentence *The chair of the committee presented* is incomplete without the complement *his plans*. There are four different types of complements: direct object, indirect object, subject complement, and object complement. A **direct object** usually receives the action expressed by the verb. It appears after the verb.

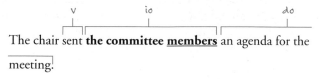

The committee members questioned **the chair.**

An **indirect object** also comes after the verb. It generally indicates to whom or for whom something is done.

The chair sent **the committee members** an agenda for the meeting.

A **subject complement** describes, identifies, or classifies the subject. Like a direct or indirect object, it follows the verb.

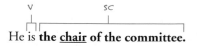

He is **the chair of the committee.**

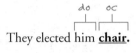

The chair of the committee is **<u>reasonable</u>**.

An **object complement** follows a direct object, describing, identifying, or classifying it.

They elected him **<u>chair</u>**.

They consider him **quite <u>reasonable</u>**.

Being able to identify the main word in subjects and complements is useful, especially when you are checking for agreement (see chapter **6**). The main word in each of the examples above is underlined. Sometimes, a main word is a noun that consists of more than one word. Examples of such **compound nouns** are *Labor Day, swimming pool,* and *ice cream.*

Subjects and complements are generally pronouns, nouns, or noun phrases. The term **noun phrase** refers to the main noun and any modifiers that provide additional information about the noun (see **1f**). A pronoun can stand in for an entire noun phrase. In fact, you can use a pronoun test to help you recognize subjects and objects: Simply substitute a pronoun for the noun phrase. Common pronouns used for this test are *he, she, it, they, him, her, them, this,* and *that.*

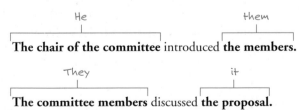

The chair of the committee introduced **the members.**

The committee members discussed **the proposal.**

(1) Subjects are usually pronouns, nouns, or noun phrases.

Grammatically complete sentences contain a subject. Except for imperatives, in which the subject, *you,* is understood, most subjects take the form of a pronoun, noun, or noun phrase.

> **My best friend** is a nutritionist. [noun phrase]
> **She** works at a clinic. [pronoun]
> Eat plenty of fruits and vegetables. [understood *you*]

To identify the subject of a sentence, find the verb and then use it in a question beginning with *who* or *what,* as shown in the following examples.

Jennifer works at a clinic.	Meat contains cholesterol.
Verb: **works**	Verb: **contains**
WHO works? **Jennifer**	WHAT contains? **Meat**
(not the clinic) **works.**	(not cholesterol) **contains.**
Subject: **Jennifer**	Subject: **Meat**

Some sentences begin with the **expletive** *there* or *it.* This word occurs in the subject position, forcing the true subject to follow the verb.

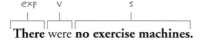

A subject following the expletive *it* is often a noun clause rather than a noun phrase. You will learn more about this type of clause in **1g**.

```
expv                                    s
| |.|
```
It is essential **that children learn about nutrition at an early age.**

In sentences beginning with the expletive *there,* the verb comes before the subject. The verb *are* is often hard to hear, so be careful that you do not omit it (see **22b**).

are
There ˄ many good books on nutrition.

(2) Objects are usually pronouns, nouns, or noun phrases.

Objects complete the meaning begun by the subject and verb.

My roommate writes **movie scripts.** [The object *movie scripts* completes the meaning of the sentence.]

Whether an object is required in a sentence depends on the meaning of the verb. Some sentences have no objects at all; others have one or even two objects.

The robins are migrating. [A sentence with no object.]

She lent **me** her **laptop.** [*Me* is one object; *laptop* is another.]

(a) Direct objects

The direct object of a verb showing action either receives the action or shows the result of the action.

I. M. Pei designed **the East Building of the National Gallery.**

Steve McQueen invented **the bucket seat** in 1960.

Compound direct objects include a connecting word, usually *and.*

Thomas Edison patented **the phonograph and the microphone.**

To identify a direct object, find the subject and the verb and then use them in a question ending with *what* or *whom.*

Marie Curie discovered radium.	They hired a new engineer.
Subject and verb: **Marie Curie discovered**	Subject and verb: **They hired**
Marie Curie discovered WHAT? **radium**	They hired WHOM? **a new engineer**
Direct object: **radium**	Direct object: **a new engineer**

Some direct objects are clauses (see **1g**).

> Researchers found **that patients responded favorably to the new medication.**

(b) Indirect objects

Some verbs can have both a direct object and an **indirect object.** Indirect objects are typically pronouns, nouns, or noun phrases that name the recipient of the direct object. Verbs that commonly take indirect objects include *bring, buy, give, lend, offer, sell,* and *send.*

> The supervisor gave **the new employees** computers.
>
> She sent **them** contracts in the mail.

Indirect objects can also be compound.

> She offered **Elena and Octavio** a generous benefits package.

(3) Subject and object complements are usually pronouns, nouns, noun phrases, adjectives, or adjectival phrases.

Like objects, complements can be pronouns, nouns, or noun phrases. However, they can also be adjectives or **adjectival phrases,** phrases in which the main word is an adjective.

(a) Subject complements

A **subject complement,** which identifies, classifies, or describes the subject, follows a linking verb (see **1a(1)** and **7c**). The most common linking verb is *be*; other linking verbs are *become, seem, appear,* and the sensory verbs *feel, look, smell, sound,* and *taste.*

> The game is **a test of endurance.** [noun phrase]
>
> The winner is **you.** [pronoun]
>
> The game rules sound **quite complicated.** [adjective phrase]

(b) Object complements

An **object complement** identifies or describes the direct object. Object complements help complete the meaning of verbs such as *call, elect, make, name,* and *paint.*

> Sports reporters called the rookie **the best player of the year.**
> [noun phrase]
>
> News of the strike left the fans **somewhat disappointed.**
> [adjective phrase]

Beyond the Rule

VERBS AND NOUNS

The verb you choose affects how many and what kinds of nouns are in a sentence. Some verbs, such as *sleep,* are never followed by an object. Other verbs take an object in some contexts (*I passed the exam*) but not in others (*Time passed slowly*). For more information, visit www.harbrace.com.

(4) Vocatives or appositives usually consist of pronouns, nouns, or noun phrases.

Sometimes, the pronouns, nouns, or noun phrases in a sentence are not subjects or complements. If they are used to address someone directly, they are **vocatives.** If they are placed near other nouns to identify them or otherwise supplement their meaning, they are **appositives.**

Arlese, would you repeat your question? [vocative]

Arlese, **my elder sister,** attends college. [appositive]

Exercise 5

Review the sentences in exercise 2, identifying all direct objects, indirect objects, subject complements, and object complements. Then, write five sentences that contain either expletives, vocatives, or appositives.

1e | There are five basic sentence patterns.

Understanding basic sentence patterns and variations will help you recognize subjects and complements. The following box summarizes the five basic sentence patterns. Each pattern is based on the type of verb in the sentence. You have already been introduced to linking verbs (such as *be, seem, sound,* and *taste*). Linking verbs are followed by subject complements. Verbs that are not linking are either transitive or intransitive (see 7c(1)). Notice that *trans* in the words *transitive* and *intransitive* means "over or across." Thus, the action of a **transitive verb** carries across to an object, but the action of an **intransitive verb** does not. Intransitive verbs have no complements, although they are often followed by adverbs or phrases functioning as adverbs.

BASIC SENTENCE PATTERNS

Pattern 1 SUBJECT + INTRANSITIVE VERB

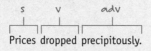

Prices dropped precipitously.

Pattern 2 SUBJECT + TRANSITIVE VERB + DIRECT OBJECT

A Chinese skater won a gold medal.

Pattern 3 SUBJECT + TRANSITIVE VERB + INDIRECT OBJECT
+ DIRECT OBJECT

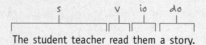

The student teacher read them a story.

Pattern 4 SUBJECT + TRANSITIVE VERB + DIRECT OBJECT + OBJECT
COMPLEMENT

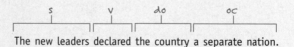

The new leaders declared the country a separate nation.

Pattern 5 SUBJECT + LINKING VERB + SUBJECT COMPLEMENT

Dr. Vargas is the discussion leader.

Some languages have sentence patterns similar to those you have learned for English. These languages are called SVO (subject-verb-object) languages, even though not all sentences have objects. The patterns for other languages vary. SOV (subject-object-verb) languages and VSO (verb-subject-object) languages are also common. Keep the SVO pattern in mind to help guide you through English sentences.

When declarative sentences, or statements, are turned into questions, the auxiliary verb is moved to the front of the sentence, before the subject.

Statement: A Chinese skater (has) won a gold medal.

Question: Has a Chinese skater won a gold medal?

When a question word, such as *what* or *why,* opens an interrogative sentence, the auxiliary verb still comes before the subject.

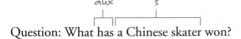
Question: What has a Chinese skater won?

If a statement does not include an auxiliary verb or a form of the linking verb *be,* then a form of *do* is added to the question. Again, the auxiliary verb is placed in front of the subject.

Statement: A Chinese skater won a gold medal.

Question: Did a Chinese skater win a gold medal?

English is one of a few languages in which subject and verb are inverted in questions. Most languages rely on intonation to indicate that a question is being asked, without a change in word order. (English speakers occasionally use uninverted questions to ask for clarification or to indicate surprise.) Another frequently occurring option for making a statement into a question is to add a particle, such as the Japanese *ka*.

As you study sentences more closely, you will find other patterns besides these basic five. For example, some patterns require mention of a destination or location. The sentence *I put the documents* is incomplete without a phrase such as *on your desk.* Phrases that are not essential, but do add pertinent information, can sometimes be moved. For example, the phrase *on Friday* can be placed either at the beginning or at the end of a sentence.

I finished my assignment **on Friday.**

On Friday, I finished my assignment.

To learn how to write effective sentences by varying their structure, see chapters **29** and **30**.

Exercise 6

Identify the basic pattern of each sentence in exercise 2. Note any nonessential phrases. Then, write a question corresponding to each of the sentences.

1f | A phrase is a group of words that can function as a single unit in a sentence.

Within a sentence, groups of words form phrases and clauses. Like single words, these larger units function as specific parts of speech: nouns, verbs, adjectives, or adverbs. By understanding how word groups function, you will be able to make your sentences clear, concise, and complete. You will also be able to vary sentence structure so that your paragraphs are rhythmic and cohesive.

Beyond the Rule

DEFINITION OF *PHRASE*

There are two definitions of the word *phrase*. The traditional definition is that a *phrase* is a sequence of grammatically related words without a subject or a predicate. However, linguists define a *phrase* as a unit that has one word as its main part. This word is called the *head* of the phrase. A noun phrase, then, is a phrase with a noun (or a pronoun) as its head. Technically, *people, a shy person, everyone in the room,* and *me* are all noun phrases. The traditional definition allows only multiword groupings to be phrases; the linguists' definition also allows phrases consisting of single words. In most composition handbooks, including this one, the traditional definition is used. For more information on phrases, visit www.harbrace.com.

(1) A noun phrase consists of a main noun and any accompanying determiners *(a, an, the, that)*, adjectives, or other modifiers.

Noun phrases serve as subjects and complements. They can also be objects of prepositions such as *in, of, on, at,* and *to.* (See **1f**(4) for a longer list of prepositions.)

The heavy frost killed **many fruit trees.** [subject and direct object]

My cousin is **an organic farmer.** [subject and subject complement]

His farm is in **eastern Oregon.** [subject and object of the preposition *in*]

In these sentences, the determiners *the* and *an* as well as the adjectives *heavy, fruit, organic,* and *eastern* add specificity. For example, the noun phrase *an organic farmer* tells the reader more than *farmer* alone would. By choosing nouns and noun phrases carefully, you will make your sentences more precise.

Much of Greenland lies within the Arctic Circle. ~~The area~~ is _{This large island}

owned by Denmark. Its ∧ name is Kaballit Nunaat. _{native}

[*The area* could refer to either Greenland or the area within the Arctic Circle. *This large island* clearly refers to Greenland. *Its native name* is more precise than just *Its name*.]

In noun phrases with nouns referring to individual items that can be counted (**count nouns**), such as *student* and *document,* some determiners are chosen according to whether the nouns are singular or plural:

a student, **an** opportunity, **that** opportunity [determiners used with singular count nouns]

some students, **few** students, **those** opportunities [determiners used with plural count nouns]

Determiners such as *less* and *much* are used with nouns representing concepts or masses that cannot be counted (**noncount nouns**):

less time, **less** water, **much** energy, **much** coffee [determiners used with noncount nouns]

Some nouns, especially abstract or plural generic nouns, do not have any determiners.

Patience is a virtue. [abstract noun]

Customers can be demanding. [plural generic noun]

Other languages that have determiners may not use them as they are used in English. For example, in Italian, the definite article, equivalent to the English *the,* is used with abstract nouns.

La pazienza è una virtù. [The definite article *La* precedes the noun *pazienza*.]

For more information on the use of determiners, see **22a.**

(2) A verb phrase is an essential part of the predicate.

The predicate says something about the subject and contains a verb (see **1b–c**). Besides a main verb, a verb phrase may also include auxiliaries, sometimes called *helping verbs,* such as *be, have, do, will,* and *should.*

The trees **blossomed.** [main verb]

The fruit **has ripened.** [auxiliary verb + main verb]

For a complete discussion of verb structure, see chapter **7.** For more information on using verbs to convey meaning effectively, see **22b, 23d, 29d,** and **30d.**

(3) Verbal phrases may be used as nouns or as modifiers.

Verb forms used as nouns or as adjectives or adverbs (see chapter **4**) are called **verbals.** Because of their origin as verbs, verbals in phrases often have their own objects and modifiers.

He wanted **to finish the task quickly.** [The object of the verbal *to finish* is *the task. Quickly* is a modifier.]

Verbal phrases are divided into three types: gerund phrases, participial phrases, and infinitive phrases.

Central to **gerund phrases** are *-ing* verb forms (see **7a**). Gerund phrases function as nouns, usually serving as subjects or objects.

Writing a bestseller was her only goal. [subject]

My neighbor enjoys **writing about distant places.** [object]

Because gerund phrases act as nouns, pronouns can replace them.

> **That** was her only goal.
>
> She enjoys **it.**

Participial phrases can be divided into two subtypes. The first includes a present participle (-*ing* form). The second subtype includes a past participle (*-ed* form for regular verbs or another form for irregular verbs). (See **7a** for more information on verb forms.)

> <u>Planning</u> **her questions carefully,** she was able to hold fast-paced and engaging interviews. [present participle]
>
> <u>Known</u> **for her interviewing skills,** she was asked to host her own radio program. [past participle]

Participial phrases function as modifiers. They may appear at various points in a sentence: beginning, middle, or end.

> **Fearing a drought,** all the farmers in the area used less irrigation water.
>
> All the farmers in the area, **recognizing the signs of drought,** used less irrigation water.
>
> Farmers used less irrigation water, **hoping to save water for later in the season.**

The commas setting off each participial phrase in the preceding examples signal that the phrase is not necessary for identifying the noun it modifies. Instead, the phrase adds extra information to the sentence. Sometimes, however, the participial phrase is essential for meaning. The details it provides help the reader identify the noun being referred to.

> The reporter **providing the most accurate account of the war** was once a soldier. [The participial phrase helps distinguish this reporter from others.]

A present participle (*-ing* form) cannot function alone as the main verb in a sentence. When an *-ing* form is the main verb, it is generally preceded by a form of *be* (*am, is, are, was,* or *were*).

They~~ ~~**thinking** about the future.
$\quad$ *are*

Infinitive phrases serve as nouns or modifiers. The form of the infinitive is distinct: the infinitive marker *to* followed by the base form of the verb.

The company intends **to hire twenty new employees.** [direct object]

To attract customers, the company changed its advertising strategy. [modifier of the verb *changed*]

We discussed his plan **to use a new packing process.** [modifier of the noun *plan*]

When an infinitive follows a form of *make* or sometimes a form of *have,* the marker *to* is omitted.

The coach **made** the new recruit **repeat** the drill.

The coach **had** the new recruit **run** an extra lap.

For advice on the punctuation of verbal phrases, see **12b** and **12d–e**.

The infinitive marker *to* does not follow modal auxiliaries.

You **should to** revise your paper.

They **must to** address the need for more energy sources.

Some verbs in English are followed by a gerund, by an infinitive, or by either one.

Verbs followed by a gerund

admit	deny	finish
avoid	dislike	miss
consider	enjoy	suggest

Example: She enjoys playing the piano.

Verbs followed by an infinitive

agree	hope	prepare
decide	need	promise
deserve	plan	seem

Example: She promised to play the piano for us.

Verbs followed by a pronoun, noun, or noun phrase

advise	encourage	persuade
allow	invite	require
cause	order	teach

Examples: Her father taught her to play the piano. A good friend persuaded the young pianist to audition for the city orchestra.

Verbs followed by either a gerund or an infinitive

begin	like	remember
continue	love	stop
hate	prefer	try

Examples: She likes to play the piano. She likes playing the piano.

Although both gerund phrases and infinitive phrases can serve as direct objects, their meanings may be different.

We stopped **discussing the plan.** [The discussion has ended.]

We stopped **to discuss the plan.** [The discussion has not yet started.]

Beyond the Rule

SPLIT INFINITIVES

Some grammarians advise against putting words between the infinitive marker *to* and the base form of the verb.

Be sure **to ~~carefully~~ proofread** your paper ∧ *carefully*.

This advice is based on Latin grammar, which says that infinitives are never split. And it is good advice to remember if the intervening words create a cumbersome sentence.

∧ *Under the circumstances, the* ~~The~~ jury was unable **to, ~~under the circumstances,~~ convict** the defendant.

However, most writers today recognize that an adverb splitting an infinitive can provide emphasis.

It was a relief **to finally finish** my history project.

For more information on split infinitives, visit www.harbrace.com.

(4) Prepositional phrases are generally used as modifiers.

Prepositional phrases provide information about time, place, accompaniment, cause, manner, and so on.

> **With great feeling,** Martin Luther King expressed his dream **of freedom.** [*With great feeling* describes the way the speech was delivered, and *of freedom* specifies the kind of dream.]
>
> King delivered his most famous speech **at a demonstration in Washington, D.C.** [Both *at a demonstration* and *in Washington, D.C.* provide details about place.]

A prepositional phrase consists of a preposition and a noun, noun phrase, or pronoun (**object of the preposition**). Such a phrase modifies another element in the sentence.

> The professor's lecture **on censorship** stirred controversy. [*On censorship* modifies the noun phrase *the professor's lecture*.]
>
> Everyone **in the class** was upset. [*In the class* modifies the pronoun *everyone*.]
>
> Some students met the professor **after class.** [*After class* tells when the action of the verb occurred.]

A prepositional phrase can also occasionally serve as a subject.

> **After supper** is too late!

When the object of the preposition is a pronoun such as *whom* or *what,* the preposition may follow rather than precede its object, especially in questions.

> **What** was the book **about?** [The object of the preposition is *what.* COMPARE The book was about what?]

SOME COMMON PREPOSITIONS

about	behind	during	off	to
above	below	except	on	toward
across	beneath	for	out	under
after	beside	from	outside	unlike
against	between	in	over	until
among	beyond	inside	past	up
around	by	into	regarding	upon
as	concerning	like	round	with
at	despite	near	since	
before	down	of	through	

Phrasal prepositions consist of more than one word.

Except for the last day, it was a wonderful trip.

PHRASAL PREPOSITIONS

according to	due to	in spite of
along with	except for	instead of
apart from	in addition to	out of
as for	in case of	with regard to
because of	in front of	with respect to
by means of	in regard to	with the exception of

Some pairs of prepositions, such as *by/until* and *except/ besides,* pose special problems. *Until* indicates a continuing situation that will come to an end in the future. *By* indicates an action that will happen prior to a specified time in the future.

I will be away **until** next Tuesday.

I will finish my work **by** six o'clock.

Besides means "in addition to" or "plus," and *except* means "but" or "minus."

Besides a salad, we had soup and crackers. [We ate soup and crackers in addition to salad.]

Everyone **except** Alice attended the luncheon. [Everyone but Alice was there.]

For other information about prepositions, consult the **Glossary of Usage**.

 In English, some verbs, adjectives, and nouns combine with prepositions to form idiomatic expressions (see **20c**).

Verb + Preposition	Adjective + Preposition	Noun + Preposition
apply to	fond of	interest in
rely on	similar to	dependence on
trust in	different from	fondness for

For more information on such combinations, consult a specialized dictionary such as those listed on pages 291–292. Specialized dictionaries include commonly occurring combinations with the entries for verbs, adjectives, and nouns.

(5) An appositive can expand the meaning of a noun or noun phrase.

Appositives (usually nouns or noun phrases) identify, explain, or otherwise supplement the meaning of other nouns or noun phrases. When appositives provide essential information, no commas are used.

> Jonathan Weiner's book *The Beak of the Finch* won a Pulitzer Prize. [The appositive identifies the book being referred to.]

When an appositive phrase provides extra details, commas set it off.

> *The Beak of the Finch*, **a book by Jonathan Weiner,** won a Pulitzer Prize. [The appositive gives details about the book.]

By using appositives carefully, you will add variety to your writing (see **30a–b**). For more information on how to punctuate nonessential appositives, see **12d**.

(6) Absolute phrases provide descriptive details or express causes or conditions.

An **absolute phrase** is usually a noun phrase modified by a participial phrase or a prepositional phrase.

> She left town at dawn, **all her belongings packed into a Volkswagen Beetle**. [*Belongings* is the main noun; *packed into a Volkswagen Beetle* is the modifying verbal phrase.]
>
> **Her guitar in the front seat,** she pulled away from the curb. [*Guitar* is the main noun; *in the front seat* is the modifying prepositional phrase.]

These absolute phrases provide details. An absolute phrase can also express cause or condition.

> **More vaccine having arrived,** the staff scheduled its distribution.

To learn how to use absolute phrases to make your writing concise, see **21b**. For information on how to punctuate absolute phrases, see **12d**.

Exercise 7

Add details to the following sentences, using prepositional phrases, verbal phrases, appositive phrases, and absolute phrases. Then, label the phrases you added.

1. The team ran onto the field.
2. The president delivered his speech.
3. The detective slowly opened the door.
4. I slept late.
5. Roy pushed the button.

1g | A clause is a group of related words that contains a subject and a predicate.

(1) Independent clauses can stand alone.

An **independent clause,** sometimes called a *main clause,* has the same grammatical structure as a simple sentence: Both contain a subject and a predicate.

> The students earned high grades. [The complete subject is *the students.* The complete predicate is *earned high grades.*]

> They were able to apply for scholarships. [The complete subject is *they.* The complete predicate is *were able to apply for scholarships.*]

Independent clauses combine with other clauses to form longer, more detailed sentences.

(2) Dependent clauses are attached to an independent clause.

A **dependent clause** also has a subject and a predicate. However, it cannot stand alone; it must be attached to an independent clause. A dependent clause functions as a noun, an adjective, or an adverb.

noun clause

We know **who won the gold medal**.

adjectival clause

The athlete **who won the gold medal** was from Argentina.

adverbial clause

Maria received the gold medal **because her performance was flawless.**

(a) Dependent clauses used as subjects or objects

Clauses that serve as subjects or objects are called **noun clauses** (or *nominal clauses*). They are introduced by *if, that,* or a *wh*-word such as *why, what,* or *when.* Notice the similarity in usage between noun phrases and noun clauses.

Noun Phrases	Noun Clauses
The testimony may not be true. [subject]	**What the witness said** may not be true. [subject]
We do not understand **their motives.** [direct object]	We do not understand **why they did it.** [direct object]
Send the money to **a charity.** [object of the preposition]	Send the money to **whoever needs it most.** [object of the preposition]

When no misunderstanding would result, *that* can be omitted before a noun clause.

The scientist said **she was moving to Australia.** [*that* omitted]

However, *that* should always be retained when there are two noun clauses.

The scientist said **that she was moving to Australia** and **that her research team was disbanding.** [*that* retained in both noun clauses]

(b) Dependent clauses used as modifiers

Two types of dependent clauses—adjectival clauses and adverbial clauses—serve as modifiers. Any clause that answers the question *Which one?* or *What kind of . . . ?* about a noun or a pronoun is an **adjectival clause.** Such clauses, which nearly always follow the words they modify, usually begin with a relative pronoun (*who, whom, that, which,* or *whose*) but sometimes begin with a relative adverb (*when, where,* or *why*). Notice the similarity in usage between adjectives and adjectival clauses.

Adjectives	Adjectival Clauses
Nobody likes **malicious** gossip. [answers the question *What kind of gossip?*]	Nobody likes news reports **that pry into people's private lives.** [answers the question *What kind of news reports?*]
Some **diligent** students begin their research early. [answers the question *Which students?*]	Students **who have good study habits** begin their research early. [answers the question *Which students?*]
The **public** remarks were troubling. [answers the question *Which remarks?*]	The remarks **that were made public** were troubling. [answers the question *Which remarks?*]

As objects in adjectival clauses, relative pronouns can be omitted as long as the meaning of the sentence is still clear.

Mother Teresa was a woman **the whole world admired.**
[*Whom,* the object in the adjectival clause, is omitted.]

She was someone **who cared more about serving than being served.** [*Who,* the subject in the adjectival clause, is not omitted.]

The relative pronoun cannot be omitted when the clause is set off by commas.

Mother Teresa, **whom the whole world admired,** cared more about serving than being served.

An **adverbial clause** usually answers a question about a verb: *Where? When? How? Why? In what manner?* Adverbial clauses are introduced by subordinating conjunctions such as *because, although,* and *when.* (For a list of subordinating conjunctions, see page 41.) Notice the similarity in usage between adverbs and adverbial clauses.

Adverbs	Adverbial Clauses
Occasionally, the company hires new writers. [answers the question *When?*]	**When the need arises,** the company hires new writers. [answers the question *When?*]
She acted **selfishly.** [answers the question *How?*]	She acted **as though she cared only about herself.** [answers the question *How?*]

In an adverbial clause that refers to time or establishes a fact, both the subject and any auxiliary verb or linking verb are frequently omitted.

While fishing, he saw a rare owl. [The subject *he* and the auxiliary verb *was* have been omitted.]

Though tired, they continued to study for the exam. [The subject *they* and the linking verb *were* have been omitted.]

When using such **elliptical clauses**, be sure that the omitted subject is the same as the subject of the independent clause.

While reviewing your report, *I thought of* a few questions ~~occurred to me~~.

For more information on the use of elliptical clauses, see **21d**.

(3) Conjunctions and conjunctive adverbs link and relate clauses.

Conjunctions are connecting words used to signal transitions such as addition, comparison, and contrast. For a list of transitional connections, see **31d**.

Coordinating conjunctions join single words and phrases, but they also link clauses. See page 10 for a list of coordinating conjunctions.

> tired **yet** excited [The coordinating conjunction *yet* joins two adjectives and signals contrast.]
>
> in the boat **or** on the pier [The coordinating conjunction *or* joins two phrases and marks them as alternatives.]
>
> We did not share a language, **but** somehow we communicated. [The coordinating conjunction *but* joins two independent clauses and signals contrast.]

Coordinating conjunctions can also join sentences.

> In the more open places are little lavender asters, and the even smaller-flowered white ones that some people call beeweed or farewell-summer. **And** in low wet places are the richly flowered spikes of great lobelia, the blooms an intense startling blue, exquisitely shaped.
>
> —**WENDELL BERRY,** *Home Economics*

Correlative conjunctions, consisting of two or more words, join single words, phrases, and clauses. See **1a(7)** for more on correlative conjunctions.

> **either** you **or** I [The correlative *either . . . or* joins two words and marks them as alternatives.]
>
> **neither** on Friday **nor** on Saturday [The correlative *neither . . . nor* joins two phrases and marks them as negative alternatives.]

Not only did they run ten miles, **but** they **also** swam twenty laps. [The correlative *not only . . . but also* joins two independent clauses and signals addition.]

Generally, a correlative conjunction links similar structures. The following sentence has been revised because the correlative conjunction was linking a phrase to a clause.

     did he save
Not only ~~saving~~ the lives of the accident victims, **but** he **also** prevented any spinal injuries.

For more information on ensuring clarity when using correlative conjunctions, see **22a**.

 A **subordinating conjunction** marks a clause as dependent and signals a connection between the dependent clause and the main clause.

She studied Spanish **so that** she would be able to work in Costa Rica. [*So that* signals a purpose.]

Unless the project receives more funding, the research will stop. [*Unless* signals a condition.]

For a list showing the types of transitions signaled by subordinating conjunctions, see **31b**.

SUBORDINATING CONJUNCTIONS

after	if	so that
although	in case	than
as if	in that	though
as though	insofar as	unless
because	no matter how	until
before	now that	when, whenever
even if	once	where, wherever
even though	provided (that)	whether
how	since	while

Conjunctive adverbs—such as *however, nevertheless, then,* and *therefore*—link independent clauses. These adverbs signal relationships such as cause, condition, and contrast. Some conjunctive adverbs may appear in the middle or at the end of a clause.

Heat the oil; **then** add the onions. [*Then* begins the clause and signals another step in a sequence.]

He made copies of the report for members of the committee. He **also** sent copies to the city council. [*Also* appears in the middle of the clause and signals an additional action.]

My parents have differing political views. They rarely argue, **however.** [*However* ends the clause and signals contrast.]

For more information on conjunctive adverbs, see **3c** and **4b**. For specific information on punctuation, see **14a**.

Exercise 8

A. Identify the dependent clauses in the following paragraph. Specify whether each is a noun clause, an adjectival clause, or an adverbial clause.
B. Identify all coordinating conjunctions, correlative conjunctions, subordinating conjunctions, and conjunctive adverbs.

[1]With the goal of crossing the North Pole alone, Børge Ousland started his 1,240-mile trek on March 3, 2001. [2]Although Ousland had prepared for the most grueling triathlon imaginable, he had no way of predicting what he would have to endure. [3]One night huge chunks of ice forced upward from the packed surface almost destroyed his camp, and the next morning he had to search hard for snow that he could melt into fresh water. [4]About a week into his trip, Ousland's sledge started to break down. [5]Ousland considered canceling his trip at that point, but instead he steeled himself

and ordered a new sledge, which did not arrive until several days later. [6]Ousland also had to swim across leads, shoot at approaching polar bears, and endure the pain of frostbite and strained tendons. [7]Despite all the misery, Ousland continually took cues from his surroundings. [8]Whenever he came to a lead, he asked himself what a polar bear would do. [9]When crossing treacherous pack ice, he thought as a fox would, making each step count. [10]Ousland said the key to surviving such a rigorous journey was perseverance.

1h	Identifying clauses helps you understand the types of sentences they form.

You can identify the form of a sentence by noting the number and kinds of clauses it contains.

(1) A simple sentence consists of a single independent clause.

A **simple sentence** is equivalent to one independent clause. Essentially, then, it must have a subject and a predicate.

> The lawyer presented her final argument. [The complete subject is *the lawyer*. The complete predicate is *presented her final argument*.]

However, you can expand a simple sentence by adding prepositional phrases or verbal phrases.

> The lawyer presented her final argument **in less than an hour.** [A prepositional phrase adds information about time.]
> **Encouraged by the apparent sympathy of the jury,** the lawyer presented her final argument. [A verbal phrase adds detail.]

(2) A compound sentence consists of at least two independent clauses but no dependent clauses.

Two or more independent clauses form a **compound sentence.** The independent clauses are most commonly linked by a coordinating conjunction. However, punctuation may sometimes serve the same purpose. (See **14a** and **17d.**)

> The Democrats proposed a new budget, **but** the Republicans opposed it. [The coordinating conjunction *but* links two independent clauses and signals contrast.]

> The Democrats proposed a new budget; the Republicans opposed it. [The semicolon serves the same purpose as the coordinating conjunction.]

(3) A complex sentence has one independent clause and at least one dependent clause.

Sentences consisting of an independent clause and at least one dependent clause are called **complex sentences.** The dependent clause may be a noun clause, an adjectival clause, or an adverbial clause.

> **Because he was known for architectural ornamentation,** no one predicted **that the house <u>he designed for himself</u> would be so plain.** [This sentence has three dependent clauses. *Because he was known for architectural ornamentation* is an adverbial clause. *That the house he designed for himself would be so plain* is a noun clause. *He designed for himself* is an adjectival clause within the noun clause. The relative pronoun *that* has been omitted.]

(4) A compound-complex sentence consists of at least two independent clauses and at least one dependent clause.

The combination of a compound sentence and a complex sentence is called a **compound-complex sentence.** This type of sentence contains two or more independent clauses and one or more dependent clauses.

> **Because it had snowed hard in October that year,** the ski resorts opened early, **and** the skiers and snowboarders flocked to them. [*Because* signals the dependent clause; *and* connects the two independent clauses.]

Exercise 9

Return to exercise 8, and identify each sentence in the paragraph as simple, compound, complex, or compound-complex.

Exercise 10

A. Write a sentence exemplifying each type listed below. (If you do not understand the terms *declarative, interrogative, imperative,* and *exclamatory,* see page 3.)

1. a declarative simple sentence
2. a declarative compound sentence
3. a declarative complex sentence
4. an imperative simple sentence
5. an imperative compound sentence
6. an imperative complex sentence
7. an interrogative simple sentence
8. an interrogative complex sentence
9. a declarative compound-complex sentence
10. an exclamatory simple sentence

B. In each of your sentences from part A, bracket the dependent clause. Label it as a noun clause, an adjectival clause, or an adverbial clause. Circle and label the coordinating and subordinating conjunctions. Your instructor may ask you to identify phrases as well.

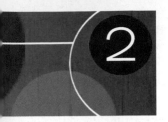

2 Sentence Fragments

This chapter can help you

- revise fragments resulting from incorrectly punctuated phrases (**2a**) and clauses (**2b**) and
- recognize effective fragments (**2c**).

As its name suggests, a **sentence fragment** is only a piece of a sentence; it is not complete. Whereas a complete sentence consists of a complete subject and a complete predicate (see **1b**), a fragment may be missing either or both of these parts. Notice how the following boldfaced fragments have been revised.

Magazines often include articles about alternative
medicine. ~~Usually~~ *, usually* **covering both the benefits and the**
drawbacks of particular methods.

Occasionally, alternative medical treatment includes
hypnosis~~.~~ *, the* **~~The~~ placement of a patient into a sleeplike state.**

Most patients, however, respond better when in a normal
state of consciousness~~.~~ *, according* **~~According~~ to most psychiatrists**
practicing today.

Alternatively, a fragment may have the essential sentence components but begin with a subordinating conjunction or a relative pronoun (see **1g**).

Subordinating Conjunction

Most people can be hypnotized easily. **Although the depth** *, although* **of the trance for each person varies greatly.**

Relative Pronoun

Hypnosis is usually induced by a hypnotist. **Who gives** *, who* **repetitive, monotonous commands.**

Because a fragment generally depends on the sentence preceding it to be meaningful, it can often be connected to that sentence. It can also be rewritten as a complete sentence.

Fragment: Most people can be hypnotized easily. Although the depth of the trance for each person varies greatly.

Revision: Most people can be hypnotized easily. However, the depth of the trance for each person varies greatly.

Note that imperative sentences (see chapter **1**) are not considered fragments. Although not written, the subject *you* is implied. In fact, the subject of an imperative sentence is often called the *understood you*.

Find out as much as you can about alternative treatments. [*You* find out as much as you can about alternative treatments.]

In some languages, subject pronouns are dropped when there is no risk of misunderstanding. In Spanish, the verb form reveals information about the subject; unless needed for clarity or emphasis, a subject pronoun can be dropped, as in *Trabajo en un banco* ("I work in a bank"). However, subject pronouns must be included in all English sentences, except imperative sentences (see chapter **1**).

> *Be* verbs (*am, is, are, was, were, been*) can be omitted in
> some languages. In English, however, they are necessary.
>
> Sentence without an auxiliary verb: The population ^is^ growing.
>
> Sentence without a linking verb: It ^is^ quite large.
>
> For more information on auxiliary verbs and linking verbs, see
> **7a** and **7c**.

If you have trouble with fragments, you should not rely on a
grammar checker to identify them in your writing. The grammar
checker used in producing this chapter recognized only half of
the fragments serving as examples.

If you have trouble recognizing fragments, try one or more
of the following four methods:

1. Read each paragraph backwards, sentence by sentence.
   When you read your sentences out of order, you may more
   readily note the incompleteness of a fragment.

2. Locate the essential parts of each sentence. First, find the
   main verb and any accompanying auxiliary verbs.
   Remember that verbals cannot function as main verbs (see
   1f(3)). After you find the main verb, find the subject by
   asking *Who?* or *What?* (see **1d(1)**). Finally, check to see
   that the sentence does not begin with a relative pronoun
   or a subordinating conjunction (see **1g**).

   Test sentence: Striving to provide educational opportunities for African Americans.

   Test: Main verb? *None. "Striving" and "to provide" are both
   verbals.* Subject? *None.*

[Because there is no subject or main verb, this test sentence is a fragment.]

Test sentence: Striving to provide educational opportunities for African Americans, Mary McLeod Bethune opened a small school in 1904.

Test: *Main verb?* Opened. Subject? *Mary McLeod Bethune.* Relative pronoun or subordinating conjunction? *None.*

[This test sentence contains a subject and a verb, and it does not begin with a relative pronoun or subordinating conjunction. It is therefore complete.]

3. Put any sentence you think might be a fragment into this frame: They do not understand the idea that _____ . Only a full sentence will make sense in this frame. If a test sentence, other than an imperative, does not fit into the frame, it is a fragment.

Test sentence: Depending on availability of food.

Test: They do not understand the idea that *depending on availability of food.*

[The sentence does not make sense; therefore, the test sentence is a fragment.]

Test sentence: The number of tiger sharks grows or shrinks depending on availability of food.

Test: They do not understand the idea that *the number of tiger sharks grows or shrinks depending on availability of food.*

[The sentence does make sense; therefore, the test sentence is a complete sentence.]

4. Rewrite any sentence you think might be a fragment as a yes/no question. Only full sentences can be rewritten this way.

Test sentence: Which is made from the leaves of the foxglove plant.

Test: *Is which made from the leaves of the foxglove plant?*

[The question does not make sense; therefore, the test sentence is a fragment.]

Test sentence: Some heart patients take digitalis, which is made from the leaves of the foxglove plant.

Test: *Do some heart patients take digitalis, which is made from the leaves of the foxglove plant?*

[The question does make sense; therefore, the test sentence is a complete sentence.]

Exercise 1

Identify the sentence fragments in the following paragraph. Revise the fragments by attaching them to related sentences or by recasting them as full sentences.

[1]One of the most versatile American sculptors of the twentieth century, Alexander Calder (1898–1976) is best known for his mobiles. [2]Playfully balanced arrangements of abstract or organic forms. [3]As a young man, Calder first studied mechanical engineering. [4]Even though he came from a family of sculptors. [5]It was not until four years after he earned his degree that he enrolled in an art school. [6]Shortly thereafter, Calder moved to Paris. [7]Where his wire sculptures won him worldwide recognition. [8]During the 1930s, he began to experiment with motion. [9]Eventually developing the mode of sculpture that most people think of when they hear the name Calder.

2a | **Fragments are often phrases incorrectly punctuated as sentences.**

Certain types of phrases (see **1f**) may be mistakenly written as sentence fragments. You can revise such a fragment by attaching it to a related sentence, usually the one preceding it. This method creates a strong link between the fragment and the independent clause it follows. If you are unsure of the correct punctuation to use with phrases, see **12b** and **12d**.

Verbal Phrase

Early humans valued color. ~~C~~reating permanent colors with natural pigments.

[edit marks: comma inserted, "creating" lowercase]

Prepositional Phrase

For years, the Scottish have dyed sweaters with soot. ~~Origi~~nally from the chimneys of peat-burning stoves.

[edit marks: comma inserted, "originally" lowercase]

Compound Predicate

Arctic foxes turn white when it snows. ~~A~~nd thus conceal themselves from prey.

[edit marks: "and" lowercase]

Appositive

During the Renaissance, one of the most highly valued pigments was ultramarine. ~~A~~n extract from lapis lazuli.

[edit marks: dash, "an" lowercase]

Appositive List

In order to derive dyes, we have always experimented with what we find in nature. ~~S~~hells, roots, insects, flowers.

[edit marks: colon inserted, "shells" lowercase]

Absolute Phrase

The deciduous trees of New England are known for their brilliant autumn color. ~~S~~ugar maples dazzling tourists with their deep orange and red leaves.

[edit marks: comma inserted, "sugar" lowercase]

Instead of attaching a fragment to the preceding sentence, you can recast the fragment as a full sentence. This method of revision elevates the importance of the information conveyed in the fragment.

Fragment: Early humans valued color. **Creating permanent colors with natural pigments.**

Revision: Early humans valued color. They created permanent colors with natural pigments.

Fragment: Humans painted themselves for a variety of purposes. **To attract a mate, to hide themselves from game or predators, or to signal aggression.**

Revision: Humans used color for a variety of purposes. For example, they painted themselves to attract a mate, to hide themselves from game or predators, or to signal aggression.

Exercise 2

Revise each fragment by attaching it to a related sentence or by recasting it as a full sentence.

1. At one time in Europe, mummy was a popular pigment. Made by crushing the remains of Egyptian mummies.
2. Many food producers package their products in red. Believing that it attracts consumers.
3. One of Marie Antoinette's favorite shades was puce. The French word for "flea."
4. At times, the pigment saffron was quite popular. And worth its weight in gold.
5. The pigment carmine was in high demand. Spanish conquistadors making vast fortunes on its production.

2b | Fragments are often dependent clauses
incorrectly punctuated as sentences.

A dependent clause that is punctuated as if it were an independent clause is sentence fragment. Such a fragment can be revised by attaching it to a related sentence, usually the sentence
preceding it. By linking the fragment to the independent
clause, you explicitly indicate their relationship.

Adverbial Clause

The iceberg was no surprise. ~~Because~~ *because* **the *Titanic*'s wireless**

operators had received reports of ice in the area.

Adjectival Clause

More than two thousand people were aboard the

Titanic. ~~Which~~ *, which* **was the largest ocean liner in 1912.**

The shipbuilders first constructed the keel. ~~Which~~ *, which* **was**

considered the backbone of the ship.

Two other methods can be used to revise these types of fragments. You can recast the fragment as a full sentence by re-
moving the subordinating conjunction or relative pronoun and
supplying any missing elements. This method of revision draws
more attention to the information conveyed in the fragment.

Revision: The iceberg was no surprise. The *Titanic*'s wireless
operators had received reports of ice in the area.

Revision: More than two thousand people were aboard the *Titanic.* In 1912, this ocean liner was the largest ever to have been
built.

You can also reduce the fragment to a participial phrase (see 1f (3)) or to an appositive phrase (see 1f (5)) and then attach the phrase to a related sentence. When you link a phrase to a sentence, you establish a certain relationship between the two.

> Revision: More than two thousand people were aboard the *Titanic,* the largest ocean liner in 1912. [reduced to an appositive phrase]

> Revision: The shipbuilders first constructed the keel—considered the backbone of the ship. [reduced to a participial phrase]

If you are unsure of the correct punctuation to use with phrases or dependent clauses, see chapter 12.

Exercise 3

Revise each fragment by attaching it to a related sentence or by recasting it as a full sentence.

1. The iceberg was hard to see. Because there was no wind causing waves to splash against it.
2. The lookouts on the *Titanic* did not spot the iceberg. Until it was too late.
3. The name given to the large ocean liner was *Titanic.* Which means "of great size."
4. One of the most reliable eyewitnesses was Jack Thayer. Who gave his report shortly after he was rescued.
5. Moviegoers raved about the film *Titanic.* Which was based on the ship's story.

2c | **Fragments can be effective when used judiciously.**

When used judiciously, fragments—like short sentences—emphasize ideas, add surprise, or enhance the rhythm of a paragraph.

Fragments are not appropriate for all types of writing, however. They are generally permitted only when the rhetorical situation allows the use of an intimate or playful tone.

> The room is full of sunlight. **Yellow. Cream. Gold. White.** These colors cover two-thirds of its surface, which is also awash with lavenders and reds falling in sun-filled stripes from the curtains, the walls, the man, the table, the chair, the dresser.
>
> —**ELAINE SCARRY,** *On Beauty and Being Just*

> Narrow, shoulderless highway 61 looked as if a tar pot had overturned at the summit and trickled a crooked course down. **A genuine white-knuckled road.**
>
> —**WILLIAM LEAST HEAT-MOON,** *Blue Highways*

Beyond the Rule

SENTENCE FRAGMENTS

You encounter sentence fragments every day—in conversations, in email messages, and even in some instructional materials. In conversation, someone might ask you, "Going anywhere tonight?" And you might respond, "Maybe." When preparing a meal, you have probably read instructions similar to these: "Just heat and serve." "Cook to golden brown." The writers of such instructions expect you to know what is to be heated or browned. These kinds of fragments, in which words that can be understood from the context are omitted, are called *abbreviated sentences*. For other examples of abbreviated sentences, visit www.harbrace.com.

Exercise 4

Advertisements often contain sentence fragments. Find a newspaper or magazine advertisement that contains several fragments. Rewrite the advertisement so that it consists of complete sentences; then, write a short paragraph explaining why you think the advertiser may have used the fragments.

Exercise 5

Follow the guidelines in this chapter to locate and revise the fragments in the following passage. If you find it necessary, make other changes to enhance the paragraph as well. Be prepared to explain your revisions.

[1]A giant hairy animal has caught the fascination of many people. [2]Including normally skeptical citizens and scientists. [3]They are all interested in the phenomenon of Sasquatch. [4]Also commonly called Big Foot. [5]*Sasquatch* comes from the Salish word *saskehavas*. [6]The North American Sasquatch has a counterpart. [7]The Himalayan Yeti. [8]Both have been studied by cryptozoologists. [9]Who research undiscovered animals. [10]In our country, most sightings of Sasquatch occur in the Pacific Northwest. [11]From northern California to central Alaska. [12]Although reports have come from almost every state. [13]During the settlement of the United States, stories of hairy ape-men were told by Native Americans. [14]And later on by trappers. [15]Teddy Roosevelt recorded one such story.

Comma Splices and Fused Sentences

Comma splices and fused sentences are similar sentence-level mistakes; both result from weak or missing punctuation between two sentences. Such errors are sometimes hard to find because the content and purpose of the sentences are closely related. Nonetheless, because comma splices and fused sentences do not follow punctuation conventions, they may distract your readers from understanding what you have written.

This chapter will help you

- recognize comma splices and fused sentences (**3a**) and
- learn ways to revise them (**3b**, **3c**, **3d**).

Although grammar checkers identify many comma splices and some fused sentences, they routinely miss many others. In fact, a grammar checker could not reliably identify the comma splices and fused sentences in this chapter. See Using a Grammar Checker on page 2.

A **comma splice,** or *comma fault,* refers to the incorrect use of a comma to separate two independent clauses (see **1g(1)**).

Most stockholders favored the merger, the management did not.

Because a comma is a weak mark of punctuation (see chapter **12**), it is not conventionally used to join independent clauses.

For this purpose, you should use connecting words, stronger marks of punctuation, or both.

> Most stockholders favored the merger, **but** the management did not.
> OR
> Most stockholders favored the merger; the management did not.

A **fused sentence** consists of two independent clauses run together without any punctuation at all. This type of sentence is sometimes called a *run-on sentence*.

> The first section of the proposal was approved however the budget will have to be resubmitted.

To revise a fused sentence, all you have to do is include appropriate punctuation and any necessary connecting words.

> The first section of the proposal was approved; **however,** the budget will have to be resubmitted.

In case you are unfamiliar with or unsure about the conventions of punctuating independent clauses, here is a short review:

- A comma and a coordinating conjunction can join two independent clauses (see **1g**). The coordinating conjunction indicates the relationship between the two clauses. For example, *and* signals addition, whereas *but* and *yet* signal contrast. The comma precedes the conjunction.

  [Independent clause], **and** [independent clause].

  The new store opened this morning, **and** the owners greeted everyone at the door.

- A semicolon can join two independent clauses that are closely related. A semicolon generally signals addition or contrast.

  [Independent clause]; [independent clause].

One of the owners comes from this area; the other grew up in Costa Rica.

- A semicolon may also precede an independent clause that begins with a conjunctive adverb such as *however* or *nevertheless*. A comma follows this type of connecting word.

  The store will be open late on Fridays and Saturdays; however, it will be closed all day on Sundays.

- A colon can join two independent clauses. The second clause usually explains or elaborates the first.

  [Independent clause]: [Independent clause].

  The owners extended a special offer: Anyone who makes a purchase during the opening will receive a ten percent discount.

- A period separates clauses of unequal length, different structure, or unrelated content.

  [Independent clause]. [Independent clause].

  The store is located on the corner of Pine Street and First Avenue. It was formerly an insurance office.

- Occasionally, commas are used (instead of semicolons or periods) between independent clauses, but only when the clauses are short, parallel in form, and unified in meaning.

  They came, they shopped, they left.

- Commas are also used to separate a statement from an attached question (also called a *tag question*).

  You went to the grand opening, didn't you?

For more information on punctuating sentences, see chapters 12, 14, and 17.

> **3a** | **Two different methods can be used to identify comma splices and fused sentences.**

If you have trouble recognizing comma splices or fused sentences, try one of the following methods.

1. Locate a sentence you are unsure about. Put the sentence in this frame: They do not understand the idea that _____. Only complete sentences will make sense in this frame. If only part of a test sentence fits into the frame, you have probably located a comma splice or a fused sentence.

   Test sentence: The wild Bactrian camel, a two-humped camel living in the Gobi Desert, can drink salt water.

   Test: They do not understand the idea that *the wild Bactrian camel, a two-humped camel living in the Gobi Desert, can drink salt water.* [The sentence makes sense. No revision is necessary.]

   Test sentence: Male proboscis monkeys have oddly shaped large noses, they also have unusual webbed paws.

   Test: They do not understand the idea that *male proboscis monkeys have oddly shaped large noses, they also have unusual webbed paws.* [The sentence does not make sense because there are two sentences completing the frame, rather than one. Therefore, the test sentence needs to be revised: *Male proboscis monkeys have oddly shaped large noses. They also have unusual webbed paws.*]

2. Locate a sentence you are unsure about. Try to rewrite it as a question with a yes or no answer. If only part of the sentence makes sense, you have likely found a comma splice or a fused sentence.

   Test sentence: The Arctic tern migrates from the Arctic to Antarctica.

Test: Does the Arctic tern migrate from the Arctic to Antarctica? [The question makes sense. No revision is necessary.]

Test sentence: Meerkats use their claws to forage for food they frequently prey on scorpions.

Test: Do meerkats use their claws to forage for food they frequently prey on scorpions? [The question does not make sense because only one of the two sentences has been made into a question. The test sentence should be revised: *Meerkats use their claws to forage for food. They frequently prey on scorpions.*]

Once you have identified a problematic sentence, you can determine whether the problem is a comma splice or a fused sentence by following these steps.

1. Notice how many pairs of grammatical subjects and verbs are in the sentence (see **1b–c**).

   a. Find the verbs.

   b. Match verbs to subjects.

   (1) Male proboscis monkeys have oddly shaped large noses, they also have unusual webbed paws. [two pairs]

   (2) Meerkats use their claws to forage for food they frequently prey on scorpions. [two pairs]

2. Look for the punctuation that separates the pairs of subjects and verbs (if there are at least two). Sentence (1) has a comma. Sentence (2) has no punctuation.

3. If no punctuation separates the pairs, you have found a fused sentence, unless there is a dependent clause present (see **1g(2)**). Sentence (2) is a fused sentence.

   Meerkats use their claws to forage for food. They frequently prey on scorpions.

Note, however, that the following sentence includes a dependent clause and is not fused.

> Meerkats use their claws to forage for food, which frequently consists of scorpions.

4. If a comma separates the pairs of subjects and verbs, you may have found a comma splice.

   a. If a comma is followed by a coordinating conjunction or a nonessential (nonrestrictive) dependent clause (see **12d**), the sentence does not contain a comma splice.

   > Male proboscis monkeys have oddly shaped large noses, and they also have unusual webbed paws.

   > A male proboscis monkey has an oddly shaped large nose, whose size may attract mates.

   b. If there is not a coordinating conjunction or a nonessential dependent clause, the sentence does contain a comma splice. Sentence (1) contains a comma splice.

   > Male proboscis monkeys have oddly shaped large noses, they also have unusual webbed paws.

   [handwritten correction: ". They" replacing ", they"]

You can also find comma splices and fused sentences by remembering that they commonly occur in certain circumstances:

- With transitional words and phrases such as *however, therefore,* and *for example* (see also **3c**)

  > Comma splice: The director is not able to meet with you this week, however next week she will have time on Monday and Tuesday. [Note that a semicolon replaces the comma.]

  [handwritten: semicolon after "week" and comma after "however"]

- When an explanation or an example is given in the second sentence

Fused sentence: The cultural center has a new collection of spear points, ~~many~~ . Many of them were donated by a retired anthropologist.

■ When a positive clause follows a negative clause

Comma splice: A World Cup victory is not just an everyday sporting event, ~~it~~ . It is a national celebration.

■ When the subject of the second clause is a pronoun whose antecedent is in the preceding clause

Fused sentence: Lake Baikal is located in southern Russia, it . It is 394 miles long.

3b | **A comma splice or a fused sentence can be revised in a number of ways.**

If you find comma splices or fused sentences in your writing, try one of the following methods to revise them.

1. Link clauses by using a comma and a coordinating conjunction such as *and* or *but.* By linking clauses in this way, you signal the relationship between them (addition or contrast, for example).

   Fused sentence: Joseph completed the first experiment he will complete the other by Friday.

   Revision: Joseph completed the first experiment, **and** he will complete the other by Friday.

   Comma splice: Some diplomats applauded the treaty, others opposed it vehemently.

   Revision: Some diplomats applauded the treaty, **but** others opposed it vehemently.

2. Link clauses by using a semicolon (see **14a**) or a colon (**17d**), or separate them with a period (**17a**). When you link clauses with a semicolon, you signal their connection indirectly. There are no explicit conjunctions to serve as cues. A semicolon usually indicates addition or contrast. When you link clauses with a colon, the second clause serves as an explanation or an elaboration of the first. A period indicates that each clause is a complete sentence, distinct from surrounding sentences.

Comma splice: Our division's reports are posted on our Web page, hard copies are available by request.

Revision 1: Our division's reports are posted on our Web page; hard copies are available by request.

Revision 2: Our division's reports are posted on our Web page. Hard copies are available by request.

Fused sentence: His choice was difficult he would either lose his job or betray his ethical principles.

Revision: His choice was difficult: He would either lose his job or betray his ethical principles.

3. Rewrite one clause as a phrase (see **1f**) or as a dependent clause (**1g**). A dependent clause includes a subordinating conjunction such as *although* or *because*, which indicates how the clauses are related. Phrases suggest relationships less directly because they do not include conjunctions.

Comma splice: The wind had blown down trees and power lines, the whole city was without electricity for several hours.

Revision 1: **Because of the downed power lines,** the whole city was without electricity for several hours. [using a phrase]

Revision 2: **Because the wind had blown down power lines,** the whole city was without electricity for several hours. [using a dependent clause]

4. Integrate one clause into the other. When you integrate clauses, you generally choose the important details and omit or change some words in one of the clauses.

Fused sentence: The proposal covers all but one point it does not describe how the project will be assessed.

Revision: The proposal covers all the points except assessment procedures.

As you edit fused sentences and comma splices, you will find that you are refining the connections between your sentences, making them clearer and more cohesive. By taking the time to revise, you will be helping your readers follow your train of thought. For more information on joining clauses, see chapter 24.

The following checklist will help you find and fix comma splices and fused sentences.

CHECKLIST for Comma Splices and Fused Sentences

1 Common Sites for Comma Splices or Fused Sentences

- With transitional words and phrases such as *however, therefore,* and *for example*
- When an explanation or an example occurs in the second clause
- When a positive clause follows a negative clause
- When the subject of the second clause is a pronoun whose antecedent is in the preceding clause

2 How to Identify a Comma Splice or a Fused Sentence

1. Notice how many pairs of grammatical subjects and verbs (see 1b–c) are in the sentence.
   a. Find the verbs.
   b. Match verbs to subjects.
2. Look for the punctuation that separates the pairs of subjects and verbs (if there are at least two).
3. If no punctuation separates the pairs, you have found a fused sentence.

(Continued on page 66)

(Continued from page 65)

4. If a comma separates the pairs, you may have found a comma splice.
   a. If there is a coordinating conjunction or a nonessential dependent clause, there is no comma splice.
   b. If there is no coordinating conjunction or nonessential dependent clause, there is a comma splice.

3   How to Fix Comma Splices and Fused Sentences

- Link the clauses with a comma and a coordinating conjunction.
- Link the clauses by using a semicolon or a colon.
- Separate the clauses by punctuating each as a sentence.
- Make one clause dependent.
- Reduce one clause to a phrase.
- Rewrite the sentence, integrating one clause into the other.

Exercise 1

Connect each pair of sentences in two of the following ways: (a) join them with a semicolon or colon, (b) join them with a coordinating conjunction, (c) reduce one to a phrase or dependent clause, or (d) integrate one clause into the other.

1. Our national parks offer a variety of settings. They attract millions of visitors every year.
2. The Grand Teton National Park includes a sixteen-peak mountain range. It offers extensive hiking trails and wildlife-viewing opportunities.
3. Yellowstone National Park is generally full of tourists. The geysers and cliffs are worth the visit.

4. Hikers especially enjoy their vacations at Yellowstone National Park. The park consists of two million acres of backcountry perfect for hiking.

5. Vacationers enchanted by cascading water should visit Yosemite National Park. The waterfalls at Yosemite reach heights of more than two thousand feet.

Exercise 2

Revise each comma splice or fused sentence. Do not edit a sentence that is correctly punctuated.

1. Many bats shriek and listen for returning echoes to determine the location of prey, this is the most common type of echolocation.

2. To avoid deafening themselves, these bats shriek in pulses.

3. Leaf-nosed bats have a more sophisticated location system they emit a continuous sound that does not require listening for echoes.

4. The majority of bats eat insects, they live in tropical regions, where insects are abundantly available.

5. Bats that roost in colonies produce huge amounts of guano, in the past phosphorus and nitrogen extracted from bat droppings were used to make explosives.

3c	Transitional words and phrases can be used to join independent clauses.

Another way to revise comma splices and fused sentences is to use transitional words (**conjunctive adverbs**) or transitional phrases (see list below). These words and phrases may begin new sentences.

Fused sentence: Sexual harassment is not just an issue for women ₌ After all, men can be sexually harassed too.

Transitional words or phrases may also join two clauses into one sentence. In these sentences, a semicolon appears after the first clause (before the transition); a comma appears after the transition. If a sentence contains a transitional word or phrase without the appropriate punctuation, it may be a fused sentence or contain a comma splice.

Comma splice: The word *status* refers to relative position within a group ; however , it is often used to indicate only positions of prestige.

Conjunctive Adverbs

also	however	next
anyhow	incidentally	otherwise
anyway	indeed	similarly
besides	instead	still
consequently	likewise	then
finally	meanwhile	therefore
furthermore	moreover	thus
hence	nevertheless	

Beyond the Rule

PUNCTUATING SENTENCES WITH CONJUNCTIVE ADVERBS

A comma used to set off a conjunctive adverb is sometimes omitted when there is no risk of misreading.

The sea was unusually hot; **thus** the coral turned white. [No misreading is possible, so the comma can be omitted.]

He was so nervous that his stomach was churning. **However,** he answered the question calmly and accurately. [The comma is needed. Without it, *however* might be interpreted as meaning "in whatever way" rather than "in contrast." COMPARE However he answered the question, he would offend someone.]

For more examples, visit www.harbrace.com.

Transitional Phrases

after all	even so	in fact
as a result	for example	in other words
at any rate	in addition	on the contrary
at the same time	in comparison	on the other hand
by the way	in contrast	that is

A transitional word or phrase may either begin a clause or take another position within it. When it appears within the clause, the transitional word or phrase is set off by commas.

> She believed that daily exercise has many benefits; **however**, she couldn't fit it into her schedule. [The conjunctive adverb begins the second independent clause and is positioned after a semicolon and before a comma (see also 14a).]

> She believed that daily exercise has many benefits; she couldn't, **however**, fit it into her schedule. [The conjunctive adverb appears later in the second clause. In this position, it is set off by commas.]

Exercise 3

Connect each pair of sentences by including a transitional word or phrase and any necessary punctuation.

1. Discoveries in neuroscience have yielded many benefits. Researchers have developed medication for schizophrenia and Tourette's syndrome.
2. The average human brain weighs about three pounds. The average brain of a sperm whale weighs seventeen pounds.
3. Researchers studying brain hemispheres have found that many professional musicians process music in their left hemisphere. The notion that musicians and artists depend on the right side of their brain is considered outmoded.
4. The brain needs water to function properly. Dehydration commonly leads to lethargy and hinders learning.
5. The body of a brain cell can move. Most brain cells stay put, extending axons outward.

3d | Divided quotations require special attention.

When you divide quotations (see **16a**) with **attributive tags** such as *he said* or *she asked,* be sure to use a period between independent clauses.

> Comma splice: "Beauty brings copies of itself into being," states
>
> Elaine Scarry, "it makes us draw it, take photographs of it, or
>
> describe it to other people."

[Both parts of the quotation are complete sentences; thus, the attributive tag is attached to the first, and the sentence is punctuated with a period. The second sentence stands by itself.]

A comma separates two parts of a single quoted sentence.

> "Musing takes place in a kind of meadowlands of the imagination," writes Rebecca Solnit, "a part of the imagination that has not yet been plowed, developed, or put to any immediately practical use."

[Because the quotation is a single sentence, a comma is used.]

Exercise 4

Revise the following paragraph so that no comma splices remain. Some sentences may not need revision.

1In the introduction to his book of true stories, *I Thought My Father Was God,* Paul Auster describes how he was able to collect these accounts of real and sometimes raw experience.

[2]In October 1999, Auster, in collaboration with National Public Radio, began the *National Story Project,* during an interview on the radio program *Weekend All Things Considered,* he invited listeners to send in their stories about unusual events—"true stories that sounded like fiction." [3]In just one year, over four thousand stories were submitted, Auster read every one of them. [4]"Of the four thousand stories I have read, most have been compelling enough to hold me until the last word," Auster affirms, "Most have been written with simple, straightforward conviction, and most have done honor to the people who sent them in." [5]Some of the stories Auster collected can now be read in his anthology, choosing stories for the collection was difficult, though. [6]"For every story about a dream or an animal or a missing object," explains Auster, "there were dozens of others that were submitted, dozens of others that could have been chosen."

Adjectives and Adverbs

Adjectives and adverbs are modifiers; that is, they qualify, restrict, or intensify the meaning of other words. They also describe degrees of comparison.

This chapter will help you

- recognize adjectives and understand how to use them (**4a**),
- recognize adverbs and understand how to use them (**4b**),
- use the comparative and superlative forms correctly (**4c**),
- know when to use a group modifier (**4d**), and
- revise double negatives (**4e**).

Adjectives modify nouns and pronouns; **adverbs** modify verbs, adjectives, and other adverbs.

Adjectives	**Adverbs**
a **quick** lunch	eat **quickly**
armed squads	**heavily** armed squads
She looked **angry.**	She looked **angrily** at me.

In traditional grammar, the determiners *a, an,* and *the* are often classified as adjectives since they identify or describe a noun. See **22a(1)** for the use of articles.

Because adjectives and adverbs work as modifiers, can be similar in form, and generally occur near one another, they can be difficult to tell apart. If you need to distinguish an adjective from an adverb, you consider the form of the word and its function in the particular sentence.

> **4a** | Adjectives either modify nouns or pronouns or function as complements.

Adjectives answer any of several questions: *What kind? How many? Which one(s)?*

What kind?	**simple** one
How many?	**several** men
Which one?	**writing** class

Beyond the Rule

A TEST FOR ADJECTIVES

If you need to determine whether a word is an adjective, you can use a simple test. To learn more about this test, which can identify many but not all adjectives, visit www.harbrace.com.

 In some languages, adjectives and nouns agree in number. In Spanish, for example, when a noun is plural, the adjective is plural as well: *vistas claras.* In English, however, adjectives do not have a plural form: *clear views.*

Sometimes a verbal (see **1f(2)**), for instance, an infinitive or a participle, serves as an adjective.

a chicken **to eat**   a determin**ed** effort
a determin**ing** factor

Do not omit the *-d* or *-ed* ending of a past participle used as an adjective. (See 7a(1)–(2).)

The dog was too frighten_{ed} to go to him.

 Both present participles and past participles are used as adjectives; however, they cannot be used interchangeably. To express emotion, you use a present participle with a noun referring to someone or something that is the cause of the emotion. In the phrase *the exciting tennis match,* the tennis match is the cause of the excitement. You use a past participle with a noun referring to someone who experiences the emotion. In the phrase *the excited crowd,* the crowd is experiencing the excitement.

Here is a list of commonly confused participles:

annoying, annoyed
boring, bored
confusing, confused
embarrassing, embarrassed
frustrating, frustrated
interesting, interested
surprising, surprised
tiring, tired

Adjectives generally, but not always, come before the words they modify.

When I write, I appreciate a **quiet** house.
Tom found the house **quiet.**

In English, two or more adjectives modifying the same noun are used in a particular order based on their meanings. (The use of more than three consecutive adjectives is rare.) The following list shows the usual order of adjectives and gives examples. Notice that determiners precede all of the adjectives.

Determiner	a, an, the, this, these, those, my, our, much, many, five
Evaluator	fascinating, painful, sad
Size	large, small, tiny, miniscule
Shape	square, round, triangular
Age	young, old, aged, newborn, antique
Color	black, white, green, brown
Nationality or geography	Arabian, Cuban, Peruvian, Slavic
Religion	Jewish, Catholic, Protestant, Buddhist
Material	silk, paper, pine, rubber

We stayed in **a simple old country** inn.

Have you seen **those large pine** trees?

Marquita wrapped **three blue silk** scarves around the post.

(1) Adjectives can often be recognized by their endings.

Because many adjectives are formed from other parts of speech, you can often determine that a word is an adjective by looking at its ending: *-able, -al, -ful, -ic, ish, -less,* and *-y* are commonly used to make an adjective from a noun or a verb.

accept**able**	rent**al**	event**ful**	angel**ic**
sheep**ish**	effort**less**	sleep**y**	

Certain adjectives formed from nouns have the ending *-ly* (*cost, costly*).

(2) Adjectives used as subject or object complements are easily confused with adverbs.

An adjective used as a **subject complement** completes the meaning of the verb by describing the subject of the sentence. A common error is to use an adverb as a subject complement.

The actor looked **angrily.** [*Angry* is an adjective that tells
~~angrily~~ ^{angry}

something about *actor.*]

The actor looked up **angry.** [*Angrily* is an adverb that tells
~~angry~~ ^{angrily}

something about *looked up.*]

He felt **bad** about the mistake. [Using *badly* in this sentence would be a *hypercorrection*—introducing an error in an attempt to be correct.]

His leg hurt **badly** after he broke it. [an acceptable use of *badly*]

Adjectives that modify the direct object in sentences with such verbs as *call, consider, find, make,* and *name* are **object complements.** (See **1d(3).**)

They *named* the baby **Fred.**

They *considered* the restaurant **expensive.** [The adjective *expensive* refers to the direct object *restaurant* and completes the meaning of the verb *considered.*]

Exercise 1

Using adjectives as complements, write two sentences that illustrate each of the following patterns.

Oranges	*taste*	*good.*	
Subject	+ linking verb	+ subject complement	

They	*called*	*us*	*friendly.*
Subject	+ verb	+ direct object	+ object complement

4b	Adverbs modify verbs, adjectives, and other adverbs.

Adverbs answer any of several questions: *How? When? Where?*

How did Vassily answer her?   Vassily answered her **playfully.**
When did she plan to leave?   She planned to leave **early.**
Where did I put the cat?   I put the cat **outside.**

An adverb that modifies a verb commonly describes the circumstances—how (manner), when (time), or where (place)—under which an action or event occurred.

Manner   We walked **quietly.**
Time   We arrived **later.**
Place   We walked **home.**

Adverbs of frequency (such as *always, never, sometimes,* and *often*) appear before one-word verbs.

He **rarely** <u>goes</u> to horror movies.

However, these frequency adverbs appear after a form of *be* when it is the main verb.

Movies based on Stephen King novels <u>are</u> **always** popular.

When a sentence contains more than one verb in a verb phrase, the adverb of frequency is placed after the first auxiliary verb.

My friends <u>have</u> **never** <u>seen</u> *The Shining.*
I <u>have</u> **seldom** <u>been</u> frightened by a movie.

Adverbs can also modify verbals (gerunds, infinitives, or participles) or whole clauses. (See **1g**.)

Walking rapidly is good for you. [The adverb *rapidly* modifies the gerund *walking,* which is the subject.]

Whole clauses can even function as adverbs. (See **1g**.)

When I was seven years old, my family began our tradition of spending every summer in Colorado. [The adverbial clause of time modifies the verb *began*.]

Infinitives can also serve as adverbs.

studied **to pass**   happy **to leave**   afraid **to speak**

Beyond the Rule

KINDS OF ADVERBS

Adverbs can be said to have four basic relationships to other words in a sentence. *Subjuncts* (such as *very* and *only*) are those adverbs that expand, intensify, or diminish the subject, verb, or complement. *Adjuncts* (such as *quietly, outside,* and *under the table*) give additional information about other sentence elements. *Disjuncts* are adverbs (such as the sentence modifier *Yes* in *Yes, they were late*) that are not clearly attached to other elements of a sentence. *Conjuncts* (such as *however* and *therefore*) show relationships between parts of a sentence. For additional information, visit www.harbrace.com.

Because many adverbs are formed by adding -*ly* to an adjective, you can often spot an adverb by looking for that ending.

Monique wrote her name **carefully.** [The adverb *carefully* modifies the verb *wrote*.]

The plane departs at an **unpleasantly** early hour. [The adverb *unpleasantly* modifies the adjective *early.*]

The computer was priced very **reasonably.** [The adverb *very* modifies the adverb *reasonably.*]

If an adverb is formed from an adjective ending in *-y,* the *-y* is changed to *-i* before *-ly* is added.

eas**y** [adjective]   eas**ily** [adverb]

If an adjective ends in *-le,* the *-le* is dropped before *-ly* is added.

sim**ple** [adjective]   sim**ply** [adverb]

The *-ly* ending is usually associated with adverbs formed from adjectives. A few adverbs have two acceptable forms (*quick, quickly; slow, slowly*). When in doubt, look in a dictionary for the label *adv* and any usage notes.

A number of words—for example, *fast* and *well*—can function as either adjectives or adverbs. When in doubt, consult a dictionary for the labels *adj* and *adv* and any usage notes.

She likes **fast** cars. [adjective]

We ran **fast** to catch the bus. [adverb]

Most dictionaries still label *sure* for *surely, real* for *really,* and *good* for *well* as *colloquial* (see **19e**), meaning that you may hear them in conversation but should avoid using them in your writing.

| **Conversational** | Marcy is a **real good** swimmer. [The usual meaning of *real* is "not artificial" rather than "very."] |
| **Written** | Marcy swims **really well.** [appropriate in both written and conversational usage; see **19c(2)**] |

Exercise 2

Revise the following sentences to use adverbs considered conventional in college writing. Replace any that are colloquial or unconventional. Do not change any sentence that does not need editing.

1. The boat's engine roared loud throughout Puerto Vallarta Bay.
2. We were looking for the local known island protected as a wildlife refuge.
3. The man next to me explained that he didn't scuba dive as regular as he would like.
4. With everyone participating in scuba diving and snorkeling, the boat seemed abnormal quiet.
5. My sister and I certainly enjoyed watching everyone.

> **4c** Many adjectives and adverbs change form to show relative quality, quantity, or manner (the degree of comparison).

Degree refers to the quantity, quality, or manner of items being compared. Both adjectives and adverbs show the quality, quantity, or manner of a single element (positive) or the relationship between two elements (comparative) or among three or more elements (superlative).

Positive	Comparative	Superlative
large	larger	largest
quickly	more quickly	most quickly

It can be difficult to know when to add the suffix *-er* or *-est* to show degree and when to use *more/less* or *most/least,* but the following guidelines can help you.

Generally, the endings *-er* for the comparative and *-est* for the superlative are added to one-syllable adjectives and adverbs. Two-syllable adjectives with the stress on the first syllable sometimes take *-er* and *-est*. (If the base word ends in *-y*, don't forget to change the *-y* to *-i* when adding the comparative or superlative ending: *lucky, luckier, luckiest*. See **18d(4)**.) Other two-syllable adjectives, longer adjectives, and most adverbs use *more* (or *less*) for the comparative and *most* (or *least*) for the superlative.

> tall, taller, tallest [one-syllable adjective]
>
> fast, faster, fastest [one-syllable adverb]
>
> pretty, prettier, prettiest [two-syllable adjective with stress on the first syllable]
>
> quickly, more/less quickly, most/least quickly [two-syllable adverb]
>
> fortunate, more/less fortunate, most/least fortunate [three-syllable adjective]
>
> rapidly, more/less rapidly, most/least rapidly [three-syllable adverb]

For some two-syllable adjectives, the comparative and the superlative can be formed in both ways. Examples are *able, angry, clever, common, cruel, friendly, gentle, handsome, narrow, polite, quiet,* and *simple*. Use *the* rather than *a* or *an* with the superlative.

A few common modifiers have irregular forms.

> little, less, least
>
> good/well, better, best
>
> bad/badly, worse, worst
>
> far, further/farther, furthest/farthest (See the **Glossary of Usage**.)

When in doubt, consult a dictionary.

(1) The comparative denotes two elements in a comparison.

The **comparative** is used with two elements in a comparison. Make sure to complete every comparison (see 22c), and always make clear what the first element is being compared with. The conjunction *than* often signals the second element being compared.

> The metropolitan area is much **bigger** now **than** it was five years ago.

> Dried apples are **more** nutritious per pound **than** fresh apples. [a comparison of two groups]

The comparison may be implied by the context.

> She wrote **two** papers, and the instructor gave her a **better** grade on the second.

The comparative form used with *other* sometimes refers to more than two.

> Bert can run **faster** than the *other* players can.

(2) The superlative denotes three or more elements in a comparison.

The **superlative** shows the relationship among three or more elements in a comparison.

> Bert is the **fastest** of the three runners.

> OR

> Bert is the **fastest** runner of all.

The superlative occasionally refers to fewer than three, as in "Put your *best* foot forward!"

Beyond the Rule

ABSOLUTE MODIFIERS

General usage and dictionaries accept comparative forms of many adjectives or adverbs with absolute meanings, as in *a more perfect society, the deadest campus,* and *less completely exhausted.* But careful writers rarely use such comparisons. Also, most still consider *unique* an absolute adjective—one without degrees of comparison—and thus do not write *more unique* or *most unique.* For more information, visit www.harbrace.com.

(3) A double comparative or superlative is redundant.

This bus stop is **more** cold**er** than the one around the corner.

That was the **most** smart**est** thing anybody ever said.

Exercise 3

Provide the correct comparative or superlative form of each modifier within parentheses.

1. Amphibians can be divided into three groups. Frogs and toads are in (common) group.
2. Wormlike caecilians are (common) of the amphibians.
3. Because they do not have to maintain a specific body temperature, amphibians eat (frequently) than mammals do.
4. Reptiles may look like amphibians, but their skin is (dry).
5. During the Devonian period, (close) ancestors of amphibians were fish with fins that looked like legs.

6. In general, amphibians have (few) bones in their skeletons than other animals with backbones.

7. Color markings on amphibians vary, though the back of an amphibian is usually (dark) than its belly.

8. Frogs are known for their leaping ability. (Long) jump recorded is seventeen and a half feet.

9. The skin on a frog is usually (smooth) than the dry, warty skin of a toad.

10. Once fairly common, frogs of many species are becoming (rare) due to the effects of pollution.

4d | **A noun or a word group can be used as a modifier.**

Many nouns or word groups effectively modify other nouns (as in *reference manual, windfall profits tax, House Ways and Means Committee*), especially when appropriate adjectives are not available. Avoid such forms, however, when they are awkward or confusing.

Many candidates entered the president~ial~ race.

~~The~~ Representative Landor~'s~ ~~recess~~ maneuvers during the recess led to victory.

Occasionally, a group of words linked with hyphens (a compound adjective) modifies a noun. (See **18f(1)**.)

I threw away the **half-eaten** apple.

The students did very well on a **harder-than-average** examination.

Nouns used as modifiers are almost always singular: *sophomore students, executive decision.*

4e | A double negative is redundant.

Most words that express negation are modifiers. The term **double negative** refers to the use of two negative words within a sentence or clause to express a single negation.

He didn't keep ~~no~~ records. OR He ~~didn't keep~~ no records.

(handwritten: "any" above "no"; "kept" above "didn't keep")

Beyond the Rule

THE ORIGINAL DOUBLE NEGATIVES

In spoken and written English several centuries ago, two—or even three, four, or five—negative words were used to make a negative statement more emphatic. In the eighteenth century, grammarians decided that this practice was incorrect because the second negative was redundant at best and likely to be confusing (based on the mathematical idea that two negatives make a positive). Double negatives are common in many other languages and in some nonprestige English dialects and song lyrics ("I can't get no satisfaction"). For more information, visit www. harbrace.com.

Because *hardly, barely,* and *scarcely* denote severely limited or negative conditions, using *not, nothing,* or *without* with any of these modifiers creates a double negative.

I could**n't hardly** quit in the middle of the job.

OR

I could**n't** ~~**hardly**~~ quit in the middle of the job.

The motion passed with ~~not scarcely~~ a protest.

OR

The motion passed with ~~not scarcely a~~ protest.
little ∧

Rarely, emphasis in a sentence requires the use of two negatives, and such a construction is not considered a double negative.

It would**n't** be safe **not** to install smoke detectors. [This construction is permissible when *not* is being emphasized. Otherwise, the sentence should be revised. COMPARE It would be dangerous not to install smoke detectors.]

Exercise 4

Using what you have learned in this chapter, revise the following sentences to remove modifier errors.

1. As a woman in the twentieth century, Gertrude Bell led an unusual life.
2. She was among the first women to graduate from Oxford and couldn't hardly be satisfied with domestic life.
3. Bell traveled to what were considered the most remotest countries in the world and explored the Iraqi desert.
4. The war in Iraq didn't give Bell no time to pursue her research.
5. She became an Arab rebellion supporter.
6. In 1921, Winston Churchill invited Bell to a conference in the Middle East because the other Great Britain conference participants knew little about Iraq.

Pronouns and Case

This chapter will help you

- identify the various kinds of pronouns (**5a**),
- determine the forms of pronouns (**5b**), and
- know how to use *who* and *whom* (**5c**).

A **pronoun** is commonly defined as a word that can replace either a noun or a phrase acting as a noun. Unlike nouns, which change form only to become plural or possessive, pronouns change form to show their relationship to other words in a sentence. Each of a pronoun's forms is a **case.** You can see how a pronoun changes form (case) in the examples that follow. When a pronoun changes case, that change signals a different relationship.

He wants his cousin to help him.	**Hugh** wants his cousin to help him.
He wants **his** cousin to help him.	He wants **Hugh's** cousin to help him.
He wants his cousin to help **him.**	He wants his cousin to help **Hugh.**

 Grammar checkers often provide minimal help in identifying case errors. A grammar checker found nothing wrong with this sentence: *Carol and me agree that Mark is a good athlete.* And it identified a word order problem, not a case error, in this sentence: *Me and Carol agreed that Mark is a good*

athlete. In addition, grammar checkers miss as many errors involving *who/whom* as they find (see **5c(2)**), and they almost never find problems with pronoun-antecedent agreement (**6b**). See **Using a Grammar Checker** on page 2.

5a	Being familiar with the various kinds of pronouns helps writers use them correctly.

English has several different kinds of pronouns: personal, relative, interrogative, and reflexive pronouns.

(1) Personal pronouns identify the speaker, the person spoken to, and the person or thing spoken about.

The first-person pronoun (*I* or *we*) identifies the speaker, the second-person pronoun (*you*) identifies the person spoken to, and the third-person pronoun (*he, she, it,* or *they*) identifies the person or thing spoken about. Personal pronouns change form to reflect their relationship to other words in a sentence. The subject of a sentence appears in the subjective case, the object appears in the objective case, and a word showing possession appears in the possessive case. (See **15a.**)

Person	Subjective Singular	Subjective Plural	Objective Singular	Objective Plural	Possessive Singular	Possessive Plural
First person	I	we	me	us	my mine	our ours
Second person	you	you	you	you	your yours	your yours
Third person	he she it	they	him her it	them	his hers its	their theirs

Notice that the second-person pronoun *you* has the same form for both singular and plural and for the subjective and objective cases. The third-person pronoun *it* has the same form for the subjective and objective cases. The possessive form of *it* is *its,* without an apostrophe (*it's* means "it is"). All the other personal pronouns reflect person, number, and case. (And the third-person singular forms also reflect the last vestige of gender in English usage. See **6b(1)** and **19d(1)**.)

Beyond the Rule

THE TERRITORIES OF CASES

It can be useful to think in terms of territories to distinguish the subjective and objective cases. That is, the part of a sentence before the verb is "subject territory," and pronouns in that position appear in subjective case. The rest of the sentence is "object territory," and the pronouns in that part of the sentence almost always appear in objective form. The only exception occurs when the verb is a form of *be*. For additional information on case, visit www.harbrace.com.

(2) A relative pronoun relates a dependent clause to a noun in the main clause.

Relative pronouns (*who, whom, whoever, whomever, which, whose,* and *that*) introduce clauses that refer to a noun in a main clause.

> **Mike Schildt, who** carved my stone bear, lives in Taos.
>
> Mike Schildt, about **whom** I know only that he lives in Taos, carved my stone bear.

Graham explained his invention to **whoever** would listen.
[*Whoever* is the subject of its own clause.]

Graham explained his invention to **whomever** he could get to
listen. [*Whomever* is the object of the preposition *to.*]

Who, whose, and *whom* ordinarily refer to people; *which* refers
to things; *that* refers to either people or things. The possessive
pronoun *whose* (used in place of the awkward *of which*) sometimes refers to things.

The poem, **whose** author is unknown, has recently been set to
music. [COMPARE The poem, of which the author is unknown,
has . . .]

	Refers to people	Refers to things	Refers to either
Subjective	who	which	that
Objective	whom	which	that
Possessive			whose

Do not confuse *who's* and *whose*. *Who's* is a contraction for *who
is*, and *whose* indicates possession.

(3) Interrogative pronouns introduce questions.

Like their relative counterparts, the interrogative pronouns *who*
and *whom* change form to reflect their grammatical use in a
sentence. *Which* and *that* do not change form.

Who asked the question? [*Who* is the subject of the sentence.]
Whom did she give the book to? [See **5c(2)** for the approved
use of the subjective case in such sentences.]

(4) Reflexive pronouns direct the action back on the subject or the agent; intensive pronouns are used for emphasis.

Reflexive and intensive pronouns are formed by combining personal pronouns with *-self*. The reflexive pronouns (*myself, himself, themselves,* and so on) refer to the subject of the clause in which they appear. Intensive pronouns are used primarily for emphasis and are indistinguishable from the reflexive forms.

> Jake saw a picture of **himself.** [reflexive]
>
> Jake, **himself,** brought the plant here. [intensive]

When these pronouns refer to a noun or pronoun already mentioned in the sentence, they always immediately follow the person or thing to which they refer.

Do not use *myself* or *me* in place of *I* in a compound subject.

> Jake and ~~**myself**~~ brought the plant here.
> _∧ ^I
>
> Jake and I
> _∧~~**Me and Jake**~~ brought the plant here.

Hisself and *theirselves,* although logical forms for reflexive pronouns (possessive plus *-self* as in *myself, yourself,* and *herself*), are inappropriate in college or professional writing. Instead, use *himself* and *themselves.*

> Tommy and Mike painted the house by ~~**theirselves.**~~
> themselves

Attempts to create a gender-neutral singular reflexive pronoun have resulted in such forms as *themself;* these forms are also inappropriate in college or professional writing.

5b Pronouns change form to indicate the subjective, objective, or possessive case.

In English, most of what there is to say about case applies to the pronouns that change form to show their relationship to other words in a sentence. For example, the different cases of the boldfaced pronouns below, all referring to the same person, show their different uses.

> **He** [the subject] wants **his** [modifier showing possession] cousin to help **him** [direct object].

He, the subject, is in the *subjective* case; *his,* showing possession, is in the *possessive* case; and *him,* the object, is in the *objective* case.

Pronouns also have singular and plural forms.

> **They** [plural subject] want **their** [plural modifier showing possession] cousins to help **them** [plural direct object].

(1) Subjects and subject complements with linking verbs are in the subjective case.

A **subject complement** is a word that renames the subject. A **linking verb** is a form of *be* (*am, is, are, was, were*), a verb expressing sensation (*look, sound, feel, taste, smell*), or a verb conveying a state or condition (*become, grow, prove, remain, seem, turn*). A linking verb relates the subject to the subject complement. (See **7c(1)**.) Pronouns that are subject complements or subjects are in the subjective case.

> The ones in charge were ~~him and me~~ ^{he and I}. [compound subjective complement, *he and I,* in the subjective case]

Russell and ~~me~~ were in charge. [compound subject of the sen-
<u>I</u>

tence, *Russell and I,* in the subjective case]

"It's *me*" (or *him, her, us,* or *them*) is acceptable in conversation.

 In some languages, a noun and a pronoun can both be
the subject of a clause. In English, though, only one of
these can be in the subject position.

My roommate ~~he~~ works in the library for three hours a week.

(2) All objects are in the objective case.

All pronouns that are objects—direct or indirect objects or objects of prepositions—take the **objective case.**

Direct object	Miguel loves **her.** [The direct object, *her,* is in the objective case. COMPARE Miguel loves Martha.]
Indirect object	Miguel gave **her** his love. [The indirect object, *her,* is in the objective case. COMPARE Miguel gave Martha his love.]
Object of a preposition	Miguel cares deeply for **her.** [The object of the preposition, *her,* is in the objective case. COMPARE Miguel cares deeply for Martha.]

(3) The possessive case indicates ownership.

Modifiers that indicate ownership or a comparable relationship
are in the **possessive case.** A few possessive pronouns (such as
mine and *theirs*) sometimes function as nouns.

That book is **mine.** [COMPARE That book is my book.]

Their and *they* can be confused in spoken English. *Their* is the possessive pronoun; *they* is in the subjective case. These must be distinguished in written English.

their
~~they~~ book   ~~they~~ house
    ^   ^

See the Glossary of Usage to clear up confusion among *their*, *there*, and *they're*.

Beyond the Rule

CASE MATTERS

When an offending pronoun is in the possessive or objective case, people notice the lack of agreement (see 6b) more often and find it more objectionable than when the incorrect pronoun is in the subjective case. For examples, visit www.harbrace.com.

> **5c** | The use of a pronoun in its own clause determines its case.

(1) Pronouns in compound constructions have the same case as they would if the construction were not compound.

Pronouns in compound subjects or subject complements are in the subjective case.

> I thought **he or Dad** would come to my rescue. [*He* is part of the compound subject of the clause that acts as the direct object. COMPARE I thought **he** would come to my rescue.]

> It was **Maria and I** who solved the problem. [compound subject complement; see 5b(1)]

> **She and her father** buy groceries on Saturday morning. [compound subject containing two pronouns, one subjective and one possessive]

You can test the case of any pronoun in a compound construction by eliminating the accompanying noun or pronoun and the conjunction.

> (Lou and) I like to watch *Star Wars* movies. [subject]
>
> They elected (George and) me to the board. [direct object]
>
> Gabriel gave it to (Edwyn and) me. [object of the preposition]

The first-person pronoun *I* occurs last in a compound construction. (See **20d** for ways to use the first-person pronoun effectively.)

> ~~Me and~~ Ricardo_∧ *and I* are good friends.

As compound objects of prepositions, pronouns are in the objective case.

> between him and ~~I~~ *me*   with Amanda and ~~he~~ *him*

Beyond the Rule

YOU AND ME, OR YOU AND I?

The subjective case has come to be viewed as more formal and thus more prestigious than the objective case. Perhaps in an effort to lend more prestige to their speech, some people incorrectly use *I* as the second element in compound objects.

> The supervisor asked John and ~~I~~ *me* to lead the discussion.
>
> Between you and ~~I~~ *me*, he talks too much.

For additional information, visit www.harbrace.com.

Compound objects of verbs or verbals and subjects of infinitives are also in the objective case.

> Clara may appoint **you or me.** [direct object]
>
> They lent **Tom and her** ten dollars. [indirect object]
>
> He gets nowhere by scolding **Bea or him.** [object of the gerund]
>
> Dad wanted **Sheila and me** to keep the old car. [subject of the infinitive in a verbal phrase, which is the direct object of the sentence]

If an appositive (a word that renames a noun or pronoun) follows a pronoun, normal case rules apply.

> We
> ~~Us~~ students need this.
>   ∧
>   us
> The director told we extras to go home.
>   ∧

To test the case of a pronoun that is followed by an appositive, remove the appositive.

> We
> ~~Us students~~ need this.
> ∧
>   us
> The director told ~~we extras~~ to go home.
>   ∧

Exercise 1

Revise the following paragraph, using appropriate cases for pronouns. Some sentences may not require editing.

[1]When I was twelve, my family lived in Guatemala for a year. [2]My parents taught English at a university; me and my younger brother went to a local school. [3]Although the Spanish language was new to both Sam and I, we learned to speak it quickly. [4]After we learned to ask and answer some basic questions, we started making friends, whom eventually introduced us to they're own version of Spanish. [5]Sam and me learned the language so quickly because, unless we were with our parents or by ourself, we listened to it, read it, wrote it, and spoke it all day long.

(2) *Who/whoever* and *whom/whomever* are often misused.

You may be able to avoid confusion about the correct usage of *who/whoever* and *whom/whomever* if you remember that the case of any pronoun is determined by its grammatical function in the clause in which it appears. The subject of a verb in a dependent clause takes the subjective case, even if the whole clause is used as an object.

> I remembered **who** won the Academy Award that year. [*Who* is the subject of the clause *who won the Academy Award that year.* The clause is the object of the verb *remembered.*]

> She offered help to **whoever** needed it. [*Whoever* is the subject of the clause *whoever needed it.* The clause is the object of the preposition *to.*]

When the pronoun is the direct object or the object of a preposition, *whom* is *always* the correct form. See **1d(2)**.

> They helped the people ~~who~~ they liked. [direct object]
> *(whom)*

> Gabriel happily greeted ~~whoever~~ he met that day. [direct object]
> *(whomever)*

> This is a friend ~~who~~ I write to once a year. [*Whom* is the object
> *(whom)*
> of the preposition *to.* COMPARE I write to him once a year.]

> Hemingway's seventh novel is titled *For **Whom** the Bell Tolls.*

> [objective case for the object of a preposition]

Whom may be omitted (or replaced by *that*) in sentences where no misunderstanding would result.

> The friend he relied on moved away. [*Whom* has been omitted after *friend.*]

> The friend *that* he relied on moved away. [*That* has been substituted for *whom.*]

Beyond the Rule

WHO AND WHOM

Although many writers still prefer the objective case, *whom* or *whomever,* dictionaries have approved the use of *who* or *whoever* when the pronoun begins a clause.

> I wondered **who** she gave the book to.
>
> Give the book to **whoever** he wants to have it.
>
> **Who** do you plan to vote for?
>
> **Who** were you speaking of?

In college writing, it is better to use *whom* as the object even when it is the first word in a sentence or a clause.

> **Whom** will they elect president?

For additional information, visit www.harbrace.com.

Exercise 2

Use the guidelines for college and professional writing to choose the appropriate form of each pronoun in parentheses. Remember to use *whom* when the pronoun functions as an object and *who* when it functions as a subject or a subject complement.

1. The United States Equestrian Team's training program allows visits by interested individuals (who/whom) arrive when the stables are open.

2. The organization considers supporting (whoever/whomever) can provide their own horses and exhibit the skills to win.

3. Amateurs and professionals (who/whom) apply to the United States Equestrian Team are evaluated by (whoever, whomever) the organization accepts as skilled judges.

4. The American Horse Shows Association can nominate a professional rider (who/whom) it thinks would be an asset to the United States Equestrian Team.

5. (Whoever/Whomever) the organization finances for competition must surely be thankful that supporters, (whoever/whomever) they may be, were able to make contributions to the United States Equestrian Team.

(3) The use of *who* or *whom* with an interpolated expression depends on the pronoun's grammatical function.

Such interpolated expressions as *I think, he says, she believes,* and *we know* can follow either *who* or *whom.* The case of the pronoun still depends on its grammatical function in the clause. To make sure you have used the correct form, delete the intervening phrase.

Walter picked Jan, **who** he knows speaks well. [*Who* is the subject of the verb *speaks.*]

Walter picked Jan, **whom** he knows we all respect. [*Whom* is the object of the verb *respect.*]

(4) The choice of pronoun form can determine the meaning of the sentence.

In sentences with implied (rather than stated) elements, the pronoun form can determine the meaning of the sentence.

She likes Clarice more than **I.** [subjective case, meaning "more than I like Clarice"]

She likes Dana more than **me.** [objective case, meaning "more than she likes me"]

He talks to Jerry as much as **her.** [objective case, meaning "as much as he talks to her"]

(5) Pronouns used with infinitives are in the objective case.

A pronoun grouped with an infinitive takes the objective case.

They wanted Dave and me to help **him.** [object of the infinitive, in the objective case]

Bill wanted **us** to play more music that features the bassoon. [subject of the infinitive, in the objective case]

(6) A pronoun that precedes a gerund takes the possessive case.

Just like a noun, a pronoun follows the convention of taking a possessive form when it occurs before a **gerund** (a verb form ending in *-ing* and used as a noun).

I appreciated Tom's helping Denise.

I appreciated ~~him~~ ^{his} helping Denise.

The *-ing* ending marks both gerunds and participles. A **participle** is a verbal used as an adjective.

The man **sitting** [participle modifying *man*] at the next table annoyed us. [The participle *sitting* tells more about which man annoyed us.]

A gerund is a verbal used as a noun.

The man's **sitting** [gerund acting as subject] at the desk annoyed us. [The gerund *sitting* indicates that it was the act of sitting that annoyed us.]

Notice that the possessive case is used before gerunds, but not before participles.

Exercise 3

Revise the following sentences, using correct pronoun cases. Some sentences may not require editing.

1. The board of directors has asked you and I to conduct a customer survey.
2. They also recommended us hiring someone with extensive experience in statistical analysis.
3. You understand statistics better than me.
4. Although the board asked me to be in charge, I would like you to recruit and interview candidates.
5. The directors recognize your expertise and will surely approve of you taking the lead.

Agreement

A subject and a verb agree, or match, when both are either singular or plural. A pronoun and its antecedent (the noun to which the pronoun refers) agree when both are singular or plural and both have the same gender. This chapter will help you recognize and fix agreement problems

- between subjects and verbs (6a) and
- between pronouns and their antecedents (6b).

6a | Verbs must agree with their subjects.

A verb must agree with its subject in **number.** That is, when a subject is plural, the verb must have a plural form; when the subject is singular, the verb must have a singular form. The subject and verb must also agree in **person.** First-person subjects require first-person verb forms, second-person subjects require second-person verb forms, and third-person subjects require third-person verb forms.

Singular   The **car** in the lot **looks** new. [*Car* and *looks* are both singular.]

Plural   The **cars** in the lot **look** shabby. [*Cars* and *look* are both plural.]

You can refer to the following subsections for guidance on ensuring subject-verb agreement in particular situations:

- when words come between the subject and the verb (**6a(1)**),
- when two or more subjects are joined by conjunctions (**6a(2)–(3)**),
- when word order is inverted (**6a(4)**),
- when the subject is a relative pronoun (**6a(5)**), an indefinite pronoun (**6a(6)**), or a collective noun (**6a(7)**), and
- when the subject is a noun that is plural in form but singular in meaning (**6a(8)**).

Standardized English requires the addition of *-s* to mark most nouns as plural but most verbs as third-person singular. (Modal auxiliaries are the exception.) Be careful not to confuse the verb ending and the noun ending.

The **students** need attention. [noun + *-s*]
The student **needs** attention. [verb + *-s*]

Except for *be*, verbs change form to indicate the number and person of their subjects only in the simple present tense.

Simple present tense of *be*: *am, is, are*

Simple past tense of *be*: *was, were*

Simple present tense of other verbs: base form or base form + *-s* or *-es* (*read/reads, push/pushes*)

Because of the possibility of confusing the two forms, most problems with subject-verb agreement occur when the present tense is used. When you edit your writing, watch for the following potential pitfalls.

(1) Agreement errors are likely when other words come between the subject and the verb.

The **rhythm** of the pounding waves **is** calming. [*Waves* is the object of the preposition *of.*]

Certain phrases commonly occur between the subject and the verb; however, they do not affect the form of the verb:

accompanied by   along with   as well as   in addition to
not to mention   no less than   including   together with

Her **salary,** together with tips, **is** just enough to live on.
Tips, together with her salary, **are** just enough to live on.

(2) Subjects joined by *and* usually take a plural verb.

Writing on a legal pad and **writing with a computer are** not the same at all.

A compound subject that refers to a single person or thing takes a singular verb.

The **founder and president** of the art association **was** elected to the board of the museum.
Red beans and rice is the specialty of the house.

(3) Agreement errors are common when subjects are joined by *or* or *nor*.

When singular subjects are linked by *or, either/or,* or *neither/nor,* the verb is singular as well.

The provost or the dean usually **presides** at the meeting.
Neither the car nor the motorcycle **is** for sale.
Either her accountant or her lawyer **has** the will.

If one subject is singular and one is plural, the verb agrees with the subject closer to the verb.

> Neither the basket nor the **apples were** expensive.
>
> Neither the apples nor the **basket was** expensive.

The verb also agrees in person with the nearer subject.

> Either Frank or **you were** going to make the announcement.
>
> Either you or **Frank was** going to make the announcement.

(4) Inverted word order may lead to agreement errors.

In most sentences, the subject precedes the verb.

> The large **cities** of the Northeast **were** the hardest hit by the subzero temperatures.

The subject and verb can sometimes be inverted for emphasis (see **29f**); however, they must still agree.

> Hardest hit by the subzero temperatures and snow **were** the large **cities** of the Northeast.

When the expletive *there* begins a sentence, the subject and verb are also inverted; the verb still agrees with the subject, which follows it (see **1d(1)**).

> There **are** several **cities** in need of federal aid.

(5) Adjectival clauses are common sites for agreement errors.

In an adjectival clause (see **1g(2)**), the subject may be a relative pronoun (*that, who,* or *which*). To determine whether a relative pronoun is singular or plural, you must find its antecedent (the noun it refers to). When the antecedent is singular, the relative pronoun is singular; when the antecedent is plural, the relative pronoun is plural.

> singular singular
> antecedent verb
>
> This is the only **store that gives** triple coupons.

> plural plural
> antecedent verb
>
> Those are the **books that are** out of print.

> singular singular
> antecedent verb
>
> It is not bigger discounts but better **service that makes** a store successful.

> plural plural
> antecedent verb
>
> The Starion is one of the new **models that include** air conditioning as standard equipment.

Beyond the Rule

ONE AS A POSSIBLE ANTECEDENT

According to traditional grammar, in sentences containing the pattern *one* + *of* + plural noun + adjective clause (such as the example just before this box), the antecedent for the relative pronoun (*that,* in this case) is the plural noun (*models*). The verb is thus plural as well. However, professional writers often consider *one,* instead of the plural noun, to be the antecedent of the relative pronoun and thus make the verb singular:

> The Starion is **one** of the new models that **includes** air conditioning as standard equipment.

For more information on this variation, visit www.harbrace.com.

(6) Agreement errors frequently occur with indefinite pronouns.

The indefinite pronouns *each, either, everybody, one,* and *anyone* are considered singular and so require singular verb forms.

>**Either** of them **is willing** to lead the discussion.

>**Each has bought** a first-class ticket.

>**Everybody** in our apartment building **has** a parking place.

Other indefinite pronouns, such as *all, any, some, none, half,* and *most,* can be either singular or plural, depending on whether they refer to a unit or quantity (singular) or to individuals (plural).

> plural   plural
> antecedent   verb

>My sister collects comic **books; some are** very valuable.

> singular   singular
> antecedent   verb

>The bank would not take all the **money** because **some was** foreign.

Singular subjects that are preceded by *every* or *each* and joined by *and* require a singular verb.

>**Every** cat **and** dog in the county **has** to be vaccinated.

>**Each** fork **and** spoon **has** to be polished.

However, placing *each* after a plural subject does not affect the verb form. The verb should agree with the plural subject.

>Colleges and vocational schools **each have** their advantages.

When an indefinite pronoun is followed by a prepositional phrase beginning with the preposition *of* (see **1f(4)**), the verb agrees in number with the object of the preposition.

> plural   plural
> object   verb

>**None** of **those are** spoiled.

singular singular
object verb

None of the **food is** spoiled.

singular singular
object verb

More than **half** of the **population** in West Texas **is** Hispanic.

plural plural
object verb

More than **half** of the **people** in West Texas **are** Hispanic.

Beyond the Rule

AGREEMENT WITH *NONE*

Some grammarians reason that, like *no one, none* is singular and thus should be followed by a singular verb:

None of the grant requests **has** been rejected.

Nonetheless, many reputable writers have used *none* with plural verbs, leading to the widespread acceptance of this usage:

None of the grant requests **have** been rejected.

For more information, visit www.harbrace.com.

(7) Collective nouns and measurement words often cause agreement difficulties.

Collective nouns and measurement words require singular verbs when they refer to groups or units. They require plural verbs when they refer to individuals or parts.

Singular (regarded as a group or unit)	Plural (regarded as individuals or parts)
The **majority rules.**	The **majority** of us **are** in favor.

Ten million gallons of oil **is** more than enough.	**Ten million gallons** of oil **were spilled.**
The **number is** insignificant.	A **number** of workers **were** absent.

Although the use of *data* and *media* as collective nouns has gained currency, treat *data* and *media* as plural in most academic writing. (See the Glossary of Usage.)

> The data **are** in the appendix.

> The media **have** shaped public opinion.

(8) Words ending in -s are sometimes singular.

Individual titles that are plural in form (for example, *Star Wars* and *Dombey and Son*) are treated as singular because they refer to a single book, movie, recording, or other work.

> ***Lilo and Stitch* is** now out on video and DVD.

A reference to a word is also considered singular.

> ***Beans* is** a slang word for "a small amount": I don't know beans about football.

A few nouns ending in *-s* are actually singular. Examples are *linguistics, news,* and *Niagara Falls.*

> The **news is** encouraging.

Some nouns (such as *athletics, politics, electronics, measles,* and *deer*) can be either singular or plural, depending on their meanings.

Singular	**Plural**
Statistics is an interesting subject.	**Statistics are** often misleading.
A **series** of natural disasters **has** occurred recently.	Two **series** of natural disasters **have** occurred recently.

Although grammar checkers do flag agreement errors, they are only occasionally correct, and they frequently flag acceptable sentences and recommend bizarre alternatives. For instance, one grammar checker flagged *What I think is my own business,* suggesting that *is* should be changed to *am* to agree with *I.* Because a grammar checker cannot distinguish separate clauses, it first compares *think* to *I* and finds agreement, but then compares *is* with *I* as well and finds a problem. For more information about grammar checkers, see Using a Grammar Checker on page 2.

Exercise 1

In each sentence, choose the correct form of the verb in parentheses. Make sure that the verb agrees with its subject.

1. Neither time nor affluence (remove/removes) memories of childhood poverty.
2. Experiences of poor children (illustrate/illustrates) how significant money and status (is/are) in our society.
3. Some adults (think/thinks) their mother or father (was/were) responsible for their attitudes about money.
4. Their current understanding of their parents' past problems with money often (provide/provides) little solace.
5. A number of adults (overcome, overcomes) the stigma of having been poor as children.
6. There (is/are) affluent children who also (develop/develops) unhealthy attitudes about money.

Exercise 2

Complete the following sentences, making sure that subjects and verbs agree.

1. Applying for college and enrolling in courses . . .
2. Erik is one of the students who . . .
3. Either of them . . .
4. Neither the president nor the senators . . .
5. The list of volunteers . . .
6. There . . .
7. Hidden beneath the stairs . . .
8. The teacher, along with her students, . . .
9. Ten months . . .
10. Politics . . .

6b | **A pronoun and its antecedent agree when they have the same number and gender.**

A pronoun and the noun or other pronoun to which it refers, the **antecedent,** must agree in number (singular or plural).

Singular   A **wolf** has **its** own language. [*Wolf* and *its* agree.]

Plural   **Wolves** have **their** own language. [*Wolves* and *their* agree.]

A pronoun also agrees with its antecedent in gender (masculine, feminine, or neuter).

the **boy** and **his** sister [masculine antecedent]

the **girl** and **her** brother [feminine antecedent]

the **garden** and **its** weeds [neuter antecedent]

The possessive pronouns (*his, her, its, their, my, our,* and *your*), sometimes called *possessive determiners,* agree with their antecedents, not with any noun they modify.

Ken Carlson brought ~~her~~ young daughter to the office today.
^{his}

[The possessive pronoun *his* agrees with the antecedent, *Ken Carlson,* not with the following noun, *daughter.*]

(1) Agreement is still necessary when the antecedent is an indefinite pronoun or a generic noun.

Indefinite pronouns are generally singular.

Everybody has to live with ~~themselves~~. [OR Rephrase using the plural: *People have* to live with themselves.]
^{himself or herself}

Each student has the combination to ~~their~~ own locker.
^{his or her}

Because many readers consider the use of *his or her* awkward, it is usually best to rewrite your sentence so that a generic noun is plural.

Singular   A lawyer represents **his or her** clients.
Plural   Lawyers represent **their** clients.

A pronoun that refers to one of the following words should be singular: *man, individual, woman, person, everybody, one, anyone, each, either, neither, sort,* and *kind.*

Each of these companies had ~~their~~ books audited.
^{its}

When the gender of the antecedent is clear, use the appropriate personal pronoun.

Masculine   John represents **his** clients.
Feminine   Mary represents **her** clients.

When the gender of the antecedent is not clear or when the noun could refer to either gender, rewrite the sentence to make the noun plural or use a form of *his or her* or *himself or herself.*

> College students who support **themselves** have little free time. [COMPARE A college student who supports *himself or herself* has . . . .]

When using a word such as *student,* which can refer to either a man or a woman, you can avoid agreement problems by dropping the pronoun, making the antecedent plural, or, as a last resort, rewriting the sentence using the passive voice. (See 7c.)

> Each student has the combination to a private locker. [no pronoun]
>
> Students have the combinations to their private lockers. [plural]
>
> The combination to a private locker is issued to each student. [passive voice]

In spoken English, a sentence such as the following is considered easy and natural; in college and professional writing, however, it is not accepted.

> who
> Everyone ̱was invited to dinner, but they had already eaten.
>
> [The revision avoids the agreement problem.]

Beyond the Rule

INCLUSIVE USE OF PRONOUNS

Be careful not to introduce errors into your writing because you are trying to avoid sexist usage. (See 19d(1).)

> s   s
> Whenever a driver lets their license expire, they have to take the driving test.

For more information on pronouns and nonsexist usage, visit www.harbrace.com.

(2) The pronoun agrees with the nearer of two antecedents joined by *or* or *nor*.

Did **Mark or Gordon** lose **his** enthusiasm?

If one of two antecedents joined by *or* or *nor* is singular and the other is plural, the pronoun usually agrees with the nearer antecedent.

Neither the **president nor** the **senators** had announced **their** decision. [*Their* is closer to the plural antecedent *senators*.]

When gender makes it awkward to follow the rule, as in *Roger or Betty will bring his or her book,* recast the sentence to avoid the problem: *Roger will bring his book, or Betty will bring hers.*

(3) Agreement with collective nouns as antecedents can be tricky.

When the antecedent is a collective noun, take care to avoid treating it as both singular and plural in the same sentence.

The choir is writing ~~their~~ its own music. [Because the choir is working as a unit, *choir* is regarded as singular.]

The group of students disagree on methods, but **they** unite on basic aims. [Because the students in the group are behaving as individuals, *group* is regarded as plural.]

PRONOUN-ANTECEDENT AGREEMENT

Antecedent	Singular Pronoun	Plural Pronoun	Option
Indefinite pronoun such as *anybody, each, everyone, either,* or *someone*	✔		

(Continued on page 116)

(Continued from page 115)

Antecedent	Singular Pronoun	Plural Pronoun	Option
Collective noun such as *committee* or *audience*	✔	(✔ only if referring to individuals within a group)	
Word that refers to a member of a class, such as *student* or *employee*	✔		
Compound construction such as *brother and sister* or *family and friends*			✔ (refers to nearest element)

Exercise 3

Revise the following sentences so that they have correct agreement between pronouns and antecedents.

1. A researcher relies on a number of principles to help him make ethical decisions.
2. Everyone should have the right to participate in a study only if she wants to.
3. A team of researchers should provide its volunteers with informed-consent forms, in which they describe to the volunteers the risks involved in participation.
4. Every participant should be guaranteed that the information they provide will remain confidential.
5. Institutions of higher education require that a researcher address ethical issues in their proposal.

Verbs

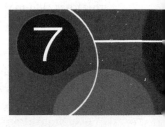

Choosing precise verbs to convey what you observe or think is the first step toward writing clear and effective sentences. The next step is to ensure that the verbs you choose conform to the conventions your audience expects you to follow.

This chapter will help you

- identify conventional verb forms (7a),
- use verb tenses to provide information about time (7b),
- distinguish between active and passive voice (7c), and
- use verbs to signal mood (7d).

7a | A verb has three or more forms.

Most English verbs have four forms, following the model for *walk.*

walk, walks, walking, walked

However, English also includes irregular verbs, which may have as few as three forms or as many as eight forms:

let, lets, letting   be, am, is, are, was, were, being, been

(1) Regular verbs have four forms.

A regular verb has a **base form.** This is the form you find in a dictionary. *Talk, act,* and *serve* are all base forms.

The second form of a regular verb is the **-s form.** To derive this form, add to the base form either *-s* (*talks, acts, serves*) or, in some cases, *-es* (*marries, carries, tries*). See **18d** for information on spelling changes that accompany the addition of *-es*.

The third form of a regular verb is the **-*ing* form,** also called the **present participle.** It consists of the base form and the ending *-ing* (*talking, acting*). Depending on the verb, spelling changes may occur (*changing, chatting*). (See **18d**.)

The fourth form of a regular verb consists of the base form and the ending *-ed* (*talked, acted*). Again, spelling may vary when the suffix is added (*served, chatted*). (See **18d**.) The *-ed* form has two names: When it is used without the auxiliary verb *have* or *be*, it is called the **past form** (*We **talked** about the new plan*). When the *-ed* form is used with one of these auxiliary verbs, it is called the **past participle** (*We **have talked** about it several times*).

Verb Forms of Regular Verbs

Base Form	-s Form	-*ing* Form (Present Participle)	-*ed* Form (Past Form or Past Participle)
work	works	working	worked
watch	watches	watching	watched
apply	applies	applying	applied
stop	stops	stopping	stopped

When verbs are followed by words that begin with similar sounds, you may find their endings (*-s* and *-ed*) difficult to hear. In addition, these verb endings may seem unfamiliar because your dialect does not have them. Nonetheless, you should use *-s* and *-ed* when you write for an audience that expects these endings:

She **seem** satisfied with the report.

He **live** seven blocks from the university.

I **use** to play the saxophone.

We were **suppose** to receive the results yesterday.

(2) Irregular verbs have from three to eight forms.

Some irregular verbs, such as *write,* have forms similar to some of those for regular verbs: base form (*write*), *-s* form (*writes*), and *-ing* form (*writing*). However, the past form (*wrote*) and the past participle (*written*) vary from the regular forms. In fact, some irregular verbs have two acceptable past forms and/or past participles. Other irregular verbs have only three forms because the same form serves as the base form, the past form, and the past participle. The following chart illustrates these differences.

Verb Forms of Irregular Verbs

Base Form	-s Form	-ing Form (Present Participle)	Past Form	Past Participle
awake	awakes	awaking	awaked, awoke	awaked, awoken
bear	bears	bearing	bore	borne, born
begin	begins	beginning	began	begun
break	breaks	breaking	broke	broken
bring	brings	bringing	brought	brought

(Continued on page 120)

(Continued from page 119)

Base Form	-s Form	*-ing* Form (Present Participle)	Past Form	Past Participle
choose	chooses	choosing	chose	chosen
come	comes	coming	came	come
dive	dives	diving	dived, dove	dived
do	does	doing	did	done
drink	drinks	drinking	drank	drunk
drive	drives	driving	drove	driven
eat	eats	eating	ate	eaten
fall	falls	falling	fell	fallen
forget	forgets	forgetting	forgot	forgotten
freeze	freezes	freezing	froze	frozen
get	gets	getting	got	gotten, got
give	gives	giving	gave	given
go	goes	going	went	gone
hang (suspend)	hangs	hanging	hung	hung
hang (execute)	hangs	hanging	hanged	hanged
know	knows	knowing	knew	known
lay (see the Glossary of Usage)	lays	laying	laid	laid
lead	leads	leading	led	led

Base Form	-s Form	-ing Form (Present Participle)	Past Form	Past Participle
leave	leaves	leaving	left	left
lend	lends	lending	lent	lent
lie (see the Glossary of Usage)	lies	lying	lay	lain
pay	pays	paying	paid	paid
rise (see the Glossary of Usage)	rises	rising	rose	risen
see	sees	seeing	saw	seen
set (see the Glossary of Usage)	sets	setting	set	set
sit (see the Glossary of Usage)	sits	sitting	sat	sat
speak	speaks	speaking	spoke	spoken
stand	stands	standing	stood	stood
strike	strikes	striking	struck	struck
swim	swims	swimming	swam	swum
take	takes	taking	took	taken
teach	teaches	teaching	taught	taught
wear	wears	wearing	wore	worn
write	writes	writing	wrote	written

Beyond the Rule

IRREGULAR VERBS

Irregular verbs follow seven basic patterns. Once you know these patterns, you can predict the forms for most irregular verbs. For more information on irregular verb patterns, visit www.harbrace.com.

The verb *be* has eight forms.

be	**Be** on time!
am	I **am** going to arrive early tomorrow.
is	Time **is** of the essence.
are	They **are** always punctual.
was	The meeting **was** scheduled for 10 A.M.
were	We **were** only five minutes late.
being	He is **being** delayed by traffic.
been	How long have we **been** here?

(3) A phrasal verb consists of a main verb and an adverbial particle.

A **phrasal verb** is a combination of a verb and an **adverbial particle** such as *up, out,* or *on.* Such a verb + particle unit is often idiomatic, conveying a meaning that differs from the common meanings of the individual words. For example, the definitions that first come to mind for the words *blow* and *up* are not likely to help you understand the phrasal verb *blow up* when it means "to enlarge": *She **blew up** the photograph so that she could see the faces better.* However, the meanings of other phrasal verbs are similar to common definitions; the adverbial particles just add a sense of completion: *They **finished up** the report by six o'clock.* The particle *up* in *finish up* does not refer to a direction; instead, it emphasizes the completion of the report. Other phrasal verbs retain the common meanings of the verb and the particle: *The protesters **hung up** a banner.*

Most phrasal verbs may be separated by short noun phrases or pronouns.

> She **called** the meeting **off.**
>
> The student **turned** it **in** yesterday.

Some phrasal verbs are not separable, however.

> The group **went over** the proposal.
>
> I **came across** an interesting fact.

Adverbial particles that add little meaning are often deleted, especially if they seem redundant.

> I **sent ~~out~~** the invitations.

 You may have trouble finding the definitions for phrasal verbs in conventional dictionaries. Instead, use a specialized dictionary that provides both definitions and information about the separability of these verbs. See pages 291–292 for a list of dictionaries.

---

(4) Auxiliary verbs combine with main verbs.

The auxiliary verbs *be, do,* and *have* combine with main verbs, both regular and irregular:

be	*am, is, are, was, were writing*
do	*does, do, did call*
have	*has, have, had prepared*

Be, do, and *have* are not just auxiliary verbs, though. They may be used as main verbs as well.

be   I **am** from Texas.

do   He **does** his homework early in the morning.

have   They **have** an apartment near a park.

A sentence may even include one of these verbs as both an auxiliary and a main verb.

They **are being** careful.

Did you **do** your taxes by yourself?

She **has** not **had** any free time this week.

Another type of auxiliary verb is called a **modal auxiliary.** By combining a modal auxiliary such as *will, should,* or *could* with the base form of a main verb, you can make a request, give an instruction, or express certainty, doubt, obligation, or possibility: *we shall overcome, she must sleep, they should laugh.*

 Although English verbs are often followed by the infinitive marker *to* (as in *want to go* and *plan to leave*), modal auxiliaries do not follow this pattern.

We **should to** finish our report by Friday.

Each modal auxiliary has more than one meaning. For example, *may* can indicate permission or probability.

The instructor said we **may** have an extension. [permission]

The weather **may** improve by tomorrow. [probability]

The box provides examples of the use of modal auxiliaries to convey common meanings.

COMMON MEANINGS OF MODAL AUXILIARIES

Meaning	Modal Auxiliary +	Main Verb	Example
Ability	can, could	afford	They can afford to buy a small house.
Certainty	will	succeed	We will succeed by dint of our hard work.
Obligation	must	return	You must return your books by the due date.
Advice	should	talk	He should talk with his counselor.

When a modal auxiliary occurs with the auxiliary *have* (*should have known*), *have* frequently sounds like the word *of*. When you proofread, be sure that modal auxiliaries are not followed by *of*.

> have
> They **could of taken** another route.
>   ∧

Writers generally do not combine modal auxiliaries unless they want to portray a regional dialect.

> be able to
> We **might could** plan the meeting for after the holidays.
>   ∧

English also has **phrasal modals,** or auxiliary verbs consisting of more than one word. They have meanings similar to those of one-word modals.

be able to (ability): We **were able to** find the original document.

have to (obligation): To complete the application, you **have to** include your test results.

Other common phrasal modals are *be going to, be supposed to, had better, used to,* and *ought to.* Most phrasal verbs have more than one form (*am able to, is able to, were able to*). Only *had better, ought to,* and *used to* have a single form.

(5) Participles are accompanied by auxiliary verbs.

Present participles (*-ing* verb forms) are used with the auxiliary verb *be* (*We **were waiting** for the next flight*). Depending on the intended meaning, past participles can be used with either *be* or *have* (*We **have waited** for an hour. The first flight **was canceled***). If a sentence contains only a participle, it is probably a fragment (see **2a**).

We were dreaming
∧ ~~Dreaming~~ of far-off places.

When a participle is part of a verbal phrase, it often appears without an auxiliary verb (see **1f(3)**).

Swatting at mosquitoes and **cursing** softly, the campers quickly packed up their gear.

Exercise 1

Supply the correct form of each verb in parentheses.

1. I (awake) early that morning.
2. Jason said we were (suppose) to leave at 5:00 A.M.

3. I wasn't (use) to getting up before dark, but I (manage) to be at the bus stop on time.

4. The sun was just (begin) to rise.

5. My backpack (be) heavy, so I (lay) it next to the other gear that was (lie) in a heap.

6. Without my pack on, though, I (be) cold.

7. I had (forget) how chilly mornings (be) in the desert.

8. Jason (see) me shivering and (lend) me his jacket.

9. "(Be) you okay?" he (ask).

10. "Yes," I (lie). It (be) early, it (be) cold, and I (be) nervous.

Exercise 2

Revise the following sentences. Explain any changes you make.

1. The Lewis and Clark Expedition began in May 1804 and end in September 1806.

2. The Fates must of smiled on the explorers for there were no fatalities under their leadership.

3. Lewis and Clark lead the expedition from St. Louis to the Pacific Ocean and back.

4. By 1805, the Corps of Discovery, as the expedition was call, included thirty-three members.

5. The Corps might of lost all maps and specimens had Sacajawea, a Native American woman, not fish them from the Missouri River.

6. The success of the expedition depend on its members' willingness to help one another.

Verb tenses provide information about time. For example, the tense of a verb may indicate that an action took place in the past or that an action is ongoing. Verb tenses are labeled as present, past, or future; they are also labeled as simple, progressive, perfect, or perfect progressive. The chart shows how these labels apply to the tenses of *walk*.

Verb Tenses

	Present	Past	Future
Simple	walk, walks	walked	will walk
Progressive	am, is, are walking	was, were walking	will be walking
Perfect	has, have walked	had walked	will have walked
Perfect progressive	has, have been walking	had been walking	will have been walking

Some of the tenses have more than one form because they depend on the person and number of the subject. **Person** refers to the role of the subject. First person (*I, we*) indicates that the subject of the verb is the writer or writers. Second person (*you*) indicates that the subject is the audience. Third person (*he, she, it, they*) indicates that the subject is someone or something other than the writer or audience. **Number** indicates whether the subject is one or more than one (*I/we, building/ buildings*). In the following subsections, conjugation tables are used to show how person and number influence the forms of the regular verb *work*.

(1) Simple tenses have many uses, not all related to specific points in time.

The conjugation for the simple present tense includes two forms of the verb: the base form and the *-s* form. Notice that the third-person singular form is the only form with the *-s* ending.

Simple Present Tense

	Singular	Plural
First person	I **work**	We **work**
Second person	You **work**	You **work**
Third person	He, she, it **works**	They **work**

Tense is not the same as time. Although the words *present, past,* and *future* may lead you to think that these tenses refer to actions happening now, in the past, and in the future, this strict separation does not always hold. For example, the simple present tense is used to indicate a current state, a habitual action, or a general truth.

We **are** ready. [current state]

Dana **uses** common sense. [habitual action]

The sun **rises** in the east. [general truth]

The simple present tense is also commonly used to add a sense of immediacy to historical actions and to discuss literary and artistic works (see **42e**).

In 1939, Hitler's armies **attack** Poland. [historical present]

Joseph Conrad **writes** about what he sees in the human heart. [literary present]

On occasion, the simple present tense is used to refer to future time.

My bus **leaves** in twenty minutes.

The simple past tense of regular verbs has only one form: the base form with the -*ed* ending. The past tense for irregular verbs varies (see 7a(2)).

Simple Past Tense

	Singular	Plural
First person	I **worked**	We **worked**
Second person	You **worked**	You **worked**
Third person	He, she, it **worked**	They **worked**

The simple past tense is used to refer to completed past actions or events.

He **traveled** to the Philippines. [past action]

The accident **occurred** several weeks ago. [past event]

Like the simple past tense, the simple future tense has only one form: the base form accompanied by the auxiliary *will.*

Simple Future Tense

	Singular	Plural
First person	I **will work**	We **will work**
Second person	You **will work**	You **will work**
Third person	He, she, it **will work**	They **will work**

The simple future tense refers to future actions or states.

> I **will call** you after work today. [future action]
>
> The video **will be** ready by Friday. [future state]

(2) Progressive tenses indicate that events have begun but have not been completed.

The present progressive tense consists of a form of the auxiliary verb *be* and the present participle (*-ing* form) of the main verb.

Present Progressive Tense

	Singular	Plural
First person	I **am working**	We **are working**
Second person	You **are working**	You **are working**
Third person	He, she, it **is working**	They **are working**

Notice that the present participle remains the same regardless of person and number, but the auxiliary *be* appears in three forms: *am*, *is*, and *are*.

The present progressive tense signals an activity in progress or a temporary situation.

> The doctor **is attending** a conference in Nebraska. [activity in progress]
>
> We **are living** in a yurt right now. [temporary situation]

The present progressive tense can refer to a future event when it occurs with a word indicating time.

> Tomorrow we **are leaving** for Alaska. [*Tomorrow* indicates a time in the future.]

Like the present progressive, the past progressive tense is a combination of the auxiliary verb *be* and the present participle (*-ing* form) of the main verb. However, the auxiliary verb is in the past tense, rather than in the present tense.

Past Progressive Tense

	Singular	Plural
First person	I **was working**	We **were working**
Second person	You **were working**	You **were working**
Third person	He, she, it **was working**	They **were working**

The past progressive tense signals an action or event that occurred in the past and was repeated or ongoing.

The new member **was** constantly **interrupting** the discussion. [repeated past action]

We **were eating** dinner when we heard the news. [ongoing past action]

The future progressive tense has only one form. Two auxiliaries, *will* and *be,* are used along with the *–ing* form of the main verb.

Future Progressive Tense

	Singular	Plural
First person	I **will be working**	We **will be working**
Second person	You **will be working**	You **will be working**
Third person	He, she, it **will be working**	They **will be working**

The future progressive tense refers to actions that will occur in the future.

> She **will be giving** her report at the end of the meeting.
> [future action]

 Some verbs that do not express actions but rather mental states, emotions, conditions, or relationships are not used in the progressive form. These verbs include *believe, belong, contain, cost, know, own, prefer,* and *want.*

The book ~~is containing~~ contains many Central American folktales.

He ~~is knowing~~ knows many old myths.

(3) Perfect tenses indicate action performed prior to a particular time.

The present perfect tense is formed by combining the auxiliary *have* with the past participle of the main verb.

Present Perfect Tense

	Singular	Plural
First person	I **have worked**	We **have worked**
Second person	You **have worked**	You **have worked**
Third person	He, she, it **has worked**	They **have worked**

The participle remains the same regardless of person and number; however, the auxiliary has two forms: *has* and *have*. The present perfect tense signals a time prior to the present. It can refer to a situation originating in the past but continuing into the present. It can also refer to a past action that has current relevance.

> They **have lived** in New Zealand for twenty years. [situation originating in the past and still continuing]
>
> I **have read** that book already. [past action that is currently relevant]

The past perfect tense is formed by combining the past tense of the auxiliary *have* with the past participle of the verb. There is only one form of the past perfect for regular verbs.

Past Perfect Tense

	Singular	Plural
First person	I **had worked**	We **had worked**
Second person	You **had worked**	You **had worked**
Third person	He, she, it **had worked**	They **had worked**

The past perfect tense refers to an action completed at a time in the past prior to another past time or past action.

> Before 1990, he **had worked** in a shoe factory. [past action prior to a given time in the past]
>
> I **had studied** geology before I transferred to this school. [past action prior to another past action]

The future perfect tense consists of two auxiliaries, *will* and *have,* along with the past participle of the main verb. There is only one form of the future perfect tense.

Future Perfect Tense

	Singular	Plural
First person	I **will have worked**	We **will have worked**
Second person	You **will have worked**	You **will have worked**
Third person	He, she, it **will have worked**	They **will have worked**

The future perfect tense refers to an action that is to be completed prior to a future time.

By this time next year, I **will have finished** medical school.

(4) Perfect progressive tenses combine the forms of the progressive and the perfect tenses.

The present perfect progressive tense consists of two auxiliaries, *have* and *be,* plus the present participle of the main verb.

Present Perfect Progressive Tense

	Singular	Plural
First person	I **have been working**	We **have been working**
Second person	You **have been working**	You **have been working**
Third person	He, she, it **has been working**	They **have been working**

The form of the auxiliary *have* varies with person and number. The auxiliary *be* appears as the past participle. The present perfect progressive signals that an action, state, or event originating in the past is ongoing or incomplete.

I **have been feeling** tired for a week. [ongoing state]

We **have been organizing** the conference since April. [incomplete action]

The past perfect progressive tense follows the pattern *had +
been* + present participle (*-ing* form) of the main verb. The auxiliary *have* is in the past tense.

Past Perfect Progressive Tense

	Singular	Plural
First person	I **had been working**	We **had been working**
Second person	You **had been working**	You **had been working**
Third person	He, she, it **had been working**	They **had been working**

The past perfect progressive tense refers to a situation or action
occurring over a period of time in the past prior to another past
action or time.

> She **had been living** so frugally all year that she saved enough
> money for a new car. [past situation prior to another past
> action]

The future perfect progressive tense follows the pattern
will + have + been + present participle of the main verb.

Future Perfect Progressive Tense

	Singular	Plural
First person	I **will have been working**	We **will have been working**
Second person	You **will have been working**	You **will have been working**
Third person	He, she, it **will have been working**	They **will have been working**

The future perfect progressive tense refers to action that is occurring in the present and will continue to occur for a specific
amount of time.

In one more month, I **will have been working** on this project for five years.

(5) The auxiliary verb *do* is used to question, negate, or emphasize.

Unlike *be* and *have,* the auxiliary verb *do* does not occur with other verbs to indicate tense. Instead, it is used to question, negate, or emphasize.

Do you have any questions? [question]

I **do** not have any questions. [negation]

I **do** have a few questions. [emphatic sentence]

The auxiliary *do* is used only in the simple present (*do, does*) and the simple past (*did*).

Exercise 3

Explain what the verb tenses used in the following paragraph reveal about the time or duration of the actions expressed by the main verbs.

[1]Professor Alex Cohen and his literature students are leaving on Friday for Oxford University. [2]While there, they will study Keats and Wordsworth. [3]Although they have been studying these poets since September, Professor Cohen believes that the students will gain greater insight into English poetry because they will have access to important archives. [4]Professor Cohen studied in Oxford when he was an undergraduate, earning a degree in English and classics. [5]This is the first trip he has planned for students. [6]However, with the help of a university grant, he will be planning many more. [7]He is already exploring the possibility of taking students from his mythology class to Greece next year.

Exercise 4

In a paragraph from one of your recent writing assignments, underline all the verbs and identify the tenses you used. Explain why they are appropriate.

(6) Tense forms should appear in logical sequence.

When you combine tense forms in a single sentence, you give readers information about how actions and events are related in time and duration.

> Whenever he **calls** on me, I **stutter** nervously. [Both forms indicate habitual actions.]

> When the speaker **had finished,** everyone **applauded.** [The past perfect tense *had finished* indicates a time before the action expressed by *applauded.*]

Infinitives and participles (see **1f(3)**) can be used to express time relations within a sentence. The present infinitive (*to* + base form) of a verb expresses action occurring at the same time as or later than the action expressed by the main verb.

> We **like to write** about sports. [Both actions occur at the same time.]

> They **want to design** a new museum. [The action of designing will take place in the future.]

The perfect infinitive (*to* + *have* + past participle) signals that an action did not occur.

> The governor **would like to have postponed** the vote. [The postponement did not occur.]

The present participle (*-ing* form) indicates simultaneous or previous action.

> **Laughing** loudly, the old friends **left** the restaurant arm in arm. [The friends were laughing as they were leaving.]

> **Hearing** that she was distressed, I **rushed** right over. [The action of hearing occurred first.]

The perfect participle (*having* + past participle) expresses action completed before that conveyed by the main verb.

> **Having learned** Spanish at an early age, she **spoke** to the Mexican diplomats in their native language.

The past participle can be used to express either simultaneous action or previous action.

> **Led** by a former Peace Corps worker, the volunteers **provided** medical assistance. [Both actions occur simultaneously.]

> **Encouraged** by job prospects, he **moved** to Atlanta. [The encouragement preceded the move.]

Exercise 5

Revise the following sentences so that all verbs occur in logical sequences.

1. We expected the storm to have bypassed our town, but it didn't.
2. We would like to have prior notice; however, even the police officers were taken by surprise.
3. Not having known much about flooding, the emergency crew was at a disadvantage.
4. Having thrown sandbags all day, the volunteers had been exhausted by 5 P.M.
5. They went home, succeeding in preventing a major disaster.

7c | **Voice indicates the relationship between a verb and its subject.**

When a verb is in the **active voice,** the subject is generally a person or thing performing an action. When a verb is in the **passive voice,** the subject is the *receiver* of the action.

Susan Sontag **wrote** the essay. [active voice]

The essay **was written** by Susan Sontag. [passive voice]

(1) Verbs may be linking, intransitive, or transitive.

A **linking verb** relates the subject and a word referring to the subject (the complement). (See **1d**.) A linking verb may be a verb referring to the senses or a verb that indicates being, seeming, remaining, or becoming.

Claudia **is** studious.

She **sounds** authoritative.

She **seems** responsible.

Linking verbs are used only in the active voice.

An **intransitive verb** does not take an object; there is no noun following the verb and receiving its action.

Claudia **studies** hard.

Intransitive verbs are used only in the active voice.

A **transitive verb** takes a direct object; that is, a noun follows the verb and receives its action.

Claudia **wrote** the prize-winning essay.

Transitive verbs can be used in the passive voice. When they are, the recipient of the action is the subject, not the object.

The prize-winning essay **was written** by Claudia.

(2) The active voice emphasizes the actor and the action.

Sentences that have the active voice are more vigorous than their passive counterparts. To use the active voice to emphasize actor and action, first make the actor the subject of the sentence; then choose verbs that show your readers what the actor is doing.

> Passive voice: The graduation ceremony was planned by a group of students. A well-known columnist was invited to give the address.
>
> Revised: A group of students planned the graduation ceremony. They invited a well-known columnist to give the address.

For more information on using the active voice to write forceful sentences, see **29d**.

(3) The passive voice highlights the recipient of the action.

The passive voice differs from the active voice in three ways. First, the subject is the recipient of the action, not the actor.

> The **construction** of the Guggenheim Museum was finished in 1959.

Second, if an actor is mentioned, that noun or pronoun is placed in a prepositional phrase beginning with the preposition *by.*

> The Guggenheim Museum was designed by **Frank Lloyd Wright.**

Finally, the verb form is different. A verb in the passive voice consists of a form of the auxiliary verb *be* and the past participle. Depending on the verb tense, the auxiliaries *have* and *will* may appear as well. The following are the most common tense forms for the passive voice for *call.*

> Simple present: *am called, is called, are called*
> Simple past: *was called, were called*

Simple future: *will be called*

Present progressive: *am being called, is being called, are being called*

Past progressive: *was being called, were being called*

Present perfect: *has been called, have been called*

Past perfect: *had been called*

Future perfect: *will have been called*

Use the passive voice when you want to stress the recipient of the action, rather than the actor, or when the actor's identification is unimportant or unknown. For example, you may want to emphasize the topic of a discussion.

Tuition increases will be discussed at the next board meeting.

Or you may be unable to identify the actor who performed some action.

The lights were left on in the building last night.

Exercise 6

Identify the voice in each sentence as active or passive.

1. Archaeologist William Saturno recently discovered the oldest known Maya mural.
2. The mural was found in a room used by looters.
3. The mural was dated to about 150 years before the beginning of the Maya Classic period.
4. For protection from further looting, the research crew posted guards outside the room.
5. The details of the mural have not yet been interpreted.

Exercise 7

Rewrite the sentences in exercise 6, making active verbs passive and passive verbs active. Add or delete actors when necessary. If one version of a sentence is better than the other, explain why.

> **7d** | The mood of a verb expresses the writer's attitude toward an action, a state, or an event.

The mood of a verb expresses the writer's attitude toward the factuality of what is being expressed. The **indicative mood** is used for statements and questions regarding fact or opinion. The **imperative mood** is used to give commands or directions. The **subjunctive mood** is used to state requirements, make requests, express wishes, and signal hypothetical situations.

Indicative	We will be on time.
Imperative	Be on time!
Subjunctive	The director insists that we be on time.

(1) Verb forms signal moods.

Verb forms for the indicative mood are described in **7b**. The verb form for the imperative is simply the base form. Verb forms used for the subjunctive mood are the present subjunctive, the past subjunctive, and the perfect subjunctive. The **present subjunctive** is the base form of the verb.

> The doctor recommended that he **go** on a diet.
>
> The curator requested that I **be** at the museum by five o'clock.

In the passive voice, the present subjunctive form consists of *be* and the past participle of the main verb.

> We demanded that you **be reimbursed.**

The **past subjunctive** has the same form as the simple past (for example, *had, offered, found,* or *wrote*). However, the past subjunctive form of *be* is *were,* regardless of person or number.

> If they **offered** me the job, I would take it.

> She acts as if she **were** the employer rather than the employee.

To form the passive voice of the past subjunctive, use *were* and the past participle.

> Even if he **were given** a large amount of money, he would not change his mind.

Although it is labeled "past," the past subjunctive refers to the present or the future.

The **perfect subjunctive** has the same form as the past perfect tense: *had* + past participle. The perfect subjunctive signals that a statement is not factual.

> I wish I **had known** about the scholarship competition.

To form the passive of the perfect subjunctive, add the past participle to *had been.*

> If she **had been awarded** the scholarship, she would have quit her part-time job.

(2) The subjunctive is mainly used in dependent clauses.

Although you may not use the subjunctive when you are speaking with your friends, using it in your writing shows your readers how you feel about your claims. The following guidelines should help you avoid pitfalls in the use of the subjunctive.

TIPS FOR USING THE SUBJUNCTIVE

In clauses beginning with *as if* and *as though,* use the past subjunctive or the perfect subjunctive.

He acts as if he *was* the owner.
were ^

She looked at me as though she **heard** this story before.
had ^

In nonfactual dependent clauses beginning with *if*, use the past subjunctive or the perfect subjunctive. Avoid using *would have* in the *if* clause.

If I *was* rich, I would buy a yacht.
were ^

If the driver ~~would have~~ **checked** his rearview mirror, the
had ^

accident would not have happened.

In dependent clauses following a verb that expresses a wish, requirement, or request, use the past subjunctive or the perfect subjunctive.

I wish I *was* taller.
were ^

My brother wishes he **studied** harder years ago.
had ^

Beyond the Rule

STATUS OF THE SUBJUNCTIVE MOOD

Some linguists believe that certain subjunctive forms are disappearing from the English language. For more information, visit www.harbrace.com.

Grammar checkers catch some missing verbs, some mismatches between auxiliary verbs and main verbs, and some missing -*ed* endings on verbs, but they skip over at least as many as they find. Furthermore, they can identify some misused infinitives but seldom find misused present participles or gerunds (see **1f(3)**). They cannot distinguish between a true passive construction, such as *have been seen,* and a form of *be* followed by an adjective, such as *have been healthy*; thus, they incorrectly flag the latter as a passive construction. In addition, they cannot tell when passive constructions are appropriate and so generally advise writers to "correct" them. They cannot identify improper tense forms or problems with conditional clauses, and they occasionally flag properly used subjunctives as agreement errors (see **6a**). For more information about grammar checkers, see **Using a Grammar Checker** on page 2.

Exercise 8

Use subjunctive verb forms to revise the following sentences.

1. The planners of Apollo 13 acted as if the number 13 was a lucky number.
2. Superstitious people think that if NASA changed the number of the mission, the astronauts would have had a safer journey.
3. They also believe that if the lunar landing would have been scheduled for a day other than Friday the Thirteenth, the crew would not have encountered any problems.
4. The crew used the lunar module as though it was a lifeboat.
5. If NASA ever plans a space mission on Friday the Thirteenth again, the public would object.

Mechanics

8 E-documents

Delivery is the visual design or format that gives readers the cues that lead them to the information they require and that makes your writing as readable as possible.

This chapter will help you

- compose a Web page (**8a**),
- use visual elements in Web design (**8b**),
- integrate graphics in Web design (**8c**),
- format documents to enhance content (**8d**), and
- format documents for readability (**8e**).

Delivery is important from the time you begin conceptualizing your document. Keeping in mind how you will present your ideas helps you develop them. Thus, delivery is closely related to arrangement (see **32d**), whether your document is intended for print or electronic distribution.

Visual design can invite readers to explore at the same time as it reflects the rhetorical purpose. Consider the message that the uncluttered and inviting visual design of the award-winning Web page in figure 8.1 sends to those who view it.

One of the guiding principles of organization (see **31b** and **32d**) is grouping the parts of a document that go together, whether it is a paper document or an electronic one. Notice how the designer of the British Airways Web site organized the information about types of travelers by embedding it in several clickable images. Make sure that there is a focal point for the reader's eye. In print, blocks of text—such as paragraphs (see

Figure 8.1. Award-winning British Airways Web site.

chapter **31**) and block quotations (**39d**)—provide focal points. On the British Airways Web page, the focal point is the line of five images across the middle. The content flows from that focal point. Ample white space signals openness and availability by drawing the reader's eye to a focal point. White space on a page frames the material on the page and contributes to the balance. In print, a tightly packed page with narrow margins signals difficult material. Notice that the British Airways Web page has lots of white space, contributing to a user's impression that this page is easy to use and well organized.

8a | Composing for the Web puts all of your rhetorical skills to use.

Notice how Aaron Munk, the author of the Web page shown in figure 8.2, establishes his credibility by announcing from the very first that he admires the courage and determination of African American soldiers who served in segregated units of the U.S. military before 1948. He continues that theme throughout this home page as well as on the other pages of

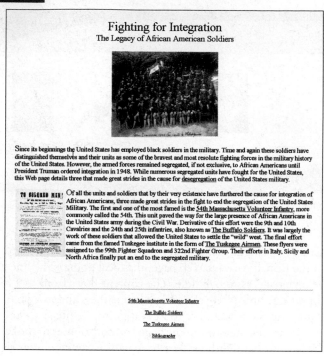

Figure 8.2. Home page of "Fighting for Integration."

the site (see **8d**). Munk's text appeals to a varied audience, composed partly of people of color and partly of military historians but also including any person who believes segregation was demeaning and inhumane. The attitudes so clearly displayed here contribute to Munk's credibility, help users of the site identify with his emotions, and support the logic that makes the site rewarding for those users. (See also **35d**.)

The home page of Munk's site introduces the main topics—the 54th Massachusetts Volunteer Infantry, the Buffalo Soldiers, and the Tuskegee Airmen—each of which is the subject of a separate page. (See page 163.) Notice also that the arrangement (see 32d) of the site is clear and easy to use: "Fighting for Integration" has links to all pages in the site at the bottom of each page, an example of how delivery can enhance content. Arrangement is involved in linking the word *desegregation* to a page of the Truman Library's Web site, which describes the events preceding and immediately following desegregation of the military. Finally, the centered picture at the top of the home page shows clearly that before 1948 soldiers of color served in the U.S. military in segregated units—a combining of arrangement and delivery. Another example of this blending is the image in the lower-left corner, which demonstrates that the U.S. military was actively recruiting for those segregated units.

(1) The rhetorical situation for a Web document expands the audience and the context.

When you plan a Web page or site, you make the same kinds of rhetorical choices you make when you plan an essay or a research paper: You identify your audience and your purpose, determine how they are affected by the context—time and place, writer, and medium (see 32a)—and decide how you want to present your material. The rhetorical situation for a Web page or site differs from that for an essay or paper mainly in the expansion of audience and context.

The potential audience for e-writing on the Web is vast—the number of possible readers far exceeds the number in any classroom, interest group, or club. So you may need to consider audience differently as you plan and put together a Web page or site. You also want to make appropriate decisions so that your document will achieve your intended purpose (see 32a), much as you would for a paper document. The advantages of hypertext (see 8a(2)) and visual elements (8b) for presenting information constitute part of the context for a Web document, as do your background, your attitudes and beliefs, and your credibility.

In addition to traditional considerations about audience, purpose, and context, you may wish to consider the following questions as you develop a Web document and seek guidance from your instructor if necessary.

CHECKLIST for Creating a Web Document

- Who is likely to visit my page or site?

- How might the fact that audiences other than my intended audience may view my page or site affect my purpose?

- Are there potential audiences I haven't considered?

- What influences do time and place have on the development of my page or site?

- What am I doing to take advantage of the fact that I am creating a Web document rather than a paper document?

- In what specific ways can a Web document help me achieve my purpose and reach my audience?

- Do I have particular strengths that I can use to advantage in developing this page or site?

---

(2) Planning Web documents involves working out an arrangement for presenting ideas.

It is important to distinguish between a Web page and a Web site. A Web page is a single document, or *node,* that can be displayed by a Web browser. While the user may need to scroll down the screen to read it all, a page can often be displayed in one screen. In some ways, constructing a Web site is a matter of constructing a set of related Web pages, and constructing a Web page requires you to think about arrangement (see **32d**) in ways that are significantly different from the ways in which you arrange your conventional print documents.

The key element of presentation in Web documents is **hypertext**—a way of linking text, pictures, and sound into your document seamlessly. A true electronic document is planned and drafted with hypertext as well as images and even sound as integral parts of its arrangement and content, and it is delivered with all of those elements integrated into the content. Such a document is never intended to appear in print form. A document converted from print is first written on paper in the conventional way, then transformed into a Web page. Both kinds of Web documents allow you to use **hyperlinks** (elements that take you to another place in a Web site or to a different Web site); thus, a hypertextual document is significantly different from a print document because its arrangement allows for structuring and linking text and other kinds of elements in ways that are not available in conventional print documents.

Beyond the Rule

USING HTML

To create a Web page, you do not have to understand the computer codes that allow a browser to display your text. There are many programs that will do such coding for you automatically. But some writers find that knowing some of the basic HTML commands can be useful for troubleshooting a Web page. A number of tutorials are available on the Web. For additional information on HTML, visit www.harbrace.com.

Several important considerations will influence your use of hypertext as you work to create an effective Web document:

- Since the interests and personalities of those who read your Web document will prompt them to move through, or navigate, it in different ways, you will need to consider how user differences may affect the intended purpose of your document and arrange it accordingly.

- Because the inclusion of hyperlinks transfers control of the sequence of information from the writer to the reader, planning and composing a Web page or site requires a more fluid arrangement of the material than is typical in an essay. Since users may click links in any order they choose, Web documents offer them unlimited options for ordering the content.

- The visual elements included in a Web page or site may eliminate the need for some text or create a need for additional text. For instance, the second image on Aaron Munk's home page (see figure 8.2) relieves him of the necessity to comment specifically about the role of the U.S. government in recruiting men of color for segregated military units.

Audience concerns will lead you to think about what you can expect users of a page or site to want. Considering information and purpose will lead you to ask how much and what kind of detail you will provide and what you are trying to achieve with your page or site. The answers to those questions can also involve content—both verbal and visual—as well as matters of how you will arrange it and what kinds of visual design and layout you will choose. You will also want to accommodate users who lack sophisticated equipment or fast Internet connections by keeping the design simple and using a limited number of graphical elements. These accommodations will make a Web site accessible to the greatest number of users.

You need to think about which ideas or information you
wish to emphasize and how to arrange your Web document to
convey those effectively. You might decide what supplementary
links you want to use at the same time as you are generating material. But you don't have to do everything at once. You can
fine-tune the visual design later. When you plan a Web site, you
may find it helpful to create a visual representation (sometimes
called a *storyboard*) of it. You can sketch plans on a sheet of paper or in a word-processing file if your site is fairly simple, or
you can use index cards tacked to a bulletin board if it is more
complex; you can also use the graphical capabilities of your
word-processing program to help you map out your site. For instance, it is easy to draw a representation of how a linear site
might be set up (see figure 8.3). Hierarchical and radial
arrangements are more complex to develop. The hierarchical
arrangement branches out at each level (figure 8.4), and the radial arrangement, in which individual pages can be linked in a

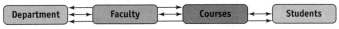

Figure 8.3. Linear model of a Web site.

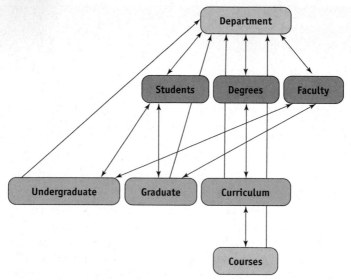

Figure 8.4. Hierarchical model of a Web site.

CHECKLIST for Planning a Web Site

- How will the arrangement of your site help you accomplish your purpose with your intended users?
- Should you devote each page to a single main idea or combine several ideas on one page?
- Can single pages be used to highlight the most important ideas or items of information?
- What will be the most effective way for users to navigate the site?
- What key connections between ideas or pieces of information might be emphasized through the use of hyperlinks?
- Where will key visual elements be placed to be most effective?

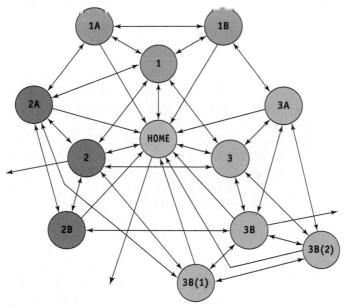

Figure 8.5. Radial model of a Web site.

variety of sequences (figure 8.5), allows the user to determine the sequence in which pages are viewed.

You can see that the possibilities for organizing a Web site are endless. The most important consideration is how the arrangement of your site will affect a user's experience in navigating it. However you decide to organize your site, try to represent each main element in your plan. You will find a good plan invaluable as you draft text, incorporate visual elements, and refine your arrangement.

(3) Hyperlinks help fulfill the rhetorical purpose of a Web document.

One of the distinguishing features of Web pages and sites, hyperlinks can be valuable tools for Web authors. Some basic principles can help you use hyperlinks effectively in your Web documents.

(a) Hyperlinks help make a Web document coherent.

Hyperlinks between pages of a site can provide transitions based on key words, ideas, or divisions of the document. In other words, because these links provide coherence and help readers navigate your Web site, they are powerful rhetorical tools that aid you in creating an effective arrangement for your site. Consider carefully where you will place these navigational tools, especially those that appear on the home page of a site that contains several pages. Users should be able to locate hyperlinks quickly, and they should be able to get to any part of your site easily from every page within it. However, avoid peppering your pages with unnecessary links.

(b) Hyperlinks provide focus as well as coherence.

For example, on the home page in figure 8.2, the key phrases "The Buffalo Soldiers" and "The Tuskegee Airmen" are hyperlinks that reinforce the coherence of the site. Similarly, the key term "desegregation" links from this page chronicling the segregated military units to a page on another Web site that addresses the general topic of desegregation of the U.S. military. Such a link makes a rhetorical connection through the subject matter of both pages and allows users to navigate between those pages. But you may also want to have other links to pages that present information that is central to the purpose of your site. And at the top or bottom of every page in a site, you need to provide links to every other page in the site. Collectively, such links provide focus for your site and contribute to making it effective.

(c) Hyperlinks can be textual or graphical.

You can use individual words, phrases, or even entire sentences as textual hyperlinks. You can also use icons or other graphical elements instead of text. If you do use graphical links, be sure their appearance is appropriate for the kind of link you are making. On his home page, Aaron Munk could have made the recruiting poster a graphical link, but a photo of a buffalo would not have been an appropriate link for this page.

(d) External links can enhance Web documents.

Consider very carefully how many and what kind of external hyperlinks to include. Make sure that you have a clear reason for using each link. For example, on his Web site, Aaron Munk provides a link to the Truman Library page on desegregating the military because he felt that the library had done a good job of presenting the steps the Truman administration followed between 1945 and 1950. The link explains what finally happened to the segregated military units—the end of the story.

When choosing external links, be sure to select those sites containing relevant, accurate, and well-presented information. You should also use any contact information on a site to ask permission to link to it and check your links periodically to be sure they are still active.

Above all, no matter how extensive a Web site is, it should be easy to use. As you develop your site, keep the following tips in mind.

TIPS FOR MAKING A WEB SITE EASY TO USE

- Make sure visitors to your site can easily find the information they are looking for without having to search through the entire site or click on many links to get to the page they want.

- If you know how to use frames, which allow you to divide the screen into several smaller screens and manipulate the content of each screen independently, they can help you organize your site and help users navigate it. But frames can diminish the size of the content window, can make it difficult for users to backtrack, and can make a site slow to download.

- Always provide navigational links that take users back to the home page of your site.

CHECKLIST for Developing a Web Site

- How would you like a user to navigate your Web site? For what purpose?
- What information or ideas should a user take away from your site?
- Will a user who follows external links be able to get back to your page?
- Will the experience of navigating the Web site be exciting and informative for the user?
- How might different users react to the arrangement of the site?
- Have you used Web-specific resources in creating your Web site so that it has more impact than a paper document?
- Do you need graphics—charts, graphs, pictures, cartoons, clip art, animations, and so on—to enhance the site so that it will accomplish your purpose?

Exercise 1

Plan and write out the information for a Web page that supports a paper you are writing for one of your classes. If you have access to a program that converts your document to a Web page, try that. Then, critique your page.

8b | The visual elements of a Web document should serve a rhetorical purpose.

Web documents can be effective if you keep some basic principles in mind: Photographs and other kinds of visual elements can illustrate a key idea, present information, or help make a point, but these elements should not be merely decorative; they should be integral to achieving your purpose. Using a carefully chosen image can be a powerful way to evoke a feeling or make an argument. Similarly, a dramatic font style can be used to emphasize an idea. All the design elements of a Web document, like the tone and style of a printed one, are rhetorical tools that help you achieve your purpose and reach your intended audience. When you choose design elements such as photographs, try to anticipate how your audience may react.

To optimize the appearance of a Web document, keep five basic design principles in mind: balance, proportion, movement, contrast, and unity.

SOME BASIC DESIGN PRINCIPLES

Balance involves the way in which elements in the design are spatially related to each other. Web pages with a symmetrical arrangement of elements convey a formal, static impression, whereas asymmetrical pages are informal and dynamic.

Proportion has to do with the relative sizes of elements in a design. For example, large elements attract more attention than small ones and will be perceived as more important.

Movement concerns the way in which our eyes scan a page for information. Most of us are accustomed to looking at the upper-left corner of a page first and the lower-right corner last. Therefore, the most important information on a Web page should appear in those locations. Vertical or horizontal arrangement of elements on a page implies stability; a diagonal or zigzag arrangement suggests movement.

Contrast between elements can be achieved by varying the focus or the size. For instance, a Web page on the dog breed the Siberian Husky might show the dog in sharp focus while blurring the background. The dog might also appear large relative to other elements on the page. You can also use contrasting fonts to emphasize an idea. For instance, a

(Continued on page 162)

(Continued from page 161)

display font such as **kids** that looks like a child's writing or an elegant script font such as *Edwardian Script* might be used to highlight a contrast with something simpler and more direct. (Remember, though, that older Web browsers may not display all fonts properly.)

Unity refers to the way all the elements (and pages) of a site combine to give the impression that they are parts of a complete whole. For instance, choose colors and fonts to reflect the tone you want to convey and use them consistently throughout your site. Creating a new design for each page of a Web site is almost certain to make the site seem chaotic and ineffective.

(1) Visual elements should be integrated with text in a Web document.

Rhetorically, Web pages are as much visual as they are verbal, and the most effective Web documents integrate both types of elements in such a way that they complement each other. Images and other visual elements extend and enhance the content of a Web document. Visual elements can be powerful tools, but selecting them and using them judiciously can be difficult. Too many visual elements may overwhelm viewers. Keep in mind that the basic design unit for a Web document is the computer screen, and put only as much on a page as a user can easily grasp within the space of a single screen. If you have too many images (or too much information) for one page, put some on another page or delete what is not essential.

Keep in mind that the visual impact of your Web site should be appropriate to its subject. Not only are the images on the pages from the "Fighting for Integration" site appropriate for an informative site, but they also help to tell the story and to involve readers in that story by arousing emotions, as the photo of the lone Tuskegee airman in figure 8.6 does. Furthermore, in figure 8.7, the prominently placed painting of the Black soldiers

The Tuskegee Airmen

During World War II another experiment was begun involving black soldiers. This experiment was begun by the Army Air Corps in Tuskegee, Alabama, in order to train Black Americans as military pilots. The school chosen to train these pilots was none other than the famed Tuskegee Institute (now University). The Tuskegee Institute was selected as the training center because the institute already had a commitment to aeronautical training, and so it already had the facilities and instructors. Furthermore, the Institute was located in Alabama where the climate was good for year-round flying. Prior to 1940 Black men were not allowed to fly in the military. The program at the Tuskegee institute was the direct result of pressure from civil right groups working to change this.

Cadets took their primary flight training at Tuskegee's Moton Field, and then were moved to Tuskegee Army Air Field to complete their training. This allowed the airmen to make the conversion from civilian to combat aircraft.

When done with their training, the airmen were assigned to the 99th Fighter Squadron and the 322nd Fighter Group. These units saw action in North Africa and the Mediterranean, primarily in Italy and Sicily. The units made up of the Tuskegee Airmen received a total of three Presidential Unit Citations for their role in air support

Figure 8.6. The Tuskegee Airmen page.

The 54th Massachusetts Volunteer Infantry

While the 54th Massachusetts Infantry did posses a commendable battle history, most notably the assault on the Fort Wagner Battery and the rearguard action at the battle of Olustee, it is not the service record of the unit that made it famous. Rather the fame of the unit largely stemmed from the reason for its inception and the composition of its forces.

The 54th was composed mainly of free blacks from the northern states. The regiment came into existence through pressure that abolitionists placed on President Lincoln who as a result opened up the Military for black soldiers. Furthermore, several members of the 54th were the children of some of these same abolitionists. The organizing and commanding officer of the 54th, Robert Gould Shaw, was the son of prominent Boston abolitionists Francis Gould and Sarah Sturgis Shaw. Within the ranks of the recruits were two sons of Fredrick Douglass, a former slave and prominent abolitionist. The first was Sergeant-Major Lewis Douglas and the second, Charles Douglass. The assault on Fort Wagner was also where Sergeant William H. Carney earned his Congressional Medal of Honor saving the regiment's union flag from capture. He was the first African-American to receive such an honor.

The 54th had a clear purpose of helping to turn the war from one about state's rights to one about human rights. The regiment was as much a symbol as it was a fighting

Figure 8.7. The 54th Massachusetts Volunteer Infantry page.

fighting under the Union flag emphasizes that this regiment fought extremely hard in battle and was especially valorous, and it helps connect this page with the other pages on the site.

Because image files tend to be very large, they may download slowly on a user's Web browser, especially if the user has a slow connection to the Internet. For this reason, be sure that any image you include serves an important rhetorical purpose, especially if it is a large file.

Web sites often incorporate audio or video elements. If you design a site devoted to rap music, for instance, you might want to include links to audio clips of rap songs featured on the site. Or you might link to a video clip of a political speech on a site for a political science class.

(2) Color and background play an important rhetorical role in a Web document.

Color and background can be used in a Web document to achieve various visual effects. Current Web standards allow the display of a wide array of colors for background, text, and frames. And it is easy to find thousands of background graphics on the Internet or to create them with special software. Like the other elements of a Web document, however, color and background should be considered rhetorical tools.

When deciding how to use color in your Web documents, keep the following considerations in mind:

- Designers recommend using no more than three main colors for a document (although you can use varying intensities, or shades, of a color). Using more than three colors can make your Web pages unappealing or confusing.
- Color can contribute to specific effects you wish to achieve. For example, bright colors such as red and yellow are more noticeable than light blue or brown. Some colors have asso-

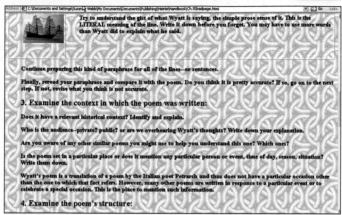

Figure 8.8. Example of poor Web page design.

ciations you may wish to take advantage of. For instance, reds can suggest danger or an emergency.

■ Usually, textual hyperlinks appear in a color different from the surrounding text on a Web page. Also, a link that has not yet been clicked is one color, and a link that has already been clicked is a different color.

The background can also enhance your Web document, but there are some pitfalls to avoid when choosing one:

■ A dark background can create a dramatic appearance, but it often makes text difficult to read and hyperlinks more difficult to see. A dark background can also cause a printout of a Web page to be blank.

■ A background with a pattern can also be dramatic but can make a Web page very difficult to read. If you want to use a pattern for your background, check the readability of the text. You may need to change the color of the text to make it easier to see. Notice how difficult it is to read the Web page in figure 8.8.

- You can use different background colors or patterns for different pages of your Web site, but be aware that doing so can create confusion, even if you have a good rhetorical reason to alter the background from page to page.

For more detailed help with designing a Web site, you might look at some of the following.

Tim Berners-Lee, the creator of the World Wide Web, is the author of the following Web-based design manual: www.w3.org/Provider/Style/Introduction.html

Jeff Glover, the Web manager for XOOM.com, has good advice to offer at his Web site: jeffglover.com/ss.html

Check out library science professor Alastair Smith's list of nearly four dozen Web site evaluation guides: www.vuw.ac.nz/~agsmith/evaln/

If any of these Web addresses change, you may still be able to find the page by dropping the last element of the address and trying again. If that doesn't work, run a search (see 37c) or look at the links on other Web sites.

Beyond the Rule

HTML

Web pages are written in a fairly simple language called HyperText Markup Language (HTML). You insert HTML codes in a document to instruct a browser how to display the information in the document. For more information about HTML, visit www.harbrace.com.

CHECKLIST for Designing a Web Site

- Have you created a template to use for all of the pages in the Web site so that all of them are consistent?

- Have you chosen the background and text colors so that users can easily print copies of your pages?

- Have you used no more than three colors, but perhaps varied the intensity of one or more of them?

- Does a background pattern on your page make the text difficult to read?

- Have you chosen a single, easy-to-read font such as Times Roman for most of your text? If you use display fonts for titles or headings or for emphasis, are they suitable for the content and purpose? Are the type styles (bold, italic, and so on) used consistently throughout the document?

- Have you used visual elements sparingly? Are any image files larger than 30K, making it likely that they will take a long time to transfer? If so, can you shrink them by using a lower resolution or a smaller size?

- Are points indicated graphically by using bullets or numbers or by being divided into short blocks?

- Is any page crowded? Can users scan the information quickly on a single screen?

- Is there a site map or list of the site's sections on your main page? Are there links to get back to the main page from every other page in your site?

- Is the site too "text heavy"—that is, does each screen contain text of about the same density as in a book? If so, can you revise to provide more white space?

- Have you made sure that all links work?

- Have you identified yourself as the author and noted when the site was created or last revised?

- Have you run a spell checker?

Exercise 2

Using the Save as Web Page option of your word processor, create a simple Web page to accompany one of the papers you have written. Keep track of your reasons for each design decision. State the rhetorical purpose for each visual element.

8c | Graphics enhance understanding.

Visual elements help most readers understand complex information more readily. Word-processing software makes graphics easy to use. For assignments in the natural and social sciences, business (see chapter 43), and education, tables, graphs, and charts are often essential. The danger, of course, is that visual elements can be overused. Becoming familiar with the creation and use of these elements will help you produce better documents for courses in these disciplines.

(1) Tables organize information to show relationships clearly.

When you design a table, be sure to label all of the columns and rows accurately and to provide a title and a number (see table 8.1). Table number and title appear above the table, but any notes or source information should be placed below it.

Word-processing programs let you determine how many rows and columns a table will have, and you can also size each row and each column appropriately for the information it will hold. Tables can also be used to enhance page design.

(2) Charts and graphs demonstrate relationships.

Charts and graphs demonstrate relationships among data and show spatial concepts or call attention to particular informa-

TABLE 8.1
Modified Monthly Tornado Statistics

Month	2002 Prelim.	2001 Final	2000 Final	1999 Final	3-Year Average
Jan	8	5	16	212	77
Feb	2	30	56	22	32
Mar	30	34	103	56	66
Apr	114	131	136	177	140
May	130	235	241	311	256
Jun	?	147	135	289	219
Jul	?	123	148	102	128
Aug	?	69	52	79	62
Sep	?	85	47	56	58
Oct	?	121	63	17	60
Nov	?	112	48	7	37
Dec	?	?	26	15	16
Total	290	1212	1071	1343	1151

Source: National Weather Service.

tion or comparisons. In Web documents, they often substitute for text. (See page 154.) In paper documents, they should be used to support your text, not to replace any of it. If you need many charts or graphs in a paper, consider placing all of them in an appendix.

Charts and graphs are often referred to as **figures.** Each figure in a document should be numbered and have a title. The figure number and title, as well as any source note, should be placed below the illustration.

Pie charts are especially useful for showing the relationship of parts to a whole (see figure 8.9).

Graphs show relationships over time. For instance, a graph can show the progression of sleep stages during a night (see figure 8.10), increases or decreases in student achievement or annual rainfall, or trends in financial markets.

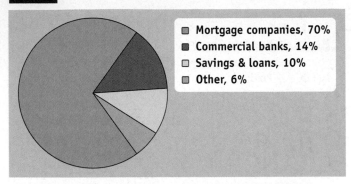

Figure 8.9. Pie chart showing issuers of mortgage-backed securities.
Source: GMAC Mortgage-Backed Securities.

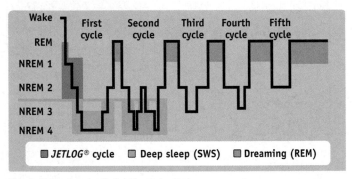

Figure 8.10. Graph of nightly sleep stages.
Source: Jetlog 24x7.

Bar charts show other kinds of correlations. A bar chart might illustrate gross national product for several nations, the relative speeds of various computer processors, or statistics about the composition of the U.S. military (see figure 8.11).

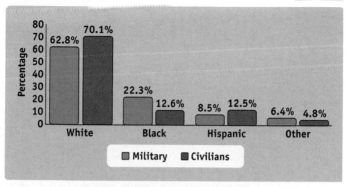

Figure 8.11. Bar chart illustrating the composition of the military.
Source: Seattle Times (seattletimes.nwsource.com/.../ military/new_military.html), 7/17/02.

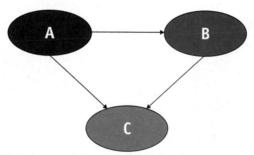

Figure 8.12. A diagram of the process from A to C.

(3) Diagrams, drawings, maps, and other illustrations help explain concepts.

Diagrams or drawings (see figure 8.12), maps (figure 8.13), and other kinds of illustrations help readers understand processes or concepts and visualize spatial dimensions and relationships, as well as other details pertinent to the topic of a document. Photographs can also have visual or emotional impact (see figure 8.14), and cartoons can add humor (figure 8.15).

Figure 8.13. A map showing Starbucks locations in China.
Source: Modified from *CIA Fact Book*.

Figure 8.14. A photograph that could add impact to a document.
Source: Courtesy of Roland Schlager.

"Indeed, your class attendance does give new meaning to the term 'distance learning.'"

Figure 8.15. A cartoon that brings humor to the discussion of a concept.
Source: Chronicle of Higher Education, 1999.

8d A well-designed document format contributes to the rhetorical purpose.

Creating a balanced page and grouping related parts of a document are essential to good design. The advice here follows MLA guidelines. If your instructor has specified another style manual, check the most recent edition of that manual. (See the list of style manuals on pages 602–603.) In general, if your instructor asks you to use a particular style, follow the instructions for that style exactly.

(1) Indentation signals a change of ideas.

The first line of every paragraph should be uniformly indented. You can set your word-processing software to automatically indent the first line of a paragraph one-half inch. Indent block quotations one inch from the left margin (see figure 8.16).

If you use the tab key or space bar to create indentations, the format can change if you transfer your document to another computer or save it as a Web page. Thus, it is a good idea to learn to use the formatting controls in your word processor.

(2) All pages should be numbered.

Place arabic numerals—without parentheses or periods—on each page of a document. According to Modern Language Association (MLA) style, the number appears at the right margin, one-half inch from the top of the page. Put your last name immediately before the page number so that your instructor can identify any page that gets misplaced. (Notice the way the page number and last name appear in figure 8.16.) Similarly, American Psychological Association (APA) style calls for the page number to appear in the upper-right corner of the page immediately after the running head (see 40c). *The Chicago Manual of Style* (CMS) does not specify the placement of page numbers, so ask your instructor for directions.

(3) The first page of a document has a distinctive format.

Unless your instructor requires that you use a different style, follow MLA guidelines and place your name, your instructor's name, the course and section number, and the date in the top left-hand corner of the first page of a paper (one inch from the

the first outlet opened across from the city's famous opera house. Once some success is accomplished, Starbucks buys enough of the foreign-owned branch to control the company, and proceeds to enlarge rapidly throughout the country (Burke, Smith, and Wosnitza 47).

Vienna, considered by many to be the birthplace of the coffeehouse tradition, is legendary for its coffee culture. The first Viennese coffeehouses appeared after invading Turks left sacks of coffee outside the city walls as they fled in 1683 (Pendergast 10). Intellectual life abounded in elegant cafés by the nineteenth century, as they became meeting places for early modernists such as Sigmund Freud and Gustav Klimt, as well as for notable exiles such as Vladimir Lenin and Leon Trotsky. In Vienna, the people take pride in the history and enjoy the culture that surrounds the coffeehouse tradition. Austrians received the opening of Starbucks with mixed emotions:

> Many Viennese sniff that their culture has been infected, that Viennese use their 1,900 or so coffee shops to linger and meet, smoke and drink, savor the wonders of pastries with cream and marzipan, ponder the world, write books and read free newspapers. They drink from china cups and order from a waiter, usually in a stained black dinner jacket. (Erlanger B3)

Skeptics found it difficult to believe that an American brand such as Starbucks could survive in an environment steeped in its own local history of coffee and pride in its heritage, but these skeptics seem to have underestimated Starbucks.

There are several fundamental differences between the Starbucks experience and the traditional experience found in Viennese coffeehouses. Instead of ordering through a server, Starbucks patrons order at an American-style coffee bar. As opposed to more traditional offerings such as Sachertorte and hot goulash, Starbucks sells American-style sweets like blueberry muffins and chocolate-chip cookies. Furthermore, patrons are not allowed to smoke in any Starbucks outlet in order to allow the aroma of coffee to fill each store. Smoking, however, is a large part of the European coffeehouse experience.

These differences add up to two coffee cultures at a crossroads in Vienna. Traditional American offerings are pitted against the offerings of Viennese coffeehouses that have

Figure 8.16. Example of indentation format.

top and one inch from the left edge of the page), double-spacing after each line. You should also double-space between the lines of a long title or between a main title and a subtitle. Center all lines of titles. Do not triple- or quadruple-space after the title. (See figure 8.17.) Begin your first paragraph on the second line below the title (the first double-spaced line). (See also the models in chapters 33, 36, 40, and 42.)

Most papers do not require a title page, but if you use one, follow your instructor's directions about the format. The title

Andy Pieper

Professor Miller

English 299, Section 4

27 November 2002

Starbucks in Vienna: Coffee Cultures at a Crossroads

From St. Paul to Sao Paulo, from Rome to Riyadh, and from Johannesburg to

Jakarta, world citizens are increasingly being pushed toward a global culture. We are

being affected internationally through the media we experience, the food we eat, and the

products we consume as multinational corporations act on a world stage (Rothkopf 38).

People with disposable incomes can watch MTV in India, catch a Hollywood-produced

movie in Australia, purchase a Mickey Mouse doll in Oman, use an Icelandic cell phone

to call a friend in Malaysia, send an e-mail from an IBM computer in Russia, and

purchase a bucket of Kentucky Fried Chicken in Japan.

All of these examples are signs of <u>globalization</u>, a term coined to describe the

increasingly prominent role of large companies in the world marketplace. At the forefront

of globalization is the multinational corporation, which David Korten, author of <u>When</u>

<u>Corporations Rule the World</u>, defines as a business that takes "on many national

identities, maintaining relatively autonomous production and sales facilities in individual

countries, establishing local roots and presenting itself in each locality as a good local

citizen" (125). Many of these multinationals originate and are headquartered in the

United States or other Western nations, but they have means of production or outlets in

countries all over the world.

Proponents of globalization claim that this process is advantageous because it

makes business efficient and helps foster international ties. Opponents argue that local

cultures are damaged and that globalization primarily benefits wealthy corporations in

nations already rich. The Starbucks Coffee Corporation is one example of a multinational

company involved in globalization. No matter what the long-term advantages or

disadvantages of globalization prove to be, investigating how a Western company like

Figure 8.17. First page of a paper in MLA style.

page shown in CMS style in figure 8.18 may be suitable for use
with an MLA-style paper if your instructor wants a title page.
Figure 8.19 shows a first page that follows APA style.

(4) Headings help organize complex information.

Headings are necessary to help readers manage information in
research papers, technical and business reports, and other kinds
of complex documents. Headings highlight the organization of

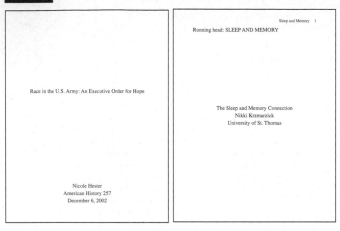

Race in the U.S. Army: An Executive Order for Hope

Nicole Hester
American History 257
December 6, 2002

Sleep and Memory 1
Running head: SLEEP AND MEMORY

The Sleep and Memory Connection
Nikki Krzmarzick
University of St. Thomas

Figure 8.18. Title page in CMS style.   **Figure 8.19. Title page in APA style.**

a long block of information and make it easy to combine several related statements. They are more commonly used for writing in the sciences and social sciences than in the humanities.

Short papers rarely require headings. If you use headings in a longer paper, make them consistent throughout your document. APA style has specific requirements for formatting headings. (See 40c–d.) If you have two or more levels of headings, treat all occurrences of each level alike. For instance, headings in this book follow a pattern similar to that of an outline. The main sections are identified by a number and letter set at the left margin. Subsections are identified by numbers in parentheses, and subdivisions of these, where they appear, are indicated by letters in parentheses.

8e | A well-designed format enhances a document's readability.

Several formatting principles will help make your documents as attractive and easy to read as possible.

(1) Documents should follow a consistent format.

The conventions of academic writing require that all papers be double-spaced. Set margins of at least one inch (no more than one and one-half inches) on all sides of the text block to give your reader room for comments and to prevent a crowded appearance, and use eleven- or twelve-point type. Also, resist the impulse to justify the right margin (i.e., to make it straight), unless a document will be printed without being reformatted, as is sometimes the case with business documents or documents intended for desktop publishing.

If you submit your work electronically (for instance, by email, in a Web document, or on a removable medium), follow your instructor's directions exactly. Check with your instructor about any special requirements, such as the need to provide your document in PC or Mac format. Always label files and disks clearly. Employers will have their own formatting requirements and the equipment to produce your documents in the form they require.

(2) Type fonts are best kept simple.

Although word-processing software makes it easy to use a variety of different type sizes and fonts on a single page, using a variety detracts from your content. Most academic papers should be printed using a font that looks like typewriter type, such as Courier, or a simple proportional font, such as Times Roman. It is usually best to avoid sans serif fonts (those, such as Arial, in which letters lack cross-bars at the ends of strokes) and fancy display fonts, such as Old English and *Script*, because blocks of text printed in such fonts are hard to read.

Although ink-jet printers offer the option of printing text in color, you should not do so unless there is some purpose to formatting in this way (as when creating a flyer or announcement). Most professors prefer that you use black ink (and a font such as Times Roman) for traditional academic assignments because it produces clear, dark text that is easy to read.

CHECKLIST for Formatting Paper Documents

- Have you used proper margins? Are the margins at least one inch wide or set according to your instructor's specifications?
- Is the first line of each paragraph indented one-half inch?
- Is each page numbered?
- Does the first page have the appropriate title and heading?
- Is the print dark, clean, clear, and legible?
- Are the lines double-spaced?
- Are all listed items numbered sequentially?

Exercise 3

Review the formatting decisions you have made for a paper that you have submitted or are planning to submit. What, if anything, do you think needs to be changed? Why?

Capitals

Capital letters designate such things as names, peoples and their languages, geographical names, and organizations.

This chapter will help you

- capitalize proper names (**9a**),
- use capitals for titles of persons (**9b**),
- capitalize words in titles of works (**9c**),
- capitalize the first word of directly quoted speech (**9d**), and
- avoid unnecessary capitalization (**9e**).

Rhetorically, capitalization contributes to clarity when it marks the beginning of a sentence; writers also capitalize proper nouns naming persons or organizations.

When you are uncertain whether to capitalize a particular word, look it up in a good, recent dictionary (see **19e**). Dictionaries list not only words and abbreviations that begin with capitals but also acronyms that use full capitals. (For more about acronyms, see **9a(9)** and **11e**.)

Tom Cruise   California   Italians   Federal Express   EPA

A recent dictionary is also useful when the capitalization of a word depends on a particular meaning in context.

| mosaic pictures | BUT | Mosaic law |
| on earth | BUT | the planet Earth |

A style manual for the discipline in which you are writing is another useful guide for capitalization. (See pages 602–603.)

When you can choose whether or not to capitalize a word, it is important to follow one style consistently.

sunbelt OR Sunbelt   a.m. OR A.M. OR A.M.

When you type a final draft, you may notice that the AutoCorrect function of your word-processing program capitalizes letters that you want in lowercase form. For instance, it may capitalize items in a list that you intend to be part of a series completing a sentence—like those in the list at the beginning of this chapter. You may wish, therefore, to turn off any automatic style or formatting function.

9a Proper names are capitalized and so, usually, are their abbreviations and acronyms.

As you study the following examples, notice that common nouns like *college, company, park,* and *street* are capitalized only when they are essential parts of proper names.

(1) Names and nicknames of persons or things and trade names are capitalized.

Zora Neale Hurston	Flight 224	Honda Accord
John Paul II	Academy Award	USS *Cole*
Skylab	Nike	Microsoft Word

(2) Names of peoples and their languages are capitalized.

African Americans	Asians	Latinos	Poles
English	Swahili	Korean	Urdu

Blacks, Whites OR blacks, whites [Whichever you choose, be consistent.]

(3) Names of geographical features and of bridges, monuments, and buildings are capitalized.

Arctic Circle	Havana	Golden Gate Bridge
China	Iowa	Empire State Building
Ellis Island	Lincoln Memorial	Seventh Street

When referring to two or more geographical features, however, do not capitalize the generic term: *Lincoln and Jefferson memorials, Yellowstone and Grand Canyon national parks.*

(4) Names of organizations, government agencies, institutions, and companies are capitalized.

Congress of Racial Equality	Howard University
Phi Beta Kappa	New England Patriots
Internal Revenue Service	Ford Motor Company

When used as common nouns, *service, company,* and *university* are not capitalized.

(5) Names for days of the week, months, and holidays are capitalized.

Wednesday	August	Fourth of July	Labor Day

The names of the seasons—spring, summer, fall, winter—are not capitalized unless followed by a year: *Spring 2004.*

(6) Designations for historical documents, periods, events, and movements are capitalized.

Declaration of Independence	Gulf War	Renaissance
Impressionism	Stone Age	World Series

(7) Names of religions, their adherents, holy days, titles of holy books, and words denoting the Supreme Being are capitalized.

Buddhism, Christianity, Islam, Judaism

Buddhist, Christian, Muslim, Jew

Bodhi Day, Easter, Ramadan, Yom Kippur

Sutras, Bible, Koran, Talmud [BUT biblical, talmudic]

Buddha, God, Allah, Yahweh

Some writers always capitalize pronouns referring to the Supreme Being (except *who, whom, whose*). Others capitalize such pronouns only when capitalization is needed to prevent ambiguity, as in "The Lord commanded the prophet to warn His people."

(8) Words derived from proper names are capitalized.

Americanize [verb]   Orwellian [adjective]   Marxism [noun]

When a proper name becomes the name of a general class of objects or ideas, it is no longer capitalized.

zipper [originally a capitalized trademark]

blarney [derived from the Blarney Stone]

A word derived from a brand name, such as Xerox, Kodak, Polaroid, or Kleenex, should be capitalized. Because the corporations that own these brand names object to their use for generic purposes, use *photocopy, camera, instant snapshot,* or *tissue* instead. If you are not sure whether a proper name has come to stand for a general class, look in a dictionary. Many such words can be either capitalized or not.

French windows OR french windows

Roman numeral OR roman numeral

Beyond the Rule

CAPITALIZATION STYLE

Most style books recommend that initial letters of words derived from proper names not be capitalized. *Merriam-Webster's Collegiate Dictionary* **comments that such words are often capitalized, but it shows most of them in lowercase. For more information on capitalization styles, visit www.harbrace.com.**

(9) Abbreviations and acronyms often appear in capitals.

These forms are derived from the initial letters of capitalized word groups:

AMEX, AT&T, CBS, CST, JFK, NFL, OPEC, UNESCO, YMCA

(See also chapter 11 and 17a(3).)

> **9b** | **Titles that precede the name of a person are capitalized but not those that follow it or stand alone.**

Governor Peter Dunn	Peter Dunn, the governor
Captain Machado	Machado, our captain
President Lincoln	the president of the United States

Words denoting family relationships are capitalized only when the words substitute for proper names.

Tell Mother I'll write soon. [COMPARE My mother wants me to write.]

9c | The first, last, and all major words in titles of works are capitalized.

All words in titles and subtitles of literary and artistic works are capitalized, except articles (*a, an,* and *the*), coordinating conjunctions (*and, but, for, nor, or, so,* and *yet*), prepositions (see the list on page 33), and the infinitive marker *to* (unless it is the first or last word in the title). (See also **10a** and **16b**.) APA style requires capitalizing any word that has four or more letters, including prepositions (except in references entries). (See **40c**.)

The Scarlet Letter	"How to Be a Leader"
From Here to Eternity	"What This World Is Coming To"

Southwestern Pottery from Anasazi to Zuni [MLA and CMS]

Southwestern Pottery From Anasazi to Zuni [APA]

MLA, APA, and CMS recommend capitalizing all words of any hyphenated compound in a title, except for articles, coordinating conjunctions, and prepositions.

"The Building of the H-Bomb" [noun]

"The Arab-Israeli Dilemma" [proper adjective]

"Stop-and-Go Signals" [lowercase the conjunction]

Single-word compounds (*undercover, decommission*) in titles follow the normal rules of capitalization. However, if misreading could occur (as with *Un-ionized* or *Re-cover*), MLA and APA capitalize both elements if the second element begins with a capital letter (*pre-Columbian*) or if the compound contains a doubled letter that could be hard to read (*anti-intellectual*). CMS capitalizes only those words that are proper nouns or adjectives.

"Colonial Anti-Independence Poetry" [MLA]

"Anti-Independence Behavior in Adolescents" [APA]

"Anti-independence Activities of Delaware's Tories" BUT
"Pre-Columbian Artifacts in Peruvian Museums" [CMS]

9d

9d | The first word of every sentence (or any unit written as a sentence) and of any directly quoted speech is capitalized.

Experienced cooks are usually ready to try something new. (You can learn from them.) [parenthetical sentence]

Oh, really! Not right now. [units written as sentences]

Beth got out of the car and shouted, "Home at last!" [directly quoted speech]

"Stop dieting," he says, "and start exercising." OR "Stop dieting," he says. "And start exercising." [directly quoted speech in a single sentence and directly quoted speech in separate sentences]

I have only one rule: Pay attention. [independent clause following a colon; see 17d]

A series of questions following an introductory element are usually capitalized when the intent is to draw attention to the questions. Otherwise, they may be set in lowercase.

How do we distinguish the legal codes for families? For individuals? For genetic research?

Are interest rates on car loans down to six percent? five? three?

9e | Unnecessary capitals are distracting.

(1) Capitalizing common nouns can distract your readers.

Do not confuse a common noun with a proper noun naming a specific entity. A common noun preceded by the indefinite article *a* or *an* or by a modifier such as *every* or *several* is not capitalized.

a speech course in theater and television [COMPARE Speech 324: Theater and Television] a university, my high school [COMPARE University of Michigan, Hickman High School]

However, always capitalize proper nouns, even when they are preceded by *a* or *an* or by a modifier such as *every* or *several*.

a St. Bernard   every Virginian   several Canadians

(2) Using capitalization to indicate emphasis requires caution.

Occasionally, a common noun is capitalized for emphasis.

The motivation of many politicians is Power.

If you use capitals for emphasis, do so sparingly; overuse will weaken the effect. For other ways to achieve emphasis, see chapter **29**.

STYLE SHEET FOR CAPITALIZATION

Capitals	No Capitals
the West [geographical region]	driving west [compass point]
Southerners [a group of people]	the southern plains
a Chihuahua [a breed of dog named after a state in Mexico]	a poodle [a breed of dog]
Washington State University [a specific institution]	a state university
German, Italian, Japanese [specific languages]	a language course
Revolutionary War [a specific war]	an eighteenth-century war
the U.S. Army OR US Army [a national army]	a peacetime army [an army of any nation]
Declaration of Independence [title of a document]	a declaration of independence
May [specific month]	spring [general season]

Memorial Day [specific day]	a holiday
two Democratic candidates [a specific political party]	democratic procedures [a form of government]
a Ford tractor [brand name]	a farm tractor
Parkinson's disease [a disease named for a person]	flu, asthma, leukemia
Dr. Katherine Kadohata [a person's title]	every doctor, my doctor

Exercise 1

Write a sentence using each of the following words correctly.

1. president   5. north   9. republican
2. President   6. North   10. Republican
3. company   7. street   11. mountains
4. Company   8. Street   12. Mountains

Exercise 2

Insert capitals wherever needed.

[1]when i went back to school after being in the navy, i began to see why i had had problems in school three years earlier. [2]as a first-year student, i was delighted to be out from under my parents' supervision, and i spent more time and money at the college inn's perpetual party than i did studying german and zoology. [3]roger gibson, my roommate that year, was from denver, colorado, and he drove a very fast pontiac firebird. [4]we had some wonderful friday nights in that car when we should have been studying. [5]when i flunked out in june, i joined the navy. [6]basic training was a real eye-opener.

[7]lieutenant davis, my commanding officer, helped me understand how to use self-discipline. [8]as i neared the end of my military service, i consulted a copy of *peterson's guide to colleges and universities.* [9]i applied to laughlin state university because they offered two things that were important to me: a major in game theory and a cooperative education program. [10]cooperative education allows me to apply some of my work experience for credit and to earn money to supplement the scholarship i get from the department of defense—often called the g.i. bill.

Italics

When you use italics, you let readers know that you are using a word or a group of words in a special way. For example, the following sentence is ambiguous.

The linguistics students discussed the word stress.

Does this sentence mean that the students discussed a particular word or that they discussed an accent pattern? By italicizing *stress,* the writer indicates that it was the word, not the accent pattern, that the students discussed.

The linguistics students discussed the word *stress.*

This chapter will help you use italics for

- the titles of separate works (**10a**),
- foreign words (**10b**),
- the names of legal cases (**10c**),
- the names of ships, submarines, aircraft, spacecraft, and satellites (**10d**),
- words, letters, or figures used as such or as statistical symbols or variables in algebraic expressions (**10e**), and
- emphasis of words (**10f**).

Word-processing programs make it easy to use italics. In handwritten or typewritten documents, you can indicate italics by underlining.

Richard Russo's novel *Empire Falls* won a Pulitzer Prize.
Richard Russo's novel <u>Empire Falls</u> won a Pulitzer Prize.

Although the use of italics instead of underlining is widely accepted in business writing, conventions for academic writing vary. The MLA recommends underlining, but the APA prefers italics. If in doubt, follow the convention your audience expects. Remember that in email and on Web pages, an underlined word or phrase often indicates a hyperlink. If you are unable to format your email or other electronic text with italics, use an underscore before and after words you would normally italicize.

Richard Russo's novel _Empire Falls_ won a Pulitzer Prize.

10a | Italics indicate titles of separate works.

A **separate work** is one published (or produced) as a whole rather than as part of a larger work. A newspaper, for example, is a separate work, but an editorial is not. Different conventions are used for indicating the title of the newspaper and the title of the editorial. (See **9c** and **16a**.) These conventions help readers realize the nature of a work and the relationship of one work to another.

Helen Keller's "Three Days to See" originally appeared in the *Atlantic Monthly*. [an essay in a magazine]

The titles of the following kinds of separate works are italicized.

Books	*The Bluest Eye*	*The God of Small Things*
Magazines	*Wired*	*National Geographic*
Newspapers	*USA Today*	*Wall Street Journal*
Plays, films	*Death of a Salesman*	*A Beautiful Mind*
Television and radio shows	*Friends*	*A Prairie Home Companion*

Recordings	*A Day without Rain*	*Great Verdi Overtures*
Works of art	*American Gothic*	*David*
Long poems	*Paradise Lost*	*The Divine Comedy*
Pamphlets	*Saving Energy*	*Tips for Gardeners*
Comic strips	*Peanuts*	*Doonesbury*

When you include an italicized title in a sentence, switch to nonitalic type to indicate that another title of a separate work is embedded within it.

> The class read various selections from *Twentieth Century Interpretations of* Paradise Lost.
> [COMPARE We studied various interpretations of *Paradise Lost* last quarter.]

Titles are not italicized when they stand alone, for example, on a title page, a book cover, or a newspaper masthead. The title of a paper or report (unless it is also the title of a separate work) should not be italicized. (See also 9c.)

Neither italics nor quotation marks are necessary for titles of major historical documents or religious texts.

> The Bill of Rights contains the first ten amendments to the U.S. Constitution.
> The Bible, which is a sacred text just as the Koran or the Torah is, begins with the Book of Genesis.

According to the guidelines in the *MLA Handbook for Writers of Research Papers* and those in *The Chicago Manual of Style,* an initial *the* in a newspaper or periodical title is not italicized. It is not capitalized either, unless it begins a sentence.

> The story was leaked to a journalist at the *New York Times.*

Also recommended is the omission of an article (*a, an,* or *the*) at the beginning of such a title when it would make a sentence awkward.

> The report will appear in Thursday's ~~the~~ *Wall Street Journal.*

10b | Italics indicate foreign words.

> Side by side, hunched low in the light rain, the two outcasts dip up *tsampa,* the roasted maize or barley meal, ground to powder and cooked as porridge or in tea, that is subsistence food in the Himalaya. **—PETER MATTHIESSEN**

The Latin words used to classify plants and animals according to genus and species are also italicized.

Homo sapiens   *Rosa setigera*

Countless words borrowed from other languages have become part of English and are therefore not italicized. The more familiar a word becomes, the less likely it is to be italicized.

bayou (Choctaw)	karate (Japanese)	spaghetti (Italian)
cliché (French)	arroyo (Spanish)	curriculum vitae (Latin)

10c | Italics identify the names of legal cases.

Miranda v. Arizona   *Roe v. Wade*

The abbreviation *v.* (for "versus") may appear in either italic or nonitalic type, as long as the style is used consistently. Italics are also used for the shortened name of a well-known legal case.

> According to the *Miranda* decision, suspects must be informed of their right to remain silent and their right to legal advice.

Italics are not used to refer to a case by other than its official name.

> All the major networks covered the O. J. Simpson trial.

10d | Italics identify the names of specific ships, submarines, aircraft, spacecraft, and satellites.

USS *Enterprise*   USS *Hawkbill*   *Enola Gay*   *Atlantis*

The names of trains and the trade names of aircraft are not italicized.

Orient Express   Boeing 747   Concorde

10e | Italics indicate words, letters, or figures referred to as such or used as statistical symbols or as variables in algebraic expressions.

The *p* in *ptarmigan* is silent.

The *8* on the sign has faded, and the *5* has disappeared.

The Pythagorean theorem is expressed as $a^2 + b^2 = c^2$.

According to the APA style manual, volume numbers in reference lists are italicized (see **40c**): *Memory & Cognition, 3,* 635–647.

10f | Used sparingly, italics can emphasize words.

When you think a sentence may be misunderstood, you can italicize words that you want readers to stress.

These *are* the right files. [The italicized word receives more stress than it normally would.]

Italics can also emphasize emotional content.

We have to go *now*. [The italicized word signals urgency.]

If overused, italics will lose their impact. Instead of italicizing words, try substituting more specific or forceful words (see chapters **20** and **29**).

Exercise 1

Identify all words that should be italicized in the following sentences. Explain why italics are necessary in each case.

1. Information about museum collections can be found in special sections of magazines and newspapers such as Smithsonian Magazine and the New York Times.

2. The Web site for the Metropolitan Museum of Art has pictures of Anthony Caro's sculpture Odalisque and Charles Demuth's painting The Figure 5 in Gold.

3. The title page of Blake's Songs of Innocence is included in Masterpieces of the Metropolitan Museum of Art.

4. This book includes a photograph of a script used in the Koran; the script is known as the maghribi, or Western, style.

5. The large Tyrannosaurus rex discovered by Sue Hendrickson is on display at the Field Museum.

6. The International Museum of Cartoon Art provides information about the designers of such comic strips as Blondie, Peanuts, Mutt and Jeff, and Li'l Abner.

7. The Great Train Robbery, It Happened One Night, and Grand Illusion are in the collection at the Celeste Bartos Film Preservation Center.

8. The Songwriters Hall of Fame honored John Williams, who has written music for Jaws, Star Wars, and E.T.

9. The Smithsonian Institution's National Air and Space Museum houses an impressive collection of aircraft and spacecraft, including Spirit of St. Louis and Gemini 4.

10. The digital collection listed on the Web site Experience Music Project includes music from the albums Fresh Cream and Bluesbreakers with Eric Clapton.

Abbreviations, Acronyms, and Numbers

Abbreviations, acronyms, and numbers facilitate communication in both academic papers and business documents.

Abbreviations usually contain periods. Acronyms do not. An abbreviation is a shortened version of a word or phrase: *assn.* (association), *dept.* (department), *B.C.E.* (before the common era). An acronym is formed by combining the initial letters and/or syllables of a series of words: *AIDS* (**a**cquired **i**mmune **d**eficiency **s**yndrome), *sonar* (**so**und **na**vigation **r**anging).

This chapter will help you learn

- how and when to abbreviate (**11a–d**),
- when to explain an acronym (**11e**), and
- whether to spell out a number or use numerals (**11f–g**).

11a | Abbreviations appear before or after proper names.

Designations such as *Ms., Mr., Mrs., Dr.,* and *Prof.* appear before proper names because they are a way of addressing people.

Ms. Lopez	Mrs. Marcus	St. Peter
Mr. Rodriguez	Dr. Redshaw	Prof. Yagelski
Capt. Hoffner	Sen. Kennedy	Rev. Burns

Designations such as *Jr., Sr., III,* and *M.D.* appear after proper names because they provide information about the individuals' status and are not a form of address.

Samuel Levy, Jr.	Delia Hvidsten, M.D.	Henry VIII
Mark Ngo, Sr.	Erika Schuerer, Ph.D.	Putman Amory III

Avoid redundant designations.

> Dr. Carol Ballou OR Carol Ballou, M.D. [NOT Dr. Carol Ballou, M.D.]

Most abbreviations form plurals by adding *-s* alone, without an apostrophe: *Drs. Ballou and Hvidsten.* Exceptions are made when adding *-s* would create a different abbreviation, such as for *Mr.* and *Mrs.* When this is the case, consult a dictionary.

11b | Abbreviations are used for addresses in correspondence.

Although words such as *Street, Avenue, Road, Company,* and *Corporation* are usually written out when they appear in sentences, they are abbreviated when used in the address on an envelope. Similarly, the names of states are also abbreviated when they are part of an address.

Sentence	Derson Manufacturing Company is located on Madison Street in Watertown, Minnesota.
Address	Derson Manufacturing Co. 200 Madison St. Watertown, MN 55388

When addressing correspondence within the United States, use the abbreviations designated by the U.S. Postal Service for the names of the states. (No period follows these abbreviations.)

Beyond the Rule

POSTAL ABBREVIATIONS

The abbreviations of states' names required for U.S. mail always consist of two letters. For a list of these abbreviations, visit www.harbrace.com.

11c	**Abbreviations are used in bibliographies and other citations of research sources.**

The *MLA Handbook for Writers of Research Papers,* the *Publication Manual of the American Psychological Association,* and *The Chicago Manual of Style* all provide lists of abbreviations for writers to use when citing research sources in bibliographies, footnotes, and endnotes. (See also chapter 40.) Common abbreviations include the following (not all citation styles accept all of these abbreviations).

Bibliographies and Notes

anon.	Anonymous
biog.	biography, biographer, biographical
bull.	bulletin
c.	circa, about (for example, *c. 1920*)
col., cols.	column, columns
cont.	contents OR continues, continued
et al.	*et alii* ("and others")
fig.	figure
fwd.	foreword, foreword by
gen. ed.	general editor
illus.	illustrated by, illustrator, illustration
intl.	international
introd.	introduction, introduction by

(Continued on page 198)

(Continued from page 197)

ms., mss.	manuscript, manuscripts
natl.	national
n.d.	no date
n.p.	no page number
no., nos.	number, numbers
p., pp.	page, pages
P, Pr.	Press
pref.	preface
trans.	translation, translated by
U, Univ.	University

Computer Terms

CD-ROM	compact disc read-only memory
DVD	digital video disc
FTP	File Transfer Protocol
HTML	HyperText Markup Language
http	hypertext transfer protocol
MB	megabyte
MOO	Multiuser domain, Object-Oriented
URL	Uniform Resource Locator
WWW, www	World Wide Web

Divisions of Government

Cong.	Congress
dept.	department
div.	division
govt.	government
GPO	Government Printing Office
HR	House of Representatives

Months

Jan.	January
Feb.	February
Mar.	March
Apr.	April
Aug.	August
Sept.	September
Oct.	October
Nov.	November
Dec.	December

Although abbreviations are usually too informal for use in sentences, some are acceptable substitutes for words.

When writing sentences, use abbreviations if they have become so familiar that readers can read them aloud easily. This is the case when abbreviations are used in place names, such as *St.* for Saint (as in *St. Louis*) or *Mt.* for mount or mountain (as in *Mt. Hood*). Similarly, titles of address (see **11a**) can be used in sentences. Other examples follow.

(1) Words that are abbreviated for special purposes are usually written out when they appear within sentences.

For ease of reading, the names of months, days of the week, and units of measurement are usually written out, not abbreviated, when they are included in sentences, as are abbreviations for words such as *Street* and *Corporation* (see **11b**).

> On a Tuesday in September, we drove ninety-nine miles to San Francisco, California, where we stayed in a hotel on Market Street.

Similarly, words such as *volume, chapter,* and *page* are written out within sentences, even though they are abbreviated in bibliographies and other citations of research sources (see **11c**).

> I read the introductory chapter and pages 82–89 in the first volume of the committee's report.

(2) A *clipped form* is a word shortened from a longer word.

Because it functions as a word, a **clipped form** does not end with a period. Some clipped forms—such as *rep* (for representative), *exec* (for executive), and *info* (for information)—are too informal for use in college writing. Others—such as *exam, lab,* and *math*—have become acceptable because they have been used so frequently that they no longer seem like abbreviations.

(3) Abbreviations designate time periods and zones.

82 B.C. [OR B.C.E.] for before Christ [OR before the common era]

A.D. 95 [OR 95 C.E.] for *anno Domini* [OR the common era]

7:40 a.m. [OR A.M. OR A.M.] for *ante meridiem*, before noon

4:52 EST [OR E.S.T.] for Eastern Standard Time

Words designating units of time, such as *minute* and *month,* are written out when they appear in sentences. They can be abbreviated in tables or charts.

sec. min. hr. wk. mo. yr.

(4) The abbreviation for the United States (U.S.) should be used only as an adjective.

the U.S. Navy, the U.S. economy [COMPARE The United States continues to enjoy a strong economy.]

In MLA style, use US rather than U.S. (The MLA recommends omitting periods in abbreviations made up of all capital letters, except after initials used for personal names.)

(5) Some individuals are widely known by their initials.

JFK LBJ E. B. White B. B. King

In most cases, however, first and last names should be written out in full.

Phyllis D. Miller

(6) Some abbreviations stand for expressions in Latin.

Certain abbreviations for Latin expressions are common in academic writing.

cf. [compare]   et al. [and others]   i.e. [that is]

e.g. [for example]   etc. [and so forth]   vs. OR v. [versus]

11e | **Acronyms are usually spelled out the first time they are used.**

Some acronyms have been used so frequently that they are likely to be recognized without explanation.

NASA   NATO   UNICEF

The ability to identify a particular acronym will vary from one audience to another. Some readers know that NAFTA stands for the North American Free Trade Agreement; others may not. By spelling out acronyms the first time you use them, you are being courteous and clear.

The Federal Emergency Management Administration (FEMA) was criticized . . . .

 When you use an abbreviation, an acronym, or a number, you sometimes need an indefinite article. Choose *a* or *an* based on the pronunciation: Use *a* before a consonant sound and *an* before a vowel sound.

I have **an IBM** computer. [*IBM* is pronounced as three letters.]

The reporter interviewed **a NASA** engineer. [*NASA* is pronounced as one word.]

My friend drives **a 1964** Mustang. [*1964* is pronounced "nineteen sixty-four."]

> **11f** | **Depending on their use, numbers are treated in different ways.**

When writing for general purposes, spell out numbers from one through one hundred (*nine employees, nineteen employees, ninety-one employees*). If one of these numbers is followed by a word such as *hundred, thousand,* or *million,* it should also be spelled out (*nine hundred years, ninety-one million years*). Use a numeral for any other number, unless it begins a sentence.

> The register recorded 164 names.

> One hundred sixty-four names were recorded in the register. [Notice that *and* is not used in numbers greater than one hundred. NOT One hundred and sixty-four names . . . .]

In a discussion of related items involving both single- and double- or triple-digit numbers, use figures for all numbers.

> Only 5 of the 134 delegates attended the final meeting.

In scientific or technical writing, use numerals before symbols, measurement words, and abbreviations (*24%, 3 inches* or *3″, 30 cubic centimeters* or *30 cc*).

> Style manuals differ in their treatment of numbers. The general guidelines given here are from *The Chicago Manual of Style.* Consult a manual for the specific discipline to be sure that you are following the appropriate conventions.

> **11g** | **Some numbers follow special conventions.**

(1) Specific times of day can be expressed in either numbers or words.

4 P.M. OR four o'clock in the afternoon

9:30 A.M. OR half-past nine in the morning OR nine-thirty in the morning [Notice the use of hyphens.]

(2) Dates are usually indicated by both numbers and words.

May 20, 1976 OR 20 May 1976 [NOT May 20th, 1976]

the fourth of December OR December 4

the fifties OR the 1950s

the fourteenth century OR the 14th century

from 1999 to 2003 OR 1999–2003 [Use an en dash, not a hyphen, in number ranges.]

 Many cultures invert the numbers for the month and the day: *14/2/2003* or *14 February 2003*. In American practice, the month generally precedes the day: *2/14/2003* or *February 14, 2003*.

(3) Addresses require the use of numbers.

25 Arrow Drive, Apartment 1, Columbia, MO 78209
OR 25 Arrow Dr., Apt. 1, Columbia, MO 78209

459 East 35 Street OR 459 East 35th Street

(4) Identification numbers are indicated with figures.

Channel 10   Edward III   Interstate 40   Room 311

(5) Pages and divisions of books and plays are indicated with figures.

page 15   chapter 8   in act 2, scene 1 OR in Act II, Scene I

(6) Decimals and percentages are expressed numerically.

a 2.5 average   12 percent   0.853 metric ton

(7) Large round numbers can be expressed with either figures or words or both.

five million inhabitants OR 5 million inhabitants [Figures are often used for emphasis.]

(8) In legal or commercial writing, numbers are often stated in two ways.

The lawyer's fee will exceed two million (2,000,000) dollars.

OR

The lawyer's fee will exceed two million dollars ($2,000,000).

Cultures differ in their use of the period and the comma with numbers. In American usage, a decimal point (period) indicates a number or part of a number that is smaller than one, and a comma divides larger numbers into units of three digits (thousands).

10,000 (ten thousand)   7.65 (seven and sixty-five one-hundredths)

In some other cultures, the decimal and the comma are reversed.

10.000 (ten thousand)   7,65 (seven and sixty-five one-hundredths)

Exercise 1

Edit the following sentences to correct the usage of abbreviations and numbers.

1. A Natl. Historic Landmark, Hoover Dam is located about 30 miles s.e. of Las. Vegas, Nev.

2. The dam is named after Herbert Hoover, the 31st pres. of the U.S.

3. It is administered by the U.S. Dept. of the Interior.

4. Built by the fed. gov. between nineteen thirty-three and 1935, this dam is still considered one of the greatest achievements in the history of civ. engineering.

5. Construction of the dam became possible after several states (namely, AZ, CA, CO, NV, NM, UT, and WY) agreed on a plan to share water from the river.

6. The concrete used in the dam would have built a highway 16 ft. wide, stretching all the way from San Francisco to NYC.

7. 3,500 men worked on the dam during an average month of construction; this work translated into a monthly payroll of $500,000.

8. Spanning the Colorado River, Hoover Dam created Lake Mead—a reservoir covering 247 sq. miles.

9. A popular tourist attraction, Hoover Dam was closed to the public after terrorists attacked the U.S. on 9/11/01.

10. Today, certain pts. on the dam remain closed to the public as part of the effort to improve U.S. security.

Punctuation

The Comma

Punctuation signals meaning. It lends to written language the flexibility that facial expressions, pauses, and variations in voice pitch give to spoken language. For instance, a pause after *called* in the first of the following examples would make it clear that the spoken sentence refers to only two people: the recruiter and Kenneth Martin. In the second example, a pause after *Kenneth* would let the listener know that the sentence refers to three people: the recruiter, Kenneth, and Martin. In written text, the same meanings can be established by commas.

When the recruiter called, Kenneth Martin answered.

When the recruiter called Kenneth, Martin answered.

But pauses are not a reliable guide for comma use because commas are often called for where speakers do not pause and pauses occur where no comma is called for. Knowing some basic principles of comma usage works better.

Beyond the Rule

HISTORY OF THE COMMA

Ancient Greeks referred to a short section of a speech as a *comma*. During the Middle Ages, scribes used a special mark to signal a pause in speech. By 1566, a mark recognizable as a comma was being used in Italy to clarify relationships between phrases and clauses. For more information about the history of the comma, visit www.harbrace.com.

This chapter will help you understand that commas

- come before coordinating conjunctions when they link independent clauses (**12a**),
- follow introductory clauses and, usually, introductory phrases (**12b**),
- separate items in a series (**12c**),
- set off nonessential (nonrestrictive) elements (**12d**),
- set off parenthetical elements (**12e**), and
- contribute to ease in reading (**12f**).

12a | A comma comes before a coordinating conjunction that links independent clauses.

A comma must come before a coordinating conjunction (*and, but, for, nor, or, so,* or *yet*) that links two independent clauses. An **independent clause** is a group of words that can stand as a sentence (see **1g(1)**).

INDEPENDENT CLAUSE,	CONJUNCTION	INDEPENDENT CLAUSE.
	and	
	but	
	for	
Subject + predicate,	nor	subject + predicate.
	or	
	so	
	yet	

American pottery of the Southwest reveals an artistic heritage, **and** it unlocks the history of the indigenous people of the region.

Most Southwestern pottery comes from Arizona and New Mexico, **but** some also comes from Nevada, Utah, Colorado, and Texas.

Pottery provides important archaeological artifacts, **for** it is abundant, identifiable, and well preserved.

No one knows exactly how many types of Southwestern pottery there are**, nor** is there a list of even the most common.

A classification system based on culture and historical period has been developed**, so** archaeologists can at least establish a time-line.

Studying pottery seems simple at first**, yet** it has challenged archaeologists and art historians for decades.

No matter how many clauses are in a sentence, a comma comes before each coordinating conjunction.

No one knows exactly how many types of Southwestern pottery there are**, nor** is there a list of even the most common**, but** scientists are working to change that.

When the independent clauses are short, the comma can be omitted before *and, but,* or *or,* but not usually before *for, nor, so,* or *yet.*

I liked my lessons **but** Annie hated hers.

Howie worked hard on calculus**, for** he wanted to be an engineer.

Sometimes a semicolon instead of a comma separates two independent clauses, especially when the second one already contains commas or when it reveals a contrast. (See also 14a–b.)

Most archaeologists study the pottery in connection with a particular culture; **but** it should be possible, I think, to study one type of pottery across several cultures.

Not all coordinating conjunctions, however, are preceded by commas. A common error is to place one before *and* when that conjunction links parts of a compound predicate rather than two clauses. (See 1g.)

She **slapped** the hamburger patty onto the grill **and seasoned** it liberally before taking my order. [no comma before *and* in a compound predicate]

Exercise 1

A. Combine the following sentences by using coordinating conjunctions and inserting commas where appropriate. (Remember that not all coordinating conjunctions link independent clauses and that *but, for, so,* and *yet* do not always function as coordinating conjunctions.)

B. Explain why you used each of the conjunctions you chose.

1. Dinosaurs lived for 165 million years. Then they became extinct.

2. No one knows why dinosaurs became extinct. Several theories have been proposed.

3. Some theorists believe that a huge meteor hit the earth. The climate may have changed dramatically.

4. Another theory suggests that dinosaurs did not actually become extinct. They simply evolved into lizards and birds.

5. Yet another theory suggests that they just grew too big. Not all of the dinosaurs were huge.

12b | A comma usually follows an introductory word, phrase, or clause.

(1) A comma follows an introductory clause that precedes an independent clause.

INTRODUCTORY CLAUSE,   INDEPENDENT CLAUSE.

When you write, you make a sound in the reader's head.
—RUSSELL BAKER

Although the safest automobile on the road is expensive, the protection it offers makes the cost worthwhile.
[dependent clause preceding independent clause]

Although you can always include a comma after any introductory clause, you can omit one if the clause is short.

> **If I shout** someone will hear me.

(2) A comma follows an introductory phrase that appears before an independent clause.

> **INTRODUCTORY PHRASE,** subject + predicate.
> **OR**
> **INTRODUCTORY WORD,** subject + predicate.

(a) Introductory prepositional phrases

> **From our porch,** I could not hear what my father was saying, but I could hear the sound of my mother's laughter, throaty and rich with joy.

If the comma after an introductory prepositional phrase is not necessary to prevent misreading, it can be omitted.

> For safety the university installed call boxes linked directly to campus security.

(b) Other types of introductory phrases

> **Having traveled nowhere,** she believed the rest of the world was like her own small town; **having read little,** she had no sense of how other people think. [participial phrases before both independent clauses; see **1f–g**]

> **The language difference aside,** life in Germany doesn't seem much different from life in the United States. [absolute phrase; see **12e(4)**]

Commas are not used after phrases that begin inverted sentences. (See **29f.**)

> With marriage came responsibilities. [COMPARE Responsibilities came with marriage.]

Of far greater concern than censorship of bad words is censorship of ideas. —DONNA WOOLFOLK CROSS

(c) Introductory words

Well, come on in and join the party. [interjection]

Yes, I have a valid inspection sticker. **No,** I did not forget to renew it. [introductory *yes* or *no*]

Exercise 2

Insert commas wherever necessary in the following paragraph. Explain why each comma is needed. Some sentences may not require editing.

[1]If you had to describe sound would you call it a wave? [2]Although sound cannot be seen people have described it this way for a long time. [3]In fact the Greek philosopher Aristotle believed that sound traveling through air was like waves in the sea. [4]Envisioning waves in the air he hypothesized that sound would not be able to pass through a vacuum because there would be no air to transmit it. [5]Aristotle's hypothesis was not tested until nearly two thousand years later. [6]In 1654 Otto von Guericke found that he could not hear a bell ringing inside the vacuum he had created. [7]Thus Guericke established the necessity of air for sound transmission. [8]However although most sound reaches us through the air it travels faster through liquids and solids.

 A grammar checker can be helpful for discovering places where you may have skipped a necessary comma. For instance, a grammar checker found two of the missing commas in exercise 2. Be sure to use your own comma sense when you proofread. For Web sites that can give you help with commas, visit www.harbrace.com.

> **12c** | Commas separate parallel elements, such as items in a series.

A **series** contains three or more parallel elements. (To be parallel, elements must be grammatically equal. See chapter **26**.) The punctuation of a series depends on its form.

The sky was cloudless, bright, and blue. [A comma is preferred before *and.*]

The sky was cloudless, bright, blue. [A comma is essential when *and* is omitted.]

The sky was cloudless, bright and blue as a sapphire. [This sentence does not contain a series.]

(1) Commas separate words, phrases, or clauses in a series.

A comma appears after each item in a series except the last one.

Many dogs are affectionate, trusting, obedient, and intelligent. [words in a series]

My job allows me to start work at 7 A.M., to drive to three charming villages every day, and to be home by 4 P.M. [phrases in a series]

My idea of a great vacation spot is one where no telephone rings, someone else fixes me great food, and I sit in the cool shade all day and read mystery novels. [clauses in a series]

If items in a series contain internal commas, you can make the meaning clear by separating the items with semicolons. (See **14b**.)

The main reasons our ancestors smiled were to reinforce social bonds; to reduce tensions in stressful situations; and, most of all, to express pleasure.

For emphasis, writers sometimes use commas when coordinating conjunctions link all the items in a series.

We cannot put it off for a month, or a week, or even a day.

(2) Commas separate coordinate adjectives.

Two or more adjectives that modify the same noun or pronoun are called **coordinate adjectives.** One way to test for coordinate adjectives is to switch them; another is to put *and* between them. If the meaning does not change, the adjectives are coordinate.

Crossing the **rushing, shallow** creek, I stepped on a rock and sank above my boot tops into a **small, still** pool. [*Rushing* and *shallow* modify *creek,* and *small* and *still* modify *pool.*]

Commas separate coordinate adjectives only when the adjectives are not linked by a coordinating conjunction.

The pool of water that I stepped in was small and still.

Exercise 3

Using commas where necessary, write sentences in which coordinate adjectives modify any three of the following six words.

EXAMPLE

metric system   Most countries use the familiar, sensible metric system to measure distances.

1. bagel   3. steak   5. software
2. music   4. painting   6. college

12d | **Commas set off nonessential (nonrestrictive) elements.**

Nonessential (nonrestrictive) clauses or phrases give supplemental information about a noun or pronoun. To set off a nonessential word or word group, use two commas, unless the element is at the beginning (see **12b**) or end of the sentence. Of course, not all words preceded and followed by commas are nonessential.

Some people lie, **as my grandmother observed,** because
they don't know how to tell the truth. [COMPARE As my
grandmother observed, some people lie because they don't
know how to tell the truth. OR Some people lie because they
don't know how to tell the truth, as my grandmother
observed.]

Restrictive clauses or phrases follow and limit the words
they modify. They are essential to the clear identification of
the word or words they refer to. Restrictive clauses make the
meaning more specific. When a restrictive clause follows an
independent clause, a comma is unnecessary.

Dinosaurs may have become extinct because their habitat was
destroyed. [*Because,* a subordinating conjunction, introduces a
dependent clause.]

If a dependent clause is not essential to understanding the sentence, a comma can precede it.

My neighbor is now retired, **although she works every day
at the food bank.**

Beyond the Rule

NONESSENTIAL ELEMENTS

**If you are having difficulty deciding whether a particular clause
or phrase is nonessential, visit www.harbrace.com.**

(1) Commas set off nonessential elements used as modifiers.

Clauses and phrases that *describe* the meaning of a noun or pronoun but are not essential to that meaning are supplemental

(nonrestrictive). Set off by commas, they are nonessential elements that could be omitted without changing the meaning of the sentence.

> My sister, who lives in Denver, is visiting me. [I have only one sister, and she happens to live in Denver.]
>
> We climbed Mt. McKinley, which is over 15,000 feet high. [There is only one Mt. McKinley, so it doesn't need further identification.]

Clauses and phrases that *limit* a noun or pronoun by providing essential identifying information are restrictive. Not set off by commas, they identify the noun or pronoun they modify by telling which specific one (or ones). Restrictive clauses and phrases are essential elements that may not be omitted from a sentence.

> My sister who lives in Denver is visiting me. [I have several sisters, and the one who is visiting is the one who lives in Denver.]
>
> We climbed a mountain that is over 15,000 feet high. [There are many mountains, so the identification of a rare characteristic of this mountain is essential.]

As in the examples about the sisters above, sometimes only the omission or the use of commas indicates whether a modifier is restrictive or supplemental and thus signals the writer's exact meaning. That is, only the presence or the absence of the commas in those examples reveals whether the writer's only sister is visiting and she happens to live in Denver or the particular sister who lives in Denver is visiting, not the one who lives, say, in Miami.

The placement of a comma often has consequences and can actually reverse the meaning of a sentence. The two example sentences that follow illustrate such a reversal. In the first sentence, the one without the comma, the committee that oversees the budget opposes only a certain kind of spending. In the sentence with the comma, the committee opposes spending of any kind because all spending would increase the deficit.

> The committee that oversees the budget opposes spending which would increase the deficit.
>
> The committee that oversees the budget opposes spending, which would increase the deficit.

Although writers have traditionally used *that* at the beginning of restrictive clauses, *which* has become acceptable if, as in the example below, it does not cause confusion. Grammar checkers, however, do not recognize this option and will instruct you to change *which* to *that*.

> I like to drive a car *which* has fast acceleration and nimble handling.

(2) Commas set off supplemental appositives.

Appositives can supply supplemental, nonessential (nonrestrictive) details about nouns or pronouns, or they can limit the meaning of nouns or pronouns by indicating which one is meant (restrictive).

> Even Milo Papadupolos, **my friend,** let me down. [Knowing more than one person with this name is unlikely; therefore, identifying Milo as a friend is not essential.]
>
> Even **my friend** Milo Papadupolos let me down. [Presumably the writer has more than one friend, so the identification is essential here.]

Abbreviations of titles or degrees after names are treated as supplemental appositives.

> Was the letter from Frances Evans, Ph.D., or from F. H. Evans, M.D.?

Increasingly, however, *Jr., Sr., II,* and *III* are being treated as part of the name rather than as appositives, and hence the comma after the name is occasionally omitted. (See also chapter 11.)

William Homer Barton, Jr. OR William Homer Barton Jr.

Exercise 4

Set off nonessential clauses, phrases, and appositives with commas.

1. Maine Coons long-haired cats with bushy tails have adapted to a harsh climate.
2. These animals which are extremely gentle despite their large size often weigh twenty pounds.
3. Most Maine Coons have exceptionally high intelligence for cats which enables them to recognize language and even to open doors.
4. Unlike most cats Maine Coons will play fetch with their owners.
5. According to a legend later proven to be false Maine Coons developed from interbreeding between wildcats and domestic cats.

12e | Commas set off parenthetical elements.

Parenthetical elements are nonessential words or phrases.

Witches'-broom fungus and black pod rot, **however,** threaten the world's chocolate supply.

An airline ticket, **for example,** can be delivered electronically.

When they cause little or no pause in reading, expressions such as *also, too, of course, perhaps, at least, therefore,* and *likewise* need not be set off by commas.

> My awareness of the absurd has therefore grown in recent years.

(1) Commas set off contrasted elements.

Commas separate sentence elements in which such words as *never* and *unlike* express contrast.

> A planet**,** **unlike** a star**,** reflects rather than generates light.

In sentences in which contrasted elements are introduced by *not* and *but,* some writers put a comma before *but* and others do not. Generally, the comma before *but* emphasizes the contrast.

> I disagree with people**,** but I base my opinion on facts, not on emotion.
> Automatic aircraft are flown**,** not by humans but by computers.

(2) Commas set off geographical names and items in dates and addresses.

See also **11b**.

> **Nashville, Tennessee,** is the largest country-and-western music center in the United States.
> Martha left for Peru on **Wednesday, February 12, 2003,** and returned on March 12.
>
> OR
>
> Martha left for Peru on **Wednesday, 12 February 2003,** and returned on 12 March. [The comma is omitted when the date precedes rather than follows the month.]
> I had to write to **Ms. Melanie Hobson, 2873 Central Avenue, Orange Park, FL 32065.** [There is no comma between the state abbreviation and the ZIP code.]

(3) Commas set off mild interjections and terms of direct address.

A direct address, also called a **vocative,** is a word or phrase that speaks directly to some person, group, or thing.

> **Ah,** that's what they mean by a firm mattress. [interjection]
> Now is the time, **my friend,** to stop smoking. [vocative]

(4) Commas set off absolute phrases.

An **absolute phrase** is a part of a sentence that is not grammatically connected to any other part.

> **Their income being what it is,** I don't expect them to fly home for Christmas.
> She was staring at the stranger, **her heart pounding louder and louder.**

12f | **Commas are occasionally needed for ease in reading.**

Some commas are necessary to prevent misreading. Without the commas, the following sentences would confuse readers, if only temporarily.

> Still, air is often polluted by diesel motors. [COMPARE Still air is often polluted . . . .]
> The week after, I saw him at the supermarket. [COMPARE I saw him at the supermarket the week after.]
> In 2003, 600 building permits were issued. [COMPARE In the first quarter of 2003 600 . . . .]

Sometimes a comma replaces a clearly understood word or group of words.

> Scholars often see the humor in mistakes, pedants, never.

Exercise 5

Explain the reason for each comma used in the following sentences, and point out any commas whose use is optional or a matter of stylistic preference.

1. Alvar Nuñez Cabeza de Vaca, unlike most other Spanish conquistadors, came to perceive Native Americans as equals.
2. On February 15, 1527, Cabeza de Vaca was appointed to an expedition headed for the mainland of North America.
3. The expedition landed near present-day Tampa Bay, Florida, sometime in March, 1528.
4. Devastated by misfortune, the expedition dwindled rapidly; Cabeza de Vaca and three other members, however, survived.
5. His endurance now tested, Cabeza de Vaca lived as a trader and healer among Native Americans of the Rio Grande Basin, learning from them and eventually speaking on their behalf to the Spanish crown.

Exercise 6

For humorous effect, the writer of the following paragraph deliberately omits commas. Identify where commas might be inserted to make reading easier. Compare your version with someone else's and comment on any differences you find.

[1]The commas are the most useful and usable of all the stops. [2]It is highly important to put them in place as you go along. [3]If you try to come back after doing a paragraph and stick them in the various spots that tempt you you will discover that they tend to swarm like minnows into all sorts of crevices whose existence you hadn't realized and before you know it the whole long sentence becomes immobilized and lashed up squirming in commas. [4]Better to use them sparingly, and with affection precisely when the need for one arises, nicely, by itself.   —**LEWIS THOMAS,** *The Medusa and the Snail*

Unnecessary Commas 13

Although a comma ordinarily signals a pause, not every pause calls for a comma. As you read the following sentence aloud, you may pause naturally at several places, but no commas are necessary.

> Heroic deeds done by ordinary people inspire others to act in ways that are not only moral but courageous.

13a | A comma does not separate a subject and its verb or a verb and its object.

Although speakers often pause after the subject or before the object of a sentence, such a pause should not be reflected by a comma.

> Rain at frequent intervals⊙ can produce mosquitoes.
> [separation of subject (*rain*) and verb (*produce*)]

> The accountant said⊙ that I couldn't deduct my trip.
> [separation of verb (*said*) and direct object (a noun clause, *that I couldn't . . .*)]

13b | Commas do not follow coordinating conjunctions, and they immediately precede them only when the conjunctions link independent clauses.

It is incorrect to use a comma after a coordinating conjunction (*and, but, for, nor, or, so,* or *yet*). Writers also sometimes put an unnecessary comma before a coordinating conjunction that does not link independent clauses. (See also chapter **1** and **12a**.)

> We worked very hard on her campaign for state representative but⊙the incumbent was too strong in the northern counties. [separation of coordinating conjunction (*but*) and subject of the clause (*the incumbent*)]
>
> He parked the car⊙ and closed the garage door. [separation of compound verbs (*parked* and *closed*)]

13c | Commas set off words and short phrases only if they are clearly parenthetical.

Parenthetical words and phrases are those that are nonessential—such as asides or interpolations. (See also **12e**.)

> Zoe was born⊙ in Chicago in 1985. [The phrase *in Chicago* modifies *born* and is an integral part of the sentence.]
>
> Perhaps⊙ the thermostat is not set correctly. [*Perhaps* is not a parenthetical element.]

13d | Commas do not set off restrictive (essential) clauses, phrases, or appositives.

A restrictive clause, phrase, or appositive is essential to the meaning of the sentence. (See also **12d**.)

> Everyone⊙ who has a mortgage⊙ is required to have fire insurance. [The clause beginning with *who* is essential; people who do not have mortgages are not required to have fire insurance.]
>
> The spectators watched two skaters⊙ dressed in identical black uniforms⊙ battle for the puck. [The skaters dressed in identical black uniforms were being watched, not any skaters dressed in uniforms of another color.]

13e A comma does not precede the first item of a series or follow the last (including the last of a series of coordinate adjectives).

She was supposed to eat lots of green vegetables, such as⊙ broccoli, peas, and green beans. [No comma is needed before the first noun of the series (*broccoli*).]

Lamont is the most attractive, intelligent, and pleasant⊙friend I have. [No comma is needed after the last adjective in the series (*pleasant*).]

Exercise 1

Explain the use of each comma in the following paragraph.

[1]Contrails, which are essentially artificial clouds, form when moisture in the air condenses around particles in jet exhaust. [2]Like ordinary clouds, contrails block incoming sunlight and trap heat radiated from Earth's surface. [3]This process reduces daytime highs and increases nighttime lows, narrowing the temperature range. [4]Multiple contrails can cluster together and obscure an area as large as Iowa, Illinois, and Missouri combined, magnifying the effect. [5]Although they may not alter the overall climate, contrails could still have environmental consequences.

—LAURA CARSTEN, "Climate on the Wing"

14 The Semicolon

The semicolon may be the most rhetorical of the punctuation marks because it clarifies the relationship the writer wants the reader to make between ideas in a sentence. A stronger mark of punctuation than the comma, the semicolon connects grammatically equal elements such as two independent clauses (see **1g(1)**) and separates grammatically equal elements that contain internal commas. Two related independent clauses can be linked by a semicolon, connected by a comma and one of the coordinating conjunctions (*and, but, for, nor, or, so,* or *yet*), or punctuated as separate sentences. The method you choose depends to a large extent on your conscious rhetorical decision as well as on your sense of the way your ideas are connected.

This chapter will help you understand that semicolons

- link closely related independent clauses (**14a**),
- separate parts of a sentence containing internal commas (**14b**), but
- do not connect independent clauses with phrases or dependent clauses (**14c**).

Mary said she was hungry; Hugh thought she wanted to go out to dinner. [linking closely related clauses]

Watching silly, sentimental, dull soap operas; eating junk food like french fries, cheeseburgers, and milkshakes; and just doing nothing are my favorite ways to relax. [separating parts containing internal commas]

14a A semicolon connects independent clauses not linked by a coordinating conjunction.

The semicolon can be a valuable resource for writers who sense that two "sentences" are so closely related that they belong in a single sentence but do not lend themselves to being joined by a coordinating conjunction. Sometimes, a conjunctive adverb such as *however* or *therefore* (see 3c) accompanies the semicolon and further establishes the exact relationship between the ideas.

Beyond the Rule

THE HISTORY OF THE SEMICOLON

The term *semicolon* comes from a Greek word, *kolon,* which meant "a unit of meaning," similar to a modern sentence. For more information on the history of the semicolon, visit www.harbrace.com.

1. **INDEPENDENT CLAUSE**	**.**	**INDEPENDENT CLAUSE**
Many Web sites are interesting	**.**	Some are not accurate.
2. **INDEPENDENT CLAUSE**	**, (and** OR **but)**	**INDEPENDENT CLAUSE**
Many Web sites are interesting	**, but**	some are not accurate.
3. **INDEPENDENT CLAUSE**	**; (however** OR **therefore),**	**INDEPENDENT CLAUSE**
Many Web sites are interesting	**; however,**	some are not accurate.
4. **INDEPENDENT CLAUSE**	**;**	**INDEPENDENT CLAUSE**
Many Web sites are interesting	**;**	some are not accurate.

If you read the sentences in the box aloud, you can probably hear different intonations for them. For instance, when you read the two sentences in the first pattern, your voice probably drops as you come to the end of the first one. That drop signifies the end of one statement and the beginning of another. When you read the second sentence pattern, your voice does not drop as much at the comma as it did at the period, and it rises when you say "but." That rise indicates that there is still some separation between the two ideas. When you read the third pattern, you probably keep your voice level as you say "interesting" but drop it as you say "however." That drop indicates that more is to come and that it will be related to what you have already said. When you read the last pattern, your voice maintains the same level when you say "interesting" and when you say "some." That lack of change in intonation indicates that the two ideas are closely related. These patterns also apply in sentences that combine different kinds of clauses (compound-complex sentences). (See **1e** and **14b**.)

> Researchers now think that language functions as a kind of index for memories; events that occurred before we acquired language apparently aren't indexed, and so we cannot retrieve those memories at will.

A semicolon (instead of the usual comma) sometimes comes before a coordinating conjunction when a writer wants to emphasize the contrast between the two ideas being joined. (See also **12a**.)

> Regular exercise is good for the body; but such exercise alone does not make us healthy.

Occasionally, a comma separates short, very closely related main clauses.

> Victory was ours, the war was over.

A semicolon comes before a transitional word or phrase or a conjunctive adverb (such as *for example, however, on the con-*

tary, or therefore) that occurs between independent clauses. (See **3c**, especially the lists on pages 68 and 69.)

> Some glaciers are melting; **for example,** the Athabascan glacier has retreated a thousand feet in the last fifty years.

A comma can be omitted after a conjunctive adverb or a transitional expression if the adverb is essential to the sentence or if the comma is not needed to prevent misreading.

> Like jazz, hip-hop is a uniquely American form of music; indeed it can be said that both forms are fundamentally African American.

When the second independent clause explains or expands the first, a colon is sometimes substituted for the semicolon. Either is acceptable. (See **17d(1)**.)

| **14b** | **Semicolons separate elements that themselves contain commas.** |

When a series of phrases or clauses contain commas, semicolons indicate where each element ends and the next begins.

> To survive, mountain lions need a large range area; a steady supply of deer, skunks, raccoons, foxes, and opossums; and plenty of room to mate and raise litters.

Exercise 1

Revise the following sentences, using semicolons to separate independent clauses and elements that contain internal commas.

1. Homelessness used to be typical only of the hardcore unemployed, but it is becoming more frequent among the working poor, some of whom earn the minimum hourly wage of $5.15, and few of whom can ever expect to earn

the $14 hourly wage that would enable them to pay for a two-bedroom apartment.

2. The last time the minimum wage was raised was in 1997, however, housing costs went up an average of about 20 percent in one year, which means they could have doubled since the last time the minimum wage was increased.

3. In some homeless families, even though both adults work full-time, their pay is low, they often cannot afford even the least expensive housing, and they require state assistance, a form of welfare, to provide minimum shelter in a motel room for their children.

4. Such families are very crowded, living four, five, or six to a room, rarely having more than two double beds, a chair, and perhaps a roll-away bed, and lacking a place to keep the children's toys and school books.

5. These families eat at soup kitchens, they have no money for anything other than rent and basic clothing.

| **14c** | Semicolons do not connect sentence elements that are grammatically unequal, such as phrases and clauses. |

Semicolons do not connect clauses with phrases. (See **1f–g.**)

We consulted Alinka Kibukian; the local meteorologist.

Needing them to provide summer shade; we planted two of the largest trees we could afford.

Do not use a semicolon to connect an independent clause with a dependent clause.

I learned that he would not graduate this term; which really surprised me.

I really should trade this car in; although I can still drive it.

Exercise 2

Replace any semicolon used between grammatically unequal sentence elements with the appropriate punctuation mark. Do not change properly used semicolons.

1. Every morning I take vitamins; a multivitamin and sometimes extra vitamin C.
2. I used to believe that I could get my vitamins from a balanced diet; then I found out that diet may not provide enough of some vitamins, such as folate.
3. By eating a balanced diet, getting plenty of exercise, and keeping stress to a minimum; I thought I would stay healthy.
4. New research suggests that multivitamins are beneficial; when our diets don't provide all the recommended amounts of every vitamin every day; our health can suffer.
5. Although taking one multivitamin tablet a day is a healthy habit; we don't need to buy the most potent or most expensive vitamins available.

Exercise 3

Find or compose one sentence to illustrate each of the following uses of the semicolon.

1. To link two related independent clauses
2. To connect a sentence element containing at least one dependent clause and one independent clause with another independent clause
3. To create a sharp division between two independent clauses
4. To separate clauses in a sentence containing a conjunctive adverb such as *however* or *therefore*
5. To separate elements that contain commas

The Apostrophe

Apostrophes serve a number of purposes. For example, you can use them to show that someone owns something (*my neighbor's television*), that someone has a specific relationship with someone else (*my neighbor's children*), or that someone has produced or created something (*my neighbor's recipe*). Apostrophes are also used in contractions (*can't, don't*) and in certain plural forms (*B.A.'s, M.D.'s*).

This chapter will help you use apostrophes to

- indicate ownership and other relationships (**15a**),
- mark omissions of letters or numbers (**15b**), and
- form certain plurals (**15c**).

| **15a** | **Apostrophes indicate ownership and other relationships.** |

An apostrophe most commonly indicates ownership or origin.

> Fumi's computer, Dr. Smith's office, the photographer's camera [ownership]
>
> Einstein's ideas, the student's decision, Murphy's Law [origin]

An apostrophe indicates other relationships as well. For example, you use an apostrophe to show how people are related or what physical or psychological traits they possess.

> Linda's sister, my roommate's teacher, the employee's supervisor [human relationships]

Mona Lisa's smile, the author's ego, the team's determination [physical or psychological traits]

An apostrophe also indicates traits or features of animals, plants, objects, and abstract nouns.

the dog's ears, the tree's branches, the chair's legs, tyranny's influence

Words used to identify certain tools, buildings, events, and other things also include apostrophes.

tailor's scissors, driver's license, bachelor's degree

St. John's Cathedral, Parkinson's disease, Valentine's Day

You can also use an apostrophe with some forms of measurement.

a day's wages, an hour's delay, five dollars' worth of chocolates

A noun usually follows a word with an apostrophe. However, occasionally, the noun is omitted when it is understood from the context.

Is this Ana's or LaShonda's? [COMPARE Is this Ana's book or LaShonda's book?]

 In many cases, you can use either a word with an apostrophe and an *s* or a prepositional phrase beginning with *of.*

Louise Erdrich's novels, the novels **of** Louise Erdrich

the plane's arrival, the arrival **of** the plane

However, the apostrophe is more commonly used with nouns referring to people, and the prepositional phrase is used with most nouns referring to location.

(Continued on page 234)

(Continued from page 233)

> my **uncle**'s workshop, **Jan**'s car, the **student**'s paper [nouns referring to people]
>
> the **end** of the movie, the **middle** of the day, the **front** of the building [nouns referring to location]

(1) Most singular nouns, indefinite pronouns, abbreviations, and acronyms require -'s to form the possessive case.

the dean's office   Parrish's paintings   Yeats's poems

anyone's computer   someone's birthday

Walter Bryan Jr.'s letter [To avoid confusion, no comma precedes *Jr.'s* here, although *Jr.* is sometimes set off by commas; see **12d(2)**.]

the NFL's reputation   OPEC's price increase

Unlike the possessive forms of nouns and indefinite pronouns, possessive pronouns *(my, mine, our, ours, your, yours, his, her, hers, its, their, theirs,* and *whose)* are not written with apostrophes (see **5b**).

Japanese democracy differs from **ours.**

The committee concluded **its** discussion.

Be careful not to confuse possessive pronouns with contractions. Whenever you write a contraction, you should be able to substitute the complete words for it without changing the meaning.

Possessive Pronoun	Contraction
Its motor is small.	**It's** [it is] a small motor.
Whose turn is it?	**Who's** [who is] representing us?

To form the possessive of most singular proper nouns, you add an apostrophe and an *s: Iowa's governor.* When a singular proper noun already ends in *-s*, though, you need to consult the publication guide for the discipline in which you are writing. To avoid confusing singular and plural forms, the *MLA Handbook for Writers of Research Papers* recommends always using *-'s*, as in *Illinois's legislature, Dickens's novels, Ms. Jones's address,* and *Descartes's reasoning. The Chicago Manual of Style,* however, notes some exceptions to this rule. An apostrophe without an *s* is used with the names *Jesus* and *Moses* and with names ending in a syllable pronounced "eez": *Jesus' parable, Sophocles' poetry, Hermes' message.*

(2) Plural nouns ending in -s require only an apostrophe for the possessive form.

the boys' game   the babies' toys   the Joneses' house

Plural nouns that do not end in *-s* need both an apostrophe and an *s.*

men's lives   women's health   children's projects

The addition of an apostrophe does not make a noun plural. To make most nouns plural, add *-s* or *-es*. Add an apostrophe only to signal ownership, origin, relationships, and so on.

The ~~protesters'~~ protesters met in front of the conference center.

Likewise, to form the plural of a family name, use *-s* or *-es*, not an apostrophe.

The ~~Johnson's~~ Johnsons participated in the study. [COMPARE The Johnsons' participation in the study was crucial.]

The trophy was given to the ~~James's~~ Jameses. [COMPARE The Jameses' trophy is on display in the lobby.]

(3) To show joint ownership or collaboration, add -'s or an apostrophe to the second noun only.

the carpenter and the **plumber's** decision [They made the decision collaboratively.]

Olga and **Nadia's** stocks [They jointly own more than one stock.]

the Becks and the **Lopezes'** cabin [They own one cabin jointly.]

(4) To show separate ownership or individual contributions, add -'s or an apostrophe to each noun.

the **carpenter's** and the **plumber's** proposals [They each made a proposal.]

Olga's and **Nadia's** apartments [They have different apartments.]

the **Becks'** and the **Lopezes'** cars [Each family owns a car.]

(5) Add -'s to the last word of compound nouns.

my brother-in-**law's** friends, the attorney **general's** statements [singular]

my brothers-in-**law's** friends, the attorneys **general's** statements [plural]

To avoid awkward constructions such as the last two, writers often rephrase them using a prepositional phrase beginning with *of: the statements of the attorneys general.*

(6) Add -'s or an apostrophe to nouns that come before gerunds.

Lucy's **having** to be there seemed unnecessary. [gerund]

The family appreciated the lawyers' **handling** of the matter. [gerund]

Sometimes you may find it difficult to distinguish between a gerund and a participle (see **1f(3)**).

Our successful completion of the project depends on Terry's **providing** the illustrations. [gerund]

I remember my brother **telling** me the same joke last year. [participle]

Notice the difference in meaning. In the sentence containing a gerund, the emphasis is on the action; in the sentence containing a participle, the emphasis is on the person.

 When a gerund appears after a noun ending with -'s or with just an apostrophe, that noun is usually the subject of the gerund phrase.

Lucy has to be there → Lucy's having to be there

The **lawyers** handled the matter → The lawyers' handling of the matter

The gerund phrase may serve as the subject or object in the sentence (see **1d** and **1f(3)**).

      subject
Lucy's having to be there seemed unnecessary.

            object
The family appreciated **the lawyers' handling of the matter.**

(7) Follow an organization's preference for its name or the name of a product; follow local conventions for a geographical location.

Consumers Union	Actors' Equity	
Shoppers Choice	Taster's Choice	
Devil's Island	Devils Tower	Devil Mountain

Exercise 1

Following the pattern of the examples, change the modifier after each noun to a possessive form that precedes the noun.

EXAMPLES

proposals made by the committee   *the committee's proposals*

poems written by Keats   *Keats's poems*

1. the day named after St. Patrick
2. a leave of absence for six months
3. the position taken by HMOs
4. the report given by the eyewitness
5. the generosity characteristic of the Halvorsons
6. an article coauthored by Gloria and Alan
7. the weights of the children
8. the spying done by the neighbors
9. the restaurants in New Orleans
10. coffee roasted by Starbucks

15b | **Apostrophes mark omissions in contractions, numbers, and words mimicking speech.**

do not → don't

they will → they'll

class of 2006 → class of '06

you all → y'all

singing → singin'

Contractions are not always appropriate for formal contexts. Your audience may expect you to use full words instead (for example, *cannot* instead of *can't* and *will not* instead of *won't*).

A grammar checker will often flag problems with possessives, marking them as "possible" errors but not telling you whether the apostrophe goes before the *s* or after it, or whether you need an *s* at all. A grammar checker is usually right, however, about missing apostrophes in contractions such as *can't* and *don't*. See Using a Grammar Checker on page 2.

| **15c** | An apostrophe is not required in plurals of letters, numbers, abbreviations, and words referred to as words. |

Although an apostrophe was used in the past to form the plurals of letters, numbers, abbreviations, and words used as words, it is now used only rarely. These plurals are generally formed by simply adding *-s*.

> *x*s and *y*s   1990s   fours and fives   YWCAs   three *and*s

The MLA differs from this style in recommending the use of apostrophes for the plurals of letters (*x*'s and *y*'s or *A*'s *and B*'s).

Some abbreviations are still written with periods. These abbreviations are made plural by adding *-'s* (see chapter **11**).

> He has two Ph.D.'s.
> Everyone liked Mr. G.'s class.

Exercise 2

Insert apostrophes where needed in the following sentences. Be prepared to explain why they are necessary.

1. Whose responsibility is it to see whether its working?
2. Hansons book was published in the early 1920s.

3. They hired a rock n roll band for their wedding dance.
4. NPRs fund drive begins this weekend.
5. Youll have to include the ISBNs of the books youre going to purchase.
6. Only three of the proposals are still being considered: yours, ours, and the Wilbers.
7. Few students enrolled during the academic year 98–99.
8. There cant be more *x*s than there are *y*s.
9. The students formed groups of twos and threes.
10. The M.D.s disagreed on the patients prognosis.

Quotation Marks

Quotation marks are always used in pairs. The first pair indicates the beginning of the quotation, and the second indicates the end. This chapter will help you use quotation marks

- with direct quotations (**16a**),
- with titles of short works (**16b**),
- for words used ironically (**16c**), and
- in combination with other punctuation (**16d**).

16a | Quotation marks set off direct quotations.

Double quotation marks set off direct quotations, including those in dialogue, but not indirect ones. Single quotation marks enclose a quotation within a quotation.

(1) Double quotation marks enclose words that are direct quotations.

"Like branding steers or embalming the dead," writes David Sedaris, "teaching was a profession I had never seriously considered." [Quotation marks enclose only the quotation, not any expression such as *she said* or *he replied*. Place the period inside the quotation marks.]

In direct quotations, reproduce all quoted material exactly as it appears in the original, including capitalization and punctuation.

(See **39d**.) To learn how to set off long quotations as indented blocks, see pages 173, 640, and 670.

(2) Quotation marks are not used for paraphrases or for indirect quotations.

David Sedaris claims that he never wanted to become a teacher any more than he wanted to become a cowboy or mortician. [a paraphrase]

Dr. Schurman said that we wouldn't have class tomorrow. [an indirect quotation]

(3) Single quotation marks enclose quotations within quotations.

"We have been going together for two years, and now all of a sudden she says, 'Let's just be friends,' " Derek complained. [The comma appears inside the quotation within a quotation; the period goes at the end of the sentence. (When a direct quotation appears within an indented block quotation, use double quotation marks.)]

 British English and some other languages reverse the positions of single and double quotation marks; they also sometimes place punctuation outside quotation marks. For college and professional writing within the United States, follow the American English convention. (See also **16d**.)

British and other usage	In class, we compared Wordsworth's 'Upon Westminster Bridge' with Blake's 'London'.
American English	In class, we compared Wordsworth's "Upon Westminster Bridge" with Blake's "London."

(4) Dialogue is enclosed in quotation marks.

Dialogue is directly quoted conversation. When quoting a dialogue, write what each person says, no matter how short, giving a separate paragraph to each speaker, and changing paragraphs whenever the speaker changes. Expressions such as *he said,* as well as closely related bits of narrative, can be included in the same paragraph as a direct quotation.

> Jack Maggs listened only fitfully, for he was more concerned with Mercy Larkin, and the mischief he imagined in those sleepy eyes.
>
> "He wants us now," cried Percy Buckle, pushing away his buttered toast.
>
> "I cannot go now, Sir."
>
> "Yes you can, Sir," winked Mr. Buckle. "I would not miss this for the world."
>
> "You're coming with me, Sir?"
>
> Mr. Buckle stood, slurping down his tea. "Wild horses couldn't stop me." Mercy Larkin made a hand signal Jack Maggs did not understand.   —PETER CARY, *Jack Maggs*

When quoting more than one paragraph by a single speaker, put quotation marks at the beginning of each new paragraph. However, use only one set of closing quotation marks, at the end of the last paragraph.

(5) Thoughts are enclosed in quotation marks.

Quotation marks set off thoughts reported directly within a narrative.

> "I want to bake that cake again," I thought.

Quotation marks do not set off thoughts presented as ideas within an essay or other written text.

> I think that evening classes would attract students who work during the day.

(6) Short excerpts of poetry included within a sentence are enclosed in quotation marks.

When quoting fewer than four lines of poetry, enclose them in quotation marks and use a slash (see **17i**) for each line division.

> After watching a whale swim playfully, the speaker in "Visitation" concludes, "What did you think, that joy / was some slight thing?"

16b | Quotation marks enclose the titles of short works, such as stories, essays, poems, and songs.

Lon Otto's *Cover Me* contains such wonderful stories as "Winners" and "How I Got Rid of That Stump." [short stories]

Annie Dillard's "Living Like Weasels" is frequently included in anthologies for college writing courses. [essay]

Did you read William Gibson's "Disneyland with the Death Penalty" when it appeared in *Wired?* [article in a periodical]

"Big Black Car," by Lynn Emanuel, showed me how a good poem can make the ordinary seem extraordinary. [short poem]

I always laugh when I hear "Big Girls Don't Cry." [song]

Coral Browne starred in "An Englishman Abroad," part of the *Great Performances* series. [episode in a television series]

Use double quotation marks around the title of a short work that appears within a longer italicized (or underlined) title. Use single quotation marks for a shorter title within a longer title that is enclosed in double quotation marks.

Interpretations of "A Good Man Is Hard to Find" [long work discussing a short story by Flannery O'Connor]

"Irony in 'The Sick Rose'" [short work discussing a poem by William Blake]

16c | Quotation marks are sometimes used around a word or phrase to convey an ironic tone.

Writers sometimes use quotation marks to indicate that they are using a word or phrase ironically.

His "gourmet" dinner turned out to be processed turkey and instant mashed potatoes. [COMPARE His so-called gourmet dinner turned out to be processed turkey and instant mashed potatoes. The use of *so-called* eliminates the need for quotation marks.]

If you emphasize a questionable word choice, however, readers might wonder why you did not substitute another word or phrase.

He is too much of a "wimp" to be a good leader.
[COMPARE He is too indecisive to be a good leader.]

Putting a cliché (see **20b**) in quotation marks gives it emphasis. Readers could conclude that you lacked the imagination to substitute a fresh expression for the hackneyed one.

16d | Placement of other punctuation marks relative to quotation marks depends on the context.

(1) Commas and periods are placed inside quotation marks.

Commas go inside closing quotation marks. Periods go inside the closing quotation marks if the quotation ends the sentence.

"Amanda," she said, "we need to talk." [commas and period inside the quotation marks]

Jason admitted, "I didn't finish 'Sonny's Blues.' " [period inside the closing quotation marks, both single and double]

The period goes at the end of the sentence if other words follow the end of the quotation.

"I don't know why my CD player doesn't work," she said. [comma inside the closing quotation marks and period at the end of the sentence]

(2) Semicolons and colons are placed outside quotation marks.

Semicolons and colons always go outside the quotation marks.

She spoke of "the gothic tale"; I immediately thought of "The Dunwich Horror": H. P. Lovecraft's masterpiece is the epitome of "gothic."

(3) Question marks, exclamation points, and dashes are placed outside quotation marks unless they are part of the quotation.

When a question mark, an exclamation point, or a dash is part of the quoted material, it goes *inside* the quotation marks. When it is not, it goes *outside* the quotation marks. When a quotation containing one of these marks ends a sentence you have written, do not add an additional end punctuation mark either inside or outside the quotation marks.

Inside the Quotation Marks

Pilate asked, "What is truth?"

Gordon shouted "Congratulations!"

"Achievement—success!—" states Heather Evans, "has become a national obsession."

Why do children keep asking "Why?" [Use one question mark inside the quotation marks when a question ends with a quoted question.]

Outside the Quotation Marks

Who wrote "The Figure a Sentence Makes"?

Stop playing "Dancing Queen"!

She exclaimed, "I'm surprised at you!"—understandable under the circumstances.

Exercise 1

Insert quotation marks where they are needed in the following sentences. Do not alter sentences that are written correctly.

1. Have you read Ian Buruma's essay The Joys and Perils of Victimhood?

2. Buruma writes, The only way a new generation can be identified with the suffering of previous generations is for that suffering to be publicly acknowledged, over and over again.

3. When my reading group met to talk about this essay, I started our discussion by noting that the word *victim* is defined in my dictionary as anyone who is oppressed or mistreated.

4. So how can we tell who the real victims are? asked Claudia.

5. Cahit responded, I think that both the Israelis and the Palestinians are victims of violence.

6. Yes, agreed Claudia, I worry especially about the women and children in that part of the world. I wish I could say to them, Do not give up hope!

7. According to Tony, the situation in the Middle East would improve if people could learn to live and let live.

8. Using the events of September 11, 2001, as an example, Kyle argued that victims can be of any race, nationality, religion, or gender.

9. Rachel agreed but added that victims can be of different ages as well, pointing out that child abuse is a growing concern.

10. I see many victims of abuse when I volunteer at the Center for the Family, Mai explained, but we must be careful not to confuse abuse with discipline.

The Period and Other Punctuation Marks

Periods, question marks, exclamation points, colons, dashes, parentheses, brackets, ellipsis points, and slashes help clarify writing, usually by conveying tone and speech inflections. (For use of the hyphen, see **18f**.) Notice how the punctuation marks in the sentences below signal meaning and intonation.

> What a beautiful view! Mountains inspire awe. Don't you feel it?

> Maia Weinstock reviews Michael Corballis's *From Hand to Mouth: The Origins of Language* (2002), saying that Corballis developed a new theory of how language began: A complex sign language "developed 2 million years ago . . . [H]umans made the transition to speech just 50,000 years ago."

> Emily Dickinson—a much admired American poet—penned the lines "I found the phrase to every thought / I ever had, but one."

This chapter will help you understand how to use

- the end punctuation marks (the period (**17a**), the question mark (**17b**), and the exclamation point (**17c**)),
- the colon (**17d**),
- the dash (**17e**),
- parentheses (**17f**),
- brackets (**17g**),
- ellipsis points (**17h**), and
- the slash (**17i**).

To accommodate computerized typesetting, both CMS and the APA style manual call for only one space to follow a period, question mark, exclamation point, colon, ending parenthesis or bracket, and each of the periods in ellipsis points. No spaces precede or follow a hyphen or dash. The MLA style manual uses only one space after ending punctuation marks but permits two if used consistently.

17a | Periods punctuate sentences and abbreviations.

Rhetorically and grammatically, the period indicates completion.

(1) A period marks the end of a declarative sentence or a mildly imperative one.

Global warming is a serious problem. [declarative sentence]

Respect the environment. [mildly imperative sentence COMPARE Watch out!]

"Be careful," he warned. [declarative sentence with a quotation containing an imperative]

She asks whether global warming really exists. [declarative sentence containing an indirect question]

"Does global warming really exist?" she asked. [declarative sentence containing a direct quotation that happens to be a question]

"It's a huge problem!" he shouted. [declarative sentence with a quotation containing an exclamation]

(2) A period follows an indirect question.

Indirect questions are phrased as statements, and therefore they end with periods.

They want to know what Ruth is doing. [COMPARE What is Ruth doing? (See **17b**.)]

(3) Periods follow some abbreviations.

Dr. Jr. A.M. P.M. vs. etc. et al.

Periods are not used with some other abbreviations (for example, *MVP, mph,* and *FM*). (See chapter **11**.) If you do not know whether an abbreviation uses a period, check a dictionary. Dictionaries often list options, such as *USA* or *U.S.A.* and *CST* or *C.S.T.*

Only one period follows an abbreviation that ends a sentence.

The study was performed by Ben Werthman et al.

17b | **A question mark follows a direct (but not an indirect) question.**

Rhetorically, the question mark indicates uncertainty. A request is also sometimes stated as a question and is followed by a question mark: *Would you pass the salt?*

What in the world is Shahri doing? [direct question]

Did you hear them ask, "What is Shahri doing?" [A direct question quoted within a direct question is followed by one question mark inside the closing quotation marks. See **16d**.]

What is Shahri doing? thinking? hoping? [A series of questions having the same subject and verb can be treated as elliptical; that is, only the first item needs to include both the subject and the verb.]

Declarative sentences sometimes contain direct questions.

He asked, "Did David recommend a good mortgage company?" [Put a question mark inside the quotation marks when it concludes a direct question. See **16d(3)**.]

When the question Why don't you invest in the stock market? comes up, we answer that we live on a budget. [A question mark follows the embedded question, which begins with a capiral letter but is not enclosed in quotation marks. The comma follows the introductory clause (see **12b**).]

A question mark inside parentheses shows that the writer is not sure whether the preceding word, figure, or date is correct.

Chaucer was born in 1340 (**?**) and died in 1400.

Do not punctuate an indirect question with a question mark. (See **17a(2)**.)

Indirect questions are written as declarative sentences. The subject and verb are not inverted as they would be in the related direct question.

We do not know when ~~will~~ the meeting will end.

17c | An exclamation point shows strong feeling.

Although the exclamation point can mark the end of a sentence—the same grammatical function as the other two end punctuation marks—its primary use is rhetorical, to create emphasis.

Wow! Amazing! That was the best movie I've ever seen!

When an exclamation point at the end of a sentence designates that sentence as emphatic, most writers replace the exclamation point with a period and rewrite the sentence to show the emphasis in other ways. When a direct quotation ends with an exclamation point, no comma or period is placed immediately after it.

"Get off the road!" he yelled.
He yelled, "Get off the road!"

Use the exclamation point sparingly. Overuse diminishes its value, and emphasis can be achieved in better ways (see chapter **29**). A comma is preferred after mild interjections, and a period works better after mildly exclamatory expressions and mild imperatives.

Somebody give me a pencil, please.

How moving that final scene was.

Exercise 1

Compose and punctuate brief sentences of the following types.

1. a declarative sentence containing a quoted exclamation
2. a mild imperative
3. a direct question
4. a declarative sentence containing an indirect question
5. a declarative sentence containing a direct question

17d | A colon calls attention to what follows and also separates figures in time references, parts of scriptural references, and titles from subtitles.

A colon generally signals that what follows is important. An independent clause precedes a colon. Leave only one space after a colon.

Beyond the Rule

STYLISTIC USES OF THE COLON

For information about stylistic uses of the colon, visit www.harbrace.com.

(1) A colon directs attention to an explanation or summary, a series, or a quotation.

> I am always seeking the answer to the eternal question: How can we be joined to another person—spouse, parent, child— yet still remain ourselves?

A colon can introduce a second independent clause that explains or expands the first.

> For I had no brain tumor, no eyestrain, no high blood pressure, nothing wrong with me at all: I simply had migraine headaches, and migraine headaches were, as everyone who did not have them knew, imaginary. —JOAN DIDION

> They were concerned mainly about speed: Not only did they want a very fast computer, but they also had to have a very fast Internet connection.

Style manuals are fairly consistent on whether the first word following a colon is capitalized (see 9d). All style manuals agree that after a colon you should capitalize the first letter of a rule or principle or of a quoted sentence. APA requires a capital letter when a complete sentence follows a colon. When other material follows a colon, MLA, CMS, and APA all recommend the use of a lowercase letter.

> I was finally confronted with what I had dreaded for months: The ultimate, balloon payment on my car loan was due. [complete sentence]

> I was finally confronted with what I had dreaded for months: the due date for that ultimate, balloon payment on my car loan. [phrase]

A colon is not used between a verb and its complement, between a verb and its object, between a preposition and its object, or after *such as*.

> The winners were: Asa, Vanna, and Jack.

> Many vegetarians do not eat dairy products, such as: butter and cheese.

A colon may introduce a list.

> There were three winners: Asa, Vanna, and Jack.
> OR   The winners were as follows: Asa, Vanna, and Jack.
> BUT   The winners included Asa, Vanna, and Jack.

(2) A colon separates titles from subtitles as well as figures in time references and in citations of scripture.

> I just read *Women's Ways of Knowing: The Development of Self, Voice, and Mind.*
> We are to be there by 11:30 A.M.

Many writers use a colon in scriptural references.

> He quoted from Psalms 3:5.

However, MLA recommends periods (Psalms 3.5), and recent biblical scholarship follows this practice as well. CMS accepts either format.

(3) Colons have specialized uses in business correspondence.

A colon follows the salutation of a business letter and any notations.

> Dear Dr. Horner: Dear Maxine: enc:

A colon introduces the headings in a memo.

> To: From: Subject: Date:

(4) The colon is also used in bibliographical entries.

(See chapters 39–40.)

Exercise 2

Insert colons where they are needed in the following sentences.

1. Before we discuss marketing, let's outline the behavior of consumers Consumer behavior is the process individuals go through as they select, buy, or use products or services to satisfy their needs and desires.

2. The process consists of six stages recognizing a need or desire, finding information, evaluating options, deciding to purchase, purchasing, and assessing purchases.

3. Many consumers rely on one popular publication for product information *Consumer Reports.*

4. When evaluating alternatives, a consumer uses criteria; for example, a house hunter might use some of the following criteria price, location, size, age, style, and landscaping design.

5. The postpurchase assessment has one of two results satisfaction or dissatisfaction with the product or service.

| 17e | A dash marks a break in thought, sets off a parenthetical element for emphasis or clarity, or follows an introductory list or series. |

You can use your keyboard to form a dash by typing two hyphens with no spaces between, before, or after the hyphens. Most word-processing programs can be set to convert these hyphens automatically to an em dash (—).

Dashes signal a specific meaning, so use them purposefully rather than as easy or automatic substitutes for commas, semicolons, or colons.

(1) A dash marks a sudden break in thought, an abrupt change in tone, or a faltering in speech.

I was awed by the almost superhuman effort Stonehenge represents—but who wouldn't be?

I know who she is, Mrs.—Mrs.—Mrs. Somebody—the Mayor of Gilpin—or Springtown.

(2) A dash sets off a parenthetical element for emphasis or (if it contains commas) for clarity.

In many smaller cities of this nation, cable television operators—with the connivance of local government—have a virtual monopoly.

The trail down into the Grand Canyon—steep, narrow, winding, and lacking in guard rails—is treacherous.

(3) A dash occurs after an introductory list or series.

The main part of the following sentence sums up the meaning of the list.

Eager, determined to succeed, and scared to death—all of these describe my emotions the first day on the job.

17f | **Parentheses set off nonessential matter and enclose numerals or letters used for lists.**

Use parentheses to set off information that mainly illustrates or supplements the main part of the sentence or that is nonessential (parenthetical).

I accepted his explanation (up to a point) and set out to enjoy the evening. [an explanatory parenthetical expression]

In general, a sound argument contains (1) a clear statement of its point placed near the beginning and (2) a refutation of opposing positions, usually right after the point statement. [In long sentences especially, parenthetical enumeration highlights the points.]

The Search for Extraterrestrial Intelligence (SETI) uses the Very Large Array (VLA) outside Sicorro, New Mexico, to scan the sky. [first-time use of an acronym; see **11e** and the **Glossary of Terms**]

In the next example, an entire sentence is parenthetical.

If we refuse to talk "like a lady," we are ridiculed and criticized for being unfeminine. ("She thinks like a man" is, at best, a left-handed compliment.) —**ROBIN LAKOFF**

Use parentheses sparingly; the elements they enclose should still read smoothly in the sentence as a whole.

Beyond the Rule

PARENTHETICAL RHETORIC

Although dashes and parentheses are both used to set off parenthetical material within sentences, their use is almost entirely rhetorical. They express different degrees of emphasis and are seldom used for any other purpose.

- Dashes set off parenthetical elements sharply and usually emphasize them.
- Parentheses usually deemphasize the elements they enclose.
- Commas also separate elements, usually without emphasizing them.

To see how a sentence can be punctuated in each of these ways, visit www.harbrace.com.

> **17g** Square brackets set off additions or alterations to quoted matter and replace parentheses within parentheses.

Parker Pilgrim has written, "If he [Leonard Aaron] ever disapproved of any of his children's friends, he never let them know about it." [An unclear pronoun reference is explained by the bracketed addition.]

Not every expert agrees. (See, for example, Katie Hafner and Matthew Lyon's *Where Wizards Stay Up Late* [New York: Simon, 1996].) [Brackets replace parentheses within parentheses.]

[I]f the network was ever going to become more than a test bed . . . , word of its potential had to spread.

—KATIE HAFNER AND MATTHEW LYON

[In CMS style, the brackets indicate that the capital *I* was a lowercase letter in the original. To avoid the awkwardness of this usage of brackets, construct the sentence so that it does not begin with the quotation: Hafner and Lyon note that "if the network . . . ."]

Another kind of brackets, angle brackets (< >), often enclose Web addresses so that punctuation in the sentence is not confused with the dot(s) in the URL:<http://www.harbrace.com>.

> **17h** Ellipsis points indicate an omission from a quoted passage or a reflective pause or hesitation.

(1) Ellipsis points mark an omission within a quoted passage.

Whenever you omit anything from material you quote, make sure your omission does not change the meaning of the orig-

inal. Replace the omitted material with **ellipsis points**—
three equally spaced periods.

Omission within a quoted sentence

Original

A satire is supposed to make fun of whatever it is attacking. But
there is no humor in *Natural Born Killers*. It is a relentlessly
bloody story designed to shock us and to further numb us to
the senselessness of reckless murder. The film wasn't made with
the intent of stimulating morally depraved young people to
commit similar crimes, but such a result can hardly be a
surprise.   —**JOHN GRISHAM**, "Unnatural Killers"

Noting that *Natural Born Killers* "wasn't made with the intent
of stimulating . . . similar crimes," John Grisham points out
that copy-cat behavior has, nevertheless, been one result.

Omission at the beginning or end of a quoted sentence   If the
initial part of a quoted sentence is omitted, neither ellipsis
points nor a capital letter is used at the beginning of the
quotation, whether it is run into the text or set off in a block
(see **39d(2)**).

John Grisham points out that "satire is supposed to make
fun of whatever it is attacking." [The first word of the
sentence has been omitted.]

An omission that coincides with the end of the sentence requires
an end punctuation mark (a period, a question mark, or an exclamation point) in addition to the ellipsis points. Put a space after
the last word quoted and before the three spaced periods. Place the
end punctuation mark after the ellipsis points. If the quoted material is followed by a parenthetical source or page reference, the
period comes after the second parenthesis.

John Grisham points out that the film "is a relentlessly bloody
story designed to shock us . . . ." OR "shock us . . ." (2).
[MLA style]

Omission of a sentence or more Omission of a sentence or more (even a paragraph or more) within a quoted passage is indicated by a period before the ellipsis points. A comma preceding the ellipses indicates the omission of part of one sentence and part or all of another.

Original

Cacao doesn't flower, as most plants do, at the tips of its outer and uppermost branches. Instead, its sweet white buds hang from the trunk and along a few fat branches, popping out of patches of bark called cushions, which form where leaves drop off. They're tiny, these flowers. Yet once pollinated by midges, no-see-ums that flit in the leafy detritus below, they'll make pulp-filled pods almost the size of rugby balls. The big, colorful, exuberant pods flop around the tree's trunk and dangle from its branches in a shameless display of ripeness—low-hanging fruit for forest animals that eat the juicy, satin-white pulp inside and disperse its bitter-tasting seeds, the magic beans. —**PATRICIA GADSBY**, "Endangered Chocolate"

Cacao flowers "hang from the trunk and along a few fat branches, popping out of patches of bark called cushions, which form where leaves drop off. . . . The big, colorful, exuberant pods flop around the tree's trunk and dangle from its branches in a shameless display of ripeness." [Two sentences have been omitted from the original, and a sentence comes before and after the period and ellipsis points.]

Patricia Gadsby says of cacao flowers that, although "tiny, . . . once pollinated . . . they'll make pulp-filled pods almost the size of rugby balls." [Three words have been omitted from the first sentence and eleven from the second. The first set of ellipsis points links the sentences.]

To avoid excessive use of ellipses, you can also recast a sentence.

Although cacao flowers are small, as Patricia Gadsby notes, "once pollinated . . . they'll make pulp-filled pods almost the size of rugby balls."

You can also paraphrase a passage rather than editing it heavily. (See **39d(3)**.)

To indicate the omission of a full line or more in quoted poetry, use spaced periods covering the length of either the line above it or the omitted line.

> The yellow fog that rubs its back upon the window-panes,
>
> . . . .
>
> Curled once about the house, and fell asleep.
>
> —T. S. ELIOT, "The Love Song of J. Alfred Prufrock"

(2) Ellipsis points can occasionally mark a reflective pause or a hesitation.

> Keith saw four menacing youths coming toward him • • • and ran. [Alternatively, you could use a dash to indicate the pause in this sentence.]

| 17i | The slash is used to mark line divisions in quoted poetry and between terms to indicate that either term is applicable. |

There are no spaces before and after a slash used between terms, but a space is inserted before and after a slash used between lines of poetry.

> Wallace Stevens refers to the listener who, "nothing himself, beholds / Nothing that is not there and the nothing that is."

Extensive use of the slash to indicate that either of two terms is applicable (as in *and/or* and *he/she*) can make writing choppy. You might want to use *or* instead of the slash.

When two terms combine to modify a noun, link the terms with a hyphen: *East-West differences.* (See **18f**.)

Exercise 3

Add appropriate dashes, parentheses, slashes, and brackets to the following sentences. Be ready to explain the reason for every mark you add.

1. Researchers in an exciting field (Artificial Intelligence AI) are working on devices to assist the elderly.
2. One such device is Pearl a robotic nurse that helps around the house.
3. Another application is cooking software that checks for missing and or incorrect ingredients.
4. Researchers are even investigating Global Positioning Systems GPS as a way to track Alzheimer patients' daily routines.
5. The actual cost of such devices expensive now but more affordable later is yet to be determined.

Exercise 4

Punctuate the following sentences with appropriate end marks, commas, colons, dashes, parentheses, and ellipsis points. Do not use unnecessary punctuation. Give a justification for each mark you add, especially where more than one type of mark (for example, commas, dashes, or parentheses) is acceptable.

1. Many small country towns are very similar a truck stop a gas station a crowded diner and three bars
2. If you don't want to miss pure Americana as you roar down the interstate, you'd better shout whoa
3. Why do we never see these quaint examples of pure Americana when we travel around the country on the interstates

4. The simple life, a nonexistent crime rate, and down-home values these are some of the advantages little towns offer

5. Rolling across America on one of the big interstates I-20, I-40, I-70, I-80, or I-90 you are likely to pass within a few miles of a number of these towns

6. These towns almost certainly will have a regional or perhaps an ethnic flavor Hispanic in the Southwest Scandinavian in the North

7. When I visit one of these out-of-the-way places, I always have a sense of well really a feeling of safety

8. I think a town like that might be the very best place to live in the whole world

9. There's one thing I can tell you Small town life is not boring

10. My one big question however is what do you do to earn a living there

Spelling and Diction

18 Spelling, the Spell Checker, and Hyphenation

People often decide whether you are intelligent or well informed based on how well you write and, in particular, how well you spell. But you don't always have access to a spell checker. You want to spell correctly on in-class assignments so that your teacher gets a good impression of your ability. Employers may also evaluate your competence by your ability to spell correctly in job-related writing. And you need to spell correctly when searching the Web. For these reasons, a basic knowledge of spelling is always important.

This chapter will help you

- use a spell checker (**18a**),
- spell words according to pronunciation (**18b**),
- spell words that sound alike (**18c**),
- use affixes (prefixes and suffixes) correctly (**18d**),
- deal with *ei* and *ie* (**18e**), and
- use hyphenation to link and divide words (**18f**).

Beyond the Rule

SHAPING UP YOUR SPELLING

Typically, misspellings result from carelessness, lack of shape recognition, confusion of words that sound alike, or a learning disability. If you're a poor speller who is serious about improving, visit www.harbrace.com to learn about resources available to you.

If you have trouble with spelling, use a dictionary. Dictionaries may list two unlabeled ways to spell a word—for example, *fulfill* and *fulfil*. In such cases, either form is correct, although the first option listed is often more commonly used. Whatever spelling you choose, use it consistently.

18a | Spell checkers can be valuable tools.

The spell checker can catch many errors, but it will not alert you to words you may have confused, such as *principal* and *principle*, because it cannot know which meaning you intend.

THE TRUTH ABOUT SPELL CHECKERS

A spell checker finds errors by checking the words in a document against the words in its dictionary. When it finds a word that does not match any words in its dictionary, it flags that word as misspelled. Thus, a spell checker will usually catch

- misspellings of common words,
- misspellings of irregular words,
- words in which a vowel changes when a suffix is added,
- a letter dropped or added when a prefix is added, and
- obvious typographical errors, such as *tge* for *the*.

However, a spell checker cannot determine whether a correctly spelled word is used incorrectly (for example, *there* in place of *their*), and it cannot determine whether a word that is not in its dictionary is incorrectly spelled. Therefore, a spell checker generally will *not* catch

- typographical errors that make correctly spelled words (such as *was* for *saw*),

(Continued on page 268)

(Continued from page 267)

- misuses of correctly spelled words that result from mistaking words not stressed in speech (such as *could of* or *would of* for *could have* or *would have*),

- words that are correctly spelled but incorrectly used (such as *affect* for *effect*), and misuses of words that sound alike, such as *course* and *coarse*.

Furthermore, a spell checker may provide erroneous advice by suggesting incorrect alternative words, or it may offer no alternatives at all. Therefore, you should always evaluate any choices provided by a spell checker. You can also try the following strategies to help you use a spell checker effectively:

- Keep a separate file of words you tend to misspell. When you edit a document, use the Search and Replace feature to find and correct any misspellings of those words.

- If a spell checker regularly flags a word (or a name) that is not in its dictionary but is spelled correctly, you can give it a command to add that word to its dictionary. When you run the spell checker, it will be able to check for that word.

It is also best to reject any offers your spell checker may make to correct all instances of a particular error. Getting to know what the spell checker can and cannot do is the best way to use it effectively. And you should always proofread your writing yourself, never relying on a spell checker to locate all of the spelling errors.

18b | Spelling does not necessarily reflect pronunciation.

Many words are not spelled the way they are pronounced, so pronunciation is not a reliable guide to correct spelling. Sometimes, people skip over an unstressed syllable, as when *February* is pronounced "Febary," or they slide over a sound that is hard to articulate, as when *library* is pronounced "libary." Other times, people add a sound—for instance, when they pronounce *athlete* as "athalete." And people also switch sounds around, as in "irrevelant" for *irrelevant*. Such mispronunciations can lead to misspellings. As an aid to remembering, it may be helpful to consider the spelling of the root word—for example, the root word for *irrelevant* is *relevant*.

TIPS FOR SPELLERS

Fixing Pronunciation Problems

- Check for unstressed syllables.
- Consider the spelling of the root word.
- Consider alternative pronunciations as spelling clues.

Beyond the Rule

WHEN PRONUNCIATION IS UNRELIABLE

For a list of words that are usually not pronounced the way they are spelled, visit www.harbrace.com.

The words *have, and,* and *than* are often not stressed in speech and are thus misspelled. A spell checker will not catch these misspellings.

       have   than   and
I would ~~of~~ rather had fish ~~then~~ soup ~~an~~ salad.

18c | **The meanings of words that sound alike are determined by their spelling.**

Pairs of words such as *forth* and *fourth* or *sole* and *soul* are **homophones:** They sound alike but have different meanings and spellings. The spell checker cannot identify words that are correctly spelled but incorrectly used. If you are unsure about the difference in meaning between any pair of words, consult a dictionary. A number of frequently confused words are listed with explanations in this handbook's **Glossary of Usage**.

Single words and two-word phrases that consist of the same letters but have different meanings can also be troublesome. Following are some examples.

He wore **everyday** clothes.	He wears them **every day.**
They don't fight **anymore.**	I can't eat **any more.**

Other examples are *awhile/a while, everybody/every body, everyone/every one, maybe/may be,* and *nobody/no body.*

A lot and *all right* are still spelled as two words. *Alot* is always considered incorrect; *alright* is considered incorrect except in newspapers and magazines. (See the **Glossary of Usage**.)

Singular nouns ending in *-nce* and plural nouns ending in *-nts* are easily confused.

Assistance is available.	I have two **assistants.**
My **patience** is frayed.	Some **patients** waited for hours.

Contractions and possessive pronouns are often confused. In contractions, an apostrophe indicates an omitted letter (or letters). In possessive pronouns, there is no apostrophe. (See **5b** and **15a**.)

Contraction	Possessive
It's my turn next.	Each group waits **its** turn.
You're next.	**Your** turn is next.
There's no difference.	**Theirs** is no different.

TIPS FOR SPELLERS

Fixing Problems with Homophones

- Distinguish between possessives and contractions (*your* versus *you're*).

- Distinguish between single words and two-word phrases (*maybe* versus *may be*).

- Distinguish between the endings *-nce* and *-nts* (*instance* versus *instants*).

- Distinguish between other words that sound alike (*accept* versus *except*).

18d | **Prefixes change a word's meaning; suffixes may change its spelling.**

A **prefix** is added to the beginning of a base word, called the **root.**

> necessary, **un**necessary
> moral, **im**moral

No letter is added or dropped when a prefix is added: *grand + daughter.*

Adding a **suffix** to the end of a base word often changes the spelling.

> beauty, beaut**iful**
> describe, descri**ption**
> BUT resist, resist**ance**

Although spellings of words with suffixes are irregular, they follow certain conventions. Misspellings that result from adding prefixes or suffixes are usually detected by a spell checker.

(1) Dropping or retaining a final *e* depends on whether the suffix begins with a vowel.

- If a suffix begins with a vowel, the final *e* of the base word is dropped:

  bride, brid**al**   come, com**ing**   prime, prim**ary**

- If a suffix begins with a consonant, the final *e* of the base word is retained:

  entire, entire**ly**   rude, rude**ness**   place, place**ment**

  Some exceptions are *argument, awful, ninth, truly,* and *wholly.*

- To keep the /s/ sound in *ce* or the /j/ sound in *ge,* retain the final *e* before *-able* or *-ous:*

  notice**able**   courage**ous**

(2) A final consonant is usually doubled when a suffix begins with a vowel.

Double the final consonant before a suffix beginning with a vowel if (1) the consonant ends a one-syllable word or a stressed syllable or (2) the consonant is preceded by a single vowel. If the suffix does not begin with a vowel, the consonant is not doubled.

drop, dro**pp**ing   BUT   droop, droo**p**ing
admit, admi**tt**ed   BUT   picket, picke**t**ed

(3) A final *y* is changed or retained depending on whether the suffix begins with a vowel.

Change a final *y* to *i* before adding a suffix—except *-ing.*

defy: de**fies,** de**fied,** de**fiance**   BUT   def**ying**
modify: modi**fies,** modi**fied,** modif**ier**   BUT   modif**ying**

Most verbs ending in *y* preceded by a vowel do not change the *y* before adding *-s* or *-ed: stay, stays, stayed.* Similarly, some nouns, such as *joy* and *day,* retain the *y* when *-s* is added. The following spelling irregularities are especially troublesome: *lays, laid; pays, paid; says, said.*

(4) A final *l* is retained when *-ly* is added.

cool, coo**ll**y   formal, forma**ll**y   real, rea**ll**y   usual, usua**ll**y

(5) The plural of nouns is formed by adding *-s* or *-es* to the singular.

scientist**s**   sister**s**-in-law [chief word pluralized]

toy**s**   the Smith**s** [proper name]

- For nouns ending in *f* or *fe,* change the ending to *ve* before adding *-s* when the sound of the plural changes from *f* to *v:*

  thie*f,* thie**ves**   life, li**ves** BUT *roof, roofs*

- For nouns ending in *s, z, ch, sh,* or *x,* add *-es* when the plural adds another syllable:

  box, box**es**   peach, peach**es**   the Rodriguez**es**

- For nouns ending in *y* preceded by a consonant, add *-es* after changing the *y* to *i:*

  company, compan**ies**   ninety, ninet**ies**   territory, territor**ies**

- Although usage varies, most nouns ending in *o* preceded by a consonant add *-es.* Some can add *-s* or *-es:*

  motto**s,** mott**oes**   zero**s,** zer**oes**

- Certain irregular nouns do not add *-s* or *-es* for the plural:

  wom*a*n, wom**e**n   goose, g**ee**se   sheep, sheep   child, child**ren**

TIPS FOR SPELLERS

Fixing Problems with Affixes

- Recognize prefixes *(moral/immoral)*.
- Recognize suffixes:

    dropping a final *e (bride/bridal)*
    doubling a final consonant *(drop/dropping)*
    changing *y* to *i (defy/defies)*
    retaining a final *l (real/really)*
    forming plurals *(toy/toys, box/boxes, man/men, criterion/criteria)*

Beyond the Rule

WORDS BORROWED FROM OTHER LANGUAGES

Words borrowed from Latin or Greek generally form their plurals as they did in the original language. If you aren't sure about how to make any word plural, look in a dictionary.

| **Singular** | criterion | alumnus, -a | analysis | datum | species |
| **Plural** | criteria | alumni, -ae | analyses | data | species |

Some words are spelled differently in Great Britain and the United States. When writing for American readers, use the American form.

| **American** | theater | fertilize | color | connection |
| **British** | theatre | fertilise | colour | connexion |

For further information, visit www.harbrace.com.

Exercise 1

Supply plural forms (including any optional spellings) for the following words. If a word is not covered by the rules, use a dictionary.

1. half	7. genius
2. woman	8. passerby
3. potato	9. halo
4. theory	10. leaf
5. radius	11. phenomenon
6. speech	12. church

18e | *Ei* and *ie* are often confused.

When the sound of the letters is /ē/ (as in *me*), write *ie* except after *c,* where you should write *ei:*

ch**ie**f, pr**ie**st, y**ie**ld BUT conc**ei**t, perc**ei**ve, rec**ei**ve [after *c*]

When the sound is other than /ē/, you should usually write *ei:*

eight, for**ei**gn, h**ei**r, r**ei**n, th**ei**r, w**ei**ght

Some exceptions are *either, neither, friend, species,* and *weird.*

18f | Hyphens can link or divide words.

Hyphens not only link, or make a compound of, two or more words that function as a single word, but they also divide words at the ends of lines.

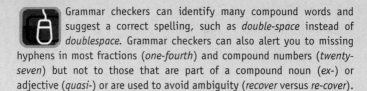

Grammar checkers can identify many compound words and suggest a correct spelling, such as *double-space* instead of *doublespace*. Grammar checkers can also alert you to missing hyphens in most fractions (*one-fourth*) and compound numbers (*twenty-seven*) but not to those that are part of a compound noun (*ex-*) or adjective (*quasi-*) or are used to avoid ambiguity (*recover* versus *re-cover*).

(1) Hyphens sometimes link two or more words that form a compound functioning as a single word.

Nouns   We planted forget-me-nots and Johnny-jump-ups.

Verbs   I double-checked. He hard-boiled the egg.

Some compounds are listed in the dictionary with hyphens (*eye-opener, cross-examine*), others are written as two words (*eye chart, cross fire*), and still others are written as one word (*eye-witness, crossbreed*). When in doubt, consult a dictionary.

- Do not confuse the hyphen with the dash, which is key-boarded as a double hyphen with no spaces before and after. (See **17e**.)
- Use a hyphen to link two or more words serving as a single adjective before a noun: *self-imposed* exile, a *well-built* house [COMPARE a house that is well built].
- In a series of compound adjectives, a space may follow the hyphen in every item except the last one: *first- and second-degree burns.*
- Omit the hyphen after an adverb ending in -*ly* (*quickly frozen foods*), in names of chemical compounds (*sodium chloride solution*), and in a modifier using a letter or numeral as the second element (*group C homes, type IV virus*).
- Hyphenate to avoid ambiguity or an awkward combination of letters or syllables between a prefix and a base word: *anti-intellectual, de-emphasize, re-sign the petition* [COMPARE *resign the position*].

■ In addition, hyphenate between a prefix and a capital letter and between a noun and the suffix *-elect: anti-American, President-elect.* Otherwise, do not use hypens with prefixes or suffixes.

Exercise 2

Convert the following word groups using the pattern of the examples.

EXAMPLES

a movie lasting two hours   *a two-hour movie*
colors used with water   *watercolors*

1. a brush for teeth
2. diplomats who solve problems
3. cereal in the shape of an *O*
4. a house twenty years old
5. a garage for three cars
6. a light used at night
7. a highway with four lanes
8. lightbulbs costing ten dollars

---

(2) Hyphens break words at the ends of lines.

If you must divide a word at the end of a line, use a hyphen to separate it between syllables.

In dictionaries, dots usually divide entries into syllables: **re·al·ly, pre·fer, pref·er·ence, sell·ing, set·ting.** But not every division between syllables is an appropriate place for dividing a word. Following are some general guidelines.

■ Do not divide abbreviations, first and middle initials, capitalized acronyms, or one-syllable words.

p.m. [NOT p.-m.]   USAF [NOT US-AF]
through [NOT thr-ough]   UNESCO [NOT UNES-CO]

- Do not divide a word after the first letter or before the last or last two letters, even if they form a syllable.

  omit   able   boa   dated   doesn't   safely   gravel
  o·mit   a·ble   bo·a   dat·ed   does·n't   safe·ly   grav·el

- Divide hyphenated words only at the hyphen.

  mass-|produce   father-|in-law OR father-in-|law

- Divide words between consonants, except when the division does not reflect pronunciation.

  pic-|nic   dis-|cuss   thun-|der   set-|ting   plan-|ning

  [COMPARE the pronunciation of *co-|bra* with that of *sell-|ing,* in which the base word already has a double consonant.]

Exercise 3

Edit the following paragraph to correct misspellings and the usage of hyphens.

¹My friend and I recently watched a videotape of *First-Knight* that she had recieved for her birthday; its a movie that is principly located in the make believe city of Camelot. ²Of course, we had all heard the story of Lancelot and Guinevere, definately too of the most famous lovers in all of fiction, and there trouble relationship with King Arthur. ³We liked the movie alot because it successfully depictted conflict between love and loyalty. ⁴In fact, all of the issues concerning love and loyalty portrayed in the movie's storyline are timeless ones and will be as importent in the twenty first century as they were in the eighth. ⁵Nevertheless, although the filmmaker did a good job of teling the story, some of my friends didn't like the fact that the costumes worn by the acters and actresses were historicly inaccerate.

Good Usage

Using the right words at the right time can make the difference between having your ideas taken seriously and seeing them brushed aside. In academic or professional writing, it is important for you to sound well informed and respectful. In conversation with friends, it is just as important to sound casual; otherwise, your friends may think that you are cold or snobbish. Whatever the occasion, choosing the right words will help you connect with your audience. Effective writers avoid sounding too casual or too stuffy, and they usually avoid slang and jargon (see **19c**) when writing for a diverse audience (**32a**)). But for an academic or professional audience, they use a specialized vocabulary, thus enhancing their credibility (see **38a**). When you edit your writing, be sure that your words can be understood by everyone in your audience.

This chapter will help you

- understand how word choice is related to the rhetorical situation (**19a**),
- write in a clear, straightforward style (**19b**),
- choose words that are appropriate for the audience, the purpose, and the context (**19c**),
- use inclusive language (**19d**), and
- realize the benefits of dictionaries (**19e**) and thesauri (**19f**).

19a | Language varies according to audience, purpose, and context.

The words you use vary from situation to situation. How you talk to a loan officer differs from how you talk to your best friend. A discussion with a loan officer would probably be relatively formal, while a conversation with a friend would be less so. Understanding such differences in tone and making word choices that reflect them are especially important in writing because readers cannot see your body language, hear the inflections of your voice, or interrupt to say that they are having trouble following you. Instead, readers respond to the words on the page or the screen. You can help them understand your ideas by choosing words that they know (or that you can explain to them) and that also help you fulfill your purpose in a particular context.

When drafting (see chapter 32), use words that come immediately to mind. Sometimes, these words will be good choices. When revising (see chapter 33), you can identify any that need to be replaced. Remembering your rhetorical situation (see 32a) will help you use the right word at the right time.

19b | A clear, straightforward style is easy to read.

Although different styles are appropriate for different situations—depending, for example, on purpose, audience, and context (see 32a)—you should usually keep your writing simple and straightforward. An ornate and wordy style takes more time to read and could make you seem stuffy or pretentious.

Ornate   The majority believes that the approbation of society derives primarily from the diligent pursuit of allocated tasks.

Simple   Most people believe that success results from hard work.

A simple writing style does not indicate that you are a simplistic thinker. Instead, it shows that you can write clearly and do not want to waste your readers' time. Active, forceful verbs can help you to create this style (see **29d**). Using words that are precise (see **20a**) and sentences that are concise (chapter **21**) will also help you write simply and directly.

Beyond the Rule

THE PLAIN STYLE

Western rhetoricians have discussed the advantages of a plain, straightforward style for thousands of years, while also recognizing the advantages of an ornate style. The plain style became dominant in the twentieth century, influenced by the value people in the modern era placed on efficiency. In the future, new standards for usage will emerge as style preferences evolve. For more information about the history of style, visit www.harbrace.com.

19c | Making appropriate word choices establishes common ground with your readers.

Unless you are writing for a specialized audience and have good reason to believe that this audience would welcome slang (and other kinds of informal language) or jargon, the following advice can help you achieve good usage.

(1) Slang is effective in only a few rhetorical situations.

Slang is usually defined as words used primarily by people in a particular age group, locality, or profession. Slang, in fact, covers a wide range of words that are variously considered casual, facetious, or fashionable—any of which can either appeal to readers or alienate them. For example, using *shrink* for "psychiatrist" may convey disrespect for a field of medicine. Although such words are often used in private conversation, they are not appropriate for academic or professional writing (see chapters **41–43**). A clear sense of your audience is essential if you want to use slang effectively. If a slang word or expression is newly coined, your audience may not understand what you mean. If it has been around for a long time, your use of it can make you seem out of touch with popular culture. Frequent use of *whatever, awesome,* or *dude,* for example, can make you sound as if you are still living in the twentieth century.

(2) Conversational (or colloquial) words are usually too informal for academic and professional writing.

Words labeled *colloquial* in a dictionary (see **19e**) are fine for casual conversation and can be used by writers when composing dialogue or a personal essay on a light topic. Such words may sometimes be used for special effect in academic writing, but you should usually replace them with more appropriate words. For example, conversational terms such as *dumb, belly button,* and *kid* can be replaced by *ignorant, navel,* and *tease.*

Contractions (such as *you'll* for "you will" and *she's* for "she is") reflect the sound of conversation and can be useful for engaging a specific audience in a particular context (see **15b**). Some readers find them too informal for academic or professional writing.

(3) Regionalisms can be fun to read.

Regionalisms—such as *tank* for "pond" and *sweeper* for "vacuum cleaner"—can make writing lively and distinctive, but they are effective only when the audience can understand them in a specific context. Moreover, many readers consider regionalisms too informal for use in academic and professional writing (see chapters **41 43**). Consider your rhetorical situation (see **32a**) before using regionalisms.

CHECKLIST for Assessing Usage within a Rhetorical Situation

- Do your words convey the meaning you intend?
- Can your audience understand the words you have used?
- Do you explain any words your audience might not understand?
- Have you used any words that could irritate or offend members of your audience?
- Do any of your words make you sound too casual or too formal?
- Do your words help you to fulfill your rhetorical purpose?
- Are your words appropriate for the context in which you are writing?
- Are your words appropriate for the context in which they will be read?

---

(4) Technical words are essential when writing for specialists who understand them.

When writing for a diverse audience (see **32a**), an effective writer will not refer to the need for bifocals as *presbyopia*. However, technical language is appropriate when the audience can understand it (as when one physician writes to another) or when the audience needs to learn the terms in question.

Jargon is technical language tailored specifically for a particular occupation. Jargon can be an efficient shortcut for conveying specialized concepts, but you should use it only when you can be sure that you and your readers share an understanding of the terms. *Splash,* for example, does not always refer to water or an effect (as in *making a splash*); the word also signifies a computer screen that can appear after you click on a Web site but before you view its opening page. Keep in mind that spell checkers cannot recognize jargon.

19d | Using inclusive (nonprejudiced) language increases your credibility.

By making word choices that are inclusive rather than exclusive, you invite readers into your writing. Not only does prejudiced or derogatory language have no place in academic or professional writing, using it undermines your authority as a writer. Even if you are writing for one person you think you know well, do not assume that you know everything about that person. A close colleague at work might have a gay uncle, for example, or his sister might be married to someone of a different race or religion. Do not try to justify demeaning language on the grounds that you meant it as a joke. Take responsibility for the words you use.

(1) Nonsexist language respects both men and women.

Effective writers show equal respect for men and women. For example, they avoid using *man* to refer to people in general because they feel that the word excludes women.

Man's achievements in science are impressive.

Sexist language has a variety of sources, such as contempt for the opposite sex and the unthinking repetition of words used by others. Words that characterize someone in terms of sexual attraction (such as *babe, hunk,* and *hottie*) can be demeaning, even if they could be taken as compliments in some contexts.

Stereotyping can also lead to sexist language. Women, like men, can be *firefighters* or *police officers*—terms that are increasingly used as gender-neutral replacements for *firemen* and *policemen*. Even though some sexist usage remains embedded in the English language, it is gradually being reduced, as illustrated by the widespread avoidance of the once common practice of using *he* or *mankind* to refer to both men and women.

A grammar checker can find sexist words ending in *-ess (authoress)* or *-man (policeman)* and almost always flags *mankind*. Unfortunately, it also erroneously identifies as sexist many appropriate uses of the words *female, woman,* and *girl,* but not similar uses of *male, man,* and *boy*.

Being alert for sexist language and knowing how to revise it will help you gain acceptance from your audience, whatever its demographics. As the following box shows, revising to remove sexist language is relatively straightforward.

TIPS FOR AVOIDING SEXIST LANGUAGE

When you review your drafts, revise the following:

- **Generic *he*:** A doctor should listen to *his* patients.

  A doctor should listen to **his or her** patients. [use of the appropriate form of *he or she*]

  Doctors should listen to **their** patients. [use of plural forms]

  By listening to patients, **doctors gain information they can use in their diagnoses.** [elimination of the pronoun by revising the sentence]

(Continued on page 286)

(Continued from page 285)

- **Occupational stereotype:** Glenda, a female engineer at Howard Aviation, won the best-employee award.

  Glenda, an engineer at Howard Aviation, won the best-employee award. [removal of the unnecessary gender reference]

- **Terms such as *man* and *mankind* or those with *-ess* or *-man* endings:** Labor laws benefit the common *man*. *Mankind* benefits from philanthropy. The *stewardess* brought me some orange juice.

  Labor laws benefit **working people.** [replacement of the stereotypical term with a neutral term]

  Everyone benefits from philanthropy. [use of an indefinite pronoun]

  The **flight attendant** brought me some orange juice. [use of gender-neutral language]

- **Stereotypical gender roles:** I was told that the university offers free tuition to faculty *wives*.

  I was told that the university offers free tuition to faculty **spouses.** [replacement of the stereotypical term with a neutral term]

- **Inconsistent use of titles:** *Mr. Holmes* and his *wife,* Mary, took a long trip to China.

  Mr. and Mrs. [or Ms.] Holmes took a long trip to China. [consistent use of titles]

  OR **Peter and Mary Holmes** took a long trip to China. [removal of titles]

  OR **Peter Holmes** and **Mary Wolfe** took a long trip to China. [use of full names]

- **Unstated gender assumption:** Have your *mother* make your costume for the school pageant.

  Have your **parents** provide you with a costume for the school pageant. [replacement of the stereotypical term with a neutral term]

Languages vary in the ways they indicate gender, so translations may result in unintentionally sexist usage. For example, the German word *Mann* means both "man" and "husband." However, in English, *man and wife* is considered sexist because the word *wife* indicates a woman's relationship to a man as well as her gender, whereas the word *man* indicates a person's gender only. The unbiased version of this expression is *husband and wife.* If you are unsure of the possible bias in a gender-marked word, ask a teacher, classmate, or colleague for advice.

Exercise 1

Make the following sentences inclusive by eliminating sexist language.

1. The ladies took a tour of the city while the executive managers met for a business conference.
2. The old boys run the city's government.
3. Mothers should read to their small children.
4. Some fans admired the star because he was a hunk; others praised him for his environmental activism.
5. For six years, he worked as a mailman in a small town.

(2) Nonracist language promotes social equity.

Rarely is it necessary to identify anyone's race or ethnicity in academic or professional writing, unless you are writing about demographics, racial inequities, or the history of a particular ethnic group. Because language changes, the terms used to refer to various racial and ethnic groups also change. Although Americans of African descent are no longer referred to as *colored* or *Negro,* those terms persist in the names of important organizations such as the National Association for the Advancement of Colored People and the United Negro College

Fund. And whether to refer to *African Americans* or *Blacks* is now sometimes determined by the generation to which your audience belongs. People of Spanish-speaking descent in different parts of the United States have preferences concerning the usage of *Latino/Latina, Chicano/Chicana, Hispanic, Latin American, Mexican American,* or *Puerto Rican.* Many descendants of indigenous peoples prefer *Native American* to *American Indian,* and *Asian American* has supplanted *Oriental.* Use the term the group or individual prefers on those infrequent occasions when you need to identify race or ethnicity.

Many writers now use *person(s) of color* to describe individuals who are other than white. Writers of any race or color should also be mindful that *white* is widely considered a race even if different cultures have had different criteria for deciding who is "white." Racist terms for white people are no more acceptable than racist terms for people of any other color.

(3) Respectful writers do not use homophobic language.

Terms such as *faggot* or *dyke* should never be used to describe a man or a woman who is gay, lesbian, bisexual, or transgendered—or to demean heterosexuals who appear or act as though they may be other than heterosexual. Like sexist and racist language, homophobic language is inappropriate for academic or professional writing.

Words associated with sexual orientation often function better as adjectives than as nouns. Describing a man as *a gay,* for example, implies that he is defined by his sexuality. When used as one among other identifying adjectives, however, *gay* (or *lesbian, bisexual,* or *transgendered*) functions simply as one of the words describing someone: *a conservative, gay, white attorney.*

Beyond the Rule

INCLUSIVE LANGUAGE

Members of a social minority may choose to reclaim as their own words that have been used against them. For more information about prejudicial language and the power people have to change usage that hurts them, visit www.harbrace.com.

(4) Respectful writers are sensitive to matters of ability, age, class, religion, and occupation.

Although referring to persons with physical disabilities as *handicapped* may be insensitive, being overly cautious about references to disabilities can be demeaning. Someone who is blind might object to being called *visually impaired* because the phrase is imprecise. Many older people dislike being called *senior citizens* (imagine how most young people would resent being called *junior citizens*). Labels such as *preppie* and *redneck* are clearly class-based references that reduce individuals to stereotypes.

A secular calendar that marks Christmas and Easter with no mention of Yom Kippur or Ramadan is exclusionary. Although some attempts to enhance the prestige of manual labor (such as making up a term like *deforestation technician* to describe a member of a logging team) could be considered patronizing, using the terms that are preferred by the people who perform the labor shows sensitivity. In all instances, avoid the stereotyping that careless use of language can create.

Exercise 2

Find a short piece of writing that includes words or phrases that bother you because they are unclear, unnecessarily ornate, or potentially hurtful. Share your choice with a group of peers or colleagues, explaining what you dislike and why.

19e | Dictionaries can help you make good writing decisions.

A good dictionary is an indispensable tool for writers. Desk dictionaries such as *The American Heritage Dictionary* and *Merriam-Webster's Collegiate Dictionary* do much more than provide the correct spellings of words; they also give meanings, parts of speech, plural forms, and verb tenses, as well as information about pronunciation and derivation (how a word originated and how its meaning evolved). In addition, a reliable dictionary also includes labels that can help you decide whether words are appropriate for the purpose, audience, and context of your writing. Words labeled **dialect, slang, colloquial, nonstandard,** or **unconventional**, as well as those labeled **archaic** or **obsolete** (meaning that they are no longer in common use), are usually inappropriate for college and professional writing. If a word has no label, you can safely assume that it can be used in writing for school or work. But whether the word is appropriate depends on the precise meaning a writer wants to convey (see **20a**).

Because language is constantly changing, it is important to choose a dictionary with a recent copyright date. Many dictionaries are available—in print, online, or on CD-ROM. Pocket dictionaries, which are useful for checking spellings and definitions, omit important information on usage and derivation. The dictionaries incorporated into most word-processing programs are equivalent to pocket dictionaries and may be out of date.

(1) Words and expressions labeled *nonstandard* or *colloquial* should not be used in college and professional writing, except possibly in direct quotations.

For example, *ain't* should not be used for *am not,* nor should *irregardless* be used for *regardless.* Usage such as this might be appropriate, however, if you are quoting someone you interviewed (see 37e) or a character from a piece of literature (42e).

(2) Using words labeled archaic can make you sound silly or pretentious.

All dictionaries list (and give meanings for) words that have long since passed out of general use. Such words as *rathe* ("early") and *yestreen* ("last evening") are still found in dictionaries because they occur in literature from the past and so must be defined for the modern reader; these words are no longer used, however. A number of obsolete or archaic words—such as *worser* (for *worse*) or *holp* (for *helped*)—are still in use but are considered nonstandard.

(3) Consulting an unabridged or special dictionary can enhance your understanding of a word.

Unabridged Dictionaries
The Oxford English Dictionary. 2nd ed. 20 vols. 1989– . CD-ROM. 1994.
Webster's Third New International Dictionary of the English Language. 1995.

Special Dictionaries
Cowie, A. P., and R. Mackin. *Oxford Dictionary of Current Idiomatic English.* Vols. 1–2. 1975, 1984.
Follett, Wilson. *Modern American Usage: A Guide.* 1998.
Morris, William, and Mary Morris. *Harper Dictionary of Contemporary Usage.* 2nd ed. 1985, 1992.

Partridge, Eric, and Paul Beale. *Dictionary of Catch Phrases.* 1992.

Dictionary of American Slang, 3rd ed. 1994.

Merriam-Webster's Dictionary of English Usage. 1994.

The following dictionaries are recommended for non-native speakers of English.

Collins Cobuild Dictionary. 1995

Longman Dictionary of Contemporary English. 1996.
(*Longman Dictionary of American English,* 1997, is the American abridgment.)

Longman Dictionary of English Language and Culture. 2000.

The Newbury House Dictionary of American English. 4th ed. 2004.

Oxford Advanced Learner's Dictionary of Current English. 1998. (*Oxford ESL Dictionary,* 1994, is the American edition.)

Two excellent resources for ESL students are the following:

Longman Language Activator. 1993. (This book supplies definitions, usage, and sample sentences: It is a cross between a dictionary and a thesaurus.)

Swan, Michael. *Practical English Usage.* 1995. (This is a practical reference guide to problems encountered by those who speak English as a second language.)

---

(4) Reading the introductory material and noting any special abbreviations will help you understand the information a dictionary provides.

Figure 19.1 shows sample entries from the tenth edition of *Merriam-Webster's Collegiate Dictionary.* The type of information these entries provide can be found in almost all desk

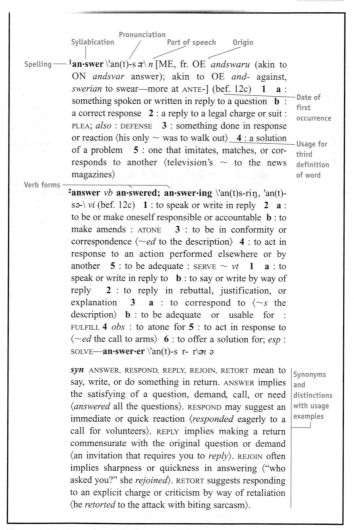

Spelling

Syllabication

Pronunciation

Part of speech

Origin

Date of first occurrence

Usage for third definition of word

Verb forms

¹**an·swer** \'an(t)-s ɑ\ *n* [ME, fr. OE *andswaru* (akin to ON *andsvar* answer); akin to OE *and-* against, *swerian* to swear—more at ANTE-] (bef. 12c) **1 a** : something spoken or written in reply to a question **b** : a correct response **2** : a reply to a legal charge or suit : PLEA; *also* : DEFENSE **3** : something done in response or reaction ⟨his only ~ was to walk out⟩ **4** : a solution of a problem **5** : one that imitates, matches, or corresponds to another ⟨television's ~ to the news magazines⟩

²**answer** *vb* **an·swered; an·swer·ing** \'an(t)s-riŋ, 'an(t)-sə-\ *vi* (bef. 12c) **1** : to speak or write in reply **2 a** : to be or make oneself responsible or accountable **b** : to make amends : ATONE **3** : to be in conformity or correspondence ⟨~*ed* to the description⟩ **4** : to act in response to an action performed elsewhere or by another **5** : to be adequate : SERVE ~ *vt* **1 a** : to speak or write in reply to **b** : to say or write by way of reply **2** : to reply in rebuttal, justification, or explanation **3 a** : to correspond to ⟨~*s* the description⟩ **b** : to be adequate or usable for : FULFILL **4** *obs* : to atone for **5** : to act in response to ⟨~*ed* the call to arms⟩ **6** : to offer a solution for; *esp* : SOLVE—**an·swer·er** \'an(t)-s r- r\ɔr ə

syn ANSWER, RESPOND, REPLY, REJOIN, RETORT mean to say, write, or do something in return. ANSWER implies the satisfying of a question, demand, call, or need ⟨*answered* all the questions⟩. RESPOND may suggest an immediate or quick reaction ⟨*responded* eagerly to a call for volunteers⟩. REPLY implies making a return commensurate with the original question or demand ⟨an invitation that requires you to *reply*⟩. REJOIN often implies sharpness or quickness in answering ⟨"who asked you?" she *rejoined*⟩. RETORT suggests responding to an explicit charge or criticism by way of retaliation ⟨he *retorted* to the attack with biting sarcasm⟩.

Synonyms and distinctions with usage examples

Figure 19.1. Example of dictionary entries.

dictionaries, although sometimes in a different order. Notice that *answer* is listed twice—first as a noun, then as a verb.

(a) Spelling, syllabication, and pronunciation

Dictionaries describe both written and spoken language. You can check spelling and word division (syllabication), as well as pronunciation of an unfamiliar word. A key to sound symbols appears at the bottom of each page and also in the introduction. Alternative pronunciations usually represent regional differences.

(b) Parts of speech and inflected forms

Dictionaries identify the possible functions of words in sentences—for instance, *n* for "noun" or *vi* for "intransitive verb." Meanings will vary depending on the part of speech identified. Dictionaries may also identify inflected forms, especially irregular ones: *fly, flew, flown, flying, flies* or *good, better, best.*

(c) Word origin, or etymology

The origin of a word—also called its *derivation* or *etymology*—can be useful in understanding its meaning. It can also lead to an appreciation of the many cultures that have influenced, and continue to influence, the English language.

(d) Date of first occurrence

A date in parentheses (such as *bef. 12c* for "before the twelfth century" in the examples in figure 19.1) is the first known occurrence of the word in written English.

(e) Definition(s)

The order of definitions varies from dictionary to dictionary. In figure 19.1, the oldest meaning is listed first. Often, however, meanings are ordered according to how common they are.

(f) Usage

Most dictionaries give guidance on usage and include quotations showing how the word has been used in several contexts.

(g) Synonyms

Dictionaries always list synonyms and sometimes provide detailed explanations of subtle differences in meaning. When such lists of synonyms are used in conjunction with a thesaurus, they are extremely helpful. Notice in figure 19.1 that the second entry for *answer* lists four one-word synonyms (following *syn*) and provides information about their meanings and usage.

Exercise 3

Study the definitions for the pairs of words in parentheses. Then, choose the word you think best completes each sentence. Be prepared to explain your answers.

1. Sixteen prisoners on death row were granted (mercy/clemency).
2. The outcome of the election (excited/provoked) a riot.
3. The young couple was (covetous/greedy) of their neighbors' estate.
4. While she was traveling in Muslim countries, she wore (modest/chaste) clothing.
5. The president of the university (authorized/confirmed) the rumor that tuition would be increasing next year.

19f | **A thesaurus provides alternatives for frequently used words.**

Unlike a dictionary, which explains what a word means, a thesaurus provides only a list of words that serve as possible **synonyms** for each term it includes. A thesaurus can be useful, especially when you want to jog your memory about a word you know but cannot recall. You may, however, use a word incorrectly if you simply pick it from a list in a thesaurus. If you find an unfamiliar word that intrigues you, look it up in a dictionary before you use it.

Several thesauri are available in print. Among them are *Roget's International Thesaurus* (1999) and *Merriam-Webster's Collegiate Thesaurus* (1995). Most word-processing programs include a thesaurus, and other thesauri are available online. Remember that you must take responsibility for the language you use. Learning new words is beneficial. Using them accurately (see chapter **20**) is essential.

Exercise 4

Review two or three of your recent papers, and look for a word you used frequently. Look up that word in a thesaurus, and then check each possible synonym in a dictionary. Use one of these synonyms appropriately in a sentence, and explain your usage. If you are unable to find an adequate synonym, explain why the words listed in the thesaurus are inappropriate.

Exactness

Make words work for you. By choosing the right word and putting it in the right place, you can communicate exactly what you mean and make your writing memorable. When drafting (see chapter **32**), choose words that express your ideas and feelings. Then, when revising (see chapter **33**), make those words exact, fresh, and natural. Use the words you already know effectively, but add to your vocabulary regularly so that you will be able to pick the exact word that suits your purpose, audience, and context.

This chapter will help you

- master the denotations and connotations of words (**20a**),
- use fresh, clear expressions (**20b**),
- understand how to use idioms (**20c**),
- use the first- and second-person pronouns appropriately (**20d**), and
- compose clear definitions (**20e**).

20a | Accurate and precise word choice conveys meaning clearly.

(1) Denotations establish precision.

The **denotation** of a word refers to what it names, not what it suggests. In other words, denotations are definitions of words, such as those that appear in dictionaries (see **19e**). For example, the noun *beach* denotes a sandy or pebbly shore. Select words that convey your point exactly.

> The Alaskan wilderness is ~~really great~~. [Because *great* can mean "extremely large" as well as "outstanding" or "powerful," its use in this sentence is imprecise.]

astonishingly beautiful

> The speaker ~~inferred~~ that the team attracted many new fans this year. [*Infer* means "to draw a conclusion from evidence," as in *From the figures before me, I **inferred** that the team attracted many new fans this year. Imply* means "to suggest," so *implied* is the exact word for the sentence as drafted.]

implied

(2) Connotations enrich meaning.

The **connotation** of a word is what the word suggests or implies. *Beach,* for instance, may connote natural beauty, surf, shells, swimming, tanning, sunburn, or crowds. The context affects the connotations a word evokes. In a treatise on shoreline management, *beach* has scientific and geographic connotations; in a fashion magazine, it evokes images of bathing suits. Most readers carry with them a wealth of personal associations that can influence how they respond to the words on a page. The challenge for writers is to choose the words that are most likely to evoke the appropriate connotations from their readers in the given context.

> One of the reasons I am recommending Mr. Krueger for this job is that he is so ~~relentless~~. [*Relentless* has negative connotations that are inappropriate for a recommendation.]

persistent

> I love the ~~odor~~ of freshly baked bread. [Many odors are unpleasant; *aroma* sounds more positive, especially in association with food.]

aroma

He gets into trouble sometimes because he is so *innocent*. [naive inserted above, *innocent* struck through]

[*Innocent* suggests virtue; *naive* suggests a lack of judgment.]

 Your ability to recognize connotations will improve as your vocabulary increases. When you learn a new word that seems to mean exactly what another word means, study the context in which each word is used. Then, to help you remember the new word, create a phrase or a sentence in which the word is used in an appropriate context. If you are confused about the connotations of specific words, consult an ESL dictionary or ask a native speaker for help.

(3) Specific, concrete words provide readers with helpful detail.

A **general word** is all-inclusive, indefinite, and sweeping in scope. A **specific word** is precise, definite, and limited in scope.

General	Specific	More Specific/Concrete
food	fast food	cheeseburger
entertainment	film	*Gladiator*
place	city	Atlanta

An **abstract word** refers to a concept or idea, a quality or trait, or anything else that cannot be touched, heard, or seen. A **concrete word** signifies a particular object, a specific action, or anything that can be touched, heard, or seen.

Abstract	democracy, evil, strength, charity
Concrete	mosquito, hammer, plastic, fog

Some writers use too many abstract or general words, making their writing vague and lifeless. As you select words to fit your context, you should be as specific and concrete as you can. For example, instead of the word *bad,* consider using a more precise adjective.

bad neighbors: rowdy, snobby, nosy, fussy, sloppy, dangerous

bad meat: tough, tainted, overcooked, contaminated

bad wood: rotten, warped, scorched, knotty, termite-ridden

To test whether or not a word is specific, you can ask one or more of these questions about what you want to say: *Exactly who? Exactly what? Exactly when? Exactly where? Exactly how?* In the following examples, notice what a difference specific, concrete words can make in expressing an idea and how adding details can expand or develop it.

Vague	She has kept no reminders of performing in her youth.
Specific	She has kept no sequined costume, no photographs, no fliers or posters from that part of her youth. —LOUISE ERDRICH
Vague	He realized that he was running through the cold night.
Specific	He found himself hurrying over creaking snow through the blackness of a winter night. —LOREN EISELEY

As these examples show, sentences with specific details are often longer than sentences without them. But the need to be specific does not necessarily conflict with the need to be concise. (See chapter **21**.) Simply substituting one word for another can often make it far easier for your readers to see, hear, taste, or smell what you are hoping to convey.

I ~~had an accident~~ while trying to ~~catch a fish~~.
_{fell out of the canoe}   _{land a muskie}

Writers use general and abstract words successfully when such words are vital to communicating ideas, as in the following sentence about what happens when a plague comes to an end.

We expect a catharsis, but we merely find a transition; we long for euphoria, but we discover only relief, tinged with, in some cases, regret and depression. —ANDREW SULLIVAN

Abstract words are exact when they are used to express abstractions—such as *spirit, compassion, sacrifice, endurance, freedom,* and *terrorism.* When you use abstract words, make sure you do so deliberately and with good reason.

(4) Figurative language can contribute to exactness.

Commonly found in nonfiction prose as well as in fiction, poetry, and drama, figurative language involves using words in an imaginative rather than a literal sense. Similes and metaphors are the chief **figures of speech.** A **simile** is the comparison of dissimilar things using *like* or *as.* A **metaphor** is an implied comparison of dissimilar things without *like* or *as.*

Similes

He was **like a piece of rare and delicate china which was always being saved from breaking and finally fell.**

—ALICE WALKER

She sat **like a great icon** in the back of the classroom, tranquil, guarded, sealed up, watchful. —REGINALD MCKNIGHT

Metaphors

His **money was a sharp pair of scissors** that snipped rapidly through tangles of red tape. —HISAYE YAMAMOTO

The injured **bird was a broken handled flag** waving in the grass. —TRACY YOUNGBLOM

Single words can be used metaphorically.

These roses must be **planted** in good soil. [literal]

Keep your life **planted** wherever you can put down the most roots. [metaphorical]

Similes and metaphors are especially valuable when they are concrete and describe or evoke essential relationships that cannot otherwise be communicated. Similes and metaphors can also be extended throughout a paragraph of comparison, but be careful not to mix them. (See **23c**.)

Exercise 1

Study the paragraph below and prepare to discuss in class your response to the author's choice of words—his use of both exact and figurative language to communicate his ideas.

[1]A single knoll rises out of the plain of Oklahoma, north and west of the Wichita range. [2]For my people, the Kiowas, it is an old landmark, and they gave it the name Rainy Mountain. [3]The hardest weather is there. [4]Winter brings blizzards, hot tornadic winds arise in the spring, and in summer the prairie is an anvil's edge. [5]The grass turns brittle and brown, and it cracks beneath your feet. [6]There are green belts along the rivers and creeks, linear groves of hickory and pecan, willow and witch hazel. [7]At a distance in July or August the steaming foliage seems almost to writhe in fire. [8]Great green and yellow grasshoppers are everywhere in the tall grass, popping up like corn to sting the flesh, and tortoises crawl about on the red earth, going nowhere in plenty of time.

—N. SCOTT MOMADAY, "The Way to Rainy Mountain"

Exercise 2

Choose five of the items below, and use them as the bases for five original sentences containing figurative language, exact denotations, and appropriate connotations.

1. the look of someone's hair
2. a hot summer day
3. studying for an exam
4. your favorite food
5. buying a car
6. an empty street
7. college athletes
8. a heavy rain
9. a traffic jam
10. the way someone talks

20b | Fresh expressions can capture the attention of readers.

Such expressions as *bite the dust, breath of fresh air,* and *smooth as silk* were once striking and effective. Excessive use, however, has drained them of their original force and made them **clichés.** Faddish or trendy expressions such as *to put a spin on something* and *to think outside the box* have also lost their vitality because they are overused. Many political slogans and the catchy phrases used in advertisements have also become hackneyed. Some **euphemisms** (pleasant-sounding substitutions for more explicit but possibly offensive words—for example, *correctional facility* for *jail* or *pre-owned* for *used*) are not only trite but wordy or awkward.

Clichés are so much a part of the language, especially the spoken language, that nearly every writer uses them from time to time. But effective writers often give a fresh twist to an old saying.

> I seek a narrative, a fiction, to order days like the one I spent several years ago, on a gray June day in Chicago, when I took a roller-coaster ride on the bell curve of my experience.
>
> —GAYLE PEMBERTON
>
> [Notice how much more effective this expression is than frequent references elsewhere to "being on an emotional roller coaster."]

Variations on familiar expressions from literature, many of which have become part of everyday language, can often be used effectively in your writing.

> Now is the summer of my great content.
>
> —KATHERINE LANPHER
>
> [This statement is a variation on Shakespeare's "Now is the winter of our discontent. . . ."]

Good writers, however, do not rely too heavily on the words of others; they choose their own words to communicate their ideas.

Beyond the Rule

CLICHÉS

Some scholars have defended clichés on the grounds that they convey widely accepted ideas in a direct way and can thus help writers to communicate effectively with certain readers in specific rhetorical situations. For information about this position, visit www.harbrace.com.

Exercise 3

From the following list of trite expressions, select five that you often use or hear and replace them with carefully chosen words or phrases. Then, use the replacements in sentences.

EXAMPLES

beyond the shadow of a doubt   *undoubtedly*

slept like a log   *slept deeply*

1. a crying shame
2. after all is said and done
3. at the crack of dawn
4. bored to tears/death
5. in the last analysis
6. avoid like the plague
7. beat around the bush
8. the powers that be
9. in this day and age
10. the bottom line

| 20c | Exact word choice requires an understanding of idioms. |

An **idiom** is an expression whose meaning is peculiar to a community or class or differs from the individual meanings of its word parts. Most academic and professional writing assignments call for the use of idiomatic Standardized English, not unidiomatic approximations. *She talked down to him* is idiomatic. *She talked up to him* is not. Occasionally, the idiomatic use of prepositions can be difficult. If you do not know which preposition to use with a given word, check the dictionary. For instance, *agree* may be followed by *about, on, to,* or *with.* The choice depends on the context. Writers sometimes have trouble with the idioms in the following list.

MASTERING IDIOMS

Instead of	Use
abide **with**	abide **by** the decision
according **with**	according **to** the source
bored **of**	bored **by** it
comply **to**	comply **with** rules
conform **of/on**	conform **to/with** standards
differ **to**	differ **with** them
in accordance **to**	in accordance **with** policy
independent **to**	independent **of** his family
happened **on**	happened **by** accident
plan **on**	plan **to** go
superior **than**	superior **to** others
type **of a**	type **of** business

Many idioms—such as *all the same, to mean well,* and *to pay attention to*—cannot be understood from the individual meanings of their words. Others—such as *turning something over in one's mind*—are metaphorical. Such expressions cannot be meaningfully translated word for word into another language. Used every day, they are an important part of the English language. As you encounter idioms that are new to you, master their meanings just as you do for words you are adding to your vocabulary.

Grammar checkers can find some unidiomatic expressions but will not find all of them. Further, although a grammar checker will not flag a nonsense sentence such as *These books must be broiled in the hope,* it will flag *Is a squirrel in the tree* and point out "*Is* usually begins a question." The problem with this sentence, however, may not be an omitted question mark but rather an omitted expletive such as *there.* You must decide for yourself when and how to correct an unidiomatic expression.

When learning how to use idioms, study how writers use them. The context in which idioms appear can often help you understand their meaning. For example, if you read *I never eat broccoli because I can't stand it,* you would probably understand that *not to be able to stand something* means "to dislike something intensely." As you learn new idioms from your reading, make a list of them, and then use them in your writing. If you are confused about the meaning of a particular idiom, check a dictionary of idioms (see pages 291–292.)

Exercise 4

Write sentences using each of the following idioms correctly. Use your dictionary when necessary.

1. hang up, hang out
2. differ from, differ with
3. wait on, wait for
4. get even with, get out of hand
5. on the go, on the spot

20d | **The use of first- and second-person pronouns can help writers be exact.**

Using *I* is appropriate when you are writing about personal experience. In academic and professional writing (see chapters 41–43), the use of the first-person singular pronoun is also a clear way to distinguish your own views from those of others or to make a direct appeal to readers. However, if you frequently repeat *I feel* or *I think,* your readers may start to feel that you do not understand much beyond your own experience or that you are more interested in talking about yourself than about your topic.

We, the first-person plural pronoun, is trickier to use correctly. When you use it, make sure that your audience can tell which individuals are included in this plural. For example, if you are writing a paper for a college professor, does *we* mean you and the professor, you and your fellow students, or some other group (such as all Americans)? If you are using *we* in a document you are drafting in the workplace, are you intending to include the entire company, your group within it, or you and a specific individual? When drafting (see chapter 32), you may inadvertently use *we* when you are thinking of more than one group of people. You will confuse readers if you move carelessly from one kind of *we* to another. When editing (see **33d**), check to see whether you have used the first-person plural pronoun consistently and, if not, revise or clarify any change of meaning.

Beyond the Rule

WHO IS PART OF *WE*?

Writing specialists have been discussing how the use of *we* can blind writers to differences of gender, race, religion, region, class, and sexual orientation. Readers sometimes feel excluded from works in which the first-person plural pronoun has been used carelessly. For more information about this debate, visit www.harbrace.com.

Using the second-person pronoun (*you*) is a way to address readers. When using this pronoun, be sure that you have specific readers in mind, that you are not using it to refer to anyone outside your audience, and that you are not accidentally shifting from a reference to a single member of your audience to the audience as a whole. Consider your rhetorical situation (see **32a**) to determine if the second-person pronoun is appropriate for the work you are drafting.

If you are not allowed to use first- or second-person pronouns in a particular rhetorical situation and feel frustrated by this restriction, you might be able to relax and draft successfully by giving yourself temporary permission to use *I, we,* or *you.* Later, when revising and editing (see chapter **33**), you can find replacements for these words or eliminate the need for using them.

Exercise 5

Revise the following paragraph to eliminate the use of the first- and second-person pronouns.

[1]In my opinion, some animals should be as free as we are. [2]For example, I think orangutans, African elephants, and Atlantic bottlenose dolphins should roam freely rather than be held in captivity. [3]We should neither exhibit them in zoos nor use them for medical research. [4]If you study animals such as these you will see that, like us, they show emotions, self-awareness, and intention. [5]You might even find that some use language to communicate. [6]It is clear to me that they deserve the right to freedom.

20e | Definitions help establish exact meanings.

Because words often have more than one meaning, you must clearly establish which meaning you have in mind. Definitions of terms help make your writing exact.

> In this paper, I use the word *communism* in the Marxist sense of social organization based on the holding of all property in common.

By stipulating your meaning in this way, you set the terms of the discussion.

A formal definition first states the term to be defined, then puts it into a class, and finally differentiates it from other members of that class.

> A *phosphene* [term] is a luminous visual image [class] that results from applying pressure to the eyeball [differentiation].

You can use a short dictionary definition to define a term or convey a meaning unfamiliar to readers. (See **19e.**)

Here *galvanic* means "produced as if by electric shock."

Giving a synonym may also clarify the meaning of a term. Such synonyms are often used as appositives.

Machismo, confidence with an attitude, can be a pose.

Writers frequently show—rather than tell—what a word means by giving examples.

Many homophones (such as *be* and *bee, in* and *inn,* or *see* and *sea*) are not spelling problems.

You can also formulate your own definition of a concept you wish to clarify.

Clichés could be defined as thoughts that have hardened.

Placing a predicate with a subject that is not logically connected to it is **faulty predication.** (See **23d.**) Combining *is* or *are* with *when, where,* or *because* is often illogical because forms of *to be* signify identity or equality between the subject and what follows.

Faulty   The Internet is when you look at text and images from across the world.

Revised   The Internet allows you to look at text and images from across the world.

Exercise 6

Using your own words, define any two of the following terms in full sentences.

1. collaboration   3. party   5. globalization
2. honesty   4. style   6. terrorism

Conciseness

Using words economically is fundamental to writing clearly because unnecessary words or phrases distract readers and blur meaning. Good writers know how to make their points concisely. This chapter will help you

- make each word count (**21a**),
- combine and simplify phrases and clauses (**21b**), and
- avoid unnecessary repetition (**21c**) and (**21d**).

In some situations, repeating a word or a phrase can be useful. (See **29e** and **31b(2)**.) In most cases, however, repetition is inefficient.

Wordy	In the early part of August, a hurricane was moving threateningly toward Houston.
Concise	In early August, a hurricane threatened Houston.
Repetitious	This excellent baker makes excellent bread.
Concise	This baker makes excellent bread.

21a Every word should count; omit words or phrases that add nothing to the meaning of a sentence.

Many people feel overwhelmed by the huge amount of information that technology has made easily available (see chapters **8** and **37**). You show respect for others by not asking them to read ten pages when five would make your point.

(1) Redundancy contributes to wordiness.

Restating a key point in different words can help readers understand it. (See **39d**.) But there is no need to rephrase readily understood terms. If you do, your work will suffer from redundancy—repetition for no good reason.

Ballerinas auditioned ~~in the tryouts~~ for *The Nutcracker*.

Each actor has a unique talent ~~and ability that he or she uses in his or her~~ acting. *for*

Although they are often small ~~in size~~, women gymnasts are extremely strong.

USELESS WORDS IN COMMON PHRASES

yellow [in color]	circular [in shape]
at 9:45 A.M. [in the morning]	return/refer [back]
[basic] essentials	rich [and wealthy] nations
bitter[-tasting] salad	small[-size] potatoes
connect [up together]	[true] facts
because [of the fact that]	was [more or less] hinting
[really and truly] fearless	by [virtue of] his authority
fans [who were] watching TV	the oil [that exists] in shale

You should also avoid grammatical redundancy, as in double subjects (*my sister [she] is*), double comparisons ([*more*] *easier than*), and double negatives (*could*[*n't*] *hardly*).

Review your adjectival clauses to make sure that they do not include a personal pronoun as well as a relative pronoun referring to the same antecedent.

The drug that we were testing ~~it~~ has not been approved by the Food and Drug Administration.

The principal investigator, whom we depended on ~~her~~ for guidance, had to take a medical leave before the project was completed.

(2) Delete unnecessary words.

Watch for empty or vague words such as *area, aspect, element, factor, feature, field, kind, situation, thing,* and *type.* They may signal wordiness.

Effective
~~In an employment situation, effective~~ communication is essential at work.

If   voters will complain
~~In the event that~~ taxes are raised, ~~expect complaints on the part of the voters~~.

SOME ONE- OR TWO-WORD REPLACEMENTS FOR COMMON EXPRESSIONS

at all times	**always**
at this point in time	**now**
by means of	**by**
for the purpose of	**for**
in an employment situation	**at work**
in spite of the fact that	**although**
on account of the fact that	**because**
somewhere in the neighborhood of $2,500	**about $2,500**

One exact word can say as much as several inexact ones. (See 20a.)

spoke in a low and hard-to-hear voice	**mumbled**
persons who really know their particular field	**experts**

(3) The constructions *there are* and *it is* can often be deleted.

There followed by a form of *be* is an **expletive**—a word that signals that the subject of the sentence will follow the verb. (See 29f.) Because expletives shift emphasis away from the subject, they can result in unnecessary words. They can also be imprecise because they substitute a form of *be* for a forceful verb.

Three
∧ ~~There were three~~ children ∧playing in the yard.
                                were

When the pronoun *it* has no word to refer to and is followed by a form of *be*, *it* also is an expletive.

Learning to ski
∧ ~~It is easy~~ ~~to learn to ski~~.

Exercise 1

Substitute one or two words for each of the following phrases, and use your choice in a sentence.

1. in this day and age
2. has the ability to sing
3. was of the opinion that
4. in a serious manner
5. prior to the time that
6. did put in an appearance
7. located in the vicinity of
8. has a tendency to break
9. during the same time that
10. involving too much expense

21b | Combining sentences or simplifying phrases and clauses can eliminate needless words.

Notice how the following sentences have been edited to make every word count.

> ~~A carpet of blue-green grass~~
> ^The grass was like a carpet. It~~ covered the whole playing field.
> ~~The color of the grass was blue-green.~~

> Some ~~phony~~ unscrupulous brokers are ~~taking money and~~
> cheating
> ~~savings from~~ elderly ~~old~~ people ~~who need that money because~~
> out of their pensions.
> ~~they planned to use it as a retirement pension.~~

21c | Repetition is useful only when it contributes to emphasis, clarity, or coherence.

> ~~One week was like the next week.~~ Each week was as boring as the last.
>
> She hoped Alex understood that ~~the complaint she made did~~
> her comment did not reflect her feelings.
> ~~not mean she was complaining because she disliked him.~~

In the preceding examples, repetition serves no useful purpose; in the following example, it provides emphasis.

> We will not rest until we have pursued **every** lead, inspected **every** piece of evidence, and interviewed **every** suspect. [The repetition of *every* is effective because it emphasizes the writer's determination.]

(See also **26b**, **29e**, and **31b(2)**.)

> **21d** Using pronouns and elliptical constructions can eliminate unnecessary repetition.

Instead of repeating a noun or substituting an inexact synonym, you can use a pronoun as long as the reference is clear (see chapter 28).

> The hall outside the office was empty. ~~The hall~~ _It_ had dirty floors, and the walls ~~of this corridor~~ _its_ were covered with graffiti.

An **elliptical construction** (the omission of words that are readily understood) helps make the following sentence concise.

> Speed is the goal for some swimmers, endurance [is the goal] for others, and relaxation [is the goal] for still others.

Sometimes, as an aid to clarity, commas mark omissions in elliptical constructions.

> My family functioned like a baseball team: My mom was the coach; my brother, the pitcher; and my sister, the shortstop.

As these examples show, parallelism reinforces elliptical constructions. (See chapter 26.)

Exercise 2

Revise the following paragraph to eliminate wordiness and needless repetition.

[1]When I look back on my high school career, I realize that I wasn't taught much about international affairs in the world in spite of the fact that improved communications, the media, the Internet, travel, trading with different foreign countries, and immigration have made the world smaller. [2]Nonetheless, because both international affairs and business interest me,

I decided to major in political science now that I am in college and to study marketing as my minor. [3]There are advantages to this combination of a major and a minor in my job situation at work as well, for I am now currently working part-time twenty hours a week for a company that imports merchandise into the United States and exports products to other countries. [4]Eventually, at some future time, when I have graduated and received my bachelor's degree, I may go on to law school and pursue my interest in politics, unless, on the other hand, my supervisor makes the recommendation that I develop my skills in marketing by spending time overseas in one of the company's foreign offices. [5]The opportunity to work overseas would provide me with a knowledge, an understanding, and an appreciation of the world economy. [6]Such an understanding is essential for anyone hoping to succeed in business.

22 Clarity and Completeness

Clarity in writing depends on more than grammar. Clarity results at least as much from critical thinking (see chapter **35**), logical development (chapter **32**), and exact diction (chapter **20**) as it does from correct grammar. However, grammatical slips can mar what would otherwise be clear writing. This chapter will help you

- use articles, conjunctions, or prepositions effectively (**22a**),
- include all necessary verbs and auxiliaries in a sentence (**22b**), and
- complete comparisons (**22c**) and intensifiers (**22d**).

22a | Articles, conjunctions, or prepositions are sometimes necessary for clarity.

(1) Omitting an article (a, an, or the) can confuse your audience.

The following sentence is ambiguous. Without the indicated revision, it could mean that either one person or two people are standing nearby.

A friend and͜ₐhelper stood nearby.

The indefinite articles *a* and *an* classify the singular nouns they precede. Use *a* before a consonant sound (*a* yard, *a* university). Use *an* before a vowel sound (*an* apple, *an* hour).

The teacher asked me to buy **a** writing journal.

In this sentence, *a journal* is a general term meaning a certain type or class of notebook; it does not refer to a specific journal. Indefinite articles are used for classification in the following common contexts.

- With the first mention of a noun: Use an indefinite article when you introduce a singular noun for the first time.

    I bought **a** writing journal for my English class.

- With the expletive *there:* Use an indefinite article when you introduce a topic that includes a singular noun.

    There is **a** good reason for practicing your English.

- For a generalization: When you are referring to a singular noun in a general way, use an indefinite article.

    A journal is a notebook for you to write in.

If a noun is plural or if it cannot be counted, no article is needed.

Journals are useful.

Writing is an important skill.

The definite article *the* can precede singular or plural nouns. It is used for identification.

The students in the class write in their journals daily.

(Continued on page 320)

(Continued from page 319)

The students referred to in this sentence are identified as specific students. The definite article is used for identification in the following common contexts.

- For a subsequent mention: Once a noun has been introduced, use the definite article to refer back to it.

   I wrote an entry about whales. **The** entry included facts about the size, shape, and color of whales.

- Subsequent mention does not always involve exact repetition of a noun. However, the noun used in the subsequent mention must be clearly related to the content of the previous clause or sentence.

   The teacher grades us on our work, but **the grade** isn't based on grammatical correctness. [*The grade* is close in meaning to the verb *grades*.]

- For shared knowledge: When a reference is to something that is part of common knowledge, use the definite article.

   One teacher asked her students to write about **the** moon.

   The moon is considered part of common knowledge because there is only one and everyone knows what is meant by a reference to it. Other nouns like *moon* include *universe, solar system, sun, earth,* and *sky.*

- For abstract classes: *The* is used with a noun that refers to an abstract class.

   The writer's journal has become a mainstay in the composition classroom.

(2) When conjunctions or prepositions are omitted, clarity suffers.

In sentences like the following example, *of* is often omitted in speech but never in writing.

We had never tried that brand ^of^ film before.

We discussed a couple ^of^ issues at the meeting.

When a sentence has a compound verb (two verbs linked by a conjunction), you may need to supply a different preposition for each verb to make your meaning clear.

I neither believe ^in^ nor approve of those attitudes.

In the following sentence, use a comma when the conjunction *and* is omitted.

Habitat for Humanity built the house, (**and**) then later painted it. [COMPARE Habitat for Humanity built the house and later painted it. (See **12f**.)]

22b | **Verbs sometimes omitted in speech are necessary in writing to clarify meaning.**

When speaking, we sometimes drop—or "swallow"—unemphatic words. If you try to write like you talk, you may mistakenly omit words from your writing because you simply do not hear them. These words are necessary in writing, however, to make your sentences complete.

She ^has^ seen the movie three times.

A grammar checker will sometimes alert you to a missing word, but it will just as often fail to do so. It may also tell you that an article is missing when it is not. You are better off proofreading your work yourself. (See **33e**.)

Providing all necessary verbs eliminates the awkwardness in the following sentence.

Voter turnout has never ^been^ and will never be 100 percent.

Although forms of the verb *be* may not be used in speech, they should be included in writing.

Lamont ^is^ strong and very tall.

In sentences with two short clauses that include the same verb, the second instance of the verb can be omitted (see **21d**).

The storm was fierce and the thunder (**was**) deafening.

Beyond the Rule

SPEECH AND WRITING

Although a good piece of writing sounds fine when it is read aloud, a good speech does not necessarily read well if written down exactly as it was spoken. For more information about how speech and writing differ, visit www.harbrace.com.

22c | **Complete comparisons are needed to convey meaning if it is not provided by the context.**

Comparisons can be completed by words or phrases later in the sentence, by other sentences in the paragraph, or by the context.

He is taller **than his brother.**

Most people think television is more violent **than it used to be.**

Occasionally, an incomplete comparison can be understood by readers.

Craig is exercising more.

Most readers will interpret this to mean that Craig is exercising more than he used to exercise, not that he is exercising more than someone else. However, if there is any chance that a reader could misunderstand a comparison, be sure to make it complete.

Craig is exercising more than he did last season.
OR
Craig is exercising more than the rest of the team.

22d | The intensifiers *so, such,* and *too* require a completing phrase or clause.

My hair is **so** long **that I must get it cut today.**
Julian has **such** a hearty laugh **that we all laugh, too.**
It is just **too** much **for me to try to do.**

When writers approximate speech, they sometimes omit a completing phrase after the intensifier *so, such,* or *too* when it is used for emphasis.

My hair is **so** long.
Julian has **such** a hearty laugh.
It is just **too** much.

In academic and professional writing, *so* and *such* are usually considered too informal. In these contexts, use another intensifier, such as *very, unusually,* or *extremely.* (See chapter 4.)

Exercise 1

Revise the following sentences to make them clear and complete. Some sentences may not require editing.

1. To design the character of Darth Maul for *The Phantom Menace,* Iain McCaig started by sketching a picture of his worst nightmare.
2. He drew generic male face with metal teeth and long red ribbons of hair falling in front of it.
3. This drawing did not satisfy the movie's producer, George Lucas, who asked McCaig to think of another nightmare.
4. Although McCaig always found the painted faces of clowns frightening, he decided to draw masks instead.
5. The preproduction period was such a long time. It lasted three years, so in the end McCaig had time to experiment with designs for both masks and painted faces.
6. Ralph McQuarrie sketched designs for R2-D2 and Darth Vader, including his mask. McCaig wanted to create something scarier.
7. He designed a face that looked as though it been flayed.
8. The evil visage of Darth Maul was so horrible. To balance the effect, McCaig added elegant black feathers.

Effective Sentences

Sentence Unity

Good writing is unified (see **31a**). It is composed of unified sentences that have no unnecessary shifts in structure, tone, style, or person. If you want to write unified sentences, this chapter can help you

- recognize unrelated ideas (**23a**),
- avoid excessive detail (**23b**),
- revise mixed metaphors and constructions (**23c**), and
- correct faulty predication (**23d**).

> **23a** | **Relating ideas clearly in a sentence helps readers understand your meaning.**

Occasionally, a sentence needs more information to establish such relationships as time sequence, location, and cause.

Unrelated	Jason gave his girlfriend a bracelet for her birthday, and she went out to dinner.
Related	Jason gave his girlfriend a bracelet for her birthday, and she **wore it when they** went out to dinner. [The additional information establishes why the bracelet and the dinner belong in the same sentence.]
Unrelated	An endangered species, tigers live in India, where there are many people.

Related	An endangered species, tigers live in India, **where their natural habitat is shrinking because of population pressure.** [The revised clause clarifies the cause-and-effect relationship between the tigers' habitat and their endangerment.]

Exercise 1

Rewrite the sentences to indicate a logical relationship between apparently unrelated ideas. If you cannot establish a close relationship, put the ideas in separate sentences.

1. Firefighting is a dangerous job, but there are many high-tech devices and fire-resistant materials.
2. Wildfires can trap firefighters. Fire shelters are being developed to withstand temperatures of 2,000 degrees.
3. NASA developed Uninhabited Aerial Vehicles. Firefighters need accurate information fast.
4. Firefighters have difficulty seeing through smoke. A thermal imaging camera detects differences in heat and distinguishes between humans and surrounding objects.
5. Opticom is a traffic-control system, so firefighters can get to a fire quickly. They can change a red light to green from 2,000 feet away.

23b | **Choosing and arranging details can make sentences clear and complete.**

Details help you create effective sentences (see **31c**). If you try to include too many details within a single sentence, however, your readers may lose sight of your main point. Include only those details that develop your point.

| Excessive | When I was only sixteen, I left home to attend a college in California that my uncle had graduated from twenty years earlier. |
| Clear | I left home when I was only sixteen to attend college in California. [If the detail about the uncle is important, include it in another sentence. If not, delete it.] |

When considering how much detail to include, remember that lengthiness alone does not make a sentence ineffective. Sometimes you may need a long sentence in which every detail contributes to the central thought. Parallel structure (see chapter 26), balance, rhythm, and effective repetition of connecting words can make a lengthy sentence interesting and coherent. The challenge is to make no sentence more complex than it has to be to fulfill your rhetorical purpose (see 32a).

Exercise 2

Revise each sentence in the following paragraph to eliminate excessive detail.

[1]Shortly before the end of the year 1997, I returned to the place where I had lived for years as a child with my father, mother, and our two cats, an old farm that had been built decades before my birth, which actually took place there. [2]The farm had been passed along by various family members such as my uncle Rick and aunt Louise and later by my cousins Sam and Bernie, who, though they all cherished living there, had done little in the way of upkeep and improvement. [3]The farmhouse had been considered a model of technological advances in 1950, and it was probably coveted by neighboring farmers, but when I lived there with my family, it was in need of paint and repair. [4]Because it was so dilapidated, though not because of our lack of care, my parents decided to renovate it completely, which meant that we had to move

to an apartment in a dreary suburb of a nearby city. [5]The renovation of the house lasted only a year, though it seemed much longer than that, and I remember constantly asking my mother when it would be finished. [6]Still, watching the slow transformation of the house made me appreciate the care that had gone into its original construction, which many people fail to recognize when they look at old houses.

23c | **When revising, writers correct mixed metaphors and mixed constructions.**

(1) A mixed metaphor combines different images and creates an illogical comparison.

Mixed	If you are on the fast track up the corporate ladder, it is best to keep your nose to the grindstone.
Revised	If you are on the fast track to a brilliant corporate career, it is best to keep working as hard as you can.
	OR
	If you are trying to become a successful business executive quickly, you will need to work as hard as you can.

As this example shows, mixed metaphors often include clichés (see 20b), which may be at odds with each other, as in the image of someone quickly climbing a ladder while his or her nose is held against a grindstone. Mixed metaphors are not limited to clichés, however; they can arise when you create your own metaphors if you don't think about what you are asking readers to picture. Every metaphor should be fresh. When revising a mixed metaphor, don't simply remove one cliché and leave another in place.

(2) Mixed constructions are illogical.

A sentence that begins with one kind of construction and shifts to another is a **mixed construction** (see also **23d**). Mixed constructions often omit the subject or the predicate.

Mixed	By practicing a new language every day will help you become proficient.
Revised	Practicing a new language every day will help you become proficient.
	OR
	Daily practice with a new language will help you become proficient.
Mixed	It was a young, frisky puppy but which was generally well behaved.
Revised	It was a young, frisky puppy, but it was generally well behaved.

23d | In a good sentence, the predicate follows logically from the subject.

When drafting, writers sometimes compose sentences in which the subject cannot logically perform the action of the predicate, a problem called **faulty predication.** You can fix faulty predication by changing either the subject or the predicate.

Faulty	One book I read believes in eliminating subsidies. [A book does not believe.]
Revised	The author of one book I read believes in eliminating subsidies.
Faulty	One kind of discrimination is a salesclerk who refuses to help an elderly customer. [The refusal of help, not the salesclerk, is an example of discrimination.]
Revised	One kind of discrimination is a salesclerk's refusal to help an elderly customer.

Subordination and Coordination

24

Subordination and coordination help readers understand the relative importance of different ideas by making the structure of sentences clearer. This chapter will help you

- combine short, choppy sentences (24a),
- revise long, stringy sentences (24b), and
- avoid faulty or excessive subordination (24c).

Coordinate means "being of equal rank." When two ideas are expressed in coordinate structures—in two independent clauses, for example—they are grammatically equal and thus seem of equal importance.

Independent Clause		Independent Clause
SUBJECT + PREDICATE,	Coordinating Conjunction	**SUBJECT + PREDICATE.**
The company was losing money,	**but**	**the employees knew nothing about it.**

Coordinate structures can also give equal importance to words and phrases.

a **stunning** and **unexpected** conclusion [coordinate adjectives]

in the attic or **in the basement** [compound prepositional phrases]

Subordinate means "being of lower rank." Subordinate structures make the ideas they express seem less important than the ideas expressed in the structures to which they are subordinate, regardless of which structure comes first in a sentence. In the following sentences, two facts of potentially equal importance are alternately made subordinate by being placed in dependent clauses.

Dependent Clause	Independent Clause
Although the company was losing money,	**the employees knew nothing about it.**
Although the employees knew nothing about it,	**the company was losing money.**

Notice that when the clauses are reversed, the emphasis changes. The first sentence subordinates the financial problem; the second subordinates the employees' knowledge. In addition to dependent clauses, phrases and appositives are often used as subordinate structures. (See **1f–g** for an explanation of the differences between phrases and clauses and between independent and dependent clauses.)

24a | Subordination can help you combine two or more short, related sentences into one effective sentence.

Short sentences can be effective (see **29h**), but too many of them in a row can make your writing seem choppy.

Choppy   I was taking eighteen hours of course work. I wanted to graduate in three years. Such a schedule turned out to be impossible for me. I also had a full-time job at a newspaper office. I just did not have enough time to finish my homework. I had to make a decision. I had to decide what was important. Was money more important? Or was graduating early more important? I really had hoped to have a degree in three years. Then, I decided to drop a course. That way, I could keep my job. I could also pay for tuition.

Revised   I was taking eighteen hours of course work because I wanted to graduate in three years. However, such a schedule turned out to be impossible for me. Since I already had a full-time job at a newspaper office, I did not have enough time to finish my homework. So I had to decide whether money or early graduation was more important. Even though I had hoped to have a degree in three years, I decided to drop one course so that I could both keep my job and pay for tuition.

When combining related sentences, select the main idea, express it in the structure of a simple sentence (subject + predicate), and use any of the following subordinate structures to relate the other ideas to the main one.

(1) Related sentences can be reduced to single words or phrases.

Choppy   The lake was surrounded by forest. It was large and clean. It looked refreshing.

Better   **Surrounded by forest,** the **large, clean** lake looked refreshing. [participial phrase and coordinate adjectives]

Choppy   Season the ground beef with garlic and Italian herbs. Use a lot of garlic. Go lighter on the herbs. Brown it over low heat.

Better	**After seasoning** the ground beef **heavily** with garlic and **lightly** with Italian herbs, brown it **slowly.** [prepositional phrase and adverbs]
	OR
	Season the ground beef **heavily** with garlic and **lightly** with Italian herbs, and brown it **slowly.** [adverbs]
Choppy	His face was covered with white dust. So were his clothes. The man looked like a ghost.
Better	**His face and clothes white with dust,** the man looked like a ghost. [The first two sentences are combined in an absolute phrase (see **1f(6)**).]
Choppy	Philip's behavior consisted of a series of foolish acts. They were noticed. But they were not criticized.
Better	Philip's behavior—**a series of foolish acts**—**was noticed** but **not criticized.** [An appositive phrase and a compound predicate reduce the choppiness.]

(2) A related sentence can become a dependent clause.

Dependent clauses are linked to main clauses by subordinating conjunctions or relative pronouns. These subordinators signal how a dependent clause is related to the main idea: in terms of **time** (*after, before, since, until, when, while*), **place** (*where, wherever*), **reason** (*as, because, how, since, so that*), **condition** (*although, if, unless, whether*), or **additional information** (*that, which, who, whose*). (See pages 41 and 90 for lists of subordinating conjunctions and relative pronouns.)

Choppy	The thunderstorm ended. Then we saw a rainbow. It seemed to promise a happy future.
Better	**When the thunderstorm ended,** we saw a rainbow, **which seemed to promise a happy future.** [adverbial clause and adjectival clause]

If English is not your native language, be sure to check your adverbial clauses to make sure that you have used a subordinating conjunction rather than a preposition.

My friend lived in Mexico for a year **because of** he wanted to improve his Spanish.

Because is a subordinating conjunction; *because of* is a two-word preposition that should be followed by a noun or noun phrase.

24b | Using subordination or coordination is preferable to stringing independent clauses together.

If you overuse coordinating conjunctions (*and, but, or,* and *so*), your writing may lack emphasis (see chapter **29**) and variety (chapter **30**). Methods of subordination that apply to combining two or more sentences also apply to revising faulty or excessive coordination in a single sentence.

(1) Subordination makes one idea less prominent than another.

When information is strung out over a series of independent clauses, readers may not be able to tell what really matters to the writer. Effective writers usually put what they consider the most important information in an independent clause and place minor points or supporting details in a dependent clause.

In the following examples, the independent clauses are boldfaced; the dependent clauses are italicized. Notice how the ideas expressed in the dependent clauses in the revisions are subordinate to the ideas in the independent clauses.

Stringy | **It was Friday,** and **the crew leader picked us up early,** and **we ate breakfast together at a local diner.**

Better   *On Friday, after the crew leader picked us up
        early,* **we ate breakfast together at a local
        diner.** [one dependent clause and one
        independent clause]

Sometimes, however, the most important information appears
in an embedded dependent clause that is an essential part of the
independent clause.

The weather service announced *that a tornado was headed
straight for town.* [The dependent clause is the direct object of
the sentence.]

Beyond the Rule

SUBORDINATING IMPORTANT IDEAS

Writers sometimes use subordination to draw attention away
from information whose importance they want to play down. For
more information about this strategy, visit www.harbrace.com.

(2) Coordinate elements give ideas equal importance.

The band came back onstage, and the audience was pleased.
[Independent clauses place equal emphasis on the band and
the audience.]

COMPARE The audience was pleased when the band came
back onstage. [Subordinating the action of the band
emphasizes the reaction of the audience.]

OR The band came back onstage, pleasing the audience.
[Subordinating the reaction of the audience emphasizes the
action of the band.]

(3) Choosing precise conjunctions enhances readability.

The meanings of some conjunctions are more specific than those of others. For example, the coordinating conjunction *so* indicates a cause-and-effect relationship better than *and* does.

The rain continued to fall, ~~and~~ so the tournament was canceled.

Accurate coordination calls for precise coordinating conjunctions. Similarly, effective subordination requires carefully chosen subordinating conjunctions. In the following sentence, the use of *as* is distracting because it can mean either "because" or "while."

Because
~~As~~ time was running out, I randomly filled in the remaining

circles on the exam sheet.

When introducing an adjectival clause, do not use *but* or *and* before *which, who,* or *whom.*

It was a large can of olive oil, ~~and~~ which was very expensive.

 In English, connections between clauses are signaled with coordinating conjunctions or subordinating conjunctions but not with both.

Even though I took aspirin, ~~but~~ I still have a sore shoulder.
Because he had a severe headache, ~~so~~ he went to the health center.

Alternatively, coordinating conjunctions, rather than subordinating conjunctions, can be used to connect clauses.

I took some aspirin, but I still have a sore shoulder.
He had a severe headache, so he went to the health center.

24c | **Faulty or excessive subordination can confuse readers.**

Faulty subordination	Chen was a new player, winning more than half of his games.
Better	Although Chen was a new player, he won more than half of his games. [*Although* establishes the relationship between the ideas in the sentence's two clauses.]
Excessive subordination	Some people who are insecure and who act superficially miss opportunities for making interesting friends.
Better	Some insecure, superficial people miss opportunities for making interesting friends. [The ideas in two subordinate clauses are reduced to adjectives.]

Exercise 1

Using coordination and subordination, revise the sentences in the following paragraph so that they emphasize the ideas you think are important.

¹The Lummi tribe lives in the Northwest. ²The Lummis have a belief about sorrow and loss. ³They believe that grief is a burden. ⁴According to their culture, this burden shouldn't be carried alone. ⁵After the terrorist attack on the World Trade Center, the Lummis wanted to help shoulder the burden of grief felt by others. ⁶Some of the Lummis carve totem poles. ⁷These carvers crafted a healing totem pole. ⁸They gave this pole to the citizens of New York. ⁹Many of the citizens of New York had family members who were killed in the terrorist attacks. ¹⁰The Lummis escorted the totem

pole across the nation. [11]They also offered songs. [12]The Lummis don't believe that the pole itself heals. [13]Rather, they believe that healing comes from the prayers and songs said over it. [14]For them, healing isn't the responsibility of a single person. [15]They believe that it is the responsibility of the community.

Exercise 2

Revise the following sentences to eliminate faulty or excessive subordination. Be prepared to explain why your sentences are more effective than the originals.

1. The Duct Tape Guys usually describe humorous uses for duct tape, providing serious information about the history of duct tape on their Web site.

2. Duct tape was invented for the U.S. armed forces during World War II to keep the moisture out of ammunition cases because it was strong and waterproof.

3. Duct tape was originally called "duck tape" as it was waterproof and ducks are too and because it was made of cotton duck, which is a durable, tightly woven material.

4. Duck tape was also used to repair jeeps and aircraft, its primary use being to protect ammunition cases.

5. When the war was over, house builders used duck tape to connect duct work together, so the builders started to refer to duck tape as "duct tape" and eventually the color of the tape changed from the green that was used during the war to silver, which matched the ducts.

Misplaced Parts and Dangling Modifiers

Keeping related parts of a sentence together and avoiding modifiers that do not logically refer to other words in a sentence (dangling modifiers) make your meaning clear to your reader. This chapter will help you

- place modifiers near the words they modify (**25a**) and
- make sure modifiers refer to another sentence element (**25b**).

> **25a** | **Placing modifiers near the words they modify clarifies meaning.**

The meaning of the following sentences changes according to the position of the modifier.

Butch **just** sat down at the table with his hat on.

Just Butch sat down at the table with his hat on.

Butch sat down at the table with **just** his hat on.

The student **who fell** had tried to help his friend.

The student had tried to help his friend **who fell.**

To keep the meaning clear, place modifiers such as *almost, even, hardly, just, merely, nearly,* and *only* immediately before the words they modify.

The flight ~~only~~ costs $\overset{\text{only}}{\wedge}$ \$380.

Drew ~~even~~ spent $\overset{\text{even}}{\wedge}$ his tuition money.

Similarly, prepositional phrases and adjective clauses should be placed so that what they modify is clear.

in the first stanza

Bobby Joe sings ∧ that his heart is broken ~~in the first stanza~~.

Constructions that could modify either of two elements in a sentence should be revised so that they refer clearly to either a preceding or a following element.

The next day he

∧ ~~He~~ agreed ~~the next day~~ to pay what he owed.

the next day

He agreed ~~the next day~~ to pay what he owed ∧.

Exercise 1

Improve the clarity of the following sentences by moving the modifiers.

1. In 1665, Sir Isaac Newton devised three laws about moving objects that are still discussed today.
2. According to one of the laws, an object only moves when force is applied.
3. Once in motion, something must force an object to slow down or to speed up; otherwise, it will continue at a constant speed.
4. Another of Newton's contributions is the law about action and reaction that engineers use to plan rocket launchings.
5. Scientists still use the laws of motion formulated by Newton over three hundred years ago to understand moving objects.

25b | Modifiers that refer to no particular element in a sentence need to be revised.

Although any misplaced word, phrase, or clause can be said to dangle, a dangling modifier is generally a verbal phrase that does not refer clearly and logically to another word or phrase in a sentence. The words in the sentence can be rearranged, or words can be added, to make the meaning clear.

Dangling participial phrases have no clear word to which to refer.

millions of voters listened to

Tuning the television to CNN, the State of the Union speech ~~reached millions of voters~~.

Because they tuned

Tuning the television to CNN, the State of the Union speech reached millions of voters.

Placed after the main independent clause, the participial phrase in the first revision below refers to the subject, but the revision changes the emphasis of the sentence. The second revision clarifies the relationship between the main clause and the modifier.

We passed the

~~The~~ afternoon ~~passed~~ very pleasantly, **lounging in the shade and reminiscing about our childhood.** [shifts the focus to *we*]

while we were

The afternoon passed very pleasantly, lounging in the shade and reminiscing about our childhood. [maintains the focus on *afternoon,* as in the original sentence]

A dangling modifier containing a gerund or an infinitive needs a logical word to refer to. (See **1f(3).**)

Theo was surprised at

On **entering** the stadium, the size of the crowd ~~surprised Theo~~.

a person must read

To write well, good books ~~must be read~~.

Elliptical clauses often dangle because they imply words that are not stated. (See **1g(2).**)

I was

When only a small boy, my father took me with him to

∧

Chicago. [The elliptical clause in the original sentence refers to

father, not to the speaker.]

Sentence modifiers and absolute phrases are not considered to be dangling. (See **1f (6)** and the **Glossary of Terms.**)

Marcus played well in the final game, **on the whole.**

Considering all she's been through this year, Marge is remarkably cheerful.

Grammar checkers rarely catch problems with dangling or misplaced modifiers. A grammar checker identified no problems with the sentences in exercises 1 and 2 in this chapter. Careful proofreading, not the use of a grammar checker, is the best way to avoid problems with modifiers. For more information about grammar checkers, see Using a Grammar Checker on page 2.

E x e r c i s e   2

Revise the following sentences to eliminate misplaced and dangling modifiers.

1. Climbing a mountain, fitness becomes all-important.
2. Having set their goals, the mountain must challenge the climbers.
3. Taking care to stay roped together, accidents are less likely to occur.
4. Even when expecting sunny weather, rain gear should be packed.
5. Although adding extra weight, climbers should not leave home without a first-aid kit.

26 Parallelism

Parallelism contributes to clarity by making ideas that are parallel in meaning parallel in structure. It also gives your writing rhythm. This chapter will help you

- balance similar grammatical elements (**26a**),
- use parallel structures within sentences (**26b**),
- use parallel structures to link sentences (**26c**),
- establish parallelism with correlative conjunctions (**26d**), and
- use parallelism for emphasis (**26e**).

Parallel elements frequently appear in lists or series.

I like **running, hiking,** and **swimming.**

Their goals are **to raise awareness of the natural area, to build a walking path near the creek running through it,** and **to construct a nature center at the east end of the parking lot.**

Parallel elements are often linked by a coordinating conjunction (such as *and, but,* or *or*) or by a pair of correlative conjunctions (such as *neither/nor* or *whether/or*), sometimes referred to as *correlatives.* In the following examples, the conjunctions are in italics, and the parallel elements are in boldface.

She is both **smart** *and* **efficient.** [A coordinating conjunction links two adjectives.]

Whether **mortgage rates** rise *or* **building codes change,** the real estate market should remain strong this spring. [Correlative conjunctions join two clauses.]

To learn *a new language* is **to understand** *another culture.* [Verbals in parallel form are used as subject and subject complement.]

Ideas that are equal in importance should be presented in parallel structures.

We are not so much what we eat as ~~the thoughts~~ we think.
 [*what* inserted above "the thoughts"]

OR

We are not so much ~~what~~ we eat as the thoughts we think.
 [*the food* inserted above "what"]

If elements are not parallel in meaning, you may have to add words or otherwise revise rather than just changing the form of existing words.

His favorite activities are playing golf, baseball, and watching television.
 [*coaching* inserted above before "baseball"]

26a	Similar grammatical elements should receive similar treatment.

To achieve parallelism, balance grammatical elements—nouns with nouns, prepositional phrases with prepositional phrases, adjectival clauses with adjectival clauses, and so on. In the examples that follow, repetition emphasizes the balanced structures.

(1) Balance parallel words and phrases.

I traded **wealth for simplicity,**
  and **smugness for satisfaction.**

The dean emphasized his commitment to **academic freedom,**
$$\text{\textbf{professional}}$$
$$\text{\textbf{development,}}$$
$$\text{\textbf{cultural diversity,}}$$
and **social justice.**

(2) Balance parallel clauses.

Eventually, she came to understand Ted,
> **who longed for love,**
> **who worried about rejection.**

(3) Balance parallel sentences.

When I interviewed for the job, I tried not to sweat.

When I got the job, I managed not to shout.

Making sentences parallel can help make paragraphs coherent.
(See **31b.**)

Exercise 1

Write two sentences that illustrate each of the following structures: parallel words, parallel phrases, and parallel clauses. Use the examples in this section as models.

26b | **Parallel structures help readers grasp ideas within a sentence.**

Repeating a preposition, an article, the infinitive marker *to,* or the introductory word of a phrase or clause can improve the parallel structure in a sentence and clarify meaning.

For about fifteen minutes, I have been stalking about my house,
> hands **on** my hips,
> a scowl **on** my face,

        trying to remember where I put my car keys,
        trying to retrace my movements last night.

The satisfaction came not **from the money**
                but **from the recognition.**

The team vowed **that they would stick together,**
                that they would play their best,
        and **that they would win the tournament.**

26c | Parallel structures can establish a relationship between two or more sentences.

Repeating a pattern emphasizes the relationship of ideas (see **23a**). The following example comes from the conclusion of "Letter from Birmingham Jail" (see **36e**).

> **If I have said anything** in this letter **that overstates the truth and indicates an** unreasonable **impatience, I beg you to forgive me. If I have said anything that understates the truth and indicates** my having **a patience** that allows me to settle for anything less than brotherhood, **I beg God to forgive me.** —MARTIN LUTHER KING

Almost every structure in the second sentence is parallel with a structure in the first. To create this parallelism, King repeats some words and phrases. But the second sentence would still be parallel with the first if some of its words were changed. For example, substituting *written* for the second *said* and *reveals* for the second *indicates* would result in a sentence that was still parallel with the first sentence—although these changes would lessen the impact of the passage.

In addition to using parallelism to establish the relationship between sentences in a paragraph, you can also use it to create a transition between paragraphs by making the first sentence of a paragraph parallel with the last sentence of the preceding paragraph (see **31b**).

26d | Correlative conjunctions require parallel structures.

Correlative conjunctions (or *correlatives*) are pairs of words that link ideas of equivalent importance:

>both . . . and
>either . . . or
>neither . . . nor
>not only . . . but also
>whether . . . or

Readers expect these pairs to be associated with parallel structures.

> *Either* **you pass the final** *or* **you repeat the course.**

> *Whether* **at home** *or* **at work,** she was always busy.

> The team not only practices
> ~~Not only practicing~~ at 6 A.M. during the week, but ~~the team~~
>
> also scrimmages on Sunday afternoons.

OR

> does the team practice   it
> Not only ~~practicing~~ at 6 A.M. during the week, but ~~the team~~ also
>
> scrimmages on Sunday afternoons.

26e | Parallel structures can help you emphasize key ideas.

Although parallel structures could be used to link all the sentences in a paragraph, readers are likely to grow bored with a pattern that is repeated too many times. The use of parallel structures can contribute to emphasis (see **29g**). But if you try to emphasize every point you make, none of your points will stand out from the rest. Using parallelism is especially effective when you are writing the conclusion of a paragraph or of an essay.

The first of the following examples comes from the conclusion of an article criticizing the amount of attention many Americans give to trying to look young; the second is from the conclusion of an essay on cowboys.

> Advances in **science** and **medicine** have come to this: **the tattooing of permanent eyeliner, the bleaching of teeth, the lasering of sun spots.**
>
> —**ANNA QUINDLEN,** "Leg Waxing and Life Everlasting"

> **Because these men work** with **animals,** not **machines, because they live** outside in landscapes of torrential beauty**, because they are confined** to **a place** and **a routine** embellished with awesome variables, **because calves die** in the arms that pulled others into life, **because they go** to the mountains as if on a pilgrimage to find out what makes a herd of elk tick, **their strength** is also a **softness, their toughness,** a rare **delicacy.**
>
> —**GRETEL EHRLICH**

Similarly, parallel structures can be effective in the introduction to an essay or as the topic sentence of a paragraph (see **31a**).

The following example is the first paragraph in a chapter of a book about how advertising affects women.

> **While men are encouraged to fall in love with their cars, women are more often invited to have a romance,** indeed an erotic experience, with **something** closer to home, **something** that truly does pump the valves of our hearts—**the food we eat.** And the consequences become even more severe as we enter into the territory of **compulsivity** and **addiction.** —JEAN KILBOURNE

Contrasting men with women, the author establishes that the chapter will discuss the relationship between women and food. Departing from the use of parallel structures after "romance," the author builds some suspense before introducing her topic.

During this break, however, a degree of parallelism is maintained by the repeated use of "something."

COMPARE While men are encouraged to fall in love with cars, women are encouraged to fall in love with food.

Although this sentence is more completely parallel than the original, it lacks some of the playfulness of that version. The key point is that you can use parallelism effectively without necessarily making every word or phrase parallel with another one. But a break in parallelism should contribute to the effect you are trying to achieve—rather than undermining that effect by appearing to be a careless slip.

Beyond the Rule

PARALLELISM AND POLITICS

Because parallelism helps make ideas easy to grasp and remember, it is frequently used by politicians when giving speeches. Some parallel structures have been used so often that they have become clichés. But others have helped win elections or define important moments in world history. For examples, visit www.harbrace.com.

Exercise 2

Make the structures in each sentence parallel.

1. Helen was praised by the vice-president, and her assistant admired her.
2. Colleagues found her genial and easy to schedule meetings with.

3. When she hired new employees for her department, she looked for applicants who were intelligent, able to stay focused, and able to speak clearly.

4. At meetings, she was always prepared, participating actively yet politely, and generated innovative responses to department concerns.

5. In her annual report, she wrote that her most important achievements were attracting new clients and revenues were higher.

6. When asked about her leadership style, she said that she preferred collaborating with others to work alone in her office.

7. Although dedicated to her work, Helen also recognized that parenting was important and the necessity of cultivating a life outside of work.

8. She worked hard to save money for the education of her children, for her own music lessons, and investing for her retirement.

9. However, in the coming year, she hoped to reduce the number of weekends she worked in the office and spending more time at home.

10. She would like to plan a piano recital and also have the opportunity to plan a family vacation.

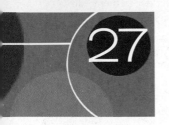

Consistency

Abrupt, unnecessary shifts—for example, from past to present, from singular to plural, from academic language to slang, or from one perspective to another—may confuse your readers and obscure your meaning. This chapter will help you avoid shifts

- in tense and mood (**27a**),
- in person and number (**27b**),
- between direct and indirect discourse (**27c**), and
- in tone and style (**27d**).

27a | **Shifts in verb tense or mood interfere with clarity.**

Verb tense should be kept consistent, unless the actions the verbs are expressing occur at different times. Make sure you do not confuse your readers by switching needlessly from past to present tense or from indicative to subjunctive mood.

Roger **lifted** one side of the table while Betty **lifts** the other. [Both verbs should be in the same tense.] _(lifted)_

If I **were** not so inexperienced and he **was** not so naive, we would have known better. [Both verbs should be in the subjunctive mood.] _(were)_

When using the literary or historical present (see **7b(1)**), avoid slipping into the past tense.

> Hamlet **sees** his father's ghost, **kills** Polonius, and ~~died~~ dies in the final act. [All three verbs should be in the present tense.]

27b | Consistent person and number contribute to ease in reading.

> If ~~a person is~~ you are looking for a job, **you** should have a solid résumé. [Both subjects are in the second person.]

> The **team** is counting on winning ~~their~~ its game. [Both *team* and *its* are singular.]

27c | Shifts between direct and indirect discourse make writing less clear.

Direct discourse is an exact quotation from another source. **Indirect discourse** is a report of what another source says, not a direct quotation from that source. Similarly, a **direct question** is phrased as a question, and an **indirect question** is phrased as a statement. (See also **17b**.)

> My professor told me, "You're late." [direct discourse]

> My professor told me that I was late. [indirect discourse]

> Janet heard that Alex won the contest and wondered why ~~didn't he~~ he didn't tell her himself. [indirect question]

27d | Consistent tone and style make reading easier.

When writers shift tone or style, they signal a different attitude toward their topic or their readers.

It seemed to Romeo, as he gazed up at the balcony, that Juliet's face was as white as ~~a fish belly~~ a lily.

Exercise 1

Revise the following paragraph to eliminate all unnecessary shifts.

[1]In a cool, pivotal scene of *The Fellowship of the Ring*, Gandalf is fighting a Balrog on a bridge in the mines of Moria. [2]He struck the bridge with his staff, the bridge cracks, and the Balrog fell to his death. [3]As it falls, though, you can see its whip curl around Gandalf's legs and pull him toward the abyss. [4]Just before he falls, Gandalf advised the others to "Fly, you fools!" [5]For a brief moment, no one moved; they are too horrified by what has just happened. [6]Not only have they witnessed a death, but they also lost their leader. [7]Then, Aragorn steps forward and tells everyone to "Come! I will lead you now." [8]He showed them the way up long, steep stairs; Boromir guards the rear of the group. [9]If Aragorn were not so clear-minded and courageous, and if Boromir was not supportive, the end of the fellowship would be at hand.

Pronoun Reference

The main rhetorical principle to keep in mind regarding pronoun reference is clarity. This chapter will help you maintain clarity by making sure that your pronoun references are not

- ambiguous or unclear (**28a**),
- remote or awkward (**28b**),
- broad or implied (**28c**), or
- impersonal (**28d**).

Each boldfaced pronoun in the following clearly refers to an italicized noun or pronoun—its **antecedent**—which can be a word group or a single word.

> Nevertheless, the same dedication to family that has always tied *women* to the home today urges **them** into the workplace.

> Our ranching operation keeps *cattle* year-round in the same pastures where **they** are bred, born, and raised.

> *Losing weight* has become more than a national occupation; **it** is a national obsession.

Without any loss of clarity, a pronoun can often refer to a noun that follows it.

> Unlike **their** ancestors, the *soldiers* of today do not travel on their feet.

The meaning of each pronoun in a sentence should be immediately obvious. To avoid confusion, repeat the antecedent, use a synonym for it, or rewrite the sentence so that the pronoun and the antecedent are clearly related.

> **28a** | Ambiguous or unclear pronoun references can confuse readers.

When a pronoun could refer to either of two possible antecedents, the ambiguity confuses, or at least inconveniences, your readers. To make the antecedent clear, replace the pronoun with a noun or rewrite the sentence.

Sue pointed out ~~to Lou that since her~~ *that because Lou's* cat was shedding, ~~she~~ *Lou*

had cat hair all over her suit. [In the unrevised sentence, it is

not clear who owns the cat and who has cat hair on her suit.]

A pronoun may clearly refer to two or more antecedents.

Jack and Jill lost **their** tickets.

> **28b** | Remote or awkward references can cause readers to misunderstand.

If a pronoun is too far away from its antecedent, the reader may have to backtrack to get the meaning. A pronoun that refers to a **modifier** (a word that explains or gives more details about another word) or to another pronoun in the possessive case (see **5b(3)**) can also obscure the meaning. Rewriting the sentence to bring a pronoun and its antecedent closer together or substituting a noun for the obscure pronoun will clarify the meaning.

The **sophomore** *who was not a joiner of organizations* found herself the unanimously elected

president of a group of animal lovers, ~~who was not a joiner of organizations~~. [*Who* is too far removed from its antecedent,

sophomore. See **25a**.]

The Kiwanis Club sells tickets for the **fireworks** ~~on the~~
on the Fourth of July
~~Fourth of July~~ **that** it sponsors. [The pronoun refers to a

distant antecedent.]

28c | **Broad or implied references can make writing vague.**

Pronouns such as *it, such, this, that,* and *which* may refer to a
specific word or phrase or to the sense of a whole clause, sentence, or paragraph.

> The weight of the pack was manageable, once I became used to
> **it.** [*It* refers specifically to *weight.*]

> Large corporations may seem to be more trustworthy than in-
> dividuals, but **that** is not true. [*That* refers to the sense of the
> whole first clause.]

When used carelessly, broad references can interfere with clear
communication. To ensure clarity, make each pronoun refer to
a specific word. Unless the meaning is clear, avoid reference to
the general idea of a preceding clause or sentence.

> When class attendance is compulsory, some students feel that
> perception
> education is being forced on them. This is not true. [*This* has
> no clear antecedent.]

Express the idea referred to rather than merely implying it.

> He wanted his teachers to think he was above average, as he
> his intelligence his
> could have been if he had used it to advantage. [*It* has no
> expressed antecedent.]
> Teaching music
> My father is a music teacher. It is a profession that requires
> much patience. [*It* has no expressed antecedent.]

> **28d** | The use of the impersonal pronoun *it* can result in wordiness or ambiguity.

The use of *it* without a specific antecedent postpones the actual subject of the sentence and can be wordy or awkward.

Trying useless
~~It~~ was ~~no use~~ trying.
 ^   ^

Avoid placing *it* near another *it* with a different meaning.

Staying in the old apartment
~~It~~ would be simpler ~~to stay in the old apartment~~, but it is
 ^

too far from my job. [The first *it* is an expletive (see the

Glossary of Terms); the second *it* refers to *apartment*.]

Exercise 1

Edit the following sentences to make all references clear. Some sentences may not require editing.

1. It is remarkable to read about Lance Armstrong's victories.
2. A champion cyclist, a cancer survivor, and a humanitarian, it is no wonder that Lance Armstrong is one of the most highly celebrated athletes in the world.
3. By the time he was twenty-five, Armstrong was ranked as the top cyclist in the world.
4. Not long afterward, because of intense pain, he sought medical attention, and they told him he had testicular cancer that had spread to his lungs and brain.
5. Armstrong underwent dramatic surgery and aggressive chemotherapy; this eventually helped him recover.

Emphasis 29

You can emphasize ideas by using subordination and coordination (see chapter 24), parallelism (chapter 26), exact word choice (chapter 20), and concise sentence structure (chapter 21).

There are several other ways to add emphasis to your writing. This chapter will help you

- place words where they receive emphasis (**29a**),
- use periodic sentences (**29b**),
- arrange ideas in climactic order (**29c**),
- use active, forceful verbs (**29d**),
- repeat words effectively (**29e**),
- invert word order in sentences (**29f**),
- balance similar grammatical elements (**29g**), and
- vary sentence length (**29h**).

29a Placing words at the beginning or the end of a sentence emphasizes them.

Words at the beginning or the end of a sentence—especially the end—receive emphasis.

> ~~In today's society, most good~~ Good jobs today require a college education ~~as part of the background you are supposed to have~~.

Traffic roared

~~I could hear the roar of traffic~~ outside my hotel room in
Chicago ~~when I was there~~.

As these examples show, you can often make sentences more concise (see chapter **21**) by revising them so that important words fall at the beginning or the end. Sometimes, however, you may need to add a few words to make a sentence emphatic.

Because the semicolon (see chapter **14**) is a strong mark of punctuation, most often used to separate independent clauses, the words placed immediately before and after it tend to be emphasized. Either a colon or a dash also often precedes an emphatic ending. (See also **17d–e**.)

> By "power" I mean precisely the capacity to do what force always does: coerce assent.   **—CYNTHIA OZICK**

> By 1857, miners had extracted 760 tons of gold from these hills—and left behind more than ten times as much mercury, as well as devastated forests, slopes and streams.
>
> **—REBECCA SOLNIT**

Exercise 1

Find the most important idea in each set of sentences. Then, combine each set into one sentence so that the most important idea is emphasized. Be prepared to explain your changes.

1. Snowboarding is a new sport. It debuted at the Olympics in 1998. The Olympics were held in Nagano, Japan.
2. The inventor of the snowboard is hard to identify. People have been sliding down hills on sleds for a long time.
3. Some sources credit M. M. "Jack" Burchet. Burchet tied his feet to a piece of plywood in 1929.

4. Most claim that Sherman Poppen invented the snowboard. His Snurfer went into production in 1966. (The name is a combination of the words *snow* and *surf*.)

5. Poppen created the Snurfer for his daughter. He bound two skis together. He also fixed a rope at the nose.

29b | A periodic sentence can contribute to emphasis.

In a **cumulative sentence,** the main idea (the independent clause, or sentence base) comes first; less important ideas or details follow. In a **periodic sentence,** however, the main idea comes last, just before the period.

Cumulative   History has amply proved that large forces can be defeated by smaller forces superior in arms, organization, morale, and spirit.

Periodic   That large forces can be defeated by smaller forces superior in arms, organization, morale, and spirit is one important lesson of history.

Cumulative   Memory operates by way of the senses, by way of detail, which is the stuff of fiction, the fabric of good stories.   —DAVID HUDDLE

Periodic   In a day when movies seem more and more predictable, when novels tend to be plotless, baggy monsters or minimalist exercises in interior emotion, it's no surprise that sports has come to occupy an increasingly prominent place in the communal imagination.
—MICHIKO KAKUTANI

Both types of sentence can be effective. Because cumulative sentences are more common, however, the infrequently encountered periodic sentence is often more emphatic.

> **29c** | When ideas are arranged from least to most important, the last idea receives the most emphasis.

Arranging your ideas in **climactic order**—from least important to most important—encourages your audience to read the entire sentence. If you place your most important idea first, the sentence may seem to trail off. If you place it in the middle, readers may not recognize its full significance.

They could hear the roar of the artillery, the crash of falling timbers, the shrieks of the wounded.

The applicants relaxed when they saw that she was charming, friendly, and kind.

Beyond the Rule

PLACING THE LEAST IMPORTANT IDEA LAST

Placing the least important idea last can be effective when you are trying to be humorous, as in the following example:

Contemporary man, of course, has no such peace of mind. He finds himself in the midst of a crisis of faith. He is what we fashionably call "alienated." He has seen the ravages of war, he has known natural catastrophes, he has been to singles bars.

—WOODY ALLEN

For additional examples, visit www.harbrace.com.

Exercise 2

Arrange the ideas in the following sentences in the order you consider to be least to most important.

1. Juan is known for his wisdom, humor, and efficiency.
2. He became a social worker because he wanted to understand people, inspire them, and influence them.
3. In his work, he has found that alcoholism destroys families, ruins health, and leads to erratic behavior.
4. His clients include abused children, single mothers, crack addicts, ex-convicts, and laid-off workers.
5. Unless the city invests more money in social services, several neighborhoods will become dangerous, unattractive, and unlivable.

29d | Active, forceful verbs can add emphasis to sentences.

(1) Active voice is more emphatic than passive voice.

Active voice emphasizes the *doer* of the action by making that actor the subject of the sentence. **Passive voice** emphasizes the *receiver* of the action, minimizes the role of the doer, and results in wordier sentences. (See 7c.) One sign of a passive construction is the addition of a form of the verb *to be* to the main verb. The preposition *by* before a noun also often indicates the passive voice.

Active   Sylvia won the race.

Passive   The race **was** won **by** Sylvia.

Active	All citizens should insist on adequate medical care.
Passive	Adequate medical care should **be** insisted on **by** all citizens.

Because whoever or whatever is responsible for the action is not the subject, a sentence in the passive voice is often less precise. It is grammatically correct but stylistically undesirable to write *The requirement was waived.* Such a sentence does not tell the reader *who* waived the requirement. Politicians sometimes favor the passive voice because it allows them to avoid responsibility—by using constructions like *a meeting has been called* and *your taxes have been raised.*

The passive voice is appropriate, however, when the person or thing performing the action is unknown or unimportant to the main idea of the sentence.

Passive	My television set was stolen. [The thief is unknown, or there is a reason to withhold the person's identity.]
Passive	We couldn't watch the Super Bowl because our television set had been stolen. [Given the emphasis of the sentence, the identity of the thief is unimportant.]

Unless they have a rhetorical reason for using the passive voice, effective writers prefer the active voice because it is clearer and more emphatic.

(2) Action verbs and forceful linking verbs are more emphatic than forms of *have* or *be*.

When used without an action verb, forms of *have* or *be* rob your writing of energy and forcefulness. In sentences lacking an action verb, the action is often suggested by a noun or a verbal phrase.

Our college ~~is~~ always $\overset{wins}{\underset{\wedge}{\text{the winner of}}}$ the conference. [The action suggested by the noun *winner* is conveyed more forcefully by the action verb *win*.]

The meat $\underset{\wedge}{\overset{smells}{\text{has a}}}$ rotten ~~smell~~. [The action is more directly expressed by the linking verb *smells* than by the noun *smell*.]

You can ~~be~~ $\underset{\wedge}{\overset{solve}{\text{more effective at solving}}}$ a problem $\underset{\wedge}{\overset{more\ effectively\ if\ you\ understand}{\text{by understanding}}}$ it first. [The verbals (*solving* and *understanding*) contain the action, which main verbs can convey more forcefully.]

Exercise 3

Make each sentence more emphatic by changing passive voice to active (you may have to invent an actor) or by substituting a more forceful verb for a form of *have* or *be*.

1. Both teachers and parents acknowledged that every student has the right to high-quality education.
2. All the teachers in our district will have the responsibility for more students next year.
3. A petition is being circulated to reduce class size in elementary schools.
4. To cover the costs of more students and smaller classes, a tax increase was recommended by the school board.
5. The outcome of a referendum on school funding will be decided by voters in the fall.

29e | Repeating important words gives them emphasis.

Although effective writers avoid *unnecessary* repetition (see chapter **30**), they also understand that *deliberate* repetition emphasizes key words or ideas.

> We **forget** all too soon the things we thought we could never **forget**. We **forget** the loves and betrayals alike, **forget** what we whispered and what we screamed, **forget** who we are.
>
> —JOAN DIDION

In this case, the repetition of *forget* emphasizes how easy it is to forget things, reinforcing the author's point.

When you decide to repeat a word for emphasis, make sure that that word conveys an idea central to your rhetorical purpose. (See **32a**.)

29f | Inverting word order in a sentence provides emphasis.

> At the back of the crowded room sat a newspaper reporter. [COMPARE A newspaper reporter sat at the back of the crowded room.]

> Fundamental to life in New York is the subway. [COMPARE The subway is fundamental to life in New York.]

When you invert standard word order (subject before predicate) for emphasis, you should make sure that the sentence has not become so awkward or artificial that it is difficult to read.

English sentences are inverted in various ways. Sometimes, the main verb in the form of a participle is placed at the beginning of a sentence. The subject and the auxiliary verb(s) are then inverted.

part   aux   s

<u>Lying</u> under the doormat <u>was</u> <u>a house key</u>.
[COMPARE A house key was lying under the doormat.]

part   aux   s

<u>Carved</u> into the bench <u>were</u> <u>someone's initials</u>.
[COMPARE Someone's initials were carved into the bench.]

An adjective may also begin a sentence. In this type of sentence, the subject and the linking verb are inverted.

adj   linking verb   s

<u>Crucial</u> to our success <u>was</u> <u>the dedication of our employees</u>.
[COMPARE The dedication of our employees was crucial to our success.]

In other inverted sentences, the auxiliary verb comes before the subject. Sentences beginning with a negative adverb (such as *never, seldom, rarely,* or *barely*) require this type of inversion.

aux s

Rarely <u>have</u> <u>we</u> experienced such bad weather!

Both the auxiliary and the main verb, in normal order, can be placed before the subject in sentences beginning with prepositional phrases and containing verbs of location.

aux   v   s

On top of the chimney <u>was</u> <u>perched</u> <u>a huge owl</u>.

29g | Balanced construction gives a sentence emphasis.

A sentence is balanced when similar grammatical elements—often parallel independent clauses—express contrasting or similar ideas. (See 26a.) The length and rhythm of different parts of a balanced sentence mirror each other, thus emphasizing the contrast or similarity of ideas.

> Gospel is for the mornings; jazz is for the evenings. Gospel inspires you; jazz relaxes you.

29h | A short sentence following one or more long ones gains emphasis.

Readers often grasp the meaning of a sentence more easily if it is short than if it is long. If all your sentences are short, however, no single sentence will stand out, and your writing may seem choppy (see 30a). To give a short sentence emphasis, lead up to it with a long sentence.

> After organizing the kitchen, buying the groceries, slicing the vegetables, mowing the lawn, weeding the garden, hanging the decorations, and setting up the grill, I was ready to have a good time when my guests arrived. Then the phone rang.

Exercise 4

Add emphasis to the following sentences by repeating words, inverting words, using balanced constructions, or using short sentences after long ones. You may have to add some words and delete others.

1. Wilma Rudolph was in leg braces in 1946. In 1960, she was on the Olympic podium.

2. Rudolph tied the world records in the 100-meter race and the 400-meter relay. She broke the record in the 200-meter race. She also won the hearts of fans from around the world.

3. Some sports reporters described Rudolph as a gazelle because of her beautiful stride.

4. Rudolph's Olympic achievement is impressive, but her victory over a crippling disease is even more spectacular.

5. Rudolph was born prematurely, weighing only four and one-half pounds. As a child, she suffered from double pneumonia, scarlet fever, and then polio.

6. Every day, her brothers and sister massaged her legs. In addition, her mother drove her to a hospital for frequent therapy sessions.

7. Her siblings' willingness to help was essential to her recovery, as were her mother's vigilant care and her own determination.

8. After she recovered, her passions became basketball and track.

9. Rudolph set a scoring record in basketball and an Olympic record in track. She also established the standard for future track and field stars.

10. Since Rudolph's time, other female athletes, such as Florence Griffith Joyner and Jackie Joyner-Kersee, have won Olympic medals and broken Olympic records. Many of them have said that Wilma Rudolph was an inspiration.

30   Variety

Relying too heavily on a few familiar sentence structures can make your writing seem predictable and repetitious. Varying the kinds of sentences you use can make your writing seem lively and distinctive. For example, if most of your sentences follow the familiar pattern subject + predicate + object, varying your sentence structure may help you keep your readers' attention.

This chapter will help you

- combine choppy sentences (**30a**),
- vary the beginnings of sentences (**30b**),
- revise ineffective compound sentences (**30c**),
- insert words or phrases between a subject and a verb (**30d**), and
- use questions, commands, or exclamations instead of statements (**30e**).

Both of the following paragraphs express the same ideas in virtually the same words, both use acceptable sentence patterns, and both are grammatically correct. Variety in the structure and length of the sentences, however, gives one paragraph more rhythm and impact than the other.

Sentences Not Varied

I am going to start with taste. I want you to imagine your first taste of honey or sugar on your tongue. I want you to imagine it as an astonishment. I want you to imagine it as intoxication. I'm thinking of my son's first experience with sugar. It was in the icing on the cake on his first birthday. I have the testimony of Isaac's face to go by. I also know that he was determined to repeat the experience. It was plain that his first encounter with sugar had intoxicated him. He was in ecstasy, in the literal sense of the word. He was beside himself with pleasure. He was no longer here with me. He was in a different time and space. He gazed at me between bites. He was on my lap. His mouth was gaping. I was feeding him ambrosial forkfuls. His expression showed that he was surprised to taste something sweet. He also seemed to want to dedicate his life to eating sweet food. (He has done that basically.) I remember thinking that desire like this is not minor. I wondered if sweetness could be the prototype of *all* desire.

The paragraph becomes much more interesting if sentence variety is employed.

Variety in Sentence Structure and Length

Start with the taste. Imagine a moment when the sensation of honey or sugar on the tongue was an astonishment, a kind of intoxication. The closest I've ever come to recovering such a sense of sweetness was secondhand, though it left a powerful impression on me even so. I'm thinking of my son's first experience with sugar: the icing on the cake at his first birthday. I have only the testimony of Isaac's face to go by (that, and his fierceness to repeat the experience), but it was plain that his first encounter with sugar had intoxicated him—was in fact an ecstasy, in the literal sense of the word. That is, he was beside himself with the pleasure of it, no longer here with me in space and time in quite the same way he had been just a moment before. Between bites Isaac gazed up at me in amazement (he was on my lap, and I was delivering the ambrosial forkfuls to his gaping mouth) as if to exclaim, "Your world contains *this*? From this day forward I shall dedicate my life to it." (Which he basically has done.) And I remember thinking, this is no minor desire, and then wondered: Could it be that sweetness is the prototype of *all* desire?   —**MICHAEL POLLAN**, *The Botany of Desire*

In addition to commands and questions, the second paragraph has simple sentences, complex sentences, and a compound-complex sentence—as well as a sentence fragment (see chapter 2).

Moreover, the sentences begin in different ways and have different lengths. The content remains the same, but now a paragraph about pleasure *sounds* pleasurable. Repetitious sentence structure made the first version predictable; the revision is surprising.

If you have difficulty distinguishing between various types of sentence structures, review the fundamentals in chapter 1.

Although a grammar checker will flag long sentences, it cannot determine whether they contribute to variety. But identifying long sentences can allow you to decide if you have used them effectively. See **Using a Grammar Checker** on page 2.

30a | A series of short, simple sentences sounds choppy.

To avoid the choppiness produced by a series of short sentences, you can lengthen some of them by using subordination or co-ordination to show how the ideas are related. (See chapter 24.)

Choppy   Minneapolis and St. Paul are called the Twin Cities. The Mississippi River is a boundary between them. They differ in many ways.

Effective   Separated only by the Mississippi River, Minneapolis and St. Paul are called the Twin Cities even though they differ in many ways. [use of subordination to combine sentences]

Choppy   Some people study everything on the menu. Next, they ask about how various dishes are made. Then, they contemplate the possibilities for a few minutes. Finally, they order exactly what they had the last time. The idea is to seem interested in food without taking any risks.

Effective   To seem interested in food without taking any risks, some people study everything on the menu, ask how various dishes are made, contemplate the possibilities, and end up ordering exactly what they had the last time. [use of subordination and coordination to combine sentences]

Beyond the Rule

THE VIRTUE OF BREVITY

Occasionally, a series of brief sentences can be used for special effect. For example, a writer may have a rhetorical reason for conveying a sense of abruptness; thus, what might seem choppy in one situation seems dramatic in another. For examples, visit www.harbrace.com.

Exercise 1

Convert each set of short, simple sentences into a single longer sentence. Use no more than one coordinating conjunction in the revised sentence.

1. It was the bottom of the ninth inning. The score was tied. The bases were loaded. There were two outs.

2. A young player stepped up to the plate. This was his first season. He had hit a home run yesterday. He had struck out his last time at bat.

3. He knew the next pitch could decide the game. He took a practice swing. The pitcher looked him over.

4. The pitch came in high. The batter swung low. He missed this first pitch. He also missed the second pitch.

5. He had two strikes against him. The young player hit the next ball. It soared over the right-field fence.

30b | **Writing sounds monotonous when too many sentences begin the same way.**

Most writers begin more than half of their sentences with the subject. Although this pattern is common for English sentences, relying on it too heavily can make your writing dull. Experiment with the following alternatives for beginning your sentences.

(1) Begin with an adverb or an adverbial clause.

Immediately, the dentist stopped drilling and asked me how I was doing. [beginning with an adverb]

Although the company offers only two weeks of paid vacation time, it offers other benefits that appeal to employees. [beginning with an adverbial clause]

When you use email to correspond with someone you are dating, you can get the impression that you are more involved than you really are. [beginning with an adverbial clause]

(2) Begin with a prepositional or verbal phrase.

In the auditorium, electricians installed a new lighting system. [beginning with a prepositional phrase]

To win, candidates need to convey a clear message to voters. [beginning with an infinitive phrase]

Looking south from the top of the Empire State Building, we can still imagine where the twin towers of the World Trade Center once stood. [beginning with a participial phrase]

(3) Begin with a connecting word—a coordinating conjunction, a conjunctive adverb, or a transitional phrase.

In each of the following examples, the connecting word shows the relationship between the ideas in the pair of sentences. (See also **31b**.)

Many restaurants close within a few years of opening. **But** others, which offer good food at reasonable prices, become well established. [*But* is a coordinating conjunction.]

Difficulty in finding a place to park is one of the factors that prevent people from shopping downtown. **Moreover,** public transportation has become too expensive. [*Moreover* is a conjunctive adverb.]

This legislation will hurt the economy. **In the first place,** it will cost thousands of jobs. [*In the first place* is a transitional phrase.]

(4) Begin with an appositive, an absolute phrase, or an introductory series.

A town of historic interest, Santa Fe also has many art galleries. [beginning with an appositive; see **1f(5)**]

His fur bristling, the cat attacked. [beginning with an absolute phrase; see **1f(6)**]

Light, water, temperature, minerals—these affect the health of plants. [beginning with an introductory series; see **17e**]

Exercise 2

Rewrite each sentence so that it begins with anything except the subject.

1. John Spilsbury was an engraver and mapmaker from London who made the first jigsaw puzzle in about 1760.

2. He pasted a map onto a piece of wood and used a fine-bladed saw to cut around the borders of the countries.

3. The jigsaw puzzle was first an educational toy and has been a mainstay in households all over the world ever since its invention.

4. The original puzzles were quite expensive because the wooden pieces were cut by hand.

5. Most puzzles are made of cardboard today.

30c | Varying the structure of compound sentences is often effective.

Writers who draft a series of short, simple sentences sometimes revise them by using a conjunction such as *and* or *but* to turn two simple sentences into a compound sentence. This technique works well if the two ideas are of equal importance (see 24b(2)). Frequently, however, one idea is less important than another; when this is the case, subordination (see 24a) is a creative way to add variety in sentence structure and retain readers' interest. To revise an ineffective compound sentence, you can use one of the following methods.

(1) Make a compound sentence complex.

Compound	Seafood is nutritious, and it is low in fat, and it has become available in greater variety.
Complex	Seafood, which is nutritious and low in fat, has become available in greater variety.

(2) Use two or more verbs with the same subject.

Compound	Marie quickly grabbed a shovel, and then she ran to the edge of the field, and then she put out the fire before it could spread to the trees.
Simple	Marie quickly grabbed a shovel, ran to the edge of the field, and put out the fire before it could spread to the trees.

(3) Use an appositive.

Compound	Matthew Shepard was a college student in Wyoming, and his brutal murder captured national attention.
Simple	The brutal murder of Matthew Shepard, a college student in Wyoming, captured national attention.

(4) Add a prepositional or verbal phrase.

Compound   The snow was thick, and we could not see where we were going.

Simple   In the thick snow, we could not see where we were going.

Compound   The plane pulled away from the gate on time, and then it sat on the runway for two hours.

Simple   After pulling away from the gate on time, the plane sat on the runway for two hours.

Compound   The town is near the interstate, and it attracted commuters, and it grew rapidly.

Simple   The town, located near the interstate, attracted commuters and thus grew rapidly.

Beyond the Rule

REPETITION OF CONJUNCTIONS

Effective writers sometimes add stylistic interest by exaggerating what could be considered a flaw. By using a number of conjunctions in close succession, you can slow the pace and dignify material that might otherwise seem unremarkable. Rhetoricians call this technique *polysyndeton*. For examples, visit www.harbrace.com.

Exercise 3

Revise the following paragraph, using any of the methods for varying compound sentences.

¹Onions are pungent, they are indispensable, and they are found in kitchens everywhere. ²China is the leading producer of this vegetable. ³Libya is the leading consumer, and on average a Libyan eats over sixty-five pounds a year. ⁴One hundred billion pounds of onions are produced each year, and they make their way into a variety of foods. ⁵Raw onions add zest to salads, but they also add zest to burgers and salsas. ⁶Cooked onions give a sweetness to pasta sauces, and they can also be added to soups and curries. ⁷The onion is a ubiquitous ingredient, yet its origin remains unknown.

30d | Separating the subject and the verb in a sentence can introduce variety.

Although it is usually best to keep the subject next to the verb so that the relationship between them is clear (see **1c**), breaking this pattern on occasion can lead to variety. In the following examples, subjects and verbs are in boldface.

Subject-verb	**Great Falls was** once a summer resort, but **it has become** a crowded suburb.
Varied	**Great Falls,** once a summer resort, **has become** a crowded suburb.
Subject-verb	The **fans applauded** every basket and **cheered** the team to victory.
Varied	The **fans,** applauding every basket, **cheered** the team to victory.

An occasional declarative sentence with inverted word order can also contribute to sentence variety. (See **29f**.)

There but for the grace of God go I.

> **30e** | **When surrounded by declarative statements, a question, an exclamation, or a command adds variety.**

When you have written a long series of declarative statements, you can vary the paragraph by introducing another type of sentence: *interrogative, exclamatory,* or *imperative.* (See page 3.)

(1) Raise a question or two for variety.

> If people could realize that immigrant children are better off, and less scarred, by holding on to their first languages as they learn a second one, then perhaps Americans could accept a more drastic change. What if every English-speaking toddler were to start learning a foreign language at an early age, maybe in kindergarten? What if these children were to learn Spanish, for instance, the language already spoken by millions of American citizens, but also by so many neighbors to the South?   —**ARIEL DORFMAN**

You can either answer the question or let readers answer it for themselves, according to your rhetorical situation (see **32a**).

(2) Make an exclamation for variety.

> But at other moments, the classroom is so lifeless or painful or confused—and I so powerless to do anything about it—that my claim to be a teacher seems a transparent sham. Then the enemy is everywhere: in those students from some alien planet, in the subject I thought I knew, and in the personal pathology that keeps me earning my living this way. What a fool I was to imagine that I had mastered this occult art—harder to divine than tea leaves and impossible for mortals to do even passably well!
>
> —**PARKER PALMER**

Effective writers make their sentences exciting without always resorting to exclamation points (see **17c**). As a result, the introduction of an exclamatory sentence can contribute to variety.

(3) Include a command for variety.

> Now I stare and stare at people shamelessly. Stare. It's the way to educate your eye.   —WALKER EVANS

In this case, a one-word imperative sentence provides variety. Because few people enjoy being ordered around, use commands with care.

Exercise 4

Consider how you could improve sentence variety in one of your recent papers. Identify the kind of sentence you use most frequently. Then, revise three of those sentences by using one of the strategies discussed in this chapter.

Exercise 5

Prepare for a class discussion on the sentence variety in the following paragraph.

¹It is too much that with all those pedestrian centuries behind us we should, in a few decades, have learned to fly; it is too heady a thought, too proud a boast. **²**Only the dirt on a mechanic's hands, the straining vise, the splintered bolt of steel underfoot on the hangar floor—only these and such anxiety as the face of a Jock Cameron can hold for a pilot and his plane before a flight, serve to remind us that, not unlike the heather, we too are earth-bound. **³**We fly, but we have not "conquered" the air. **⁴**Nature presides in all her dignity, permitting us the study and the use of such of her forces as we may understand. **⁵**It is when we presume to intimacy, having been granted only tolerance, that the harsh stick falls across our impudent knuckles and we rub the pain, staring upward, startled by our ignorance.   —BERYL MARKHAM, *West with the Night*

Writing

31 Working with Paragraphs

Effective writers know that each individual paragraph enhances the overall quality of their writing. Whether a paragraph introduces, concludes, supports, or advances the main points in a piece of writing, it is an essential unit of information that relates to and fits within the context of all the paragraphs that surround it. Many single paragraphs exhibit specific patterns of development that apply to entire essays (see chapters **32** and **33**). This chapter will help you write

- unified paragraphs (**31a**),
- coherent paragraphs (**31b(1)–(2)**),
- transitions within and between paragraphs (**31b(3)–(4)**), and
- well-developed paragraphs (**31c**).

Good paragraphs create unity, coherence, and clear organization within a piece of writing, just as good sentences contribute to those qualities within a paragraph. (See **31b–c**.) The beginning of a paragraph is indented (or preceded by an extra line of white space) to signal the reader that a new unit of information or a new direction for an idea follows.

31a | When revising, make sure your paragraphs are unified.

When revising the body of a essay, writers are likely to find opportunities for further development (see **31c**) within each paragraph. In addition, each paragraph should be **unified;** that is, every sentence within the paragraph should relate to a single main idea, which most often appears in a topic sentence. After weeding out unrelated sentences, writers concentrate on **coherence,** ordering the sentences so that ideas progress logically and smoothly from one sentence to the next. A successful paragraph, then, is well developed, unified, and coherent.

(1) A topic sentence expresses the main idea of a paragraph.

Much like the thesis statement of an essay, a **topic sentence** states the main idea of a paragraph and comments on that main idea. Although the topic sentence is usually the first sentence in a paragraph, it can appear in any position within the paragraph—or not at all. Sometimes, the topic sentence is implied by information from all of the sentences in the paragraph. If you are new to writing or are making a special effort to improve your paragraphing, you might want to keep your topic sentences at the beginning of your paragraphs. Not only will they serve to remind you of your focus, but they're also obvious to your readers, who will grasp your main ideas immediately. More experienced writers try to avoid repeating the same paragraph patterns; they organize the sentences differently within different paragraphs.

When you announce your general topic and then provide specific support for it, you are writing **deductively.** Your topic sentence appears first, like the one in italics in paragraph 1, which announces that the author will discuss the purpose of topic sentences. (For ease of reference, all the sample paragraphs in this chapter are numbered.)

1   *Topic sentences establish a focus of attention at the beginning of a paragraph.* In a well-designed paragraph, the reader should be able to anticipate what is to come in the rest of the paragraph. Topic sentences orient readers by identifying what the paragraph is about and how it will be developed. When writers stay within the limits they establish, paragraphs are easier to follow. They feel unified, since they don't seem to digress or run off the point.

—**JOHN TRIMBUR**, *The Call to Write*

If you want to emphasize the main idea of a paragraph or give its organization some extra support, you can begin and conclude the paragraph with two versions of the same idea. This strategy is especially useful for long paragraphs—it gives readers whose attention may have wandered a second chance to grasp the main idea. In paragraph 2, both the first sentence and the last convey the idea that the perfect relationship is probably an illusion.

2   *We should not assume that there is a perfect relationship and that if only we could achieve it we would find, at least in this one place in the world, peace and contentment.* Rather, let us start by facing what seems to be a fact of modern life: Relationships are becoming more and more difficult. We might, as suggested, do well to ask why we attempt them at all. Phrased another way, what is loving another person all about? If we dwell on this question, we realize that expecting relationships to be completely free of fear may be the doorway through which fears enter our connections with others, because that expectation is an illusion. It is the illusion of imagining that people are not deeply hurt, that their past has been ideal, that no trauma has touched us, that all of our troubles will disappear once we have found the right relationship. Through this opening fear gets hold of us, compels us to try to make sure we get

what we need from others, and allows us to lose sight of the basic spiritual dimension of relating—that we form bonds to be of help to others, not to ourselves. *We can begin to change this expectation by imagining being in a relationship exactly as we are, with all that we bring, by not expecting the relationship to heal the past, and by working to discover how we can love out of our woundedness.*

—**ROBERT SARDELLO**, *Freeing the Soul from Fear*

As you prepare to revise a draft, try underlining the topic sentences you can identify. If you cannot find a topic sentence, add a sentence stating the main idea of that paragraph. If you find that you open every paragraph with a topic sentence, you might try experimenting with another pattern, revising a paragraph so that the topic sentence appears at the end, as in paragraph 3.

3   I have been to big-money tribal casinos on both coasts and in Minnesota, and they tend to run together in the mind. They are of a sameness—the vast parking lots, the low, mall-like, usually windowless buildings, the arbitrary Indianish décor, the gleeful older gamblers rattling troves of quarters in their bulging pants pockets, the unromantic expressions in the employees' eyes. Also, going to a major Indian casino is so much like going to a non-Indian one, in Atlantic City or someplace, that you may have to remind yourself exactly why Indian casinos enjoy tax advantages non-Indian casinos don't. The idea of Indian tribal sovereignty, a bit elusive to begin with, can fade out entirely behind the deluge of generic gambling dollars. In the last few years, some state and federal legislators have begun to view tribal casinos in just this skeptical way. Their renewed attacks on tribal sovereignty usually include a lot of rhetoric about the supposed great gambling wealth of Indian tribes nowadays. Regrettably, the resentment against Indian casinos, whose largest benefits go to only a few tribes, may end up threatening the sovereignty of all tribes. Many Indians have worried more about loss of sovereignty since the casino boom began. Some say that entering into compacts with the states is itself a wrong idea, because it accepts state jurisdiction where none existed before. Concern for sovereignty has been a main reason why the Navajo have rejected casino gambling. *A Navajo leader said that tribes who accept outside oversight of their gambling operations have*

allowed a violation of tribal sovereignty; he added, "The sovereignty of the Navajo nation and the Navajo people is not and should never be for sale." —IAN FRAZIER, *On the Rez*

Placing the topic sentence toward or at the end of the paragraph works well when you are moving from specific supporting details to a generalization about those ideas, or writing **inductively.** Effective writers try to honor the expectations of their readers, which often include the anticipation that the first sentence will be the topic sentence; however, writers and readers alike enjoy an occasional departure from the expected.

(2) In a unified paragraph, every sentence relates to the main idea.

Paragraphs are **unified** when every sentence relates to the main idea; unity is violated when something unrelated to the rest of the material appears. Consider the obvious violation in paragraph 4.

4   New York has a museum to suit almost any taste. The Metropolitan Museum and the Museum of Modern Art are famous for their art collections. Other important collections of art can be found at the Frick, Guggenheim, and Whitney Museums. Visitors interested in the natural sciences will enjoy the Museum of Natural History. Those interested in American history should visit the Museum of the City of New York. *Getting around the city to visit the museums is easy once you have mastered the subway system.* Part of Ellis Island has become a museum devoted to the history of immigration. Exhibits devoted to social and cultural history can also be found at the Jewish Museum and the Asia Society.

Easy to delete, the italicized sentence about the subway system violates the unity of a paragraph devoted to New York's museums. If the overall purpose of the essay includes an explanation of how to use the city's public transportation for sightseeing, then the writer can simply develop "Getting around the city is easy . . ." into a separate paragraph.

As you revise your paragraphs for unity, the following tips may help you.

TIPS FOR IMPROVING PARAGRAPH UNITY

Identify Identify the topic sentence for each paragraph. Which topic sentences are stated? Which are implied?

Relate Read each sentence in a paragraph, and decide if and how it relates to the topic sentence.

Eliminate Any sentence that violates the unity of a paragraph should be cut (or saved for use elsewhere).

Clarify Any sentence that "almost" relates to the topic sentence should be revised until it does relate. You may need to clarify details or add information or a transitional word or phrase to make the relationship clear.

Rewrite If more than one idea is being conveyed in a single paragraph, either rewrite the topic sentence so that it includes both ideas and establishes a relationship between them or split the paragraph into two.

31b | Clearly arranged ideas and effective transitions make for coherent paragraphs.

Some paragraphs are unified (see **31a**) but not coherent. In a unified paragraph, every sentence relates to the main idea of the paragraph. In a **coherent** paragraph, the relationship among the ideas is clear and meaningful, and the progression from one sentence to the next is easy for readers to follow. The following paragraph has unity but lacks coherence.

5   The inside of the refrigerator was covered with black mold, and it smelled as if something had been rotting in there for years. I put new paper down on all the shelves, and my roommate took care of lining the drawers. The stove was as dirty as the refrigerator. *When we moved into our new apartment, we found that the kitchen was in horrible shape.* We had to scrub the walls with a wire brush and plenty of Lysol to get rid of the grease. The previous tenant had left

behind lots of junk that we had to get rid of. All the drawers and cabinets had to be washed.

Although every sentence in paragraph 5 concerns cleaning the kitchen after moving into an apartment, the sentences are not arranged coherently. This paragraph can easily be revised so that the italicized topic sentence controls the meaningful flow of ideas—from what they saw to what they did:

6   *When we moved into our new apartment, we found that the kitchen was in horrible shape.* The previous tenant had left behind lots of junk that we had to get rid of. The inside of the refrigerator was covered with black mold, and it smelled as if something had been rotting in there for years. The stove was as dirty as the refrigerator. [New sentence:] So we set to work. All the drawers and cabinets had to be washed. I put new paper down on all the shelves, and my roommate took care of lining the drawers. We had to scrub the walls with a wire brush and plenty of Lysol to get rid of the grease.

Paragraph 6 is coherent as well as unified.

To achieve coherence and unity in your paragraphs, study the following patterns of organization (chronological, spatial, emphatic, and logical), and consider which ones you might easily adopt as your own.

(1) Organization helps foster coherence.

(a) Using chronological order, according to time

When you use **chronological order,** you arrange ideas according to the order in which things happened. This organizational pattern is particularly useful in narrations.

7   When everyone was finished, we were given the signal to put our silverware on our plates. Each piece of silverware had its place—the knife at the top of the plate, sharp edge toward us; then the fork, perfectly lined up next to the knife; then the spoon—and any student who didn't put the silverware in the right place couldn't leave the table. Lastly, our napkins were refolded and put

in their original spot. When we stood, we pushed our chair under the table and waited for the signal to turn right. Then we marched outside, single file, while the kitchen staff started to clean the dining room.   —ANNE E. BOLANDER AND ADAIR N. RENNING, *I Was #87*

(b) Using spatial order, according to the movement of the eye

When you arrange ideas according to **spatial order,** you orient the reader's focus from right to left, near to far, top to bottom, and so on. This organizational pattern is particularly effective in descriptions. Often the organization is so obvious that the writer can forgo a topic sentence, as in the following paragraph.

8   The stores on Tremont Avenue seemed to be extensions of my domestic space. Each one had sensory memories that I associate with my mother. On the corner was the delicatessen. From its counter, which was like a bar complete with a brass footrest, came the deeply dark smell of cured meats, the tang of frankfurters, with the steaming background scent of hot knishes on the griddle.

—LENNARD J. DAVIS, *My Sense of Silence*

(c) Using emphatic order, according to importance

When you use **emphatic order,** you arrange information in order of importance, usually from least to most important (see **29c**). Emphatic order is especially useful in expository and persuasive writing (see **32a** and chapter **36**), both of which involve helping readers understand logical relationships (such as what caused something to happen or what kinds of priorities should be established).

In paragraph 9, the author emphasizes the future as the most important site for change.

9   Among the first things Goldsmith had taught the executive was to look only to the future, because, whatever he had done to make people angry, he couldn't fix it now. "Don't ask for feedback about the past," he says. Goldsmith has turned against the notion of feedback lately. He has written an article on a more positive methodology, which he calls "feedforward." "How many of us have wasted

much of our lives impressing our spouse, partner, or significant other with our near-photographic memory of their previous sins, which we document and share to help them improve?" he says. "Dysfunctional! Say, 'I can't change the past—all I can say is I'm sorry for what I did wrong.' Ask for suggestions for the future. Don't promise to do everything they suggest—leadership is not a popularity context. But follow up on a regular basis, and you know what's going to happen? You will get better."

—**LARISSA MACFARQUHAR**, "The Better Boss"

(d) Using logical order, moving from specific to general or from general to specific

Sometimes the movement within a paragraph follows a **logical order,** from specific to general or from general to specific. A paragraph may begin with a series of details and conclude with a summarizing statement, as paragraphs 3 and 10 do, or it may begin with a general statement or idea, which is then supported by particular details, as occurs in paragraphs 6 and 11.

10   It was not the only disappointment my mother felt in me. In the years that followed, I failed her so many times, each time asserting my own will, my right to fall short of expectations. I didn't get straight As. I didn't become class president. I didn't get into Stanford. I dropped out of college.

—**AMY TAN**, "Two Kinds"

11   This winter, I took a vacation from our unfinished mess. Getting back to it was tough, and one morning, I found myself on my knees before the dishwasher, as if in prayer, though actually busting a water-pipe weld. To my right were the unfinished cabinets, to my left the knobless backdoor, behind me a hole I'd torn in the wall. There in the kitchen, a realization hit me like a 2-by-4: for two years I'd been working on this house, and there was still no end in sight. It had become my Vietnam.

—**ROBERT SULLIVAN**, "Home Wrecked"

(?) Grammar contributes to coherence.

In addition to arranging your sentences in a clear pattern, you can also create a coherent paragraph by ensuring that each new sentence builds on either the subject or the predicate of the preceding one. (See chapter 1.) In one common pattern, links are established between the subject of the topic sentence and all subsequent sentences in the paragraph, as the diagram in figure 31.1 suggests.

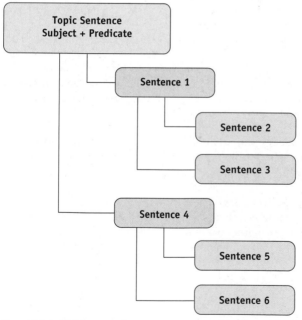

Figure 31.1. Linking a topic sentence to the rest of a paragraph.

Repeating or restating key words and phrases (or using synonyms and pronouns) is one grammatical way to build coherence in paragraphs. Note how many of the sentences in paragraph 12 refer back to *never*, the subject of the topic sentence.

12   ***Never*** is the most powerful word in the English language, or perhaps any language. It's magic. Every time I have made an emphatic pronouncement invoking the word ***never***, whatever follows that I don't want to happen happens. **Never** has made a fool of me many times. The first time I remember noticing the powerful effect of this word I was a student at Indian school. My best friend, Belinda Gonzalez, and I were filling out our schedules for spring semester. She was Blackfeet, a voice major from Yakima, Washington. I was a painting major and checking out times for painting and drawing courses. She suggested I sign up for drama class with her. I said no, I will **never** get on a stage. Despite my initial protest I did sign up for drama class and soon was performing in one of the first all-native drama and dance troupes in the country, and now I make my living performing. **Never** is that powerful.   —JOY HARJO, "The Power of Never"

You can also link each new sentence to the preceding one by linking predicates or, as Annie Dillard does in paragraph 13, by creating links through both subjects and predicates.

13   Sir Robert Falcon Scott, who died on the Antarctic peninsula, was never able to bring himself to use dogs, let alone feed them to each other or eat them. Instead he struggled with English ponies, for whom he carried hay. Scott felt that eating dogs was inhumane; he also felt, as he himself wrote, that when men reach a Pole unaided, their journey has "a fine conception" and "the conquest is more nobly and splendidly won." It is this loftiness of sentiment, this purity, this dignity and self-control, which makes Scott's farewell letters—found under his body—such moving documents.

Subject Links	Predicate Links
Sir Robert Falcon **Scott,** who died on the Antarctic peninsula,	was never able to bring himself **to use dogs,** let alone feed them to each other or **eat them.**
Instead *he*	struggled with English ponies, for whom he carried hay.
Scott felt that **eating dogs**	was inhumane;
he also felt, as he himself wrote, that when men reach a Pole unaided, their journey	has "a fine conception" and "the conquest is more nobly and splendidly won."
It is this **loftiness of sentiment, this purity, this dignity and self-control,**	which makes Scott's farewell letters—found under his body—such moving documents.

—ANNIE DILLARD, "An Expedition to the Pole"

(3) Transitions improve coherence within and between paragraphs.

Sentences can be arranged in a seemingly clear sequence, but a single paragraph may lack internal coherence and a series of paragraphs may lack overall coherence if transitions are abrupt or nonexistent. When revising your writing, you can improve the coherence by using transitional elements such as pronouns, repetition, conjunctions, transitional phrases, and parallel structure.

(a) Pronouns help establish links between sentences.

In paragraph 14, the writer explains the similarities of identical twins raised separately. She mentions their names only once, but uses the pronouns *both, their,* and *they* to keep the reference to the twins always clear.

14   Jim Springer and Jim Lewis were adopted as infants into working-class Ohio families. **Both** liked math and did not like spelling in school. **Both** had law enforcement training and worked part-time as deputy sheriffs. **Both** vacationed in Florida, **both** drove Chevrolets. Much has been made of the fact that **their** lives are marked by a trail of similar names. **Both** married and divorced women named Linda and had second marriages with women named Betty. **They** named **their** sons James Allan and James Alan, respectively. **Both** like mechanical drawing and carpentry. **They** have almost identical drinking and smoking patterns. **Both** chew their fingernails down to the nubs.

—**CONSTANCE HOLDEN**, "Identical Twins Reared Apart"

(b) Repetition of words, phrases, or ideas can link a sentence to those that precede it.

In paragraph 15, the repetition of the key word *wave* links the sentences and also provides emphasis. (See **29e**.)

15   The weekend is over, and we drive down the country road from the cottage to the pier, passing out our last supply of **waves.** We **wave** at people walking and **wave** at people riding. We **wave** at people we know and **wave** at people who are strangers.

—**ELLEN GOODMAN**, "Waving Goodbye to the Country"

Repeating a key word and using parallel constructions (see chapter **26**) are other common ways of establishing transitions between paragraphs, as in paragraphs 16 and 17.

16   I want a **wife** who will take care of *my* physical needs. I want a **wife** who will keep my house clean. A **wife** who will pick up after my children, a **wife** who will pick up after me. I want a **wife** who will keep my clothes clean, ironed, mended, replaced when

need be, and who will see to it that my personal things are kept in their proper place so that I can find what I need the minute I need it. I want a **wife** who cooks the meals, a **wife** who is a *good cook*. I want a **wife** who will plan the menus, do the necessary grocery shopping, prepare the meals, serve them pleasantly, and then do the cleaning up while I do my studying. I want a **wife** who will care for me when I am sick and sympathize with my pain and loss of time from school. I want a **wife** to go along when our family takes a vacation so that someone can continue to care for me and my children when I need a rest and change of scene.

17   I want a **wife** who will not bother me with rambling complaints about a **wife's** duties. But I want a **wife** who will listen to me when I feel the need to explain a rather difficult point I have come across in my course of studies. And I want a **wife** who will type my papers for me when I have written them.

—**JUDY BRADY**, "I Want a Wife"

In this case, the author wished to stress the expectations many people have about the role of a wife; by using *wife* fourteen times, she emphasizes how many details of a comfortable domestic life are often attended to by the wife.

(c) Conjunctions and other transitional words or phrases also contribute to coherence.

Conjunctions and transitional words or phrases demonstrate the logical relationship between ideas. In the following sentences, in which two clauses are linked by different conjunctions, notice the subtle changes in the relationship between the two ideas.

He laughed, **and** she frowned.

He laughed **while** she frowned.

He laughed **because** she frowned.

He laughed, **so** she frowned.

He laughed; **later** she frowned.

The following list of frequently used transitional connections, arranged according to the kinds of relationships they establish, can help you with your critical reading as well as your writing.

TYPES OF TRANSITIONAL CONNECTIONS

Alternative	or, nor, and, and then, moreover, besides
Addition	further, furthermore, likewise, also, too, again, in addition, even more important, next, first, second, third, in the first place, in the second place, finally, last
Comparison	similarly, likewise, in like manner
Contrast	but, yet, or, and yet, however, still, nevertheless, on the other hand, on the contrary, conversely, even so, notwithstanding, in contrast, at the same time, although this may be true, otherwise, nonetheless
Place	here, beyond, nearby, opposite to, adjacent to, on the opposite side
Purpose	to this end, for this purpose, with this object, in order to
Result or cause	so, for, therefore, accordingly, consequently, thus, thereupon, as a result, then, because, hence
Summary	to sum up, in brief, on the whole, in sum, in short, in any event
Repetition	as I have said, in other words, that is, to be sure, as has been noted
Exemplification	for example, for instance, to show, to see, to understand, in the case of
Intensification	in fact, indeed, to tell the truth
Time	meanwhile, at length, soon, after a few days, in the meantime, afterward, later, now, then, in the past, while

(d) Coherence can also be achieved through the use of parallel structures.

Parallelism is a key principle in writing coherent sentences and paragraphs. (See chapter 26.)

> Human beings are more alike than unalike, and what is true anywhere is true everywhere, yet I encourage travel to as many destinations as possible for the sake of education as well as pleasure.
>
> —**MAYA ANGELOU**, *Wouldn't Take Nothing for My Journey Now*

(e) Transitions establish the relationship between paragraphs.

Transitions between paragraphs are as important as transitions between sentences and are achieved by many of the same devices: repetition of words or ideas and use of conjunctions, transitional phrases, and parallel structures. Such devices are often evident in the first sentence of a paragraph.

One of the easiest ways to create a transition is to repeat a word or an idea from the last paragraph in the first sentence of the new one, as in paragraphs 18 and 19 (italics added to highlight the repetition).

18   For those who pray or chant with great perseverance, there is the suggestion that their *waiting* has been converted into purposefulness.

19   Of course, we do not just *wait* for love; we *wait* for money, we *wait* for the weather to get warmer, colder; we *wait* for the plumber to come and fix the washing machine . . . .

> —**EDNA O'BRIEN**, "Waiting"

Paragraphs 20 and 21 show how you can use a transitional phrase (italicized) to connect paragraphs.

20   Children need help in becoming civic-minded citizens of the digital age, in figuring out how to use the machinery in the service of some broader social purpose than simple entertainment. They need guidance in managing their new ability to connect instantly

with other cultures. They need reminders about how to avoid the dangers of elitism and arrogance.

21   But *more than anything else,* it's time to extend to children the promise of the fundamental idea that Locke, Thomas Paine, Thomas Jefferson, and others introduced to the world three centuries ago: That everyone has rights. That everyone should be given as great a measure of freedom as possible. That all should get the opportunity to rise to the outer limits of their potential.

—JON KATZ, "The Rights of Kids in the Digital Age"

You can use parallel structures to establish relationships between paragraphs, as in paragraphs 22 and 23.

22   I understood that when I graduated
           I would get a job at *Glamour* or *Mademoiselle*
              where I would meet a dashing young lawyer,
                 fall in love,
                 get married,
                 have 2.5 children, and
                 play bridge all day
                    like my mother did.
           But the Sixties gave me new goals.
23   I discovered that when I married,
           I had to keep my job at *Rolling Stone*
              where I met my unemployable poet-husband,
                 got promoted,
                 had 1 child, and
                 did the housework late at night
                    like my mother's maid had.

—SUSAN ALLEMEIR, "Divorcaversarey"

Sometimes a transitional paragraph serves as a bridge between two paragraphs, as paragraph 25 does for 24 and 26. Ordinarily, such a paragraph is short (often consisting of only one sentence) because the writer intends it to be merely a signpost.

24   I'd met him, and his girlfriend, at a Valentine's party given by a mutual friend. For months I had arisen at dawn each Saturday and

Sunday to bike fourteen miles across the busy city to reach his house. I spent the day with him and rode back. He came to visit me in his car (a souped-up, cherry red GTO in need of a new muffler—I heard the muffler's growl two blocks distant and my heart executed an involuntary backflip). After he left, I lectured myself. *I'm in control. We're just friends.*

25   Then he began to visit my dreams.

26   Too many of these dreams and I biked fourteen miles to his house, then invited him to go on a bike ride. I rode as far as we could go and farther to exhaust myself and him, and when I had ridden past exhaustion I found I was still driven by the energy of love and I sat down and said, "There's something I have to tell you. Something you ought to know."

—**FENTON JOHNSON**, *Geography of the Heart*

31c | Draft your essay by writing well-developed paragraphs

You compose a draft by developing the paragraphs that will constitute the essay as a whole. If you are working from an outline, especially a topic or sentence outline (see **32d**), you can anticipate the number of paragraphs you will probably write and what you hope to accomplish in each paragraph. If you are working from an informal working plan (see **32d**), you will have a sense of where you want to take your ideas but may be uncertain about the number and nature of the paragraphs you will need. In both cases, however, you need to develop each paragraph fully and then ask yourself whether any additional paragraphs (or additional supporting information within any paragraph) would help your audience understand the main idea of your essay.

Paragraphs have no set length. Typically, they range from 50 to 250 words, and paragraphs in books are usually longer than those in newspapers and magazines. There are certainly times when a long paragraph makes for rich reading, as well as times when a long paragraph exhausts a single minor point, combines too many points, or becomes repetitive. On the other hand, short, one-sentence paragraphs can be effectively used for emphasis (see chapter **29**) or to establish transition (see **31b**). Short paragraphs can also, however, indicate inadequate development. There will be times when you can combine two short paragraphs as you revise (see chapter **33**), but there will be many more occasions when you need to lengthen a short paragraph by developing it with specific details or examples.

Experienced writers don't worry much about paragraph length; rather, they concentrate on getting words on the paper or on the screen, knowing that all paragraphs can be shortened, lengthened, merged, or otherwise improved later in the writing process. So think of revising and developing your paragraphs as a luxury, an opportunity to articulate exactly what you want to say without anyone interrupting you—or changing the subject.

(1) You can develop a paragraph with details.

A good paragraph gives readers something to think about. You will disappoint them if you end a paragraph too soon. Consider paragraph 27.

27   My liberated hair made me happy. No longer was I addicted to the beauty shop; I was charmed by my own creativity with my own hair—no Korean-hair extensions, no relaxers, no dyes.

This paragraph is short, and it promises details that remain unmentioned: How exactly did her hair make the writer happy? What had happened at the beauty shop? How exactly did the writer's hair show off her creativity?

Now consider a well-developed paragraph by Alice Walker.

28   *I stood in front of the mirror and looked at myself and laughed.* My hair was one of those odd, amazing, unbelievable, stop-you-in-

your-tracks creations—not unlike a zebra's stripes, an armadillo's ears, or the feet of the electric-blue-footed boobie—that the Universe makes for no reason other than to express its own limitless imagination. I realized I had never been given the opportunity to appreciate hair for its true self. That it did, in fact, have one. I remembered years of enduring hairdressers—from my mother onward—doing missionary work on my hair. They dominated, suppressed, controlled. Now, more or less free, it stood this way and that. I would call up my friends around the country to report on its antics. It never thought of lying down. Flatness, the missionary position, did not interest it. It grew. Being short, cropped off near the root, another missionary "solution," did not interest it either. It sought more and more space, more light, more of itself. It loved to be washed; but that was it.

—**ALICE WALKER**, "Oppressed Hair Puts a Ceiling on the Brain"

Notice how the series of details in paragraph 28 supports the main idea (italicized), the topic sentence (see **31a**). Readers can easily see how one sentence leads into the next, creating a clear picture of the hair being described.

(2) You can develop a paragraph by providing examples.

Like details, examples contribute to paragraph development by making specific what otherwise might seem general and hard to grasp. Details describe a person, place, or thing; examples illustrate an idea with information that can come from different times and places. Both details and examples support your ideas in terms of the rhetorical situation. (See **36d**.)

The author of paragraph 29 uses several closely related examples (as well as details) to support the main idea with which he begins.

29 *Illiterates live, in more than literal ways, an uninsured existence.* They cannot understand the written details on a health insurance form. They cannot read the waivers that they sign preceding surgical procedures. Several women I have known in Boston have entered a slum hospital with the intention of obtaining a tubal

ligation and have emerged a few days later after having been sub-
jected to a hysterectomy. Unaware of their rights, incognizant of
jargon, intimidated by the unfamiliar air of fear and atmosphere of
ether that so many of us find oppressive in the confines even of the
most attractive and expensive medical facilities, they have signed
their names to documents they could not read and which nobody,
in the hectic situation that prevails so often in those overcrowded
hospitals that serve the urban poor, had even bothered to explain.

—**JONATHAN KOZOL**, "The Human Cost of an Illiterate Society"

You can also use one striking example, as in paragraph 30, to illustrate your main idea.

30   Glamour's lethal effect on the psyche is also caught in the language that commonly describes its impact: "dressed to kill," "dev-
astating," "shattering," "stunning," "knockout," "to die for."
Perhaps it's not surprising that Rita Hayworth's famous pinup pose
in which she's kneeling in a silk negligee on satin sheets was taped
to the bomb that was dropped on Hiroshima.

—**JOHN LAHR**, "The Voodoo of Glamour"

When revising an essay, you must consider the effectiveness
of the individual paragraphs at the same time as you consider
how those paragraphs work (or don't work) together to achieve
the overall purpose. Some writers like to revise at the paragraph
level before addressing larger concerns; other writers cannot
work on the individual paragraphs until they have grappled
with larger issues related to the rhetorical situation (overall purpose, attention to audience, and context; see **32a**) or have fi-
nalized their thesis (**32c**). All experienced writers use a process
to write, but they do not all use exactly the same process. Since
there's no universal predetermined order to the writing process,
you can follow whichever steps work best for you at the time
you are revising. Be guided by the principles and strategies discussed in this chapter, but trust also in your own good sense.

The following checklist can guide you in revising your paragraphs.

> **CHECKLIST for Revising Paragraphs**
>
> - Does the paragraph have a clear topic sentence (31a)? Does it need one?
> - Do all the ideas in the paragraph belong together? Do sentences link to previous and later ones? Are the sentences arranged in chronological, spatial, emphatic, or logical order? Or are they arranged in some other pattern (31a)?
> - Are sentences connected to each other with effective transitions (31b)? What transitions are used?
> - How does the paragraph link to the preceding and following ones (31b)?
> - Is the paragraph adequately developed? How do you know? What idea or detail might be missing (31c)? What rhetorical methods have been used to develop each of the paragraphs (32e)?

Exercise 1

Examine some of your own writing—such as an essay you have recently drafted or entries in your journal—and select one paragraph that holds potential interest. Revise the original paragraph, developing it with additional details or examples.

32 Planning and Drafting Essays

Experienced writers understand that writing is a process. Think of the writing you do out of school, and you'll realize how experienced in that process you already are. When you make a gift-giving list, for example, you consider the recipients, the gift ideas, and the appropriateness of each gift for the occasion; then, while you shop, you may cross off some items, move some around, add new ones, and make annotations. Whether in or out of school, you continually consider your purpose, audience, and context. You revise and edit what you write (see chapter 33).

This chapter will help you

- understand the rhetorical situation (**32a**),
- find good topics (**32b(1)**),
- focus your ideas (**32b(2)**),
- write a clear thesis statement (**32c**),
- organize your ideas (**32d**),
- use various strategies to develop an essay (**32e**), and
- write a first draft (**32f**).

Effective writers begin any writing project by focusing on these steps one at a time. As they work, they may revisit an earlier stage of the writing process at the same time as they begin working on the next stage. They know that the stages are sometimes separate and sometimes overlapping.

As you plan and draft an essay, you may need to return to a specific activity several times. Experienced writers expect the writing process to provoke new ideas and to reveal places that need improving. (See chapter 33.)

32a | **Critical readers and effective writers understand the rhetorical situation.**

Critical readers and effective writers have a clear sense of the **rhetorical situation,** that is, the context for which they are interpreting a reading or creating a piece of writing. Components of the rhetorical situation are the sender (or writer), the receiver (intended audience or reader), the message itself, and the context (see figure 32.1). The sender's purpose arises out of the particular rhetorical situation. As you read and write, then, you'll want to consider the following issues:

- The nature and the receptiveness of the intended **audience,** whoever will be reading the piece of writing

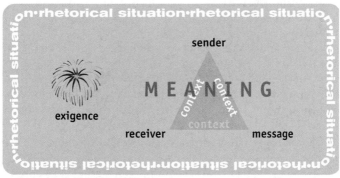

Figure 32.1. The rhetorical situation.

- The author's relationship with that audience, the writer's **credibility** as an author
- The particular need or situation that inspires this piece of writing, also called the **exigence**
- The author's goal, or **purpose,** what the author hopes to achieve in a piece of writing
- The **message,** the contents and delivery of the piece of writing itself
- Whatever else (opposing or supporting views) has already been said on the subject, part of the **context.** When and where (and through what medium) the exchange between writer and reader takes place are also part of the context.

(1) *Purpose* means your reason for writing.

The clearer your purpose, the better your writing is likely to be. To clarify your purpose, it helps to ask yourself whether you want to

- express how you feel about something,
- create a mood,
- amuse or entertain,
- report information,
- explain or evaluate the significance of information,
- analyze a situation,
- clarify a point or situation, or
- argue a point or argue for or against a course of action.

Depending on the overall purpose, writing can be described as expressive, expository, or argumentative. Any of these types of writing can be used to help you fulfill your overall purpose.

Expressive writing emphasizes the writer's feelings and reactions to people, objects, events, and ideas. The following example (paragraph 1) comes from an essay designed to convey how the author feels about the relationship he had with his father. (For ease of reference, each of the sample paragraphs in this chapter is numbered.)

1   At just about the hour when my father died, soon after dawn one February morning when ice coated the windows like cataracts, I banged my thumb with a hammer. Naturally I swore at the hammer, the reckless thing, and in the moment of swearing I thought of what my father would say: "If you'd try hitting the nail it would go in a whole lot faster. Don't you know your thumb's not as hard as that hammer?" We were both doing carpentry that day, but far apart. He was building cupboards at my brother's place in Oklahoma; I was at home in Indiana putting up a wall in the basement to make a bedroom for my daughter. By the time my mother called with the news of his death—the long distance wires whittling her voice until it seemed too thin to bear the weight of what she had to say—my thumb was swollen. A week or two later a white scar in the shape of a crescent moon began to show above the cuticle, and month by month it rose across the pink sky of my thumbnail. It took the better part of a year for the scar to disappear, and every time I noticed it I thought of my father.
                            —**SCOTT RUSSELL SANDERS**, "The Inheritance of Tools"

Expository writing focuses on objects, events, or ideas, rather than on the writer's feelings about them. When you report, explain, clarify, or evaluate, you are practicing exposition. Paragraph 2 comes from an essay that explains how paleoanthropologists—in this case, a paleoanthropologist named Mac—discover their prizes.

2   Searching only in the most promising areas isn't the key to [Mac's] success; perseverance is. He walks the same territory over and over again, changing courses around obstacles, and he tells his people to do the same. If you walked to the left around this bush yesterday, then walk to the right today. If you walked into the sun yesterday, then walk with the sun at your back today. And most of all, walk, walk, walk, and *look* while you are doing it. Don't daydream; don't scan the horizon for shade; ignore the burning sun even when the temperature reaches 135°F. Keep your eyes on the ground searching for that elusive sliver of bone or gleaming tooth that is not just any old animal, fossilized and turning to rubble, but a hominid. Those are the prizes we seek; those are the messengers from the past.
                            —**ALAN WALKER AND PAT SHIPMAN**, *The Wisdom of the Bones*

Argumentative writing is intended to influence the reader's attitudes and actions. Most writing is to some extent an argument; however, writing is usually called argumentative if it clearly supports a specific position (see chapter 36). In paragraph 3, note how the author calls for students to claim their own educations.

3   The first thing I want to say to you who are students, is that you cannot afford to think of being here to *receive* an education; you will do much better to think of yourselves as being here to *claim* one. One of the dictionary definitions of the verb "to claim" is: *to take as the rightful owner; to assert in the face of possible contradiction.* "To receive" is *to come into possession of; to act as receptacle or container for; to accept as authoritarian or true.* The difference is that between acting and being acted-upon, and . . . it can literally mean the difference between life and death.
   —ADRIENNE RICH, "Claiming an Education," *On Lies, Secrets, and Silence*

Writers need to identify their overall purpose for each piece of writing, knowing that they can tap different methods of development (such as narration, description, and cause-and-consequence analysis; see 32e), all of which have specific purposes or subpurposes, to work toward that overall goal. Although you may mix methods of development, you should be sure to align your method or methods with your overall purpose for writing. The following checklist may assist you.

CHECKLIST for Assessing Purpose

- If you are writing in response to a specific assignment, what does your instructor want your writing to do? Talk to your instructor or reread your assignment sheet to see what goals (and limits) have been set for you.

- Has your instructor provided a purpose for your writing, or can you define your own?

- Are you trying primarily to express how you feel? Are you writing to improve your self-understanding or trying to help others understand you better?

- Are you trying to be entertaining or inspiring? What do you hope to accomplish by treating your subject humorously?

- Are you writing primarily to convey information? Are you trying to teach others something they do not know or to demonstrate that you have knowledge in common?

- Are you writing primarily to argue a course of action? Do you want your readers to stop a certain behavior or to undertake a specific action?

- Do you have more than one purpose in writing? Which one is primary? How can the other purposes help you achieve your primary one? Or are some of your purposes in conflict?

- Are you trying to demonstrate that you have specific writing skills and are knowledgeable about your subject?

(2) *Audience* refers to those who will read your writing.

Understanding your audience—their values, concerns, and knowledge—helps you tailor your writing in terms of length, quality and quantity of details, the kind of language to use, and the examples that will be most effective. Some writers like to plan and draft essays with a clear sense of audience in mind; others like to focus on the audience primarily when they are revising. (See chapter 33.) At some point, whether during drafting or during revising, you must think clearly about who will be reading what you write and ask yourself whether your choices are appropriate for that audience.

(a) Specialized audience

A **specialized audience** has a demonstrated interest in your subject. If you were writing about the harm done through alcohol abuse, members of an organization such as Alcoholics

Anonymous or Mothers Against Drunk Driving would constitute a specialized audience, as would nutritionists, police officers, or social workers. These audiences would have different
areas of expertise and possibly different agendas, so it would be
unwise to address each of them in exactly the same way.

As you consider your relationship with a specialized audience—what its members know that you do not, how much and
what sorts of information you might provide them, and how best
to develop your information—you can continue to think about
your overall purpose. You'll be writing to experts, so you'll want
to establish common ground with them by acknowledging that
you recognize their expertise and mentioning areas of agreement,
adjusting your tone and language choices as you tailor your writing to their knowledge and attitudes. (See chapter **19**.) The average reader would probably be confused by the language in
paragraph 4 because it was written for a specialized audience of
rhetoricians who are already familiar with the terminology of
their discipline.

4   Rhetoric as persuasive discourse is still very much exercised
among us, but modern students are not likely to have received
much formal training in the art of persuasion. Frequently, the only
remnant of this training in the schools is the attention paid to argumentation in a study of the four forms of discourse: Argumentation, Exposition, Description, and Narration. But this study of
argumentation usually turns out to be an accelerated course in
Logic. For the classical rhetorician, logic was an ancillary but distinct discipline. Aristotle, for instance, spoke of rhetoric as being
"an offshoot" or "a counterpart" of logic or, as he called it, dialec-
tics. The speaker might employ logic to persuade the audience, but
logic was only one among many "available means of persuasion."
So those who study argumentation in classrooms today are not really exposed to the rich, highly systematized discipline that earlier
students submitted to when they were learning the persuasive art.

—**EDWARD P. J. CORBETT,** *Classical Rhetoric for the Modern Student*

Since no one knows everything about a subject, members of
a specialized audience will usually enjoy thinking about their

subject in a new way, even if they're not learning new information. So writing for a specialized audience doesn't mean you have to know more than your audience does; it may be sufficient to demonstrate that you understand the material and can discuss it appropriately.

(b) Diverse audience

A **diverse audience** consists of readers with different levels of expertise and interest in your subject. For example, if you are writing about upgrading computer software in a report that will be read by various department heads of a company or about the responsibilities of public schools for your local newspaper, you should be aware that some of your readers probably know more about software or schooling than others. When writing for a diverse audience, you can usually assume that your readers have interests different from yours. Paragraph 5 helps a diverse audience of readers understand how critical teaching functions within U.S. schools.

5   Critical teaching aims to transform. That ambition is both subversive and entirely common, akin, that is, to the aim of any teaching. Schools, after all, accept the burden of assisting the nation's young people to become responsible and productive citizens. Hence, teaching is always a transformative act: students aren't expected to leave their classrooms thinking, knowing, judging, living in the ways they did before they entered them—fundamentalist students encounter evolution in biology class; students raised on television read literature; students from "liberal" backgrounds study growing crime rates in sociology and the cost of assistance programs in economics; "conservatives" study the women's movement in history class or Marxism in philosophy. The choices teachers make in their classrooms are always, in part, choices about what children "ought" to become, what the nation "ought" to aspire to through the productive action of succeeding generations. These are political choices: the question is, what indeed *should* students become and who should have the power to say so? What indeed *should* the nation aspire to, and who should compose the stories about that aspiration? Critical

teaching differs from other sorts primarily in its answers to these questions and in its self-consciousness about the political nature of schools (including its own practices). It presumes that American citizens should understand, accept, and live amicably amidst the realities of cultural diversity—along axes of gender, race, class, and ethnicity—that are the hallmarks of American society. It presumes that people are entitled to fairness in their social and economic lives. It presumes that a critical citizenry, willing as well as able to take responsibility for the nation's future, is preferable to a passive, unengaged citizenry that lets government, business, and mass media do its thinking. Finally, it presumes that no one group is exclusively entitled to the privilege of representation, but that each has a right to tell its story, critique other stories, and participate in forming a community responsive to the needs of all its members.

—C. H. KNOBLAUCH AND LIL BRANNON,
Critical Teaching and the Idea of Literacy

To attract the attention of a diverse audience, you'll want to establish what its members are likely to have in common despite their differences. In the previous example, you might consider whether all the readers have the same knowledge of critical teaching, the same experiences in critical literacy. The key to communicating successfully with diverse readers is to find some way to draw them together on common ground and to join them there. In the previous example, then, the author considered all members of the audience to be educated readers, interested in the relationship among teaching, learning, and participatory democracy. That consideration enabled the author to make appropriate choices in diction (see chapters 19–22) and detail (see 31c and 32e(2)).

There will be times, however, when you simply won't know much about your audience. When this is the case, you can often benefit from imagining a thoughtful audience of educated adults, with whom you may even share common ground. Such an audience is likely to include people with different backgrounds and cultural values (see 36d(2)). To a considerable extent, the language you use will determine whether diverse readers feel included in or excluded from your work. Be careful to avoid jargon or unexplained technical terms that would be understood only by a specialized audience. (See 19c and 19e.)

(c) Multiple audiences

Writers often need to address multiple audiences. The readers in a multiple audience can have distinctly different expectations. If, for example, you are asked to evaluate the performance of an employee you supervise and send copies to both that person and your boss, one part of your audience is probably looking for praise while the other is looking to see whether you are a competent supervisor.

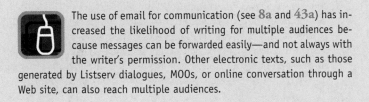

The use of email for communication (see 8a and 43a) has increased the likelihood of writing for multiple audiences because messages can be forwarded easily—and not always with the writer's permission. Other electronic texts, such as those generated by Listserv dialogues, MOOs, or online conversation through a Web site, can also reach multiple audiences.

When writing essays in college, you may also find yourself writing for multiple audiences. For example, you'll write essays that you'll not only share with your writing group but submit to your instructor; you may take a linked or team-taught course in which you'll submit written work for evaluation by two instructors; or you may write an essay for a diverse audience and submit it to an instructor who is a specialist on your subject. In each of these cases, you are writing for multiple audiences. The following checklist may help you assess your audience.

CHECKLIST **for Assessing the Audience**

- Who is going to be reading what you write?
- What do you know about the members of this audience? What do they have in common? How are they different?
- What values do you share with them?
- How do you differ from them?
- How much do they already know about your topic?
- What kind of language is appropriate for this audience?
- How open are the members of this audience to views that may be different from their own?
- What level of expertise will they expect from you?
- What do you *not* know about this audience? What assumptions would be risky?
- Are you writing with one audience in mind and then expecting a different audience to read what you have written? If so, have you clearly indicated the intended audience so that you can address that audience specifically, in the hope that your readers will imagine they are part of it?

Exercise 1

Take notes during a class or at a meeting you regularly attend. Using those notes and your memories of the class or meeting, write a one-page essay in which you describe that occasion to one of the following: (1) a member of your family, (2) an instructor or supervisor, or (3) the dean of the school or a department head. Then write a second, one-page description that is to be read by all three.

(3) *Context* means the circumstances under which writer and reader communicate.

Context includes time and place, writer and audience, and medium. An essay written outside of class may be very different from one written in the classroom, even if both are written for the same instructor and in response to the same question. Your instructor is likely to expect more from you when you have had advanced coursework, more time to write, and better conditions for writing.

Context is also influenced by social, political, religious, and other cultural factors. Your background and beliefs often shape the stance (or attitude) you take when writing. An essay written shortly before your school's winter break, for example, could be influenced by both your anticipation of a combined religious holiday and family reunion and whether or not you think your audience shares that anticipation. Writers who consider their audience as well as the context in which they are writing are more likely to communicate their ideas effectively.

The medium for which you are writing can be considered part of the context as well. Writing material for a Web page or another online medium may require you to think differently about organization and style and may also require more or less time than writing a traditional academic essay or business letter.

When you read the work of other writers, you will sometimes find that the context is specifically stated. Often, however, the context must be inferred. Whether you choose to identify your context or not, it is essential that you consider it.

> **CHECKLIST for Assessing the Context**
>
> - If you are free to choose the time and place in which to write, have you set aside a time and found a place where you can work without distractions?
>
> - Under what circumstances will your writing probably be read? For example, if it is going to be one of many reports in a pile on a manager's desk, can you help that person quickly see the purpose and thrust of your work?
>
> - How has your response to the assigned task been influenced by other things going on in your life? Can you make any changes in your schedule that will allow you to focus more attention on your writing?
>
> - Have you been asked to write an essay of a specific length? If length has not been specified, what seems appropriate for your purpose and audience?
>
> - What document design (see chapter 8) is appropriate for this context?

(4) *Exigence* means the circumstance that compels you to write.

Exigence is the particular need or situation that calls for writing. A parking ticket, a birth or marriage, a winning lottery ticket—these are all events that may compel you to write. As soon as you know that you can use words to address a particular need or situation, you can decide whether your words will solve a problem, explain a point, make a claim, or entertain. Once you determine the exigence for your writing, you'll be better able to gauge all the elements of your writing (from word choice to organizational pattern) in terms of your overall purpose.

Beyond the Rule

EXIGENCE

Historical events often serve as the exigence for writing. The September 2001 terrorist attacks on New York City and Washington, D.C., provided many people—from journalists to schoolchildren—with a reason to write. The collapse of the Quecreek Mine in Somerset, Pennsylvania, in July 2002 offered another occasion for many people to write. For more information, visit www.harbrace.com.

32b | **Writers find appropriate subjects and decide how to focus them.**

Whether you are assigned a subject or are free to choose one, you must consider what you already know—or would like to learn about—and what is likely to interest your audience (see **32a(2)**). You must also decide how to narrow your general **subject** into a more specific **topic** so that you can develop that topic adequately within the time and page limit available to you.

When you take a writing course, you might be asked to choose your own subject. More often, however, you will be asked to write essays about subjects outside your personal experience but within your academic experience. For instance, you may be assigned an essay for a course in ancient history. You should make an effort to find material that interests you and begin focusing on a topic. Look in your textbook; go through your lecture notes or marginal annotations you've made for the course. Ask yourself if there are any details of the subject that have surprised, annoyed, or pleased you—something you feel strongly about and would like to explore further.

(1) There are several ways to explore subjects.

If you have a hard time finding something to write about—or have so many ideas that you have trouble choosing among them—try some of the following invention exercises: **keeping a journal, freewriting, listing,** and **questioning.** Discussing assignments with classmates, friends, or an instructor can also help you generate ideas and decide which ones are likely to yield good essays, the kind that are interesting to write. In other words, to generate ideas, use whatever methods produce results for you.

(a) Keeping a journal

Keeping a journal is a good way to generate subjects for essays. You will benefit from writing in a personal journal or a writer's notebook every day.

In a **personal journal,** you reflect on your experiences. Instead of simply listing activities, meals, or weather reports, you use writing to explore how you feel about what is happening in your life. Writers who keep a personal journal usually write for their own benefit, but in the process of writing the journal—or reading it—they may discover subjects they can use for essays.

Like a personal journal, a **writer's notebook** includes responses to experiences. In this case, however, the emphasis is on recording and exploring material for future projects. You can often benefit from keeping a writer's notebook in which you list quotations and observations that invite development. When time allows, you might also draft the opening pages of an essay, outline an idea for a story, or experiment with writing a poem.

Some writers keep both a personal journal and a writer's notebook. Others use only one of these types—or create a combination of the two. Still others prefer to keep a **reading jour-**

nal (see 35b(3)). You might find it convenient to keep your journal in a word-processing file on your computer, especially if you use a laptop. In any case, feel free to write quickly, without worrying about spelling or grammar.

Because you don't have to worry about grammatical correctness when writing journal entries, you can pay more attention to your ideas. In fact, if writing in English sometimes slows you down, try using your native language instead. You can decide later which parts of your journal entries are worth translating into English. A journal can also be a place to experiment with sentence patterns and vocabulary. You can begin learning new words and phrases by listing in your journal those that you read or hear in your classes.

(b) Freewriting

When freewriting, writers record whatever occurs to them, without stopping—often for no more than ten minutes. They do not worry about whether they are repeating themselves or getting off track; they simply write to see what comes out. Freewriting is another good way to generate ideas for a writing project because no matter what you write, it will contain ideas and information you didn't realize you had.

In *directed freewriting,* you begin with a general subject and record whatever occurs to you about this subject during the time available. Some writers use colored marking pens (or change the font in their word-processing program) to identify different topics generated by this activity. When Melissa Schraeder's English instructor asked her to write for five minutes, assessing some of the main challenges to being a happy and successful college student, she produced the freewriting on page 420. (This freewriting represents the first step toward her essay, three different versions of which appear in chapter 33.)

As the color shading shows, Melissa's freewriting generated several possible topics for an essay about being a successful college student: managing stress, finding creative approaches to studying, and balancing work and school.

Sometimes I feel like being successful in school and simultaneously remaining sane, much less happy, are incompatible goals. Schoolwork can be very stressful and it requires important sacrifices to stay on top of your studies. Especially when working on those classes that I don't particularly enjoy such as my math or science classes, it is often difficult for me to keep a positive attitude while studying. But I have learned that it takes both time and commitment to do well in school and that oftentimes sacrifices are well-invested and hard work usually leads to good results.

This is why I have had to be creative in my study habits and patterns, a challenge that I have come to surmount only with lots of experience and practice. An example of one of the small compromises I make with myself in order to feel more at ease when studying is to invite a friend along to study with me. Studying seems less gloomy when done in pairs since it is comforting and motivating to know that you are not the only one who is working hard.

Probably the biggest challenge I face in maintaining my success and happiness as a college student though is the balancing act between my schoolwork and my part-time job. With tuition so high and all the extra expenses such as books and technology fees that accompany a modern college education, most students find that they have to work in order to stay afloat and I am certainly not exempt from this rule. Even though I usually only work around 15 hours a week, those 15 hours can be quite crucial in the midst of exams and papers with strict deadlines. Since I always try to put my schoolwork first, there are definitely some weeks where I wish I didn't have to work at all!

(c) Listing

One way to gather ideas about a writing topic is to make an informal list, a process also known as **brainstorming.** The advantage to listing is that, like outlining, it lets you see individual items at a glance rather than having to pick them out of a block of writing. It also encourages the establishment of relationships. Jot down any ideas that come to you while you are thinking about your subject. Devote as much time as necessary to making your list—perhaps ten minutes, perhaps an entire evening. The point is to collect as many ideas as you can.

Melissa made the following list after she had decided to focus her essay on the challenge of balancing schoolwork with a part-time job.

> Need to place schoolwork first
>
> Part-time job can be career experience
>
> Part-time job can also be motivating to do well in school so you don't always have to stay at this job
>
> You will value your education more if you have had to work hard for it
>
> Part-time job can also remind you that your personal stress is not the only thing in the world, nor the most important
>
> Need to have understanding employers who value employing good students
>
> Need to have flexibility in scheduling job hours, especially for exam and paper weeks
>
> Having a part-time job forces you to keep on top of schoolwork, to be consistent in your studies

This list may appear chaotic, but earlier items suggest later ones, and a review of the whole list may indicate items that need to be rearranged, added, or deleted. As you look through the list, you will note that some ideas are closely related and can be grouped together. Melissa has used several words and phrases that are clearly related to balancing schoolwork and a job: "flexibility," "motivating," "keep on top of schoolwork," and "be consistent in your studies." Order and direction are beginning to emerge.

(d) Questioning

You can also explore a subject by asking yourself some questions. **Journalists' questions**—*Who? What? When? Where? Why?* and *How?*—are easy to use and can help you discover ideas about any subject. Using journalists' questions to explore the subject of balancing schoolwork and a job could lead you to think about it in a number of ways: *Who* typically has to work part-time while in college? *What* should college students look for in a part-time job? *When* should students work? *Where* should students work? *Why* can part-time work be an important part of the college experience? And *how* can students balance part-time work with good schoolwork?

Kenneth Burke's **pentad** consists of five points of consideration; he calls it a dramatistic pentad because it uses the drama of being a human being as the basis for exploring any subject.

Act	What is happening?
Actor	Who is doing it?
Scene	What are the time, place, and conditions in which the act occurred?
Agency	How was the act accomplished?
Purpose	How and why did act, actor, scene, and agency come together?

This method can help you discover relationships among the various features of your general subject. For example, consider "remaining sane"—one of the ideas generated by Melissa Schraeder in the freewriting on page 420. What is the relationship between the act (remaining sane) and the actor (Melissa)? Does she sometimes feel sane because she's balancing school and a job? Because she's pleased with the good results of her efforts?

Word-processing programs can facilitate brainstorming activities, such as freewriting, listing, and questioning. Some writers like to keep files of their brainstorming activities, which they can consult later when they begin drafting. Sometimes, freewriting or listing can yield phrases, sentences, or even paragraphs that a writer decides to use in a rough draft. If those phrases, sentences, or paragraphs are saved in a word-processing file, they can easily be copied and pasted directly into the rough draft. In addition, you might consider brainstorming online with friends or classmates. You can use instant messaging sites, chat rooms, or MOOs (Multiuser dimension, Object-Oriented virtual spaces) to exchange ideas about a topic. In fact, your instructor may have set up a discussion board or created a forum for your class to use.

(2) Writers need to focus their subject ideas into specific topics.

Exploring a subject will suggest not only productive strategies for development, but also a direction in which to focus a topic. Some ideas will seem worth pursuing; others will seem inappropriate for your purpose, audience, or context. You will find yourself discarding ideas even as you develop new ones and determine your topic.

For example, "balancing work and school" is too large and general a subject to make a good topic for a college essay. However, some of the ideas that emerged in the freewriting (see page 420) and the list (page 421) on this subject can be grouped to form a topic that is both interesting and manageable. Or a single idea, if well chosen, might lead to a sharply focused essay of some depth.

In addition to reviewing the ideas you have generated through strategies such as freewriting and listing, you can also achieve focus by thinking in terms of how strategies you might use for developing your ideas (see 32e) can take you in different directions. Working with "balancing a part-time job with schoolwork" as a large subject that she needed to narrow into a topic, Melissa considered it in terms of the following development strategies:

- *Narration.* What kind of story can I tell about part-time work for college students?
- *Description.* What kind of part-time job do I have? What is my place of work like? How do my employers treat me?
- *Process.* How have I gone about balancing my own part-time job with my schoolwork?
- *Cause and consequence.* What have been the causes of my success in balancing my job with my schoolwork? Concentration? Commitment? What were some of the consequences when I have made mistakes in balancing these two in the past? Exhaustion? Frustration? What is the primary cause? What are contributory causes?
- *Comparison and contrast.* How do my study habits and academic skills compare with those of students who do not work and those of students who do? How does my work-and-school lifestyle compare to my previous school-only lifestyle?
- *Classification and division.* How can I classify the different types of jobs that college students take on? How can I divide up the desirable qualities of jobs and employers? How many jobs are listed in the classified ads each day? How many college students feel they must take a job?
- *Definition.* How do I define "success" in college? Is career experience as important as good grades? What constitutes a "good attitude" toward your education?

The following sentence suggests a focus on comparison and contrast:

Before I came to college and took on a part-time job, I spent all of my free time either studying or hanging out with friends.

This sentence focuses on cause and consequence:

Now that I'm working part-time and taking classes full-time, I have little free time to spend with my friends or relax.

Because writing is a form of thinking and discovering, your focus might not emerge until after you've written your first draft. When you compare the draft of Melissa's essay on working while attending school (see pages 462–468) with the final version of it (pages 474–479), you will see how drafting and revising can sharpen a writer's focus.

Whatever method you use to bring a topic into focus, your choice should be determined not only by your interests but also by your purpose, the needs of your audience, and the time and space available. The following checklist may help you assess your topic.

CHECKLIST for Assessing a Topic

- Is the topic appropriate for your writing task?
- Can you do justice to the topic in the time and space available to you? Should you narrow it?
- Do you know enough about the topic to write a paper of the length your instructor requires? If not, how will you get additional information?
- Are you interested in the topic and willing to learn more about it?
- Can you interest your audience in the topic?

Exercise 2

Choose one experience from your earlier education that has potential as an appropriate writing topic. In one paragraph, explain why that experience is worth sharing with others. Identify the audience that would most benefit from understanding the experience, and then write a second paragraph describing how much information you would need to include to ensure that this audience understands and appreciates its significance. Set some limits for yourself in terms of your needs as well as those of your audience: What details do you wish to keep private? What details make your experience unique? What details are essential to your telling? Or are common to everyone who has shared this experience?

Exercise 3

Explore the experience from exercise 2 by experimenting with one of the following strategies: freewriting, listing, or questioning. Then consider how you could focus the ideas you have generated to form a topic. To illustrate the different directions you could follow, depending on your focus, ask and answer five questions about your subject—either the journalists' questions or the pentad.

32c | A clearly stated thesis conveys your main idea.

Once you have focused your subject, you've gone a long way toward developing a controlling idea for your content and your approach. By this point, you've probably also established your purpose for writing, whether to explain, teach, analyze, argue, or compare. Your subject, purpose, and focus all come together in a controlling idea, or **thesis,** which is appropriate for your audience and context (see 32a). In the first draft or two, your thesis may be only tentative. By your final draft, however, you'll have developed a clear thesis statement.

(1) Essays usually include a thesis statement.

Most pieces of writing have a **thesis statement,** an explicit declaration (usually in one sentence) of the main idea. Your thesis statement, then, will convey a single idea, clearly focused and specifically stated, that has grown out of your exploration of a subject. A thesis statement can be thought of as an assertion or a claim (see **36c**)—that is, it indicates what you claim to be true, interesting, or valuable about your topic.

An explicitly formulated thesis statement identifies the topic, the approach, and, in some cases, the plan of development.

The following thesis statement (in two sentences) divides student excuses into five kinds, using humor to make a point.

> With a show of energy and creativity that would be admirable if applied to the (missing) assignments in question, my students persist, week after week, semester after semester, year after year, in offering excuses about why their work is not ready. Those reasons fall into several broad categories: the family, the best friend, the evils of dorm life, the evils of technology, and the totally bizarre.
>
> —**CAROLYN FOSTER SEGAL,** "The Dog Ate My Disk, and Other Tales of Woe"

The main idea in an argumentative essay usually carries a strong point of view, as in the following, which unmistakably argues for a specific course of action.

> Amnesty International opposes the death penalty in all cases without exception.
>
> —**AMNESTY INTERNATIONAL,** "The Death Penalty: Questions and Answers"

You will probably try out several tentative thesis statements as you explore your topic. It's just as important for you to allow your thesis statement to remain tentative in the early stages of writing as it is to allow your essay to remain flexible. Rather than starting with a preconceived thesis, then, which you must struggle to support, you should let your final thesis statement grow out of your thinking and discovery process as you draft and revise. Your goal should be a statement that is neither too obvious nor too general. The following tips might help you develop a thesis statement.

TIPS FOR DEVELOPING A THESIS STATEMENT

- Decide which feature of the topic interests you most.
- Write down your point of view or assertion about that feature.
- Mark the passages in your freewriting, journal, or rough draft that support your position.
- Draft a thesis statement, and consider whether you can address the full scope of this tentative thesis in your essay or whether it's still too broad to be developed sufficiently.
- After your first or second draft, if your essay has grown beyond your thesis (or vice versa), revise your thesis to widen or narrow its scope in the direction your essay has taken.
- If you're unhappy with the results, start again with the first tip, and be even more specific.

A clear, precise thesis statement helps unify what you write; it's a promise to your readers that you'll stay with the topic you've declared. Thus, your thesis statement will guide not only your decisions about which details to keep and which to toss out but also your search for appropriate additional information to strengthen your points or support your assertions. No matter what thesis statement you develop, you'll need enough relevant information to support it credibly and clearly.

As you write and revise, check your thesis statement frequently to see whether you have drifted away from it. Do not hesitate to tweak your thesis, however, if you find a more productive course to pursue. When you revise, test everything you retain against the thesis statement you have finally decided on—your original or a new version you have developed—and scrupulously discard anything that does not help you keep your promise to your readers (see chapter 33).

As you clarify your thesis statement, resist using such vague qualifiers as *interesting, important,* and *unusual.* For example, in the thesis statement "My education has been very unusual," the vague word *unusual* may indicate that the idea itself is weak and that the writer needs to find a sharper focus. The following examples show how vague thesis statements can be clarified and sharpened.

Vague	It is hard to choose a major.
Better	Choosing a major is difficult for me because I enjoy so many different classes, and I usually end up with more courses each semester than I can responsibly handle.
Vague	Bobby Knight is a unique individual.
Better	A successful college basketball coach with an uncontrollable temper, Bobby Knight has earned his place in the media spotlight.
Vague	Young people are too influenced by the media.
Better	The frequent use of unusually thin models in television and magazine advertisements has contributed to the rise of eating disorders among adolescent girls and boys in the United States.

Thesis statements appear most often in the first or second paragraph of an essay, although you can put yours anywhere that suits your purpose—occasionally even in the conclusion. The advantage of putting the thesis statement in the first paragraph, however, is that readers know from the beginning what you are writing about and where the essay is going. This technique helps readers who are searching for specific information to locate it easily. If the thesis statement begins the introductory paragraph, the rest of the sentences in the paragraph usually support or clarify it, as is the case in paragraph 6.

6   America is suffering from overwork. Too many of us are too busy, trying to squeeze more into each day while having less to show for it. Although our growing time crunch is often portrayed as a personal dilemma, it is in fact a major social problem that has reached crisis proportions over the past 20 years.

—**BARBARA BRANDT**, "Less Is More"

If the thesis statement is the last sentence of the opening paragraph, the preceding sentences will build toward it, as is the case in paragraph 7.

7   The story of zero is an ancient one. Its roots stretch back to the dawn of mathematics, in the time thousands of years before the first civilization, long before humans could read and write. But as natural as zero seems to us today, for ancient peoples zero was a foreign—and frightening—idea. An Eastern concept, born in the Fertile Crescent a few centuries before the birth of Christ, zero not only evoked images of a primal void, it also had dangerous mathematical properties. Within zero there is the power to shatter the framework of logic.

—**CHARLES SEIFE**, *Zero: The Biography of a Dangerous Idea*

(2) A main idea is necessary even when a thesis statement is not required.

Some kinds of writing do not require an explicit thesis statement, but they still have a main, or controlling, idea. Writing without a thesis statement is sometimes acceptable when the work is narrative or descriptive. A memoir or a journal, for example, is unlikely to have a thesis statement. And reports of information, such as news stories or business memos, frequently do not require a thesis statement. Yet, even in cases such as these, readers should be able to sense a clear direction and focus.

Most of the writing done for college courses contains an obvious thesis statement. The following checklist may help you assess the thesis of an essay.

CHECKLIST for Assessing a Thesis

- Is your thesis clear? What comment are you making about your topic? What promise are you making to your readers?

- If your thesis is vague or too broad, how can you make it more specific? (See pages 428–429.)

- How does your thesis relate to or interest your audience?

- Is your thesis an accurate reflection of what you believe to be true about your topic?

- Where is your thesis located in your essay? Would your readers benefit from having it stated earlier or later?

- Does your thesis make a claim that is not obvious or too general to support in the length of your essay?

- What specific support (examples, illustrations, or experiences) can you think of to support your assertions?

In some cultures, the type of thesis statement described in this chapter may seem overly direct, even rude. In the United States, however, directness is expected. If you do not state your thesis or main idea clearly, readers may think that you are unprepared or unqualified to write about your subject.

32d | Arranging ideas requires choosing an appropriate method or combination of methods.

Many writers need a working plan to direct their ideas and keep their writing on course. Some use informal written lists; others use formal outlines. Such methods are especially helpful when writing lengthy papers (see chapters 40–42) and when writing under pressure (chapter 34). Whatever method you choose for organizing your writing, remember that you can always change your plan to suit any new direction your writing takes.

(1) Informal working plans can be composed quickly.

An informal working plan need be little more than an ordered list that grows out of a collection of ideas. Melissa Schraeder made such an informal working plan as she prepared to write on balancing work and school. Before she started to write her first draft, Melissa reexamined her freewriting (see page 420) and her first list of ideas (page 421). She decided to focus on the value of learning to balance work and school. She formulated a tentative thesis statement and made an ordered list to chart one possible direction for her essay.

TENTATIVE THESIS STATEMENT: Balancing a part-time job with success in schoolwork is not only a manageable task, but also a valuable experience contributing to growth as a student and as a growing individual.

1. account of my own experiences with balancing work and school

2. describe how I am able to work and maintain success in my studies

3. the importance of having understanding employers who allow for flexible scheduling

4. stress need to make schoolwork top priority

5. part-time work can offer career experience or motivate you to do well in school in an effort to move beyond the work you do part-time

6. working to fund your education means that you will value it more and stay on top of your studies

When you make such a list, ideas might overlap. Some ideas may be discarded, and others may occur to you as you draft. But a list can be the beginning of an overall plan.

As Melissa continued to work on her essay, she made several changes in her original plan. For example, she decided to discuss the consequences of balancing work and school right at the start of her essay, before concentrating on her reasons for working. She also decided to write a conclusion that included recommendations for incoming students: reasons why working is a valuable experience and ways to balance work and school. Because writing is a process, changes of this sort are natural.

(2) Rough outlines can help writers develop ideas.

Writers sometimes find themselves required to follow a plan of organization that has been determined for them, either by their instructor or by the discipline in which they are writing. The simplest way to consider an organizational pattern, or arrangement, is to think of Aristotle's claim that every speech needs a "beginning, a middle, and an end." Your essays need those features as well.

Often, however, your arrangement grows out of your early drafts, for it's much easier to arrange information you have in front of you than to spin an outline out of nothing in particular. Some writers develop excellent plans early in the writing process, turning a working list into a formal outline; others discover after they have done some writing that they need to rethink their original plan. But whether it is written before the first draft or after it, a rough outline is often helpful for analyzing a draft and preparing to revise it.

Although rough, an outline offers an essay a structure. Like the framework of a house, a rough outline can quickly become more elaborate and detailed. As you work and think, an outline becomes a visual image of your thinking. The main points form the major headings, and the supporting ideas form the subheadings. An outline of Melissa's essay might look something like the following.

TENTATIVE THESIS STATEMENT: Balancing a part-time job with success in schoolwork is not only a manageable task, but also a valuable experience contributing to growth as a student and as an individual.

I. Balancing work with school is manageable
   A. Your own sacrifices will determine success
      1. Time with friends
      2. Use breaks at work wisely
      3. Get a good handle on your school schedule and determine how far ahead you need to start assignments
   B. Best if you have an understanding employer
      1. An employer who puts school first and values scholarship
      2. Take advantage of university-run work programs
   C. Flexibility in scheduling hours
      1. Plan ahead around exam and paper weeks
      2. Often need to sacrifice weekend time in order to get in hours
II. Balancing work with school is valuable experience for students
   A. Provides discipline
      1. In prioritizing schoolwork, those students who work part-time jobs often have a good handle on their academic schedules and stay on top of their studies
      2. Working students learn the importance of time management and set realistic goals and timelines for themselves
   B. Working to pay for education leads students to place more respect and value on their education
      1. More serious about schoolwork
      2. Realize the importance of timely completion of degree
         a. Sleep becomes a priority
         b. Exercise seems less important
   C. Part-time work can offer career experience
      1. Internships
      2. Career-related work
   D. Part-time work can motivate students to achieve excellence in school as a means of moving beyond the scope of part-time work
      1. Face boredom or monotony in job

2. Face low wages

3. Constructive use of potential negativity

The types of outlines most commonly used are topic and sentence outlines. The headings and subheadings in a topic outline are expressed in grammatically parallel phrases; a sentence outline contains headings and subheadings that are complete and usually parallel sentences. The headings in a sentence outline can often serve as tentative topic sentences in a first draft. The following is a sentence outline Melissa might create from her rough outline.

TENTATIVE THESIS STATEMENT: Balancing a part-time job with success in schoolwork is not only a manageable task, but also a valuable experience contributing to growth as a student and as an individual. Since so many students need to work while going to school, I hope to show them that while holding a part-time job and doing well in school may seem difficult at first, in many ways these two undertakings are quite compatible.

I. Balancing work with school is a manageable task.
   A. As with most things in life, your own individual sacrifices in this balancing act will determine your success.
      1. You will often need to limit or carefully schedule the time that you spend with friends.
      2. Bringing along your books to work, you can get a heads up on nightly work by using your work breaks as study time.
   B. You can minimize the pressure put on yourself by choosing a job where you work for an understanding employer.
      1. You should look for an employer who understands the need to put schoolwork first and who values scholarship in employees.
      2. A good place to look for such an employer is in university-run businesses where supervisors are advised to view employees as students first and foremost.

II. The challenge of balancing work with school can be a valuable learning and growing experience for college students.

    A. This challenge provides students with a degree of self-discipline as working students need to prioritize their schoolwork carefully, thus learning the importance of realistic goal-setting and time management.

    B. Students who work to support their own education often develop a heightened sense of respect, value, and responsibility for it.

    C. Certain types of part-time work such as internships or major-area work programs can give students valuable career experience.

    D. Other types of part-time work, such as factory, food service, or maintenance work, while less directly valuable to the education process, often have positive motivating effects on students' academic attitudes.

Regardless of the type of outline you use, you need enough headings to develop your topic fully within the boundaries promised in your thesis.

You can create an outline quickly and easily with a word-processing program; some programs even have functions to help you work with outlines. These functions can be especially useful if your instructor has asked you to submit an outline with your first draft. If you are using a newer word-processing program, consult the Help document for instructions on how to use the outline functions.

32e | Experimenting with different strategies can help you develop your ideas.

Certain strategies can be used to frame entire essays by providing a way to organize ideas. Often referred to as **rhetorical methods,** these strategies for developing paragraphs (and essays) are already second nature to you. Every day you use one or more of them to define a concept, narrate a significant incident, supply examples for an assertion, classify or divide information into specific parts, compare two or more things, analyze a process, or identify a cause or consequence. You use rhetorical methods to generate ideas, to focus your topic (see **32b**), and to clarify your meaning for your audience. Writers have the option of tapping one, two, or several of these rhetorical methods to fulfill their overall purpose. For example, a formal definition can be developed through both comparison and contrast, and narration can be developed through description. Using one of these methods—or some combination of them—will help you develop your paragraph (or essay) and eventually fulfill the needs of your rhetorical situation (see **32a**): your purpose, the expectations of your audience, and the specific context in which you are writing.

(1) Narrating a series of events tells readers what happened.

A narrative discusses a sequence of events, normally in **chronological order** (the order in which they occur), to develop a particular point or set a mood. This rhetorical method usually uses transition words or phrases such as *then, later, that evening,* or *the following week* to help guide readers from one incident to the next. Drawn from Charles Darwin's journal, written during his voyage on the *Beagle,* paragraph 8 uses narrative to convey a sense of wonder at the power of nature.

8   The day has been memorable in the annals of Valdivia, for the most severe earthquake experienced by the oldest inhabitant. I happened to be on shore, and was lying down in the wood to rest myself. It came on suddenly, and lasted two minutes, but the time appeared much longer. The rocking of the ground was very sensible. The undulations appeared to my companion and myself to come from due east, whilst others thought they proceeded from the southwest. This shows how difficult it sometimes is to perceive the direction of vibrations. There was no difficulty in standing upright,

but the motion made me almost giddy; it was something like the movement of a vessel in a little cross-ripple, or still more like that felt by a person skating over thin ice, which bends under the weight of his body. —**CHARLES DARWIN**, "Great Earthquake"

(2) Describing something to show how it looks, sounds, smells, or feels adds useful detail.

By describing a person, place, object, or sensation, you can make your material come alive. Often descriptions are predominantly visual, but even visual descriptions can include the details of what you hear, smell, taste, or touch.

Description should suit your purpose and audience. In describing your car, for example, you would emphasize certain features to a potential buyer, others to a mechanic who is going to repair it, and still others to a friend who wants to borrow it. In paragraph 9, Kathleen Murphy (writing for movie fans) makes her description of Clint Eastwood vivid by blending visual and auditory images and suggesting tactile sensations.

9   His gait is that of a ghost or a predator, his poncho'd torso remaining strangely still, propelled ahead by the long legs, as though swimming upright in slow motion. Paradoxically, the hands of the remorseless gunfighter are those of a musician or a painter: elegant, long-fingered, with graceful wrists. In these formative stages of the Eastwood persona, his often nearly whispered vocal tones seem too pressured for ordinary speech. The silky, then increasingly abrasive sibilance of his drawl, like sand or gravel shifting in water, works best for epigrams, cryptic ripostes, up-close seduction.
      —**KATHLEEN MURPHY**, "The Good, the Bad, and the Ugly"

(3) Explaining a process shows readers how something happens.

Process paragraphs, in explaining how something is done or made, often use both description and narration. You might describe the items used in a process and then narrate the steps chronologically. Add an explanation of a process to a draft if doing so can illustrate a concept that might otherwise be hard for your audience to grasp. In paragraph 10, Garrison Keillor explains how to get started on a letter.

10 The first step in writing letters is to get over the guilt of *not* writing. You don't "owe" anybody a letter. Letters are a gift. The burning shame you feel when you see unanswered mail makes it harder to pick up a pen and makes for a cheerless letter when you finally do. *I feel bad about not writing, but I've been so busy,* etc. Skip this. Few letters are obligatory, and they are *Thanks for the wonderful gift* and *I am terribly sorry to hear about George's death* and *Yes, you're welcome to stay with us next month,* and not many more than that. Write those promptly if you want to keep your friends. Don't worry about the others, except love letters, of course. When your true love writes *Dear Light of My Life, Joy of My Heart, O Lovely Pulsating Core of My Sensate Being,* some response is called for.

—**GARRISON KEILLOR**, "How to Write a Personal Letter"

(4) Analyzing cause or consequence establishes why something happens or predicts results.

Writers who analyze cause or consequence raise the question *Why?* and must answer it to the satisfaction of their audience, differentiating the **primary cause** (the most important one) from **contributory causes** (which contribute to but do not directly cause a situation) or the **primary consequence** (the most important one) from **secondary consequences** (which occur because of an event but are less important than the primary consequence). Writers who analyze cause or consequence usually link events along a time line. Always keep in mind, though, that just because one event occurs before—or after—another event, doesn't necessarily make it a cause—or a consequence—of that event (see **35f(9)**). In paragraph 11, humorist Dave Barry uncovers a historical cause for the male tendency "to do extremely little in the way of useful housework."

11   Somewhere during the growth process, a hormonal secretion takes place in women that enables them to see dirt that men cannot see, dirt at the level of *molecules,* whereas men generally don't notice it until it forms clumps large enough to support agriculture. This can lead to tragedy, as it did in the ill-fated ancient city of Pompeii, where the residents all got killed when the local volcano erupted and covered them with a layer of ash twenty feet deep. Modern people often ask, "How come, when the ashes started falling, the Pompeii people didn't just *leave?*" The answer is that in Pompeii, it was the custom for the men to do the housework. They never even *noticed* the ash until it had for the most part covered the children. "Hey!" the men said (in Latin). "It's mighty quiet around here!" This is one major historical reason why, to this very day, men tend to do extremely little in the way of useful housework.

—**DAVE BARRY**, "Batting Clean-up and Striking Out"

Writers can also demonstrate effects, as in paragraph 12, which explores the effects automobiles have had on our society by asking us to imagine life without them.

12   Let us imagine what life would be like in a carless nation. People would have to live very close together so they could walk, or, for healthy people living in sunny climes, bicycle to mass transit stops. Living in close quarters would mean life as it is now lived in Manhattan. There would be few free-standing homes, many row houses, and lots of apartment buildings. There would be few private gardens except for flowerpots on balconies. The streets would be congested by pedestrians, trucks, and buses, as they were at the turn of the century before automobiles were common.

—**JAMES Q. WILSON**, "Cars and Their Enemies"

(5) Comparing or contrasting helps readers see similarities or differences.

A **comparison** points out similarities, and a **contrast** points out differences. When drafting, consider whether a comparison might help your readers see a relationship they might otherwise miss or whether a contrast might help them establish useful distinctions. In paragraph 13, Jane Tompkins uses descriptive details in her revealing comparison of her two kindergarten teachers.

13   The teachers, Miss Morget (pronounced *mor-zhay*) and Miss Hunt, were tall and thin but unalike in every other way. Miss Hunt was young and attractive. She had chestnut brown hair, stylishly rolled, hazel eyes, and a prominent chin. At first, her smart outfits and polished good looks fooled me into thinking she was the nice one. But there was a twist to her mouth sometimes and a troubled look in her eyes that frightened me, and when she spoke to the children, there was iron in her voice. Miss Morget was old and kind. Her frizzled white hair stuck out, softening her sharp nose; and her pale eyes, which held a twinkle, made me pretty sure she wasn't going to do or say anything mean. She spoke in a gentle, cracked voice that was never angry; but the children knew when she meant business, and they minded.

—JANE TOMPKINS, *A Life in School*

(6) Classifying or dividing material can give order to it.

To classify is to categorize things into groups based on certain common characteristics. **Classification** is a way to understand or explain something by establishing how it fits within a category or group. For example, a book reviewer might classify a new novel as a mystery—leading readers to expect a plot based on suspense. **Division,** in contrast, separates an object or group into smaller parts and examines the relationships among them. Divided into chapters, a novel can also be discussed according to components such as plot, setting, and theme (see chapter 42).

Classification and division represent two different perspectives: Ideas can be put into groups (classification) or split into subclasses (division) on the basis of a dividing principle. In paragraph 14, for example, classification and division work together to help clarify the differences among the kinds of pressures college students endure. Like most paragraphs, this one mixes rhetorical methods; the writer uses definition as well as classification to make his point.

14 I see four kinds of pressure working on college students today: economic pressure, parental pressure, peer pressure, and self-induced pressure. It is easy to look around for villains—to blame the college for charging too much money, the professors for assigning too much work, the parents for pushing their children too far, the students for driving themselves too hard. But there are no villains, only victims. **—WILLIAM ZINSSER,** "College Pressures"

(7) Defining an important concept or term clarifies meaning.

By defining a concept or a term, writers efficiently clarify their meaning and develop their ideas. Definitions are usually constructed in a two-step process: The first step locates a term by placing it in a class; the second step differentiates this particular term from other terms in the same class. For instance, "A concerto [*the term*] is a symphonic piece [*the class*] consisting of three movements performed by one or more solo instruments accompanied at times by an orchestra [*the difference*]." Paragraph 15 defines volcanos by putting them into a class ("landforms") and by distinguishing them ("built of molten material") from other members of that class. The definition is then clarified by examples.

15 Volcanos are landforms built of molten material that has spewed out onto the earth's surface. Such molten rock is called lava. Volcanos may be no larger than small hills, or thousands of feet high. All have a characteristic cone shape. Some well-known mountains are actually volcanos. Examples are Mt. Fuji (Japan), Mt. Lassen (California), Mt. Hood (Oregon), Mt. Etna and Mt. Vesuvius (Italy), and Paricutín (Mexico). The Hawaiian Islands are all immense volcanos whose summits rise above the ocean, and these volcanos are still quite active.

—**JOEL AREM,** "Rocks and Minerals"

Use the rhetorical methods just described to make your essay as a whole more understandable to your audience. Make sure, however, that you are using them to support your thesis and fulfill your overall purpose. If a paragraph or two developed with one of the methods is contributing to the main idea of your draft, then it is contributing to your purpose. If the development of a paragraph doesn't support the thesis, then you need to revise or delete it (see chapter 33).

32f | **Your first draft allows you to continue exploring your topic and to clarify what you think.**

When writing a first draft, get your ideas down quickly. Spelling, punctuation, and correctness are not important in the first draft; ideas are. Experienced writers know that the most important thing about a first draft is to have done it, for it gives you something to work on—and against. If you're not sure how to begin, look over some of the journal writing, listing, or rough outlining you've already done, and try to state a tentative thesis. Then write out some main points you'd like to develop, along with some of the supporting information for that development. Keep your overall plan in mind as you draft. You may find that you need to revise your plan—or you may need to rethink your topic. Experienced writers expect a change in plan as they write and revise.

If you feel stuck, move to another spot and draft paragraphs that might appear later (see 34c). Doing so may help you restart your engine, for when you're actually writing, you think more efficiently. You can then move on to another part that's easier to write—another supporting idea, an introduction, a conclusion. But don't worry about writing a provocative introduction or a sensible conclusion at this point. Later, when you're revising, you can experiment with ways of introducing and concluding an essay (see 33b). What's important at this stage is to begin writing, and then keep writing as quickly as you can. Save this early work so that you can refer to it as you revise (see chapter 33). Finally, remember that writing is a form of discovering, understanding, and thinking. As you draft, you're likely to discover that you have more to say than you ever thought you would.

Although some writers like to draft in longhand, using a word-processing program when drafting offers distinct advantages: You can easily move from one part of a piece to another. Knowing that you can scroll up or down easily allows ideas to flow. And when you save a draft in an electronic file, you are well positioned for making revisions later.

Revising and Editing Essays

Revising, which literally means "seeing again," lies at the heart of all successful writing. **Revising** entails rethinking what you've already written in terms of your overall purpose: how successfully you've addressed your audience, how clearly you've stated your thesis, how effectively you've arranged your information, how thoroughly you've developed your assertions. **Editing,** on the other hand, focuses on issues that are smaller in scale. When you're editing, you're polishing your writing: You choose words more precisely (see chapter **20**), shape prose more distinctly (chapter **21**), and structure sentences more effectively (chapters **23–24**, **26–27**, and **29–30**). While you're editing, you're also **proofreading,** focusing even more sharply to eliminate surface errors in grammar, punctuation, and mechanics. Revising and editing often overlap (just as drafting and revising do), but they are distinct activities that concentrate on large-scale and small-scale issues, respectively.

As you revise and edit your essays, this chapter will help you

- consider your work as a whole (**33a(1)–(2)**),
- evaluate your tone (**33a(3)**),
- compose an effective introduction and conclusion (**33b**),
- benefit from reviewers' comments (**33c**),
- edit to improve style (**33d**),
- proofread to eliminate surface errors (**33e**), and
- submit a final draft (**33f**).

33a Revision is essential to good writing.

In truth, you're revising throughout the writing process. Even in the earliest planning stages, you're revising when you consider possible subjects and discard them in favor of more appropriate ones. You're also revising after you've chosen a subject, when you decide to change your focus or emphasize some new feature of the subject. And of course, you're revising when you realize that the sentence or paragraph you've just written doesn't work there and decide to move or delete it.

Even though revision occurs throughout the writing process, you will do most of your revising after you've completed a draft. You may rewrite specific sentences and paragraphs as well as reconsider the draft as a whole. A few writers prefer to start revision immediately after drafting, while their minds are still fully engaged by their topic. But most writers like to let a draft "cool off," so that when they return to it, they can assess it more objectively, with fresh eyes.

Using word-processing software, writers sometimes print each draft as they complete it, labeling and dating the drafts to keep track of their progress. However, most newer word-processing programs enable you to track your revisions easily without printing, a feature that is especially useful if a peer group is reviewing your drafts. If your word-processing program does not have this feature, you can save each new version of your work in a separate file.

(1) Anything and everything on the page can be revised.

As you reread your essay as a whole, you will want to recall your purpose, restate your thesis, and reconsider your audience. Does your main point come through clearly in every paragraph, or do some paragraphs digress, repeat information, or contradict what has come before (see **32d**)?

In addition to taking care of your main idea, you'll also want to revise in terms of audience expectations. How does your overall purpose connect with the expectations of your audience? How will your audience respond to your thesis statement? Which of your assertions will your audience immediately understand or accept? Which examples or details will interest your audience? Which of your language choices were aimed expressly at this audience? In other words, revising successfully requires that you examine your work both as a writer and as a reader.

As you read and revise for your overall purpose, you'll also be reading and revising paragraph by paragraph, making sure each paragraph is well developed (see **32c**), as well as unified and coherent (**31a–b**). You'll be assessing whether each paragraph leads smoothly to the next, whether you need to rearrange any, and whether your transitions are effective (see **31b**). It's especially important to recheck the transitions after you've deleted, added, or rearranged paragraphs.

(2) What is not on the page can be more important than what is on the page.

Writers are always on the lookout for what they've put on the page—and what they may have left out. What information might the audience be expecting? What information might strengthen this essay? Your best ideas will not always surface in your first draft; you will sometimes have an important new idea only after you have finished that draft and taken a good look at it, asking yourself whether something is missing. You might share your draft with a classmate or colleague who is working on the same assignment, asking that person to mark confusing or unclear passages (see **33c**).

(3) Your tone helps you fulfill your purpose.

Tone reflects a writer's attitude toward a subject, so you'll want to make sure that your tone is appropriate to your purpose, audience, and context (see **32a**). When revising, consider how your writing sounds. If you want to present yourself as confident, well informed, and fair-minded, then you'll want all of your words and sentences to convey that tone. Your challenge is to make sure that your tone contributes to eliciting from your readers the desired response.

Consider the difference in tone between the following two writers, both of whom grew up in the South and are describing the expectations for women in their family. Paragraph 1 is by a black woman who is a celebrated anthropologist and writer; paragraph 2 is by a white woman, who is a prize-winning novelist and essayist. (For ease of reference, each of the sample paragraphs in this chapter is numbered.)

1   Mama exhorted her children at every opportunity to "jump at de sun." We might not land on the sun, but at least we would get off the ground. Papa did not feel so hopeful. Let well enough alone. It did not do for Negroes to have too much spirit. He was always threatening to break mine or kill me in the attempt. My mother was always standing between us. She conceded that I was impudent and given to talking back, but she didn't want to "squinch my spirit" too much for fear that I would turn out to be a mealy-mouthed rag doll by the time I got grown. Papa always flew hot when Mama said that. I do not know whether he feared for my future, with the tendency I had to stand and give battle, or that he felt a personal reference in Mama's observation. He predicted dire things for me. The white folks were not going to stand for it. I was going to be hung before I got grown. Somebody was going to blow me down for my sassy tongue. Mama was going to suck sorrow for not beating my temper out of me before it was too late. Posses with ropes and guns were going to drag me out sooner or later on account of that stiff neck I toted. I was going to tote a hungry belly by reason of my forward ways. My older sister was meek and mild. She would always get along. Why

couldn't I be like her? Mama would keep right on with whatever she was doing and remark, "Zora is my young'un, and Sarah is yours. I'll be bound mine will come out more than conquer. You leave her alone. I'll tend to her when I figger she needs it." She meant by that that Sarah had a disposition like Papa's, while mine was like hers.   —ZORA NEALE HURSTON, "Dust Tracks on a Road"

2   The women of my family were measured, manlike, sexless, bearers of babies, burdens, and contempt. My family? The women of my family? We are the ones in all those photos taken at mining disasters, floods, fires. We are the ones in the background with our mouths open, in print dresses or drawstring pants and collarless smocks, ugly and old and exhausted. Solid, stolid, wide-hipped baby machines. We were all wide-hipped and predestined. Wide-faced meant stupid. Wide hands marked workhorses with dull hair and tired eyes, thumbing through magazines full of women so different from us they could have been another species.

—**DOROTHY ALLISON,** *Two or Three Things I Know for Sure*

Exercise 1

Reread paragraphs 1 and 2 by Zora Neale Hurston and Dorothy Allison, and then write a short analysis of how each of these women sounds. Be sure to identify specific words and phrases that led you to attribute this tone to each of them.

The thesaurus and grammar checker in your word-processing program may give you advice that can affect the tone of your writing. For example, a grammar checker may suggest that you change a word you have intentionally repeated in order to achieve a specific effect and create a certain tone. If you are using these features of your word-processing program as you revise your writing, give the suggestions they make careful consideration.

33b | Introductions and conclusions guide readers in responding to your entire essay.

Your introduction and conclusion play a special role in helping readers understand your essay as a whole. In fact, readers look for and read these parts of an essay carefully, expecting guidance and clarification from them.

(1) An effective introduction arouses the reader's interest and establishes your topic and tone.

Experienced writers know that the opening paragraph is important; it is their best chance to "hook" their readers with tantalizing information that establishes the topic as worthy of their time and the writer as worthy of their trust. Effective introductions make readers want to read on. Mark Twain built on the success of *Tom Sawyer* when he wrote the introduction for *Huckleberry Finn,* using Huck to speak directly to the readers:

> You don't know about me without you have read a book by the name of *The Adventures of Tom Sawyer;* but that ain't no matter. That book was made by Mr. Mark Twain, and he told the truth, mainly. There was things which he stretched, but mainly he told the truth.

Twain's lively introduction connects with the audience and establishes that the story is being told by an uneducated boy. For any piece of writing that is long and complex, an especially good introduction orients the reader as to the direction the work will take.

Introductions have no set length; they can be as brief as a couple of sentences or as long as a couple of paragraphs or more. The only feature of introductions that remains the same, regardless of their tone or length, is their location. Introductions always appear first—but they are often drafted and revised much later in the writing process, for introductions and the

thesis statements they so often contain (see 32c) evolve naturally as writers revise their material, sharpening its focus and developing it to fulfill the overall purpose.

You can arouse the interest of your audience by writing introductions in a number of ways.

(a) Opening with an unusual fact or statistic

3   The most recent statistics from the U.S. Substance Abuse and
Mental Health Services Administration's National Household Survey on Drug Abuse indicate that nearly 7 million youths between
the ages of 12 and 20 binge-drink at least once a month. And despite the fact that many colleges have cracked down on drinking,
Henry Wechsler of the Harvard School of Public Health says that
two of every five college students still binge-drink regularly. For a
male that means downing five or more drinks in a row; for a female
it means consuming four drinks in one session at least once in a
two-week period.   —BERNICE WUETHRICH, "Getting Stupid"

(b) Opening with an intriguing statement

4   After smiling brilliantly for nearly four decades, I now find myself trying to quit. Or, at the very least, seeking to lower the wattage
a bit.   —AMY CUNNINGHAM, "Why Women Smile"

(c) Opening with an anecdote

5   10:00 P.M. Time for the nightly lockdown and head count. The
heavy metal door to my cell lets out an ominous grinding sound,
then slides abruptly shut with a loud clang. I hear other doors
clanging almost simultaneously down the cellblock. The walls re-
verberate, as do my nerves. Even though I know it's about to happen, at the sudden noise my skin jumps. I'm always on edge in
here, always nervous, always apprehensive. I'd be a fool not to be.
You never let your guard down when you live in hell. Every sudden sound has its own terror. Every silence, too. One of the
sounds—or one of those silences—could well be my last, I know.
But which one? My body twitches slightly at each unexpected foot-
fall, each slamming metal door.   —LEONARD PELTIER, *Prison Writings*

(d) Opening with a question your essay will answer

6   You ask me what is poverty? Listen to me. Here I am, dirty, smelly, and with no "proper" underwear on and with the stench of my rotting teeth near you. I will tell you. Listen to me. Listen without pity. I cannot use your pity. Listen with understanding. Put yourself in my dirty, worn out, ill-fitting shoes, and hear me.

—**JO GOODWIN PARKER,** "What Is Poverty?"

(e) Opening with an appropriate quotation

7   Wordsworth said we "half perceive and half create" the beauty we find in nature, and I guess that's what I'm saying, too. On the one hand I see the forest differently now because of the ideas and knowledge I bring to it. I accept it because I know more and am more confused about notions I used to take for granted. On the other hand my sense of this landscape, my pleasure in it, seems to come from outside, too, unbidden and uncontrolled, surprising. I didn't expect to feel the way I do and even resisted it. Satisfaction is the feeling actually produced in me when I walk here over time. Enjoyment is what I experience in the presence of these trees and these openings, just empirically, prior to thoughts and theories.

—**CHRIS ANDERSON,** "Life on the Edge"

(f) Opening with an example

8   Libby Smith knows what it is like to be a victim of gay bashing. First, there were the harassing telephone calls to her home. Then, one evening last March as she went to get her book bag out of a locker at the University of Wisconsin at Eau Claire, she was attacked by two men.   —**MARY CRYSTAL CAGE,** "Gay Bashing on Campus"

(g) Opening with general information about the topic or with background on how you came to choose it

9   I fell in love with it—college basketball, that is—at a drafty old barn in Lincoln Square in Worcester, Massachusetts, not far from where one of my great-uncles once owned a saloon. This Worces-

ter Memorial Auditorium was square and huge, and it had tower-
ing murals depicting men loading shells into the big guns of a
dreadnought and firing artillery along the banks of the Somme.
You had to walk up broad staircases to see the murals in their entirety, and I didn't have the courage for that until I was nearly ten.
I continued to love it—the whole raucous, tumbling parade of
it—through my undergraduate days at Marquette University,
where Al McGuire put together a delightfully rambunctious program. I even loved it when I covered it for five years, more or less
full-time, for the *Boston Herald*. I have missed one Final Four
since 1982, and I can tell you exactly where and when I stopped
loving college basketball: I stopped loving it in a hotel in Indianapolis in 1999, on a Saturday afternoon, before the national
semifinals.   —**CHARLES P. PIERCE,** "ConMen"

(h) Opening with a thesis, simply stated

10   Complaining was great when I was a kid. Well, maybe not great,
just better than now. When you are a kid, your sense of entitlement
is more intact. At least that's how it seems from this distance. Things
are supposed to be a certain way—*yours.* Oh sure, things are supposed to go your way as an adult, but it's not always appropriate to
mention this.   —**CARRIE FISHER,** "The Art of Complaining"

Whatever type of introduction you choose to write, use your
opening paragraph to indicate your topic, engage your readers'
attention, and establish your credibility (see **38a**).

(2) An effective conclusion helps readers recognize the most important points of your essay and understand why those points are significant.

Just as a good introduction tantalizes readers, a good conclusion satisfies them. It wraps up the essay in a meaningful, often thought-provoking way. Some suggestions for writing
effective conclusions follow.

(a) Concluding by rephrasing the thesis and summarizing the main points

11   The Endangered Species Act should not take into account economic considerations. Economics doesn't know how to value a species or a forest. Its logic drives people to exploit resources to the point of extinction. The Endangered Species Act tells us that extinction is morally unacceptable. It was enacted by a Congress and president in a wise mood, to express a higher value than a bottom line.   **—DONELLA MEADOWS,** "Not Seeing the Forest for the Dollar Bills"

(b) Concluding by calling attention to larger issues

12   Nonetheless, the greatest growth industry in this country is the one dedicated to the mirage of good grooming as the road to immortality. Immigrants past built bridges and schools, gilded the cherubim in the corners of churches. Today an entire immigrant class makes a living painting toenails and opening pores. Advances in science and medicine have combined to offer this: the tattooing of permanent eyeliner, the bleaching of teeth, the lasering of sun spots. The waning days of a great nation can be charted only in hindsight. But surely it is a danger sign of some sort when a country is no longer able to care for its own cuticles.

   —ANNA QUINDLEN, "Leg Waxing and Life Everlasting"

(c) Concluding with a call for a change in action or attitude

13   Our medical care system is in trouble and getting worse. While the experts try to figure out how to achieve utopian goals at affordable prices, let's do something practical about the suffering on our doorsteps. Primary care is the most affordable safety net we can offer our citizens. By all means, let's continue the debate about universal, comprehensive insurance to cover all medical costs, but, in the meantime, let's provide primary health care to all uninsured Americans—now!

   —GORDON T. MOORE, "Caring for the Uninsured and Underinsured"

(d) Concluding with a vivid image

14   At just past 10 A.M., farm workers and scrap-yard laborers in Somerset County looked up to see a large commercial airliner dipping and lunging as it swooped low over the hill country of southern Pennsylvania, near the town of Shanksville. A man driving a coal truck on Route 30 said he saw the jet tilt violently from side to side, then suddenly plummet "straight down." It hit nose first on the grassy face of a reclaimed strip mine at approximately 10:05 Eastern Daylight Time and exploded into a fireball, shattering windowpanes a half-mile away. The seventy-two-year-old man who was closest to the point of impact saw what looked to him like the yellow mushroom cloud of an atomic blast. Twenty-eight-year-old Eric Peterson was one of the first on the scene. He arrived to discover a flaming crater fifty feet deep. Shredded clothing hung from the trees, and smoldering airplane parts littered the ground. It did not look much like the site of a great American victory, but it was.
—**RANDALL SULLIVAN**, "September 11th, 2001 Somewhere over Pennsylvania"

(e) Concluding by connecting with the introduction

Introduction

15   In the Prelude to *Middlemarch,* George Eliot lamented the unfulfilled lives of talented women: "Some have felt that these blundering lives are due to the inconvenient indefiniteness with which the Supreme Power has fashioned the natures of women: if there were one level of feminine incompetence as strict as the ability to count three and no more, the social lot of women might be treated with scientific certitude." Eliot goes on to discount the idea of innate limitation, but while she wrote in 1872, the leaders of European anthropometry were trying to measure "with scientific certitude" the inferiority of women. . . .

In the essay that follows this introduction, Steven Jay Gould focuses on anthropometry (the measuring of skulls) and then loops back to Eliot for his conclusion.

Conclusion

16 George Eliot well appreciated the special tragedy that biological labeling imposed upon members of disadvantaged groups. She expressed it for people like herself—women with extraordinary talent. I would apply it more widely—not only to those whose dreams are flouted but also to those who never realize that they may dream—but I cannot match her prose. —**STEVEN JAY GOULD**, "Women's Brains"

Whatever technique you choose for your conclusion, provide readers with a sense of closure. Bear in mind that they may be wondering, "So what? Why have you told me all this?" Your conclusion gives you an opportunity to address that concern. Use your conclusion to clarify why you have asked them to read what they have just read (see **36f(6)**).

Exercise 2

Thumb through a magazine you enjoy, and skim the introductions of all the articles. Select two introductions that caught your attention. Consider the reasons *why* they interested you. What specific techniques for an introduction did the authors use? Next, look through the same or another magazine for two effective conclusions. Analyze their effectiveness as well.

33c | **Writers benefit from having others read their drafts.**

Because writing is a form of communication, writers benefit from checking whether they are communicating their ideas effectively to their readers. Instructors are, of course, one set of readers, but they are often the last people to see your writing. Experienced writers *always* consult a trusted reader before they submit their work for evaluation. You, too, can consult with readers—at the writing center or in your classes—asking them for honest responses to your concerns. Both writers and readers benefit from sharing and responding to writing; both gain a clearer sense of how they can improve their work.

(1) Clearly defined evaluation standards help both writers and reviewers.

Although you'll always write within a rhetorical situation (see 32a), you'll often address that situation in terms of an assigned task with specific evaluation standards. Instructors usually indicate their evaluation standards in class, on assignment sheets, or on separate handouts. Whether you're working with a small writing group from class or a single reader, such as a classmate or writing center tutor, you need to review evaluation criteria at the beginning of a working session and use them to indicate where you should focus your attention. For example, if your instructor has told you that your essay will be evaluated primarily in terms of whether you have a clear thesis (see 32c) and adequate support for it (36d), then those aspects should be your primary focus. Other concerns will be secondary.

If you are developing your own criteria for evaluation, the following checklist can help you get started. Based on the elements of the rhetorical situation, this checklist can be easily adjusted so that it meets your specific needs for a particular assignment.

CHECKLIST for Evaluating a Draft of an Essay

- What is your purpose in the essay (32a(1))? Does the essay fulfill the assignment?
- Does the essay address a specific audience (32a(2))? Is that audience appropriate for the assignment?

(Continued on page 458)

(Continued from page 457)

- What is the tone of the essay (33a(3))? How does the tone align with the overall purpose, the intended audience, and the context for the writing (32a)?

- Is your topic sufficiently focused (32b)? What is the thesis statement (32c)?

- What assertions do you make to support the thesis statement? How do you support these assertions? What specific evidence do you provide?

- Are paragraphs arranged in an effective sequence (32d)? What order do you use? Is each paragraph thoroughly developed (31c)?

- Is the introduction effective (33b(1))? How do you engage the reader's attention?

- Is the conclusion appropriate for the essay's purpose (33b(2))? Does it draw the essay together, or does it seem disconnected and abrupt?

(2) You can help readers review your work by telling them about your purpose and your concerns.

When submitting a draft for review, you can increase your chances of getting the kind of help you want by indicating what your concerns are. You can provide such an orientation orally to a writing group, tutor, or peer reviewer in just a few minutes.

Or, when doing so is not possible, you can attach a cover letter consisting of a paragraph or two, especially if you are submitting it online. In either case, adopting the following model can help reviewers give you useful responses.

SUBMITTING A DRAFT FOR REVIEW

Topic and Purpose

State your topic and why you have chosen it. Explain what you hope to accomplish by writing about it. Describe your exigence for writing (see **32a**). Indicate your thesis (**32c**), and explain in a sentence or two why you have taken this position. Providing this information gives reviewers useful direction.

Strengths

Mark the passages of the draft you are confident about. Doing so directs attention away from areas you do not want to discuss.

Concerns

Being clear about your concerns is essential to the review process. Put question marks by the passages you find troublesome and ask for specific advice. For example, if you are afraid that one of your paragraphs may not fit the overall purpose, direct attention to that particular paragraph. You are most likely to get the kind of help you need when you ask for it specifically.

(3) When you submit a draft for peer review, some responses may be more helpful than others.

Before asking for responses to a draft you are planning to revise, you may find it useful to remind both your readers and yourself that the work in question is *only a draft*. In fact, you may wish to type "DRAFT" onto the paper. Then, your readers know that it is safe for them to criticize, and you feel reassured that they are responding to a piece that is not yet finished.

Reviewers don't always know exactly how to help—or what to say that might be helpful—which is the best reason for you to provide some guidelines. Whether the advice is helpful or not, try to listen to or read what your reviewers have to say about your work. After the reviewers have finished, however, you are responsible for evaluating their comments—rejecting those that would take you in a direction you do not want to pursue and applying those that will help you fulfill your purpose (see 33c(1)). You have the final say about what goes into an essay with your name on it.

(4) You can help other writers by giving thoughtful responses to their work.

When you are asked to read a draft written by someone else, ask what concerns the writer has about it and how the writer would like you to respond to those concerns. Then, before you respond, read the draft carefully—at least twice. Be sure to respond to the concerns the writer has expressed. If you see a major problem in the draft that the writer hasn't mentioned, ask the writer if she or he wants to discuss it at this time; if not, honor that decision. Be sure to praise whatever the writer has done well and to identify specific passages you think could be improved and *how.*

Whenever possible, frame your comments like those of a colleague rather than a judge. For example, if you tell a writer, "Your second page is confusing," you are making a judgment and putting yourself in the position of speaking for all readers. If, on the other hand, you say, "I have trouble following your organization on page two," you alert the writer to a potential problem while speaking only for yourself. Remember, then, that it is possible to be honest without being unkind. As a reviewer, your job is to help writers write the essays they want to write, not the ones you want to write.

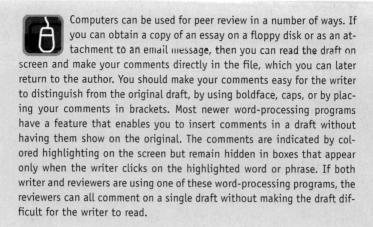

Computers can be used for peer review in a number of ways. If you can obtain a copy of an essay on a floppy disk or as an attachment to an email message, then you can read the draft on screen and make your comments directly in the file, which you can later return to the author. You should make your comments easy for the writer to distinguish from the original draft, by using boldface, caps, or by placing your comments in brackets. Most newer word-processing programs have a feature that enables you to insert comments in a draft without having them show on the original. The comments are indicated by colored highlighting on the screen but remain hidden in boxes that appear only when the writer clicks on the highlighted word or phrase. If both writer and reviewers are using one of these word-processing programs, the reviewers can all comment on a single draft without making the draft difficult for the writer to read.

(5) Peer review usually improves as writers gain experience and build trust.

After freewriting, listing, and organizing her ideas into a working plan (see **32d**), Melissa Schraeder submitted a draft for peer review in a first-year writing course. Melissa worked with a classmate, who was working on the same assignment, and a peer tutor from the university's writing center as she drafted and revised her essay, using set criteria for peer evaluation. These students' comments represent the range of responses you might receive in a similar situation. As members of writing groups gain experience and learn to employ the strategies outlined in **33c(1)–(4)**, their advice usually becomes more helpful.

As you read the assignment and then Melissa's draft, remember that it is only a first draft—not a model of perfect writing—

and also that this is the first time the peer reviewers, Bob Geiger and Michelle Clewell, responded to it. Melissa sent her draft electronically to Bob and Michelle, who used Track Changes (a Word editing function that can be found on the pulldown menu under Tools) to add suggested changes and comments throughout the essay.

The assignment Draft a three- to four-page, double-spaced essay in which you analyze the causes or consequences of a choice you have had to make in the last year or two. Whatever choice you analyze, make sure that it concerns a topic you can develop with confidence and without violating your own sense of privacy. Moreover, consider the expectations of your audience and whether the topic you have chosen will help you communicate something meaningful to readers. As you draft, then, establish an audience for your essay, a group that might benefit from or be interested in any recommendation that grows out of your analysis.

Melissa A. Schraeder   Bob

English 15   *Michelle*

Professor Glenn

Draft—Working toward a Degree

When I first decided to pursue my college education at Penn State University, a key factor in my decision was that as a state university, Penn State offered a relatively low tuition. This first sentence doesn't seem to have much grounding. Maybe develop your own experience with choosing a school more, or use a different opening. Adding this factor to the giving financial support of my parents and my fortune at receiving several grants and scholarships, I initially believed that my college education would be easily affordable. When I started classes however, I soon found that with all the additional expenses of school such as the cost of books, technology fees, and spending money, going to school meant finding a job. Though hesitant at first about how holding a job might affect my studies, I soon took on a part-time job ~~where I worked~~ , *working* about fifteen hours a week. *Up until this point your sentences seem sort of long. Maybe you can condense these introductory sentences into a central idea that will get us more quickly to your thesis statement. See my suggestion.* Based on my own experience, I feel confident in saying that balancing a part-time job with success in schoolwork is not only a manageable task, but also a valuable experience contributing to growth as a student and as an individual. ~~Since so many students of today need to work while going to school, I hope to show them that while holding a part-time job and doing well in school may seem difficult at first, in many ways these two undertakings are quite compatible.~~ *This sentence seems repetitive to me—I don't think it is needed.*

If you have the right attitude and some good advice about finding a part-time job, you will find that working while going to school *does not have to be a scary experience.* ~~is not as scary as it may sound at first.~~ As college students, the most important thing ~~that we need~~ to remember is that ~~our~~ schoolwork must always be *your* ~~our~~ first priority. *I think you should keep your pronouns consistent. Since you started with the second-person voice, why not stick with it?* Keeping this in mind, as with most things in life, your own individual sacrifices in this balancing act will determine your success. One of the sacrifices that you might have to make is the need to limit or carefully schedule the time that you spend with your friends. *Since you are trying to show how work at school is both manageable and beneficial for a college student, maybe you shouldn't begin your evidence* with such a negative example. Keep a consistent tone. Not all sacrifices need to be so difficult though. A small sacrifice you can make is to bring your schoolbooks along with you to work and utilize your work breaks to get a ~~heads up~~ head start on your nightly schoolwork. In addition, ~~since part of your time is already committed to your employers, You~~ you will need to get a good handle on your school schedule and plan ahead ~~to determine the time you need to work on various assignments~~. *This section seems kind of vague. I think it would be better if you gave some of your own personal experiences with planning in order to show specific examples of this point.* This sacrifice however will have positive repercussions as it will encourage you to form early study and time management habits. This is a good point, but I wonder if it might fit better on page three where you begin to discuss the positive repercussions of part-time work on the college experience.

While it is important to make such sacrifices in balancing a part-time job with success in school, you need not put all of the pressure on yourself. In fact, a key factor in minimizing such pressure is to choose a job where you work for an understanding employer. I don't like the way this is worded, it implies that you are putting pressure on the employer. Maybe rephrase "there are ways to limit the pressure that you might feel." This is not always an easy task and is certainly easier said than done. You can, however, take advantage of the resources available to you such as older students, advisors, and internship coordinators in finding a student-friendly employer. You should look for an employer that understands the need to put schoolwork first and who values scholarship in employees. A good place to look for such an employer is in university-run businesses where supervisors are advised to view employees as students first and foremost. Planning ahead around exam or paper weeks, you should also look for a job that offers flexibility and variability in scheduling hours. Again, this is a feature that can be found in most university-related businesses or services since many of these follow the academic calendar in their hours of operation. For the understanding and flexibility that such jobs offer, you should take advantage of the many positions available within your own college or university. *This paragraph seems to repeat itself a little bit. I think you should condense this material and use a personal experience to drive home your point about university employment.* This paragraph is where you start to sound too "preachy." You say "you should" a few times. How about changing this to "I would recommend" or "based on my experiences, the following methods have been helpful" in order to make your tone less presumptuous?

Now that I have shown how college students can manage their schoolwork with a part-time job, I want to move on to demonstrating the ways in which the challenge of balancing work with school can be a valuable learning and growing experience for college students. First, this challenge provides students with a degree of self-discipline as working students need to prioritize their schoolwork carefully, thus learning the importance of realistic goal-setting and time management. *The tone of this is too definite. Remember that your previous paragraphs give good examples but are not the ultimate method for everyone.* Second, students who work to support their own education often develop a heightened sense of respect, value, and responsibility for that education. *Great point!* This means that working students often take their studies rather seriously and realize the importance of a timely completion of their degree. These two examples represent large-scale attitudes and outlooks on education, but part-time work can also have more immediate effects on the academic career of a college student.

Such immediate effects of part-time work can be categorized into two types of experiences ~~with part-time work~~, work which offers career experience and work which fuels academic and career motivation. The former category includes but need not be limited to arranged, paid internships or focused work programs implemented or overseen by your college or university. Career experience is also found in more unexpected ways, such as when a management student gets to observe her manager at work or when a communications student practices his skills in a sales job. While many students will be fortunate to have such experiences, others will find themselves working at jobs that have very little to do with their projected career goals. In such cases, there are still valuable lessons to be learned. Certain types of part-time work, such as factory, food service, or maintenance work, while less directly valuable to the education process, often have positive motivating effects on students' academic attitudes. A working student who faces boredom, monotony, or low wages in her or his part-time job, will often be motivated to achieve academic excellence as a means of moving beyond the scope of this part-time work. *I think you should add some personal experience here. Did you work at a job related to your major or that was monotonous yet motivating?*

With the right attitude and outlook, part-time work can have many positive effects on the experiences of a college student. Even the potential negativity of facing boredom or monotony at work can be used constructively to motivate students to do their best schoolwork. If your college years are the best and most important of your life, I assure you that combining work with academics will enrich that importance, as it will give you a greater appreciation for the education you worked doubly hard to receive. I like your conclusion. I think it is good that it ends on a very positive note and that it relates back to your title about "Working toward a Degree."

Melissa,

Generally, I think this is a very good essay. The overall progression of the paper going from "how to work and do well in school" to "why it is beneficial to work while in school" makes logical sense to me. I like that you emphasize the benefits of holding a job beyond just the obvious point of making money. I also think that you have strong credibility and show good will since you have personal experience with your topic. This credibility makes for a strong argument. Maybe it would behoove you to include specific examples of your working experiences in college. Although your credibility is strong, you might want to avoid being too "preachy" in your tone. I feel that this self-assured tone tends to weaken your argument. I do like, however, the way you note in your paper that not all work has to apply directly to your major in order for it to be valuable. And the way your working experience reinforce this point. Finally, I like the point you make in the concluding paragraph about monotonous work motivating students to appreciate schooling and thus work harder at their education, as this is something that many college students don't think about. This is especially true for freshmen since many often take attending college for granted as they see it as the next logical step following high school.

—Bob Geiger

Melissa,

Your paper is well thought out and focused, yet combining several sentences and limiting the wordiness would intensify your point. The validity of the paper is strengthened because of your personal experience of holding a part-time job while attending college—tie some of these specific examples into your paper rather than using generic and general examples. This is a great draft—keep working, developing, and improving. Here are some specific suggestions for improvement.

—Michelle Clewell

- First paragraph suggestion: "Because I decided to attend a state university, was fortunate to receive several grants and scholarships, and had the financial support of my parents, I initially believed my college education would be easily affordable. However, with all the additional expenses, such as the cost of books, technology fees, and spending money, going to school meant finding a part-time job."

- Paper has good structure and flow.

- Limit prepositional phrases and repeating yourself.

- Great points made about time management and valuing one's education.

- First half of the paper "you" is used talking directly to the student reading the paper, but the second half is written in a more generic third person. Try to be consistent with point of view.

- Add personal experiences and examples to strengthen points.

Before revising, Melissa considered the comments she received from Bob and Michelle. Since she'd asked both of them to respond to her overall essay, addressing both big issues and small, she had to weigh all the comments and use the ones that seemed to be most useful for her next draft.

Exercise 3

Compose an evaluation sheet, with specific questions and guidelines, to use with another writer as you review each other's draft for an assignment you're working on. You'll want to have questions about fulfilling the assignment, the overall purpose of the essay, the intended audience, and the thesis, among others.

After Melissa had time to reconsider her first draft and to think about the responses she received from readers (including the ones reprinted here), she made a number of large-scale changes concerning her attention to audience, improved her introduction and conclusion, and edited some of her paragraphs to make them more effective and clear. She also dealt with sentence-level issues of punctuation and word choice. To view these revisions, visit **www.harbrace.com**.

After more revision, more peer review, and some careful editing and proofreading, Melissa was ready to submit her essay to her instructor. Her final draft is on pages 474–479.

33d | Editing makes ideas, sentences, and paragraphs clearer and more engaging.

If you are satisfied with the revised structure of your essay and the content of your paragraphs, you can move to the process of editing individual sentences for clarity, effectiveness, and variety (see chapters **21–23** and **29–30**). Your writing group or tutor may have already alerted you to some of these editing issues, but if not, you can work alone. Consider combining choppy or unconnected sentences and reworking long, overly complicated ones. If you overuse some structures, say, introductory prepositional phrases, try experimenting with other patterns (see chapter **30**). Eliminate any needless shifts in grammatical structures, tone, style, or point of view (see chapter **27**).

Examine your diction, and make sure the words you have used are appropriate for this particular essay (see chapters **19** and **20**). If any words leap out as much more formal or informal than your language as a whole, replace them with words that are more consistent with your style. Eliminate any redundant or repetitive words (see chapter **21**). If you have experimented with words new to your vocabulary, make sure that you have used them accurately.

Check whether your punctuation is correct and whether you have followed standard conventions for mechanics. Even if you have already used a spell checker (see **18a**), use it again because new errors may have been introduced in the revision process. Remember also that such software is never foolproof. Double-check that you are using such words as *there* or *their* and *who's* or *whose* correctly—and remember that even words that are spelled correctly might be the wrong words in a specific sentence.

The following checklist for editing contains cross-references to other chapters where you can find more specific information.

CHECKLIST for Editing

1 Sentences

- What is the unifying idea of each sentence (**23**)?
- Are ideas given appropriate emphasis within each sentence (**29**)?
- Are the sentences varied in length and in type (**30**)?
- Are there any fragments (**2**)? Are there any comma splices or fused sentences (**3**)?
- How many of your sentences use subordination? Coordination? How are the ideas related in each of the sentences using these constructions (**24**)?

- Do any of your sentences have structures that should be parallel but are not (26)?

- Do any sentences contain misplaced or dangling modifiers (25)?

- Do any of your sentences shift in tone, style, or grammatical structure (27)? Is the shift intentional?

- Is every verb form appropriate (7)? Does each verb agree with its subject (6a)? Does every pronoun agree with its antecedent (6b)?

2 Diction

- Have you repeated any words? Is your repetition intentional? Are your word choices exact, or are some words vague or imprecise (20a–b)? Have you used idioms correctly (20c)?

- Can you justify the necessity for every word or phrase (21)? Have any necessary words been left out by mistake (22)?

- Is the vocabulary you've chosen appropriate for your audience, purpose, and context (19 and 32a)?

- Have you defined any technical or unfamiliar words for your audience (20e)?

3 Punctuation and Mechanics

- Is all punctuation correct (12–17)? Are any marks missing?

- Are all words spelled correctly (18)?

- Is capitalization correct (9)?

- Are titles identified by either quotation marks (16b) or italics (10a)?

- Are abbreviations appropriate and correct (11b–d)?

33e | Proofreading can make your final draft free from error.

Once you have revised and edited your essay, it's your responsibility to format it carefully and properly (see **8d–e**) and proofread it. Proofreading means making a special search to ensure that the final product you submit is free from error, or nearly so. An error-free essay allows your reader to read for meaning, without encountering spelling or punctuation errors that interfere with meaning. As you proofread, you may discover problems that call for further revision or editing, but proofreading is usually the last step in the writing process.

With a computer, you can easily produce professional-looking documents. Showing that you care about presentation indicates respect for your audience. (See **8d–e**.) However, no matter how professional your paper looks when you print it, proofread it carefully. Mechanical mistakes can undermine your credibility.

Because the eye tends to see what it expects to see, many writers miss errors—especially minor ones, such as a missing comma or apostrophe—even when they think they have proofread carefully. To proofread well, then, you need to read your work more than once, to read it aloud, or read it backwards.

An extra pair of eyes can also be helpful, so you might ask another writer for help. If someone else helps you proofread, this check should be in addition to your own. Moreover, if you ask someone to proofread your work, remember that you are asking for an error check only. If you want a more thoughtful response that could help you revise, you need to ask for it at an earlier point in the process (see **33c(2)**).

When using the proofreading checklist that follows, you may find it helpful to refer to the chapters and sections cited. Also, keep your dictionary at hand (see **19e**) to look up any words that puzzle you.

CHECKLIST for Proofreading

1 Spelling (18)

- Have you double-checked the words you frequently misspell and any the spell checker might have missed (for example, homonyms or misspellings that still form words, such as *form* for *from*)?
- Have you double-checked the spelling of all foreign words and all proper names?

2 Punctuation (12–17) and Capitalization (9)

- Does each sentence have appropriate closing punctuation, and have you used only one space after each end punctuation mark (17)?
- Is all punctuation within sentences used appropriately and placed correctly (commas (12), semicolons (14), apostrophes (15), other internal marks of punctuation (17d–i), and hyphens (18f))?
- Are quotations carefully and correctly punctuated (16a)? Where have you placed end punctuation with a quotation (16d)? Are quotations capitalized properly (16a and 9d)?
- Are all proper names, people's titles, and titles of published works correctly capitalized (9a–c)?

Beyond the Rule

EDITING AND PROOFREADING

Editing and proofreading share many features: Both processes function to ensure a clear and error-free essay. For more information about the differences between the two processes, visit www.harbrace.com.

33f | The final draft reflects the care the writer took.

Melissa continued to revise and edit her essay. Each subsequent draft became stronger. The following is the essay that Melissa ultimately submitted to her teacher.

Melissa A. Schraeder

English 15

Professor Glenn

Working Toward a Degree

With many private universities approaching $40,000 per year for tuition, it is all too obvious that getting a higher education is expensive. Fortunately, financial aid programs and state-funded schools, where tuition costs are normally less than half of the average private school, have made higher education more affordable for Americans. When I decided to attend Penn State University, I was fortunate to receive several grants and scholarships as well as the promise of financial support from my parents. Little wonder that I initially believed that my college education would be easily affordable. When I started classes however, I soon found that with all the additional expenses of school such as the cost of books, technology fees, and spending money, going to school meant finding a job—even for someone with financial support. Though hesitant about how holding a job might affect my studies, I soon took on a part-time job at the Penn State Creamery where I work about fifteen hours a week— and continue to do well in my coursework. Based on my experience, I feel confident in assuring hardworking students that not only can they balance a part-time job with success in schoolwork, but that the experience can be a valuable, life-long lesson, contributing to their growth as students and individuals.

If you have the right attitude and some good advice about finding a part-time job, you will find that working while going to school does not have to be an overwhelming experience. As a college student, the most important thing to remember is that schoolwork must always be your first priority. After all, like most things in life, your individual sacrifices in this balancing act will determine your success. One of the first sacrifices you might have to make is to limit, schedule, or reimagine the free time you have with your friends. After you start working, you won't be able to spend long hours in the coffee shop with your friends, but you can study with them. Not all sacrifices are difficult, though. Another small sacrifice might be to take your schoolbooks along with you to work and consistently think of your work breaks as pre-scheduled time to spend on your nightly coursework. Using work breaks for study time will also help you plan ahead in terms of your various assignment deadlines. I usually set up a calendar where I indicate the dates of all my major exams and due dates for papers and then tailor my work schedule around these dates.

Such small sacrifices can lead to big gains: you quickly learn how to manage your time so you work and study efficiently.

While it is important to make such sacrifices in balancing a part-time job with success in school, you need not put all of the pressure on yourself. One key factor in reducing pressure will be your ability (or luck) in finding a job that includes an understanding employer. Doing so is not easy, so you might want to take advantage of some of the on-campus or campus-sponsored job opportunities. Older students, academic advisors, and internship coordinators can help you locate a student-friendly employer, one that expects you to be a reliable employee at the same time that your employer accepts the fact that your major responsibility is your studies. In fact, it was my academic advisor who told me about openings at the Creamery, a university-run business where supervisors are advised to view employees as students first and foremost. Supervisors at the Creamery release a monthly newsletter in which they highlight the academic achievements of student employees as a means of encouragement. The Creamery is also one of a number of on-campus businesses that offer flexibility and variability in scheduling hours, especially during holiday breaks and finals' week. This scheduling feature can be found in most university-related businesses or services since they usually follow the academic calendar in their hours of operation. For the understanding and flexibility that such jobs offer, I recommend that you try to take advantage of the many positions available within your own college or university.

Once you meet the challenge of balancing your college studies with the obligations of part-time work, you'll find that the balancing act has its own rewards: it can be a valuable learning and growing experience for you. First, this challenge can provide you with self-discipline, the self-discipline that comes with prioritzing your schoolwork, setting realistic goals, managing your time, and becoming a reliable employee. Second, students who work to support their own education often develop a heightened sense of respect, value, and responsibility for that education because we've worked and paid (or helped pay) for it. Because we take more responsibility for our educations, we usually study seriously enough to graduate on time, even early. We realize the importance of the timely completion of a degree. These two examples represent forward-looking attitudes and outlooks, but part-time work can also have more immediate effects on your academic career as well.

Such immediate effects of part-time work can be categorized into two types of experiences with part-time work: work that offers career experience and work that fuels academic and career motivation. The former category includes but need not be limited to arranged, paid internships or focused work programs implemented or overseen by your college or university. But career experience can also be found in more unexpected ways, such as when a management student gets to observe her manager at work or when a communications student practices his skills in a sales job. While many student-workers will be fortunate to have such experiences, others, like me, will find themselves working at jobs that have very little to do with their projected career goals. My experiences with work at college have fallen into the latter category, but there are still valuable lessons to be learned. Although the food service work I perform at the Creamery has little relevance to my English and History majors, I enjoy my time there as a release from my studies. Working at the Creamery has also motivated me to do my best schoolwork, since I recognized that a food service job would not be fulfilling to me as a life-long career. If you find that the part-time work available to you is not directly related to your education, such work can still have positive motivating effects on your academic attitudes. A working student who faces boredom, monotony, or low wages in her or his part-time job will often be motivated to achieve academic excellence as a means of moving beyond the scope of this part-time work.

With the right attitude, you might gain work experiences that are as positive as your academic ones. There are likely to be many jobs available within your university community that are student-friendly and may even be directly related to your major area of studies. If that is not the case, you can use the less-than-fulfilling aspects of the work as motivation to do your best academic work in order to move steadily through your requirements and graduate on time. Any kind of employment may help you appreciate your career goals more than someone who isn't working their way through school. Everyone tells us that our college years are the best years of our life—and so far I think they're right. By combining part-time work with academics, we're not only earning a greater appreciation for our education, one we've worked doubly hard to receive, but we are also helping to pay for that education.

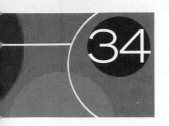

34 Writing under Pressure

You won't always have the luxury of planning, drafting, revising, getting feedback from others, and editing a piece of writing over a stretch of days or weeks. Frequently, your college instructor or employer will ask you to produce an essay or report during a class period or within a day or two.

No matter how much time they have between an assignment and a due date, most writers feel some pressure. Some writers, however, experience added anxiety when they're asked to write quickly and on demand. If you belong to either or both of these groups of writers, you'll want to follow some general strategies for reducing stress: freewriting frequently (see **32b**), making writing a part of your daily routine by keeping a journal (**32b**), and remembering that most rhetorical situations allow time for the writing process (chapters **32** and **33**). The focus of this chapter, however, is how to write well when faced with time constraints, especially when you feel as though you have only one shot at success.

This chapter will help you

- work within deadlines (**4a**),
- abbreviate the writing process (**4b**),
- manage writer's block (**4c**), and
- take essay examinations (**4d**).

It is not always possible to engage in a writing process that stretches over a period of days or even weeks. Sometimes writers must respond almost immediately to email or prepare a proposal for presentation at a hastily convened meeting. Few college students devote as much time as they ideally should to every writing assignment—especially if they're also working or parenting. The key to succeeding in such situations is to use the available time as efficiently as possible.

34a | Deadlines can help you organize your work.

You will almost always be working with deadlines—whether for essays, business plans, or grant proposals with a specified due date or on in-class writing assignments, essay exams, or time-sensitive documents. Because missing deadlines often leads to penalties, you'll want to learn some techniques for managing your time wisely.

Preparing ahead of time always helps. Even though an in-class essay exam may not be scheduled until midterm, start preparing on the first day of class. As you read your assignments and participate in class discussions, try to determine what is most important about the material you are learning. Pay attention to indications that your instructor considers certain material especially important. Read instructions or questions carefully, asking questions until you know exactly what is expected of you. If an assignment is open-ended or general, start right away imagining how you might best respond to it. Devise your own reason (or exigence) for writing and your own guidelines for the assignment.

The best preparation for writing assignments is to write frequently for your own benefit—note taking (during class, meetings, or reading), regular journal writing, and freewriting. By writing regularly, you will be able to write more fluently when forced to write quickly.

The best preparation for a writing assignment with a longer deadline, such as a research project or a progress report, is to start early. If you are choosing your own topic, begin early to narrow down your ideas (see 34b). The sooner you identify a subject (even if you continue to focus it more sharply), the sooner you can discuss it with your instructor or supervisor. For an important project or report, you might even set yourself intermediate deadlines for writing an introduction with a thesis statement (see **33b(1)**), composing a first draft, meeting with a classmate or colleague for review, revising your draft, and editing.

Whatever the deadline for a writing assignment, think about the form of the assignment and the best way to approach it. In fact, if you have the space to spread out your preliminary work (e.g., notes, research findings, relevant books and articles), you'll find that your mind will keep working on the assignment, whatever you're doing. If you carry a small notebook or hand-held computer with you, you'll always have a place to jot down notes and ideas.

34b | It may sometimes be necessary to abbreviate the writing process.

No matter how dependent you are on writing as a process, sometimes, you'll need to abbreviate that process. When given little advance notice for writing, you can quickly focus on a topic. You might decide to write about something you already know about or an idea you already feel comfortable with—whatever doesn't require time-consuming library research. If you can adjust the assignment in such a way that it allows you to write from personal or professional knowledge, so much the better. Faced with a short deadline, try to narrow the topic to a manageable scope or to relate the assignment to past or present academic or work experiences, or personal knowledge or experience—but stay away, if possible, from a topic that requires much research. Once you have a focused topic, you can write a thoughtful, in-depth analysis. Finishing the writing assignment can be a simple matter of organizing and presenting your ideas about that topic.

The following tips will help you abbreviate the writing process.

TIPS FOR ABBREVIATING THE WRITING PROCESS

- If at all possible, brainstorm about the assignment or topic with a friend or colleague (see 32b). That person can help you clarify your thinking, discover flawed reasoning, or develop counter-arguments (see 33c and 36d). As you brainstorm, take notes.

- Draft an introductory paragraph that frames your position or approach and includes a clear thesis statement. At this point, you might want to email your paragraph to your instructor, a colleague, or a friend to make sure that the paragraph addresses the right audience and is on track.

- If your thesis statement and basic approach have been approved, write down the main points you want to make and try to flesh them out with examples and supporting text.

- Read your draft aloud, slowly. Make sure that your topic sentences or bulleted points are clear. If your writing needs transitional words or phrases to help your reader along, now is the time to insert those.

- Write a strong conclusion, one that reiterates your main points but also suggests their implications, the directions in which they might point.

- Proofread one last time. Examine your writing closely to make sure that you've "pulled everything together"—that your writing fulfills the assignment you were given. Reread your introduction and conclusion to see whether they frame your piece. Reconsider your topic sentences and supporting paragraphs to make sure that they provide a shape for the piece, and to assess the overall effect on your audience.

- Submit your work on time.

You can use your computer to help you manage writing
tasks efficiently.

- If you don't have much time for revising and editing, the grammar
  checker and spell checker can help you proofread, even while you
  are drafting (see 33e). You can usually adjust the settings on these
  functions so that errors or usage problems will be automatically highlighted (usually with colored squiggly underlining).

- Keeping your notes in a word-processing file will enable you to use
  the Search function to find key words or phrases quickly.

- A program such as Microsoft's Outlook can be used to schedule
  tasks and keep a calendar. You can set the Alarm function of this
  type of program to remind yourself of a deadline.

- Many on-campus writing centers can receive drafts of student
  writing via email or through a Web site, and writing tutors can
  often respond to a draft within twenty-four hours with helpful
  advice on short notice.

34c You can manage writer's block.

Writer's block can affect any writer at any time, no matter how
experienced, no matter what the writing assignment. It helps to
recognize writer's block for what it is and what it is not. First, it
is not limited to inexperienced or unskilled writers. Many experienced and successful writers suffer from writer's block,
which is nothing more than the inability to begin or continue
writing for reasons other than lack of skill or commitment.

Plan your time carefully. The stress that results from a loom-
ing deadline can be a major contributor to writer's block, and
procrastination is one symptom of this problem. Of course, you
have a good many demands on your time, but even if you

budget your time carefully, you may not be able to give as much time to every assignment as you would like.

A number of factors can contribute to writer's block: You may not think you're a very good writer; you want the words to be "just right"; you cannot decide on a thesis statement, because there seem to be so many angles you could take; and a host of others. Whenever you experience writer's block, try to identify its cause. The sooner you identify what you're worrying about, the sooner you can work to overcome it. One of the most common causes for writer's block is striving for perfection, but you must keep in mind that perfection is a goal rarely attained, even by experienced writers.

CHECKLIST **for Managing Writer's Block**

- Prioritize your responsibilities, and allow time for each.
- Establish regular writing habits; write at the same time and in the same place whenever possible.
- For an out-of-class assignment, do not worry about getting the wording exactly right in the first draft or about mechanical problems (spelling or punctuation). You can check such errors later.
- For an essay exam, read each question slowly and jot ideas in the margin as you read down the page.
- When writing under pressure in the workplace, stay put at your keyboard. You need to get something on the screen that you can revise.

Like experienced writers, you'll be better off turning in completed work that is less than perfect than submitting no work at all. When other responsibilities have claimed more of your time than you had planned or you haven't been able to muster much enthusiasm for the assigned topic, it's time to do the very best you can, given your circumstances, and then move on. The deadline or due date is a reality that must be honored by all writers.

34d | You can prepare for essay examinations.

Essay exams have two basic parts: each individual question and your answer to each question. If your instructor has asked a question in such a way that you know what to write about, in what manner, and for how long, you're home free. All you have to do is write out your answer, framing it with a thesis statement, main points, and supporting arguments or examples. However, if a question does not make clear what is called for, ask your instructor for clarification (see 34d(5)). The steps described in this section will help you improve your ability to take essay examinations.

(1) Set up a time schedule.

If the exam has more than one question, the first thing to do is to figure out how much time to allot to each question. If you're faced with two questions that are worth the same number of points, the answer's easy: You give half the time to one and half to the other. If there are three questions to complete in a fifty-minute class period, and one of them is worth half of the total points while the rest of the points are split between the other two, allow about twenty minutes for the more heavily weighted question and ten minutes for each of the others. That strategy leaves you about ten minutes to go back over your answers, revising and proofreading. When you have used up the time you have allotted for a question, leave room to complete it later and go on to the next, whether you are finished or not. Partial answers to all questions will usually gain you more points than complete answers to only some of the questions. Furthermore, you can use the ten minutes you saved to put the finishing touches on any incomplete answers, even if you have to draw arrows to the margins or the back of the page, even if you have to supply rough notes (see **34d(6)**). Your instructor will probably appreciate the extra effort. Don't spend precious time recopying any of your answers.

(2) Read instructions and questions carefully.

Students who take time to read instructions carefully almost always do better than those who don't. Before you start writing, read the instructions carefully and note any specific directions. For example, realizing that you must "answer questions A *and* B" is very different from believing that you must "answer question A *or* B."

Most questions contain specific instructions about how, as well as what, to answer. Be alert for words such as *compare, define, argue,* and *cause,* which identify the writing task and provide specific cues for organizing your response (see chapter **32**). Other words, such as *discuss* and *explain,* are less specific, so try to determine exactly what it is your instructor wants you to do. When these more general directions appear, be tuned in to such accompanying words as *similar* or *differ* (which signal, respectively, a comparison or a contrast), *identify* (which signals a definition or description), and *why* (which signals the need to identify causes). Words such as *think, defend,* and *opinion* signal that you are to frame a thesis (see **32c**) and support it. Most essay exam questions use one of the words in the following list to indicate the approach your instructor expects you to take.

TERMS USED IN ESSAY QUESTIONS

Compare (or **contrast**)	Examine the points of similarity (compare) or difference (contrast) between two ideas or things. See $32e(5)$.
Define	State the class to which the item to be defined belongs (see $32e(6)$), and clarify what distinguishes it from the others of that class ($32e(7)$).
Describe	Use details in a clearly defined order to give the reader a clear mental picture of the item you are being asked to describe. See $32e(2)$.
Discuss	Examine, analyze, evaluate, or state pros and cons—in short, this word gives you wide latitude in addressing the topic and is thus more difficult to handle than some of the others, since you must choose your own focus. It is also the term that, unfortunately, appears most frequently. See $31c$ and $32e$.
Evaluate	Appraise the advantages and disadvantages of the idea or thing specified. See $36c(2)$.
Explain	Clarify and interpret (see $32e(7)$), reconcile differences, or state causes (see $32e(4)$).
Illustrate	Offer concrete examples, or, if possible, create figures, charts, or tables that provide information about the item. See $31c$.
Summarize	State the main points in a condensed form; omit details, and curtail examples. See $33b(2)$.
Trace	Narrate a sequence of events that show progress toward a goal or comprise a process. See $32e(1)$ and $32e(3)$.

(3) Decide how to organize your response.

When answering an essay exam question, you should be able to find time to draft a rough outline or jot down a few phrases for an informal working plan (see $32d$). Identify your thesis; then list the most important points you plan to cover. You might later decide to rearrange them, but the first step is to get some ideas down on paper. Before you begin to write the answer, quickly review the list, deleting any irrelevant or unimportant points and adding any better ones that come to you—keeping your time schedule in mind. Number the points in a logical sequence determined by chronology (reporting events in the order in which they occurred), by causation (showing how one thing led to another), or by order of importance (going from the most important point to the least important). Although arranging points in order of increasing importance is often effective, it can be risky in an exam situation because you might run out of time and not get to your most important point.

Sometimes, the language of the question will tell you how you should organize your answer. Consider this example:

> Discuss how the two-party political system of the United States influenced the outcome of the Bush-Gore presidential election.

At first glance, this exam question might seem to state the topic without indicating how to organize a discussion of it. *To influence,* however, is to be responsible for certain consequences. In this case, the two-party political system is a cause, and you are being asked to identify its effects (see 32e(4)). Once you have recognized this, you might decide to discuss different effects in different paragraphs.

There is almost always more than one way to organize a thoughtful response. Devoting at least a few minutes to organizing your answer can help you better demonstrate what you know.

(4) State main points clearly.

If you state your main points clearly, your instructor will see how well you have understood the assigned material and the important points in that material. Identify your main points to make them stand out from the rest of the answer. Use transitional words such as *first, second,* and *third.* You might even create headings to separate your points. By the time you have outlined your essay exam answer, you should know which points you'll want to highlight, even if the points change slightly as you begin drafting. Use your conclusion to summarize your main points.

(5) Stick to the question.

Always answer each essay exam question as directly as you can, perhaps using some of the instructor's language in your thesis statement. If your thesis statement implies an organizational plan, follow that plan as closely as possible. If you move away from your original thesis because better ideas have occurred to you as you write, simply go back and revise your thesis statement (see **32c**). If you find yourself drifting into irrelevant material, simply draw a line through it.

If you find yourself facing a vague or truly confusing question, construct a clear(er) question and then answer it. Rewriting the instructor's question can seem like a risky thing to do, especially if you've never done it before. But figuring out a reasonable question that is related to what the instructor has written is actually a responsible move if you can answer the question you've posed.

(6) Revise and proofread each answer.

Save a few minutes to reread each answer. Make whatever deletions and corrections you think are necessary. If time allows, think about what is not on the page: Ask yourself if there is anything you have left out that you can still manage to include (even if you have to write in the margins or on the back of the page). Unless you are certain that your instructor values neatness more than knowledge, do not hesitate to make additions and corrections. Simply draw a caret (∧), marking the exact place in the text where you want an addition or correction to be placed. Making corrections will allow you to focus on improving what you have already written, whereas recopying your answer just to make it look neat is an inefficient use of time. Finally, check spelling, punctuation, and sentence structure (see 33d).

Exercise 1

Consider an exam you've taken in another course. Analyze the wording of each question in terms of what it asks—and how the answer is to be organized. Then describe how you went about answering each question that you chose and why you avoided the other questions. If this exam posed particular difficulties for you, be prepared to identify and discuss them.

Reading and Thinking Critically

You read and think critically every day—even if you don't realize it. You read accounts of sporting events to analyze why one team won or lost; you read leases to see if you can abide by the terms. In short, every day you employ many of the same critical reading strategies you need to succeed in college. When you read and think critically, you are actively engaging a text. Reading critically offers you the opportunity to evaluate key points and the amount of support each merits, what needs to be said, and what is purposefully left unsaid.

This chapter will help you learn how to read and think critically by

- previewing a text (**35a**),
- distinguishing a text's content from your personal response to that content (**35b**),
- distinguishing fact from opinion (**35c**),
- recognizing inductive and deductive reasoning (**35d**),
- using the Toulmin model to analyze a text's argument (**35e**), and
- recognizing rhetorical fallacies that a writer may purposely or unintentionally employ (**35f**).

35a | Critical readers preview a text to understand its rhetorical situation.

In order to understand a text fully, critical readers often **preview** it, determining ahead of time the features of its rhetorical situation (author, audience, exigence, purpose, and context) as well as how difficult the text will be to understand, how interesting it is, and what they are likely to learn from it.

You preview reading all the time—when you thumb through a newspaper or a magazine looking for articles that stir your interest. Sometimes a simple preview helps you identify a topic you're interested in reading more about; sometimes, the preview leads you to an article that you decide not to finish. As you preview a text, you might try using the following features to make your reading time more efficient.

FEATURES OF A TEXT FOR PREVIEWING

Title

Titles and subtitles can reveal the focus of a text and sometimes even its thesis. If the title provides little information, look at other parts of the text to get a clearer sense of the work as a whole.

Author

Sometimes the author's name alone is an indication of the expertise or tone she or he brings to the topic. You'll want to consider anything you already know about the author. For instance, if Dave Barry is the author, you can expect the essay to be humorous; but if Ellen Goodman is the author, you can expect the essay to be political and thought-provoking.

Directories

Books usually have features that direct readers to specific sections within them. A *table of contents* identifies the chapters and often the main sections within a book; an *index* lists the specific topics covered. A *bibliography* indicates how much research was involved in writing the book; it can also direct you to other useful sources. Using information from the directories, you can decide how much or what sections of a book you want to read.

(Continued on page 494)

(Continued from page 493)

Length

Considering a text's length allows you to estimate how much time you should set aside for reading. By checking length, you can also decide whether a work is long enough or too short to include useful content.

Visual Aids

A quick check for graphs and illustrations can help you decide whether the work has the kind of information you need.

Summaries

Reading a summary can help you decide whether the work as a whole will be helpful; a summary can also help you follow a difficult text because it tells you the major points in advance. Summaries can often be found in the *preface* of a book, as well as in introductory and concluding chapters. Scholarly articles often begin with a summary identified as an *abstract* (see page 557).

In addition to looking for these features within a text, look inside yourself as well so that you can prepare to engage the text critically. Assess how much you already know about the subject or the author. If you are unfamiliar with the subject matter, you might want to supplement your understanding by locating a less demanding treatment of the topic. If your values or opinions differ greatly from those of the author, you'll want to pay close attention to passages in the text that you might be tempted to skim over. Without abandoning your values, you can increase your capacity for critical reading by being alert for occasions when you might dismiss new ideas without considering them.

The following questions may help you in previewing texts.

CHECKLIST for Previewing a Reading Selection

- How long is this work? Is the organization straightforward or complex? How much time will I need to read this selection until I understand it?

- What do I already know about this subject?

- Do I have strong feelings about this subject that could interfere with my ability to understand how it is treated in this text? (See 35b.)

- Do I know anything about this author, and, if so, can I trust what he or she writes? If the author is unfamiliar to me, is any biographical information included that will help me assess the author's credibility? (See 35c and 38a.)

- What does the title tell me? The subtitle? If there are subheadings in the text, what do they reveal about the organization or the way the subject is being handled?

- What do the table of contents, index, and abstract indicate about what is in the book?

- Are there graphs, figures, or other visual aids? How might they be useful to me?

- Is there a bibliography that indicates how extensive and current the research is?

- When was the book or article published?

- Where is the author's thesis? (See 32c.)

- Has the author included a summary near the introduction or conclusion of any of the chapters or subsections?

- Would it be easier for me to understand this text if I read something simpler on the same topic first?

Besides asking yourself these questions, you can also scan the first and last sentences in every paragraph. The central idea of a paragraph can, of course, occur anywhere within the paragraph (see **31a**), but it often appears in one of these two sentences.

The main outline of a text can also be determined by words that indicate sequencing, such as "There are *three* advantages to this proposal. . . . The *first* is . . . . The *second* is . . . ." In addition, you can scan for key phrases writers use to signal important points. The phrase *in other words,* for example, signals that a writer is about to paraphrase a point just made—probably because it is important. Other key phrases include *in summary, in conclusion,* and *the point I am making,* which signal that a point is being made about the information just presented.

Previewing is a way to make reading easier and more meaningful. It can also help you select appropriate material when you do research (see chapter **37**). But remember that previewing a text is not the same as reading it for understanding.

35b	Critical readers distinguish between the content of what they read and their personal response to that material.

Reading is a transaction or exchange between a writer and a reader within the rhetorical situation (see **32a**). The writer tries to choose words that express the intended meaning and will be understood by others. The reader then tries to understand what exactly the author wanted the words to mean within the specific rhetorical situation.

Sometimes, however, communication between writers and readers breaks down. Writers may have used language carelessly, or readers may have read in haste. Critical readers and writers strive to be successful and efficient communicators by developing strategies for preventing misunderstandings.

To read a text critically, you need to ask at least four questions:

- What exactly is this writer trying to say? Why?
- Who is the writer's intended audience?
- How did the writer try to communicate the content?
- What does this text make me think or feel? How does the author want me to think or feel?

(1) Understanding content requires paying close attention to the words on the page or the screen.

Speakers of English sometimes use the same word to mean different things, depending on the context. When you read, you are the audience, the one who often determines the meanings of words and sentences from their context—the sentences, paragraphs, sections, and chapters surrounding them. On first reading a sentence, you might think you understand its meaning; but by the time you finish reading the entire paragraph, you might be able to enhance your understanding of that first sentence given the information provided in the following sentences. Your challenge as a reader, then, is to understand as much as you can but to keep that understanding flexible enough to accommodate what will come.

When reading for content, make sure you understand the words on the page. When you encounter a word that is new to you, the meaning may be defined in the text itself, or you might be able to infer the meaning from the way the word has been used. But whenever an unfamiliar term appears in a critically important position such as a thesis statement (see 32c) or a conclusion (33b(2)), look it up in a good dictionary (19e).

Transitional words indicating sequencing (see 35a) or movement within a text also help you grasp content. Transitional expressions—especially those indicating purpose, result, summary, repetition, exemplification, and intensification—alert you to important points. When reading from a book or article you own, underline, highlight, or write back to passages that interest or confuse you, or that you question. If you've borrowed a book, use sticky notes to highlight and annotate the text. With an electronic text, you can print out a hard copy, use your word-processing program to annotate, or respond to a downloaded file directly on the screen and then save both versions.

(2) Recognizing a personal response requires that you separate what a writer has said from the way you feel about the message.

Often what we hear or read provokes a reaction. We can become immediately prejudiced toward or against a speaker or text if we mishear, misread, or in other ways allow our personal responses to interfere with our ability to understand. Critical readers work hard to keep their personal responses from interfering with their ability to understand. So, in addition to reading for content (see **35b(1)**), they also keep track of how they're reacting to this content. That's not to say that they read passively; critical readers read actively, noting where they agree or disagree, become frustrated or intrigued, sympathetic or annoyed. And they keep track of what feature of the writing (or themselves) triggered each response: Was it the writer's tone (see **33a(3)**), an example that evoked a personal memory, a lapse in the organization (**32d**), the topic itself (**32b**), or a visual element such as a photo or illustration?

By noting personal responses and recognizing that they are independent of a work's content, critical readers increase their understanding of the purposeful choices writers make. Personal responses often serve as the basis for new pieces of writing (see **32b**). Good readers and writers frequently use techniques from the following checklist.

> ### CHECKLIST **for Recording Personal Responses**
>
> - Note passages that capture your attention. Underline or highlight your own copy; highlight with a different text color when reading on a computer screen.
>
> - Put a question mark in the margin when you do not understand a passage—or question its accuracy.
>
> - Put an exclamation point in the margin when a statement or example surprises you.
>
> - Write *yes* or *no* in the margin when you agree or disagree. When a passage reminds you of another passage (or of something else you have read), note that association in the margin.
>
> - Keep a reading journal (see 35b(3)). Include at least one question, compliment, or reservation about something you read each day.
>
> - Correspond by email with other people who are reading the same material (see 8a).
>
> - Talk with friends and family members about any texts you have enjoyed reading.

(3) Keeping a reading journal or participating in e-discussions about reading selections increases comprehension and generates ideas for writing.

Take opportunities to write daily. Like a personal journal or a writer's notebook (see 32b), a **reading journal** (or, in some classes, an online discussion forum) provides a daily opportunity for you to write in order to understand your reading and your reactions to your reading. Writing regularly about your reading helps to increase your comprehension and identify responses that could be the seeds from which larger pieces of writing subsequently grow.

Your reading journal can focus on the reading you're doing for one course, for all your courses, for your job—or on all the reading you do. Whatever your focus, you'll want to design your journal in such a way that you'll benefit in terms of both comprehension and creativity. One way to do this is to keep a **double-entry notebook,** a journal in which each entry has two distinct parts: summary and response. For example, if you keep your journal in a spiral notebook, you could use the left side of each page to summarize your understanding of what you've read and the right side to record your responses to it. (Or you might prefer to format computer files into columns.)

Try always to keep separate the entries devoted to summarizing content from those devoted to your personal response or reflection (see **35b(2)**). This separation will come in handy when you need to review what you have written. When you're preparing for a written examination (see **34d**), for example, you will be able to easily identify the entries that will help you remember content. And when you're involved in the brainstorming necessary for drafting an essay (see **32b**), you can turn to those entries in which you recorded your own ideas, responses, or reflections.

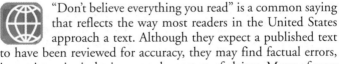

"Don't believe everything you read" is a common saying that reflects the way most readers in the United States approach a text. Although they expect a published text to have been reviewed for accuracy, they may find factual errors, inconsistencies in logic, or weak support of claims. Many of your reading and writing assignments will require you to do the same, so be prepared to question an author's ideas and test out your own.

The following list summarizes the critical reading process

FEATURES OF THE READING PROCESS

Previewing

Skim through the reading; get a sense of how the information is organized and what the reading consists of. Assess what the reading demands of you in terms of time, effort, and previous knowledge (see 35a).

Reading for Content

Determine who the author is and what you already know about him or her. Then determine what the author wants to communicate—to whom and for what specific purpose. As you read, note the author's major points, underlining or highlighting them. Talk back to the text itself as though you were carrying on a conversation with the author: Write in the margins and annotate key passages whenever you have something to say or a question to pose (see 35b(1)).

Noting Your Personal Response

Try to determine what the author thinks and why he or she holds that opinion. Then determine what *you* think and why *you* hold your opinion. In other words, what information do you agree or disagree with—and why? What passages brought to mind your own experience or expertise? What have you learned from this reading? What confuses you about this reading? What would you like to know more about (see 35b(2))?

Rereading

Check your understanding of the content. Consider why the author chose the title and how he or she presented the material to an audience; determine the specific purpose; and note how the information is organized and how supporting ideas are developed (see 8d, 32d, and 35b(1)).

When you explore your topic and consider how you want your audience to interpret it, you use both facts and opinions. It's important to distinguish between these two kinds of information so that you can use both to your advantage. **Facts** are reliable pieces of information that can be verified through independent sources or procedures. **Opinions,** on the other hand, are assertions or inferences that may or may not be based on facts. Opinions that are widely accepted, however, may seem to be factual when actually they are not.

Just because facts are reliable does not mean that they speak for themselves. Facts are significant only when they are used responsibly to support a claim; otherwise, a thoughtful and well-informed opinion might have more impact. To distinguish between fact and opinion, ask yourself questions about a statement you have read: Can it be proved? Can it be challenged? How often is the same result achieved? If a statement can consistently be proved true, then it is a fact. If it can be disputed, then it is an opinion.

> **Fact**   Milk contains calcium.
>
> **Opinion**   Americans should drink more milk.

To say that milk contains calcium is to state a well-established fact: It can be verified by consulting published studies or by conducting laboratory tests. Whether or not this fact is significant depends on how a writer chooses to use it. As an isolated fact, it is unlikely to seem significant. But to say that Americans need to drink more milk is to express an opinion that may or may not be supported by facts. When considering the statement "Americans should drink more milk," a thoughtful reader might ask: "How much calcium does a human need? Why do humans need calcium? Is milk the richest source of calcium?

Might leafy green vegetables provide a richer source of calcium? Is cow's milk good for humans?" Anticipating questions such as these can help you develop a thesis.

Because facts can change over time, writers and readers need to remain flexible as they distinguish between fact and opinion. The erroneous belief that the sun revolves around the earth was once considered a fact, and Christopher Columbus's "discovery" of America was long undisputed. Describing what can easily happen in research, a distinguished physician writes that a good scientist must be prepared for the day when his or her life's work is suddenly called into question:

> All the old ideas—last week's ideas in some cases—are no longer good ideas. The hard facts have softened, melted away and vanished under the pressure of new hard facts.
>
> —**LEWIS THOMAS,** "The Art of Teaching Science"

The most knowledgeable people are those who realize that the line between fact and opinion is not always clear. What appears to be factual (the earth is flat; earth, wind, fire, and water are the only elements; species are unchangeable) could be the result of inadequate research or assumptions that are so widely held that they have gone unchallenged. Knowledgeable people, then, are constantly assimilating new information and questioning old ideas.

Critical readers and thinkers are always prepared to interpret and assess the information before them; they evaluate the stance, the beliefs supporting such a stance, the kinds of sources used, and the objections that could be made. Careful writers and readers ask what kind of verification could establish the reliability of the information.

Whether you are considering a fact or an opinion, prepare for writing a convincing argument by asking yourself, "What kind of evidence is necessary, how can that evidence be obtained, and what will happen if conflicting evidence is discovered?"

Exercise 1

Determine which of the following statements seem to be fact and which seem to be opinion. In each case, what kind of verification would you require in order to accept the statement as reliable? Explain your decisions in writing, and be prepared to discuss your choices in class.

1. Toni Morrison won the Nobel Prize in literature in 1993.
2. Women often earn less money than men holding the same positions.
3. *The Lion King* was the best movie ever made about animals.
4. Writing well is a gift, like musical genius.
5. A college degree guarantees a good job.
6. The oldest city in the United States is Santa Fe.
7. Running is good for your health.
8. The United States won the Second World War.
9. In combination, ammonia and chlorine bleach result in poisonous gas.
10. Researchers will find a cure for AIDS.

35d | **Understanding inductive and deductive reasoning can improve your ability to read arguments critically.**

Because writers cannot argue solely on the basis of ethos, or their character, they need to understand the ways in which **logic**—the reasoning behind an argument—enhances or detracts from the argument. Studied as a separate discipline, logic entails highly specific exercises that are worked out with mathematical precision. When used in writing, however, logic is studied and used differently. When you evaluate the logic of an argument, you take into consideration the clarity of the thinking, the ethics of the reasoning, and the possible response to diverse views. Traditionally, logical arguments are classified as either inductive or deductive.

(1) Inductive reasoning is the process of using a number of specific facts or observations to make a generalization.

You use inductive reasoning on a daily basis. If you get a stomachache within fifteen minutes of eating ice cream, you might conclude that there's a connection. Perhaps you're lactose-intolerant. This use of evidence to form a generalization is called an **inductive leap,** and the leap should be in proportion to the amount of evidence gathered.

Inductive reasoning involves moving (or leaping) from discovering evidence to interpreting it, and it can help you arrive at probable, believable conclusions (but not absolute, enduring truth). Making a small leap from evidence (a stomachache) to a probable conclusion (lactose intolerance) is more effective and ethical than using the same evidence to make a sweeping claim that could easily be challenged (ice cream is bad for everyone) (see 35f(1)). Generally, the greater the weight of the evidence, the more reliable the conclusion.

When used in argument, inductive reasoning often employs facts (see 35c) and examples (see 31c). When writers cannot cite all the information that supports their conclusions, they choose the evidence that is most reliable and closely related to the point they are making.

(2) Deductive reasoning is the process of applying a generalization (or generalized belief) to a series of specific cases.

At the heart of a deductive argument is a **major premise** (a generalized belief that is assumed to be true), which the writer applies to a specific case (the **minor premise**), thereby yielding a conclusion or claim. For example, if you know that all doctors must complete a residency and that Anna is in medical school, then you could conclude that Anna must complete a residency. This argument can be expressed in a three-part structure called a **syllogism.**

Major premise	All doctors must complete a residency. [generalized belief]
Minor premise	Anna is studying to become a doctor. [specific case]
Conclusion	Anna must complete a residency. [conclusion or claim]

Sometimes premises are not stated, for the simple reason that the writer assumes a shared belief with the audience.

Anna has graduated from medical school, so she must complete a residency.

In this sentence, the unstated premise is that all doctors must complete a residency. A syllogism with an unstated premise—or even an unstated conclusion—is called an **enthymeme.** Frequently found in written arguments, enthymemes can be very effective because they presume shared beliefs or knowledge.

caution

Critical thinkers should examine enthymemes with care since the omitted statement may be inaccurate. "Racquel is from Texas, so she speaks Spanish" contains the unstated premise "Everyone from Texas speaks Spanish." This premise is unacceptable because there is no reason to assume that everyone from Texas knows how to speak Spanish—even though many people who live in Texas do speak Spanish. When you use deductive reasoning in your arguments, be sure to work from a reliable premise with which you and your audience can agree.

The conclusion of a deductive argument must be both true and valid. A **true conclusion** is based on well-backed premises generally accepted by your audience. A **valid conclusion** is based on logical thinking. The conclusion in the following syllogism is valid because it follows logically from the major and minor premises, but it is not true because the major premise is not generally accepted.

Major premise	All redheads are hotheaded.
Minor premise	Jamie is a redhead.
Conclusion	Jamie is hotheaded.

Because syllogisms can be logical without their conclusions being true and because they are too rigid and absolute to serve in arguments without absolute answers, they work more effectively as exercises in critical thinking than as outlines for written arguments.

Exercise 2

Analyze the following enthymemes, supplying the missing premise for each of them. Then, determine if the conclusion is valid, true, both, or neither.

1. He must be healthy. He always has a good tan.
2. She is a good writer. She is easy to understand.
3. We need to restrict the use of water. We are suffering from a severe drought.
4. Omtronic Company must be well managed. Its earnings have grown steadily during the past few years.
5. Dr. Kordoff must be a good teacher. Her classes always fill up quickly.

To create a working system of logic suitable for the needs of all writers, philosopher Stephen Toulmin moved away from the formal conventions of the syllogism. Instead, he defined *argument* as a logical progression, from the **data** (accepted evidence or reasons that support a claim), to the **claim** (a debatable or controversial statement), based on the **warrant** (the underlying assumption, like the major premise). If the warrant is controversial, it requires **backing** (support). Writers who assume that they are drawing their evidence from reliable authorities should be able to cite the credentials of those authorities.

Like deductive reasoning, Toulmin's method establishes a reasonable relationship between the data and the claim. The following argument may help explain the progression:

Fair trade coffee should be served at the University of St. Thomas because doing so would foster social justice.

Data (or support)	Purchasing fair trade coffee promotes social justice.
Claim	The University of St. Thomas should purchase and serve only fair trade coffee.
Warrant	The University of St. Thomas seeks to promote social justice.

The warrant establishes a relationship with the data, providing a reasonable link with the claim that follows. Of course, few arguments are as simple as this example. Qualifiers such as *usually, probably, should,* and *possibly* show the degree of certainty of the conclusion, and rebuttal terms such as *unless* indicate exceptions.

Since the University of St. Thomas seeks to promote social justice, it **should** purchase and serve only fair trade coffee, **unless** it cannot pursue this course of action at this time.

You may be able to identify the claim, the data, and the qualifiers more easily than the warrant. Like the unstated premise in an enthymeme (see 35d(2)), the warrant is often assumed and backed up by something left unsaid. In the example above, the backing is the university's mission statement, which calls for commitment to social justice. To determine your warrant, trace your thinking back to the assumptions with which you began. As you trace back, remember that warrants can take different forms. A warrant may be

- a requirement of a law or regulation (such as university regulations for student housing),
- an assumption that the data came from a reliable source (see chapters 38 and 39),
- an assumption that what is true of a sample is true of a larger group (see 35d), or
- a moral, political, or economic value that is widely accepted in the writer's culture.

Exercise 3

A. Analyze the argument in the following excerpt by asking yourself the following questions:

1. What is the claim or conclusion? Is it implied or stated?
2. What data support the claim?
3. Does the author make more than one claim?
4. What is the warrant that underlies the argument?

[1]The movement to make English the official language of the United States is in no way a put-down of other languages or cultures. [2]But it is the language used predominantly by the print and electronic media; it is the tongue in which government at every level is conducted. [3]To be an effective citizen one ought to vote, and to do so intelligently one must

be well informed. [4]Candidates, of course, present the issues and outline their platforms in English.

——**YOLANDA DE MOLA,** "The Language of Power"

B. Whatever your own position on language use may be, demonstrate that you understand the reasoning within the preceding excerpt by writing a two- to three-page essay in which you walk your reader through the steps in De Mola's argument.

35f | Rhetorical fallacies can weaken an argument.

Logical reasoning not only enhances the overall effectiveness of an argument, it also enhances the ethos of the speaker or writer. Almost as important as constructing an argument effectively is avoiding errors in argument, or **rhetorical fallacies.** Rhetorical fallacies signal to your audience that your thinking is not entirely trustworthy, that your argument is not well reasoned. Such fallacies may be lapses in logic that result from relying on faulty premises, appeals to the emotions of the reader in inappropriate situations, or misplaced emphases on the authority (or lack thereof) of the quoted sources.

Rhetoricians find it useful to distinguish among the different kinds of fallacies. As you read the arguments of others (see chapter 38) and revise the arguments you draft (chapter 33), try to keep the following common rhetorical fallacies in mind.

(1) *Non sequitur,* Latin for "it does not follow," is the basis for many fallacies.

Faulty

Eddie is smart; therefore, he'll do well in college. [This assertion is based on the faulty premise that *all* smart people do well in college. (See **35d**.)]

(2) *Ad hominem* refers to a personal attack on an opponent that draws attention away from the issues under consideration.

Faulty

She is unfit to be a minister because she is divorced. [The fact that a woman is divorced may reveal the condition of a previous marriage, but a divorce has little if anything to do with her spiritual beliefs and principles that could benefit a congregation.]

(3) *Appeal to tradition* is an argument that says something should be done a certain way simply because it has been done that way in the past.

Faulty

We should not forbid fraternity hazings because they continue to be a memorable part of the pledge process. [Times change; what was considered good practice in the past is not necessarily considered acceptable now.]

(4) *Bandwagon* is an argument saying, in effect, "Everyone's doing or saying or thinking this, so you should too."

Faulty

Everyone drives over the speed limit, so why shouldn't we raise the limit? [The majority is not always right.]

(5) *Begging the question* **is an argument that assumes what in fact needs to be proved.**

Faulty

We need to fire corrupt officials in order to reduce the city's crime rate. [If there are corrupt officials in city government, this point needs to be established.]

(6) *Equivocation* **is an assertion that falsely relies on the use of a term in two different senses.**

Faulty

We know this is a natural law because it feels natural. [In the first use, *natural* means "derived from nature or reason"; when used again, it means "easy or simple because of being in accord with one's own nature."]

(7) *False analogy* **is the assumption that because two things are alike in some ways, they must be alike in others.**

Faulty

The United States lost credibility with other nations during the war in Viet Nam, so we should not get involved in the Middle East, or we will lose credibility again. [The differences between the war in Southeast Asia in the 1960s and 1970s and the current conflict in the Middle East may well be greater than their similarities.]

(8) *False authority* **is the assumption that an expert in one field can be credible in another.**

Faulty

We must stop sending military troops into Afghanistan, as Bruce Springsteen has argued. [Springsteen's expertise in music does not automatically qualify him as an expert in foreign policy.]

(9) *False cause* is the assumption that because one event follows another, the first is the cause of the second—sometimes called *post hoc, ergo propter hoc* ("after this, so because of this").

Faulty
When Coach Joe Paterno turned 75, Penn State's football team had a losing season. [The assumption is that Paterno's age is solely responsible for the losing season, with no consideration given to the abilities and experience of the football players themselves.]

(10) *False dilemma* (sometimes called the *either/or fallacy*) is a statement that only two alternatives exist when in fact there are more than two.

Faulty
We must either build more nuclear power plants or be completely dependent on foreign oil. [Other possibilities exist.]

(11) *Guilt by association* is an unfair attempt to make someone responsible for the beliefs or actions of others.

Faulty
Jon Williams's family is a bunch of gamblers. [Several people can graduate from the same school, practice the same profession or religion, belong to the same family, or live in the same neighborhood without engaging in the same behavior.]

(12) *Hasty generalization* is a conclusion based on too little evidence or on exceptional or biased evidence.

Faulty
Ellen is a poor student because she failed her first history test. [Her performance may improve in the weeks ahead or be good in all her other subjects.]

(13) *Oversimplification* **is a statement or argument that leaves out relevant considerations in order to imply that there is a single cause or solution for a complex problem.**

Faulty

We can eliminate unwanted pregnancies by teaching birth control and abstinence. [Teaching people about birth control and abstinence does not guarantee the elimination of unwanted pregnancies.]

(14) *Red herring* **(sometimes called *ignoring the question*) means dodging the real issue by drawing attention to an irrelevant one.**

Faulty

Why worry about violence in schools when we ought to be worrying about international terrorism? [International terrorism has little if any direct relationship with school violence.]

(15) *Slippery slope* **is the assumption that if one thing is allowed, it will be the first step in a downward spiral.**

Faulty

Handgun control will lead to a police state. [Handgun control has not led to a police state in England.]

Beyond the Rule

RHETORICAL FALLACIES

What looks like a rhetorical fallacy may be acceptable under some circumstances. For examples of how and when to use rhetorical fallacies in an argument, visit www.harbrace.com.

Be alert for rhetorical fallacies in your own writing. If you find such a fallacy, be sure to moderate your claim or clarify your thinking to eliminate the fallacious point. Even if your argument as a whole is convincing, rhetorical fallacies can damage your credibility (see **36d** and **38a**).

Exercise 4

For each of the following statements, write one or two sentences in which you identify and explain the faulty reasoning. Then, identify circumstances under which you might find these statements convincing. Finally, rewrite each statement so that it avoids rhetorical fallacies, regardless of the circumstances (if possible).

1. You should go to Puerto Rico; the rest of us are going.
2. We must either build more dormitories or double up students in existing dormitories.
3. This car must be reliable; it's the kind my dentist drives.
4. If we censor neo-Nazi demonstrations, we will ultimately lose freedom of speech.
5. I know that store is badly managed. One of the salespeople there was rude to me.
6. If women dressed more conservatively, they would earn as much money as men.
7. You can't trust a guy like that; he comes from a poor family and bad neighborhood.
8. We should cut welfare because people on welfare are getting too many benefits.
9. The union is arguing for a cost-of-living raise, but its leaders are all a bunch of crooks.
10. Children would do a lot better at school if they didn't spend so much time watching television.

36 Writing Arguments

You write arguments on a regular basis. When you email your parents to ask them for a loan for a down payment, when you petition your academic advisor for a late drop, or when you demand that a mail-order company refund your money, you're writing an argument. You are expressing a point of view and then using logical reasoning to try to get a specific audience to accept that point of view or adopt a course of action. *Argument* and *persuasion* are often used interchangeably, but they differ in two basic ways. Traditionally, **persuasion** has referred to winning or conquering with the use of emotional reasoning, whereas **argument** has been linked with logical reasoning. But because much writing involves some measure of "winning"—even if it's only gaining the ear of a particular audience—and uses both emotion and reason, this book uses *argument* to cover the meanings of both terms.

When writing arguments, you follow the same process you use for all your writing: planning, drafting, revising, and designing (see chapter 8 and 31–33), as well as attending to audience and context (see 32a). Argument is considered an important way to invite exchange, understanding, cooperation, consideration, joint decision making, agreement, or negotiation of differences. Thus, argument serves three basic and sometimes overlapping purposes: to analyze a complicated issue or question an established belief, to express or defend a point of view, and to invite or convince an audience to change a position or adopt a course of action.

This chapter will help you

- determine the purpose of an argument (36a),
- establish an arguable statement (36b),
- take a position or make a claim (36c),
- provide evidence to support your claims (36d),
- appeal appropriately to the feelings of your audience (36e),
- arrange ideas (36f), and
- learn from others' arguments (36g).

36a | Different arguments have different purposes.

What is your subject? Why are you arguing about it? What is at stake? What is likely to happen as a result of your making this argument? How important are those consequences? Who is in a position to act or react in response to your argument?

Let's say that you want to talk with your insurance agent about lowering your rates. She believes that you're a reckless driver because you've received two speeding tickets in the past two years; you know that you've stopped speeding, and you would like one last chance. Expecting your agent to change her business policy is not only unrealistic but undesirable; instead, your purpose is to invite or convince the agent (your audience, in this case) to consider another point of view, to modify her position, adjust her course of action, or allow some exceptions to the policy (in other words, give you one more chance). You'll need to provide the agent with the most compelling reasons you can think of, so that she begins to consider your point of view, the first step in changing her mind. Because you cannot always hope to defeat a position outright, your aim is sometimes to encourage slight movement, not radical change.

After you establish the relationship among your subject, purpose, and audience, you need to make that relationship clear in your introduction. Your readers (or audience) always expect to find the purpose of your argument in the introduction, and sometimes in the conclusion as well.

In argument, audience is integral to purpose. In fact, in certain circumstances, your audience might shape your purpose:

- If there is little likelihood that you can convince members of your audience to change a strongly held opinion, you might still achieve a great deal by simply inviting them to seriously consider and understand your position.
- If the members of your audience are not firmly committed to a position, you might be able to convince them to agree with the opinion you are expressing or defending.
- If the members of your audience agree with you in principle, you might invite them to undertake a specific action—such as voting for the candidate you are supporting.

In any event, you must establish **common ground** with your audience, stating a goal toward which you both want to work or a belief, assumption, or value that you both share; in other words, common ground is a starting point of agreement.

36b | Argument assumes the existence of differing views.

A good deal of writing requires that you take a position on a topic, an arguable position. Almost everyone agrees that smoking is not a healthful practice—that's a widely shared belief that is nearly impossible to argue against. Such a widely held opinion could become a topic for an expressive or expository essay (see **32a**), such as "Why Smoking Is Harmful to Your Health" or "The Surgeon General's Latest Report on Smoking," but, in and of itself, this opinion lacks the element of controversy or disagreement that is essential to an argument. On the other hand, this topic could be reconceived into an arguable statement: "Smoking is not healthful, but it's nearly impossible to quit." Thus, the first step toward finding a topic for argumentation is to consider issues that inspire different opinions.

Behind any effective argument is a question that can generate more than one reasonable answer. If you ask "Is there racism in the United States?" almost anyone will agree that there is. But if you ask "Why is there still racism in the United States?" or "What can Americans do to eliminate racism?" you will hear different answers. Answers differ because people approach questions with various backgrounds, experiences, and assumptions.

When you write an argument, then, you are trying to solve a problem or answer a question—with or for an audience. When you choose a topic for argumentation, you'll want to take a stance toward that topic that allows you to question, that provides you an exigence (or reason) for writing. Whatever general subject you're writing about, you'll focus on a topic (see 32b(2)), on the part of the subject you'll address in your essay, and then pose a question. As you craft your critical question, you'll want to consider the following: (1) your own values and beliefs with respect to the question, (2) how your assumptions might differ from those of your intended audience, and (3) how you might establish common ground with members of your audience, while at the same time respecting any differences of opinion between you and them. The question you raise will evolve into your thesis, an arguable statement.

The most important criterion for choosing an arguable statement for an essay is knowledge of the topic. When you're in a position to choose your own topic, you can draw on your knowledge of current events, politics, sports, fashion, or specific academic subjects. To find a topic, you can also try methods such as freewriting and listing (see 32b(1)). To determine if a topic might be suitable, make a statement about that topic and then check to see if that statement can be argued.

TIPS FOR ASSESSING A TOPIC AND AN ARGUABLE STATEMENT

- One thing I believe strongly about this topic is _____. List every reason you can think of to support your view.

- Who or what groups might disagree with my statement? Why?

- Do I know enough about this topic to discuss other points of view? Can I find out what I need to know?

- Mine is not the only belief on this topic. Other people believe _____. List all the reasons you can think of to support these other viewpoints.

- What is my purpose in writing about this topic?

- How does my purpose relate to my audience?

- What do I want my audience to do in response to my argument? In other words, what do I expect from my audience?

If you can answer all these questions to your satisfaction, then you should feel confident about your topic and move further into the writing process. If you cannot answer any of them, then reconsider your topic, your thesis statement, or the amount of research you may need to do to support your argument.

36c | An argument takes a position or makes a claim.

When making an argument, a writer takes a position on a particular topic. Whether analyzing, questioning, expressing, defending, inviting, or convincing, a writer of an argument makes that position clear. This position, called the **claim,** or **proposition,** clearly states what the writer wants the audience to do with the information being provided. This claim is the thesis (see 32c) of the argument and usually appears in the introduction (see 33b and 36f) and sometimes again in the conclusion.

(1) Effective writers claim no more than they can responsibly support.

Claims vary in extent; they can be absolute or moderate, large or limited. A writer who makes an absolute claim needs to provide more, and more compelling, evidence than a writer who makes a moderate one. Absolute claims assert that something is always true or false, completely good or bad; moderate claims make less sweeping assertions.

Absolute claim	College athletes are never good students.
Moderate claim	Most colleges have low graduation rates for their athletes.
Absolute claim	Harry S. Truman was the best president we've ever had.
Moderate claim	Truman's domestic policies helped advance civil rights.

Moderate claims are not necessarily superior to absolute claims. But the stronger the claim, the stronger the evidence needed to support it. Be sure to consider the quality and the significance of the evidence you use (see 35c and 36e)—not just its quantity.

(2) Claims vary in kind as well as in how much they encompass.

(a) Substantiation claims assert that something exists.
Without making a value judgment, a **substantiation claim** makes a point that can be supported by evidence.

The job market for new Ph.D.'s in English is limited.

The post office is raising rates again.

(b) Evaluation claims assert that something has a specific quality.

According to an **evaluation claim,** something is good or bad, effective or ineffective, attractive or unattractive, successful or unsuccessful.

> The graduation rate for athletes at Penn State is very high compared with that at the other Big Ten universities.

> The public transportation system in Washington, D.C., is reliable and safe.

> Jennifer Lopez is a great actress.

(c) Policy claims call for a specific action.

When making **policy claims,** writers call for something to be done.

> We must find the funds to hire better qualified high school teachers.

> We need to build a light-rail system linking downtown with the airport and the western suburbs.

Much writing involves substantiation, evaluation, and policy claims. When writing about the job market, you might tap your ability to substantiate a claim; when writing about literature (see chapter 42), you might need to evaluate a character. Policy claims are commonly found in arguments about social issues such as health care, social security, and affirmative action. They also occur in daily life, where they might take the form of asking not to attend a family gathering. Policy claims often grow out of substantiation or evaluation claims: First, you demonstrate that a problem exists (traveling to and from a family gathering uses too much precious time); then, you establish the best solution for that problem (staying home to study for midterms and attending family gatherings only during vacations).

TIPS FOR MAKING A CLAIM ARGUABLE

- Write down your opinion.
- Describe the situation that produced your opinion.
- Decide who constitutes the audience for your opinion and what you want that audience to do about your opinion.
- Write down the verifiable and reliable facts that support your opinion.
- Using those facts, transform your initial opinion into a thoughtful claim that considers at least two sides to the issue under discussion.
- Ask yourself, "So what?" If the answer to this question shows that your claim doesn't lead anywhere, start over with the first tip.

Exercise 1

The following excerpt is from an argument analyzing racial strife in the United States, written by Cornel West, a scholar specializing in race relations. Evaluate the claims it presents. Are they absolute or moderate? Can you identify a substantiation or evaluation claim? What policy claim is implicit in this passage?

[1]To engage in a serious discussion of race in America, we must begin not with the problems of black people but with the flaws of American society—flaws rooted in historic inequalities and longstanding cultural stereotypes. [2]How we set up the terms for discussing racial issues shapes our

perception and response to these issues. [3]As long as black people are viewed as a "them," the burden falls on blacks to do all the "cultural" and "moral" work necessary for healthy race relations. [4]The implication is that only certain Americans can define what it means to be American—and the rest must simply "fit in."

—**CORNEL WEST**, "Introduction," *Race Matters*

36d | An effective argument is well developed.

Effective arguments are well developed and supported. Although you may sometimes be able to write an effective argument directly from your own experience and observations, you are often likely to need to do some research to gain more information (see chapter 37). In either case, you should explore your topic in enough depth to have the evidence to support your position intelligently and ethically (see **36b** and **36e**). In addition, you'll want to take into consideration the reasons why other people might disagree with you and be prepared to respond to those reasons.

(1) An effective argument clearly establishes the thinking that leads to the claim.

If you want readers to take your ideas seriously, you must establish why you think as you do. That means communicating the reasons that have led to your position, as well as the values and assumptions that support your thinking. When you are exploring your subject, make a list of the reasons that have led to your belief without trying to edit them (see **32b(1)**). For example, when Laura Klocke was working on her argumentative essay (at the end of this chapter; see pages 537–544), she listed the following reasons for her belief that fair trade coffee should be used exclusively at her school:

> The average price of coffee is $12.00/lb., while the average coffee grower is paid only 20–40 cents/lb.
>
> The average latte costs $3.50, while the average coffee farmer makes $3.00/day.
>
> University of St. Thomas is committed to producing "morally responsible individuals who combine cultural awareness and intellectual curiosity."
>
> St. Thomas could easily support only fair trade coffee.

Although it is possible to base your argument on one good reason (such as "Buying fair trade coffee is the right thing to do"), doing so can be risky. If your audience does not find this reason convincing, you have no other support for your position. When you show that you have more than one reason for believing as you do, you increase the likelihood that your audience will find merit in your argument. For example, suppose you argue that the United States is one nation that should have one language—Standardized English. Readers who are aware of the evidence showing that fluency in more than one language or dialect enriches cognitive abilities will dismiss your argument even if they find it well written. In this case, you'll need to introduce other reasons for supporting the use of Standardized English. When you introduce several reasons for your claim, you make a more complex argument, one that cannot be dismissed so readily.

Sometimes, however, one good reason is stronger—and more appropriate for your audience—than several others you could advance. To develop an argument for which you have only one good reason, explore the values and assumptions that led you to take your stand. By demonstrating the thinking behind the single reason on which you are building your case, you can create a well-developed argument.

Whether you have one reason or several, be sure to provide sufficient evidence from credible sources to support your claim:

- facts,
- statistics,
- examples, and
- testimony, often from personal experience or professional expertise.

This evidence must be accurate, representative, and sufficient. Accurate information should be verifiable by others (see **35c**). Representative and sufficient information is never drawn from an exceptional case, a biased sample, or a one-time occurrence. You need to consult a wider array of sources. (See chapter **37**.)

When gathering evidence, you need to think critically about the information you find, especially the results of polls, interviews, authorities, and other statistics you plan to use. How recent and representative is the information, and how was it gathered? Is an authority you plan to quote qualified to address the topic under consideration? As you consider survey statistics, you need to keep in mind that any set of statistics can be manipulated, whether the poll is representative or not.

Whatever form of evidence you use—facts, statistics, examples, or testimony—you need to make clear to your audience exactly *why* and *how* it supports your claim. As soon as the relationship between your claim and your evidence is clear to you, make that connection explicit to your readers, helping them understand your thinking.

(2) Effective arguments respond to diverse views.

Issues are controversial because good arguments can be made on all sides. In order for your argument to be convincing, your audience must realize that you are knowledgeable about points of view other than your own. The most common strategy for addressing opposing points of view is referred to as **refutation.**

In the refutation, you introduce these diverse views and then respectfully demonstrate why you disagree with each of them. You may discover some you cannot refute, perhaps because they are based in a belief system markedly different from your own. You may also discover that some enrich your own point of view but fail to convince you. You will need to demonstrate why.

When you find yourself agreeing with a point raised on another side of the issue, you can benefit from offering a **concession.** By openly admitting that you agree with opponents on one or more specific points, you demonstrate that you are fair-minded (see **36e** and **38a**) and at the same time increase your credibility. Concessions also increase the likelihood that opponents will be inclined to find merit in your argument: If you admit that your opponents are partially right, they are more likely to admit that you could be partially right as well. In this sense, then, argument involves working with an audience as much as getting them to work with you.

Arguments that are exchanged electronically—by email or in online discussion groups—can easily become one-sided when writers consider only the text before them and not the person sitting at another computer. The flame wars that often occur in online discussion groups or chat rooms develop when participants simply state their opinions or attack the opinions of others. These flame wars are rarely genuine arguments; rather, they are characterized by the rhetorical fallacies that weaken arguments (see **35f**). Even if you cannot see your readers or do not expect to meet them face-to-face, you will be more convincing if you imagine that they are in the same room with you and that you would like to continue your acquaintance.

When deciding what points to refute or to concede in a short argument, limit yourself to a brief discussion; in a longer argument, you can explore more fully. In either case, however, think about what your audience is likely to believe. Address the most important concerns of your readers.

 Although it may seem impolite to disagree openly with authority or to state personal views frankly, most readers in the United States are accustomed to such directness. They will expect you to state your opinion clearly and support it with various kinds of evidence.

Exercise 2

The following paragraph is taken from an argument by Martin Luther King, Jr., in which he defended the struggle for civil rights against public criticism from a group of prominent clergymen. Write a short analysis of this paragraph in which you note (a) an opposing viewpoint to which he is responding, (b) a refutation he offers to this viewpoint, (c) a concession he makes, and (d) any questions this excerpt raises for you.

[1]You express a great deal of anxiety over our willingness to break laws. [2]This is certainly a legitimate concern. [3]Since we so diligently urge people to obey the Supreme Court's decision of 1954 outlawing segregation in the public schools, at first glance it may seem rather paradoxical for us consciously to break laws. [4]One may well ask: "How can you advocate breaking some laws and obeying others?" [5]The answer lies in the fact that there are two types of laws, just and unjust. [6]I would be the first to advocate obeying just laws. [7]One has not only a legal but a moral responsibility to obey just laws. [8]Conversely, one has a moral responsibility to disobey unjust laws. [9]I would agree with St. Augustine that "an unjust law is no law at all."

—MARTIN LUTHER KING, JR., "Letter from Birmingham Jail"

36e | Effective arguments use several rhetorical appeals.

Effective arguments always incorporate several appeals to the audience simply because logical reasoning—providing good reasons—is rarely enough (see 35c and 36d). Human beings do not believe or act on the basis of facts or logic alone; if we did, we would not engage in unsafe practices (speeding, smoking, unprotected sex, and so on), and we would believe only that which can be proved. In reality, however, we believe and act on the basis of our own concerns, experiences, and needs. An effective argument, then, is one that gets a fair hearing, an essential step in the argumentation process. If you want your views to be heard, understood, and maybe even acted on, you need to follow the necessary steps to gain a hearing.

(1) There are three classical rhetorical appeals.

A combination of three persuasive strategies helps speakers shape effective arguments: the rhetorical appeals of ethos, logos, and pathos. **Ethos** (an ethical appeal) establishes the speaker's or writer's credibility and trustworthiness. An ethical appeal demonstrates your goodwill toward your audience, your good sense or knowledge of the subject at hand, and your good character. Establishing common ground with your audience is another feature of ethos. When you take the time to establish common ground, your audience is more likely to continue considering your argument. But ethos alone rarely carries an argument; therefore, you also need to use **logos** (a logical appeal). Logos demonstrates your effective use of reason and judicious use of evidence, whether facts, statistics, comparisons, anecdotes, expert opinions, personal experiences, or observations. You employ logos in the process of supporting claims, drawing reasonable conclusions, and avoiding logical fallacies (see 35f). Aristotle also taught that persuasion comes about only when the audience feels emotionally stirred by the topic under discussion. Therefore, **pathos** (an emotional appeal) involves using language that will stir the feelings of the audience. If you misuse pathos in an attempt to manipulate your audience, it can backfire. But pathos can be used successfully when it establishes empathy and authentic understanding. Thus, the most effective arguments combine these three persuasive appeals responsibly and knowledgeably.

Although ethos is often developed in the introduction, logos in the body, and pathos in the conclusion, these classical rhetorical appeals often overlap and appear throughout an argument. Once you start looking for them, you'll discover that these appeals appear in much of your reading and in your writing.

(2) Rogerian appeals show other people that you understand them.

Rogerian argument derives from the work of Carl R. Rogers, a psychologist who believed that many problems are the result of a breakdown in communication arising from a natural tendency to judge and evaluate, agree or disagree. He emphasizes the importance of listening carefully to what others say and understanding their ideas. His model calls for suspending judgment until each person in a conflict is able to restate fairly and accurately what the others believe, thereby significantly reducing the likelihood of misunderstanding. This model can be initiated by a single person in a potentially explosive situation, and it can help foster personal growth.

A writer making a Rogerian argument says, in effect, "I have heard your concerns, and I am responding to them to the best of my ability. I am also offering some ideas of my own from which we can both benefit. I want to work with you and will not try to push you around." This emphasis on being fair-minded and nonconfrontational gives ethos (see **36e(1)**) an essential place in the Rogerian approach. Because this approach emphasizes the importance of listening and speaking respectfully, it is also useful when writing groups discuss how to revise drafts. (See **33c**.)

For information on how to organize a Rogerian argument, see pages 532–533.

36f | Effective arguments are purposefully arranged.

Unless your instructor asks you to demonstrate a particular type of arrangement, the decisions you make about arrangement should be based on your subject, your audience, and your purpose. (See 32a.) Writers often develop a good plan by simply listing the major points they want to make (see 32b), deciding what order to put them in, and then determining where to include refutation or concession (see 36d(2)). They must also decide whether to place their thesis statement or claim at the beginning or the end of their argument.

In addition, there are a few basic principles that may be useful.

(1) Classical arrangement works well if your audience has not yet taken a position on your issue.

Use the classical arrangement if it seems appropriate for your rhetorical situation (see 32a).

FEATURES OF THE CLASSICAL ARRANGEMENT

Introduction	Introduce your issue and capture the attention of your audience. Try using a short narrative or a strong example. (See 33b.) Begin establishing your credibility (or ethos) and common ground.
Background Information	Provide your audience with a history of the situation, and state how things currently stand. Define any key terms. Even if you think the facts speak for themselves, draw the attention of your

(Continued on page 532)

(Continued from page 531)

audience to those points that are especially important, and explain why they are meaningful.

Proposition	Introduce the position you are taking; in other words, present the argument itself, and provide the basic reasons for your belief. Frame your position as a thesis statement or claim. (See 32c and 36c.)
Proof or Confirmation	Discuss the reasons why you have taken your position. Each reason must be clear, relevant, and representative. Provide facts, expert testimony, and any other evidence that supports your claim.
Refutation	Recognize and disprove the arguments of people who hold a different position and with whom you continue to disagree.
Concession	Concede any point with which you agree or that has merit; in either case, show why this concession does not damage your own case.
Conclusion	Summarize your most important points, and appeal to your audience's feelings, making a personal connection. Describe the consequences of your argument in a final attempt to encourage your audience to consider (if not commit to) a particular course of action.

(2) Rogerian arrangement can help calm an audience strongly opposed to your position.

To write an argument informed by Rogerian appeals, you can be guided by the following plan.

FEATURES OF THE ROGERIAN ARRANGEMENT

| **Introduction** | Establish that you have paid attention to views different from your own. Build trust by stating these views clearly and fairly. |

Concessions	Reassure the people you hope to persuade by showing that you agree with them to some extent and do not think that they are completely wrong.
Thesis	Having earned the confidence of your audience, state your claim, or proposition.
Support	Explain why you have taken this position and provide support for it.
Conclusion	Conclude by showing how your audience and other people could benefit from accepting your position. Indicate the extent to which this position will resolve the problem you are addressing. If you are offering a partial solution to a complex problem, concede that further work may be necessary.

When following this plan, you will find that some parts require more development than others. For example, although you may be able to make concessions or to state your position within a single paragraph, you are likely to need several paragraphs to support your position.

(3) Refutation and concession are most effective when placed where readers will welcome them.

Classical arrangement places refutation after the proof or confirmation of the argument, an arrangement that works well for an audience familiar with this organizational model. But if you wait until the end of your confirmation to begin the refutation, to recognize views that differ from yours, it may be too late. Readers unfamiliar with classical arrangement may have decided that you are too one-sided—and may even have stopped reading. When writers are taking a highly controversial stand on a subject that has inspired strong feelings, they sometimes begin by establishing common ground and then acknowledge opposing viewpoints and respond to them. In a Rogerian argument, a writer begins by reporting opposing views fairly and identifying what is valuable about them, not to refute the views but to concede that they have merit.

However, sometimes readers may react negatively to a writer who responds to opposing views before offering any reasons to support his or her own view. These readers want to know from the start where an argument is headed. For this reason, writers often choose to state their position at the beginning of the argument and offer at least one strong reason to support it before turning to opposing views.

Unless you are required to follow a specific arrangement or organizational plan, you should respond to opposing views wherever your audience is most likely either to expect this discussion or to be willing to hear it. You must assess your readers carefully (see **32a**), determining what opinions they are likely to have about your topic and how open they are to new ideas. If your audience is receptive, you can place refutation and concession after your confirmation. If your audience adheres to a different position, you should respond to their views toward the beginning of your argument.

(4) Separate reasons are best discussed in separate paragraphs.

As you sort out the reasons supporting your argument, consider how much development each of the reasons merits within your organizational plan. Whether you follow a classical or Rogerian arrangement, you are likely to need at least one full paragraph to develop any one reason for your claim (see **36c**). You might need two paragraphs to explain an important or substantial reason. If you try to develop two separate reasons in the same paragraph, it may lack unity and coherence. (See **31a**.) However, if the purpose of a paragraph is to summarize why you hold your position, you might list several reasons in that paragraph. In fact, writers sometimes include several reasons in a single paragraph near the conclusion if these reasons consist of additional advantages that do not call for detailed discussion. When readers look at any paragraph, they should be able to see how it advances the argument that is being made.

(5) You can begin a paragraph with a view different from yours.

If you open a paragraph with an opposing view, you can use the rest of the paragraph for your response to that view. Readers will have to make only one shift between differing views. However, if you begin a paragraph with your view, then introduce an opposing view, and then move back to the development of your view, readers must shift direction twice and may miss the point you want them to get. If you use most of a paragraph to develop an opposing point of view, waiting until the very end of the paragraph to introduce your own, you may dilute the effect of your own view.

(6) Your conclusion can reinforce your purpose.

The most effective conclusions move beyond a mere summary of what has already been stated. When considering how to conclude an argument, then, you may want to imagine readers who are interested in what you've just said but remain unsure about what you expect from them. Whether your conclusion emphasizes a specific course of action you want your audience to take, an invitation to further understanding, or a purposeful restatement of your claim (see 33b(2)), it is the best place for you to introduce or reinforce an emotional, person-to-person connection with your audience (see 36e). The conclusion is your last opportunity to explain to your audience the potentially useful, wonderful, harmful, or dangerous consequences of a particular belief or action. In other words, try to conclude by answering the question "So what?" The student paper by Laura Klocke at the end of this chapter (see pages 537–544) ends with a conclusion that not only reinforces her purpose but links her purpose with the stated mission of her university.

Exercise 3

In the editorial pages of your community or college newspaper, find editorials that analyze or question an established belief, express or defend an opinion, invite consideration, or try to convince. Bring several copies of a well-argued, well-developed, and well-organized editorial to class, and be prepared to discuss its purpose, audience, use of appeals, and conclusion.

36g | You can improve your ability to write arguments by studying the written arguments of others.

The following paper was Laura Klocke's response to an assignment in argumentative writing. She was asked to write an essay that pointed to a specific problem at her living quarters, on her campus, in her town, or in the world at large, and then proposed a process, policy claim, or procedure for solving that problem.

As you read Laura's essay, consider whether—and how—she argued her case effectively. Note her use of classical rhetorical appeals (ethos, logos, and pathos) and arrangement and her inductive reasoning. Also, identify the kinds of evidence she uses (facts, examples, testimony, or authority).

Just Coffee: A Proposal in the Classical Arrangement

Laura Klocke

From the local café and the multinational chains to the gas
station and the grocery story, you can buy lattes, cappucinos,
fresh drip, and espresso. Everywhere and anywhere, it seems,
coffee is "the best part of waking up."

Introduction

Approximately 20 to 25 million people grow coffee for the
world's drinkers and rely solely on coffee production for their
income and survival. Coffee is a world beverage of choice, and
this is perhaps most clearly evident in the United States, which
consumes one-third of the world's coffee. Roughly $18 billion
dollars is spent on coffee itself; almost just as much is invested in
coffee equipment in the United States. It's not surprising, then,
that coffee is the second-largest commodity traded on the market
in the entire world, following oil (Dicum and Luttinger 3). With
these large dollar figures and millions of cups of coffee in mind,
you might wonder where all the money goes. Or, better yet, to
whom?

The answer has mostly to do with coffee plantations known
as *fincas,* a modern-day version of pre-Civil War Southern
plantations. The coffee grown and processed is taken from the
fincas and enters into what is called the "coffee chain." This chain
continues from the *finca* and its workers to a local speculator, or
"coyote." The coyote draws up a contract with an exporter, and the

Background
Information

chain proceeds to the roaster, distributor, retail outlet, and, finally, your cup. The goal of this chain, like the goal of most business transactions, is to maximize the final profit. Unfortunately for those at the beginning--the peasant farmers of the *finca*--their livelihood is not a consideration of their employer; the maximization of profit is the employer's sole concern. Grocery store gourmet coffee costs as much as $12.00 per pound, and yet some *finca* workers are paid only twenty to forty cents per pound for the coffee they harvest. When considering that the average *finca* coffee farmer makes $3.00 a day, and the average latte is priced at $3.50 or more, it is clear that something doesn't add up in this coffee chain system (Rice and McLean 22). And, because the workers do not own the land, though they live and work on it in each stage of the coffee-growing production, they have relatively little say in their pay. Something akin to the sharecroppers of the past, the situation for those living on *fincas* is a present-day injustice. The emphasis for the world's production of coffee is on profit, and a speedy profit at that, which I will explain below.

When fair trade coffee organizations are part of the coffee-growing and coffee-selling equation, the emphasis is not only on speed and profit. Fair trade coffee organizations establish personal, gradually developing, and long-term buying relationships with coffee growers and encourage the farmers to organize into cooperatives, where they are free to live, work, and

Klocke 3

grow coffee in a community supported by a guaranteed fair and
livable wage. Fair trade coffee eliminates the middle people in the
chain and thereby allocates the money that had gone to the
coyotes to the growers themselves. Instead of the twenty to forty
cents per pound they earned on the *fincas,* the workers can earn a
minimum of $1.20 per pound. This pay raise is accomplished by
eliminating the middle people and ensuring that the workers are
paid fairly for their labor--not by raising the price of coffee
noticeably. With the guarantee of a livable wage, many farmers
would be able to put money into their community, building
schools, recreation centers, churches, and businesses, improving
the lives of everyone in the region.

Though I have never traveled to a *finca,* I am aware that my
purchases are just one of the many ways that I can demonstrate
my recognition of the inherent dignity of all people. Therefore,
I do not want to support knowingly any flawed financial system
with my purchases. My university is also working to make
positive steps in its purchasing practices; however, with regard
to fair trade food products, particularly coffee, the University of
St. Thomas is not yet up to speed. In order to be fully engaged
in ethical buying practices, St. Thomas must support a fully
fair trade coffee supplier. Though the whole world may never
be converted to the philosophy of fair trade, the sizable amount
of money the university spends on coffee can still make a

Proposition

Klocke 4

difference and set an example that other universities may want
to follow.

Since the university can choose between selling fair trade or
unfairly traded coffee at every food service location on campus, I
advocate that our university sell only that coffee that has been
provided from fair trade organizations. Such a university-wide
decision will reflect the ethics and politics of the university's
buying power as well as align with the commitment of our
University Mission Statement.

The switch from coffee drinker to conscientious coffee
drinker is not difficult. The mission of the University of St.
Thomas includes a commitment to "develop morally responsible
individuals who combine . . . cultural awareness and intellectual
curiosity." In addition, the tradition of the school seeks to foster "a
value-oriented education needed for complete human
development and for responsible citizenship in contemporary
society"; an "international perspective"; and an "appreciation for
cultural diversity." Finally, "the university embraces its role and
our responsibilities in the world community," a statement that
clearly connects the University of St. Thomas and the fair trade
issue. The commitment to ethical activities in the university
supports not only a continuation of international learning and
experience, but also reflects an understanding of the inherent

Proof

dignity of work and the workers that grow and process the coffee the university serves. Not only are the workers valuable as members of the human race, but their work, also, has value to them, and to the world.

Many other groups already support the fair trade coffee movement, including the Audubon Society and the MacArthur Foundation, so the University of St. Thomas would join a wide movement of people and organizations who recognize that drinking fair trade coffee is in good taste--financially, politically, and ethically (Rice and McLean 38).

Unfortunately, this proposal for a change to a completely fair trade coffee offering at the University of St. Thomas has been met with several concerns from the administration. St. Thomas does not desire to terminate its contract with Dunn Brothers Coffee, a local Twin Cities company that currently provides several varieties of certified fair trade coffee, including Guatemalan and Mexican. Though Dunn Brothers offers these choices, they are not a solely fair trade coffee company. Through a gradual approach of switching to an entirely fair trade coffee company, Dunn Brothers would be given a chance to improve their offerings as well as help St. Thomas to address some of its major concerns, in particular, those from a cost standpoint. As a student of this university, and given my support of this mission

Refutation

statement, I prefer to approach this issue from an ethical stand. However, it is easy to show that the serving of fair trade coffee makes sense from a financial perspective as well.

First, however, to answer the concerns of the university is necessary. University administrators argue that, by supporting a small local company like Dunn Brothers, they are still using university money in an acceptable way. I argue that the university could use its money in an even better way. The fact that Dunn Brothers is not a solely fair trade company puts them at odds with the university mission. Besides, there are several local fair trade companies--Cloud Forest Initiatives and Peace Coffee, to name just two--that are small enough for the university to support at the same time that it does more with its buying power.

Next, the cost difference between fair trade and unfair trade coffee is an understandable concern for St. Thomas. While the movement continues to grow, fair trade coffee has the potential to cost slightly more (though hardly noticeably more) per pound than unfairly traded coffee. However, with an institution-sized order, many coffee cooperatives could be in a position to provide a contract that could work in the best way, financially, for both the growers and, in this case, the university. A worst-case scenario would be an increase of almost five cents more per cup. In answering this argument, however, the University of St. Thomas should recognize that the price difference for fair trade coffee is negligible when compared to the cost of unfairly traded coffee for communities, farmers, and families.

The last concern the administration of St. Thomas has expressed is the fear of losing the recognizable Dunn Brothers' name. The administration understandably wants to continue to sell coffee that is successfully marketed and doesn't yet know if students will support the move to fair trade coffee if there's no name recognition. To that objection, I would respond that relatively few students have taken an active interest in the coffee served at the University of St. Thomas (fair trade or otherwise). It is unlikely that once the switch to fair trade coffee is realized, my fellow students will notice--let alone protest against it. It seems that, at the heart, there is a discrepancy between the bottom lines in this issue. The University of St. Thomas would like to make the bottom line about cost, and yet the mission statement and foundation of the university clearly states otherwise. Also in response to this argument, it is worth mentioning that students are rarely consulted about the buying choices of the university. We live in a closed market system on campus, meaning, we have no choice about many of our food products (for example, the university is a "Pepsi" campus, and only Pepsi products are sold in beverage vending machines).

Klocke 8

We at the University of St. Thomas have the chance not only to have our concerns answered but to affirm our mission statement and be a leader in the intra-campus community. We would convey a strong message with our purchase and sales of fair trade coffee, demonstrating that we are a community of concerned citizens. Our mission guides us in decisions that affect our local community as well as our global community. St. Thomas should be a leader in social justice as well as in academics.

We must support fair trade coffee growers and their communities, and, thereby, as a university, adhere to the mission that we profess. By helping to guarantee coffee growers a livable wage, the commitment to fair trade coffee at the University of St. Thomas is clearly the just choice.

Conclusion

Klocke 9

Works Cited

Dicum, Gregory, and Nina Luttinger. <u>The Coffee Book:
    Anatomy of an Industry from Crop to the Last Drop</u>. New
    York: New Press, 1999.

Rice, Paul D., and Jennifer McLean. "Sustainable Coffee at
    the Crossroads." <u>CCC Coffee Program</u>. 15 Oct. 1999.
    Consumer's Choice Council. 23 Oct. 2001.
    <http://www.consumerscouncil.org/coffee/coffeebook/
    coffee.pdf>.

University of St. Thomas. "Mission Statement."
    <http://www.stthomas.edu>.

Exercise 4

Reread Laura Klocke's essay to establish its grounding. What
qualities or experiences of this writer have shaped the values she
reveals as she argues for fair trade coffee? In other words, what
evidence in her essay might provide an explanation for her side
of the argument? What are her unspoken but underlying values? What other sides of the argument might you be able to
provide? What values do you bring to the argument?

37 Finding Sources Online, in Print, and in the Field

Good research skills are essential when you are required to incorporate outside sources into text that is your own. An inquiring mind is the best equipment you can bring to research. But to inquire efficiently, you need to develop specific skills in accessing information. Although different projects require different strategies—depending on the nature of the topic, your familiarity with it, and the time you have for research— you will benefit from developing effective research skills.

This chapter will help you

- assess your information needs and develop a research routine (**37a**),
- frame a research question (**37b**),
- use sources on the Web (**37c**),
- use library resources such as books and periodicals (**37d**), and
- conduct field research (**37e**).

37a | Writers need information.

Because downloading material from the Web can be easy and fast (see **37c**), some people now go to it exclusively—overlooking other avenues that might give them better results. One of the advantages to searching the Web is that you can do so whenever you have access to a computer and can get online. But bear in mind that visiting a college or university library will allow you to find thousands of documents that do not appear online. You will also find librarians who are knowledgeable in specific subject areas. They can help you focus your topic and can guide you to appropriate resources for your research (see **37d**).

As you proceed with research, be aware of whether sources are primary or secondary. **Primary sources** for topics in literature and the humanities are generally documents—such as old letters and records—and literary works. In the social sciences, primary sources can be field observations, case histories, and survey data. In the natural sciences, primary sources are generally empirical—measurements, experiments, and the like. **Secondary sources** are commentaries on primary sources. For example, a review of a new novel is a secondary source and so is a discussion of adolescence based on survey data. Experienced researchers usually consult both primary and secondary sources, read them critically, and draw on them carefully. (See chapters **35** and **38**.)

In addition to examining information that has already been published, you might benefit from discussing your research topic with other people. An authority on your topic could be teaching at your college, working in the next office, or accessible via email. Thoughtful conversation about your topic could even be generated in an online discussion group or forum.

(1) Different types of resources offer different advantages.

Much of the research people do in their daily lives involves looking in various places to find answers to questions. If you plan to buy a new car, for example, you may read reviews published in magazines or on the Web, talk to people familiar with the cars that interest you, and take a test drive or two. A similar strategy may be appropriate for research assignments in school or at work: read, interview, and observe.

The following box can help you see at a glance the advantages and disadvantages of different types of resources.

RESOURCE ASSESSMENT

Web Sites (see pages 550–553)

Advantages

The Web contains an amazing amount of recent material. Many sites have links to other relevant sites. The full text of a document can be printed out.

Disadvantages

Researchers can be overwhelmed by the number of available sites. Many sites lack credibility. Sites can vanish without warning.

Library Catalog (see pages 553–556)

Advantages

A library catalog indexes its own books but may link to other catalogs. It identifies material that has been professionally selected for purchase.

Disadvantages

A library catalog lists only the library's own holdings. Books listed in the catalog may be checked out or lost.

Electronic Indexes to Periodicals (see pages 556–563)

Advantages

Electronic indexes enable you to find material focused specifically on your topic. They cover a high percentage of credible sources. The most recent citations are identified first.

Disadvantages

Electronic indexes provide article citations, but an electronic version of the full text of an article is not always available.

Interviews and Dialogues (see pages 564–566)

Advantages

Interviews or dialogues can be conducted in person, by phone, or by email. An interview allows you to focus on a point you need to clarify. A dialogue can generate new ideas when you feel stuck.

Disadvantages

Ideas can be lost if not recorded. Misreporting is common. Sources may lack credibility.

(2) Establishing a research schedule helps you use time efficiently.

Planning ahead and scheduling your time are critical when writing research papers. Make sure to allow enough time for choosing a subject (see 32b), reading extensively, taking notes (39b), preparing a working bibliography (39c), developing a thesis (32c), outlining (32d(2)), drafting (32f), revising (33a–b), and editing (33d). You must allow some time for each of these stages, no matter how much (or how little) time you have for the entire project.

37b	Researchers choose a topic and frame it as a question that needs to be answered.

When assigned a research paper, either you are given a topic, or you choose one that interests you. The methods discussed in 32b(1)—freewriting, listing, and questioning—can help you find and explore a topic. Focusing on a specific topic is important since one of your main objectives is to show your ability to write in some depth within the time allowed and the length specified. But be flexible. Even if you begin research with a focused topic already in mind, be prepared to revise it if preliminary research leads you to a related issue that is more interesting or better documented.

As you do preliminary research, bear in mind that thorough research usually incorporates different kinds of materials. Research drawn exclusively from books might overlook current information available online. Similarly, relying solely on electronic sources is unwise since there are excellent sources in print that do not appear online.

As you choose a topic, think in terms of a **research problem,** a question that can be resolved at least partly through research. Your investigation of this problem may lead you to a position you wish to argue (see chapter 36), but the question you initially pose should invite exploration rather than make a judgment. For example, the thesis statement "Animal experimentation is wrong" is not a research problem because it is a conclusion rather than a question. Someone interested in a research topic related to animal experimentation might begin with this question: "Are animals being treated responsibly in research labs?" or "Under what circumstances could animal experimentation be necessary?" Beginning with a question, rather than an answer, encourages you to look at diverse materials—not just material that reinforces what you already believe.

Exercise 1

Each of the following subjects would need to be narrowed down for a ten-page paper. To experiment with framing a research problem, compose two questions about each subject.

1. terrorism
2. the job market
3. gender differences
4. globalization
5. civil rights
6. health care

37c | Researchers understand how to navigate the Web.

The **World Wide Web** is a huge and rapidly expanding collection of information, much of which—once located—is useful for research papers. You may have been using this resource for years, but if you do not have experience with the Web, the computer center or library at your school may offer workshops on using the Web for research. The library's Web site may even offer advice and tutorials. Similarly, the company you work for may provide special training.

The easiest way to find information on the Web is to use one of the many search tools, such as AltaVista, Google, Lycos, or

Yahoo! After you type **keywords** (words that describe your research topic) into an on-screen text entry box, a search tool provides a list of electronic documents (Web sites) that meet the search criteria. Knowing how to use several search tools can make your Web searches more productive.

The opening page for Google, shown in figure 37.1, includes a space for the user to type in keyword(s) for a search. Clicking on "Google Search" after typing "Starbucks" would establish how many sites mention Starbucks and provide a list of the first ten. Clicking on "I'm Feeling Lucky" would take the user directly to the first site on the list. (When this search was made, Google listed 416,000 sites that mentioned Starbucks, demonstrating the need to narrow a keyword search.)

On the right side of Google's opening page, a link offers users an option called "Advanced Search." Undertaking an advanced search can reveal the difference between surfing the Web and searching the Web. When **surfing the Web,** you simply enter a keyword, receive a list of sites, and scan them to determine which, if any, are worth consulting. **Searching the Web,** however, demands thinking carefully about keywords,

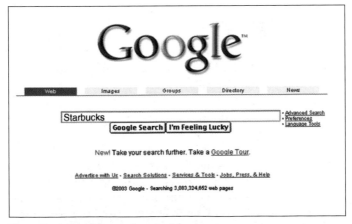

Figure 37.1. Google's opening page.

identifying authorities you would like to locate, and deciding what dates are appropriate for the kind of data you need for a specific research project.

Among the numerous tools available for searching the Web, some, like Yahoo!, are **subject directories.** These match keywords against descriptions of Web sites submitted by sponsors or creators or entered by human indexers. Other search tools are **search engines,** which use automatic programs to index the content of Web sites by searching for keywords or phrases. Search engines, such as AltaVista, tend to be larger than subject directories. However, the distinction between subject directories and search engines is blurring, since many of the directories now link directly to one or more engines.

Search tools will return different results. One may search for only the titles of documents, another may look at document links, and a few search the full text of every document they index. Furthermore, some search tools cover only the Web, whereas others go into other areas of the Internet (such as usenet newsgroups). For these reasons, one tool may be better for academic information, another for general information, and yet another for business information.

The result of a successful search will be a list of Web addresses, or **Uniform Resource Locators (URLs),** which you can use to access the sites you need. Because sites change and even disappear, scholarly organizations such as the Modern Language Association (see **40a**) and the American Psychological Association (see **40c**) require that bibliographies include both the access date and the posting date for any site listed. When you print out material from the Web, the **access date** usually appears at the top or bottom of the printout. The **posting date** (the date when the site was last modified or updated) generally appears on the site itself. Some sites do not show a posting date, however, and some printouts will not have an access date. Keeping a separate record of this information can help you later, when you need to verify information on a site or list it in a bibliography (see **39c**). If a site does not have a posting date, note in your records that it is undated; doing so will establish that you did not accidentally omit a piece of information. When you take notes directly from the screen, without making a printout, a record of sites and dates is essential.

Exercise 2

Using at least three search tools and entering different keywords in each one, look on the Web for information about a topic you are interested in researching. Then, write a one- or two-page paper describing your search.

37d | Libraries house books, periodicals, and other important sources.

Libraries provide a variety of materials, including books, periodicals (journals, magazines, and newspapers), videotapes, artwork, and unpublished documents (such as letters and manuscripts). Although information about resources in some small specialized libraries may be available only in those libraries, most large libraries provide information about their resources and services via the Web. However, if you want to borrow or consult the print resources, you will have to visit a library.

(1) Books often contain the results of extensive research.

You locate a book by consulting the library's main catalog, which gives you the **call number** you need to find the location where the book is shelved. Books put temporarily **on reserve** can be checked out for only a short period, if at all. Reference books, encyclopedias, and indexes—materials that cannot be checked out of the library—are located in the reference collection, but some of these materials may also be available online or on CD-ROMs.

Some libraries still maintain a **card catalog** consisting of cards arranged alphabetically in drawers. Most libraries, however, have **online catalogs,** which save space and make research more efficient. A library catalog, whether computerized or kept on cards, identifies books by author, title, and subject. Most online catalogs also allow researchers to locate sources by searching for other information, such as a keyword that may appear in the title or the text. In addition to providing the author, title, publisher, and date of publication, an online record also reveals the book's status—information that tells a researcher when a book has been moved to a special collection or checked out by someone else.

The example online catalog record shown in figure 37.2 was generated by the search that Nicole Hester did for her paper on desegregating the U.S. military (see **40f**). Expect to encounter variations from this example because libraries use different systems for computerizing their catalogs. The information displayed on the screen can help you decide whether you want to examine the book itself or search for other books like it. Look at the terms, sometimes called *subjects,* listed for the book; you can click on the terms to find other books that may help you answer your research question.

(2) Reference books provide useful background.

When doing research, you may need to consult a variety of reference works. A general encyclopedia, such as *Encyclopaedia Britannica* (now available by subscription on the Web at www.eb.com), can provide useful background information for the early stage of your research.

Despite the ease with which many reference works can be accessed electronically, you may need to consult a specialized encyclopedia or dictionary in your college library to identify

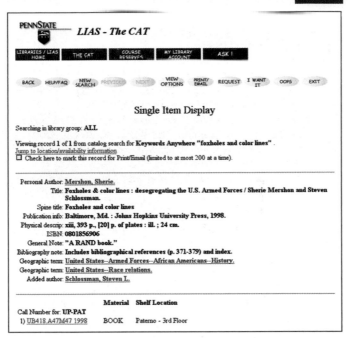

Figure 37.2. A record from an online catalog.

names and understand concepts in the books or articles you have discovered. Sources written for a specialized audience (see 32a) assume that readers do not need help with basic terminology in the field. Reference books can help you fill in the gaps that keep you from understanding the sources you have found.

For a detailed list of reference books and a short description of each, consult *Guide to Reference Books* by Robert Balay and *American Reference Books Annual* (*ARBA*). A few of the most widely used reference books are listed here with abbreviated bibliographical information. Remember that these sources are useful for background information; refer to them for help, but do not use them as major sources for your research.

Special Dictionaries and Encyclopedias

Dictionary of American History. Rev. ed. 8 vols. 1976–1978. Supplements, 1996.

Dictionary of Art. Ed. Jane Turner. 34 vols. 1996.

Encyclopedia of Psychology. Ed. Alan E. Kazdin. 2000.

Encyclopedia of U.S. Foreign Relations. Eds. Bruce W. Jentleson and Thomas G. Paterson. 4 vols. 1997.

International Encyclopedia of the Social and Behavioral Sciences. Eds. Neil J. Smelser and Paul B. Baltes. 26 vols. 2001.

McGraw-Hill Encyclopedia of Science and Technology. 8th ed. 20 vols. 1997. Yearbooks.

The New Grove Dictionary of Music and Musicians. Ed. Stanley Sadie. 2nd ed. 29 vols. 2001.

Biographies

American National Biography. Eds. John A. Garraty and Mark C. Carnes. 24 vols. 1999.

Biography and Genealogy Master Index. 1980– . Also on CD-ROM.

Current Biography Cumulated Index. 1940– .

Dictionary of Scientific Biography. 16 vols. 1970–1981. Supplements.

Notable American Women: 1607–1950. 3 vols. 1971. Supplements.

Notable Black American Women. 2nd ed. 1996.

Webster's New Biographical Dictionary. 1995.

Who's Who in America. 1899– . (See also Marquis's *Who's Who Publications: Index to All Books,* revised annually, 1976– .)

(3) Magazines, journals, and newspapers often contain recent information on a topic.

Periodicals (magazines, journals, and newspapers, in print or on microfilm) are typically held in a special section of the library. To access information in periodicals, researchers use **electronic indexes.** Many periodicals are also available online, and some allow **full-text retrieval,** the option of downloading and printing out an entire article. Periodical literature is useful not only because it is timely, but also because it has been professionally reviewed and edited. For information on how to evaluate the credibility of periodicals, see 38b(2).

Virtually every discipline and profession has its own **journals,** periodicals that generally provide much more detailed information than can be found in magazines or newspapers aimed at the general public. When conducting research on a topic, you should familiarize yourself with the indexes that direct you to work written by authorities on that topic and published in journals.

With full-text retrieval becoming increasingly available, you will often be able to obtain the complete text of an article through your computer—whether directly from a periodical you subscribe to or through an electronic index available via your library's Web site. On many occasions, however, you will need to visit a library to use an electronic or print index or to obtain a copy of an article in a periodical for which full-text retrieval is not available electronically.

(a) Choosing and using an electronic index

Electronic indexes, also frequently called *electronic databases,* can help you locate the titles and authors of articles. In addition, many of these indexes include *abstracts* (short summaries of articles; see page 494). Some can even provide you with complete texts of articles. Selecting an appropriate index requires that you locate your topic within a field (such as psychology) or discipline (a group of related fields, such as the social sciences). For example, if you are researching the nature of memory, you could go directly to PsycINFO (see page 561), which is devoted exclusively to scholarship in psychology. If you are researching cases in which students have opened fire on their high school classmates, you could also go to PsycINFO. But if you recognize that sociologists and criminologists—as well as psychologists—are likely to have studied such cases, you might turn to SocialSciIndex for a broader range of materials (see page 560).

Many indexes are available on CD-ROM as well as on the Web. A CD-ROM offers you the convenience of searching for periodical literature from a personal computer when you do not have a link from your home or office to the electronic indexes available at a college library. But CD-ROM indexes have one disadvantage: Once published, the information cannot be updated unless a continuation is issued. If you need up-to-the-minute information, you might have to search through one of the online indexes to supplement what you find on the CD-ROM.

InfoTrac College Edition is often a good place to begin your search for periodical literature. It indexes more than 10 million articles in over 3,800 full-text journals, including the following:

Scholarly journals (such as the *Journal of Business Communication* and the *Journal of Social Psychology*)

Trade journals (such as *Adhesive Technology* and *Frozen Food Digest*)

General-circulation magazines (such as *Newsweek* and *Sports Illustrated*)

The InfoTrac screens in figures 37.3 and 37.4 illustrate part of the research conducted for the paper that appears in 40d. Clicking in the box labeled "Mark" next to the article, as shown in figure 37.3, and then clicking on "text and full content retrieval choices" brought up the complete article, whose first page appears in figure 37.4.

As you continue your research, you may also benefit from consulting FirstSearch, a family of electronic indexes that is usually accessed through terminals in a school library or through personal computers linked to a school library. FirstSearch covers several broad topic areas (such as "Arts and Humanities" and "Business and Economics") and specialized databases (such as MEDLINE and GeoRefS). You will be asked to choose from among these topics and databases. FirstSearch also prompts you to enter keywords related to your topic.

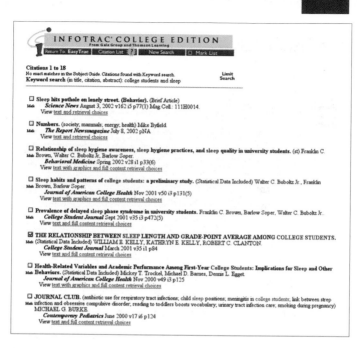

Figure 37.3. Example of an InfoTrac screen.

Beyond the Rule

USING INFOTRAC

Through an agreement between the publisher of InfoTrac College Edition and the publisher of this handbook, access to InfoTrac is available through a passcode packaged with new copies of this book. If your copy did not come with a passcode for InfoTrac and you would like to know more about this service, or if you have access to InfoTrac but have questions about it, visit www.harbrace.com.

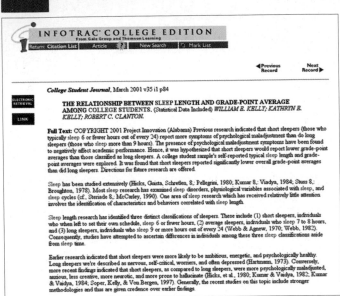

Figure 37.4. First page of an article found through InfoTrac.

Depending on the Web page you are viewing, you might have to choose a topic before choosing a database. The screen in figure 37.5 shows the choices available for "Social Sciences." By selecting "ECO," you could access a collection of scholarly journals; by clicking on "SocialSciIndex," you would also obtain journal articles, although this search might identify other kinds of articles as well. An effective search would probably include both. (Note that FirstSearch also provides access to books and Web resources through its WorldCat feature.)

The databases available through FirstSearch vary from one library to another. Similarly, the appearance of the opening screen for FirstSearch varies from one school to another. The example shown in figure 37.5 is from the library system through which Nikki Krzmarzick conducted her search.

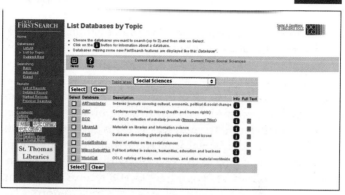

Figure 37.5. Example of a screen from FirstSearch.

Whether or not your school or library provides access to FirstSearch, check to see whether you can access other indexes or specialized databases. Some examples follow.

Literature	The MLA Bibliography indexes articles and books written in most modern languages and is essential for research in literature.
Education	ERIC indexes articles and conference papers in all areas of education.
Psychology	PsycINFO provides short summaries, or abstracts, of articles in psychology in addition to the citations that will help you find the full article.
Life sciences	MEDLINE provides abstracts of articles in medicine and biology from more than seven thousand journals.

Another important electronic index is LexisNexis, a service that indexes legal documents and newspaper articles. Because this service is updated daily, and even includes information that will not be published in print until the following day, it is especially helpful for researchers working on current events.

Many electronic indexes permit keyword searches of their entire contents, not just limited searches by topic or by **controlled terms** (a vocabulary of official descriptors used to retrieve information). Even if a keyword is not one of the controlled terms, a search may turn up potential sources that use the keyword in the title or in some other part. If your search yields no records, try substituting or adding another closely related term. If your search turns up more records than you can handle, try locating those that are most relevant by adding other words to the keyword with which you began. A search result such as "Found 2,493,508 records containing the descriptor *film*" is as useless as one that reports "No records found." To narrow or broaden a search, you can use **logical operators** (also called **Boolean operators**):

or	broadens a search (For example, "Starbucks **or** Vienna" finds all records that contain information about either keyword.)
and	narrows a search ("Starbucks **and** Vienna" returns only those records that contain both keywords.)
not	excludes specific items ("Starbucks **and** Austria **not** Vienna" excludes any records that mention Austria's capital city.)
near	finds records in which the two keywords occur in close proximity, within a preset number of words, and excludes those in which the keywords are widely separated ("Starbucks **near** globalization" lists only those records in which references to both *Starbucks* and *globalization* occur in close proximity; this option is often not available, however.)

Whether your library provides indexing and abstracting services online or on CD-ROMs, you can use the following search strategy to locate sources.

TIPS FOR CONDUCTING A SEARCH

1. Identify keywords that clearly describe the topic.
2. Determine the databases to be searched.
3. Apply a basic search logic.
4. Log on and perform the search.
5. Identify the citations you want to keep.
6. Refine your search strategy if the first search returned too many or too few citations, or (worse) irrelevant ones.
7. Obtain the articles for which you have citations.

Exercise 3

Using InfoTrac or FirstSearch, identify at least two sources that seem useful for the research you began in exercise 2. Explain how you could use the sources for the research question you have in mind.

(b) Searching indexes in bound volumes

Although searching electronic indexes is more efficient than searching through bound and printed indexes, many college libraries continue to purchase bound volumes along with the comparable electronic versions. Bound volumes provide essential backup when computers are out of service. Searching through bound volumes takes more time than searching via computer, but it is preferable to having your research disrupted. Some of the most useful printed indexes, with their dates of beginning publication, are as follows.

Applied Science and Technology Index. 1958– .
Art Index. 1929– .

Biological and Agricultural Index. 1946– .
Business Periodicals Index. 1958– .
*Cumulative Index to Nursing and Allied Health Literature
    (CINAHL).* 1982– .
General Science Index. 1978– .
Humanities Index. 1974– .
Index to Legal Periodicals. 1908– .
Music Index. 1949– .
Philosopher's Index. 1967– .
Public Affairs Information Service (Bulletin). 1915– .
Social Sciences Index. 1974– .

When they publish electronic versions of their indexes, some
publishers change the title: *Current Index to Journals in Education (CIJE)* and *Resources in Education (RIE)* are the bound
volumes for research in education, and ERIC is the electronic
version.

Consult the front of any bound volume for a key to the abbreviations used in individual entries.

(c) Using abstracting services

Although many abstracts are available through periodical indexes, others can be obtained through **abstracting services** that
support specific academic disciplines (see chapter **41**). Your library may provide access to *Academic Abstracts, Biological Abstracts, Chemical Abstracts,* and *Psychological Abstracts.* When
using one of these services, you can quickly scan the short summaries they provide and decide which articles seem likely to be
the most useful.

37e	Field research involves interviewing, corresponding, surveying, observing, and experimenting.

For some topics, you may want to do field research—which
once meant research done outside a library or office. An arche-

ologist or geologist might work outside, literally in a field, and a social worker or political scientist might do field research by going door to door interviewing people in a specific neighborhood. Thanks to the opportunities for communication that the Internet provides, field research today can also take place indoors—even at your desk. Wherever it takes place, field research requires you to uncover data that are not already available in print or online.

The most common addition to Web-based or library research is an **interview.** Since well-informed interviewers ask the best questions, you should consider an interview only after you have done some reading on your topic. Schedule the interview well in advance, and if you plan to use a tape recorder, ask permission. Record the time and date of the interview on the tape or at the beginning of your notes.

To show that you have done some preparation, avoid asking for information that is already public knowledge. For example, if you are interviewing a novelist who is visiting your campus, you should not ask, "What have you published?" Begin with questions that are broad enough to give someone room to reveal a special interest; then, follow up with more specific questions. But be prepared to depart from your list of questions whenever the person you are interviewing says something of particular interest that would be useful to pursue.

Less formal than an interview, a dialogue with other people interested in your topic can also be useful. You may be able to have such a dialogue with people on your campus or in your community. Researchers often benefit, however, from using the Internet to exchange ideas with people in other parts of the world.

Online **discussion groups** or **forums** allow you to read messages posted to all the members of a group interested in a specific topic and to post messages yourself that those members can read. Anyone who wants to discuss a topic can join a discussion list. To find out if there are any lists that might discuss the topic you are researching, visit www.topica.com, a

Web site that provides a directory for thousands of online discussion groups and instructions that can guide your search.

Electronic mailing lists can also give you a means of conducting an informal **survey,** in which you ask a number of people the same set of questions and then analyze the results. But a survey limited to people who are already familiar with a topic and have been discussing it will not yield results that are representative of other groups, such as the students at your school or the citizens of your state.

You can administer a survey orally, like an interview, or you can distribute a written questionnaire by mail or in person. If you use a written questionnaire, be sure to distribute it well in advance of your deadline. And since many people fail to respond to written surveys, send out at least twice as many questionnaires as you would like to receive back.

Once you have a clear idea of what you want to find out through a survey, you may find the following checklist helpful.

CHECKLIST for Creating Survey Questions

- Does each question relate directly to the purpose of the survey?
- Are the questions easy to understand?
- Are they designed to elicit short, specific responses that can be analyzed easily?
- Have respondents been given enough space to write their answers?

In addition to interviews, dialogues, and surveys, you may sometimes be able to draw directly on your own observations. For example, if you are doing research on dyslexia, you might benefit from getting permission to observe a session in which a reading specialist works with a group of children who have been diagnosed as having this disorder. Or if you are doing research on a species of wildlife, you might benefit from observing the animals in their natural habitat. Before making any plans, though, check with your instructor or supervisor to see whether observation is appropriate for the assignment you have been given.

You should also consult with your instructor or supervisor if you are planning to use laboratory experiments for researching a topic. When conducting laboratory experiments, chemists, physicists, and biologists use equipment that is expensive to purchase and maintain. You will almost certainly need permission to use such equipment, and you will need to schedule your use for a specific time. Other experiments, such as those conducted by biologists and psychologists, may involve the use of animals as subjects. Some researchers in the social sciences also conduct experiments using human participants. If you are planning to use equipment that does not belong to you or experiment on living subjects, you must conduct your research carefully, ethically, and legally.

Beyond the Rule

INSTITUTIONAL REVIEW BOARDS

Colleges and universities usually have committees or boards that review requests for experimentation involving animals or humans. Institutional review of this kind is intended to protect research subjects from abuse, and a researcher who proceeds to experiment with animals or humans without official permission could suffer serious penalties. For examples of review board guidelines, visit www.harbrace.com.

Evaluating Sources Online and in Print

As you search for sources that can help you resolve a research question (see **37b**), you need to be a critical reader (**35a–b**) and evaluate the credibility of the sources you discover. Credible writers are well informed and fair-minded about the topics they discuss. Credible sources are posted or published by reputable institutions, organizations, and companies. To evaluate sources, you need clear criteria for determining the credibility of authors and the works they publish. This chapter will help you

- assess authors' credibility (**38a**),
- evaluate publishers (**38b**),
- evaluate Web sites (**38c**),
- distinguish between bias and commitment (**38d**), and
- determine the relevance of a source (**38e**).

38a | Good writing conveys the author's credibility.

You can evaluate the credibility of authors by finding out how well they write, what their credentials are, and how other readers respond to their work.

(1) Authors achieve credibility through the way they write.

You can begin to determine an author's credibility by paying close attention to tone (see **33a**). If an author's tone seems thoughtful and considerate, chances are that the author is credible. If an author's tone sounds one-sided or disrespectful to readers, chances are that the author lacks credibility. However, a thoughtful tone does not necessarily indicate expertise, nor does an arrogant tone necessarily indicate unreliability. You must consider other factors in addition to tone.

To determine how credible a writer is, ask yourself the questions in the following checklist.

CHECKLIST for Evaluating an Author's Credibility

- As a reader, do you feel that you are being addressed respectfully and that the writer is trying to establish common ground with you?
- Does the writer seem knowledgeable about the topic?
- Does the writer support claims with specific evidence?
- Does the writer reveal how and where supporting evidence was obtained?
- Does the work contain signs that the author is prejudiced in any way?
- Does the writer recognize that other points of view may be legitimate?
- Do lapses in reasoning undermine the writer's case (see 35f)?
- Has the writer reached a conclusion that is in proportion to the amount of evidence produced?

---

(2) Credentials help establish an author's credibility.

When evaluating sources, consider whether the authors have credentials that are relevant to the topics they are addressing. Credentials take various forms, including academic or professional training, grants or honors, publication record, work experience, and personal experience. A college biology professor who specializes in genetics is likely to be credible when writing about genes, for example, and a civil engineer who specializes in bridges should have credibility when writing about how a particular bridge could be strengthened. However, given their areas of specialization, the biologist would not be considered a credible source of information on the foraging habits of black bears, and the engineer would not have credibility concerning the design of hydroelectric power plants.

To find information about an author's credentials, look

- on the jacket of a book,
- on a separate page near the front or back of a book,
- in the preface of a book,
- in a note at the bottom of the first or last page of an article in print,
- on a separate page devoted to providing background on contributors to a periodical, or
- through a link on a Web site.

When assessing the level of an author's expertise, ask yourself the following questions.

CHECKLIST for Assessing an Author's Credentials

- What are the extent and nature of the author's education, and how does it relate to the subject of the work?
- What is the author's job? Is the author's past or present employment related to the subject on which the author has written?
- With what institutions, organizations, or companies has the author been affiliated (see 38b)?
- What is the author's publishing record?
- Do other experts speak of the author as an authority (see 38a(3))?

Exercise 1

Find a one- to three-page article that seems credible because of the way it is written and because of the author's credentials. Distribute copies of the article to a group of fellow writers, and explain why you found the article credible.

(3) Information about authors appears in the text of works by other writers.

As you research a topic, you will often find that other writers mention authors who turned up in your preliminary search for sources. Consider how other writers refer to an author you wish to cite. If several writers offer negative evaluations of an author's work, there is a reasonable chance that it is unreliable. If, on the other hand, several writers praise the work of the author you are evaluating, you are probably considering a credible source.

(4) Information about authors appears in online sources.

You can learn more about authors by searching the Web (see 8c) for information about them. Using a search engine such as Google, you can enter an author's name or the title of a book. Even if you do not find a site dedicated to the work you are thinking about using, you may find sites containing background information on the author or bibliographical information about his or her other works. You can also use InfoTrac College Edition or other electronic periodical indexes (see 37d(3)) to locate book reviews or other articles about or by an author.

(5) Reviews contain information that can help you assess an author's credibility.

Book reviews often include useful information for readers who are looking for credible sources. Now that many reviews are available online, you can sometimes obtain a helpful review easily—especially if you are evaluating a recently published source.

When you read reviews, remember that being a credible source does not mean being a perfect source. A credible source may get some negative responses. Look for the main point of a review, and decide whether that main point amounts to a positive or negative response to the book as a whole. For example, if an author is described as "entertaining but unreliable," the negative adjective is more important than the positive one when assessing that author's credibility. Or if an author is described as "dry but nevertheless informative," the praise outweighs the complaint.

Few writers please all reviewers all the time. Be willing to consider the work of a writer who is said to include more details than are necessary or to have taken a position that differs from that of recognized authority. But dismiss from further consideration any writer whom more than one reviewer characterizes as ill-informed, careless with facts, biased (see **38d**), or dishonest in any way.

Beyond the Rule

BOOK REVIEWS

A book review might be shaped by the reviewer's religious or political affiliations, by professional rivalry, or by the requirements of a specific periodical. For additional information about the process of reviewing books, visit www.harbrace.com.

38b | Credible sources are published by reliable institutions, organizations, and companies.

When you are doing research, consider not only the credibility of authors (see 38a) but also the credibility of the media through which their work is made available to you. Some publishers hold authors accountable to higher standards than others do.

(1) You can evaluate book publishers by considering whether they are commercial or academic.

When evaluating books, you can usually assume that university presses demand a high standard of scholarship. The more prestigious the university, the more reliable a source may be—but there are exceptions. Even such distinguished presses as the Harvard University Press and the University of California Press have published some works that were subsequently questioned by serious scholars. If an author with reasonably good credentials has written a book on a topic about which there is current interest that may soon pass, editors at a university press may be less careful than they should be when checking facts.

Problems such as these occur more frequently in works published by commercial presses, so these works are sometimes taken less seriously by scholars than are works published by university presses. However, some commercial presses—such as Farrar, Straus & Giroux; Basic Books; and HarperCollins—have distinguished records. And books published by commercial presses frequently win awards such as the Pulitzer Prize and the National Book Award. Whether a commercial or university press published a work, you must judge the case individually, considering not just the publisher's reputation but also the author's credibility (see 38a). Also be aware that fine works are sometimes published by small presses with which you may not be familiar (such as Milkweed in Minneapolis or Kitchen Table in Seattle).

A directory of publishers with sites on the Web can be viewed at www.library.vanderbilt.edu/law/acqs/pubr.html, a site sponsored by Vanderbilt University.

(2) You can evaluate periodical literature by examining recent issues.

An article published in an **academic journal** is often more credible than one published in a popular magazine. Academic journals are usually published quarterly, which means that there are four issues a year; the time between issues allows for the careful selection and editing of articles. The most credible articles are usually those that appear in a **refereed journal,** which is an academic journal that publishes work recommended by external reviewers with expertise in the relevant field (as opposed to simply being chosen by the journal's editor).

Pieces that appear in **general-circulation magazines** (magazines that are published weekly or monthly and are sold in supermarkets and drugstores) may also be reliable, but they are usually written more quickly and chosen for publication by someone on the magazine's staff—not by an expert in the field. When evaluating an article in a general-circulation magazine, consider the quality of the article and the credibility of its author (see 38a). But also consider the substance and reputation of the magazine itself. Magazines such as the *Atlantic Monthly, Harper's,* and *Scientific American* publish more substantial articles than do magazines such as *GQ, People,* and *Seventeen.* For additional information about general-circulation magazines, you can visit their Web sites or use a search engine such as Google to see if other readers have offered an assessment of them.

Similarly, some newspapers have more credibility than others. For example, the *New York Times,* the *Wall Street Journal,* the *Washington Post,* the *Miami Herald,* and the *Los Angeles Times* are considered more credible than *USA Today* or the *New York Post.* If you examine different newspapers, you can gauge their credibility by considering the space devoted to various stories, the extent to which staff members (as opposed to wire services) are responsible for stories, and the tone of the commentary on the editorial pages. And, as with any informative or persuasive writing, examine the types of evidence used to support claims (see **36d**).

When evaluating periodicals or books, consider the questions in the following checklist.

CHECKLIST for Evaluating Sources in Print

■ Is the work recent enough to provide up-to-date information?

■ Does the work provide documentation to support important points? Does this documentation indicate that the work is based on solid research?

■ What can you discover about the company or organization that has published this work?

38c | Researchers need to evaluate Web sites and other online sources.

If you are evaluating periodical literature that you obtained online, you can follow the guidelines provided in (**38b(2)**). But if you are evaluating a Web site, you need to consider the nature of the site and its sponsor.

(1) You can evaluate a Web site by considering the content, timeliness, and author of the site.

When evaluating a Web site, you should consider how well the text is written (see **38a(1)**), how often the site is updated, and who produces the content. Since Web sites can easily be kept up to date, look for evidence of frequent maintenance. Consider also whether you are viewing a site put together by a single individual or a team of people working for a reputable agency, institution, or organization. A site composed by a single author may be credible if that person has relevant credentials (see **38a(2)**) and keeps the site current. A site maintained by a team of individuals may well be credible since different individuals can bring different credentials and different skills to composing and maintaining the site. However, its credibility will be weakened if it has not been updated in the past year or if it features links that lead nowhere.

The date on which a Web site was established or last updated frequently appears on the site, and the date on which you access it will usually appear on any hard copy that you print out. Do not confuse the access date with the posting date (see **37c**).

(2) You can evaluate a Web site by considering the nature of its sponsor.

Consider the origin of a Web site as well as its content and timeliness. Although many sites are created by individuals working on their own, many others are sponsored by colleges or universities, professional organizations, and commercial enterprises. Such a sponsor is typically indicated in the site's address by a suffix that represents its domain. Colleges and universities are indicated by .edu, government departments and agencies by .gov, professional organizations by .org, and businesses by .com. An address that includes any one of these domains can take you to a credible and useful site, but you should first consider whether a site with a specific type of domain is likely to have information relevant (see **38e**) to your topic, purpose, and audience.

Suppose, for example, you were writing a paper about how corporate bankruptcies in 2002 revealed serious irregularities in the work of a major accounting firm. An education site could provide a scholarly analysis of the practices in question; a government site could contain data compiled by the Securities and Exchange Commission (SEC); an organization site could give you the viewpoint of an association of accountants; and a business site could convey information from the accounting firm in question. Each of these sites would offer different content, which would be shaped by the rhetorical situation (see 32a) as envisioned by each site's sponsor. For example, the SEC is an agency of the federal government that reports to the U.S. Congress, which, in turn, represents the citizens. Accordingly, the SEC's purpose is to show its audience that it is providing careful oversight of business practices. The commercial site of an accounting firm, on the other hand, has a vested interest in making the company look good to current customers and potential clients. Depending on the nature of your research paper, you can access any or all of the various types of sites. But, as you evaluate their content, remember that every site is shaped to achieve a specific purpose.

CHECKLIST for Evaluating a Web Site

- How often is the site updated?
- What do you know about the author? If no author is identified, what can you infer about the author from the site?
- What is the purpose of the site? How might this purpose affect the kind of information included on the site?
- Is the source located at an institution or sponsored by an organization about which information is available at other sites?
- Does the site include citations for other sources or links to other reliable documents?

Additional information on evaluating sites can be found at stcloudstate.edu/~killbornj/webvalidation.html (a site created at and sponsored by St. Cloud State University in Minnesota).

Exercise 2

Write a two- or three-page paper in which you define your evaluation criteria and then evaluate one print source and one Web site on a specific topic.

38d | Evaluating sources requires understanding how *bias* differs from *commitment*.

(1) Researchers recognize bias and commitment in print publications.

Some magazines are straightforward about identifying their affiliations. For instance, *Mother Jones* reveals its political stance on its masthead, which identifies its namesake as "Mary Harris 'Mother' Jones (1830–1930), orator, union organizer, and hell-raiser," and through its diction (see chapter 19) and tone (33a).

> When the bombs explode at abortion clinics, when the tax protesters turn their guns on federal agents, the cynical politicos who mixed the cocktail of national convulsion won't be around to take the blame. In their plush backstage parlors, they will shake their heads in perfunctory pity before getting back to the business of slapping backs, trading business cards, and stirring the next round of drinks.
>
> —**WILLIAM SALETAN**, "What I Saw at the Decline of the Revolution"

Subscription forms for the *Conservative Chronicle,* the *Capitalist's Companion,* and the Conservative Book Club included in issues of the *American Spectator* reveal this magazine's political stance.

Its conservativeness is also conveyed by the language used by the authors published in any issue.

> Just when you think you've got the rules of politics figured out—that liberal Democrats won't give up the theory, rhetoric and practice of class warfare, for example, until you pry their cold, dead fingers from the wallets of the rich—along comes a one-two-three punch to send you reeling. —**TOD LINDBERG,** "Growth Democrats"

These are fairly obvious examples. In other cases, however, an apparently well-reasoned article can reflect the values built into a periodical even if those values are not readily apparent in the article itself. For example, an article on malpractice suits in the *Journal of the American Medical Association* is likely to be sympathetic to physicians.

Recognizing that periodicals are likely to reflect the political values of their owners and editors does not mean, however, that you should necessarily distrust the information they contain. Journals and newspapers can be committed to certain values and still have high standards for what they publish.

It is important to distinguish between sources that are **committed** and those that are **biased.** A committed source represents a point of view fairly; a biased source represents it unfairly. It is possible to argue ethically for ideas you believe in; it is also possible to twist facts and misrepresent events to make your point. If you read the *Wall Street Journal* over a period of several weeks, you will recognize that it has an editorial policy that is politically conservative and sympathetic to business interests. This paper is also committed to honest reporting and clear writing, however, so its articles are still generally reliable. Bias appears when politics interferes with honest reporting so that important elements of a story are ignored, distorted, or suppressed.

When distinguishing between bias and commitment, be careful not to dismiss a credible source simply because you disagree with what it says. If you immediately reject a committed source that challenges you to reconsider some of your own views, you may be displaying bias rather than thinking critically.

CHECKLIST **for Discovering Bias**

- Does the author make personal attacks on people?
- Does the author sound sarcastic or mean-spirited?
- Has the author used prejudiced language (see **19d**)?
- Does the work include sweeping generalizations unsupported by verifiable data (see **36d**)?
- Has the author oversimplified complex issues?
- Has the author ignored or belittled opposing views?

CHECKLIST **for Discovering Commitment**

- Does the author have clearly defined values?
- Are the author's values worthy of respect?
- Has the author addressed his or her audience (see **32a**) respectfully?
- Has the author provided adequate support for all claims made (see **36d**)?
- Has the author recognized that the issue in question has more than one side?
- Does the author treat opposing views fairly?

Exercise 3

Read the letters to the editor in at least three issues of your local newspaper. Choose a letter that seems biased and one that seems committed. Write a one-page paper explaining your evaluations and quoting words or passages that led you to make them.

(2) Researchers also recognize bias and commitment in online sources.

Understanding the distinction between bias and commitment is also useful when you search the Web. Many sites are created by organizations or individuals strongly committed to specific values and goals. If you visit the Web site for the American Cancer Society or the League of Women Voters, for example, you can expect to find information that advances the purpose of the organization.

Keep in mind, however, that most Web sites are not subject to review; anyone can launch a site for any purpose. Even sites that seem professional and credible may be biased or contain erroneous information. You need to read critically (see **35a–b**) and to remember that you are likely to encounter other points of view at other sites. You should not, however, assume that a site is biased just because it is committed. Look for the signs of bias described in the checklist on page 580. Much bias is the result of faulty logic, such as oversimplification or overgeneralization (see **35f**).

Sometimes, however, bias and commitment can overlap. Consider the Web page shown in figure 38.1. Anyone visiting this site sponsored by the Organic Consumers Association should expect to find the site committed to promoting the consumption of healthy, naturally produced food. This commitment is conveyed by the association's logo, which features ripe vegetables and tools more likely to be used in a home garden than on a large commercial farm. Commitment to healthy food is also conveyed by one of the demands this site makes of Starbucks: "Remove genetically engineered ingredients from their food and dairy products on a worldwide basis."

Although a credible site could be devoted to both organic food and responsible business practices, the Web page excerpted here contains a disturbing sign of bias: By adapting the Starbucks logo into a "Frankenbucks" logo, the authors of this

Figure 38.1 Web page for Fair Trade Campaign.

site evoke the idea of Frankenstein and imply that Starbucks is a kind of monster. The site might be useful for a research paper on social action, but anyone doing serious research on the kind of food products used by Starbucks would need to turn to other sites to verify the claim that Starbucks uses genetically engineered food and to discover whether this food is indeed unhealthy.

38e   Experienced researchers know how to identify relevant sources and key passages within them.

A source can be credible without being useful. It is useful when it is relevant to your research question (see **37b**). Given the huge and ever-growing amount of information available on most topics, you should not be discouraged if you find that you have located a source that seems promising but fails to give you what you need. Some writers get off track because they cannot bring themselves to abandon a source they like, even if it is no longer relevant to their topic since—as often happens—their focus has changed during the process of conducting research, taking notes, drafting the paper, and revising it.

While you may reject some sources altogether, you are likely to use only parts of others. Seldom will an entire Web site, book, or article be useful for a specific research paper. Do not assume that a source must be 100 percent relevant to be of use to you. A book's table of contents can lead you to a relevant chapter or section, and the index can lead you to relevant pages. Once you find potentially useful material, read it with your research question (see 37b) in mind.

CHECKLIST for Establishing Relevancy

- Does the table of contents, index, or directory of the work include key words related to your research question?
- Does the abstract of a journal article contain information on your topic?
- If an abstract is not available, are any of the article's topic sentences relevant to your research question?
- Do the section heads of the source include information connected to your topic?

Using Sources Responsibly

To write well using sources, you need to remember that you are a *writer,* not simply a compiler of data. *Yours* is the most important voice in a paper that has your name on it.

This chapter will help you

- determine the purpose of a research paper (**39a**),
- take notes accurately (**39b**),
- compose a working bibliography (**39c**),
- use direct quotations, paraphrase, or summarize (**39d**), and
- avoid plagiarism (**39e**).

39a | A research paper makes or proves a point.

Like any other paper, a research paper must have a purpose—and that purpose must be appropriate for its audience and context. A research paper is more than a compilation of research findings or a list of works consulted (see **39c**). In a research paper, you build on what others have discovered. You do so by drawing these sources together in a conversation in which you play an essential role. That role is to bring a specific audience to a new understanding of the paper's topic. Accordingly, a research paper is either expository or argumentative. (See **32a**.)

When you discuss a research problem (see 37b), your paper is **expository;** it explains

- the nature of the problem,
- its causes,
- its effects, or
- the way others are responding to the problem.

Your research paper is **argumentative** (see chapter 36) if it

- analyzes or questions a complicated issue,
- expresses or defends a point of view, or
- invites or convinces readers to consider another perspective or to make adjustments to their perspective.

Exposition and argumentation can overlap. You may need to explain the effects of a problem, for example, before you can convince readers to fix it. In other words, you may have more than one purpose, with the first serving to advance the second. As the writer of a research paper, you need to ask yourself, "What is the most important goal I want to achieve in this paper, and how can I best achieve that goal?" Whether your audience consists of a single instructor or some larger group, to establish your credibility as an author (see 38a), you need to

- educate yourself about the topic,
- draw accurately on the work of others (including diverse points of view),
- understand what you have discovered, and
- integrate research data into a paper that is clearly your own.

The rest of this chapter will help you fulfill these responsibilities.

39b | Taking notes demands accuracy.

Taking good notes is critical when you are preparing to write a research paper in which you attribute specific words and ideas to others while taking credit for your own ideas. Some researchers like to write notes directly on pages they have photocopied or printed out from an online source (see **37c–d**). Still others type notes directly in computer files or write them on index cards—two methods that allow notes to be rearranged easily. Each method has advantages and disadvantages, and your choice should be guided by the requirements of your project and your own work style.

(1) You can make notes on printouts and photocopies.

An easy way to take notes is to use printouts of sources from the Web (see **37c**) or photocopies of articles and excerpts from books that you think you might quote directly. On a printout or photocopy, you can mark quotable material and jot down your own ideas. Printouts from the Web almost always indicate the source and the date of access, but you should also note the date on which the site was posted or last updated (see page 552). On photocopies, make sure to record the source if this information is not shown on what you have photocopied.

The example in figure 39.1 comes from the work Nicole Hester did for her research paper on the desegregation of the U.S. military (see **40f**).

(2) You can keep notes organized in computer files.

You may find it efficient to use a computer for taking notes—recording them quickly and storing them safely. If you have a laptop, you can take it to the library or wherever you plan to work. Using a computer also makes it easy to copy and paste information into various files and ultimately into a draft of your paper.

Given the ease of computer use, it's important to identify which records are direct quotations (see **39d(2)**), which are paraphrases (**39d(3)**), and which are your own thoughts. The tips

It was the authors of the Declaration of Independence who stated the principles that all men are created equal in their rights, and that <u>it is to secure these rights that governments are instituted among men</u>.

= the purpose of gov't according to Truman

It was the authors of the Constitution who made it clear that, under our form of government, <u>all citizens are equal before the law</u>, and that the Federal Government has a duty to guarantee to every citizen equal protection of the laws.

= a radical idea for many Americans at the time

The Civil Rights Committee did more than repeat these great principles. It described a method to put these principles into action, and to make them a living reality for every American, regardless of his race, his religion, or his national origin.

background on the Civil Rights Committee link to Fahy

<u>When every American knows that his rights and his opportunities are fully protected and respected by the Federal, State, and local governments, then we will have the kind of unity that really means something</u>.

what Truman is after

Public Papers of the Presidents of the United States: Harry S. Truman, 1945–53, vol. 4 (Washington, D.C.: U.S. Government Printing Office, 1964), 923–5.

Figure 39.1. Photocopied source with notes.

in the following list can help you use your computer efficiently when taking and filing notes for a research paper.

TIPS ON USING A COMPUTER TO TAKE NOTES

- Create a separate master folder (or directory) for the paper.
- Create folders within the master folder for your bibliography, notes, and portions of drafts.

(Continued on page 588)

(Continued from page 587)

- Keep all the notes for each source in a separate file.
- Use a distinctive font or a different color to distinguish your own thoughts from the ideas of others.
- Place direct quotations in quotation marks.
- Record exactly where the information came from.
- When you discover new sources, add them to your working bibliography (see 39c). Consider using the Annotation or Comment feature of your word-processing program to keep notes on sources you are using.

(3) Note cards are easy to arrange.

In the past, researchers usually took notes on index cards (also called three-by-five cards), which can still be useful if you are working in a library without your laptop or if you prefer hand-written notes that you can rearrange as your research proceeds.

If you are using this method, each card should show the author's name (and a short title for the work if the bibliography contains more than one work by that author) and the exact page number(s) from which the information is drawn. If you put no more than one note, however brief, on each card and a heading of two or three keywords at the top, you can easily arrange your cards as you prepare to draft your paper.

Whatever method you use to create your notes, consider the questions in the following checklist.

CHECKLIST for Taking Notes

- Does every note clearly identify its source? Have you put the full bibliographic citation on the first page of every photocopy? Double-check the bibliographic information for accuracy.

- Have you taken down verbatim (that is, copied exactly every word, every capital letter, and every punctuation mark) any useful passage you think you may quote? Have you put quotation marks around any words you copied directly? Failure to do so as you take notes may lead to unintended plagiarism (see 39d–e) when you draft your paper.

- When your own written ideas are based on someone else's, have you clearly distinguished which ideas came from your source and which ideas are your own?

39c | A working bibliography lists sources.

A working, or preliminary, bibliography contains information (titles, authors, dates, and so on) about the materials you think you might use. Creating a working bibliography can help you evaluate the quality of your research. If you find that your most recent source is five years old, for example, or that you have relied exclusively on information from magazines (see 37d(3)), you may need to find some other sources.

Some researchers find it convenient to put each bibliographic entry on a separate index card; this makes it easy to add or drop a card and to arrange the list alphabetically. Others prefer to use a computer, which can sort and alphabetize automatically, making it easier to move material directly to the final draft.

It is a good idea to follow the bibliographical format you have been instructed to use right from the start. The bibliographic style of the Modern Language Association (MLA) is covered in **40a**, that of the American Psychological Association (APA) in **40c**, and that from *The Chicago Manual of Style* (CMS) in **40e**. For each Web site you use, be sure to note the URL and the date on which you accessed the site—this information must be included in the finished bibliography that will accompany your paper or report.

Exercise 1

Prepare a working bibliography consisting of at least five sources you have already located. Use the bibliographic style from chapter **40** that is appropriate for the discipline in which you are conducting your research.

39d | Integrating sources fosters mastery of information.

Writers of research papers use sources in three ways: quoting the exact words of a source, paraphrasing those words, or summarizing them. With any of these methods, be careful to integrate the material—properly cited—into your own sentences and paragraphs, and be sure to use sources responsibly.

Knowing how to evaluate sources (chapter **38**) and take notes accurately (**39b**) is essential to research, but you must also understand how to integrate the information your research uncovers into a paper that is clearly your own. In a good paper, the sources support a thesis (see **32c**) that has grown out of the writer's research. The sources do not obscure the writer's own ideas; they illuminate them.

(1) Writers introduce and discuss the sources they use.

When effective writers borrow material, they introduce it to readers by establishing the context from which the material came. A good way to introduce research is to use a phrase that indicates the importance of the information or your attitude toward it. The verbs in the following list are useful for integrating quoted, paraphrased, or summarized information with your own ideas.

Verbs for Integrating Research Information			
acknowledge	concede	explain	reason
add	conclude	express	refute
admit	concur	find	remark
advise	confirm	illustrate	report
agree	consider	imply	respond
analyze	criticize	interpret	reveal
argue	deny	maintain	show
assert	describe	note	speculate
believe	disagree	observe	state
claim	discuss	offer	suggest
comment	dispute	oppose	think
compare	emphasize	point out	write

The examples of quotation, paraphrase, and summary presented in this section use the documentation style of the Modern Language Association (MLA), which is the style most frequently required for college English courses. For additional information on MLA style, see 40a–b.

(2) Direct quotations draw attention to key passages.

Include a direct quotation in a paper only if

- you want to retain the beauty or clarity of someone's words,
- you need to reveal how the reasoning in a specific passage is flawed or insightful, or
- you plan to discuss the implications of what you quote.

Keep quotations as short as possible, and make them an integral part of your text. (For examples showing how this can be done, see **40b** and **40d**.)

Quote *accurately.* Any quotation of another person's words should be placed in quotation marks or, if longer than four lines, set off as an indented block. (See pages 611–612, and 670.) If you need to make any addition to or change in a quotation, place square brackets around the added or changed words. If you want to omit part of the quotation, use ellipsis points. When modifying a quotation, be sure not to alter its essential meaning.

Cite the source for any quotation. If you think your audience might be unfamiliar with a source, establish its authority the first time you refer to it. For example, the following sentence informs readers about Mike Rose's credentials, justifying him as a credible source.

> Mike Rose, a nationally recognized authority on education, claims that learning is facilitated not by fear but by "hope, everyday heroics, the power and play of the human mind" (242).

The citation at the end of the quotation clearly establishes that the words came from page 242 of a work by Mike Rose; additional information about that work (such as the title, the publisher, and the city and date of publication) can be found in a list of works cited at the end of the paper. (See **40a**.)

CHECKLIST **for Using Direct Quotations**

- Have you copied all the words accurately?
- Have you copied all the punctuation accurately? (See **16d**.)
- Have you used ellipsis points correctly to indicate anything you omitted? (See **17h**.)
- Have you avoided using ellipsis points before quotations that are clearly only parts of sentences?
- Have you used square brackets around anything you added to or changed in a direct quotation? (See **17g**.)
- Have you used quotations sparingly? Rather than using too many quotations, consider paraphrasing or summarizing the information instead.

(3) Paraphrasing enables you to convey another person's ideas in your own words.

A **paraphrase** is a restatement of someone else's ideas in approximately the same number of words. Paraphrasing allows you to demonstrate that you have understood what you have read; it also enables you to help your audience understand it. Paraphrase when you want to

- clarify difficult material by using simpler language,
- restate a crudely made point in more professional terms,
- use another writer's idea but not his or her exact words, or
- create a consistent tone (see **33a(3)**) for your paper as a whole.

Your restatement of someone else's words should honor two important principles. First, your version should be almost entirely in your own words, which should accurately convey the content of the original passage. Second, you must indicate where the paraphrase begins and ends.

(a) Use your own words and sentence structure.

As you compare the source below with the paraphrases that follow, note the similarities and differences in both sentence structure and word choice.

Source Cronon, William. "The Trouble with Wilderness." *Uncommon Ground: Toward Reinventing Nature.* New York: Norton, 1995. 80–81.

> This, then, is the central paradox: wilderness embodies a dualistic vision in which the human is entirely outside the natural. If we allow ourselves to believe that nature, to be true, must also be wild, then our very presence in nature represents its fall. The place where we are is the place where nature is not.

Inadequate paraphrase

Here is the main problem: wilderness embodies a dualistic vision in which people have no place. When we convince ourselves that true nature must also be wild, then nature has no people in it. This means that we could never visit nature because as soon as we got to a natural place, it would no longer be natural (Cronon 80-81).

Adequate paraphrase

William Cronon has shown why it is problematic to associate "nature" with "wilderness." Wilderness refers to a place that is unspoiled by human presence. When we describe nature as wild, we are ultimately saying that people have no place in nature (80-81).

If you simply change a few words in a passage, you have not adequately restated it. You may be charged with plagiarism if the wording of your version follows the original too closely, even if you provide a page reference for the source.

(b) Maintain accuracy.

Any paraphrase must accurately maintain the sense of the original. If you unintentionally misrepresent the original because you did not understand it, you are being *inaccurate.* If you deliberately change the gist of what a source says, you are being *unethical.* Compare the original statements below with the paraphrases.

Source Polsby, Daniel D. "Second Reading." *Reason* Mar. 1996: 33.

> Generally speaking, though, it must be said that even among enthusiasts who think about the Second Amendment quite a lot, there has been little appreciation for the intricate and nuanced way in which constitutional analysis is practiced, and has to be practiced, by judges and lawyers.

Inaccurate paraphrase

People who care about the Second Amendment don't really understand how hard judges and lawyers have to work (Polsby 33).

Unethical paraphrase

When writing about the Second Amendment, Daniel Polsby has claimed that nobody understands the issue as well as he does (33).

Accurate paraphrase

Daniel Polsby has claimed that public debate over the meaning of the Second Amendment seldom involves the kind of careful analysis that judges and lawyers have to practice when they try to interpret the Constitution (33).

(4) Summarizing enables you to convey ideas efficiently.

When you summarize, you condense the main point(s) of your source. Although a summary omits much of the detail used in the original, it accurately reflects the work's **main idea** (see 32c) and the most important support given for it.

Whereas the length of a paraphrase (see 39d(3)) is usually close to that of the original material, a summary is shorter than the material it reports. When you summarize, you present the gist of the author's ideas, without including background information and supporting details. Summaries can include short quotations of key phrases or ideas, but you must always enclose another writer's exact words in quotation marks when you blend them with your own.

Source   Kremmer, Christopher. *The Carpet Wars.* New York: HarperCollins, 2002. 197.

> Iraq was once, like the United States today, a country of firsts. Sedentary society emerged in Mesopotamia around 5000 BC when people learned to plant, irrigate and harvest crops. Three thousand years before Christ, writing based on abstract symbols was invented to label the fruits of agricultural surplus. When a potter's wheel was turned on its side and hitched to a horse, modern transportation was born. It was where time was first carved into sixty minutes and circles into three hundred and sixty degrees. When in the ninth century the Arab caliph Haroun al-Rashid wanted to demonstrate his society's superiority over Europe, he sent Charlemagne a clock.

Summary

Iraq was once a center of innovation, where new methods of agriculture, transportation, writing, and measurement were generated (Kremmer 197).

This example reduces six sentences to one, retaining the key idea but eliminating specific examples such as the clock.

Whenever you are paraphrasing or summarizing, do not interject your own opinions into a restatement of ideas you are attributing to another writer. You can convey your opinion of the material when introducing it (see page 591) or when responding to it.

Exercise 2

Find a well-developed paragraph in one of your recent reading assignments. Rewrite it in your own words, varying the sentence structure of the original. Make your paraphrase approximately the same length as the original. Next, write a one-sentence summary of the same paragraph.

39e | Plagiarism is a serious offense.

Taking someone else's words or ideas and presenting them as your own leaves you open to criminal charges. In the film, video, music, and software businesses, this sort of theft is called **piracy.** In publishing and education, it is called **plagiarism.** Whatever it is called, it is illegal.

You may know of cases in which other students or colleagues have represented as their own words or ideas that they obtained elsewhere. People who plagiarize sometimes try to rationalize what they do by saying something like "It was accidental" or "Other people are doing it" or "My boss isn't really going to read this anyway." If offered an opportunity to submit someone else's work as your own, do not compromise your integrity or risk your future.

Beyond the Rule

PLAGIARISM IN THE NEWS

If you follow the news, you may be aware of cases in which well-established writers have been accused of plagiarism. These stories demonstrate that plagiarism is not just an academic problem. For information about some of these cases, visit www.harbrace.com.

You would be putting yourself at a great disadvantage if you avoided drawing on the work of others because you felt it was unsafe to do so. One purpose of this chapter is to help you use other writers' work responsibly so that you can enter into thoughtful conversation with them. The challenge is to ensure that your audience can distinguish among the different voices that have emerged through your research.

Honoring the principles discussed in this chapter will protect you from inadvertent plagiarism. There is, however, an act of plagiarism that is so blatant that no one could do it accidentally: submitting as your own an essay or paper written by someone else—obtained from a friend or a company that sells papers or simply downloaded from the Web. The way to avoid this kind of plagiarism is clear: *Never submit as your own a paper you did not write.*

Because the Web is such an extensive and easily accessible source of information, it has become a tool both for those who plagiarize and for those who try to prevent plagiarism. Although it is fairly easy to copy material from a Web site or even purchase a paper on the Web, it is just as easy for a teacher or employer to locate that same material on the Web and determine that it has been plagiarized. Many teachers routinely use Internet search tools such as Google (see 37c) or special services such as InSite (available from Heinle) if they suspect that a student has submitted a paper that was plagiarized.

Beyond the Rule

INTELLECTUAL PROPERTY

In some countries, anyone who has purchased a book can quote from it without citing the source or requesting permission. The rationale is that the person bought the words when he or she bought the book. Anyone preparing to submit or publish a piece of writing in the United States should be mindful of this country's copyright laws. For more information about intellectual property, visit www.harbrace.com.

You must give credit for all information you use except common knowledge and your own ideas. **Common knowledge** includes well-known dates and other facts: "The stock market crashed in 1929." "Water freezes at 32 degrees Fahrenheit." It also includes information such as that reported in this sentence: "The *Titanic* sank on its maiden voyage." This event has been the subject of many books and movies, and some information about it has become common knowledge: The *Titanic* hit an iceberg, and many people died because the ship did not carry enough lifeboats. If, however, you are writing a research paper about the *Titanic* and wish to include the ship's specifications, such as its overall length and gross tonnage, you will be providing *un*common knowledge that must be documented. After you have read a good deal about a given subject, you will be able to distinguish between common knowledge and the distinctive ideas or interpretations of specific writers.

CHECKLIST of Sources That Should Be Cited

- Writings, both published and unpublished
- Opinions and judgments not your own
- Statistics and other facts that are not widely known
- Images and graphics, such as works of art, drawings, charts and graphs, tables, photographs, maps, and advertisements
- Personal communications, such as interviews, letters, and email messages
- Public electronic communication, including television and radio broadcasts, motion pictures and videos, sound recordings, Web sites, and online discussion groups or forums

Citing Sources and Submitting Final Papers

When drafting and revising a research paper, acknowledge exactly where ideas and quotations in your paper have come from, and add a bibliography that provides information about your sources. When editing a research paper, review your in-text citations and your bibliographic entries, making sure that you have followed the rules set forth by your instructor, your employer, or the appropriate professional organization.

This chapter will help you use

- MLA-style documentation (40a–b),
- APA-style documentation (40c–d), and
- CMS-style documentation (40e–f).

In addition, two complete model research papers and part of another are included so that you can see different kinds of documentation within the context of writing.

Because conventions change, the formats for citing electronic sources for all the documentation styles discussed in this chapter—MLA, APA, and CMS—are periodically updated on the respective Web sites:

MLA	www.mla.org
APA	www.apastyle.org
CMS	www.press.uchicago.edu/Misc/Chicago/cmosfaq/cmosfaq.html

Different disciplines employ different documentation styles, so there is no single way to document sources or to prepare a bibliography that can be used in every academic or professional field. The manuals listed below discuss documentation formats in detail. If you are asked to use one of these manuals, make sure that your notes and bibliography correspond exactly to the examples it provides.

Style Books and Manuals

American Chemical Society. *The ACS Style Guide: A Manual for Authors and Editors.* 2nd ed. Washington, D.C.: American Chemical Society, 1998.

American Institute of Physics. *AIP Style Manual.* 4th ed. New York: American Institute of Physics, 1990.

American Mathematical Society. *A Manual for Authors of Mathematical Papers.* Rev. ed. Providence, R.I.: American Mathematical Society, 1990.

American Psychological Association. *Publication Manual of the American Psychological Association.* 5th ed. Washington, D.C.: American Psychological Association, 2001.

Council of Biology Editors. *Scientific Style and Format: The CBE Manual for Authors, Editors, and Publishers.* 6th ed. New York: Cambridge University Press, 1994.

Gibaldi, Joseph. *MLA Handbook for Writers of Research Papers.* 6th ed. New York: Modern Language Association of America, 2003.

Turabian, Kate L. *A Manual for Writers of Term Papers, Theses, and Dissertations.* 6th ed. Chicago: University of Chicago Press, 1996.

United States Geological Society. *Suggestions to Authors of the Reports of the United States Geological Survey.* 7th ed. Washington, D.C.: U.S. Government Printing Office, 1991.

United States Government Printing Office. *Style Manual*. Washington, D.C.: U.S. Government Printing Office, 2000.

University of Chicago Press. *The Chicago Manual of Style*. 14th ed. Chicago: University of Chicago Press, 1993.

Walker, Janice R., and Todd Taylor. *The Columbia Guide to Online Style*. New York: Columbia University Press, 1998.

40a	MLA-style documentation is required for papers submitted in English and other language or literature courses.

The rules for documentation of the Modern Language Association (MLA) are used for literary analysis and for research in composition studies.

Directory of MLA-Style Parenthetical Citations

(1) Parenthetical citations tell readers that a writer has drawn material from other sources.

Give proper credit by citing your sources. The MLA recommends placing parenthetical citations directly in the text. These citations refer readers to a list of works cited at the end of the paper. The MLA suggests reserving numbered notes for supplementary or explanatory comments. Superscript numbers are inserted in the appropriate places in the text, and the notes are gathered at the end of the paper. (For examples, see pages 637 and 649.)

The basic elements of the parenthetical citation are the author's last name and the page number of the material used in the source. However, you should omit the author's name from the parenthetical citation if you have already mentioned it in the same sentence. For detailed information on parenthetical citation, study the following examples.

1. Work by one author

Set on the frontier and focused on characters who use language sparingly,

Westerns often reveal a "pattern of linguistic regression" (Rosowski 170).

In this citation, the author's name is included within the parentheses because it is not mentioned in the sentence. If there is only one work by Rosowski in the list of works cited, there is no need to place a title in the parentheses. Also included is a page number that directs readers to a specific page. Notice how the citation changes if the author's name does appear in the sentence.

Susan J. Rosowski argues that Westerns often reveal a "pattern of linguistic regression" (170).

2. Work by two or three authors

Some environmentalists seek to protect wilderness areas from further

development so that they can both preserve the past and learn from it (Katcher

and Wilkins 174).

Provide the last name of each author. Commas are necessary in a citation involving three authors, for example: (Bellamy, O'Brien, and Nichols 59).

3. Work by more than three authors

For a work by more than three authors, use either the first author's last name followed by the abbreviation *et al.* (from the Latin *et alii,* meaning "and others") or all the last names. (Do not italicize or underline the abbreviated Latin phrase.)

In one important study, women graduates complained more frequently about

"excessive control than about lack of structure" (Belenky et al. 205).

OR

In one important study, women graduates complained more frequently about

"excessive control than about lack of structure" (Belenky, Clinchy,

Goldberger, and Tarule 205).

4. Multivolume work

When you cite material from more than one volume of a multivolume work, include the volume number (followed by a colon and a space) before the page number.

As Katherine Raine has argued, "true poetry begins where human personality

ends" (2: 247).

You do not need to include the volume number in the parenthetical citation if your list of works cited includes only one volume of a multivolume work.

5. More than one work by the same author

When your list of works cited includes more than one work by the same author, parenthetical citations of those works should include a shortened title that reveals which of them is being cited in a particular instance. Use a comma to separate the author's name from the shortened title when both are in parentheses. Underline the title.

According to Gilbert and Gubar, Elizabeth Barrett Browning considered poetry by women to be forbidden and problematic (Shakespeare's Sisters 107).

That attitude was based on the conception that male sexuality is the "essence of literary power" (Gilbert and Gubar, Madwoman 4).

This passage cites two different books by the same authors. Sandra M. Gilbert and Susan Gubar wrote both *Shakespeare's Sisters: Feminist Essays on Women Poets* and *The Madwoman in the Attic: The Woman Writer and the Nineteenth-Century Literary Imagination.* Remember that the authors' names must appear in the citation if they are not mentioned earlier in the sentence.

You can often avoid cumbersome references by including information in the text that might otherwise have to appear parenthetically.

In both The Madwoman in the Attic and Shakespeare's Sisters, Sandra M. Gilbert and Susan Gubar argue that the infrequent appearance of women as literary figures is a result of the repression imposed by male sexuality.

In this case, no page numbers are necessary because reference is being made to an argument pervading both books. Titles and authors are clearly established in the sentence itself.

6. Works by different authors with the same last name

Occasionally, you will cite sources by two authors with the same last name—for example, rhetoricians Theresa Enos and Richard Enos. In such cases, use each author's first and last name.

Richard Enos includes a thirteen-page bibliography in <u>Greek Rhetoric before</u> <u>Aristotle</u> (141-54). In her collection of articles by prominent figures in modern rhetoric and philosophy, <u>Professing the New Rhetorics,</u> Theresa Enos mentions the considerable contemporary reliance on pre-Aristotelian rhetoric (25, 331-43).

In these references citing more than one page, "(141-54)" identifies continuous pages, and "(25, 331-43)" cites both a page and a set of pages.

7. Indirect source

If you need to include material that one of your sources quoted from another work and you cannot obtain the original source, use the following format (*qtd.* is the abbreviation for "quoted").

The critic Susan Hardy Aikens has argued on behalf of what she calls "canonical multiplicity" (qtd. in Mayers 677).

A reader turning to the list of works cited should find a bibliographic entry for Mayers (which was the source consulted) but not for Aikens (because the quotation was obtained indirectly).

8. Poetry, drama, and the Bible

When you refer to poetry, drama, or the Bible, you should give the numbers of lines, acts and scenes, or chapters and verses, rather than page numbers. This practice enables readers to consult an edition other than the one you have used.

Act, scene, and line numbers (all arabic) are separated by periods with no space before or after them. The MLA suggests that biblical chapters and verses be treated similarly, although some writers prefer to use colons instead of periods in such citations. In all cases, the progression is from larger to smaller units.

The following example illustrates a typical citation of lines of poetry.

Emily Dickinson concludes "I'm Nobody! Who Are You?" with a

characteristically bittersweet stanza:

> How dreary to be somebody!
>
> How public, like a frog
>
> To tell your name the livelong June
>
> To an admiring bog! (lines 5-8)

Use *line* or *lines* in the parenthetical citation for the first quotation; subsequent quotations require only numbers.

Quotations of three or fewer lines of poetry can be placed in quotation marks and not set off as a block quotation. A slash with a space on each side indicates a line break.

The following citation shows that the famous "To be, or not to be" soliloquy appears in act 3, scene 1, lines 56–89 of *Hamlet*.

In <u>Hamlet</u>, Shakespeare presents the most famous soliloquy in the history of

the English theater: "To be, or not to be . . ." (3.1.56-89).

Biblical references identify the book of the Bible, the chapter, and the pertinent verses. In the following example, the writer refers to the creation story in Genesis, which begins in chapter 1 with verse 1 and ends in chapter 2 with verse 22.

The Old Testament creation story (Gen. 1.1-2.22), told with remarkable

economy, culminates in the arrival of Eve.

Names of books of the Bible are neither underlined (see chapter 10) nor enclosed in quotation marks (chapter 16). These books are frequently abbreviated (see chapter 11).

9. Sources produced for access by computer

Although electronic sources are treated differently from print sources in the list of works cited (see 40a(3)), many can be treated identically for parenthetical documentation in the text. For example, like a printed book, an online book could have both an author and page numbers.

If an electronic source does not have page numbers but does use another system of numbers, use those numbers. If paragraphs are numbered, cite the number(s) of the paragraph(s) after the abbreviation *par.* (for one paragraph) or *pars.* (for more than one). If a screen number is provided, cite that number after the word *screen* (or *screens* for more than one).

If an electronic source includes no numbers distinguishing one part from another, you should cite the entire source. In this case, to establish that you have not accidentally omitted a number, you can avoid using a parenthetical citation by providing what information you have within the sentence that introduces the material.

Raymond Lucero's Web site offers useful advice for consumers who are

concerned about transmitting credit card information over the Internet.

OR

Raymond Lucero's <u>Shopping Online</u> offers useful advice for consumers who

are concerned about transmitting credit card information over the Internet.

The Uniform Resource Locator (URL) for this site and additional information about it would be included in the list of works cited.

(2) MLA-style documentation calls for attention to punctuation, numbers, and placement.

(a) Punctuation

A comma separates the author's name from the title: (Brown, "Olivier's Richard III: A Reevaluation"). A comma also indicates an interruption in a sequence of pages or lines: (44, 47). A hyphen indicates continuous sequences of pages or lines: (44-47) or (1-4). A colon followed by one space separates volume and page numbers: (Raine 2: 247). Periods separate acts, scenes, and lines in drama: (3.1.56-89). A period distinguishes chapters from verses in biblical citations: (Gen. 1.1). No space follows the period.

Ellipsis points (see **17h**) indicate omissions within a quotation.

"They lived in an age of increasing complexity and great hope; we in an age of

. . . growing despair" (Krutch 2).

Brackets (see **17g**) enclose added words that are not part of the quoted material.

"The publication of this novel [Beloved] establishes Morrison as one of the

most important writers of our time" (Boyle 17).

When a question mark ends a quotation (see **16d**), place it before the closing quotation marks and add a period after the parenthetical citation.

Peter Elbow asks, "What could be more wonderful than the pleasure of

creating or appreciating forms that are different, amazing, outlandish,

useless—the opposite of ordinary, everyday, pragmatic?" (542).

(b) Numbers

The MLA favors arabic numbers in all citations, except for those referring to pages identified by roman numerals in the source itself (such as a page in the front matter of a book: Garner ix).

(c) Placement of citations

Wherever possible, place a citation right before a punctuation mark.

Richard Enos provides a bibliography of sources for the study of Greek rhetoric

before Aristotle (141-54), and Theresa Enos's edited collection, <u>Professing the</u>

<u>New Rhetorics,</u> includes Michael Halloran's essay "On the End of Rhetoric,

Classical and Modern" (331-43).

The citation for Richard Enos's work falls just before a comma; that for Theresa Enos's work is just before a period. However, in a sentence such as the following, the citations follow the authors' names to keep the references separate.

Richard Enos (141-54) and Theresa Enos (25) address classical rhetoric from

very different perspectives.

(d) Lengthy quotations

When a quotation is more than four lines long, set it off from the text by indenting one inch (or ten spaces) from the left margin. Double-space the quotation. When you are quoting two or more paragraphs, indent each paragraph an extra quarter of an inch (or three spaces). Do not indent the first line of a single quoted paragraph. A colon may introduce a long quotation if the quotation is not an integral part of the structure of the preceding sentence.

In <u>Nickel and Dimed</u>, Barbara Ehrenreich describes the dire living conditions

of the working poor:

> The lunch that consists of Doritos or hot dog rolls, leading to
>
> faintness before the end of the shift. The "home" that is also a
>
> car or a van. The illness or injury that must be "worked
>
> through," with gritted teeth, because there's no sick pay or health

insurance and the loss of one day's pay will mean no groceries

for the next. These experiences are not part of a sustainable

lifestyle, even a lifestyle of chronic deprivation and relentless

low-level punishment. They are, by almost any standard of

subsistence, emergency situations. And that is how we should see

the poverty of millions of low-wage Americans—as a state of

emergency. (214)

A problem of this magnitude cannot be fixed simply by raising the minimum wage.

Note that the period precedes the parenthetical citation at the end of an indented quotation.

(3) A complete list of the sources used in a paper helps readers locate and evaluate them.

For MLA-style papers, the list of sources from which you have cited information is called **Works Cited.** The works cited list appears at the end of the paper. To prepare this list, eliminate from your working bibliography (see **39c**) any sources you did not cite in your paper.

TIPS FOR PREPARING A LIST OF WORKS CITED

- Arrange the list of works alphabetically by author.
- If a source has more than one author, alphabetize by the last name of the first author.
- Type the first line of each entry flush with the left margin and indent subsequent lines one-half inch or five spaces (a hanging indent).
- Double-space throughout.

As you study the following MLA-style entries, observe both the arrangement of information and the punctuation.

Directory of MLA-Style Entries for the Works Cited List

BOOKS

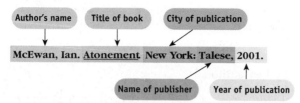

Most book entries consist of three units separated by periods:

1. *Author.* Place the last name first, following it with a comma, the first name, and a period.

2. *Title.* Underline the title of the book, and capitalize all major words. (See **9c**.) Always include a book's subtitle if it has one. Use a colon to separate a main title and a subtitle. Make underlining continuous, not separate under each word. Do not underline the final punctuation mark.

3. *Publication data.* Provide the city of publication, a shortened form of the publisher's name, and the latest copyright date shown on the copyright page. If more than one city is listed on that page, mention only the first. Use a colon after the city and a comma after the publisher. (To shorten the name of the publisher, use the principal name: Alfred A. Knopf becomes Knopf; Random House becomes Random. For books published by university presses, abbreviate *University* and *Press* without periods: Harvard University Press becomes Harvard UP.)

1. Book by one author

Halberstam, David. <u>Firehouse</u>. New York: Hyperion, 2002.

2. More than one work by the same author

Angelou, Maya. <u>A Brave and Startling Truth</u>. New York: Random, 1995.

---. <u>Kofi and His Magic</u>. New York: Potter, 1996.

If you use more than one work by the same author, alphabetize the works by the first major word in each title. Give the author's name with the first title, but substitute three hyphens followed by a period for the name in subsequent entries.

3. Book by two authors

West, Nigel, and Oleg Tsarev. <u>The Crown Jewels: The British Secrets at the Heart of the KGB Archives</u>. New Haven: Yale UP, 1999.

Invert the name of the first author, and place a comma after it. Do not invert the second name.

4. Book by three authors

Spinosa, Charles, Ferdinand Flores, and Hubert L. Dreyfus. <u>Disclosing New Worlds: Entrepreneurship, Democratic Action, and the Cultivation of Solidarity</u>. Cambridge: MIT P, 1997.

List all three authors in the same sequence used on the title page of the book.

5. Book by more than three authors

When a book has more than three authors, MLA style allows writers either to give all names in full as they appear on the title page or to use the abbreviation *et al.* (for *et alii,* meaning "and others") after the name of the first author.

Quirk, Randolph, Sidney Greenbaum, Geoffrey Leech, and Jan Svartvik. <u>A Comprehensive Grammar of the English Language</u>. London: Longman, 1985.

OR

Quirk, Randolph, et al. <u>A Comprehensive Grammar of the English Language</u>. London: Longman, 1985.

6. Book by a corporate author

Institute of Medicine. <u>Blood Banking and Regulation: Procedures, Problems, and Alternatives</u>. Washington: Natl. Acad., 1996.

Alphabetize by the first major word in the corporate name. Omit any initial article (*a, an,* or *the*) from the name.

7. Book by an anonymous author

<u>Primary Colors: A Novel of Politics</u>. New York: Warner, 1996.

Begin the entry with the title. Do not use *Anonymous* or *Anon.*

8. Book with an editor instead of an author

Kachuba, John B., ed. <u>How to Write Funny</u>. Cincinnati: Writer's Digest, 2000.

9. Edition after the first

Murray, Donald. <u>The Craft of Revision</u>. 4th ed. Boston: Heinle, 2001.

10. Work from an anthology (a collection of articles or other writings by different authors)

Bishop, Wendy. "Students' Stories and the Variable Gaze of Composition Research." <u>Writing Ourselves into the Story: Unheard Voices from Composition Studies</u>. Ed. Sheryl I. Fontane and Susan Hunter. Carbondale: Southern Illinois UP, 1993. 197-214.

Use this form for an article or essay that was first published in an anthology, as well as for a story, poem, or play reprinted in an anthology.

For an article or essay that was published elsewhere before being included in an anthology, use the following form.

Chaika, Elaine. "Grammars and Teaching." <u>College English</u> 39 (1978): 770-

83. Rpt. in <u>Linguistics for Teachers</u>. Ed. Linda Miller Cleary and

Michael D. Linn. New York: McGraw, 1993. 490-504.

Note where the essay first appeared; then show where you read it. Use the abbreviation *Rpt.* for "reprinted."

Both of these forms require that you cite the complete range of pages on which the article or essay can be found, not just the pages from which you borrowed material. In the second form, you must cite both the pages of the original publication (770-83 in this case) and the pages of the anthologized version (490-504).

11. Translated book

Garrigues, Eduardo. <u>West of Babylon</u>. Trans. Nasario Garcia. Albuquerque:

U of New Mexico P, 2002.

12. Republished book

Alcott, Louisa May. <u>Work: A Story of Experience</u>. 1873. Harmondsworth,

Eng.: Penguin, 1995.

The original work was published over a century before this paperback version. Use this form for books—even relatively recent ones—that have been reissued in a new format. (For reprinted articles, see "Work from an anthology," page 617.)

13. Multivolume work

Nowak, Ronald M. <u>Walker's Mammals of the World</u>. 2 vols. Baltimore:

Johns Hopkins UP, 1991.

Cite the total number of volumes in a work when you have used material from more than one volume. If you use only one volume, include that volume's number (preceded by the abbreviation *Vol.*).

Browning, Robert. <u>The Complete Works of Robert Browning: With Variant</u>

   <u>Readings and Annotations</u>. Ed. John C. Berkey and Allan C. Dooley.

   Vol. 6. Athens: Ohio UP, 1996.

14. Reference book

Dreyer, Edward L. "Inner Mongolia." <u>Encyclopedia of Asian History</u>. Ed.

   Ainslee T. Embree. 4 vols. New York: Scribner's, 1988.

When the author of an article in an encyclopedia is indicated only by initials, check the table of contents for a list of contributors. When an article is anonymous, begin the entry with the article title; alphabetize the entry according to the first important word in the title.

Full publication information is not necessary for a well-known reference work organized alphabetically. Begin with the article title when the author is not identified.

Petersen, William J. "Riverboats and Rivermen." <u>The Encyclopedia</u>

   <u>Americana</u>. 1999 ed.

When citing a specific dictionary definition for a word, use the abbreviation *Def.* (for "Definition"), and indicate which one you used.

"Reactive." Def. 2a. <u>Merriam-Webster's Collegiate Dictionary</u>. 10th ed. 2001.

15. Book in a series

Kelly, Richard Michael, and Barbara Kelly. <u>The Carolina Watermen: Bug</u>

   <u>Hunters and Boat Builders</u>. Twayne English Author Ser. 577.

   Winston-Salem: Blair, 1993.

When citing a book that is part of a series, provide the name of the series and, if one is listed, the number designating the work's place in it.

16. Introduction, preface, foreword, or afterword to a book

Elbow, Peter. Foreword. <u>The Peaceable Classroom</u>. By Mary Rose O'Reilley.

Portsmouth: Heinemann, 1993. ix-xiv.

Begin with the author of the introduction, preface, foreword, or afterword. Include the name of the book's author after the title. Note the pages at the end, using roman numerals if these are used in the work.

17. Pamphlet or bulletin

<u>Stucco in Residential Construction</u>. St. Paul: Lath & Plaster Bureau, 2000.

If the pamphlet has an author, begin with the author's name (last name first), as you would for a book.

18. Government publication

United States. Office of Management and Budget. <u>A Citizen's Guide to the</u>

<u>Federal Budget</u>. Washington: GPO, 1999.

When citing a government publication, identify the government body (e.g., United States, Minnesota, Great Britain, or United Nations) and the agency that issued the work. Underline the title of a book or pamphlet. Indicate the city of publication. Federal publications are usually printed by the Government Printing Office (GPO) in Washington, D.C., but be alert for exceptions.

When the name of an author or an editor appears on a government publication, insert that name after the title and introduce it with the word *By* or the abbreviation *Ed.* to describe the person's contribution.

ARTICLES

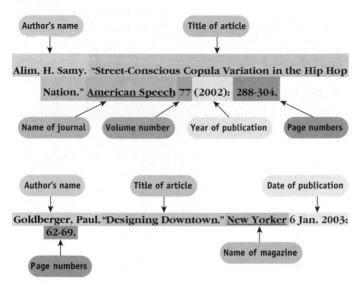

The documentation format for articles differs slightly from that for books. Notice the differences in format for title and publication information.

1. *Author.* Place the last name first, following it with a comma, the first name, and a period.

2. *Article title.* Put the article title in quotation marks with the period inside the closing quotation marks. Capitalize all major words in the title, including the first and last word. (See **9c.**)

3. *Publication data.* Provide the periodical title, the date of publication, and the page numbers on which the article appeared. Continuously underline the periodical title, and

capitalize all major words. (See 9c.) Note that no punctuation follows the periodical title and that a colon introduces the inclusive page numbers. If a periodical entry requires both a volume number and a date, put the date in parentheses.

19. Article in a journal with continuous pagination

A **journal** is a publication written for a specific discipline or profession; a **magazine** is written for the general public.

Nair, Supriya. "The Caribbean Unbound: Cross-Atlantic Discourses on

Slavery and Race." <u>American Literary History</u> 14 (2002): 566-79.

Citing a specific issue (e.g., Fall 2002) is not necessary when a journal's pages are numbered continuously throughout the year.

20. Article in a journal with each issue paginated separately

Andrews, William L. "Postmodern Southern Literature: Confessions of a

Norton Anthologist." <u>Studies in the Literary Imagination</u> 35.1 (2002):

105-12.

When an issue is paginated separately (each issue begins with page 1), put a period after the volume number and add the issue number.

21. Article in a monthly magazine

Keizer, Garret. "How the Devil Falls in Love." <u>Harper's</u> Aug. 2002: 43-51.

The names of months (except for May, June, and July) are abbreviated. Volume numbers are unnecessary because specific dates are given. A period goes between the last word in the title and the closing quotation marks, unless the title ends with a question mark or an exclamation point, which makes an additional punctuation mark redundant. A space (without punctuation) separates the name of the magazine from the date of issue.

Magazine articles are often interrupted by advertisements or other articles. If the first part of an article appears on pages 45–47 and the rest on pages 92–94, give only the first page number followed by a plus sign: 45+.

22. Article in a weekly magazine or newspaper

Klotowitz, Alex. "The Trenchcoat Robbers." New Yorker 8 July 2002: 34-39.

23. Article in a daily newspaper

Moberg, David. "The Accidental Environmentalist." Chicago Tribune 24

Sept. 2002, final ed., sec. 2: 1+.

When it is not part of the newspaper's name, the name of the city where the newspaper is published should be given in brackets after the title: *Star Tribune* [Minneapolis]. If a specific edition is not named on the masthead, put a colon after the date and then provide the page reference. Specify the section by inserting the section number or letter immediately before the page number, just as it appears in the newspaper (A7 or 7A, for example). When an article is continued elsewhere in the section (but not on the next page), add + to the page number to indicate this continuation.

24. Editorial in a newspaper or magazine

Beefs, Anne. "Ending Bias in the Human Rights System." Editorial. New

York Times 22 May 2002, natl. ed.: A27.

If the editorial is not signed, begin the entry with the title.

SOURCES VIEWED OR HEARD

25. Film

<u>My Big Fat Greek Wedding</u>. Dir. Joel Zwick. IFC, 2002.

The company that produced or distributed the film (IFC in this case) appears right before the date of release. It is not necessary to cite the city in which the production or distribution company is based.

When you want to highlight the contribution of a specific person rather than citing the film in general, put the person's name first. Other information can be included immediately after the title.

Gomez, Ian, perf. <u>My Big Fat Greek Wedding</u>. Screenplay by Nia Vardalos.

Dir. Joel Zwick. IFC, 2002.

26. Radio or television program

"'Barbarian' Forces." <u>Ancient Warriors</u>. Narr. Colgate Salsbury. Dir. Phil

Grabsky. Learning Channel. 1 Jan. 1996.

When referring to a specific episode, place quotation marks around its title. Underline the title of the program.

Finch, Nigel, dir. <u>The Lost Language of Cranes</u>. By David Leavitt. Prod.

Ruth Caleb. Great Performances. PBS. WNET, New York. 24 June

1992.

To highlight a specific contributor, begin the entry with that person's name.

27. Play performance

<u>Proof</u>. By David Auburn. Dir. Daniel Sullivan. Walter Kerr Theater, New

York. 8 Oct. 2002.

Cite the date of the performance you attended.

28. Musical composition

Puccini, Giacomo. <u>Turandot</u>.

Rachmaninov, Sergei. Symphony no. 2 in E minor, op. 27.

Begin the entry with the name of the composer and the composition. When the composition is unnamed, use the number given to it by the composer (Symphony no. 2). Add the key when it has been specified by the composer (E minor), and conclude with the work number if available (op. 27 for "opus 27").

However, if you are citing the published score of a musical composition, treat it like a book. Capitalize the abbreviations *no.* and *op.* when they are part of the title. Add the city of publication, publisher's name, and date of publication.

29. Sound recording on compact disc

Franklin, Aretha. <u>Amazing Grace: The Complete Recordings</u>. Atlantic, 1999.

Provide the full title of the compact disc, including the subtitle. For other kinds of sound recordings, identify the type (*Audiocassette* or *LP*).

Raitt, Bonnie. <u>Nick of Time</u>. Audiocassette. Capitol, 1989.

When citing a recording of a specific song, begin with the name of the performer, and place the song title in quotation marks. Identify the author(s) after the song title. If the performance is a reissue from an earlier recording, provide the original date of recording (preceded by *Rec.* for "Recorded").

Horne, Lena. "The Man I Love." By George Gershwin and Ira Gershwin.
    Rec. 15 Dec. 1941. <u>Stormy Weather</u>. BMG, 1990.

30. Lecture or presentation

Perl, Sondra. "Writing the Unwritten." Conf. on Coll. Composition and
    Communication Convention. Palmer House, Chicago. 21 Mar. 2002.

Scheiber, Andrew. Class lecture. English 215. Aquinas Hall, U of St.

> Thomas, St. Paul. 30 Apr. 2003.

Identify the site and the date of the lecture or presentation. Use the title if available; otherwise, provide a descriptive label.

31. Interview

Furstenheim, Ursula. Personal interview. 16 Jan. 2003.

Sugo, Misuzu. Telephone interview. 20 Feb. 2003.

Use these forms for interviews you have conducted, giving only the name of the person you interviewed. If the interview was conducted by someone else, add the name of the interviewer, as well as a title, if there is one, and the name of the source.

Harryhausen, Ray. Interview with Terry Gross. <u>Fresh Air</u>. Natl. Public Radio.

> WHYY, Philadelphia. 6 Jan. 2003.

SOURCES PRODUCED FOR ACCESS BY COMPUTER

The information required to cite sources such as software programs or databases that can be distributed on CD-ROM or other disks and the information required to cite online sources differ in two important ways. Citations for CD-ROM and other disks generally should identify the publisher, the place, and the date of publication. Citations for information obtained online should state the Web address and the date of access.

The main reason for citing any source is to give readers enough information so that they can consult the source on their own. Because electronic sources change more frequently than print sources do, the date given for the creation or latest modification of a Web site and the date on which you accessed it are both important. Further, because sites may disappear overnight, it is wise to print out a hard copy of any site you use as a source.

The sixth edition of the *MLA Handbook for Writers of Research Papers* (2003) recognizes that electronic sources continue to evolve—as does the style for citing them. Check the MLA's Web site (www.mla.org) for updates on formatting citations of online sources. For any Web site you use, you must provide the correct URL. By providing your readers with a complete address, including the protocol, or access identifier (**http, ftp, telnet, news**), all punctuation marks, and both path and file names, you are telling them how to locate the source.

    <http://stanfordmag.org.marapril99/>
    <ftp://beowulf.engl.uky.edu/pub/beowulf>

Although it is also important to include other information, such as the author's name, the name of the site, and the date you accessed it, the complete Web address is essential. It substitutes for the publication data that help readers find print sources. Place the address within angle brackets, < >, so that it is clearly separated from any other punctuation in your citation. Divide the address after a slash when it does not fit on a single line. Make sure that the address is accurate. Web browsers (such as Netscape) distinguish between uppercase and lowercase letters in a URL, and they recognize marks such as hyphens and underscores. Also keep in mind that the addresses of Web sites often change, which means that addresses can become out of date without warning. For that reason, double-check the URLs for any Web sites you cite before submitting your work.

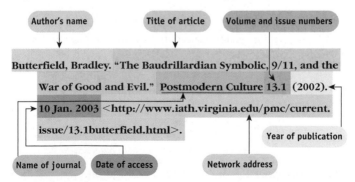

Author's name | Title of article | Volume and issue numbers

Butterfield, Bradley. "The Baudrillardian Symbolic, 9/11, and the War of Good and Evil." Postmodern Culture 13.1 (2002).

10 Jan. 2003 <http://www.iath.virginia.edu/pmc/current.issue/13.1butterfield.html>.

Year of publication

Name of journal | Date of access | Network address

The information cited varies according to the type of online source. Arrange the information in the following sequence.

1. *Author.* Place the last name first, following it with a comma, the first name, and a period.

2. *Work title.* Capitalize all major words in the title, and either underline it or place it within quotation marks (see **9a**, **10a**, and **16b**). Begin with the title when there is no author.

3. *Publication data.* For online sources, include the date of publication, the name of the sponsoring organization, the date of access, and the URL. If the URL is extremely long, you may use the URL for the site's search page instead. If there is no search page, cite the document's home page, following it with the word *Path,* a colon, and the sequence of links you used. Separate the links with semicolons. For a CD-ROM or diskette, include the city where the work was published, the name of the manufacturer, and the date of issue.

32. Online book

Ford, Jeffrey. The Empire of Ice Cream. 2003. Scifi.com. 2003. 28 Feb. 2003

    <http://www.scifi.com/originals/originals_archive/ford4/>.

In this case, the work was published in 2003 and accessed on February 28, 2003. Providing the date of publication tells readers how long the source has been available. Providing the date of access indicates how recently the site was still available, as well as the precise version used (since online sources can be updated after publication).

33. Article in an online journal

Harnack, Andrew, and Gene Kleppinger. "Beyond the MLA Handbook:

    Documenting Sources on the Internet." Kairos 1.2 (1996). 14 Aug.

    1997 <http://www.english.ttu/acw/kairos/index.html>.

The date of access follows the date of publication.

34. Article in an online magazine

Plotz, David. "The Cure for Sinophobia." <u>Slate</u> 4 June 1999. 4 June 1999

    <http://www.slate.com/StrangeBedfellow/99-06-03/

    StrangeBedfellow.asp>.

Give the date of access after the date of publication, even if you consult the source the same day it is posted.

35. Article in an online newspaper

"Tornadoes Touch Down in S. Illinois." <u>New York Times on the Web</u> 16 Apr.

    1998. 20 May 1998 <http://www.nytimes.com/aponline/a/

    AP-Illinois-Storms.html>.

When no author is identified, begin with the title of the article.

36. Review in an online newspaper

Koeppel, Fredric. "A Look at John Keats." Rev. of <u>Keats</u>, by Andrew

    Motion. <u>Nando Times News</u> 16 Apr. 1998. 27 Aug. 1998

    <http://www.nando.net/newsroom/ ntn/enter/ 041698/

    enter30_20804.html>.

37. Online government publication

United States. Dept. of State. Bur. of Democracy, Human Rights, and Labor.

    <u>Guatemala Country Report on Human Rights Practices for 1998</u>. Feb.

    1999. 1 May 1999 <http://www.state.gov/www/global/human_rights/

    1998_hrp_report/guatemal.html>.

Begin with the government responsible for the publication and the department or agency that issued it. If a subdivision of the larger organization is responsible, name that subdivision. If an author is identified, provide the name between the title and the date of issue. Place the word *by* before the name.

38. Online work of art

Vermeer, Johannes. <u>Young Woman with a Water Pitcher</u>. c. 1660.

>   Metropolitan Museum of Art, New York. 2 Oct. 2002

>   <http://www.metmuseum.org/collection/

>   view1.asp?dep=11&item=89%2E15%2E21>.

Place the date of the painting, sculpture, or photograph immediately after its title. If the precise date is not known, use the abbreviation *c.* (for *circa*) to indicate an approximate date. Include the date of access after the name and location of the institution or organization making the work available for viewing.

39. Online map

"Virginia 1624." Map. <u>Map Collections 1544-1996</u>. Library of Congress.

>   26 Apr. 1999 <http://memory.loc.gov/cgibin/map_mp/

>   ~ammmem_8kk3::&title=Virginia++>.

Include the word *Map* followed by a period immediately after the map's title.

40. Email

An email message is treated like a personal letter or memo. Provide the name of the writer, a description of the message (usually the subject line), and the name of the receiver (or use *the author* when the message is one you received directly). Conclude the message with the date. (Note that *e-mail* is hyphenated in MLA style.)

Peters, Barbara. "Scholarships for Women." E-mail to Rita Martinez.

>   10 Mar. 2003.

41. Discussion group or forum

Whenever possible, cite an archived version of a posting to an online discussion group or forum to make it easier for your readers to find the source.

Schipper, William. "Roi Quirk and Wrenn Grammar." Online posting. 5 Jan.

1995. Ansaxnet. 12 Sep. 1996 <http://www.mun.ca/Ansaxdat/>.

Identify the name of the forum (in this case, Ansaxnet, a group of scholars interested in England before 1100 A.D.) between the date of posting and the date of access.

42. Newsgroup

May, Michaela. "Questions about RYAs." Online posting. 19 June 1996.

29 June 1996 <news:alt.soc.generation-x>.

Newsgroups are open forums, unconfined by a subscription list. Most have no moderator to ensure the quality of the postings, and messages are not usually retrievable after a few weeks. Ask whether your instructor wants you to make the source retrievable by including the email address of the person who posted the item or by printing out the posting.

43. Synchronous communication

To cite a synchronous communication, include the writer's name, event description, original date, forum (e.g., Media-MOO), access date, and URL.

Galin, Jeff. Netoric's Tuesday Café discussion "Teaching Writing in the

Digital Age: What Makes Teaching Good These Days?" 10 Sept. 1996.

MediaMOO. 10 Sept. 1996 <telnet://purple-crayon.media.mit.edu/

8888>.

If the discussion is archived, substitute the URL of the archive for that of the forum itself.

Galin, Jeff. Netoric's Tuesday Café discussion "Teaching Writing in the

Digital Age: What Makes Teaching Good These Days?" 10 Sept. 1996.

MediaMOO. 12 Sept. 1996 <http://www.cs.bsu.edu/homepages/

siering/netoric.html>.

44. CD-ROM

For a source on CD-ROM, provide the author (if available), title, publication medium, place of publication, publisher, and publication date.

"About <u>Richard III</u>." <u>Cinemania 96</u>. CD-ROM. Redmond: Microsoft, 1996.

45. Publication in more than one medium

<u>English Poetry Plus</u>. CD-ROM, diskette. New York: Films for the
    Humanities and Sciences, 1995.

40b | **Studying a sample paper can help you learn the MLA style guidelines.**

Although all good writing requires attention to detail, a research paper requires extra attention to ensure that sources are cited accurately and responsibly (see chapter **39**). When preparing the final draft of an MLA-style paper, check to make sure that you have adhered to MLA conventions for punctuation (see page 610) and documentation (see **40a**).

(1) Submit a title page only if one is required.

The MLA recommends omitting a title page and instead providing the identification on the first page of the paper (see page 635). Some instructors require a final outline with a paper; this serves as a table of contents. If you are asked to include an outline, prepare a title page as well. A title page usually provides the title of the paper, the author, the instructor's name, the name of the course with its section number, and the date—all centered on the page.

A sample title page is shown in figure 40.1.

Starbucks in Vienna: Coffee Cultures at a Crossroad

Andy Pieper

English 299, Section 1

Professor Miller

27 November 2002

Figure 40.1. Sample title page for MLA-style paper.

(2) Studying a sample MLA-style paper prepares you for writing your own.

Interested in the effects of globalization, Andy Pieper decided to focus his paper on what happens when Starbucks opens coffee shops overseas. As you study his paper, notice how he develops his thesis, considers more than one point of view (see 36d(2)), and observes the conventions for an MLA-style paper.

COMMENTS

A. All pages (including the first one) are numbered with an arabic numeral in the upper right-hand corner, one-half inch from the top. The page number is preceded by the author's last name. Notice that no period follows the page number.

B. The name of the author, the name of the professor, the course number, and the date of submission—appearing in that order—begin one inch from the top of the page and flush with the left margin. A margin of one inch is provided at the left, right, and bottom.

C. Double-space between the heading and the centered title of the paper and also between the title and the first line of the text. (A title consisting of two or more lines is double-spaced, and each line is centered.)

D. Pieper provides background for his paper, establishing that Starbucks is part of a phenomenon that has economic and social consequences.

B

Andy Pieper

Professor Miller

English 299, Section 4

27 November 2002

Starbucks in Vienna: Coffee Cultures at a Crossroads   C

From St. Paul to Sao Paulo, from Rome to Riyadh, and from
Johannesburg to Jakarta, world citizens are increasingly being pushed toward
a global culture. We are being affected internationally through the media we
experience, the food we eat, and the products we consume as multinational
corporations act on a world stage (Rothkopf 38). People with disposable
incomes can watch MTV in India, catch a Hollywood-produced movie in
Australia, purchase a Mickey Mouse doll in Oman, use an Icelandic cell
phone to call a friend in Malaysia, send an e-mail from an IBM computer in
Russia, and purchase a bucket of Kentucky Fried Chicken in Japan.

All of these examples are signs of <u>globalization,</u> a term coined to
describe the increasingly prominent role of large companies in the world
marketplace. At the forefront of globalization is the multinational corporation,
which David Korten, author of <u>When Corporations Rule the World</u>, defines as
a business that takes "on many national identities, maintaining relatively
autonomous production and sales facilities in individual countries,
establishing local roots and presenting itself in each locality as a good local
citizen" (125). Many of these multinationals originate and are headquartered
in the United States or other Western nations, but they have means of
production or outlets in countries all over the world.

Proponents of globalization claim that this process is advantageous   D
because it makes business efficient and helps foster international ties.

E. The thesis statement for this paper is placed where readers can easily locate it. The thesis statement for a paper can be placed anywhere, but readers usually expect to find it at the end of the first or second paragraph. The thesis for this paper emerged during the process of writing the paper. For earlier versions of this paper, visit www.harbrace.com.

F. A superscript numeral indicates that a note gives further information. The MLA recommends placing notes that provide explanation or additional information either at the bottom of the page or on a separate page at the end of the paper.

Pieper 2

Opponents argue that local cultures are damaged and that globalization
primarily benefits wealthy corporations in nations already rich. The
Starbucks Coffee Corporation is one example of a multinational company   E
involved in globalization. No matter what the long-term advantages or
disadvantages of globalization prove to be, investigating how a Western
company like Starbucks establishes itself overseas shows that a multinational
corporation can succeed in offering its own brand of culture, despite the
strength or longevity of the local culture it enters. The introduction of
Starbucks to Vienna illustrates this point because Starbucks offers an
American-style coffee shop experience to a city that is already rich in its
own coffee traditions.

    Throughout the 1990s, Starbucks sought to dominate the American
coffee shop market, and it succeeded. The company has skyrocketed since its
stock debuted in 1992, and within ten years went from revenues of $92 million
to $2.6 billion at the end of fiscal year 2001. Today, it has achieved status as
an American brand that is nearly as familiar as Coca-Cola and McDonald's.
Starbucks has now expanded its goals to include leading the world coffee shop
market. With over 5,000 coffee shops already in operation--nearly 1,200 of
which are located outside the United States--Starbucks hopes to reach
revenues of $6 billion by 2005 (Doherty 20). In order to accomplish this, the
coffee corporation intends to open an additional 5,000 stores worldwide (Scott
1). To reach its goals, Starbucks will have to enter new markets in Africa,
Asia, and the Middle East,[1] and especially in Europe, where coffee is a staple   F
of many countries. From the sidewalk cafés of Paris to the espresso bars of
Venice, Europeans have maintained a long love affair with coffee--not only

G. Pieper shows how Starbucks operates as a multinational corporation, building on the information he provided in the third paragraph. But he continues to emphasize the introduction of Starbucks into Viennese culture. He shows how his topic (Starbucks in Vienna) relates to a larger subject (globalization) so that readers can understand why the topic deserves attention.

H. When referring to a work by three authors, Pieper correctly provides the last name for each.

with the beverage itself, but also with their own coffeehouses. Therefore, the continent represents both a challenge and an opportunity for Starbucks.

As part of its expansion plan, Starbucks had already opened European outlets in Great Britain, Germany, and Switzerland by the time it opened a store in Vienna, the capital of Austria, in the spring of 2002. Under this plan, Starbucks typically enters into a joint-venture agreement with a local firm, initially holding a minority stake in the foreign operation, usually twenty percent. This arrangement shields Starbucks from any large losses incurred **G** when stores are first opened. In this way, Starbucks presents itself as a local company, when in fact it is a multinational with similar operations throughout the globe. The local firm then sets up a few outlets, buying prime real estate and strategically placing stores near symbols of historic and cultural significance[2]--as in Vienna, where the first outlet opened across from the city's famous opera house. Once some success is accomplished, Starbucks buys enough of the foreign-owned branch to control the company, and proceeds to enlarge rapidly throughout the country (Burke, Smith, and **H** Wosnitza 47).

Vienna, considered by many to be the birthplace of the coffeehouse tradition, is legendary for its coffee culture. The first Viennese coffeehouses appeared after invading Turks left sacks of coffee outside the city walls as they fled in 1683 (Pendergast 10). Intellectual life abounded in elegant cafés by the nineteenth century, as they became meeting places for early modernists such as Sigmund Freud and Gustav Klimt, as well as for notable exiles such as Vladimir Lenin and Leon Trotsky. In Vienna, the people take pride in the history and enjoy the culture that surrounds the coffeehouse tradition. Austrians received the opening of Starbucks with mixed emotions:

I. Although the period follows the parenthetical citation in regular text, MLA style makes an exception for block quotations. For block quotations, indented one inch from the left margin, place the period before the parenthetical citation.

> Many Viennese sniff that their culture has been infected, that
> Viennese use their 1,900 or so coffee shops to linger and meet,
> smoke and drink, savor the wonders of pastries with cream
> and marzipan, ponder the world, write books and read free
> newspapers. They drink from china cups and order from a waiter,
> usually in a stained black dinner jacket. (Erlanger B3)   I

Skeptics found it difficult to believe that an American brand such as Starbucks
could survive in an environment steeped in its own local history of coffee and
pride in its heritage, but these skeptics seem to have underestimated
Starbucks.

There are several fundamental differences between the Starbucks
experience and the traditional experience found in Viennese coffeehouses.
Instead of ordering through a server, Starbucks patrons order at an American-
style coffee bar. As opposed to more traditional offerings such as Sachertorte
and hot goulash, Starbucks sells American-style sweets like blueberry muffins
and chocolate-chip cookies. Furthermore, patrons are not allowed to smoke in
any Starbucks outlet in order to allow the aroma of coffee to fill each store.
Smoking, however, is a large part of the European coffeehouse experience.

These differences add up to two coffee cultures at a crossroads in Vienna.
Traditional American offerings are pitted against the offerings of Viennese
coffeehouses that have conducted business for centuries. Both Starbucks and
independent Viennese coffeehouses sell good coffee, so the primary product
being sold is fairly similar. But two essentially different aesthetic experiences
and cultures are involved, and they now compete within the same locality. If
Austrians had wanted the Starbucks experience previously, they would have
had to seek it in other countries. Now, the Viennese cannot help but notice

J. Having decided to include a photo that illustrates the intersection of different coffee traditions in Vienna, Pieper analyzes the image so that it becomes an integral part of his paper—not just a decoration. The MLA does not require the use of images, but designing documents using a computer makes it easy for writers to include relevant graphics (see chapter 8).

K. Ellipsis points indicate that Pieper has omitted words that can be found in the original source. (See page 645.)

Pieper 5

Starbucks. The two coffee cultures have thus become intertwined--
competing against each other across not oceans, but streets.

Illustrating these differences is
the picture at right of a ticket seller
for the opera house across from the
first Viennese Starbucks. On break
from work, the man is dressed in
aristocratic attire from the
eighteenth century, but he is sipping
his Starbucks coffee out of a paper
cup rather than from the kind of
china cup he would have received in
a traditional Viennese coffeehouse.
Moreover, he is smoking a cigarette
outside instead of inside the store, as
is customary in nearly all European

Photo courtesy of Roland Schlager.

coffeehouses. At first glance, this image appears harmless; it is a combination of
new and old. Upon further examination, however, it is more than that. The
Starbucks logo, the international symbol of the American company, hangs above
the young man, with the angle of the photograph making him appear to be in a
Starbucks advertisement. The similar color green in both the man's jacket and the
Starbucks logo melts the two together even further. Also, the reflection of another
man dressed in a business suit can be seen facing the subject of the photo, and
looks to be walking straight toward him. The image can be interpreted as a sign
of the times: Starbucks and its corporate chain of coffee shops, extending their   J
reach and marching straight into the traditional independent cultures of other
countries. The photograph also shows the apparent willingness of locals to

embrace the products and service Starbucks provides even if it means abandoning a long-established cultural tradition of their own.

Starbucks has seen initial success in its Austrian operations with an estimated 100,000 patrons in its first two months of operation (Erlanger A1). This result is not uncommon since the market trend over the past decade has worked overwhelmingly in Starbucks' favor. The company has not failed in any of the markets into which it has introduced itself. A large part of the reason its expansion plans are on schedule in Europe is that Starbucks represents something different but nevertheless nonthreatening. In this case, a familiar product is being sold from one Western nation to another. The primary difference is in how that product is offered and what other products are offered along with it.

Starbucks also has played an inadvertent role in a movement that now exists throughout Europe, in which coffee shops are opening with an atmosphere noticeably reminiscent of Starbucks. Alwyn Scott, of the Seattle Times writes, "For proof of Starbucks' impact, look no further than its army of European imitators. New coffee chains are springing up with names--Chicago Coffee, San Francisco Coffee, Coffee Shop--that suggest American style, if not Seattle" (F1). Therefore, the traditional coffee cultures that reside in countries like Austria, France, and Italy compete with American culture from two fronts: Starbucks and Starbucks' imitators.

Competition alone is not necessarily bad. It is essential to capitalist economies. Without competition, there is no freedom of choice, and little innovation. People are left with the same options over and over again, while nothing new emerges. Free-market competition encourages companies to adapt to the changing needs and wants of populations. By opening stores in cities like Vienna, Starbucks could claim that it is simply offering the Viennese a choice that responds to their changing needs and that they are not compelled to accept this choice. It could even claim that it fosters diversity by increasing the options for consumers and creating an expanded coffee culture that includes not only the traditional coffeehouses but also the Americanized experience found in Starbucks and its imitators. However, Starbucks wields an immense amount of power in the regions where it establishes itself. This power is seen in its brand name--familiar from South Korea to Mexico--and in its wealth. Its coffee shops also present a powerful cultural experience, one that immerses the consumer in an American-style environment. By expanding its base to include countries all over the world, Starbucks is expanding the role of American culture abroad. This expansion diversifies the cultures of other countries, provides competition for existing coffee cultures, and offers new options to consumers. But, at some point, competition could become hegemony. In other words, the exportation of American culture occurs right along with the exportation of American products. Such expansion of American goods and services could overwhelm another culture, creating a more homogenous, Americanized culture that blurs the distinctiveness of the native one. Increasingly, foreign markets are becoming saturated with Western goods from multinational corporations, which have spread their products--whatever they may be--to places around the globe. Some suggest that this occurrence is working toward the establishment of a single global culture. According to Hugh Mackay, of the Open University, "that 'global culture' is not something which draws in any even or uniform way on the vast diversity of cultures in the world . . . but, rather, consists of the global dissemination of US or Western culture--the complete opposite of diversity" (60).

L. Pieper reaches a well-balanced conclusion in keeping with what his research has shown. Without claiming that Starbucks is damaging the coffeehouse tradition in Vienna, he nevertheless notes that other American corporations are likely to succeed in overseas markets and that the long-term results of this trend cannot be predicted.

So far, Starbucks has been able to coexist with the traditional coffee
culture in Vienna; the city's architecture, art, and beauty are likely to remain
intact no matter how many stores Starbucks opens there. Because a relatively
familiar product is passing from one Western nation to another in this case,
and people have both the means to buy it and the freedom to reject it, cultural
change may be limited to the Viennese getting used to drinking coffee out of
paper cups and standing in the street to smoke. The social and economic effects of globalization may be more serious, as Mackay suggests, when
multinational corporations operate in developing nations and limited means
give people fewer choices. The lasting effects of globalization have yet to be
seen. But it is clear that the already ubiquitous green mermaid, like the perva-
sive golden arches, is going to become even easier to find. And if Starbucks
can flourish in an environment with a well-established local coffee culture of
its own, then it is feasible that other multinational corporations will export not
only their products but also the cultural experience that accompanies those
products, no matter how strong the local culture may be.

M. Each note is coordinated with the related material in the text by a superscript number that matches the number used in the body of the paper. The number comes before the indented first line of the note. Although the MLA allows either footnotes (located on the bottom of the page) or endnotes (located on a separate page), Pieper has decided to use endnotes. He has centered the title "Notes" one inch from the top. He then double-spaces the notes, indenting them one-half inch (or five spaces) from the left margin.

Notes such as these provide writers with a way to present material they decide is too important to discard, even if they cannot incorporate it within the paper itself because they need to focus their ideas (see **32b**). However, responsible writers do not use explanatory notes to preserve everything they decide to cut from their texts. When you add explanatory notes, remember that you are asking readers to turn away from your main text in order to make a side trip. Evaluate each of these detours by asking yourself whether they help you fulfill your rhetorical purpose (see **32a**).

Visit www.harbrace.com to see an earlier draft in which Pieper included a discussion of the Middle East and Asia in the body of the paper before deciding that he needed to narrow his focus.

N. When an online source does not include page numbers, writers cannot include a page reference within the parenthetical citation for it. (See page 609.)

Notes

[1]It should be noted that in Saudi Arabia, Starbucks, along with other
multinational corporations, tries to conform to the existing cultural mores.
Upon its introduction into Riyadh, Starbucks changed its logo (normally a
crowned mermaid in a green circle) to one that did not include a depiction of a
female since any representations of females are considered pornography
(King, "Sellout"). In addition, stores make women enter through separate
doors as well as drink their coffee in separate areas. The company has defended itself by stating, "While Starbucks adheres to the local customs by providing separate entrances, service and seating, all our stores provide equal
amenities, service, menu and seating to both men and women" (King, "Arabia's" A27).

[2]In the fall of 2000, Starbucks opened an outlet in Beijing's Forbidden
City, which was built early in the fifteenth century and listed as the world's
largest imperial palace. Administrators of the site agreed to rent space to the
Starbucks Chinese affiliate as a way of improving services. After news of the
opening spread, a survey indicated that "over 70 percent of nearly 60,000
people surveyed were opposed to the café's entry . . . the main reason being
the damaging effects to Chinese cultural heritage and its atmosphere"
("Starbucks").

O. Center the title "Works Cited" one inch from the top of the page, and double-space between this title and the first entry.

P. Include only those works you cited in the paper. If you consulted other sources but did not use them, do not include them in your list. Alphabetize entries according to the author's last name. Each entry should begin flush with the left margin. Lines after the first are indented one-half inch (or five spaces).

Q. When citing two or more sources by the same author, arrange them in alphabetical order determined by the first important and distinctive word in each title. Because *Saudi* appears in both article titles by King, the words used to alphabetize are *Arabia's* in the first entry and *Sellout* in the second. (These words are also used in parenthetical citations to distinguish the sources.) The author's name is given in the first entry; the second and subsequent entries begin with three hyphens, a period, and a space.

R. Pieper's works cited list includes entries from newspapers and magazines because he needed information about an event that was current when he wrote this paper: the opening of a Starbucks in Vienna. If you write about a current event, you may need to use sources like these. For other topics, however, other kinds of sources may have more credibility (see chapter 38).

S. Demonstrating that he did not rely exclusively on information from newspapers and magazines, Pieper cited *Foreign Policy,* one of the most respected journals in the country. He also cited three books and a Web site.

Works Cited

Burke, Greg, Stacey Vanek Smith, and Regine Wosnitza. "Whole Latte
        Shakin': Can U.S. Gourmet Coffee Chain Starbucks Convert
        Continental Europe's Café Society? It's Ready to Try." Time
        International. 9 Apr. 2001: 47.

Doherty, Jacqueline. "Make It Decaf: Despite Heavy Revenue Gains,
        Starbucks' Earnings Growth Is Slowing." Barrons. 20 May 2002: 20.

Erlanger, Steven. "An American Coffeehouse (or 4) in Vienna." New York
        Times. 1 June 2002: A1+.

King, Colbert I. "Saudi Arabia's Apartheid (Cont'd)." Editorial. Washington
        Post. 19 Jan. 2002, final ed.: A27.

---. "The Saudi Sellout." Editorial. Washington Post. 26 Jan. 2002, final ed.: A23.

Korten, David C. When Corporations Rule the World. West Hartford, CT:
        Kumarian, 1995.

Mackay, Hugh. "The Globalization of Culture?" A Globalizing World?
        Culture, Economics, Politics. Ed. David Held. New York: Routledge,
        2000. 47-84.

Pendergast, Mark. Uncommon Grounds: The History of Coffee and How It
        Transformed Our World. New York: Basic, 1999.

Rothkopf, David. "In Praise of Cultural Imperialism?" Foreign Policy 107
        (1997): 38-52.

Scott, Alwyn. "A Shot of Americana; Starbucks Jolts Europe's
        Coffeehouses." Seattle Times. 19 May 2002: F1.

"Starbucks Café in Forbidden City Under Fire." People's Daily Online. 24
        Nov. 2000. 3 June 2002 <http://english.peopledaily.com.cn/
        200011/24/ eng20001124_56044.html>.

40c | APA-style documentation is appropriate for research in education and the social sciences.

The American Psychological Association (APA) publishes a manual to guide writers of papers or articles in psychology. Its documentation system (sometimes called the *author-date style*) is also used for work in other disciplines such as education, economics, and sociology.

(1) APA-style parenthetical citations include dates of publication.

In APA style, the basic elements of a parenthetical citation in the text are the author's last name, the year of publication, and the page number(s) if the reference is to a passage quoted directly from the source. If the author's name is mentioned in the text of the paper, give the date alone or the date and the page number in parentheses. In the following examples, note the details of punctuation and the treatment of the page number.

Directory of APA-Style Parenthetical Citations

1. Work by one author

A prominent neurologist has concluded, "Pushing back the age at which the widespread form of Alzheimer's strikes—from, say, age 70 to age 90—would be nearly tantamount to a cure" (Kosik, 1999, p. 17).

OR

Kosik (1999) has concluded, "Pushing back the age at which the widespread form of Alzheimer's strikes—from, say, age 70 to age 90—would be nearly tantamount to a cure" (p. 17).

APA style requires the abbreviation *p.* (or *pp.* for "pages") before the page number(s). Use commas to separate the author's name from the date and the date from the page reference.

2. Work by two authors

Whether or not children spend time in day care, their development in early childhood is determined primarily by the nature of the care they receive from parents (Darvas & Walsh, 2002).

Use an ampersand (&) to separate the authors' names. A page number is not necessary unless the sentence includes a direct quotation from the source.

3. Work by more than two authors

One study has shown that people who fear failure are not susceptible to hypnosis (Manganello, Carlson, Zarillo, & Teeven, 1985).

For works with three to five authors, cite all the authors in the first reference, but in subsequent references give only the last name of the first author followed by *et al.* ("Manganello et al." for this example). For works with six or more authors, provide only the last name of the first author followed by *et al.,* even in the first citation.

4. Anonymous work

Use a shortened version of the title to identify an anonymous work.

Chronic insomnia usually requires medical intervention ("Sleep," 2003).

In this case, the author has cited a short article identified in the bibliography as "Sleep disorders: Standard methods of treatment."

5. Two or more works by different authors in the same parenthetical citation

Opponents of animal experimentation have traditionally argued that it is both

unnecessary and cruel (Mayo, 1983; Singer, 1975).

Use a semicolon to separate citations, and arrange them in alphabetical order.

6. Two or more works by the same author in the same parenthetical citation

To determine the focus of a grammar lesson, teachers benefit from first

examining the three dimensions of a grammatical structure: form, meaning,

and use (Larsen-Freeman, 1991, 1997).

Use a comma to separate the dates of publication, and order the dates from earliest to most recent.

7. Personal communication

State educational outcomes are often interpreted differently by teachers in the

same school (J. K. Jurgensen, personal communication, May 4, 2003).

Personal communications include letters, memos, email messages, personal interviews, and telephone conversations. These sources are cited in the text only; they do not appear in the reference list.

(2) An APA-style reference list follows specific conventions.

Whether you are submitting an APA-style paper in a college course or preparing a manuscript for publication, you can be guided by the format of the following entries. Each entry should be double-spaced with a hanging indent of five to seven spaces, or one-half inch. Arrange the entries alphabetically by the author's or the first author's last name. When two entries refer to the same author, arrange them according to the date of publication, placing the entry with the earliest date first. When an author's name appears both in a one-author entry and first in a multiple-author entry, place the one-author entry first.

Directory of APA-Style Entries for the Reference List

BOOKS

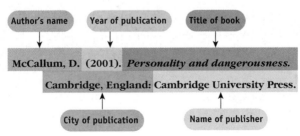

Most book entries consist of four units separated by periods.

1. *Author.* Place the author's last name first, followed by a comma and the first and middle (if used) initials. For entries that have more than one author, put commas after all last names and sets of initials, and put an ampersand (&) before the name of the last author.

2. *Date*. Place the date in parentheses after the author's name, and put a period after the closing parenthesis. By requiring the date to be near the beginning of the entry, APA style draws attention to its importance.

3. *Title*. Capitalize only the first word in titles and subtitles. Do not capitalize other words (except for proper names that would be capitalized in other contexts). For an article in an edited book, provide both the title of the article and the title of the book in which it appears. Separate a title from a subtitle with a colon, and italicize the title.

4. *Publication data.* Identify the city of publication. Add the two-letter U.S. Postal Service abbreviation for the state unless the city is one of the following: Baltimore, Boston, Chicago, Los Angeles, New York, Philadelphia, or San Francisco. When a work has been published in a city outside the United States, add the country's name unless the city is Amsterdam, Jerusalem, London, Milan, Moscow, Paris, Rome, Stockholm, Tokyo, or Vienna—in these cases, the city alone is sufficient. Give only enough of the publisher's name so that it can be identified clearly.

1. Book by one author

Simmons, R. (2002). *Odd girl out: The hidden culture of aggression in girls.*
New York: Harcourt.

Capitalize only the first word of the title and any subtitle (unless either includes a word that would be capitalized in other contexts).

2. Book by two or more authors

Beck, A. T., Emery, G., & Greenberg, R. L. (1990). *Anxiety disorders and phobias: A cognitive perspective.* New York: Basic Books.

Invert the names of all authors, and use an ampersand (&) before the name of the last author.

3. Book with editor(s)

Antony, M. M., Rachman, S., Richter, M. A., & Swinson, R. P. (Eds.).

(1998). *Obsessive-compulsive disorder.* New York: Guilford Press.

Capitalize the abbreviation for editor or editors, and place it within parentheses.

4. Edition after the first

Hostetler, J. A. (1993). *Amish society* (4th ed.). Baltimore: Johns Hopkins

University Press.

Identify the edition in parentheses immediately after the title.

5. Translation

Freud, S. (1999). *The interpretation of dreams* (J. Crick, Trans.). New York:

Oxford University Press. (Original work published 1899)

A period follows the name of the publisher but not the parenthetical note.

6. Multivolume work, published over a period of more than one year

Copleston, F. (1993–1994). *A history of philosophy* (Vols. 1–9). New York:

Doubleday.

7. Government report

National Institute of Mental Health. (1994). *Attention deficit hyperactivity

disorder* (NIH Publication No. 96-3572). Washington, DC: U.S.

Government Printing Office.

8. Selection from an edited book

Wolfe, A. (1996). Human nature and the quest for community. In A. Etzioni
(Ed.), *New communitarian thinking* (pp. 126–140). Charlottesville:
University Press of Virginia.

Italicize the book title but not the title of the selection.

9. Selection from a reference book

Wickens, D. (2001). Classical conditioning. In *The Corsini encyclopedia of
psychology and behavioral science* (Vol. 1, pp. 293–298). New York:
John Wiley.

ARTICLES IN PRINT

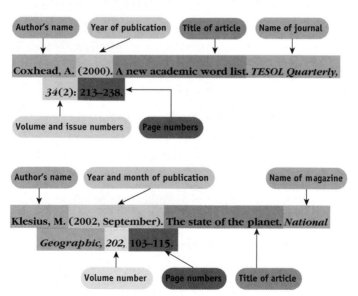

Capitalize only the first word and any proper nouns in an article title. (If the article has a subtitle, use a colon to separate the title and the subtitle, and capitalize the first word of each.) For an anonymous article, place the article title where the author's name would normally appear, and alphabetize the entry by the first important word in the title.

Each important word in the name of a journal is capitalized (in contrast to the title of an article or a book). Italicize the journal title and continue the italicizing so that it extends (without a break) to include the volume number. Include the issue number, when necessary, within parentheses, but do not italicize it. The point is to make volume and issue numbers visually distinct from page number(s).

10. Article from a journal with continuous pagination

Jazzmen, I. (2002). Previous behavioral control, self-efficacy, locus of

control, and the theory of planned behavior. *Journal of Applied Social*

Psychology, 32, 635–685.

Italicize the volume number but not the page numbers.

11. Article with two authors in a journal with each issue paginated separately

Rudisill, J. R., & Edwards, J. M. (2002). Coping with job transitions.

Consulting Psychology Journal, 54(1), 55–62.

Add the issue number within parentheses immediately after the volume number.

12. Article with three to six authors

Frost, R. O., Steketee, G., & Williams, L. (2002). Compulsive buying,

compulsive hoarding, and obsessive-compulsive disorder. *Behavior*

Therapy, 33(2), 201–213.

Include the names of all authors if the number of authors is no more than six.

13. Article with more than six authors

Reddy, S. K., Arora, M., Perry, C. L., Nair, B., Kohli, A., Lytle, L. A., et al. (2002). Tobacco and alcohol use outcomes of a school-based intervention in New Delhi. *American Journal of Health Behavior, 26,* 173–181.

After the name of the sixth author, use *et al.* to indicate that there are additional authors.

14. Article in a monthly or weekly magazine

Winson, J. (2002, June). The meaning of dreams. *Scientific American, 12,* 54–61.

For magazines published once a month, include the name of the month after the year. For magazines published weekly or bi-weekly, add the day of the issue: (2003, May 8).

15. Article in a newspaper

Liptak, A. (2002, June 16). Polygamist's custody fight raises many issues. *New York Times,* p. A20.

Include the letter indicating the section with the page number.

16. Book review

Kamil, M. L. (2002). The state of reading research [Review of the book *Progress in understanding reading: Scientific foundations and new frontiers*]. *American Journal of Psychology, 115,* 451–458.

SOURCES PRODUCED FOR ACCESS BY COMPUTER

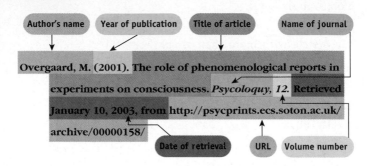

The APA suggests the following formats for reference entries for electronic sources. Notice that the APA recommends following the same sequence of information as provided for print sources. Omit any information, such as volume or page numbers, that is not available. Information about when and how the source was retrieved appears at the end. Notice that the period that normally ends an entry is omitted after a URL because trailing periods can cause difficulty in retrieving files.

17. Online article based on a print source

Lindsay, D. S., & Poole, D. A. (2001). Children's eyewitness reports after

   exposure to misinformation from parents [Electronic version]. *Journal*

   of Experimental Psychology: Applied, 7(1), 27–50.

The words in square brackets indicate that the article came from the electronic version of a journal that is also published in print.

18. Article in a journal published only online

Yu, D. L., & Seligman, M. E. P. (2002, May 8). Preventing depressive

   symptoms in Chinese children. *Prevention & Treatment, 5,* Article 9.

Retrieved June 15, 2002, from http://journals.apa.org/prevention/
    volume5/pre0050009a.html

If the article is numbered, indicate that number after the volume
number.

19. Article in an online newspaper

McGrath, C. (2002, June 15). Father time. *New York Times.* Retrieved June
    15, 2002, from http://nytimes.com/pages/science/index.html

20. Message posted to a newsgroup

Korniejczuk, V. (2002, June 11). Clinical psychology and psychiatry—
    What's the difference? [Msg 4]. Message posted to
    news://sci.psychology.theory

Provide the message number within square brackets after the message title.

21. Article from a database

Kim, Y. (2002). Spirituality moderates the effect of stress on emotional and
    physical adjustment. *Personality and Individual Differences, 32*(8),
    1377–1390. Retrieved June 21, 2002, from PsycINFO database.

Identify the database at the end of the entry.

OTHER SOURCES

22. Motion picture

Smith, M. (Producer/Writer), & Gaviria, M. (Producer/Director). (2001).
    Medicating kids [Motion picture]. (Available from the Public
    Broadcasting Service, 1320 Braddock Place, Alexandria, VA 22314)

Begin with the primary contributor(s), identifying the nature
of the contribution. Follow with the release date, the title, and
the descriptive label in square brackets. For a film with limited

distribution, provide information within parentheses about how it can be obtained. For a widely distributed film, indicate the country where it was produced and the name of the studio (e.g., United States: Paramount Pictures).

23. Television program

Holt, S. (Producer). (2002, October 1). *The mysterious lives of caves*

[Television broadcast]. Alexandria, VA: Public Broadcasting Service.

Give the title of the program in italics. If citing an entire series (e.g., *Nova*), cite the producer for the series as a whole and the network that originated it (e.g., WNET).

40d | Studying a sample paper can help you learn the APA style guidelines.

The APA makes a distinction between **final manuscript** (which a student submits to an instructor or a committee of professors) and **copy manuscript** (which an author submits to a journal for publication). Both kinds of manuscript follow the rules for documentation explained in 40c. The APA recognizes that a paper intended for publication may have to be modified so that the copy manuscript follows the requirements of the journal to which it is being submitted. Student papers may also require modification. The following section outlines the principal features and organization of a typical student paper. If you have any doubt as to what your instructor expects, find out what variations you should use.

In APA style, a **title page** includes a **manuscript page header** in the upper right-hand corner. It consists of the first two or three words of the title placed five spaces in front of the page number. The page number should be an inch from the right side of the paper and a half-inch from the top. The manuscript page header appears on all subsequent pages. The title page is considered page 1.

Below the manuscript page header but on the left-hand side of the page is the **running head,** a shortened version of the title (no more than fifty characters). Letters in the running head are all uppercase. The title appears next in upper- and lowercase letters and is centered. The **author's name** appears below the title and is followed by the author's affiliation. If an instructor asks that the course name or number be included, it generally appears where the affiliation would be. Unless the instructor specifically requires it, the instructor's name and the date the paper is due are not included. All elements on the title page are double-spaced.

The title page is followed by a page containing an **abstract,** a summary of the paper in no more than 120 words. For advice on how to summarize, see **39d**. The body of the paper, as well as the abstract, is double-spaced. A list of **references** follows the text, beginning on a separate page. This list includes only sources explicitly cited in the text. However, personal communications, such as email messages and interviews, are not listed in the reference list. Any other work that is especially pertinent or that informs the paper as a whole may be included in a separate bibliography. For additional examples of APA-style documentation, see the following student essay and the commentary printed on the left-hand pages.

COMMENTS

A. A **title page** includes five elements: the manuscript page header, the running head, the title, the author's name, and the author's affiliation. (The APA style does not include a date for the paper.) Double-space the title, the author's name, and the author's affiliation. Center the lines both horizontally and vertically on the page. For earlier versions of this paper, visit **www.harbrace.com**.

B. The **running head** is a shortened version of the title. It should not be more than fifty characters long.

C. If an instructor asks that a course name or number be included, it generally appears instead of the affiliation. Unless specifically required, the instructor's name is not included.

Running head: SLEEP AND MEMORY   B

The Sleep and Memory Connection

Nikki Krzmarzick

University of St. Thomas   C

D. An abstract is a short summary of a paper. Most papers submitted for publication in a journal include abstracts. Check with your instructor or supervisor to see whether an abstract is required for your paper.

E. An APA-style abstract should not exceed 120 words. Readers should be able to understand what a paper is about simply by reading the abstract. Devoted to summarizing the paper's content, the abstract does not include an evaluation of the paper's quality.

Abstract D

Current research indicates that sleep plays a role in learning and memory.

Results of research cited within the paper suggest that sleep affects the

acquisition of knowledge and skills needed to perform perceptual, critical, and

creative-thinking tasks. This topic's relevance to college students is addressed,

and practical application of findings to that end are discussed. Further

research is necessary to establish how the brain acquires, consolidates, and

organizes information for later retrieval. E

F. The full title is centered at the top of the page below the running head. Double-space between the running head and the title.

G. Krzmarzick introduces her thesis, a claim that she supports in the rest of her paper.

H. Following APA guidelines, Krzmarzick contacted the copyright holder for permission to reproduce the figure. (See page 672.) In addition, she provided a source note below the figure. Reproduction of a table also requires a source note indicating that permission to reproduce the table was granted by the copyright holder (who may not always be the author).

I. When more than one source is included in a parenthetical citation, semicolons separate the sources. (See page 673.)

J. The second source in this parenthetical citation includes five names. Because this is the first reference to this source, all of the authors' names are cited. Notice the comma before the ampersand.

K. A quotation of forty or more words is set off as an indented block, one-half inch from the left margin (the equivalent of an indent for a new paragraph). This example includes a citation within a citation. Krzmarzick has followed the APA rule given in the *Publication Manual:* "Do not omit citations embedded within the original material you are quoting. The works cited need not be included in the list of references (unless you happen to cite them elsewhere in your paper)" (p. 121). This example also includes numbers. The *Publication Manual* states that writers should use figures for all numbers 10 and above. Words can be used for numbers below 10, unless they indicate precise measurements or appear in a set with other numbers.

The Sleep and Memory Connection   F

It's finals week. In 24 hours, Kyle Rosemount has a biology exam. He is
not sure he is on track to pass the class, so a good grade is essential. He
regrets not starting earlier in the week but has resolved to stay up all night
reviewing course material. This method will afford him almost 16 hours of
study time. Rosemount reasons that this amount of time will be sufficient and
is almost positive he would not have spent more hours with the material had
he started exam preparations the previous week.

This scenario is all too familiar to college students, and many have used
the same logic as Rosemount in thinking that the total number of hours spent
studying is more critical than when that studying takes place. It seems to make
sense that the more time one spends studying the subject matter, the better one
will retain the information. But current research on the possibility of a
relationship between sleep and memory suggests that this assumption is not
necessarily true. In fact, irregular sleep patterns and cram sessions may
actually be sabotaging students' efforts.

If there is a connection between sleep and memory, then getting regular   G
sleep may be essential for memory consolidation and for optimal performance
on both critical- and creative-thinking tasks. An exploration of this possibility
requires a basic understanding of the sleep cycle. To an observer, a sleeping
person appears passive, unresponsive and essentially isolated from the rest of
the world and its barrage of stimuli. While it is true that humans are unaware
of most of what is happening around them during sleep, the brain is far from
inactive. It can be as active during sleep as in a waking state. While asleep, the
rate and type of neuronal firings (electrical activity) in the brain changes. The
brain cycles through four sleep stages before moving into REM sleep. All of

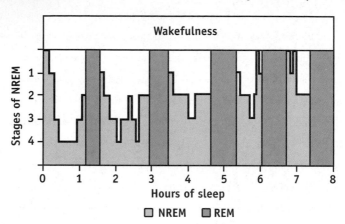

H *Figure 1.* Sleep stages. *Note.* From *Good sleep, good learning, good life,*
by Piotr Wozniak, July 2000. Retrieved September 19, 2002, from
http://www.supermemo.com/articles/sleep.htm. Reprinted with permission.

this occurs at relatively predictable intervals while the person is asleep.
Generally, it takes about 90 minutes to cycle through the four stages of sleep
and one REM episode, each with distinct neuronal characteristics (Hobson,
1989). Figure 1 graphs these stages for an 8-hour sleep period.

      The first two stages of sleep are characterized by high-amplitude, low-
frequency neural waves, aptly named slow-wave sleep. During these phases
the brain is relatively inactive and fires at a baseline rate. Wave III and wave
IV sleep are known as fast-wave sleep, recognized on an electroencepha-
logram readout by low-amplitude, high-frequency neuronal activity. REM
sleep is characterized by rapid motion of the eyes beneath closed lids. This is
the stage of sleep associated with vivid dreams, and thus it is sometimes called
dream sleep. Some dreams may occur within other stages as well, but they

lack the rich visual and emotional content of REM dreams. The function of
this fascinating phenomenon remains at least a partial mystery.

Current research examines links between sleep, or stages of sleep, and
memory or learning. Some studies suggest that all-night cram sessions, such as
the one Rosemount is planning, do not improve performance and may even have
the opposite effect (Kelly, Kelly, & Clanton, 2001; Pilcher & Walters, 1997). The
idea that sleep is linked to learning is supported by studies showing that certain
types of learning are hampered by sleep disruption or deprivation (Horne, 1988;
Karni, Tanne, Rubenstein, Askenasy, & Sagi, 1994).

Some studies implicate REM sleep as having a particularly important
role in memory consolidation (Karni et al., 1994). Early research showed the
importance of REM sleep for rats. Hunt (1989) summarizes a few of these
early studies that indicate the importance of the timing of REM sleep:

> Over the past few years Carlyle Smith (1981) has studied the REM aug-
> mentation following learning in rats over several days and has found
> that these increases occur as regular "windows" that climb steadily over
> a six-day period (Smith & Lapp, 1984). Deprivation of REM during
> these specific windows of augmentation was at its most effective in dis-
> rupting prior learning between 48 and 60 hours after training (Smith &
> Kelly, 1986). (p. 28)

Research involving human participants has yielded similar results. Karni
et al. (1994) showed that performance on a procedural task improves "neither
during nor immediately after practice but rather 8 to 10 hours after a training
session has ended" (p. 679). Hunt (1989) reports confirmation of the "window"
phenomenon by noting that in 1985 Epstein found participants in his study
reporting life events as dream content 2 or 3 days after the experiences.

L. Because Krzmarzick has already cited the full list of authors for this source (on page 5 of her paper), she follows APA style by including in this citation only the first author's name followed by *et al.* (abbreviation for the Latin phrase meaning "and others").

Epstein's findings differ in nature from those of Karni et al. (1994) in that they   L
arc more difficult to quantify because his data depend on dream recall, which
is subjective. While Epstein's observations are not the most scientifically
sound support for optimal timing of REM sleep, they are worth noting and
could be significant when pooled with other findings supporting the idea that
the brain processes new information and experiences over the course of a few
days. In addition to the timing of sleep following training, the amount of REM
sleep may play a role. Toward the end of the entire sleep cycle, time spent in
REM sleep increases. When people are deprived of REM sleep, their brains
react by going into REM sleep more frequently or by staying at the REM stage
longer during a sleep-recovery phase (Hobson, 1989).

Although there is no definitive answer as to which type of sleep is needed
for memory consolidation, studies show that lack of sleep hinders learning in
various ways. Pilcher and Walters (1997) noted its negative impact on
participant performance on a test of cognitive ability. Horne (1988) found that
participants performed creative-thinking tasks at a decreased capacity when
compared with a control group. Karni et al. (1994) observed the damaging
effect of sleep deprivation on perceptual learning.

Some studies include a self-report measure for perceived effort,
concentration, and the like (e.g., Buboltz, Brown, & Soper, 2001; Pilcher &
Walters, 1997). Participants are asked to report how confident they are in their
performance and to rate that performance. Findings from these self-report
measures are somewhat disturbing. It appears that the tendency exists, when a
person is sleep-deprived, to overestimate performance. Surprisingly, although
Pilcher and Walters (1997) noted that sleep deprivation negatively affected the
ability of participants to perform on a test, the participants overestimated their

performance. They also rated themselves as having expended more effort than participants in the control group did. Perhaps such skewed perception partially explains why college students often deprive themselves of sleep. If their perception is that performance is not hindered, there is no incentive to make sleep a priority.

The studies outlined above illustrate multiple types of learning and memory that may be affected by sleep. It is noteworthy that many of these studies used variables and methodologies that are realistic: They involve tasks similar to those that college students are asked to perform. For example, it is common for students to be asked to employ creative problem-solving skills in a classroom setting. Visual discrimination tasks, too, are common in college courses. Students may be required to recognize a painting by sight and then name the artist in an art history course. This line of research offers an obvious link between science and real-life situations.

Clearly there is a need for more research on this topic. The fact that an adequate amount of sleep is necessary for a person's health and well-being is well-established. We now have sufficient evidence to warrant a closer look at just how important the role of sleep is. Further research may establish that all stages of sleep play an important role in optimal functioning, or that one or two stages are particularly important. The exact relationship between sleep and memory is not yet known.

College students have notoriously bad sleeping habits, often because they are attempting to balance schoolwork, part-time jobs, extracurricular activities, and a social life. Known for their irregular sleep patterns, they are often sleep-deprived and/or suffer from some type of disturbed sleep (e.g., difficulty falling, or staying, asleep) (Hicks, Fernandez, & Pellegrini, 2001).

Based on the current body of research literature, it appears that there is a link between sleep and optimal functioning. For this reason, it is important for college students to manage their time in a way that allows them to study material over a period of a couple of days or longer and to have adequate sleep time in order to maximize retention. The consequences of inadequate sleep go beyond simply feeling sleepy. It is alarming that the self-reported sleep habits and quality of sleep of over 1,500 college students has worsened over the last decade (Hicks et al., 2001), indicating that necessary precautions are not being taken to ensure that at the very least students are educated regarding the importance of sleep.

It is evident that Kyle Rosemount is not doing himself any favors by delaying his studying until the last minute. Ideally, Rosemount should have studied in shorter blocks of time over a week, or at least a couple of days, allowing more time to process the information and commit it to memory. It may be that the sleep deprivation college students inflict upon themselves, particularly around finals time, may lead them to overestimate performance while actually hindering it.

M. The reference list is organized alphabetically and begins on a new page. The word *References* is centered at the top of the page. Double-space the reference list.

N. After the first line of each entry, use a hanging indent of five spaces.

O. The last name is always given first, followed by initials for the first and middle names (if available). The date of publication is always given parenthetically, immediately after the author's name. (See **40c(2)**.)

P. Observe the use of periods and commas, the capitalization for book and article titles, and the use of italics for book and journal titles. The volume number for a journal is also italicized.

References

Buboltz, W. C., Brown, F. C., Jr., & Soper, B. (2001). Sleep habits and patterns of college students: A preliminary study. *Journal of American College Health, 50*(3), 131–135.

Hicks, R. A., Fernandez, C., & Pellegrini, R. J. (2001). The changing sleep habits of university students: An update. *Perceptual and Motor Skills, 93*(3), 648.

Hobson, J. A. (1989). *Sleep.* New York: Scientific American Library.

Horne, J. A. (1988). Sleep loss and divergent thinking ability. *Sleep, 11*(6), 528–536.

Hunt, H. T. (1989). *The multiplicity of dreams: Memory, imagination, and consciousness.* New Haven, CT: Yale University Press.

Karni, A., Tanne, D., Rubenstein, B. S., Askenasy, J. M., & Sagi, D. (1994, July 29). Dependence on REM sleep of overnight improvement of a perceptual skill. *Science, 265,* 679–682.

Kelly, W. E., Kelly, K. E., & Clanton, R. C. (2001). The relationship between sleep length and grade-point average among college students. *College Student Journal, 35,* 84–86.

Pilcher, J. J., & Walters, A. S. (1997). How sleep deprivation affects psychological variables related to college students' cognitive performance. *Journal of American College Health, 46*(3), 121–126.

Wozniak, P. (2000, July), *Good sleep, good learning, good life.* Retrieved September 19, 2002, from http://www.supermemo.com/articles/sleep.htm

40e | CMS provides a widely used system for using footnotes and endnotes.

Published by the University of Chicago Press, *The Chicago Manual of Style* (CMS) provides detailed information about preparing a manuscript for submission. Although CMS encourages the use of parenthetical citations for documentation, it also shows how to use footnotes and endnotes for this purpose.

Both footnotes and endnotes require that a superscript number be placed wherever documentation of a source is necessary. The number should be as close as possible to whatever it refers to, following the punctuation (such as quotation marks, a comma, or a period) that appears at the end of the direct quotation or paraphrase.

Footnotes should be single-spaced four lines below the last line of text at the foot of the page. Double-space between footnotes if more than one appears on any page. Endnotes should be double-spaced on a separate page headed "Notes," and this heading should be at the top center of the page. Endnotes appear after the last page of text and before the bibliography. See the model CMS paper at www.harbrace.com for an example of endnotes.

Directory of CMS Note and Bibliographic Forms

BOOKS

BOOKS

Note form

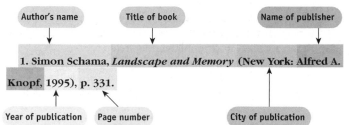

Author's name Title of book Name of publisher

1. Simon Schama, *Landscape and Memory* (New York: Alfred A. Knopf, 1995), p. 331.

Year of publication Page number City of publication

Bibliographic form

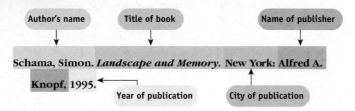

Most book entries consist of the author's name, the title of the book, and publication data (city of publication, publisher's name, and date of publication). This information appears in both footnotes and endnotes and in the bibliography at the end of the paper.

The principal differences are these:

- In a note, the author's name appears with the first name first; in a bibliographic entry, the author's name (or the name of the first author when there is more than one author) is inverted so that the last name is first.
- In a note, commas separate the author's name from the book title, and the book title from additional information (such as a translator's name) that appears before the publication data. In a bibliographic entry, periods follow the author's name and the book title.
- The publication data in a note (city of publication, publisher's name, and date) appear within parentheses. Parentheses are not used in bibliographic references.
- When information cited is found on a specific page in the text, the page number is placed at the end of the footnote or endnote. A bibliographical reference ends with the date of publication.

So that you can readily see the differences between CMS note form and CMS bibliographic form, these two forms are placed next to each other in the following pages. CMS provides no

specific requirements for indentation, so check with your instructor or supervisor.

1. Book with one author

Note form

    1. Carlo D'Este, *Eisenhower: A Soldier's Life* (New York: Holt, 2002),

417–18.

The author's name appears in normal order. Use commas to
separate the author's name from the title of the book. Put the
publication information within parentheses. Conclude with
the page number(s) on which the material being cited can be
found.

Bibliographic form

D'Este, Carlo. *Eisenhower: A Soldier's Life.* New York: Holt, 2002.

The author's last name appears first. Put a period after the author's first name and a period after the title.

2. Book with two or more authors

Note form

    2. Xue Litai, John W. Lewis, and Sergei N. Goncharov, *Uncertain*

Partners: Stalin, Mao, and the Korean War (Palo Alto, Calif.: Stanford

University Press, 1993).

Use commas after the names of the first and subsequent authors
if there are more than two. No comma follows the first author's
name if there are only two authors. In the publisher's name, do
not include words such as *Company* or *Corporation* or abbreviations such as *Co.* or *Inc.* However, CMS recommends writing
out *University Press,* although the abbreviation *Univ.* is acceptable if it is used consistently.

Bibliographic form

Litai, Xue, John W. Lewis, and Sergei N. Goncharov. *Uncertain Partners:*
   Stalin, Mao, and the Korean War. Palo Alto, Calif.: Stanford University
   Press, 1993.

Invert the order of the first author's name only. Place a comma
after this name and after subsequent authors' names. Use the
conjunction *and* before the final author's name.

3. Book with an editor

Note form

   3. Hanna Schissler, ed., *The Miracle Years* (Princeton, N.J.: Princeton
University Press, 2001).

Bibliographic form

Schissler, Hanna, ed. *The Miracle Years.* Princeton, N.J.: Princeton University
   Press, 2001.

In both forms, the abbreviation *ed.* follows the editor's name.

4. Book with an author and an editor

Note form

   4. Ayn Rand, *The Art of Fiction,* ed. Tore Boeckmann (New York: Plume,
2000).

Use the abbreviation *ed.* for "edited by."

Bibliographic form

Rand, Ayn. *The Art of Fiction.* Edited by Tore Boeckmann. New York:
   Plume, 2000.

Write out the words *Edited by.*

5. Translated book

Note form

5. Murasaki Shikibu, *The Tale of Genji,* trans. Royall Tyler (New York: Viking, 2001).

Use the abbreviation *trans.* for "translated by."

Bibliographic form

Shikibu, Murasaki. *The Tale of Genji.* Translated by Royall Tyler. New York: Viking, 2001.

Write out the words *Translated by.*

6. Edition after the first

Note form

6. Edward O. Wilson, *On Human Nature,* 14th ed. (Cambridge: Harvard University Press, 2001).

Bibliographic form

Wilson, Edward O. *On Human Nature.* 14th ed. Cambridge: Harvard University Press, 2001.

7. One volume in a multivolume work

Note form

7. Thomas Cleary, *Classics of Buddhism and Zen,* vol. 3 (Boston: Shambhala Publications, 2001), 116.

Bibliographic form

Cleary, Thomas. *Classics of Buddhism and Zen.* Vol. 3. Boston: Shambhala Publications, 2001.

8. Government document

Note form

8. Department of Commerce, Census Bureau, *Statistical Abstract of the United States,* 120th ed. (Washington, D.C., 2000), 16.

Bibliographic form

U.S. Department of Commerce. U.S. Census Bureau. *Statistical Abstract of the United States.* 120th ed. Washington, D.C., 2000.

9. Selection from an anthology

Note form

9. Elizabeth Spencer, "The Everlasting Light," in *The Cry of an Occasion,* ed. Richard Bausch (Baton Rouge: Louisiana State University Press, 2001), 171.

Bibliographic form

Spencer, Elizabeth. "The Everlasting Light." In *The Cry of an Occasion,* edited by Richard Bausch. Baton Rouge: Louisiana State University Press, 2001.

Replace the comma following the selection title with a period. Capitalize *In.* Use *edited by* instead of *ed.*

ARTICLES

Like CMS forms for books, the two forms for articles include essentially the same information, with minor differences in punctuation. The principal difference is that both the note form and the bibliographic form for articles end with page number(s). A note ends with the specific page or pages being cited; a bibliographic entry ends with the full range of pages on which the article can be found.

10. Article in a journal with continuous pagination

Note form

10. Y. C. Wong and Joe Leung, "Community-based Service for the Frail and Elderly in China," *International Social Work* 45 (2002): 212.

Use initials for first or second names only when the author's name appears that way in the original publication.

Bibliographic form

Wong, Y. C., and Joe Leung. "Community-based Service for the Frail and Elderly in China." *International Social Work* 45 (2002): 205–16.

Pages establishing the full length of the article appear at the end of the citation.

11. Article in a journal with issues paged separately

Note form

11. Andreas Schedler, "The Menu of Manipulation," *Journal of Democracy* 13, no. 2 (2002): 48.

Bibliographic form

Schedler, Andreas. "The Menu of Manipulation." *Journal of Democracy* 13, no. 2 (2002): 36–50.

12. Article in a popular (general-circulation) magazine

Note form

12. John O'Sullivan, "The Overskeptics," *National Review,* 17 June 2002, 23.

This example shows a magazine published weekly. For a magazine published monthly, include only the month and the year.

Bibliographic form

O'Sullivan, John. "The Overskeptics." *National Review,* 17 June 2002,
22–26.

13. Newspaper article

Note form

13. Rick Bragg, "An Oyster and a Way of Life, Both at Risk," *New York Times,* 15 June 2002, national edition, Sec. A, p. 14.

If the city of publication is not part of the newspaper's name, it should be added at the beginning of the name and italicized as if part of the title: *St. Paul Pioneer Press.* If the city is not well known or could be confused with another city with the same name, add the state name or abbreviation within parentheses after the city's name. If the paper is a well-known national one, such as the *Wall Street Journal,* it is not necessary to add the city of publication.

Bibliographic form

New York Times, 15 June–31 July 2002.

Unlike journal and magazine articles, items from newspapers are rarely included in a bibliography. Instead, the name of the newspaper and the run of dates used are listed.

OTHER SOURCES

14. Interview

Note form

14. Yoko Ono, "Multimedia Player: An Interview with Yoko Ono," interview by Carolyn Burriss-Krimsky, *Ruminator Review,* no. 10 (summer 2002): 28.

Bibliographic form

Ono, Yoko. "Multimedia Player: An Interview with Yoko Ono." By Carolyn

Burriss-Krimsky. *Ruminator Review,* no. 10 (summer 2002): 26–29.

Although an interview is not always listed in the bibliography, if you are required to include one, begin with the name of the person being interviewed; next, include the title of the interview and the name of the person who conducted it, followed by information about where the interview can be found.

15. Indirect (secondary) source

Note form

15. Toni Morrison, *Playing in the Dark* (New York: Vintage, 1992), 26, quoted in Jonathan Goldberg, *Willa Cather and Others* (Durham, N.C.: Duke University Press, 2001), 37.

Bibliographic form

Morrison, Toni. *Playing in the Dark,* 26. New York: Vintage, 1992. Quoted in

Jonathan Goldberg, *Willa Cather and Others* (Durham, N.C.: Duke

University Press, 2001), 37.

If you cite a work indirectly, you must cite both the original work and the secondary source in which you found it quoted. Begin with the author you have quoted, and provide information about this work (which should be available in the notes or bibliography of the indirect source you used); follow with information about the source from which you obtained the quotation.

16. Online document

Note form

16. Buzz R. Pounds, "Student-Created Contracts: Building Responsibility from the Bottom-Up," paper presented at the annual meeting of the

Conference on College Composition and Communication, Atlanta, 24–27 March 1999, available from SilverPlatter, ERIC, ED 429298.

Bibliographic form

Pounds, Buzz R. "Student-Created Contracts: Building Responsibility from the Bottom-Up." Paper presented at the annual meeting of the Conference on College Composition and Communication, Atlanta, 24–27 March 1999. Available from SilverPlatter, ERIC, ED 429298.

Follow the appropriate form for material in print, but identify the vendor, the database, and the accession or identifying number. In this case, the reference is for a paper that was obtained through ERIC, the principal database for electronic research in education.

The next edition of *The Chicago Manual of Style* is likely to include extensive coverage of how to document sources accessed by computer. You can check the CMS Web site (**www.press.uchicago.edu/Misc/Chicago/cmosfaq/cmosfaq.html**) to see whether additional examples are available.

40f Studying a sample paper can help you learn CMS style for courses in history and political science.

This section presents the first page and several entries from the bibliography of a student paper that addresses an important development in the Civil Rights movement. To read the complete paper, including the endnotes, visit www. harbrace.com Although CMS does not provide guidelines for a title page, one is shown in figure 40.2 as a sample.

Race in the U.S. Army: An Executive Order for Hope

Nicole Hester

American History 257

December 6, 2002

Figure 40.2. Sample title page for CMS-style paper.

While students of the Civil Rights movement are often familiar with the Supreme Court decision *Brown* v. *The Board of Education,* which acknowledged the inherent inequality in separate but equal practices, that decision would not happen until 1955, nearly eight years after President Harry S. Truman issued an executive order to integrate the federal government and, in particular, the United States military. Although the earlier Thirteenth (1865), Fourteenth (1868), and Fifteenth (1870) Amendments redefined freedom, citizenship, and voting, these amendments were diluted by Supreme Court decisions in the nineteenth and early twentieth centuries. In cases like *Plessy* v. *Ferguson,* the court established the precedent of "separate but equal," which legally allowed the separation of races in public facilities.[1] Thus, Truman's executive order in 1948 became an important step in the long-term struggle for civil rights.

Like American schools, the United States Army was segregated, and this segregation remained in place until after the Second World War (1941–1945). In July of 1948, by executive order, President Truman demanded equal treatment and equal opportunity in the armed forces, setting into motion a series of events that would force change, however slow it might be:

> It is hereby declared to be the policy of the President that there shall be equality of treatment and opportunity for all persons in the armed services without regard to race, color, religion or national origin. This policy shall be put into effect as rapidly as possible, having due regard to the time required to effectuate any necessary changes without impairing efficiency or morale.[2]

1

Bibliography

Billington, Monroe. Freedom to Serve: "The President's Committee on Equality of Treatment and Opportunity in the Armed Forces, 1949–1950." *Journal of Negro History* [online], 1966, vol. 51, no. 4 [cited 2002-06-20], pp. 262–74. Available from Internet: http://links.jstor.org/sici?sici=0022-2992%28196610%2951%3A4%3C262%3AFTSTPC%.

Gallup, George H. *The Gallup Poll Public Opinion 1935–1971.* Vol. 2. New York: Random House, 1972.

Gardner, Michael R. *Harry Truman and Civil Rights: Moral Courage and Political Risks.* Carbondale and Edwardsville: Southern Illinois University Press, 2002.

Humphrey, Hubert H. *Beyond Civil Rights: A New Day of Equality.* New York: Random House, 1968.

Lee, Ulysses. *The Employment of Negro Troops.* Washington, D.C.: Center of Military History, 1963.

Mayer, Kenneth. *With the Stroke of a Pen: Executive Orders and Presidential Power.* Princeton and Oxford: Princeton University Press, 2001.

McCullough, David. *Truman.* New York: Simon & Schuster, 1992.

Merrill, Dennis, ed. *Documentary History of the Truman Presidency.* Vol. 11. Bethesda, Md.: University Publishers of America, 1996.

Mershon, Sherie, and Steven Schlossman. *Foxholes and Color Lines.* Baltimore: Johns Hopkins University Press, 1998.

Nalty, Bernard C., and Morris J. MacGregor. *Blacks in the Military.* Wilmington, Del.: Scholarly Resources, 1981.

Osur, Alan M. *Blacks in the Army Air Forces During World War II.* Washington, D.C.: Office of Air Force History, 1941.

Plessy v. *Ferguson,* 163 U.S. 537 (1896).

Writing Academic Discourse

Effective communication is necessary in every academic discipline and in most professions. Professionals in every discipline—whether they work in colleges, companies, or organizations—value the basic elements of good writing: coherent organization and structure (see chapter 32), sound reasoning (chapter 36), appropriate use of evidence and detail (chapter 39), clear expression (chapters 23–30), a strong sense of audience (chapter 32), grammatical correctness (chapters 1–7), and an understanding of the conventions of the discipline or the profession.

This chapter will help you

- understand what various disciplines recognize as evidence (41a),
- understand how disciplines use evidence (41b),
- be aware that the language and writing style of disciplines differ (41c), and
- recognize the documents and formats used in several disciplines (41d).

41a | Disciplines are distinguished according to what they consider evidence to be.

Traditionally, there have been three disciplinary cultures: humanities, social sciences, and natural sciences. The way each disciplinary culture generates and delivers knowledge depends to a large extent on its values and the various sources of evidence it considers worthwhile. It's fair to say that people who work in the **humanities** focus on understanding and interpreting imagination, ideas, emotions, values, and ideals as expressed in literature and language, history, philosophy and religion, art, music, drama, and film.

People who work in the **social sciences** are interested in observing, recording, and interpreting human behavior on the basis of data they collect. The social sciences include such fields as psychology, sociology, political science, education, economics, and business.

People working in the **natural sciences** attempt to quantify and understand phenomena in the world through meticulous observation and experimentation. These problem-solving disciplines include mathematics, the biological sciences of botany and zoology, the physical sciences of chemistry and physics, and the earth sciences of geology, geography, and astronomy. The natural sciences also include the applied sciences: medicine and allied health studies, engineering, and computer science.

41b | Disciplines are distinguished according to how they use evidence.

Evidence, or **data,** includes anything that might be used to prove a point in a discipline, including language and numbers. The kind of evidence that each discipline accepts as proof depends on its specific cultural values. For instance, natural scientists consider **empirical evidence**—that is, facts that can be measured or tested—to be the only kind of evidence that leads to truth. Those working in the social sciences accept **inferences** and **opinions** as well as facts (see **35c**). Writers in the humanities accept both of these kinds of evidence as well as **logic** and **argumentation** (see chapter **35**)—the data we employ when we use language.

Natural scientists and social scientists both claim allegiance to **inductive reasoning** (see **35d–e**), but they carry out this process differently. Natural scientists generally begin an investigation with a **hypothesis,** an idea that serves as a basis for experimentation. The experiment either validates the hypothesis or shows it to be in error. Social scientists, on the other hand, collect evidence from which they develop a hypothesis. Thus, you could say that natural scientists reason from a hypothesis, and social scientists reason to a hypothesis. Both use a version of the scientific method. Humanists, however, use both inductive reasoning and **deductive reasoning** (see **35d–e**). They begin with an idea, collect evidence, and then use both types of reasoning to arrive at a conclusion—an interpretation of what the evidence means.

Disciplines also differ in their acceptance of what constitutes support. In the natural sciences, you rely on **quantitative data**—numerically based evidence—as is evident in the excerpt from Jennifer York's lab report.

**From Jennifer York's lab report,
"Sex-Linked Inheritance, Sex Determination"**

York describes her method.   Virgin female flies were mated to male flies by placing several pairs together in a vial. One week later, the parent flies were removed to prevent them from mating with their own progeny and the vial was checked for larvae to indicate that successful mating had occurred.

Week 1:

She reports quantitative data numerically.   Cross 1:

P: 3 ♂ ($++$/YB)   ×   3 ♀ (yw/yw)

Tan body, red   Yellow body, white

bar eye   round eye

Cross 2:

P: 4 ♂ (yw/YB) × 3 ♀ (++/++)

Yellow body, white   Tan body, red round

bar eye   eye

To permit readers to replicate (that is, to repeat) the results of your study, your report will generally include an introduction, a description of methods, a summary of findings, and a discussion of results. Examples of scientific reports are available online. Visit www.harbrace.com.

In the social sciences, although you may rely on quantitative data, you are also likely to use **qualitative data**—evidence based on your observations of behavior, interviews you conduct, and the like. Your report of qualitative evidence will generally include an introduction, a subject identification, a description of methods, an analysis of behaviors, and a conclusion. In an ethnographic report or case study, you might also report qualitative data in thick analysis, where you are an active agent, observing phenomena and then describing in detail what you have observed.

From Mike Demmon's field report,
"Quantitative Analysis of Diving Ducks"

With the exception of human-induced movements, it appeared that there were no significant interactions between any of the species. As may have been expected, the Buffleheads also appeared to be courting at times. The data above also show that the majority of the birds that were paired or followed by the other sex were Buffleheads.

Demmon makes an inference to produce qualitative data.

Beyond the Rule

MORE ABOUT THICK ANALYSIS

Thick analysis comes from the idea of "thick description," first introduced by philosopher Gilbert Ryle and adapted for ethnographic research by Clifford Geertz. For more information, visit www.harbrace.com.

Although you cannot generalize successfully from qualitative research studies, such studies often produce "findings" that you can then test with more control and objectivity in quantitative research studies. Examples of qualitative reports can be found online at www.harbrace.com.

In the humanities, you rely almost entirely on qualitative evidence that you derive from careful observation and analysis of texts—including musical scores and paintings or sculptures, as well as literary texts and historical documents. Josh Otis's essay on *The Things They Carried* (42f) is an example of writing in the humanities.

**From Josh Otis's essay,
"Friendship in *The Things They Carried*"**

Otis provides context for his evidence.

He presents the evidence from his source.

Just after Tim arrives in Vietnam, there is an incident in which the men find a dead farmer in an abandoned village. One by one, the soldiers go up and shake the old man's hand, but Tim refuses. His refusal makes him the object of harassment, but he persists. That night Kiowa approaches him and says, "You did a good thing today. That shaking hands crap, it isn't decent. The guys'll hassle you for a while, especially Jensen--but just keep saying no. Should've done it myself. Takes guts, I know that" (257). Kiowa's sense of what is morally sound and his support of actions in accordance with his beliefs help explain why he and Tim become so close.

Otis explains the evidence.

Each discipline has a vocabulary that you will learn when you take courses in its specific subject areas. For example, if you take a course in the social sciences, you will learn the difference between quantitative and qualitative research studies and between a field study and a laboratory study. You will also understand what is meant by the term *theory* and be able to recognize thick description. If you take a course in the natural sciences, you will learn how to collect and process quantitative data. In both the social and the natural sciences, you will learn the term *replicability* and understand its importance. In courses in the humanities, you will learn to recognize the difference between primary and secondary sources (see chapter 37). In addition to the language of a discipline, you will master a wide range of technical terms specific to its subject areas: sociology and psychology, chemistry and zoology, or literature and music, to name a few (see 19c(4)).

Learning the language of a discipline has an important benefit. The purpose of a specialized vocabulary is to make communication between those who work in a discipline precise and efficient, and it is thus the language that experts in that discipline use regularly. When you use the specialized vocabulary of a discipline, you establish yourself as knowledgeable in that discipline and as credible in writing about it; that is, you establish your professional ethos.

Each discipline has developed a distinctive writing style and tone. Writers in the natural sciences use language sparingly to convince an audience of the viability of research findings. Social scientists report ethnographic inquiry and case studies using thick descriptions, which are fundamentally rhetorical (see **41b**), but they use language more sparingly when reporting the results of surveys and experiments. In **thin descriptions,** writers in both the social and the natural sciences present themselves as impartial and objective; in doing so, they strive to avoid the first-person pronoun *I* (see **20d**), a practice that often results in the use of the passive rather than the active voice (**7c**). Writers in both the social and the natural sciences also use visual elements such as charts, graphs, and tables (see **8c**) more often than writers in the humanities do. Writers in the humanities may allow their personalities to show in their texts more than do writers in the social and natural sciences (unless the latter are using thick description). And writers in the humanities tend to see rhetorical analysis as a viable means of conducting research and rhetorical and theoretical argumentation as an acceptable way of reporting evidence.

Each discipline also has conventions for formatting documents. Writers in the humanities make minimal use of headings (see **8d(4)**), and they format documents in traditional ways. Writing in the humanities is also less dependent on a prescribed approach than is writing in the social or natural sciences, where research generally must follow specific procedures and be reported in a predetermined sequence. And writers in any discipline are expected to adhere to that discipline's approved documentation and bibliographical style (see chapter **40**). Literary studies, modern languages, and rhetoric follow the style guidelines of the Modern Language Association (MLA) (see **40a–b**). History, art, and music follow *The Chicago Manual of Style* (see **40e–f**). Linguistics and most of the social sciences use some form of the style recommended by the American Psychological Association (APA) (see 40c–d). The Council of Science Editors (formerly the Council of Biology Editors) encourages natural scientists to use either a name-date system that is similar to the APA and MLA systems or a citation-sequence system that calls for listing sources in the order in which they occur in the document.

41d Each discipline favors specific kinds of documents and formats.

In the natural sciences, you will write two important kinds of documents: the lab report and the literature review. In the social sciences, you will also write literature reviews, in addition to several kinds of reports, among them field reports, observational reports, and case studies. The excerpt from a literature review by Rebecca Abraham follows APA documentation style.

**From Rebecca Abraham's literature review,
"Thinking Styles as Moderators of Role Stressor–
Job Satisfaction Relationships"**

Sternberg and Grigorenko's (1993) 16-item, forced choice thinking styles inventory was employed. Their Cronbach alpha reliabilities for the judicial, hierarchical, global and liberal thinking styles were 0.73, 0.81, 0.83 and 0.88 and were all above the 0.70 threshold of acceptability. Sternberg and Grigorenko (1993) established construct validity through a five-factor structure accounting for 77% of the variance in the data. Factors (loadings in parentheses) elicited included legislative-executive (-0.78 and 0.58), judicial-oligarchic (0.7 each), external-internal (0.72 and 0.80), global-local (-0.82 and 0.92) and hierarchic (0.86). Convergent

▪ Abraham summarizes the work of a research team.

validity was established through correlations with the Myers-Briggs type indicator as well as the Gregorec measure of mind styles. For the former, 30 of 128 correlations were significant, whereas for the latter, 22 of 52 were significant. The judicial, global and liberal styles correlated positively with SAT math, but not with SAT verbal. Consequently, styles are largely distinct from intelligence or aptitude.

For humanities classes, you can expect to write papers that describe your experiences or argue for the correctness of your observations. These papers may be creative texts such as poems, interpretive texts that offer interpretations of literary, musical, or artistic works, or theoretical essays that attempt to understand something in a larger context (how a poem reflects the age in which it was written, for example). Remember, however, that interpretations must be logical arguments based on support and proof (chapter 36).

It is worth noting that all disciplines are dynamic entities, constantly developing new approaches and new attitudes. For instance, the acceptance of thick description in the social sciences is a relatively recent phenomenon, and such description is beginning to achieve acceptance in the natural sciences (particularly in medical writing). Similarly, writers in the humanities have borrowed techniques from the social and natural sciences. Rhetoricians report ethnographic research, musicians analyze the physiological effects of sound, and painters and sculptors discuss experiments that test the physical properties of the media they use. Generalizations made about the characteristics of specific disciplines are, like all generalizations, incomplete at best.

Exercise 1

Read an article in a professional journal on a topic you are studying in another course or one you are simply interested in. Then, answer the following questions about it.

a. What kind of evidence is the research reported in the article based on? How do you know?
b. How is the evidence presented in the article?
c. Comment on the kind of language used in the article.
d. What kind of article is it (e.g., literature review, interpretation, case study)? Identify its main characteristics.

Writing about Literature

Ever since you wrote your first book report, you've been interpreting and writing about literature, talking about plot, characters, and setting. When you write about literature in college, regardless of the literary genre involved—fiction, drama, poetry, essays, personal narratives, manifestos, or memoirs—you'll still discuss plot, characters, and setting. But you'll also apply many of the same interpretive strategies you use to write about other topics.

This chapter will help you

- recognize the various genres of literature (42a),
- use the specialized vocabulary for discussing literature (42b),
- employ various critical approaches for interpreting literature (42c),
- realize the value of a careful reading (42d), and
- apply the special conventions for writing about literature (42e).

42a | Literature can be divided into various genres.

Like all specialized fields, literature can be divided into categories, which are referred to as **genres** (from the French word for "kind" or "type"). A genre can be identified by its particular features or conventions, which develop within a specific cultural context. Some genres, such as drama and poetry, appear to be timeless and universal; others, detective fiction, for example, seem to be more recent Western cultural phenomena.

Some of the most widely studied literary genres are fiction, drama, and poetry, though many forms of nonfiction (including personal essays and memoirs, literacy narratives, and documents such as manifestos) are gaining attention in college courses. Although all imaginative literature is fiction, the term **fiction** is applied specifically to novels and short stories. These works express truth about the human condition through such components as setting, character, and plot (see **42b**).

Drama differs from other imaginative literature in one specific way: It is meant to be performed—whether on stage, on film, or on television—with the director and actors imprinting the play with their own interpretations. In a novel, you often find extensive descriptions of characters and setting, as well as passages revealing what characters are thinking. In a play, you learn what a character is thinking when he or she shares thoughts with another character in dialogue or presents a **dramatic soliloquy** (a speech delivered to the audience by an actor alone on the stage).

Poetry shares many of the components of fiction and drama. It too may have a narrator with a point of view. Dramatic monologues and narrative poems sometimes have a plot, a setting, and characters. But poetry is primarily characterized by its concentrated use of connotative language, imagery, allusions, figures of speech, symbols, sound, and rhythm.

42b	The specialized vocabulary for discussing literature helps writers understand its elements.

Like all specialized fields, literature has a unique vocabulary, which describes the various features of literary texts and concepts of literary analysis. As you learn this vocabulary, you'll learn more than just a list of terms: You'll learn how to understand, interpret, and write about literature.

(1) Characters carry the plot forward.

The **characters** are the humans or humanlike personalities (aliens, creatures, robots, animals, and so on) who carry the plot forward; they usually include a main character, called a **protagonist,** who is in external conflict with another character or an institution or in internal conflict with himself or herself. This conflict usually reveals the **theme,** or the central idea of the work (see 42b(7)).

Because writing about literature often requires character analysis, you need to understand the characters in any work you read. You can do so by paying close attention to their appearance, their language, and their actions. You also need to pay attention to what the narrator or other characters say about them. Whether you are writing about characters in novels, in plays, or in poems, you'll want to concentrate on what those characters do and say—and why.

(2) Imagery is conveyed by descriptive language.

The **imagery** in a piece of literature is conveyed by **descriptive language,** or words that describe a sensory experience. Notice the images in "Portrait," a prose poem by Pinkie Gordon Lane that focuses on the life—and death—of a mother.

> My mother died walking along a dusty road on a Sunday morning in New Jersey. The road came up to meet her sinking body in one quick embrace. She spread out like an umbrella and dropped into oblivion before she hit the ground. In that one swift moment all light went out at the age of forty-nine. Her legacy: the blackened knees of the scrub-woman who ransomed her soul so that I might live, who bled like a tomato whenever she fought to survive, who laughed fully when amused—her laughter rising in one huge crescendo—and whose wings soared in dark despair. . . .
>
> —**PINKIE GORDON LANE,** *Girl at the Window*

The dusty road, the sinking body, the quick embrace—these images convey the loneliness and swiftness of death. The blackened knees, bleeding tomato, and rising laughter, in contrast, are images of a life of work, struggle, and joy.

(3) The narrator tells the story.

The **narrator** of a literary work tells the story, and this speaking voice can be that of a specific character (or of characters taking turns telling), can seem to be that of the work's author (but should not be confused with the author), or can be that of an all-knowing presence that transcends both characters and author. Whatever the case may be, the diction and sentence structure reveal the narrator's **tone,** or attitude toward events and characters and even, in some circumstances, toward readers. By determining the tone and the impact it has on you as a reader, you can gain insight into the author's purpose. (See 33a(3).)

(4) Plot is the sequence of events and more.

The **plot** is what happens in the story, but it is more than the sequence of events or the narrative. The plot establishes how events are patterned or related in terms of conflict and resolution. Narrative answers "What comes next?" and plot answers "Why?" Consider this example:

Narrative	The king died, and then the queen died.
Plot	The queen was beheaded after she killed the king.

Plot usually begins with a conflict that sets events in motion. In the **exposition,** the author introduces the characters, setting, and background—the elements that constitute the conflict and relate to the events that follow. The subsequent series of events leads to the **climax,** which is also referred to as the **turning point** because what follows is **falling action** (or **dénouement**) that leads to a resolution of the conflict.

(5) Setting involves place and time.

Setting involves place—the physical setting and the social setting (the morals, manners, and customs of the characters). Setting involves time—not only historical time, but also the length of time covered by the narrative. Setting also includes atmosphere, or the emotional response to the situation. Being aware of these features of the setting will help you better understand the story, whether it's written in prose fiction, drama, or poetry.

(6) Symbols resonate with broader meaning.

Frequently used by writers of fiction, drama, and poetry, a **symbol** is an object, usually concrete, that stands for something else, usually abstract. A symbol is what it is, but it also stands for something more than it is, such as a moral truth or something of cultural significance.

When you write about a particular symbol, first note the lines, paragraphs, or passages in which it appears in the literary work. Then consider why it appears in those places and to what effect: What might this particular symbol mean? When you have an idea, trace the incidents in the literary work that reinforce that idea.

(7) The theme is the main idea of a literary work.

The main idea of a literary work is its **theme.** Depending on how they interpret a work, different readers may identify different themes. To test whether the idea you have identified is central to the work in question, check to see if it is supported by the setting, plot, characters, and symbols. If you can relate these components to the idea you are considering, then that idea can be considered the work's theme. The most prominent literary themes arise out of conflict: person versus person, person versus self, person versus nature, or person versus society.

Beyond the Rule

OTHER USEFUL LITERARY TERMS

As you draft and revise your essays about literature, you may want to use some of the literary terms available at www.harbrace.com.

CHECKLIST **for Interpreting a Literary Work**

- From whose point of view is the story or poem told?
- Who is the protagonist? How is his or her character developed?
- With whom or what is the protagonist in conflict?
- How are the characters depicted and distinguished through dialogue?
- What is the theme?
- How does the author use setting, plot, characters, and symbols to establish the theme?
- What symbols, images, or figures of speech does the author use? To what effect?
- How do the various elements combine to convey meaning?

42c | Critical approaches to literature can serve as the basis for interpretation.

Writing a paper about a literary work usually requires you to focus on the work itself and to demonstrate that you have read it carefully—a process known as **close reading.** Through close reading, you can offer an **interpretation** of what the work means to you. An interpretation can be shaped by your personal response to what you have read, a specific type of critical theory, or the views of other readers, which you wish to support or challenge.

Familiarity with **literary theory**—scholarly discussion that tries to explain how the meaning of literature can be determined—can enrich your reading of literature as well as your understanding of the books and essays about literature that you discover when you do research (see **37d**). Literary theory can also help you decide how you want to focus your writing about literature.

Although critical approaches to literature overlap somewhat, each has a different primary focus: the reader, some aspect of the cultural context, the text itself, or the author or characters.

(1) Reader-response theory focuses on the reader.

Reader-response theory argues that a literary work is incomplete in and of itself; a reader is necessary to complete its meaning. Readers bring different intellectual values and life experiences to a work each time they read it. Thus, meaning is not fixed on the page; meaning depends more on what each reader brings *to* the page every time he or she encounters it. Furthermore, the same reader can have different responses to the same literary work when rereading it after a number of years: A father of teenagers might find Gwendolyn Brooks's "we real cool" more disturbing than it had seemed when he first read it in high school. Although a reader-response approach to literature encourages diverse interpretations, you must be able to support your interpretation by showing how it interacts responsibly with the text to shape the meaning you describe.

(2) Both feminist and gender-based literary criticism focus on issues related to sex, gender, or sexual orientation.

Both feminist and gender-based literary criticism focus on the significance of sex, gender, or sexual orientation within a particular social context to analyze the ways the work promotes or challenges the prevailing intellectual or cultural assumptions of its day regarding issues related to gender and sexuality, including patriarchy and compulsory heterosexuality. Using a gender-based approach, a critic might focus on the positive features of the domestic relationship between Olive and Verena, two financially independent women in Henry James's *The Bostonians*; that same critic might also try to explain why Jake Barnes in Hemingway's *The Sun Also Rises* bonds with some men and is contemptuous of others.

(3) Race-based literary criticism focuses on issues related to race relations.

A useful form of race-based literary criticism, **critical race theory** focuses on the significance of race relations (race, racism, and power) within a specific historical and social setting in order to explain the experience and literary production of peoples whose history is characterized by political, social, and psychological oppression. Not only does this theoretical approach seek out previously neglected literary works, but it also illuminates the ways in which race, ethnicity, and power inform many works. Previously neglected works such as Zora Neale Hurston's *Their Eyes Were Watching God*, Rudolpho Anaya's *Bless Me, Ultima,* and Frederick Douglass's *Narrative,* each of which demonstrates how racism affects the characters' lives, have taken on considerable cultural value in the last twenty years. Closely associated with critical race theory is **postcolonial theory,** which takes into account the relationship of the colonized with the colonizer and the ways a text challenges the dominant powers at a particular time and place, asserting a drive toward the liberation of oppressed social groups. Joseph Conrad's *Heart of Darkness,* Jean Rhys's *Wide Sargasso Sea,* Daniel Defoe's *Robinson Crusoe,* and E. M. Forster's *A Passage to India* can all be read productively using postcolonial theory.

(4) Class-based literary criticism focuses on socioeconomic issues.

To explain the conflict between characters in a work of literature or between a character and a community or institution, **class-based literary criticism** draws on the work of Karl Marx, Terry Eagleton, and other theorists who have addressed the implications of social hierarchies and the accompanying economic tensions. These theorists argue that differences in socioeconomic class—in the material conditions of daily life—divide people in profoundly significant ways, much more so than differences in race, ethnicity, culture, and gender. Thus, a class-based approach can be used to explain why Bigger Thomas gets thrown into such a confused mental state in Richard Wright's *Native Son,* or why a family loses its land in John Steinbeck's *The Grapes of Wrath.*

(5) Text-based literary criticism focuses on the work itself.

Text-based literary criticism demands concentration on the piece of literature itself; with this approach, only the use of concrete, specific examples from the text validates an interpretation. The reader must pay careful attention to the elements within the literary work—plot, characters, setting, tone, dialogue, imagery, and so on (see **42b**)—to evaluate their interaction, overall effect, and meaning. The reader requires nothing more than what is contained within the text itself in order to understand and appreciate the text's unchanging meaning. Readers may change, but the meaning of the text does not. A close reading of the work is essential, then, in order to account for all of its particularities. According to text-based literary criticism, F. Scott Fitzgerald's *The Great Gatsby* is the story of unfulfilled longing, richly told with haunting imagery.

(6) Context-based literary criticism focuses on the time and place in which a work was created.

Context-based literary criticism considers the historical period in which a work was written and the cultural and economic patterns that prevailed during that period. For example, recognizing that Willa Cather published *My Antonia* during World War I can help account for the darker side of that novel; similarly, understanding that Arthur Miller wrote *The Crucible* in response to the accusations of the House Un-American Activities Committee in the 1950s helps explain why that play generated so much excitement when it was first produced. Critics who use a context-based and class-based approach known as **cultural studies** consider how a literary work interacts with economic production, socioeconomic class, and other cultural artifacts (such as songs or fashion) from the period in which it was written.

(7) Psychoanalytic theories focus on psychological factors affecting the writing and the reading of literature.

Psychoanalytic theories, which focus on the psychological state of the author and characters as well as the reader, seek to explain human experience and behavior in terms of sexual impulses and unconscious motivations. When applied to literary criticism, these theories help readers discern the motivations of characters, envision the psychological state of the author as implied by the text, and evaluate the psychological reasons for their own interpretations. Critics may apply the psychoanalytic approach to explain why Holden Caulfield rebels at school (in *Catcher in the Rye* by J. D. Salinger) or why Rochester is blinded (in Charlotte Brontë's *Jane Eyre*).

Critics who use the work of psychiatrist Carl Jung explore **archetypes** (recurring figures or patterns in literature), such as the hero, the earth mother, the scapegoat, the outcast, the cruel stepmother, the quest, the initiation, the test, and the return.

Exercise 1

Attend a film, a play, or a poetry reading at your school or in your community. Write a two- to three-page essay, using one of the theoretical approaches discussed in this chapter.

42d | Careful reading is essential to the process of writing about literature.

You can interpret and write effectively about a work of literature if you read it carefully (see chapter **35**). As you read, take notes on your personal response, either in a notebook or in the margins of your book. As you plan your essay, think critically about your impressions—and how you might interpret them.

(1) Writing about literature begins with active, personal engagement with what you read.

As you read, trust your own reactions. Which characters do you admire? Did you follow the plot? Did the work remind you of any experience of your own? Did it introduce you to a different world in terms of historical or geographical setting, or did you encounter a familiar cast of characters? Were you amused, moved, or confused? These first impressions can provide the seeds from which strong essays will grow, even if they are modified by your thinking later on.

You can also engage a text you own by **annotating** it—marking key passages and raising questions that occur as you read (see **39b**). In addition, you can benefit from **freewriting** about your first impressions (see 32b), from keeping a journal in which you record your reactions and questions (see 32b), or from practicing focusing techniques (chapter 32). These methods of exploring a subject can help you discover what you think, what you want to understand, and what you need to research.

(2) You can understand your response by considering how it is shaped by your identity.

When reflecting on your response to a work of literature, consider how your reading might be shaped by the factors that make you who you are and the critical approaches to literature you are consciously or unconsciously using (see 42c). For example, if you find yourself responding positively or negatively to a character, you could ask yourself whether this response has anything to do with your

- psychological makeup,
- political beliefs,
- gender or sexual orientation,
- race,
- social class,
- religion, or
- geographic region.

Thinking along these lines can help you decide how to focus your paper and prepare you for using one or more critical approaches (see 42c) as the basis for your interpretation.

(3) After choosing a topic, you need to develop it.

If you are choosing your own topic, your first step should be to reflect on your personal response (see 42c) and the way you've decided to narrow and focus the subject. Not only must you begin to shape a thesis, you also need to consider how to convince your readers of the validity of your interpretation and how to use specific evidence from the text to explain and support that interpretation.

For these reasons, you want to choose a topic that interests you and your readers. Apply strategies of development, singly or in combination (see 32e). You might define why you consider a character heroic, classify a play as a comedy of manners, or describe a setting that contributes to a work's meaning. You can even combine two or more development strategies when you have a clear focus.

(4) Rereading a literary work enhances your understanding of it.

A literary work can provoke different responses (see chapter 35) from different readers for different theoretical reasons (42c). Moreover, you can have a significantly different response when rereading a work—even a work you think you understand already. For instance, if you're rereading John Milton's *Paradise Lost* in order to write an essay about it, your response may differ from what you felt and thought while cramming for an exam. Reread any work you are planning to write about—or, at least, reread the passages that impressed you as especially important.

With your tentative thesis in mind, annotate the text a second time for evidence that supports *or* detracts from that thesis. To establish yourself as a credible author (see 38a), present evidence fairly.

(5) Research can reveal the ways other readers have responded to a literary work.

You will undoubtedly anchor your essay on your personal response or interpretation. But if you read literary criticism by others, visit online discussion groups or forums, participate in class discussions, or become active in a book club, you can engage in a dialogue that can enrich your own ideas at the same time as you use and give credit to outside sources (see 37c–d). Although it's tempting to lean heavily on the interpretations of experts, remember that your readers are mainly interested in your interpretation and the ways you use the sometimes conflicting interpretations of others to support your own points. To that end, you need to read critically (see chapter 35) as you formulate your thesis (32c).

Chapters 37, 38, and 39 explain how to conduct research. To locate material on a specific writer or work, consult your library's catalog (see 37d) and *The MLA International Bibliography,* an index of books and articles about literature that is an essential resource for literary studies and that can be consulted in printed volumes or online. (See page 561.)

In addition to having books and articles about specific writers, your school or public library is also likely to have a number of reference books that provide basic information on writers, books, and literary theory. Works such as *Contemporary Authors, The Oxford Companion to English Literature,* and *The Princeton Handbook of Poetic Terms* can be useful when you are beginning your research or when you have encountered terms you need to clarify.

You can also access information for an essay about a literary topic by searching the Web. Scholars and societies interested in specific writers have created Web sites. Many journals devoted to the study of literature also maintain sites that contain articles and other resources. As a general rule, however, a Web-based search should supplement but not replace a search in the *MLA Bibliography.* (See chapters 37 and 38.)

42e | Writing about literature follows certain special conventions.

Writing about literature involves adhering to several conventions.

(1) The first person is typically used.

When you're writing your analysis of a piece of literature, you can use the first-person singular pronoun, *I:*

> Although many critics believe Sethe had no choice other than to kill her daughter, I think she could have . . . .

In this case, you are showing how your opinion differs from a popular one; you are owning your opinion. But in order to own an opinion, belief, or interpretation responsibly, you must support it with specific evidence from the text itself.

(2) The present tense is used in discussions of literary works.

Use the present tense when discussing a literary work, since the author of the work is communicating to the reader at the present time. (See 7b(1).)

> In "A Good Man Is Hard to Find," the grandmother reaches out to touch her killer just before he pulls the trigger.

Similarly, use the present tense when reporting how other writers have interpreted the work you are discussing.

> As Henry Louis Gates demonstrates in his analysis of . . . .

(3) Documentation of sources follows certain formats.

When writing about a work assigned by your instructor, you may not need to give the source and publication information.

However, if you are using an edition or translation that may be different from the one your audience is using, you should indicate this. One way of doing so is to use the MLA format for listing works cited, as explained in section 40a, although in this case your bibliography will consist of only a single work—the one you are discussing. (See the example on page 723.)

You must always indicate specific references whenever you quote a line or passage. Quotations from short stories and novels are identified by page number, quotations from poems are referenced by line number, and references to plays usually give the act, scene, and line numbers (See 16d and 39d(2).)

(4) Authors' names are referred to in standard ways.

Use the full name of the author of a work in your first reference and only the last name in all subsequent references. For instance, refer to "Charles Dickens" or "Willa Cather" the first time, and after that, use "Dickens" or "Cather." Never refer to a female author differently than you do a male author: Use "Robert Browning and Elizabeth Barrett Browning" or "Browning and Barrett Browning" (not "Browning and Mrs. Browning").

42f	Study a student essay as an example of a literary interpretation.

The following student essay, which illustrates a reader-response interpretation (see 42c) of a novel by Tim O'Brien, was submitted in the first semester of a first-year English course on writing about literature. When given the opportunity to choose his own topic for a paper on O'Brien's novel, Josh Otis decided to focus (see 32b(2)) on a specific friendship that illustrates moral concerns.

Josh Otis

Professor Miller

English 199, Section 1

10 May 2002

Friendship in <u>The Things They Carried</u>

In Tim O'Brien's novel <u>The Things They Carried</u>, love blossoms in the death-filled rain forests of Vietnam. Throughout the war, soldiers are expected to remain indifferent, for unless they are indifferent they risk their own lives. Yet the friendship between Kiowa and Tim runs so deep that it can only be described as love. Their relationship shows how a soldier who preserves his morals and ability to feel compassion can help another man survive immersion in death and decadence.

Kiowa is an experienced soldier with a strong sense of self, while Tim (not to be confused with the author) is an inexperienced young man thrust into the war and unsure about whether he will succeed as a soldier. Just after Tim arrives in Vietnam, there is an incident in which the men find a dead farmer in an abandoned village. One by one, the soldiers go up and shake the old man's hand, but Tim refuses. His refusal makes him the object of harassment, but he persists. That night Kiowa approaches him and says, "You did a good thing today. That shaking hands crap, it isn't decent. The guys'll hassle you for a while, especially Jensen--but just keep saying no. Should've done it myself. Takes guts, I know that" (257). Kiowa's sense of what is morally sound and his support of actions in accordance with his beliefs help explain why he and Tim become so close.

Kiowa carries a Bible with him, and perhaps his faith is part of the reason that he is able to behave honorably during a war. Kiowa shares a religious conversation with Henry Dobbins in the chapter titled "Church." As the men are preparing to bivouac in an abandoned pagoda (a Buddhist shrine), Kiowa says, "it's bad news . . . you don't mess with churches" (133). Kiowa is a man at war, killing people, yet he still considers a foreign religious shrine sacred. During the conversation with Henry, Kiowa describes the feeling of escape he gets when he is in a church. "It feels good when you just sit there," he explains, "like you're in a forest and everything is really quiet, except there's this sound you can't hear" (136). These are the types of conversation Kiowa has in The Things They Carried, meaningful ones that deal with moral and religious issues.

When Tim kills a young boy near My Khe and freezes, staring at what he has just done, Kiowa is supportive. This is a traumatic moment for Tim. As he stares at the dead boy, he is confronted with what he has become: a killer. Although it is war, and he is there to kill the enemy, killing wasn't quite real until that moment. As a soldier, Tim has heard all the terms designed to distance men from the reality of what they are doing--"zapped," "wasted." But he fully understands that he has killed someone. It is Kiowa who tries to help him deal with the moral crisis he now faces. Kiowa knew the import of what he was looking at, that the dead boy could easily destroy his friend's moral base. Kiowa tries to comfort Tim as he stares at the boy he has just killed. "Tim, it's a war. The guy wasn't Heidi--he had a weapon, right? It's a tough thing for sure, but you got to cut out that staring" (141). That is the voice of a friend, trying to help Tim deal with what is probably the most traumatic experience of his life. He offers other words, but all had the same end: trying to help a friend he loves make sense of the horror he has just created.

If Kiowa represents the moral center of this novel, then his death represents what can happen to morals in war. Like the morals of some of the men beside whom he fought, Kiowa is also fragile. Kiowa's death is as much an accident as an act of war. A young kid makes a mistake; he turns on a flashlight and marks their position for the enemy. In an instant, Kiowa is dead; the flick of a switch triggers the mortar rounds that kill him. The morals of the soldiers could also be destroyed by small, unintentional acts. Kiowa's body sinking in the mud represents what Vietnam did to the morals of many of these men; they were sucked under all the muck and decay that surrounded them. Once their morals were sucked away, it was a tough fight to pull them back, and sometimes, no matter how hard the men pulled, their morals could not be recovered.

Tim speaks of his loss in the chapter titled "Field Trip." In this chapter, Tim goes back to the field twenty years later to take his friend's moccasins and bury them under the muck in the spot where Kiowa had died so long ago. Tim says, "In a way, maybe, I had gone under with Kiowa, and now after two decades I'd worked my way out" (212). Tim works himself out by facing the battlefield, by being able to face his painful memories instead of burying them with his friend.

Throughout the book, O'Brien creates a combination of anger, grief, and fear so that readers can begin to imagine what American soldiers experienced.

They killed and often died alongside their best friends and yet knew little about them. Most were very young and had not had their morals, faith, or emotions tested to any serious extent, let alone through killing other people and watching their friends die. These experiences created a strong bond between men of very different backgrounds. The bond between Tim and Kiowa was so strong that Tim goes back to the field twenty years later, willingly reliving the horror and death of his past, to take Kiowa his moccasins. As Tim wedges them into the muck, he thinks, "I wanted to tell Kiowa that he'd been a great friend, the very best, but all I could do was slap hands with the water" (212). Yet even that gesture was unable to capture for Tim the combined sense of love and loss he felt for his friend.

It took Vietnam veterans a long time to recover from the war, and it left some with scars that will never heal. In The Things They Carried, Tim O'Brien shows how these veterans were forced to dig long and hard through horror and squalor to make sense of what they had done. But throughout the ordeal they faced in recovering, nothing would help them more than the friendships they had forged in the fields and jungles of Vietnam.

Work Cited

O'Brien, Tim. *The Things They Carried.* New York: Penguin, 1991.

Exercise 2

Based on your reading of Josh Otis's paper on *The Things They Carried*, what personal or political values do you think this writer brought to interpreting that text? Which of the critical approaches to literature did he use as the basis for his interpretation (see 42c)? Write a one- to two-page paper analyzing Otis's interpretation of the novel.

Writing for Business

Because the writing you do in a business situation projects an image of your employer, it must be absolutely clear and correct. Writing in business therefore requires the same attention to audience, purpose, and context as does writing in any other situation.

This chapter will help you

- use email effectively (43a),
- write a business plan (43b),
- produce a professional-looking résumé (43c), and
- compose a letter of application (43d).

43a | Electronic mail (email) offers fast and easy communication.

Electronic mail has become common in the workplace, at school, and for personal communication. Because email messages are easy to create and are delivered very quickly, many people consider them superior to informal notes or letters. In business, email messages have almost entirely replaced paper memos. Email has also become the primary medium for sharing ideas and information, for exchanging documents of all kinds—including writing assignments—and for discussing and negotiating all types of business-related and course-related issues.

(1) Email responds to the rhetorical situation.

Because email's overriding purpose is rapid, concise communication with a specific audience, everything in it should serve that purpose. But the other elements of the rhetorical situation must also be considered. Audience is at least as important as purpose, and exigence influences both purpose and audience (see 32a). The ease and speed of email make it one of the most difficult media for establishing and maintaining tone—an essential consideration for addressing your audience effectively. We often assume that our audience is only the person named in the "To" line, forgetting that email can easily be forwarded to many people. And we too often hit "Send" before we have thought about how the tone of our language will be perceived without facial expressions and tone of voice to modify it.

The basic rhetorical unit of an email message is the screen—not the paragraph or the page. You have only about twenty lines in which to present the address block that automatically comes with the message, any salutation ("Hi, Bill!"), your message, and your signature line(s), so it is important to get to the point as quickly as possible. You can follow your point with a few lines of explanation or argument. The most effective email messages generally contain a single point that is identified in the subject header. If you have two points to make, it may be better to send two messages. Longer messages are appropriate for the various kinds of online communication that are devoted to specialized topics, such as those that occur in academic and professional discussion groups.

Similarly, be aware that white space also contributes to your purpose and your concern for your readers. Adequate white space makes your email message easy to read. Ease of reading will help make your purpose clear, and if the purpose is clear, you are more likely to influence your audience.

Consider the rhetorical situation for an email message, as you would for any document (see 33a(3)): Who is your audience, and what do you hope to accomplish with your message? Conversational style may be acceptable for a casual message to a coworker, but a message to your supervisor about your annual performance review should probably have a more formal style.

 Given the rapidly expanding use of email and the growing concerns about privacy, monitoring, and copyright, you should be aware that the emails you and your instructors or supervisors and other correspondents send through school or workplace accounts are neither private nor secure.

Beyond the Rule

WHO OWNS YOUR EMAIL?

Employers have been vindicated for reading employees' email, and there have been cases in which university legal counsels and administrators "confiscated" the emails of teachers or students when complaints were lodged about such things as grades. You should be sure to check your school's or employer's policy regarding the use of email. For additional information, visit www.harbrace.com.

(2) Attachments can be helpful if used with care.

Email attachments are an easy way to exchange word-processing and other kinds of files with classmates or coworkers. People send files to each other as attachments because doing so is fast and convenient and because email programs don't always preserve the formatting of text that is copied and pasted into a message. An attached document, in contrast, will arrive with paragraph breaks preserved and italics intact. Most email programs make it easy to attach a document (or an image) and send it anywhere in the world. The person receiving the attachment can then work on or respond to the document off line—giving an economical advantage if that recipient has to pay by the hour for Internet access.

When you are sending an attachment outside your company, consider the size of the file. A file created with one of the popular word-processing programs can be large enough to clog the mailbox of the person you send it to. Ask a recipient if it's all right to send a file that's larger than 50K and specify the size of the file you want to send. If necessary, break the attachment into smaller units.

You may sometimes encounter problems with attachments, for example, where you send one to someone whose software is not compatible with yours. This problem can be avoided, however, by saving the document in *rich text format* (.rtf), which preserves most formatting and is recognized by most word-processing programs.

Attachments are notorious for transmitting computer viruses. You should never open an attachment from someone you do not know. Malicious viruses are often carried in messages that appear to offer sexy pictures, love notes or poems, or "fantastic" business deals, but increasingly they accompany messages that appear normal and safe. Your best protection is to get a reliable antivirus program and keep it up to date. You can also visit Web sites such as www.symantec.com for information and updates on viruses.

Always log off after using your email account from a public location such as a university computer lab or library. You can be held liable for repairing any damage that may be caused by an unscrupulous person who gets access to your account.

Exercise 1

Analyze the rhetorical situation—intended and likely audiences, purpose, and exigence—for an email you have received. Then, analyze the rhetorical situation for an email you are sending.

43b | A business plan follows a predetermined format.

A number of widely accepted formats prescribe how business documents should look. (Visit www.harbrace.com for examples.) Although the company you work for is likely to have its own formats and style, the kind of document you are producing dictates how you handle the content. Business plans, for instance, have three main purposes: (1) to evaluate risks as well as benefits, (2) to reassure lenders and potential investors, and (3) to help the new business stay on track during its early development. The business plan Roxanne Kirkwood prepared for her advanced management class has the typical elements of any business plan. Because her plan was a course assignment, she was not required to include her personal worth in the financial data or to supply the supporting documents that would be important elements of an actual plan.

ELEMENTS OF A BUSINESS PLAN

- Cover page, including the name and address of the business
- Title page
- Table of contents
- Executive summary, a brief statement of the objectives of the business plan and a brief description of the business
- Description of the business
- Business location, including lease or sale terms and neighborhood features
- Licenses and permits
- Management, including information about managers' experience and education, the organizational structure, proposed wages, and so on
- Personnel
- Insurance
- Market, including size and potential growth, typical customers, and how the business will attract customers
- Competition
- Financial data, including a current balance sheet and income statement and projected (or actual) income statements
- Supporting documents, such as résumés, financial statements, and letters of reference for the owner(s) and letters of intent from suppliers, leases, contracts, and deeds

Roxy's   1

ROXY'S COFFEE SHOP

1819 S. University Avenue

Little Rock, AR 72204

May 25, 2002

The cover
page
contains the
business
name and
address and
the date.

Roxy's   2

Table of Contents

The table
of contents
helps
readers find
information
easily.

Executive Summary

Roxy's Coffee Shop will provide a desirable service for University of Arkansas at Little Rock (UALR) students, staff, and faculty, as well as for area residents. The purpose of this business plan is to secure financial backing for Roxy's for the first year. Roxanne Kirkwood will be the sole proprietor of the business and will be the general manager. She will hire an experienced coffee shop manager to oversee the actual operation of the business.

Students, staff, and faculty at UALR have requested an establishment like Roxy's for many years, since nothing like it exists close to the campus. The UALR campus is located in an ideal location for a coffee shop like Roxy's. It is near a main shopping area for the city and several working-class neighborhoods which are being revitalized. There is also a major hospital a block away on University Avenue. Roxanne Kirkwood is asking for a loan of $60,000 to open the shop and help with operating expenses until it makes a profit. The loan will be repaid in monthly installments beginning in the first month of the second year of business and will be secured using the borrower's home as collateral. Roxy's Coffee Shop will offer a useful, desirable service to a university community that continues to grow as well as to a revitalized neighborhood that has the potential for providing more consumers.

Roxy's   4

Roxy's will offer a somewhat limited menu. Focusing on coffee as the main sale item will allow for the greatest amount of profit. Serving a few other high-demand hot and cold drinks as well as some desserts will support the main focus on coffee. The shop will be intentionally kept small to provide the best service with the lowest prices while offering excellent quality. The research carried out for this proposal shows that Roxy's has an ideal location, is practically planned, and offers a product that is in demand.

Description of Business

This section describes the business in detail.

Roxy's will be a small, independently owned coffee shop serving regular and specialty coffee. Although juice, smoothies, hot chocolate, tea, bottled water, carbonated beverages, fruit, and desserts such as pie, cake, cookies and brownies will also be served, premium quality, free trade coffee will be marketed at a reasonable price as the primary menu item. Although Little Rock has a number of coffee shops, none are easily accessible from the UALR campus.

Roxy's primary market will be UALR students, faculty, and staff, since the restaurants on campus all close by 7:00 in the evening and the campus coffee kiosk closes at 2:00 in the afternoon. People who live close to the campus in the surrounding neighborhoods will form a secondary market.

Roxy's   5

These people will benefit from having a place nearby to enjoy coffee. In addition, Roxy's will appeal to shoppers and businesspeople frequenting the nearby malls and businesses. Situated on University Avenue, Roxy's will have an ideal location on a main thoroughfare going through the center of UALR campus, so it is convenient for morning commuter traffic.

Once financial backing for the company has been secured, all suppliers are willing to begin delivery. Restaurant supplies will be obtained through AbestKitchen.com, and a merchant account will be provided by Redwood Internet.

Business Location

This section gives details about the location of the business.

Roxy's will be located at 1819 S. University Avenue, a main thoroughfare in Little Rock. This location is one block from the main campus on University, near Highway 630, which runs through the heart of Little Rock. This location is ideal because UALR students, staff, and faculty can walk to the coffee shop from campus. In addition, tourists and businesspeople can find the location easily and park without trouble. Roxy's will be open most of the hours that the UALR library is open.

The 250-square-foot space will be leased for one year at $2,500 a month, with the option to renew and renegotiate terms at the end of that time. No walls will be moved, and electrical service and plumbing lines are to be used as is. Renovations

Roxy's 6

will involve only surface changes such as wall treatments, decorations, and furniture. The estimated cost for these changes, as noted in the financial data section of this business plan, is projected to be $5,000. Although the rent may seem high, the location of the building—only a couple of blocks from a major intersection in Little Rock offering access to traffic and potential customers—makes the cost worthwhile. It is a freestanding building located directly on the street and has a private parking lot. The building is convenient not only for UALR students, staff, and faculty, but also for shoppers from the two major malls in Little Rock as well as for staff and visitors from a major hospital located on University Avenue. On either side of University Avenue are neighborhoods consisting of mostly working-class homes. Owners are struggling to rejuvenate these neighborhoods and keep them from being overtaken by commercial and business properties. Homeowners, attempting to keep a neighborhood feel, should welcome a local spot such as Roxy's as a place to meet socially.

Licenses and Permits

All necessary licenses and permits will be obtained. The State of Arkansas leaves most decisions up to the county in which the business is located. The Little Rock Small Business Administration is gathering information on licenses and permits.

This section covers the responsibilities and compensation for the managers.

Management

Roxy's general manager will be Roxanne Kirkwood, and a business manager will be hired to assist with business operation and marketing. The general manager will work 40 hours a week for an annual salary of $30,000. The general manager will alternate day and night shifts with the business manager Monday through Friday. The business manager will work 40 hours a week for an annual salary of $25,000. Salaries will increase only when the business becomes clearly profitable.

This section summarizes personnel requirements.

Personnel

Other than the managers, Roxy's will hire two part-time employees who will work 15 hours per week at $8.00 an hour. These employees will be responsible for the shop 16 hours on Saturdays and 14 hours on Sundays, including getting ready to open and cleaning up before closing. Managers will be on call.

This section notes the extent of insurance coverage for the business.

Insurance

Roxy's will have the standard liability and property insurance. Although exact numbers are still being negotiated, costs are estimated at $100 per month. Roxy's main insurance needs include liability coverage for any accident on the property affecting customers or employees and coverage for property losses resulting from fire, theft, or vandalism. The business will not provide health insurance for employees.

Roxy's 8

The Market

Roxy's target market is UALR students, staff, and faculty. Although the campus has on-site food vendors, including a coffee vendor, these vendors close early. A large portion of UALR's student body attends night classes, which begin long after the coffee vendor's closing time of 2:00 in the afternoon. Many of these students visit the library, which is open until 11:00 on weeknights. In addition, a large neighborhood surrounds the campus, and a main street borders the campus, moving a large amount of traffic right past Roxy's. Because of Roxy's location near the intersection of 630 and University, the ability to attract shoppers, tourists, and hospital staff and visitors is guaranteed.

This section identifies the market for the proposed business.

Competition

Little Rock has not yet been inundated with coffee shops as many American cities have. There is one chain, Coffey Beanery, which has a stand in one mall and one shop halfway across town in West Little Rock, off Chenal. There are no Starbucks and only a few independently owned establishments. The other independently owned shops are located in neighborhoods nowhere near UALR or University Avenue.

This section identifies the competition for the proposed business.

A table
summarizes
the projected
financial
data for the
first year of
operation.

Financial Data

Table 1

Estimated Expenses for First Year of Operation

Expense	Startup only	Monthly	Yearly
Equipment including crockery	X		$15,000
Furniture, fixtures and remodeling	X		10,000
Inventory including coffee beans and food		$2,000	24,000
Rent		2,500	30,000
Insurance		100	1,200
Advertising	$800	100	2,000
Utilities		1,000	12,000
Licenses and permits			500
Miscellaneous		200	2,400
General manager			30,000
Business manager		2,083.33	25,000
Part-time employees		960	11,520
Total needed for first year		$11,443.33	$163,620
Total needed for startup costs		$80,000	(approximately 3 months operating costs, plus a small emergency reserve)
Total supplied by borrower		$20,000	
Total supplied by lender		$60,000	

43c | Persuasive, professional-looking résumés command attention.

A résumé lists your qualifications for a job and is enclosed with a letter of application. The résumé highlights your experience and abilities and should include

- personal data (name, mailing address, telephone number, email address, and fax number, if available),
- educational background, and
- work experience.

Like a letter of application (see 43d), a résumé is an argument (chapter 36) designed to present your qualifications for a job in the best light and get you an interview. Writing a résumé requires planning and paying attention to detail. First, make a list of the jobs you have had, the activities and clubs you have participated in, and the offices you have held. Amplify these items by adding dates, job titles, and responsibilities. Omit tangential information such as a list of hobbies.

A résumé can be organized in a number of ways. One approach is to list experience and activities in reverse chronological order, so that your most recent experience comes first. This format works well if you have a steady job history and if you want to emphasize your most recent experience. If less recent experience is more directly relevant to the job for which you are applying, you can emphasize it by giving your work history chronologically. An alternative way to organize a résumé is to list experience in terms of job skills rather than jobs held. This format, called an **emphatic résumé,** is especially useful when your work history is modest or you are applying for a position in a field in which you have skills but limited experience.

An unprofessional-looking résumé is likely to be overlooked now that computers make effective presentation so easy. Your résumé is, in effect, going to someone's office for a job interview. It is usually best to design the résumé to fit on a single page. Use

Emphatic résumé

Karen Tran
10363 East 10th Avenue
Little Rock, AR 72204
(501) 328-6974
ktran@hotmail.com

Personal data

CAREER OBJECTIVE:

A full-time management position specializing in food and beverage services.

Pertinent skills

MANAGEMENT SKILLS:

Familiarity with all contemporary models of effective management; good writing and communication skills; experience with planning and evaluating food service operations; experience with operating a coffee shop.

Relevant work experience

EXPERIENCE IN FOOD SERVICE:

Assisted in the transfer of data on development of new restaurant locations for a major restaurant development firm; developed and provided customer service information to employees; worked for three years in food service.

Brief summary

ADDITIONAL EXPERIENCE:

Worked with students, parents, and faculty at Western Ozark University as an information specialist; helped edit the yearbook; gave campus tours.

Degree and major

EDUCATION:

Western Ozark University, B.S. with honors, 2002; majored in Business Administration with an emphasis in Management; minor in Nutrition; Phi Beta Kappa.

EXTRACURRICULAR:

Active in Management Club and yearbook.

List if relevant

References available on request.

good-quality paper (preferably white or off-white) and a laser printer. Boldface type or even a different font can emphasize headings, but keep the design simple.

 Software programs that allow you to select the kind of résumé you need and then provide prompts for completing the different sections of it can be helpful. When using a computer to write your résumé, you can also view the document in its entirety on screen and redesign it if necessary.

Beyond the Rule

THE APPLICATION PACKAGE

An application package consists of a résumé and a letter of application. Both of these documents are important tools for any job search. To see a sample chronological résumé and get further information on application letters, résumés, and interviews, visit <u>www.harbrace.com</u>.

TIPS FOR RÉSUMÉ WRITING

- Make sure to include your name, address, telephone number, and an email address or fax number, if available.
- Identify your career objective simply, without elaborating on future goals. Reserve details about your plans until asked about them during an interview (and even then make sure they enhance your appeal as a candidate). Try to match your qualifications to the employer's needs.

- Mention your college or university degree and any pertinent areas in which you have had special training.

- Do not include personal data such as age and marital status.

- Even if an advertisement asks you to state a salary requirement, any mention of salary should usually be deferred until an interview.

- Whenever possible, establish a clear relationship between jobs you have had and the job you are seeking.

- The names and addresses of references are not usually listed on a résumé. Job candidates are advised to take a list of references to interviews. If there is some reason for including the names and addresses of references, provide their phone numbers and/or email addresses. List people who have agreed to speak or write on your behalf. Make sure that these individuals understand the nature of the position you are seeking.

- To show that you are well organized and thoughtful, use a clean, clear format.

- Make sure to proofread the résumé carefully.

Exercise 2

Prepare a résumé for a job that interests you.

43d Letters of application make first impressions.

Your letter of application gives a prospective employer a first impression of you. This letter usually accompanies a résumé (see 43c), and it should do more than simply repeat information that can be found there. Your letter of application provides you with the chance to sound articulate, interesting, and professional. Make the most of it.

Model letter of application

Return address and date

10363 East 10th Avenue
Little Rock, AR 72204
April 19, 2003

Ms. Roxanne Kirkwood
Roxy's Coffee Shop
1819 S. University Avenue
Little Rock, AR 72204

Inside recipient's address

Dear Ms. Kirkwood:

Salutation

    I am writing to apply for the position of Business Manager of Roxy's Coffee Shop advertised in this morning's *Arkansas Democrat-Gazette*. My education and experience are well suited to this position, and I'd welcome the chance to work full-time at making a new business successful.

    As you can see from my résumé, I majored in Business Administration with an emphasis in management; I am continuing my education by pursuing an MBA at UALR. As an assistant in the Admissions Office at Western Ozark University, I worked successfully with students, parents, alumni, and faculty. The position required both a knowledge of university regulations and an understanding of people with different needs.

Body of the letter

    I also benefited from working as an intern last summer for Brinker Enterprises, a firm that has established many different chains of restaurants around the country. This job improved my knowledge of what it takes to make a food service business successful.

    I am very much interested in putting my training to use at Roxy's because it is close to school and I can draw upon skills I already have. The location makes it possible for me to fulfill two objectives at the same time. I hope that we can schedule an interview sometime during the next few weeks. I will be here in Little Rock except for the week of May 7, but I will be checking my phone and email messages daily when I am out of town, and you should have no difficulty reaching me.

Sincerely,

Karen Tran

Karen Tran

Complimentary close

Signature
Typed name
Enclosure

enc.

Address your letter to a specific person. If you are responding to an advertisement that mentions a department without giving a name, call the company and get the name of the person who will be doing the screening. In your opening paragraph, identify the position you are applying for, explain how you learned about it, and—in a single sentence—state why you believe you are qualified to fill it. In the paragraphs that follow, describe the experience and abilities that qualify you for the job. If your experience is extensive, establish that fact and then focus on how you excelled in one or two specific situations. Try to keep your letter of application to one page or two (see chapter 21). Mention that you are enclosing a résumé, but do not summarize it. Your goal is to get a busy person, who will not want to read the same information twice, to look at your résumé.

You can show that you are a serious candidate by indicating why you are interested in the company or organization and demonstrating that you already know something about it. You can find information in annual company reports or by searching LexisNexis (see page 561) or the Web.

In your closing paragraph, offer any additional useful information, and make a specific request for an interview. Be sure to tell your reader how and where you can be reached. Indicate that you would enjoy the opportunity to exchange information.

Beyond the Rule

WRITING ON THE JOB

It is likely that you will do most of your own writing on the job, and you will always be responsible for anything that is sent from your office with your signature on it. You will need to pay particular attention to audience and purpose (see 32a) as well as to conciseness (chapter 21), correctness, and format. For further information, visit www.harbrace.com.

GLOSSARY OF USAGE

The term *usage* refers to the ways words are used in specific contexts. As you know from speaking and writing every day, the words you choose depend on your audience and your purpose. For example, you might use *guys* when you are at lunch with your friends but choose *people, classmates, employees,* or another more formal or precise word when you are writing a report. By learning about usage in this glossary, you will increase your ability to use words effectively. Many of the entries are context-specific; others distinguish between words that sound or look similar. Frequently confused words are defined in terms of their meanings (see the entry for *cite*) or their parts of speech (see the entry for *advice*).

The definitions and guidelines in this glossary will help you write clear and precise prose. Nonetheless, you should be aware that usage judgments may mask misunderstanding and prejudice. The idea of a standard potentially carries with it the assumption that any word not considered standard is inferior. Words labeled *nonstandard* are commonly condemned, even though they may be words some people have grown up hearing and using. A better way to discuss usage is to label what is conventional, or accepted practice, for a specific context. Thus, words commonly used in one context may not be appropriate in another. The words you use with your friends, for instance, likely differ from those you choose for a letter of application. This glossary uses the following labels to characterize usage.

Conventional	Words or phrases listed in dictionaries without special usage labels; generally considered appropriate in academic and professional writing.
Conversational	Words or phrases that dictionaries label *informal, slang,* or *colloquial*; although often used in informal speech and writing,

	not generally appropriate for formal writing assignments.
Unconventional	Words or phrases not generally considered appropriate in academic or professional writing and often labeled *nonstandard* in dictionaries; best avoided in formal contexts.

Because usage changes over time, attempts to redefine words are made every few years. However, agreement on usage occurs slowly, often after a period of debate. In this glossary, entries are marked ＊ when new usages have been reported by dictionary editors but may not yet be accepted by everyone. To choose between traditional and recent usage rules, you must consider your audience and your purpose (see 32a).

Beyond the Rule

ESTABLISHING USAGE RULES

To learn how usage definitions and rules are established, visit www.harbrace.com.

Grammar checkers may identify some common usage errors (such as *its* instead of *it's*), but they will not find more subtle problems. Grammar checkers also rarely distinguish between words that are spelled similarly but have different meanings. For example, a grammar checker found nothing wrong with the following sentence, even though *capitol* is used incorrectly: *The capitol of Minnesota is St. Paul.* Grammar checkers can help you with some usage problems, but you should never rely on them. See Using a Grammar Checker on page 2.

a, an Use *a* before a consonant sound: **a** house, **a** U-turn, **a** one-term president. Use *an* before a vowel sound: **an** egg, **an** M.D., **an** hour. For the differences between *a* or *an* and *the*, see **22a**.

a lot of *A lot of* is conversational for *many, much,* or *a great deal of:* They do not have ~~a lot of~~ much time. *A lot* is sometimes misspelled as *alot*.

a while, awhile *A while* means "a period of time." It is often used with the prepositions *after, for,* and *in:* We rested for **a while.** *Awhile* means "a short time." It is not used after a preposition: We rested **awhile.**

accept, except The verb *accept* means "to receive": I **accept** your apology. The verb *except* means "to exclude": The policy was to have everyone wait in line, but mothers and small children were **excepted.** The preposition *except* means "other than": All **except** Joe will attend the conference.

adapt, adopt *Adapt* means "to adjust" or "to change for a purpose": We will **adapt** to the new conditions. The author will **adapt** his short story for television. *Adopt* means "to take as one's own": The company will **adopt** a new policy.

adverse, averse *Adverse* means "unfavorable": That policy will have **adverse** effects. Usually followed by *to, averse* means "reluctant" or "opposed": I am not **averse** to making a few changes.

advice, advise *Advice* is a noun: They asked their attorney for **advice.** *Advise* is a verb: The attorney **advised** us to save all relevant documents.

affect, effect *Affect* is a verb that means "to influence" or "to touch the emotions": The lobbyist's pleas did not **affect** the politician's decision. The news of the accident deeply **affected** us. The noun *effect* means "a result": The **effect** of his decision on the staff's morale was positive and long lasting. When used as a verb, *effect* means "to produce" or "to cause": The activists believed that they could **effect** real political change.

* **aggravate** *Aggravate* means "to intensify or make worse": Lack of union representation **aggravated** the workers' discontent. Traditionally, *aggravate* was not synonymous with *annoy* or *irritate:* They

were **aggravated** annoyed by the new stringent regulations. Current dictionaries consider this usage standard but conversational.

agree on, agree to, agree with *Agree on* means "to be in accord with others about something": We **agreed on** a date for the conference. *Agree to* means "to accept something" or "to consent to do something": The customer **agreed to** our terms. The negotiators **agreed to** conclude talks by midnight. *Agree with* means "to share an opinion with someone" or "to approve of something": I **agree with** you on this issue. No one **agreed with** his position.

ain't Unconventional unless used in dialogue or for humorous effect.

all The indefinite pronoun *all* is plural when it refers to people or things that can be counted: **All** were present. It is singular when it refers to things that cannot be counted: **All** is forgiven.

all ready, already *All ready* means "completely prepared": The rooms are **all ready** for the conference. *Already* means "by or before the time specified": She has **already** taken her final exams.

* **all right** *All right* means "acceptable." The students asked whether it was **all right** to use dictionaries during the exam. *Alright* is not yet a generally accepted spelling of *all right,* although it is becoming more common in journalistic writing.

all together, altogether *All together* means "as a group": The cast reviewed the script **all together.** *Altogether* means "wholly, thoroughly": That game is **altogether** too difficult.

allude, elude *Allude* means "to refer to indirectly": The professor **alluded** to a medieval text. *Elude* means "to evade" or "to escape from": For the moment his name **eludes** me.

allusion, illusion An *allusion* is a casual or indirect reference: The **allusion** was to Shakespeare's *Twelfth Night.* An *illusion* is a false idea or an unreal image: His idea of college is an **illusion.**

alot See **a lot of.**

already See **all ready, already.**

alright See **all right.**

altogether See **all together, altogether.**

a.m., p.m. (A.M., P.M.; A.M., P.M.) Use these abbreviations only with figures: The show will begin at 7:00 **p.m.** [COMPARE The show will begin at *seven in the evening*]

* **among, between** To follow traditional usage, use *among* with three or more entities (a group): The snorklers swam **among** the fish. Use *between* when referring to only two entities: The rivalry **between** the two teams is intense. Current dictionaries also note the possibility of using *between* to refer to more than two entities, especially when these entities are considered distinct: We have strengthened the lines of communication **between** the various departments.

amoral, immoral *Amoral* means "neither moral nor immoral" or "not caring about right or wrong": Complaining that U.S. schools are **amoral,** the senator proposed the addition of prayer time. *Immoral* means "not moral": Some philosophers consider war **immoral.**

amount of, number of Use *amount of* before nouns that cannot be counted: The **amount of** rain that fell last year was insufficient. Use *number of* with nouns that can be counted: The **number of** students attending college has increased.

an See **a, an.**

and etc. See **etc.**

and/or This combination denotes three options: one, the other, or both. These options can also be presented separately with *or:* The student's application should be signed by a parent **and/or** a teacher. The student's application should be signed by a parent, a teacher, **or** both.

* **angry at, angry with** Both *at* and *with* are commonly used after *angry,* although according to traditional guidelines, *with* should be used when a person is the cause of the anger: She was **angry with** me because I was late.

another, other, the other *Another* is followed by a singular noun: **another** book. *Other* is followed by a plural noun: **other** books. *The other* is followed by either a singular or a plural noun: **the other book, the other books.**

ante-, anti- *Ante-* is a prefix meaning "before" or "earlier": They waited in the **anteroom.** *Anti-* is a prefix meaning "against": **Anti-war** riots broke out across the country.

* **anxious, eager** *Anxious* means "worried" or "nervous": They are **anxious** about the strike. *Eager* means "keenly interested": They are **eager** to see the strike end. Dictionary editors report ample evidence of *anxious* being used to mean "eager," but this usage is still considered conversational.

anymore, any more *Anymore* meaning "any longer" or "now" most frequently occurs in negative sentences: Sarah doesn't work here **anymore.** Its use in positive sentences is considered conversational; *now* is generally used instead: All he ever does ~~anymore~~ now is watch television. As two words, *any more* appears with *not* to mean "no more": We do not have **any more** time.

anyone, any one *Anyone* means "any person at all": We did not know **anyone.** *Any one* refers to one of a group: **Any one** of the options is better than the current situation.

anyplace, everyplace, someplace According to traditional usage, each of these words should be written as two words (*any place, every place, some place*). Alternatively, *-where* can be used instead of *-place* (*anywhere, everywhere, somewhere*).

anyways, anywheres Unconventional; use *anyway* and *anywhere:* We decided to go **anyways.**

as Conversational when used after such verbs as *know, say,* and *see.* Use *that, if,* or *whether* instead: I do not know ~~as~~ whether my application is complete. Also considered conversational is the use of *as* instead of *who, which,* or *that:* Many of the performers ~~as~~ who have appeared on our program will be giving a concert this evening.

as, because The use of *as* to signal a cause may be vague; if it is, use *because* instead: ~~As~~ Because we were running out of water, we decided to turn around.

* **as, like** According to traditional usage, *as* begins either a phrase or a clause; *like* begins only a phrase: My brother drives too fast, just ~~like~~ as my father did. Current dictionaries note the informal use of *like* to begin clauses, especially after verbs such as *look, feel,* and *sound.*

* **as to** Traditionally, *as to* was considered imprecise. We were certain **as to** ~~about~~ the time. But current dictionaries recognize this two-word preposition as standard.

assure, ensure, insure *Assure* means "to state with confidence, alleviating any doubt": The flight attendant **assured** us that our flight would arrive on time. *Ensure* and *insure* are usually interchangeable to mean "make certain," but only *insure* means "to protect against loss": The editor **ensured** [OR **insured**] that the reporter's facts were accurate. Physicians must **insure** themselves against malpractice suits.

at this point in time Wordy for "at this time," "at this point," "now," or "then": **At this point in time,** no one had even heard of computers.

averse See **adverse, averse.**

awful, awfully Conversational when used to mean "very."

awhile See **a while, awhile.**

back up, backup Besides "to move in a reverse direction," the verb *back up* means "to make an archival copy of work on a computer": Did you remember to **back up** your files? *Backup* is a noun that refers to such a copy: I forgot to make a **backup** of that file.

bad Unconventional as an adverb; use *badly* instead. The team played **badly** yesterday. However, the adjective *bad* can be used after sensory verbs such as *feel, look,* and *smell:* I feel **bad** that I forgot to return your book yesterday. See **4a.**

because *Because* may appear at the beginning of a sentence as long as it begins a dependent clause: **Because** the road was under construction, we had to take a detour. See also **as, because.**

being as, being that Unconventional; use *because* instead. ~~Being as~~ Because the road was closed, traffic was diverted to another route.

* **beside, besides** According to traditional usage, these two words have different meanings. *Beside* means "next to": The president sat **beside** the prime minister. *Besides* means "in addition to" or "other than": She has written many articles **besides** those on political reform. Current dictionaries report that professional writers regularly use *beside* to convey this meaning, as long as there is no risk of ambiguity.

better, had better *Better* is conversational. Use *had better* instead: We ~~better~~ had better finish the report by five o'clock.

between See **among, between.**

biannual, biennial *Biannual* means "twice in one year": An equinox is a **biannual** event. *Biennial* means "every two years": **Biennial** meetings last longer than annual meetings because they do not occur as frequently.

breath, breathe *Breath* is a noun: Take a deep **breath.** *Breathe* is a verb: **Breathe** deeply.

* **bring, take** Both words describe the same action but from different standpoints. *Bring* indicates movement toward the speaker: She **brought** me some flowers. *Take* implies movement away from the speaker: He **took** my overdue books to the library. Dictionaries report that this distinction is frequently blurred, especially when the speaker's standpoint is not relevant: He **brought** [OR **took**] her some flowers.

bunch Conversational to refer to a group: A ~~bunch~~ group of students participated in the experiment.

busted Unconventional. Use *broken* instead: Every day he walked past a ~~busted~~ broken vending machine on his way to class.

but that, but what Conversational after expressions of doubt such as *no doubt* or *did not know.* Use *that* instead: I do not doubt ~~but what~~ that they are correct.

* **can, may** According to traditional definitions, *can* refers to ability, and *may* refers to permission: You **can** [are able to] drive seventy miles an hour, but you **may** not [are not permitted to] exceed the speed limit. Current dictionaries report that in contemporary usage *can* and *may* are used interchangeably to denote possibility or permission, although *may* is used more frequently in formal contexts.

can't hardly, can't scarcely Unconventional. Use *can hardly* or *can scarcely:* The students **can't hardly** wait for summer vacation.

capital, capitol A *capital* is a governing city; it also means "funds." The **capital** of Minnesota is St. Paul. An anonymous donor provided the **capital** for the project. As a modifier, *capital* means "chief" or "principal": This year's election is of **capital** importance. It may also refer to the death penalty: **Capital** punishment is legal in some states. A *capitol* is a statehouse; the *Capitol* is the U.S. congressional building in Washington, D.C.

censor, censure, sensor As a verb, *censor* means "to remove or suppress because of immoral or otherwise objectionable ideas": Do you think a ratings board should **censor** films that have too much sex and violence? As a noun, *censor* refers to a person who is authorized to remove material considered objectionable: The **censor** recommended that the book be banned. The verb *censure* means "to blame or criticize"; the noun *censure* is an expression of disapproval or blame. The Senate **censured** Joseph McCarthy. He received a **censure** from the Senate. A *sensor* is a device that responds to a stimulus: The **sensor** detects changes in light.

center around Conversational for "to center on" or "to revolve around": The discussion **centered ~~around~~ on** the public's response to tax reform initiatives.

chair, chairman, chairperson As gender-neutral terms, *chairperson* and *chair* are preferred to *chairman*. See **19d(1)**.

cite, site, sight *Cite* means "to mention": Be sure to **cite** your sources. *Site* is a location: The president visited the **site** for the new library. As a verb, *site* also means "to situate": The builder **sited** the factory near the freeway. *Sight* means "to see": The crew **sighted** land. *Sight* also refers to a view: What an incredible **sight!**

climactic, climatic *Climactic* refers to a climax, or high point: The actors rehearsed the **climactic** scene. *Climatic* refers to the *climate:* Many environmentalists are worried about the recent **climatic** changes.

coarse, course *Coarse* refers to roughness: The jacket was made of **coarse** linen. *Course* refers to a route: Our **course** to the island was indirect. *Course* may also refer to a plan of study: I want to take a **course** in nutrition.

compare to, compare with *Compare to* means "to regard as similar," and *compare with* means "to examine to discover similarities or differences": She **compared** her mind **to** a dusty attic. The student **compared** the first draft **with** the second.

complement, complementary, compliment, complimentary *Complement* means "to complete" or "to balance": Their personalities **complement** each other. They have **complementary** personalities. *Compliment* means "to express praise": The professor **complimented** the students on their first drafts. Her remarks were **complimentary.** *Complimentary* may also mean "provided free of charge": We received **complimentary** tickets.

* **compose, comprise** *Compose* means "to make up": That collection **is composed** of medieval manuscripts. *Comprise* means "to consist of": The anthology **comprises** many famous essays. Dictionary editors have noted the increasing use of *comprise* to mean "to compose."

conscience, conscious, consciousness *Conscience* means "the sense of right and wrong": He examined his **conscience** before deciding whether to join the protest. *Conscious* means "awake": After an hour, the patient was fully **conscious.** After an hour, the patient regained **consciousness.** *Conscious* may also mean "aware": We were **conscious** of the possible consequences.

* **consensus of opinion** According to traditional usage, *of opinion* is redundant: The consensus ~~of opinion~~ was that binge drinking was adversely affecting nondrinkers as well. However, dictionary editors have questioned whether *consensus of opinion* is indeed redundant because there may also be a consensus of values or a consensus of practice.

consequently, subsequently *Consequently* means "as a result of": The surgeon made a serious mistake; **consequently,** both he and the hospital were being sued. *Subsequently* means "following": The negotiators met for several days and **subsequently** signed the treaty.

* **contact** Traditionally, this word was considered imprecise in academic writing for *telephone, see, write,* and other similar verbs: In case of an emergency, whom should we ~~contact~~ call? *Contact* is now often used to mean "communicate with."

continual, continually, continuous, continuously *Continual* means "constantly recurring": **Continual** interruptions kept us from completing the project. Telephone calls **continually** interrupted us. *Continuous* means "uninterrupted": The job applicant had a record of ten years' **continuous** employment. The job applicant worked **continuously** from 1992 to 2002.

* **convince, persuade** *Convince* means "to make someone believe something": His passionate speech **convinced** us that school reform was necessary. *Persuade* means "to motivate someone to act": She **persuaded** us to stop smoking. Dictionary editors note that many speakers now use *convince* as a synonym for *persuade.*

could care less Unconventional to express complete lack of concern. *Couldn't care less* is used in informal contexts.

could of See **of.**

council, counsel A *council* is an advisory or decision-making group: The student **council** supported the new safety regulations. A *counsel* is a legal adviser: The defense **counsel** conferred with the judge. As a verb, *counsel* means "to give advice": The new psychologist **counsels** people with eating disorders.

criteria, criterion *Criteria* is a plural noun meaning "a set of standards for judgment": The teachers explained the **criteria** for the assignment. The singular form is *criterion:* Their judgment was based on only one **criterion.**

* **data** *Data* is the plural form of *datum,* which means "piece of information" or "fact": When the **data are** complete, we will know the true cost. However, current dictionaries also note that *data* is frequently used as a mass entity (like the word *furniture*), appearing with a singular verb.

desert, dessert *Desert* can mean "a barren land": Gila monsters live in the **deserts** of the Southwest. When the second part of this word is stressed, *desert* refers to what is deserved; its plural form is frequently used: The villains received their just **deserts.** As a verb, *desert* means "to leave": I thought my friends had **deserted** me. *Dessert* refers to something sweet eaten at the end of a meal: They ordered apple pie for **dessert.**

device, devise *Device* is a noun: She invented a **device** that measures extremely small quantitites of liquid. *Devise* is a verb: We **devised** a plan that distributed the work equally.

dialogue Many readers consider the use of *dialogue* as a verb to be an example of unnecessary jargon. Use *discuss* or *exchange views* instead:

The committee chair and several community members ~~dialogued about~~ discussed the issues.

differ from, differ with *Differ from* means "to be different": A bull snake **differs from** a rattlesnake in a number of ways. *Differ with* means "to disagree": Senator Brown has **differed with** Senator Owen on several issues.

different from, different than *Different from* is generally used with nouns, pronouns, noun phrases, and noun clauses: This school was **different from** most others. The school was **different from** what we had expected. *Different than* is used with adverbial clauses; *than* is the conjunction: We are no **different than** they are.

discreet, discrete, discretion *Discreet* means "showing good judgment or self-restraint": His friends complained openly, but his comments were quite **discreet.** *Discretion* is related to *discreet:* **Discretion** is the better part of valor. *Discrete* means "distinct": The participants in the study came from three **discrete** groups.

disinterested, uninterested *Disinterested* means "impartial": A **disinterested** observer will give a fair opinion. *Uninterested* means "lacking interest": She sleepily acknowledged that she was **uninterested** in the outcome of the game.

distinct, distinctive *Distinct* means "easily distinguishable or perceived": Each proposal has **distinct** advantages. *Distinctive* means "characteristic" or "serving to distinguish": We studied the **distinctive** features of hawks.

don't Use *doesn't* instead of *don't* with *he, she,* and *it:* It ~~don't~~ doesn't make sense.

drug Unconventional; use *dragged* instead of *drug:* The settlers must have ~~drug~~ dragged these large stones from the river.

* **due to** Traditionally, *due to* was not synonymous with *because of:* ~~Due to~~ Because of holiday traffic, we arrived an hour late. However, dictionary editors now consider this usage of *due to* acceptable, noting that it is widespread.

dyeing, dying *Dyeing* comes from *dye,* meaning "to color something, usually by soaking it": As a sign of solidarity, the students are **dyeing** their shirts the same color. *Dying* refers to the loss of life: Because of the drought, the plants are **dying.**

eager See **anxious, eager.**

effect See **affect, effect.**

e.g. Abbreviation of the Latin phrase *exempli gratia,* meaning "for example." Use only within parentheses: Some herbs are highly aromatic (**e.g.,** rosemary and sage). Otherwise, replace *e.g.* with the English equivalent, *for example* or *for instance:* The nonsmoking campaign has won many battles; ~~e.g.~~ **for example,** few airlines allow smoking on their aircraft. Do not confuse *e.g.* with *i.e.,* meaning "that is."

elicit, illicit *Elicit* means "to draw forth": He is **eliciting** contributions for a new playground. *Illicit* means "unlawful": The newspaper reported their **illicit** mishandling of public funds.

elude See **allude, elude.**

emigrate from, immigrate to To *emigrate* is to leave one's own country: My ancestors **emigrated from** Ireland. To *immigrate* is to arrive in a different country to settle: The Ulster Scots **immigrated to** the southern United States.

eminent, imminent *Eminent* means "distinguished": An **eminent** scholar in physics will be giving a public lecture tomorrow. *Imminent* means "about to happen": The merger of the two companies is **imminent.**

ensure See **assure, ensure, insure.**

enthused Conversational. Use *enthusiastic* instead. Most students are ~~enthused~~ **enthusiastic** about the construction of a new student union.

especially, specially *Especially* emphasizes a characteristic or quality: Some people are **especially** sensitive to the sun. *Especially* also means "particularly": Wildflowers are abundant in this area, **especially** during April and May. *Specially* means "for a particular purpose" or "specifically": The classroom was **specially** designed for music students.

-ess This suffix has sexist connotations. Use *poet, author, actor,* and *waiter* or *server* instead of *poetess, authoress, actress,* and *waitress.* See **19d(1)**

etc. Abbreviation of the Latin phrase *et cetera,* meaning "and others of the same kind." Use only within parentheses: Be sure to bring appropriate camping gear (tent, sleeping bag, mess kit, **etc.**). Because *and* is part of the meaning of *etc.,* avoid using *and* with *etc.:* Many special events take place during orientation, including barbecues, games, and concerts~~, etc.~~

eventually, ultimately *Eventually* refers to some future time: She has made so many valuable contributions that I am sure she will **eventually** become the store supervisor. *Ultimately* refers to the final outcome after a series of events: The course was difficult but **ultimately** worthwhile.

everyday, every day *Everyday* means "routine" or "ordinary": These are **everyday** problems. *Every day* means "each day": I read the newspaper **every day.**

everyone, every one *Everyone* means "all": **Everyone** should attend. *Every one* refers to each person or item in a group: **Every one** of you should attend.

everyplace See **anyplace, everyplace, someplace.**

except See **accept, except.**

expect Conversational; use *think* or *believe* instead: I ~~expect~~ believe the answer is clear.

explicit, implicit *Explicit* means "expressed clearly and directly": Given his **explicit** directions, we knew how to proceed. *Implicit* means "implied or expressed indirectly": I mistakenly understood his silence to be his **implicit** approval of the project.

farther, further Generally, *farther* refers to geographic distance: We will have to drive **farther** tomorrow. *Further* refers to additional time or some other abstract noun: If you need **further** assistance, please let me know.

* **feel** Traditionally, *feel* was not synonymous with "think" or "believe": I ~~feel~~ think that more should be done to protect local habitat. Dictionary editors now consider such a use of *feel* to be a standard alternative.

female, male *Woman, man, girl,* and *boy* are the conventional words used to refer to gender. I interviewed two ~~females~~ women and three ~~males~~ men in my class. According to APA guidelines, *female* and *male* may be used when the age range within a group is broad: Most of the groups consisted of five **males** and five **females.** In addition, *male* and *female* may be used as modifiers when information about gender is relevant.

fewer, less *Fewer* occurs before nouns that can be counted: **fewer** technicians, **fewer** pencils. *Less* occurs before nouns that cannot be counted or before abstract nouns: **less** milk, **less** support. *Less than* may be used with measurements of time or distance: **less than** three months, **less than** twenty miles.

* **first, firstly; second, secondly** Many college instructors prefer the use of *first* and *second*. However, dictionary editors state that *firstly* and *secondly* are also well-established forms.

flunk Given the forcefulness of this term, *fail* is preferred in most contexts. She ~~flunked~~ failed the test by a slim margin.

foreword, forward A *foreword* is a preface: The **foreword** to the book provided useful background information. *Forward* refers to a frontward direction: To get a closer look, we moved **forward** slowly.

former, latter Used together, *former* refers to the first of two; *latter* to the second of two. John and Ian are both English; the **former** is from Manchester, and the **latter** is from Birmingham.

fun Conversational when used as an adjective: The children had **a fun time.**

further See **farther, further.**

get Considered conversational in many common expressions: The weather ~~got better~~ improved overnight. I did not know what he ~~was getting at~~ meant.

go, goes Unconventional for *say(s), respond(s),* and other similar words: My friends say I'm strange, and I **go** reply, "You're right!"

good, well *Good* is an adjective, not an adverb. Use *well* instead: He pitched ~~good~~ well last night. *Good* in the sense of "in good health" may be used interchangeably with *well:* I feel **good** [OR **well**] this morning.

good and Conversational to mean "very" or "quite": They were ~~good and~~ quite angry about the tax increase.

had better See **better, had better.**

had ought to, hadn't ought to Unconventional. Omit *had,* or use *should not:* We **had ought to** apologize. We ~~**hadn't ought to**~~ should not have accused him in public.

a half a, a half an Unconventional; use *half of a/an, half a/an,* or *a half:* You should be able to complete the questionnaire in **a half ~~an~~** hour.

hanged, hung *Hanged* means "to put to death by hanging": The prisoner was **hanged** at dawn. For all other meanings, use *hung:* He **hung** the picture above his desk.

hardly Unconventional when combined with a negative word such as *not.* Depending on the intended meaning, either omit *hardly* or omit the negative word: The drivers could**n't hardly** see the road.

has got, have got Conversational; omit *got:* I **have ~~got~~** a meeting tomorrow.

he Unconventional to refer to people in general or a person whose gender is unknown. Use *he or she.* See **19d(1).**

he/she, his/her As a solution to the problem of sexist language, these combinations are not universally accepted. Consider using *he or she* and *his or her.* See **19d(1).**

herself, himself, myself, yourself Unconventional as subjects in a sentence. Joe and ~~**myself**~~ I will lead the discussion. See **5a(4).**

hisself Unconventional for *himself.*

hopefully Conversational to mean "I hope": ~~**Hopefully,**~~ I hope the game will not be canceled.

hung See **hanged, hung.**

idea, ideal An *idea* is a thought: The writer's main **idea** was stated in the first paragraph. An *ideal* is a model of perfection or a standard: The politician told her audience of her democratic **ideals.**

i.e. Abbreviation of the Latin phrase *id est,* meaning "that is." Use only within parentheses: All participants in the study ran the same distance (**i.e.,** six kilometers). Otherwise, replace *i.e.* with the English equivalent, *that is:* Assistance was offered to those who would have difficulty boarding, ~~**i.e.**~~ that is, the elderly, the disabled, and parents with small children. Do not confuse *i.e.* with *e.g.,* meaning "for example."

* **if, whether** Use *if* to mean "in the event that": The ceremony will be held indoors **if** it rains. *Whether* suggests alternatives: She doesn't know **whether** the ceremony will be held outdoors. Dictionary editors report that this usage is changing, noting that the use of *if* to refer to alternatives rarely causes confusion.

illicit See **elicit, illicit.**

illusion See **allusion, illusion.**

immigrate See **emigrate from, immigrate to.**

imminent See **eminent, imminent.**

immoral See **amoral, immoral.**

* **impact** Though it is commonly used as a verb in business writing, many college teachers still use *impact* as a noun only: The new tax ~~impacts~~ affects everyone.

implicit See **explicit, implicit.**

imply, infer *Imply* means "suggest without actually stating": Though he never mentioned the statistics, he **implied** that they were questionable. *Infer* means "draw a conclusion based on evidence": Given the tone of his voice, I **inferred** that he found the work substandard.

incredible, incredulous *Incredible* means "incapable of being believed": The tale of their journey was **incredible.** *Incredulous* means "disbelieving": We responded to the story with **incredulous** smirks.

individual *Individual* is used to distinguish a person from a group: An **individual** is easily influenced by the group. Otherwise, use *person* or *someone:* We notified ~~an individual~~ someone in the payroll office.

ingenious, ingenuous *Ingenious* means "creative or shrewd": This **ingenious** design will provide inexpensive energy. *Ingenuous* means "innocent or unworldly": Though considered **ingenuous** by most of her acquaintances, she understood clearly the causes of injustice.

in regards to Unconventional; see **regard, regarding, regards.**

inside of, outside of Drop *of* when unnecessary: Security guards stood **outside of** the front door. **Inside of** a year, everyone had moved away.

insure See **assure, ensure, insure.**

irregardless Unconventional; use *regardless* instead.

* **is because, is when, is where** Traditionally, only noun clauses followed the verb *be*. Clauses beginning with *because, when,* and *where* were thought to be adverbial clauses and were thus not used: The reason the project succeeded was **because** that it had ample funding. An essay test **is when** requires students to write paragraph-long answers. An armature is **where you have** a piece of soft iron connecting the poles of a magnet. Most dictionary editors would object to the examples above but would judge acceptable examples in which the subject and the subject complement are clearly related: Midnight **is when** the bells will ring. See **23d.**

its, it's *Its* indicates possession: The committee forwarded **its** recommendation. *It's* is a contraction of *it is:* **It's** a beautiful day.

-ize Some readers object to using this ending to create new verbs: *enronize.* Some of these new verbs, however, have already entered into common usage: *computerize.*

kind, sort, type When referring to one, use *this* or *that:* **This kind** [OR **sort** OR **type**] of argument is unacceptable. When referring to more than one, use *these* or *those:* **These kinds** [OR **sorts** OR **types**] of arguments are unacceptable.

kind of a, sort of a The word *a* is unnecessary: This **kind of a** book sells well. *Kind of* and *sort of* are not conventionally used to mean "somewhat": The report was **kind of** somewhat difficult to read.

later, latter *Later* means "after a specific time" or "a time after now": The concert ended **later** than we had expected. *Latter* refers to the second of two items: Of the two versions described, I prefer the **latter.**

lay, lie *Lay* (*laid, laying*) means "put" or "place": The public **laid** the blame on the current administration. *Lie* (*lay, lain, lying*) means "rest" or "recline": I had just **lain** down when the alarm went off. *Lay* takes an object (to **lay** something), while *lie* does not. These verbs may be confused because the present tense of *lay* and the past tense of *lie* are spelled the same way.

lead, led As a noun, *lead* means "a kind of metal": The paint had **lead** in it. As a verb, *lead* means "to conduct": The guide will **lead** a tour of the ruins this morning. *Led* is the past tense of the verb *lead:* He **led** the country from 1949 to 1960.

learn Unconventional to mean "teach." My mother ~~learned~~ taught me everything I know about local herbs.

* **leave** Unconventional to mean "let": ~~Leave~~ Let the paint dry overnight. *Let* and *leave* are interchangeable in the expression *let/leave alone,* meaning "to refrain from disturbing."

led See **lead, led.**

less, less than See **fewer, less.**

liable *Liable* generally means "likely" in an undesirable sense: If they invest money in that stock, they are **liable** to lose money. With her brains, she is ~~liable~~ likely to achieve success easily.

lie See **lay, lie.**

like See **as, like.**

literally Conversational when used to emphasize the meaning of another word: I was ~~literally~~ nearly frozen after I finished shoveling the sidewalk. *Literally* is conventionally used to indicate that an expression is not being used figuratively: My friend **literally** climbs the walls after work; his fellow rock climbers join him at the local gym.

* **loan** According to traditional definitions, *lend,* not *loan,* should be used to mean "to give temporarily": My friend will ~~loan~~ lend me her notes. However, dictionary editors report that the use of *loan* to mean "lend" in the financial sense is now considered standard: Banks **loan** money for mortgages.

lose, loose *Lose* is a verb: She does not **lose** her patience often. *Loose* is chiefly used as an adjective: A few of the tiles are **loose.**

lots, lots of Conversational for *many* or *much:* He has ~~lots of~~ many friends. We have ~~lots~~ much to do before the end of the quarter.

male See **female, male.**

mankind Considered sexist because it excludes women: All ~~mankind~~ humanity will benefit from this new discovery.

many, much *Many* is used with nouns that can be counted: **many** stores, too **many** assignments. *Much* is used with nouns that cannot be counted: **much** courage, not **much** time.

may See **can, may.**

may of, might of See **of.**

maybe, may be *Maybe* is an adverb: **Maybe** the negotiators will succeed this time. *May* and *be* are verbs: The rumor **may be** true.

∗ **media, medium** According to traditional definitions, *media* is a plural word: The **media** have sometimes created the news in addition to reporting it. The singular form is *medium:* The newspaper is one **medium** that people seem to trust. Dictionary editors note the frequent use of *media* as a collective noun taking a singular verb, but this usage is still considered conversational.

might could Conversational for "might be able to": The director **might** ~~could~~ be able to review your application next week.

morale, moral *Morale* refers to a mood or spirit: **Morale** was high. *Moral* refers to ethical conduct: The government had a **moral** duty to help the victims. *Moral* may also mean "the lesson of a story": The **moral** of the story is that to live well one must treat others well.

most Unconventional to mean "almost": We watch the news ~~most~~ almost every day.

much See **many, much.**

myself See **herself, himself, myself, yourself.**

neither . . . or Conventionally, *nor,* not *or,* follows *neither:* The book is **neither** as funny ~~or~~ nor as original as critics have reported.

not . . . no/none/nothing The use of multiple negative words is unconventional: I did **not** want ~~nothing~~ anything else. Multiple negation may be used for special effect.

nothing like, nowhere near Unconventional; use *not nearly* instead: Her new book is ~~nowhere near~~ not nearly as mysterious as her previous novel.

nowheres Unconventional; use *nowhere* instead: We met for two hours, but our discussion went **nowheres.**

number of When the expression *a number of* is used, the reference is plural: **A number of** positions **are** open. When *the number of* is used, the reference is singular: **The number of** possibilities **is** limited. Make sure that the verb agrees with the subject. See also **amount of, number of.**

of Often mistaken for the sound of the unstressed *have*: They must ~~of~~ have [OR could **have,** might **have,** may **have,** should **have,** would **have**] gone home.

off of Conversational; omit *of:* He walked **off ~~of~~** the field.

OK, O.K., okay All three are acceptable spellings, but the usage of this expression is considered conversational. Choose a more specific word instead: All the passengers were ~~okay~~ uninjured.

on account of Conversational; use *because* or *because of:* The singer canceled her engagement ~~on account of~~ because of a sore throat.

on the other hand Use *however,* or make sure that the sentence or independent clause beginning with this transitional phrase is preceded by one starting with *on the one hand.*

other See **another, other, the other.**

ought See **had ought to, hadn't ought to.**

owing to the fact that Considered wordy; use *because* instead: ~~Owing to the fact that~~ Because more people came to the concert than were expected, the stage crew set up extra chairs in the aisles.

parameter Often considered an example of unnecessary jargon: We discussed the **parameters** characteristics of cross-cultural conflict.

passed, past *Passed* is the past tense of the verb *pass:* Everyone **passed** the test. *Past* means "beyond a time or location": The band marched **past** the bleachers.

people, persons In academic writing, *people* is preferred to *persons:* The reporter interviewed the **persons** people involved in the accident. *Persons* is occasionally used when emphasis is given to the individuals in a group: The person or **persons** who committed the crime will be prosecuted.

per In ordinary contexts, use *a* or *an:* You should drink eight glasses of water ~~per~~ a day.

percent, percentage *Percent* (also spelled *per cent*) is used with a specific number: **Sixty percent** of the students attended the ceremony. *Percentage* refers to an unspecified portion: The **percentage** of high school graduates attending college has increased in recent years.

perspective, prospective *Perspective* means "point of view": We discussed the issue from various **perspectives.** *Prospective* means "likely to become": **Prospective** elementary teachers visited nearby classrooms last Friday.

persuade See **convince, persuade.**

phenomena Plural of *phenomenon:* Natural **phenomena** were given scientific explanations.

plenty Conversational when used to mean "quite" or "sufficient": It was ~~plenty~~ quite humid the day we left. To mean "an adequate amount," *plenty* is followed by *of:* We have **plenty of** time.

plus *Plus* joins nouns or noun phrases to make a sentence seem like an equation: Her endless curiosity **plus** her boundless energy makes her the perfect camp counselor. Note that a singular form of the verb is required (i.e., *makes*). *Plus* is not used to join clauses: I telephoned ~~plus~~ and I sent flowers.

p.m. (P.M., P.M.) See **a.m., p.m.**

practicable, practical *Practicable* means "able to be put into practice": His plan was too complicated to be **practicable.** *Practical* means "sensible" or "useful": He read a self-help book for some **practical** advice on giving speeches.

precede, proceed To *precede* is to "go ahead of": A moment of silence **preceded** the applause. To *proceed* is to "go forward": After stopping for a short rest, we **proceeded** to our destination.

prejudice, prejudiced *Prejudice* is a noun: They were unaware of their **prejudice.** *Prejudiced* is an adjective: She accused me of being **prejudiced.**

pretty *Pretty* is used to mean "attractive" but not to mean "rather" or "somewhat": We were ~~pretty~~ rather tired after the trek to the summit.

* **previous to, prior to** Traditionally, these words were considered pretentious: ~~Prior to~~ Before our meeting, please study the reports. Dictionary editors now regard them as acceptable.

principal, principle As a noun, *principal* means "chief official": The **principal** greeted the students every day. It also means "capital": The loan's **principal** was still quite high. As an adjective, *principal* means "main": Tourism is the country's **principal** source of income. The noun *principle* refers to a rule, standard, or belief: She explained the three **principles** supporting the theory.

prior to See **previous to, prior to.**

proceed See **precede, proceed.**

prospective See **perspective.**

quotation, quote In academic writing, *quotation,* rather than *quote,* refers to a repeated or copied sentence or passage: She began her speech with a ~~quote~~ quotation from *Othello. Quote* expresses an action: My friend sometimes **quotes** lines from television commercials.

raise, rise *Raise* (*raised, raising*) means "to lift or cause to move upward, to bring up or increase": Retailers **raised** prices. *Rise* (*rose, risen, rising*) means "to get up" or "to ascend": The cost of living **rose** sharply. *Raise* takes an object (*raise* [something]); *rise* does not.

rarely ever Conversational; omit *ever:* He **rarely ever** goes to the library.

real, really *Really* rather than *real* is used to mean "very": He is from a ~~real~~ really small town. To ensure this word's effectiveness, use it sparingly.

reason is because See **is because, is when, is where.**

* **reason why** Traditionally, this combination was considered redundant: No one explained ~~the reason~~ why the negotiations failed. [OR No one explained ~~the reason~~ why the negotiations failed.] However, dictionary editors report its use by highly regarded writers.

regard, regarding, regards These forms are used in the following expressions: *in regard to, with regard to, as regards,* and *regarding* [NOT *in regards to, with regards to,* or *as regarding*].

* **relation, relationship** According to traditional definitions, *relation* is used to link abstractions: We studied the **relation** between language and social change. *Relationship* is used to link people: The **relationship** between the two friends grew strong. However, dictionary editors now label as standard the use of *relationship* to connect abstractions.

respectfully, respectively *Respectfully* means "showing respect": The children learned to treat one another **respectfully.** *Respectively* means "in the order designated": We discussed the issue with the chair, the dean, and the provost, **respectively.**

rise See **raise, rise.**

sensor See **censor, censure, sensor.**

sensual, sensuous *Sensual* refers to gratification of the physical senses, often those associated with sexual pleasure: Frequently found in this music are **sensual** dance rhythms. *Sensuous* refers to gratification of the senses in response to art, music, nature, and so on: **Sensuous** landscape paintings lined the walls of the gallery.

shall, will Traditionally, *shall* was used with *I* or *we* to express future tense, and *will* was used with the other personal pronouns, but *shall* has almost disappeared in contemporary American English. *Shall* is still used in legal writing to indicate an obligation.

should of See **of.**

sight See **cite, site, sight.**

sit, set *Sit* means "to be seated": Jonathon **sat** in the front row. *Set* means "to place something": The research assistant **set** the chemicals on the counter. *Set* takes an object (*set* [something]). *Sit* does not.

site See **cite, site, sight.**

so *So* intensifies another word when it is used with *that:* They were **so** lonely **that** they planned a trip home. Instead of using *so* alone, find a precise modifier: She was ~~so~~ intensely focused on her career.

some Conversational when used to mean "remarkable" or "memorable": She was ~~some~~ a remarkable athlete.

someplace See **anyplace, everyplace, someplace.**

sometime, sometimes, some time *Sometime* means "at an unspecified time": They will meet **sometime** next month. *Sometimes* means "at times": **Sometimes** laws are unfair. *Some time* means "a span of time": They agreed to allow **some time** to pass before voting on the measure.

sort See **kind, sort, type.**

sort of a See **kind of a, sort of a.**

specially See **especially, specially.**

stationary, stationery *Stationary* means "in a fixed position": Traffic was **stationary** for an hour. *Stationery* means "writing paper and envelopes": The director ordered new department **stationery.**

subsequently See **consequently, subsequently.**

supposed to, used to Be sure to include the frequently unsounded *d* at the end of the verb form: We are **supposed** to leave at 9:30 A.M. We **used** to leave earlier.

sure Conversational when used to mean "certainly" or "undoubtedly": That play was **sure** ~~certainly~~ amusing.

sure and Conversational; use *sure to* instead: Be **sure** ~~and~~ to have the oil checked.

take See **bring, take.**

* **than, then** *Than* is used in comparisons: The tape recorder is smaller **than** the radio. *Then* refers to a time sequence: Go straight ahead for three blocks; **then** turn left.

* **that, which** *Which* occurs in nonessential (nonrestrictive) clauses: Myanmar, **which** borders Thailand, was formerly called Burma. Both *that* and *which* occur in essential (restrictive) clauses, although traditionally only *that* was considered acceptable: I am looking for an atlas **that** [OR **which**] includes demographic information. (For more information on essential and nonessential clauses, see 12d and 13d.)

* **that, which, who** In essential (restrictive) clauses, *who* and *that* refer to people. We want to hire someone **who** [OR **that**] has had experience programming. Traditionally, only *who* was used to refer to people. *That*, as well as *which*, refers to things: He proposed a design **that** [OR **which**] will take advantage of solar energy.

their, there, they're *Their* is the possessive form of *they:* They will give **their** presentation tomorrow. *There* refers to location: I lived **there** for six years. *There* is also used as an expletive (see **21a(3)**): **There is no explanation for the phenomenon.** *They're* is a contraction of *they are:* **They're** leaving in the morning.

theirself, theirselves Unconventional; use *themselves.* The students finished the project by **theirself** themselves.

them Unconventional to mean "those" or "these": I need **them** those books for my research.

then See **than, then.**

these kind, these sort, these type, those kind See **kind, sort, type.**

they Unconventional to indicate possession: They built **they** their house near a forest.

this here, that there, these here, them there *Here* and *there* are unconventional in these combinations: **This here** number should be moved to the next column in the table.

thru *Through* is preferred in academic and professional writing: We drove **thru** through the whole state of South Dakota in one day.

thusly Unconventional; use *thus, in this way,* or *as follows* instead: He accompanied his father on archeological digs and **thusly** discovered his interest in ancient cultures.

time period Readers are likely to consider this combination redundant; use one word or the other, but not both: During this **time period,** the economy was strong.

to, too, two *To* is used in the infinitive form of a verb: She wanted **to** become an actress. *To* is also used as a preposition, usually indicating direction: They walked **to** the memorial. *Too* means "also": I voted for her **too.** *Too* also means "excessively": They are **too** busy this year. *Two* is a number: She studied abroad for **two** years.

toward, towards Although both are acceptable, *toward* is preferred in American English.

track, tract *Track* may refer to a mark left by someone or something: Deer **tracks** covered the lawn. *Track* may also refer to a course of action: You are on the right **track.** In addition, *track* may refer to awareness: I lost **track** of the time. *Tract* refers to a large area: They sold a **tract** of land near the river. *Tract* also refers to a short article expressing a strong opinion: His **tract** on radical environmentalism was published in the local paper.

try and Conversational for *try to:* The staff will **try and** to finish the project by Friday.

type See **kind, sort, type.**

ultimately See **eventually, ultimately.**

uninterested See **disinterested, uninterested.**

* **unique** Traditionally, *unique* meant "one of a kind" and thus was not preceded by a qualifier such as *more, most, quite,* or *very:* Her prose style is **quite unique.** However, dictionary editors note that *unique* is also widely used to mean "extraordinary."

usage, use *Use* is generally preferred to *usage* in nontechnical contexts: He designed the furniture for practical **usage use.**

use, utilize In most contexts, *use* is preferred to *utilize:* We **utilized used** a special dye in the experiment. However, *utilize* may suggest an effort to employ something for a purpose: We discussed how to **utilize** the new equipment we had been given.

used to See **supposed to, used to.**

very To ensure this word's effectiveness, use it sparingly. Whenever possible, choose a stronger adjective or adverb: She was **very satisfied delighted** with her new digital camera.

wait for, wait on *Wait for* means "to await": She refused to **wait on for** him. *Wait on* means "to serve": I **waited on** customers for seven years.

waive, wave *Waive* means "to give up": He **waived** his right to speak to an attorney. *Waive* also means "to refrain from enforcing": We **waived** the requirement because of her high recommendations. *Wave* means "to use a hand gesture to signal a person:" The police officer **waved** us on.

ways Conversational when referring to distance; use *way* instead: It's a long **ways way** from home.

weather, whether *Weather* refers to meteorological conditions: According to the **weather** report, it is going to snow today. *Whether* introduces alternatives: We should decide **whether** to respond.

well See **good, well.**

where Conversational for *that:* I saw on TV **where** ~~that~~ she had been elected.

where . . . at, where . . . to Conversational; omit *at* and *to:* **Where** is the library **at? Where** are you moving **to?**

whether See **if, whether.** See also **weather, whether.**

which See **that, which.** See also **that, which, who.**

who See **that, which, who.**

* **who, whom** *Who* is used as the subject or subject complement in a clause: We have decided to hire Marian Wright, **whom** ~~who~~ I believe is currently finishing her degree in business administration. [*Who* is the subject in *who is currently finishing her degree in business administration.*] *Whom* is used as an object: Jeff Kruger, **who** ~~whom~~ we hired in 2001, is now our top sales representative. [*Whom* is the object in *whom we hired.*] Dictionary editors note that in conversation *who* is commonly used as an object as long as it does not follow a preposition. See **5c(2).**

whose, who's *Whose* indicates possession: **Whose** book is this? The book was written by a young Mexican-American woman **whose** family still lives in Chiapas. *Who's* is the contraction of *who is:* **Who's** going to run in the election?

will See **shall, will.**

-wise College teachers may object to the use of this ending to create new words: *computerwise, businesswise.*

with regards to Unconventional; see **regard, regarding, regards.**

would of See **of.**

your, you're *Your* is the possessive of *you:* Let's meet in **your** office. *You're* is a contraction of *you are:* **You're** gaining strength.

yourself See **herself, himself, myself, yourself.**

GLOSSARY OF TERMS

This glossary provides brief definitions of frequently used terms. Consult the index for references to terms not listed here.

@ The "at" sign, used in email addresses to link the user name and the Internet location: <swebb@twu.edu>.

absolute phrase A sentencelike structure containing a subject and its modifiers. Unlike a sentence, an absolute phrase has no verb marked for person, number, or tense: *The ceremony finally over,* the graduates tossed their mortarboards in the air. See **1f(6)**, **12e(4)**, and **30b(4)**.

abstract A summary of the main points of a piece of writing, usually placed at the very beginning of the work. See **40d**.

abstract word A word that expresses a quality, concept, or emotion that cannot be perceived through the senses: *truth, justice, joy, future.* See **20a(3)**. COMPARE **concrete word.**

acronym A word formed by combining the initial letters or syllables of a series of words and pronounced as a word rather than as a series of letters: *OPEC* for *O*rganization of *P*etroleum *E*xporting *C*ountries. See **9a(9)**, **11e**, and **15a(1)**.

active voice See **voice.**

adjectival clause A dependent clause, sometimes called a *relative clause,* that modifies a noun or a pronoun. See **1g**, **12d**, and **25a**.

adjectival phrase A phrase that modifies a noun or pronoun. See **1d(3)** and **1f**.

adjective A word that modifies a noun or a pronoun. Adjectives typically end in suffixes such as *-al, -able, -ant, -ative, -ic, -ish, -less, -ous,* and *-y.* See **4a** and **4c**. Coordinate adjectives are two or more adjectives modifying the same noun and separated by a comma: a *brisk, cold* walk. See **12c(2)**.

adverb A word that modifies a verb, an adjective, an adverb, or a verbal. Adverbs commonly end in *-ly.* Some adverbs modify entire sentences: *Perhaps* the meeting could be postponed. See **4b–c**.

adverbial clause A dependent clause that modifies a verb, an adjective, or an adverb. See **1g(2)**, **12b**, and **30b(1)**.

adverbial particle A word such as *across, away, down, for, in, off, out, up,* or *with* that combines with a main verb to form a phrasal verb: *write down, look up.* See **7a(3)**.

adverbial phrase Phrase used as an adverb, usually indicating time, place, cause, or purpose. See **1f**.

agreement The correspondence in number and person of a subject and a verb (see **6a**) or the correspondence in number and gender of a pronoun and its antecedent (see **6b**).

analogy Reference to something familiar (and often concrete) to explain something unfamiliar (and often abstract), or a direct comparison of certain features of two things that are in most ways dissimilar. See **32e(5)**.

analysis A separation of a whole into its parts. For example, a literary work may be separated into such elements as setting, plot, and character. See **32e(4)**.

angle brackets Symbols ($< >$) used to indicate that an email address or a URL is to be understood as a single unit, without any internal spaces.

antecedent A word or group of words referred to by a pronoun. See **6b** and **28a–d**.

APA Abbreviation for *American Psychological Association.* See **40c–d**.

appeal The means of persuasion in argumentative writing, relying on reason, authority, or emotion. See **36e**.

appositive A noun or noun phrase that identifies, describes, or explains an adjacent pronoun, noun, or noun phrase. See **1d(4)**, **1f(5)**, **12d(2)**, **30b(4)**, and **30c(3)**.

article A word used to signal a noun. *The* is a definite article; *a* and *an* are indefinite articles. See **22a**.

attributive tag Short phrases that identify the source of a quotation: *according to Jones, Jones claims.* See **3d**.

auxiliary verb, auxiliary A verb that combines with a main verb. *Be, do,* and *have* are auxiliary verbs when they are used with main verbs. Also called *helping verbs.* Modal auxiliaries include *could, should,* and *may* and are used for such purposes as expressing doubt, obligation, and permission. See **1f(2)** and **7a**.

backing According to the Toulmin model, the support offered for a warrant. See **35e**.

balanced sentence A sentence in which similar elements express contrasting or similar ideas. See **29g**.

bookmark To save on a browser the address of a Web site. The saved addresses appear on a pulldown menu.

Boolean operators Words used to broaden or narrow electronic database searches. These include *or, and, not,* and *near.* Also called *logical operators.* See **37d(3)**.

brainstorming Generating ideas about a writing topic by listing ideas as they come to mind. See **32b(1)**.

browser Software that finds and displays Web pages.

case The form of a noun or pronoun that indicates the relationship of the noun or pronoun to other words in a sentence. Pronouns can be subjects or subject complements (*subjective case*), objects (*objective case*), or markers of possession and other relations (*possessive case*). See **5b**.

citation Notation of a source used in a paper. See chapter **40**.

claim A statement that a writer wants readers to accept. Also called a *proposition.* See **35d–e** and **36c**.

classification The placement of something into a category. Often used with division. See **32e(6)**.

clause A sequence of related words forming an independent unit (*independent clause*) or an embedded unit (*dependent clause* used as an adverb, adjective, or noun). A clause has both a subject and a predicate. See **1g** and chapter **24**.

cliché An expression that has lost its power to interest readers because of overuse. See **20b**.

clipped form A word that is a shortened form of another word: *bike* for *bicycle.* See **11d(2)**.

CMS Abbreviation for *The Chicago Manual of Style.* See **40e**.

coherence The principle that ideas in a paragraph or an essay should be clearly connected, one sentence leading to the next, each idea evolving from the previous one. See **31b(3)**.

collaborative writing A method of writing involving the cooperative effort of two or more writers.

collective noun A noun that refers to a group: *team, faculty, committee.* See **6a(7)**.

colloquial A label for any word or phrase that is characteristic of informal speech. *Tummy* and *belly* are colloquial words; *stomach* is used in formal contexts. See **19c(2)** and **19e(1)**.

comma fault See **comma splice.**

comma splice A punctuation error in which two independent clauses are joined by a comma only. Sometimes called a *comma fault.* See chapter **3**.

common noun A noun referring to any or all members of a class or group (*woman, city, holiday*) rather than to specific members (*Susan, Reno, New Year's Day*). COMPARE **proper noun.** See **9e(1)**.

comparative degree See **degree of comparison.**

complement A word or words used to complete the meaning of a verb. A *subject complement* is a word or phrase that follows a linking verb and renames or describes the subject. An *object complement* is a word or phrase that renames or describes a direct object when it follows such verbs as *make, paint, elect,* and *consider.* See **1d** and **4a**.

complete predicate See **predicate.**

complete subject See **subject.**

complex sentence A sentence containing one independent clause and at least one dependent clause. See **1e**, **24a–b**, and **30c(1)**.

compound-complex sentence A sentence containing at least two independent clauses and one or more dependent clauses. See **1e**.

compound predicate Predicate that has two parts joined by a connecting word such as *and, or,* or *but:* Clara Barton *nursed the injured during the Civil War* and *later founded the American Red Cross.* See **1b** and **30c(2)**.

compound sentence A sentence containing at least two independent clauses and no dependent clauses. See **1e**, **12a**, and **14a**.

compound subject Subject that has two parts joined by a connecting word such as *and, or,* or *but: Students* and *faculty* are discussing the issue of grade inflation. See **1b** and **6a**.

compound word Two or more words functioning as a single word: *ice cream, double-check.* See **18f**.

concession Agreement with an opponent on certain points of an argument. See **36d(2)** and **36f(3)**.

concrete word A word referring to what is experienced through the senses: *cologne, sunset, onions, thorns.* See **20a(3)**. COMPARE **abstract word.**

conditional clause An adverbial clause, usually beginning with *if,* that expresses a condition: *If it rains,* the outdoor concert will be postponed.

conjugation A set or table of verb forms that indicate tense, person, number, voice, and mood. See chapter **7**.

conjunction A word used to connect other words, phrases, clauses, or sentences. Coordinating conjunctions (*and, but, or, nor, for, so,* and *yet*) connect and relate words and word groups of equal grammatical rank. See **1g(3)**, **12a**, and **24a–b**. A subordinating conjunction such as *although, if,* and *when* begins a dependent clause and connects it to an independent clause. See **1g(3)** and **24a–b**. COMPARE **conjunctive adverb.**

conjunctive adverb A word such as *however, therefore,* and *nevertheless* that connects one independent clause to another. See **1g(3)**, **3c**, and **14a**. COMPARE **conjunction.**

connotation The suggested or implied meaning of a word, usually described as positive or negative. See **20a(2)**. COMPARE **denotation.**

consonant A speech sound such as /b/ or /f/ produced by a partial or complete obstruction of the air stream by the speech organs; also, a letter of the alphabet corresponding to a consonant sound. See **18d** and **22a**. COMPARE **vowel.**

context The circumstances surrounding the composition of a piece of writing: time, place, writer, audience, and medium. See **32a**. Also, the surrounding information that helps give a particular word, sentence, or paragraph its meaning; for example, *cabinet* means "a group of leaders" in a paragraph about politics and "a place for storage" in a paragraph about kitchens. See **35b**.

contraction A word formed by combining two words and adding an apostrophe to replace the omitted letter or letters: *aren't, don't*. See **15b**.

controlling idea See **main idea**.

convention, conventional Language or behavior that follows the customs of a community such as the academic, medical, or business community.

coordinate adjective See **adjective**.

coordinating conjunction See **conjunction**.

coordination The use of grammatically equivalent constructions to link or balance ideas. See **24b(2)**.

correlative conjunctions, correlatives Two-part connecting words such as *either . . . or* and *not only . . . but also*. See **1g(3)** and **26d**.

count nouns Nouns naming things that can be counted (*word, student, remark*). See **1f(1)**. COMPARE **noncount nouns**.

credibility Believability. To be trusted, writers must appear credible to their audiences. See **32a**, **36e**, and **38a–b**.

critical reading The ability to distinguish between fact and opinion, to recognize the importance of evidence and logic, to evaluate for credibility, and to avoid common fallacies. See chapter **35**.

cumulative sentence A sentence in which the subject and predicate come first, followed by modifiers: *She slept soundly, undisturbed by the noise of the party next door.* See **29b**. COMPARE **periodic sentence**.

dangling modifier A word or phrase that does not clearly modify another word or word group in the sentence. See **25b**. COMPARE **misplaced modifier**.

dangling participial phrase A verbal phrase that does not clearly modify another word or word group in the sentence. See **25b**.

database An organized collection of related information, usually in electronic form. A full-text database contains the complete, or nearly complete, text of articles. An abstract database contains summaries of articles. A bibliographic database contains limited information such as the subjects, titles, and authors of articles. See **37d**.

deductive reasoning A form of logical reasoning in which a conclusion is formed after relating a specific fact (minor premise) to a generalization (major premise). See **31a(1)**, **35d(2)**, and **41b**. COMPARE **inductive reasoning.**

degree of comparison The relative quality, quantity, or manner indicated by the form of an adjective or adverb: positive (*fast*), comparative (*faster*), or superlative (*fastest*). See **4c**.

demonstratives Four words (*this, that, these, those*) that distinguish one individual, thing, event, or idea from another. Demonstratives may occur with or without nouns: *This* [demonstrative determiner] *law* will go into effect in two years. *This* [demonstrative pronoun] will go into effect in two years.

denotation The direct or literal meaning of a word. See **20a(1)**. COMPARE **connotation.**

dependent clause See **clause.**

determiner A word that signals the approach of a noun. A determiner may be an article, a demonstrative, or a quantifier: *a reason, this reason, three reasons.* Sometimes possessives (*my, your, his, her, its, our,* and *their*) are called determiners.

development The elaboration of an idea through organized discussion supported by examples, details, and other information. See **31c**.

dialect A variety of language characteristic of a region, ethnic background, or social class. Dialects are distinguished by vocabulary, pronunciation, and syntax. See **19c**.

diction A writer's or speaker's choice of words. See chapters **19–21**.

direct address See **vocative.**

direct object See **object.**

direct quotation See **quotation.**

division Breaking a topic down into its constituent parts and showing the relationships among the parts. See **32e(6).**

documentation The provision of sources cited in a research paper according to a given style, such as MLA or APA. See chapter **40.**

domain name Part of an Internet address that follows the host name, after a period: *cwu.edu.* The Internet is organized into seven domains: commerce (.com), education (.edu), government (.gov), military (.mil), network management (.net), nonprofit organizations (.org), and the designations for other countries (.de for Germany, .uk for the United Kingdom, and so on).

double-entry notebook A journal in which each entry has two distinct parts: summary and response. See **35b(3).**

double negative The use of two negative words in one sentence. See **4e.**

download Transferring files from the Internet to a computer and saving them.

draft, drafting A working version of a piece of writing. The process of putting ideas into writing so that they can be revised and edited. See chapter **32.**

editing Reviewing a draft to improve the clarity, effectiveness, and variety of sentences. See chapter **33.**

electronic index An electronic database used to find the titles and authors of articles. Some electronic indexes include abstracts and full texts as well. See **37d(3).**

ellipsis points Three spaced periods that indicate either a pause or material omitted from a direct quotation. See **17h.**

elliptical clause A clause missing one or more words that are assumed to be understood. See **1g(2)** and **25b.**

elliptical construction The omission of an element essential to the grammar but not to the intended meaning: *Repairs will be made whenever (they are) necessary.* See **21d.**

emoticon A small icon that is made up of punctuation characters and shows how a sender wants part or all of an email message to be interpreted. For example, the emoticon :-) indicates a joke; it looks like a smiling face turned sideways.

emphatic order Arranging information according to order of importance. See **31b(1)**.

empirical evidence Facts that can be tested or measured. See **41b**.

enthymeme A syllogism with an unstated premise or conclusion. See **35d(2)**.

essential element A word or word group that modifies another word or word group, providing information that is essential for identification. Essential elements are not set off by commas, parentheses, or dashes: The woman *who witnessed the accident* was called to testify. Also called a *restrictive element.* COMPARE **nonessential element.**

ethos One of the three classical appeals; the demonstration of the writer's trustworthy character, good intentions, and substantial knowledge of a subject. Also called an *ethical appeal.* See **36e**. See also **logos** and **pathos.**

etymology The origin and historical development of a word. See **19e(4)**.

euphemism An indirect, polite expression used instead of a direct one that the writer or speaker thinks may be offensive to someone. See **20b**.

evidence Information supporting a generalization. Common types of evidence are facts, statistics, examples, testimony, sensory details, and logical inferences.

exigence The circumstance compelling one to write. See **32a**.

expletive A word signaling a structural change in a sentence, usually used so that new or important information is given at the end of the sentence: *There were over four thousand runners in the marathon.* See **1d(1)** and **6a(4)**.

expository writing Writing with the purpose of clarifying, explaining, or evaluating a subject in order to inform or instruct the reader. See **32a** and **39a**.

expressive writing Writing that emphasizes the writer's own feelings and reactions to a topic. See **32a**.

fallacy A false argument based on faulty reasoning. See **35f**.

faulty predication A sentence error in which the predicate does not logically belong with the given subject. See **20e** and **23d**.

figurative language The use of words in an imaginative rather than in a literal sense. See **20a(4)**.

figures of speech Use of language that describes things in novel ways or makes unexpected comparisons. Sometimes called *figurative language.* Metaphor, irony, and hyperbole are common figures of speech. See **20a(4)**.

first person See **person.**

fragment A group of words that begins with a capital letter and ends with a period but that lacks a subject, a predicate, or both. See chapter **2**.

freewriting A method of finding a writing topic by composing for a specified length of time without stopping to reflect, reread, or correct. See **32b**.

ftp Abbreviation for *file transfer protocol.* The guidelines that establish the format in which files can be transmitted from computer to computer. See **40a(3)**.

fused sentence Two or more sentences run together, without the punctuation required to identify them as separate sentences. Also called a *run-on sentence.* See chapter **13**.

gender The grammatical label that distinguishes nouns or pronouns as masculine, feminine, or neuter. In English, grammatical gender usually corresponds to natural gender. *Gender* also describes how people see themselves, or are seen by others, as either male or female. See **6b** and **19d**.

generalization In argument, a conclusion drawn from facts, other evidence, or both. *Overgeneralization* refers to any statement that is too broad, indefinite, or sweeping in scope. See **35d(1)**.

genre A literary category identified by its own conventions. Drama and poetry are common genres. See **42a**.

gerund A verbal that ends in *-ing* and functions as a noun: *Snowboarding* is a popular winter sport. See **1f(3)**, **5c(6)**, and **15a(6)**.

gerund phrase A verbal phrase that employs the *-ing* form of a verb and functions as a noun: Some students prefer *studying in the library.* See **1f(3)**.

helping verb See **auxiliary verb.**

home page The introductory page for a Web site.

homophones Words that have the same sound and sometimes the same spelling but differ in meaning: *their, there,* and *they're* or *capital* meaning "funds" and *capital* meaning "the top of a pillar." See **18c.**

hot link See **hyperlink.**

HTML Abbreviation for *HyperText Markup Language,* the system of codes that enables Web browsers to display Web pages.

hyperlink Embedded in a document and usually highlighted by color and underlining, a hyperlink is a Web address that allows users to move between Web pages or sites. Also called *hot link* or *link.* See **8a(2).**

hypertext Text, encoded in HTML, that allows users to move to various parts of a Web document or to other Web documents. See **8a(2).**

hypothesis A tentative assumption that is tested in an experiment. See **41b.**

idiom A language-specific expression whose meaning often cannot be derived from its elements. *Burning the midnight oil* means "staying up late studying." See **20c.**

imperative mood See **mood.**

inclusive language Language that includes all people and does not insult or ignore anyone based on age, ability, race, religion, class, gender, or sexual orientation. See **19d.**

indefinite article See **article.**

indefinite pronouns Pronouns such as *everyone* and *anything* that do not refer to specific individuals, objects, events, and so on. See **6a(6)** and **6b(1).**

independent clause See **clause**.

indicative mood See **mood**.

indirect object See **object**.

indirect question A sentence that includes an embedded question, punctuated with a period instead of a question mark: My friends asked me *why I left the party early.* See **17b**.

indirect quotation See **quotation**.

inductive reasoning The reasoning process that begins with facts or observations and moves to general principles that account for those facts or observations. See **31a(1)**, **35d–e**, and **41b**. COMPARE **deductive reasoning**.

infinitive A verbal that consists of the base form of the verb, usually preceded by the infinitive marker *to*. An infinitive is used chiefly as a noun, less frequently as an adjective or adverb: My father likes *to golf.* See **1f(3)**.

infinitive phrase A verbal phrase that contains the infinitive form of a verb: They volunteered *to work at the local hospital.* See **1f(3)**.

inflection A change in the form of a word that indicates a grammatical feature such as number, person, tense, or degree. For example, *-ed* added to a verb indicates the past tense, and *-er* indicates the comparative degree of adjectives and adverbs.

intensifier See **qualifier**.

intensive pronoun See **reflexive pronoun**.

interjection A word expressing a simple exclamation: *Hey! Oops!* When used in sentences, mild interjections are set off by commas: *Oh,* excuse me. See **12e(3)** and **17c**.

Internet An international network of computers linked through telephone and fiber-optic lines. The Internet provides access to email and the World Wide Web, among other things. See **37c**.

interpretation Explanation of meaning or significance. See **42c**.

intransitive verb A verb that does not take an object: Everyone *laughed.* See **1e** and **7c**. COMPARE **transitive verb**.

invention Using strategies to generate ideas for writing. See **32b** and **32e**.

Inversion A change in the usual subject-verb order of a sentence: *Are you* ready? See **29f**.

irony A deliberate inconsistency between what is stated and what is meant. See **16c**.

irregular verb A verb that does not take -*ed* to form both the past tense and the past participle. See **7a(2)**. COMPARE **regular verb.**

jargon Technical language appropriate as a shortcut to communication, used when an audience is knowledgeable about the topic and the terms. See **19c**.

journal A notebook in which a writer records personal responses, thoughts, and experiences. See **32b(1)** and **35b(3)**. Also, a special-interest periodical (such as *Rhetoric Review* or *Environmental Legislation*). See **37d(3)** and **40a(3)**.

keywords Specific words used with a search tool (such as Google) to find information on a research topic. See **37c**.

link See **hyperlink.**

linking verb A verb that relates a subject to a subject complement. Examples of linking verbs are *be, become, seem, appear, feel, look, taste, smell,* and *sound.* See **1d(3)**, **5b(1)**, and **7c**.

literary theory A scholarly explanation of the assumptions and values influencing the interpretation of a literary work. See **42c**.

logical operators See **Boolean operators.**

logos One of the three classical appeals; the use of language to show clear reasoning. Also called a *logical appeal.* See **36e(1)**. See also **ethos** and **pathos.**

main clause Also called *independent clause.* See **clause.**

main idea The most important idea in a paragraph or an essay; all other ideas relate to it. See **31a** and **32c**. See also **topic sentence** and **thesis.**

misplaced modifier A descriptive or qualifying word or phrase placed in a position that confuses the reader: I read about a wildfire that was out of control *in yesterday's paper.* [The modifier belongs before *I* or after *read.*] See **25a**.

mixed construction A confusing sentence that is the result of an unintentional shift from one grammatical pattern to another: When police appeared who were supposed to calm the crowds showed up, most people had already gone home. [The sentence should be written with either *appeared* or *showed up,* not with both.] See **23c.**

mixed metaphor A construction that includes parts of two or more metaphors: Her *fiery* personality *dampened* our hopes of a compromise. See **23c.**

MLA Abbreviation for *Modern Language Association.* See **40a–b.**

modal auxiliary See **auxiliary verb.**

modifier A word or word group that describes, limits, or qualifies another. See chapter **4** and **28b(2).**

mood A set of verb forms or inflections used to indicate how a speaker or writer regards an assertion: as a fact (*indicative mood*); as a command or instruction (*imperative mood*); or as a wish, hypothesis, recommendation, or condition contrary to fact (*subjunctive mood*). See **7d.**

netiquette Word formed from *Internet* and *etiquette* to name a set of guidelines for writing email messages and Listserv postings and for online behavior in general.

nominalization Formation of a noun by adding a suffix to a verb or an adjective: *require, requirement; sad, sadness.*

nominative case Also called *subjective case.* See **case.**

noncount nouns Nouns naming things that cannot be counted (*architecture, water*). See **1f(1).** COMPARE **count nouns.**

nonessential element A word or word group that modifies another word or word group but does not provide essential information for identification. Nonessential elements are set off by commas, parentheses, or dashes: Carol Murphy, *president of the university,* plans to meet with alumni representatives. Also called *nonrestrictive element.* See **12d.** COMPARE **essential element.**

nonrestrictive element See **nonessential element.**

nonstandard, nonstandardized Speech forms that are not considered conventional in many academic and professional settings. See **19e.**

noun A word that names a person, place, thing, idea, animal, quality, event, and so on: *Alanis, America, desk, justice, dog, strength, departure.* Plural nouns usually end in *-s* or *-es.* Singular possessive nouns usually end in *-'s;* plural possessive nouns usually end in *-s'.* See also **common noun, proper noun, count noun, noncount noun,** and **collective noun.**

noun clause A dependent clause used as a noun. See **1g(2).**

noun phrase A noun and its modifiers. See **1d** and **1f(1).**

number The property of a word that indicates whether it refers to one (*singular*) or to more than one (*plural*). Number is reflected in the word's form: *river/rivers, this/those, he sees/they see.* See **6a, 6b,** and **7b.**

object A noun, pronoun, noun phrase, or noun clause that follows a preposition or a transitive verb or verbal. A direct object names the person or thing that receives the action of the verb: I sent the *package.* An indirect object usually indicates to whom the action was directed or for whom the action was performed: I sent *you* the package. See **1d(2).** The object of a preposition follows a preposition: I sent the package to *you.* See **1f(4).**

object complement See **complement.**

object of a preposition See **object.**

objective case Also called *accusative case.* See **case.**

online Connected to or having access to the Internet.

online catalog A computerized database that includes information on all the holdings of a particular library. See **37d(1).**

overgeneralization See **generalization.**

parallelism The repetition of a grammatical element or structure. See chapter **26.**

paraphrase A restatement of another writer's ideas in words that differ from those in the original passage. See **39d(3).**

parenthetical citation Source information placed between parentheses. See chapter **40.**

parenthetical element Any word, phrase, or clause that adds detail to a sentence or any sentence that adds detail to a paragraph but is not essential for understanding the core meaning. Commas, dashes, or parentheses separate these elements from the rest of the sentence or paragraph. See **12e**, **13c**, and **17e–f**.

participial phrase A verbal phrase that includes a participle: The stagehand *carrying the trunk* fell over the threshold. See **1f(3)** and **25b**. See also **participle** and **phrase**.

participle A verb form that may function as part of a verb phrase (was *thinking,* had *determined*) or as a modifier (a *determined* effort; the couple, *thinking* about their past). A present participle is formed by adding *-ing* to the base form of a verb. A past participle is usually formed by adding *-ed* to the base form of a verb (*walked, passed*); however, many verbs have irregular past-participle forms (*written, bought, gone*). See **1f(3)**, **5c(6)**, and **7a**.

particle See **adverbial particle**.

parts of speech The classes into which words may be grouped according to their forms and grammatical relationships. The traditional parts of speech are verbs, nouns, pronouns, adjectives, adverbs, prepositions, conjunctions, and interjections.

passive voice See **voice**.

password A personal code that allows a user to access an Internet service account, an informational Web site, a special-topic forum, and so on. Passwords are intended to provide security against unauthorized access.

past participle See **participle**.

pathos One of the three classical appeals; the use of language to stir the feelings of an audience. Also called an *emotional appeal* or a *pathetic appeal.* See **36e(1)**. See also **ethos** and **logos**.

pentad A set of five dramatic aspects used to explore a subject: the act, the actor, the scene, the agency, and the purpose. See **32b(1)**.

perfect tenses See **tense**.

periodic sentence A sentence beginning with modifiers and ending with an independent clause: Hot, tired, yet optimistic as they neared the end of the day, the archeologists continued looking for evidence of an ancient house site. See **29b**. COMPARE **cumulative sentence**.

person The property of nouns, pronouns, and their corresponding verbs that distinguishes the speaker or writer (first person), the individuals addressed (second person), and the individuals or things referred to (third person). See **5a(1)**, **6a**, and **7b**.

personal pronoun A pronoun that refers to a specific person, place, thing, and so on. Pronoun forms correspond to three cases: subjective, objective, and possessive. See **5a(1)**.

phrasal verb A grammatical unit consisting of a verb and an adverbial particle such as *after, in, up, off,* or *out: fill in, sort out.* See **7a(3)**.

phrase A sequence of grammatically related words that functions as a unit in a sentence but lacks a subject, a predicate, or both: *in front of the stage.* See **1f**.

plagiarism The use of another writer's words or ideas without acknowledging the source. See **39e**.

plural See **number**.

point of view The vantage point from which a topic is viewed; also, the stance a writer takes: objective or impartial (third person), directive (second person), or personal (first person).

positive See **degree of comparison**.

possessive case See **case**.

predicate The part of a sentence that expresses what a subject is, does, or experiences. The complete predicate consists of the main verb, its auxiliaries, and any complements and modifiers. The simple predicate consists of only the main verb and any accompanying auxiliaries. See **1b–c**. COMPARE **subject**.

predication Stating or expressing something about the subject. See **1b** and **23d**.

prefix A small meaningful unit, usually consisting of a syllable or two, added to the beginning of a word to form a new one. Common prefixes include *re-,* meaning "again" (*review*), *pre-,* meaning "before" (*preview*), and *un-,* meaning "not" *(unbelievable).* See **18d**.

premise An assumption or a proposition on which an argument or explanation is based. In logic, premises are either major (general) or minor (specific); when combined correctly, they lead to a conclusion. See **35d**. See also **syllogism**.

preposition A word such as *at, in, by,* or *of* that relates a pronoun, noun, noun phrase, or noun clause to other words in the sentence. See **1f(4)**.

prepositional phrase A preposition with its object and any modifiers: *at* the nearby airport, *by* the sea. See **1f(4)**.

present participle See **participle**.

preview To skim a piece of writing for the main ideas. See **35a**.

prewriting The initial stage of the writing process, concerned primarily with finding good topics and focusing ideas. See **32b**.

primary source A source that provides firsthand information. See **37a**. COMPARE **secondary source**.

pronoun A word that takes the position of a noun, a noun phrase, or a noun clause and functions as that word or word group does: *it, that, he, them, mine.* See chapter **5**, **6b**, and **28a–c**.

proofreading Checking the final draft of a paper to eliminate typographic, spelling, punctuation, and documentation errors. See **33e**.

proper adjective An adjective that is derived from the name of a person or place: *Marxist* theories. See **9a**.

proper noun The name of a specific person, place, organization, and so on: *Dr. Pimomo, Fargo, National Education Association.* Proper nouns are capitalized. See **9a**. COMPARE **common noun**.

proposition See **claim**.

qualifier A word that intensifies or moderates the meaning of an adverb or adjective: *quite* pleased, *somewhat* reluctant. Words that intensify are sometimes called *intensifiers.*

qualitative data Evidence based on observations, interviews, and similar methods of data collection. See **41b**.

quantitative data Evidence that is reportable in numerical form. See **41b**.

quotation A *direct quotation* is the exact repetition of someone's spoken or written words. Also called *direct discourse.* An *indirect quotation* is a report of someone's written or spoken words not stated in the exact words of the writer or speaker. See **9d, 16a,** and **39d.**

reciprocal pronoun One of two compound pronouns—*each other* or *one another*—expressing an interchangeable or mutual action or relationship: The two roommates helped *each other* complete the assignment. The members disagreed with *one another.*

redundancy Needless repetition. See **21a(1).**

reflexive pronoun A pronoun that ends in *-self* or *-selves* (*myself* or *themselves*) and refers to a preceding noun or pronoun in the sentence: *He* added a picture of *himself* to his Web page. When used to provide emphasis, such a pronoun is called an *intensive pronoun:* The president *herself* awarded the scholarships.

refutation A strategy for addressing opposing points of view by discussing those views and explaining why they are unsatisfactory. See **36d(2)** and **36f(3).**

regular verb A verb whose past tense and past participle are formed in the same way: by adding *-ed,* or sometimes *-d* or *-t,* to the base form. See **7a(1).**

relative clause See **adjectival clause.**

relative pronoun A noun substitute (*who, whom, that, which,* or *whose*) used to introduce an adjectival clause, sometimes called a *relative clause.* See **1g(2)** and **5a(2).**

restrictive element See **essential element.**

revision Changes made to an early draft that improve its focus, content, or organization. See chapter **33.**

rhetoric The art of using language effectively, which involves the writer's purpose, the audience, the discovery and exploration of a subject, the arrangement and organization of ideas, the style and tone in which they are expressed, and the form in which they are delivered. See chapters **32, 35,** and **36.**

rhetorical methods Strategies for developing and organizing ideas within a paragraph or an essay. See **32e.**

rhetorical situation The relationship among the writer, the audience, the text, and the context. See 32a.

Rogerian argument An approach to argumentation that is based on the work of psychologist Carl R. Rogers and that emphasizes the importance of withholding judgment of others' ideas until they are fully understood. See 36e(2).

run-on sentence See **fused sentence.**

search engine A Web-based program or Web site that enables users to search the Internet for documents. Sometimes called a *search tool.* See 37c.

search tool See **search engine.**

secondary source A source that analyzes or interprets firsthand information. See 37a. COMPARE **primary source.**

sentence fragment See **fragment.**

sentence modifier A modifier related to a whole sentence, not to a specific word or word group within it: *All things considered,* the committee acted appropriately when it approved the amendment to the bylaws.

sexist language Language that arbitrarily excludes one sex or that arbitrarily assigns stereotypical roles to one sex. See 19d(1). COMPARE **inclusive language.**

simple tenses See **tense.**

singular See **number.**

slang The casual vocabulary of specific groups or cultures, usually considered inappropriate for academic and professional writing but occasionally effective if the writer carefully considers purpose and audience. See 19c.

slash The mark (/) used to separate lines of poetry or parts of an Internet address. See 17i.

spatial order The ordering of details according to how they are encountered as the observer's eye moves vertically, horizontally, from far to near, and so forth. See 31b.

split infinitive The separation of the two parts of an infinitive form by at least one word: *to completely cover.* See 1f(3).

Standardized English The style of writing expected in most academic and business settings.

subject The general area addressed in a piece of writing. See 32b. COMPARE **topic.** Also, the pronoun, noun, or noun phrase that carries out the action or assumes the state described in the predicate of a sentence. Usually preceding the predicate, the complete subject includes the main noun or pronoun and all determiners and modifiers. A simple subject consists of only the main noun or pronoun. See 1b. COMPARE **predicate.**

subject complement See **complement.**

subjective case See **case.**

subjunctive mood See **mood.**

subordinating conjunction See **conjunction.**

subordination The connection of a structure, usually a dependent clause, to an independent clause: *Even though customers were satisfied with the product,* the company wanted to improve it. See chapter 24.

suffix A small meaningful unit, usually consisting of a single syllable, added to the end of a word either to form a new word or to indicate a grammatical property such as number or degree: talk*s,* talk*ed,* fast*er,* fast*est.* See 18d.

superlative See **degree of comparison.**

syllogism Method for deductive reasoning consisting of two premises and a conclusion. See 35d. See also **premise.**

symbol A word or phrase that refers to an object, which in turn represents a concept or other abstraction. See 42b(6).

synonym A word that has a meaning similar to that of another word; *daybreak* is a synonym for *dawn.* See 19f.

syntax Sentence structure; the grammatical arrangement of words, phrases, and clauses.

synthesis Collecting and connecting information on a topic; usually involves summary, analysis, and interpretation.

tag question A question attached to the end of a related statement and set off by a comma: She came back, *didn't she?*

tense The form of a verb that indicates when and for how long an action or state occurs. Generally, simple tenses are used to report past, future, and habitual present actions. (*I wrote, I will write, I write everyday*). Progressive tenses indicate uncompleted actions (*I was writing, I will be writing, I am writing*). Perfect tenses indicate actions performed prior to another time *(I had written, I will have written, I have written)*. See **7b**.

theme The main idea of a literary work. See **42b(1)** and **42b(7)**.

thesis The central point or main idea of an essay. See **32c**.

tone The writer's attitude toward the subject and the audience, usually conveyed through word choice and sentence structure. See **33a(3)**, **33b**, and **42b(3)**.

topic The specific, narrowed main idea of an essay. See **32b(2)**. COMPARE **subject.**

topic sentence A statement of the main idea of a paragraph. See **31a(1)**.

Toulmin model A system of argumentation developed by philosopher Stephen Toulmin in which *argument* is defined as a logical progression, from data (evidence or reasons) to a claim (a debatable statement), based on a warrant (the underlying assumption connecting the two). See **35e**.

transitions Words, phrases, sentences, or paragraphs that relate ideas by linking sentences, paragraphs, or larger segments of writing. See **31b**.

transitive verb A verb that takes an object. The researchers *reported* their findings. See **1e** and **7c**. COMPARE **intransitive verb.**

truth In deductive reasoning, premises thought to be accurate, correct, realistic, and so on. See **35d**. COMPARE **validity.**

Uniform Resource Locator See **URL.**

unity A quality of writing in which all the elements contribute to the development of a single idea or thesis. A paragraph is unified when each sentence contributes to the development of a central thought. See chapter **23** and **31a(2)**.

URL Abbreviation for *Uniform Resource Locator,* which identifies an Internet address, including the domain name and often a specific file to be accessed. For example, the URL for the Harbrace Web site includes the indicator that it is on the World Wide Web (http://www), the domain name (harbrace), and the domain (com), all separated by periods: http://www.harbrace.com. A slash precedes a subpage on a Web site. For example, the URL http://owl.english.purdue.edu/lab/index.html indicates the subpage on which Purdue's Online Writing Lab posts an index of general information. See 37c.

user name The element of an email address that identifies a user to an Internet service provider.

validity In deductive reasoning, the accurate relationship between premises and a conclusion. See 35d. COMPARE **truth.**

verb A word denoting action, occurrence, or existence (state of being). See 1c, 6a, and 7a–d.

verb phrase A main verb and any auxiliaries. See 1f(2) and 7a(4).

verbal A verb form functioning as a noun, an adjective, or an adverb. See 1f(3). See also **gerund, infinitive,** and **participle.**

vocative Set off by commas, the name of or the descriptive term for the person or persons being addressed. See 1d(4) and 12e(3).

voice A property of a verb that indicates the relationship between the verb and its subject. The *active voice* is used to show that the subject performs the action expressed by the verb; the *passive voice* is used to show that the subject receives the action. See 7c and 29d.

vowel A speech sound such as /o/ produced with little obstruction of the air stream by the speech organs. A vowel is represented in writing by the letters *a, e, i, o, u,* and sometimes *y.* See 18d and 22a. COMPARE **consonant.**

warrant According to the Toulmin model, the underlying assumption connecting a claim and data. See 35e.

Web page See **World Wide Web.**

Web site See **World Wide Web.**

World Wide Web (WWW) A system of Internet servers that store documents formatted in a special computer language (HTML). These documents are called *Web pages,* and a location containing several such pages is called a *Web site.* See chapter 8.

Credits

English as a World Language Index

Entries in this index identify topics of interest to multilingual readers and writers. Numbers and letters in color refer to chapters and sections in the handbook; other numbers refer to pages.

Index

Numbers and letters in color refer to chapters and sections in the handbook; other numbers refer to pages.

(cont.)

(cont.)

(cont.)

(cont.)

THOMSON ™

INFOTRAC®
COLLEGE EDITION
The Online Library

Use the passcode inside this card to activate your

FREE 4-Month Subscription

Exclusively from Thomson Learning

Here is your FREE passcode to InfoTrac College Edition®
Only available with NEW copies of Thomson Learning textbooks

To open, detach at perforation

DO NOT DISCARD
Your Passcode to Online Library Inside

STOP

www.infotrac-college.com

InfoTrac® College Edition offers:

- More than 10 million articles from nearly 5,000 academic journals and other sources

- Daily newspapers and monthly magazines

- Online help with research papers

- Easy-to-use search features

Log On & Get Started

ISBN: 1-4130-0285-4